Susan Haradon, Ph.D., is a practicing psychotherapist in the San Diego area. She has been a provider of mental health services for over 50 years and spent many of these years also teaching, as well as monitoring dissertations, at such schools as UCSD, Alliant University, and National University. This is her third book, two previous ones being edited in conjunction with the author's material about the early days of nursing, *Care from the Heart,* and the days leading up to the battle for the Alamo, *Haley of the Rangers. When* not working as a therapist, she is an avid reader, researcher, and creative arts enthusiast.

My greatest gratitude to my children, Jennifer and Caitlin, who inspire me by their own ongoing Ingles spirit of creativity and independent thinking; and to my husband, Chuck, who believed in the magic that lies with these pages.

Susan Haradon, Ph.D.

CONNECTIONS

An Encyclopaedic Explanation of the Universe And Our Place In It

AUSTIN MACAULEY PUBLISHERS®

LONDON * CAMBRIDGE * NEW YORK * SHARJAH

Copyright © Susan Haradon, Ph.D. 2025

All rights reserved. No part of this publication may be reproduced, distributed, or transmitted in any form or by any means, including photocopying, recording, or other electronic or mechanical methods, without the prior written permission of the publisher, except in the case of brief quotations embodied in critical reviews and certain other non-commercial uses permitted by copyright law. For permission requests, write to the publisher.

Any person who commits any unauthorized act in relation to this publication may be liable to criminal prosecution and civil claims for damages.

Ordering Information
Quantity sales: Special discounts are available on quantity purchases by corporations, associations, and others. For details, contact the publisher at the address below.

Publisher's Cataloging-in-Publication data
Haradon, Ph.D., Susan
Connections

ISBN 9798891553651 (Paperback)
ISBN 9798891553668 (Hardback)
ISBN 9798891553675 (ePub e-book)

Library of Congress Control Number: 2024900494

www.austinmacauley.com/us

First Published 2025
Austin Macauley Publishers LLC
40 Wall Street, 33rd Floor, Suite 3302
New York, NY 10005
USA

mail-usa@austinmacauley.com
+1 (646) 5125767

This book is the product of twenty years of research, reading and life experiences. It would not have been possible without the patient understanding of family and friends, as I spent hundreds of hours absorbed in the process of producing these pages, or as my children called it, "Mommy typing". Many thanks to major editorial help from Gina Epstein, whose legal background and expertise in brief editing were of major assistance. As a graduate of Rutgers University, she has a brilliant outlook and a compassionate take on all the material.

She taught me even more about cohesion, clarity and style. She is a great editor and a loving friend.

Thanks also to Ani Beth Howell for the reading and comments in the Buddhism chapter.

Other past influences and mentors include Frank Schmidt, Ph.D., Thomas McGee, Ph.D., Patricia Linquist, Ph.D., Drupon Samten Ripoche, and specifically my high school English teacher, Mrs. Ross, and my brother, John Haradon, a journalist, editor and author, whose influences on my love of writing are immeasurable.

Many have contributed to the thinking that led me to start this book—ideas about the "renewal of the Renaissance" in our era and about how our need for attachment manifests on multiple levels and through an interactive theory of connection. Besides the numbers of family and friends who supported me, I especially want to thank the hundreds of students and patients over these years who encouraged me to put into writing the methodologies that seemed to work well in educating them about their own growth process. I also owe thanks to the painstaking work on the manuscript by the editors and production managers at Austin Macauley Publishers. Their assistance was invaluable.

Table of Contents

Chapter One: Our Experience of Connection	11
Chapter Two: A Philosophy of Life Influences on How We Got Here	28
Chapter Three: Revelations	45
Chapter Four: To Be a Hero	68
Chapter Five: Social Connections What Makes Us a Society?	94
Chapter Six: The Renaissance A New Historical Framework Begins	123
Chapter Seven: Growth of American Idealism	146
Chapter Eight: The Spirit and the Self How Connections Provide Us with Pathways to Comfort	175
Chapter Nine: Buddhism and the Practice of Mindfulness	201
Chapter Ten: The Neurological Universe	227
Chapter Eleven: How We Connect to Our Physical Bodies	254
Chapter Twelve: The Universe of Physics The Ultimate Cosmos?	281
Chapter Thirteen: Theories of Attachment and Personality Unified Field Theory of Development Comes to Life	305
Chapter Fourteen: Personal Growth Emotions, Personality and Self-Actualization	333
Chapter Fifteen: Developmental Issues of Adolescence Through Old Age (We Grow Up and Grow Old)	363
Chapter Sixteen: The Disconnect and Inward Suffering	383
Chapter Seventeen: Carl Jung Archetypes and the Unfolding Spirit of the Self	409
Chapter Eighteen: After Individuation Discovery, Growth and Recovery	432
Chapter Nineteen: Discovery of Self The Art and Science of Growth	451
Chapter Twenty: Self-Care as an Entry to Awareness	468
Chapter Twenty-One: A Look at Curative Factors We Find Peace	484
Chapter Twenty-Two: We Become United	503
Bibliography	532
Index	559

Chapter One
Our Experience of Connection

> Human beings are bound together by their connection with a definite portion of the environment.
> – Malinowski quoted in Sullivan, 1953

Individuals develop healthy emotional stability through the CONNECTIONS they make, with other people, and through assimilation and accommodation of new and meaningful experiences which bind them in turn to their immediate environments. These environments are CONNECTED to a greater consciousness, designed, and presented to the curious learner, first through a CONNECTION with family, then with peers and school, and finally with a larger world of work. Each of these areas of CONNECTION are ones which will be returned to repeatedly throughout the different areas of importance presented in this book. The areas represent our meaningful whole.

I have been influenced by many great writers and resources. Not the least of these were Jonas Salk (Chapter Ten), his Holiness the Dalai Lama Tenzin Gatzo (Chapter Five), Thoreau and Emerson (Chapter Three), C.G. Jung (Chapter Nine), Carl Rogers (Chapter Thirteen) and all the positive effects of the Fellowship of the 12-step programs (see Chapters 16 and others). I mention these individuals here, in addition to referring the reader to the index and bibliography, to underscore my basic concept of why the book is laid out the way it is.

Just as each developing individual gains an awareness of history, science, philosophy, psychology, and finally metaphysics, I approach each of these areas of interest through a chapter and presentation of how CONNECTIONS in each discipline/area of study advances the individual, the environment, and a global consciousness onto a higher plane of ongoing CONNECTIVITY.[1] Representation of the person's "being" presents meaning that reflects our sense of intuition and self-affirmation.

As a therapist, the transformation I see in people with whom I work generates an expression of their own internal hopes and goals for themselves. I acknowledge that psychotherapy is only one of the ways people can heal themselves [wisdom traditions are another]. This book will explore how history, philosophy, theology, science, psychology, and personality can be integrated with the Self/soul. My goal is to create a model whereby constructs personally meaningful to me (knowledge, competence, self-determination) reflect the process of growth and life span

---

[1] Take note that several words (CONNECTION, Self, Other, Outlier) are so integral to the underlying meaning of these writings that they are always capitalized to make them stand out within a sentence and to denote the unifying nature of its concept. Other words might be underlined or capitalized for emphasis only. The terms "client" and "patient" may be used interchangeably. Carl Jung (1875–1961) always capitalized the word Self because by doing so he separated his specific use of the word from meaning only one's ego, persona, or identity.

development. Each construct is integrated with all the others, creating a CONNECTION, dialectic, and global demonstration of the energy between single individual and whole systems. In this way, the establishment of goals can have a "real world" impact.

Henry James wrote The Golden Bowl in 1904. He had long been a great believer in "comparison of standpoints and collaboration". His friend and neighbor, H.G. Wells often encouraged James to stick to the "high duty of his art" (Seymour, 1988). I take this challenge to heart as I write this book.

I do not specifically reflect on socioeconomic or gender issues, nor on the influences of the arts (painting, literature, and music) because I want to avoid what would seem to be side trips into areas I lack deeper knowledge of or skill in discussing. I did not cover these subjects, even though dear to my heart, because I was trying to stay on the task of discovery of CONNECTIONS. These experiences are emotive and personal, bisecting every classification within this book (biological, historical, philosophical, psychological, and social). That is not to say that I don't highly value those areas of knowledge and social change, nor respect anyone else's need to see the subject areas in this book through their own lens from experiences in those areas.

Also, I do not have the advantage of distance in time or clarity in opinion to control reactivity in my writing about certain historical areas of interest in Chapter Seven; the readers' own perspective on more recent historical events such as the Holocaust or recent political events and the pandemic of the early 2020s are respected.

Purpose and Format

I found that I wanted to write a book about my beliefs, rather than just talk about them to students, patients, friends, and family members. I focused on relating difficult ideas in a simpler form; I created an interface and CONNECTION between the various areas of scholarly pursuit that interest me most in my own golden bowl, "a golden vessel which you flourish about with a hand of inimitable freedom" (ibid, 1988).

Although Wells warned James his "bowl" was also something "you run the risk of dropping," my commitment was to stick to my clarity of purpose. I was determined to write about the grand mysteries, both great and small, microcosmic, and macrocosmic. I didn't want to write just another popular science book, because the science in this book is supportive and not for everyone. Any one chapter may not be for everyone.

My intention is to present many ideas for many people who may then pursue further study through the resources provided here and in support of my beliefs. As Leonardo da Vinci pulled many of his ideas about physical space into a notebook called *Transformations,* which he never published, my first intention was to write down my thoughts, even if only read by friends and family. Graduate school, and the practical experience of being my mother's daughter, gave me a love of knowledge and the ability to see patterns in what I studied; I had an urge to combine many ideas in a scholarly, cumulative way.

My goal is to bring knowledge from general science, as well as behavioral science, to the attention of people who may not read journals or even understand the standards of good research. I want to make it personal as well as professional, allowing readers to assemble and apply some feedback about themselves and others. While there is a large use of direct quotations, I have tried to avoid or footnote any superfluous thoughts, sticking instead to responsible findings and a meaningful focus on the material in that chapter.

As I wrote much of this, I could hear the voice of my mother (who was also a therapist) coming through the keys as I typed. I knew she had always meant for me to understand how she felt about her experiences as a child and young adult, and how I could relate her stories and my own experiences within my early work with abused children. I learned from her. I accompanied her into the many symposiums/trainings, which provided a synthesis of feeling and thinking and gave me understanding, even as a young teenager.

I yearned for the same things she did—an engaged, comforting mother, just as my patients do. I wanted to transform my core beliefs and values into words, words that had helped me, my students, my patients, and my partners in life. I now hope that their insights will guide the reader into a synthesized understanding through what I think about how the world works and the awakenings we can have. This process of transformation takes willingness, faith in ourselves, and honesty on our part.

Because I used an encyclopedic format, I encourage the reader to make notes about interests and areas of questions as they read. Use the table of contents and index liberally. Some issues may be discussed in multiple chapters. The individual reader may choose to read only certain chapters, missing out on information in others. After finishing this first chapter, I encourage the reader to review the table of contents and pick out a topic area or two which first strikes their interest. Then as time or interest continues, proceed into secondary and tertiary areas of interest. I have tried to note where the chapter's cross-reference, but I may have missed some points of CONNECTION.

Use your ideas to develop growth and self-mastery in your areas of interest: by identifying trigger areas we can develop more discipline, character, and integrity. Be aware of any urges you might have to write about some areas yourself; that revelation would please me no end. Some of the ideas presented in this book, particularly the last five chapters or so, may touch on areas of painful memory or past therapeutic experiences. That's my goal, for you to re-experience and re-trigger old feelings if it will help you move on in areas that need growth. You can even set the book (or that chapter) aside and come back to it later.

Many questions will be raised. Most of the answers will lie within you, the reader, and your interpretation of the material that follows. Depth of CONNECTION comes from intense experiencing and the richness of interpretation you make of each experience.[2] Obviously, there will be as many

---

[2] "…as a general definition…events, relationships or transactions which give a person a sense of identity, of worth, of hope and of purpose in experience are 'inspiring,' while those that make a person feel unimportant, worthless, hopeless, low in self-esteem, isolated, and frustrated, and those that make him feel that existence is absurd and meaningless are 'dispiriting.' The hypothesis is that dispiriting events render an organism vulnerable to the always present forces of illness while inspiring events mobilize the forces of wellness latent in all organisms" (Snyder, 1967, p. 77).

responses to this material as there are individuals who read it. The goal remains constant; the goal is one of unfolding and maturing.

I write about my beliefs, interwoven with important factors that have influenced my life and choices. Philosophy, History, and Science were all strong influences on my initial studies. Now, as a psychotherapist with 50 years of experience, I want to share how I used this information, including new and exciting findings in neuroscience and psychoneuroimmunology, to help my patients become healthy and more able to direct the course of their own lives. Reflection on one's own life is an ever-changing process; I wanted, also, to reflect how my life evolved based on my willingness to make hard choices, to have faith in my Self and others, and to embrace the idea of spiritual healing at every juncture. As I wrote, my sense of myself broadened, and I began to recognize and accept certain effects of my childhood and other lost opportunities (de Salvo, 1999). I never tried to escape suffering; rather I CONNECTED to it and embraced the lessons it taught me.

I learned and grew to understand that my parents had had problems, not the least of which was my father's PTSD from being in the sixth day of landing during the D-Day invasion, and then in France and Germany later in WWII. My parents had grown up in very different ways, and yet their independent reactions to the Great Depression as they experienced it, were not the biggest family secret. Rather, it was that they were cousins, and became each's second spouse. They formed a strong working relationship, and their long-term affection for each other continued as they had two children and two very different careers, but both in psychology. My father taught me how to navigate the "real world"—its dangers and ambiguities—until I finally became pretty much fearless. My mother taught me about endurance in the face of suffering and how education and reading/writing were the world's greatest escape!

Thoreau said, "It takes two to speak the truth—one to speak and another to hear." Thank you for being my listener.

Before presenting an extensive explanation and integration of life's influences, which I call a united field theory (UFT) of development, I will spend some time exploring the philosophical bases of many of the most pertinent and useful theories already existing in modern psychology and therapeutic treatment, each of which will then be discussed further in later chapters. Theories of personality (the sum of our mental processes), as shown in Chapters Thirteen through Fifteen, are also based on UFT and philosophical backgrounds.

Building one's UFT is an additive process, in which the "index" of all experiences and features of our Selfness comes from a focus on variables across many levels of analysis, from the genetic to the social, and from which comes our continuity (Blair and Raver, 2012). All processes are CONNECTED, from experiences to the simultaneous creation of neuropathways for our memories to the neuroendocrine levels of our emotions. It is the job of our mental functioning to integrate our capacity for thought and self-control of our underlying passions. Whether we are working toward the development (eventually) of a global Self, or we are simply in the here-and-now, all experiences build a sense of CONNECTION.

In a world where the search for one's Self is sometimes overridden by belief that others will tell us who we are, it is easy to begin to believe that the others know us better than we know ourselves.³ Our mission is to replace the more illogical belief that they know how they want us to be with the knowledge of how we ourselves should develop and design our own life path. This is especially true for men, who are trained not to admit fear. Sometimes we fool ourselves for brief moments into believing that the Other has some special knowledge—a mentor of great wisdom, a friend of many years or a mate who should have only our best interests in mind. But as philosophers, shamans and even advertising executives repeatedly tell us, never seek a permanent teacher, never forget that the seat of true greatness is within. "When we have found our true individual road, we have to keep to it" (de Castillejo, 1997, p. 26). Our task is to find our wholeness by searching through the pieces, however painful.⁴ The primary focus of our CONNECTIONS is to find love and belonging, to feel heard and valued. Then we learn to trust (Brown, 2012).

Because of my belief in the basic dualism of nature, I believe man directs his actions toward a psychological explanation of how one prepares oneself for CONNECTIONS within the world and with the world. CONNECTIONS, after all, are why we're here, to CONNECT, and through these CONNECTIONS, find meaning. These CONNECTIONS are generated from, and balanced with, achieving certain developmental goals. We achieve this goal through internal CONNECTIONS with the Self, ones which overrule our deeper sense of insecurity. For the sake of fully exploring these possibilities, the Self is considered a composite of neurobiological systems as well as social-emotional ones, and the balance between one's needs biologically, psychologically, and spiritually will be addressed.⁵

---

³ "You are a puzzle to yourself as something to understand. A lifetime is all too short to bring that off. You will continue to be a puzzle to yourself. And of great interest…No one else can give you an identity—your own sensing of who and what you are" (Snyder, 1967, p. 41).

⁴ This impasse may be another in the long history of quality versus quantity arguments. Having reached a great level of understanding of Self, can the experience of the dualism of all nature, much less that needed between individuals for human survival, be quantified into how much is needed, where the individual will lose themselves if they step aside to join, or step inside to merge? The holism of Gregory Bateson (1972) puts life, love, and the other before Self, but then in reviewing Bateson's work, Berman reminds us that "quality is the issue, not quantity, and most phenomena are, at least in a special sense, alive" (ibid, 1981, p. 236). Is experiencing a qualitative experience in a few brief moments of one's life "better" than having a great quantity of parallel experiences where perhaps the CONNECTION never happens?

⁵ A look to the history of this ideology will also be addressed, particularly as found during periods of Renaissance in history, when dualism and Neoplatonic ideas were blended powerfully with science, economics, and social systems. For instance, Pascal constructed a dualism of his own: "two realms, one of the heart, and one of the mind. "Man, the unknown, is a mass of contradictions…his only solution is to listen to the promptings of his heart and embrace of God" (Bronowski & Mazlish, 1960, p. 239). Moral developmentalists, such as Kohlberg, inform us that a man can only be as morally developed as he is cognitively and emotionally prepared to handle sethical

How do we develop coping strategies and become resilient? Psychological symptoms often indicate how our adaptive strategies become maladaptive over time. Specific traumas may impair our coping skills or increase our suffering. Sometimes others can see the adverse effects of our suffering before we have labeled it as such; rather, a stress reaction may have been defended against psychologically or with the use of self-soothing behaviors and/or addictive substances.

College Background

I have been interested in the integration of ideas since my initial exposure to the study of philosophy during college (Trinity University in San Antonio, Texas). Below is a letter I wrote to my favorite professor of that time. His influence was immeasurable to the kernel of my idea for a synthesis of ideas. Inserting the letter, from 1981 or so, serves as an opportunity to share some of my own personal background.

Dear Dr. Kimmel:

I wanted to share with you the feelings I had when I saw your name. I've been having many feelings during the last 10 days of a visit back to San Antonio, and specifically, to the Trinity campus. As I have told you before, you were one of three influential people in my academic career. The first was my junior/senior English teacher at Edison High School, who taught me to write, opened my eyes to myths, poetry, Shakespeare, and survival. The second was Dr. Frank Schmidt in the Psychology Department. He taught me how to think, to structure ideas so I had the freedom to express myself. This method has carried me through many experiences including my dissertation, where I studied, the methodology of psychological assessment and the Rorschach Psychodiagnostic Test.

I proved that even the most creative or right brain functions requires a "schema", a sense of purpose, and a form of expression. I guess I also learned this in Trinity's *Integration of Abilities* Drama class, the philosophy of which I often use in my therapeutic work with clients. As you probably recall, this class encouraged us to take seven different views of any concept: self-awareness, objectification, story, art, movement, music, and transcendence experience. We had to use these discoveries in the techniques of explanation, relaxation, centeredness, projection, concretization, and shared time. Through this process I gained a concept of my Self—the origins which came from studying Plato, Freud, Jung, and Berne (and each of their views of defense mechanisms for coping) and the expression of which drew me to dance, music and art therapy. I learned how to find a Gestalt in my experiences and to use meditation, self-hypnosis, and biofeedback to engage my Self in appropriate action and decision as I gained a strong sense of Self through that process of self-analysis and personal planning.

You, Dr. Kimmel, however, gave me something additional. Through Plato, Descartes, Leibniz, Nietzsche, and Hegel, I learned about life itself. What must

---

issues, and that to insure higher moral judgment on an individual and even community level, we must invest in the emotional development of those who we may be tempted to rise above.

exist in total human experience of the universe for such thoughts by these men to manifest?[6] And how meaningfulness was not only experienced only through intellectual pursuits, but also through the affective and metaphysical levels of reality. I began to feel an obsessive ambitious urge to change my own reality, to experience more knowledge, and to be able to share it with others.

Susan

Sometimes it is hard to sort out which kind of changes were born of those subsequent years. Change occurs, of course, and I, like others, sometimes became nervous about "losing myself". I believed my Self was based on my experiences up until that point in my life. But I was also committed to a lifelong scholarship about myself, and others, which would aid in transformational experiences. As "System Theory" taught me in 1973, I needed to maintain balance, between my new thoughts and my actions, my commitments, and my sense of Self, and between my mind and body CONNECTION.

Jungian Influences

While still in college, in fact early during my studies of Psychology, I was greatly influenced by Jung [this period was only 10 years after his death in 1961]. Hayman (1999), put it best, "Jung believed in 'a general human pre-condition, the inherited and inborn biological structure which is the instinctual basis of every human being.' In political, social, and economic history, as in personal relationships, everything could be explained in these terms" (ibid, 1999, p. 400). Chapters Seventeen and Eighteen (Jung) and Nineteen (Discovery of the Self) present more to read about these factors.

For instance, Jung did not complete his great work, *Mysterium Coniunctionis,* until 1954, just seven years before he died at the age of eighty-six. "In the eighty-third year of my life I have undertaken to tell the myth of my life…my fable, my truth" (Carl Jung). Because it was written over fourteen years, and at the length of 600 pages, it sometimes loses momentum. I have taken over twenty years to finish this book; I hope I have avoided the same problem using an encyclopedic framework in the chapters which follow.

Anyone who finishes this book, or at least looks through the table of contents or index, will see Jung's influence on my thoughts, my methodology in designing this book, and my dedication to inclusiveness. From his studies, Jung came to believe in "the original non-differentiated unity of the world or of Being. His idea of the *coniunctio* was 'nothing less than a restoration of the original state of the cosmos and the divine unconsciousness of the world.'" Jung felt "paradisal unity

---

[6] The two things that filled Kant with ever-increasing admiration and awe, the starry heavens above and the moral law within us, are both our own invention-discovery. "They are the creation of an order of depth and beauty which show how artistically consciousness can affect the raw stuff of reality. The moral law, the starry heavens, Van Gogh's wheatfields at Arles, $e=mc^2$, The Magic Flute, and the Pythagorean Theorem are all examples of the aesthetic creativity we can bring to the construction of the cosmos in which we live" (LeShan, 1982, p. 26).

could be divided into two or even more parts, but it was still One; the eternal Ground of all empirical being, just as the Self is the ground and origin of the individuality, past, present, and future" (Hayman, 1999, p. 388).

Religious Influences

I was raised a Methodist, with a little Christian Scientist sprinkled in. My college studies opened my mind to certain new possibilities (see also p. 22). I studied Comparative Religions and Buddhism and, ultimately, formulated my current philosophy of life and my opinions regarding Developmental Psychology. This resulting philosophy is the basis of this book, where a dualistic view of the universe as parts and pieces parallels its quantum potential with inter-CONNECTEDNESS. The more complete my participation in life is, the more actual the "I" becomes, meaning there is a "living potentiality" in me (Martin Buber, 1970).

Just as Jung studied the CONNECTION between the nature of non-ego and conscious ego by looking into Taoism and Indian philosophy, during my two trips to India (2001, 2017) I became aware of the need to use the Tantric energies of the Chakras in my work of healing both broken bodies and the broken souls of Outliers. All along I felt the importance of using cross-cultural influences, as did Jung in his "comparative psychology of inner experience". Trained in interdisciplinary awareness and actions, I wanted to explain the multiple layers of ancestral and developmental influences on whether the individual was equipped or ill-equipped to deal with the process of individuation.[7] In the synthesis of my ideas, as stated above, I began to call my point of view a unified field theory (UFT) of CONNECTION or development. In this view, CONNECTION is defined as a "joining, or being joined; a means of joining; the relation between things that depend on, involve, or follow each other" (www.dictionary.com).

A complete Unified Field Theory touches the 'grand aim of all science,' which, as Einstein once defined it, is 'to cover the greatest number of empirical facts by logical deduction from the smallest possible number of hypothesis or axioms.' The urge to consolidate premises, to unify concepts, to penetrate the variety and particularity of the manifest world to the undifferentiated unity that lies beyond is not only the leaven of science. It is the loftiest passion of the human intellect. The philosopher and mystic, as well as the scientist, have always sought through their various disciplines of introspection to arrive at a knowledge of the ultimate immutable essence that undergirds the mutable illusory world (Barrett, 1948, p. 110).

These words, regarding relationships and systems, encouraged and validated my own attempts at integrating philosophy, history, religion, science, and

---

[7] "From the viewpoint of present-day science, there are two basic ways of organizing the knowledge of alternate realities. The social scientist works from the viewpoint: What metaphysical system (state of consciousness) does this person impose on reality? The other? Which systems are normal and which pathological?' The physicist asks: 'What metaphysical system must I use in the particular realm of experience? How can I find the laws which make different systems compatible'" (LeShan and Margenau, 1982, p.22).

psychology. The integration of processes into a UFT of my own created an underlying pathway to understand how we heal.

Awareness requires a context, of course, and we are grounded in that which touches us at our core, beyond the ego defenses developed by our UFT. Our Self incorporates that which is loved and intelligent and wonderful. The lack of CONNECTION results in confusion. The act of meditation or any looking inward closely, where we can pay attention to our sensations, feelings, and mental processes, leads us to the Truth and the sacred.

In the Western cultures, we are still vacillating in the ethnocentric point of view—that accomplishment in the here-and-now is all that is important. Rather than an ego-driving frame of experience and reality, mindfulness of the here-and-now as a resting, balance point for continual health is more Self-caring. As a therapist, and as someone who has experienced healing, I received a clearer picture of my own personal myth which gave me a perspective from which to recognize and CONNECT the basic concepts of others' individual theories of reality (UFT). I know that however I perceive reality, as a participant in my own reality, I am constantly affecting its demonstration of probabilities and outcomes (Heisenberg's Uncertainty Principle states that there is a fundamental limit to what one can know about a system).

Interactional Effects

All experience is a part of the process of synthesis. Growth, learning, understanding, and personality development are all part of the ongoing dialectical process. Growth of the personality means growth of the individual self; balance (synthesis) is required. The phenomenon of potentiation of the Self are explained in many ways; the theories deal with universals, with potentials and actualities.

My own theory, which will be explained in depth through the ideas of this book, maintains that man's interaction with his environment reflects the way he interacts with himself (a macrocosm/microcosm=unicosm point of view). Man's reflections are part social, part emotional and part intuitive. He is transcendent in "beingness", and reflects his deepest value system.

But who is aware? The "who" is defined by one's experience up to and of that moment, "who" is determined by and is a part of everything it experiences. The "who" that we are is changed by the act of definition, by the passing of a moment. The Uncertainty of this moment is the core of Heisenberg's theory in quantum physics as well.

I am also interested in how we can transcend the 'who'. How do we interact with our environment, and how do we inter-correlate these interactions with our fleeting moments of self-consciousness? These questions can be answered through analysis of the developmental processes of many core areas as noted, from the atomic level to the historical and social level as well. I am searching for what kinds of interactions have persisted, and what are the values the individual has taken on. What are the kinds of goals that are socially ingrained in us as important? What are the ways individuals spend time as they attempt to actualize the personality and values that this process has demonstrated within them?

A common theme in these questions seems to be "survival" and protection of one's values. Likewise, these thoughts about personality probably reflect my identification with Jung's concept that one's psyche becomes "projected" into a situation. I like to think of these potential "many selves" as forming a committee, an idealized reference point of response-ability and defense structure where one can pick and choose the best possible archetype to put forward in any situation. As a therapist, I am always drawn first to that which is the "Outlier behavior" in a new client; it is the source of the most information for treatment.

Again, my goal is to provide a renewal of Renaissance thinking about perceptions and emotions, to investigate the CONNECTIONS between automatic processing and cognition. Cross-disciplinary thinking and pattern-seeking were the "hallmark of the quintessential Renaissance Man," and helped those who pioneered scientific Humanism (Isaacson, 2017, p. 401). We may understand more about neuroscience than we once did, but we also may be no more in control of our actions, desires, and compulsions than we ever were.

Philosophical Influences

My core beliefs and values turned into a deeper 'philosophy of Self' by reviewing those philosophical influences which most affected my formulation of a Unified Field Theory (UFT) of CONNECTION. Borrowed from Jung's writings, I refer to *'Eudaimonia',* or a general state of happiness or welfare experienced as deeply as one's own spiritual experience. Chapter Two traces Philosophy as a state of mind from the Greeks forward; I was most influenced by the Stoics, who lived "in accordance with experience of what happens by nature."

Socrates was convinced of the virtues (self-control, justice, piety, and wisdom) necessary to have a *eudiamonic* life. He influenced Plato, who then influenced Aristotle, the one Greek philosopher whose ideas may be best known in the present. Whereas Plato, in the *Republic,* wrote that no one would give up his desires just to fulfill *eudaimonic* pursuits, Aristotle believed that the pursuit of ethics and excellence, 'practical or moral wisdom', should be the highest human good: "virtuous activity in accordance with reason, wisdom, courage, and compassion." Thus, Aristotle's theory seems to have best foretold the forthcoming Middle Ages' cultural emphasis on excellence and perfection and which influenced, and CONNECTED to, the course of European history. Many of those of European ancestry were initially involved in the formation of the United States.

Of course, at issue here may also be the personal nature of one's belief about what "highest good" really is. Is it a virtuous activity? Perhaps, as did the Epicureans (*c.* 300 BC), more recent philosophers felt that the pursuit of pleasure was the highest good. Thousands of years after the Epicureans, Kant believed that *eudaimonia* was the possession of 'good will', and the only 'unconditional good'. Nietzsche, adding his opinion to Plato, believed in the virtue of justice, even if it required the "suppression of desire."

These philosophical theories and many more will be elucidated in Chapter Two. However, I would like to put an emphasis here upon Aristotle's theory of "virtuous activity in accordance with reason." Mature moral judgments are either sentimental or rational. We consider the Other's position. We have less control over our actions and thoughts than we think.

William James discussed these ideas in terms of a "stream of consciousness". He called the "how" of picking the figure out of the ground "selective attention". He maintained that at that moment, the utilization of energy is the source and power that gives the essence its definition. In *Will to Believe* (1897), James described the act of transcendence as a feeling of sufficiency, feeling the "absoluteness of the moment". At this point, the "being vouches for itself," and there is a feeling of fluency. He believed that it was an acceptance of a "healthy-minded attitude" which could provide courage, hope, and trust, dispelling doubt, fear, worry and "all nervously precautionary states of mind". He coined the word "fearthought" to describe the state of self-imposed or self-permitted suggestion of inferiority, which he felt was "harmful, unnecessary and therefore not respectable" [see Chapter Sixteen for causes and effects of addiction] (ibid, 1897, pp. 64, 108, 112).

I use language to explain a kind of transcendence that is beyond true description with words, but the sense of which can be explained through examples and the how of which can be described through developmentally learned habits and present behaviors created by new knowledge.[8] As I have mentioned before, I maintain that both intrapsychic and interpersonal interactions take place on three levels: the social, the emotional, and the intuitive. They reflect the basic developmental learning sequence that occurs between the infant and the primary nurturing figures.

Complexification

The word "complexification" is word used by Teilhard de Chardin and others to explain how relatively simple ideas seem to help us understand otherwise complicated concepts. Complexity creates new psyche and experiential qualities that the scholar needs to embrace as a guiding light toward establishing his own values and belief system about how the universe works. For instance, Leonardo da Vinci believed in the ability to make CONNECTIONS across disciplines: arts, sciences, humanities, and technology. He was defined as an "innovator; he married observation and imagination, making clear the importance of how an innovator and misfit can use his talent" (Isaacson, 2017, pp. 3–4).

As this book goes through the various disciplines that all contribute to the understanding of how we CONNECT, we are given many keys about how to relate each event, no matter how complicated, to our own phenomenological set of

---

[8] Huxley discusses the integral relationship between our ability or inability to transcend our Self-consciousness and the degree of dependence on language that occurs. "We are like icebergs, floating in the given reality of our physiology, of our intuitions and perceptions, our pains and pleasures, but projecting at the same time into the airy world of words and notions…As the only begetter of civilization and even of our humanity, language must be taken very seriously. Seriously, too, as an instrument (when used with caution), for thinking about the relationships between phenomena. But it must never be taken seriously when it is used as being in any way the equivalents of immediate experience or as being a source of true knowledge about the nature of things" (*Tomorrow and Tomorrow and Tomorrow*, 1952, pp. 3–4, 195).

meanings about the world. This book will attempt to simplify in some cases, and expand in others, the areas covered above to include aspects of an individual as developing and connecting organism. Drives are the internal sources of motivation, produced ordinarily by bodily need states (for instance. hunger, thirst), and which stimulate or cue properties that direct behaviors. The more the drive is affected by a behavior the more reinforcing that behavior will become.

Historical Influences

Another category of development is one's sense of history. Chapters Five through Seven investigate the influence of community/CONNECTION on philosophical concerns, economics, and global development. For instance, heretical sects among the early Christians included the Gnostics, who "claimed to have a special knowledge of knowledge (gnosis)…The Gnostics believed that we were separated from God only by space and time" (Hayman, 1999, pp. 120, 131). Likewise, the Enlightenment Period of the 18th century represented the newly emerging world-centric wave of existence, with its strong belief in scientific materialism, unilinear progress, commerce, and empiricism. The result of Enlightenment movements eventually unleashed two revolutions (American and French). They emphasized "the universal rights of man (by their own logic), which were soon extended to women, slaves and children" (Wilber, 2000, p. 8). Unifying [CONNECTING] themes in myth, folklore, religion, philosophy, literature and cultural history with one's personal experience was the primary emphasis in early Psychology and Psychoanalysis. For instance, Nietzsche's influence on Freud led to the theory that "instincts which cannot be released outwards will turn inwards" (op. cit. 1999, p. 131).

I counsel my patients to achieve a balance in life. It is not easy to talk about "balance" without using dualistic terms: work/play, mental/physical, alone/together, aggressive/passive, and inner-/outer-directed activities. These pairs are often referred to as the parameters of health. I believe one creates a balance in these meaningful pairs by experiencing the cosmic whole of that which is balancing, all the little valence +/- matches that are constantly lining up within the gray areas (literally) in our neurological system. What helps most is structure; our rituals keep us in line with our various parameters and thus create health.

One of the ways we practice rituals, that which keeps us balanced and CONNECTED, is through expression of our Spirit. Group spirit is often expressed through the symbols best understood as being archetypal defenses; "archetypal defenses of the group spirit are animated by the release of these heightened emotions" (Singer, 2006, p. 7).

Family Messages

My basic beliefs about human nature and behavior are based on the rituals and values I learned from my parents. Both my mother and father were very sensitive, concerned, academic people, with inquiring minds and open hearts. The first thing I learned about life is that people care about each other, that sharing is the goal of human existence. In fact, I can remember feeling old beyond my years and a bit out of place in a Methodist Sunday school class when I proclaimed at the age of 10, "God is the experience of another human being as unique and yet part of you as you are part of them. And finding one person to love and cherish and with whom to share your life, this is the ultimate experience of God." Or as a well-respected Jungian analyst says it, "No one is lonely if God is with him" (Hannah, 1981, p. 116). As then, I now believe this process shows up in the "service of the Self"—meeting the needs of the Other.

I was also influenced by a man who was a student of Zen Buddhism and lived life as an open system. The main theme he shared with me was to be happy; one action you can take is to find someone more separate, more closed than you are and by concentrating on him/her, you will find you've both experienced some happiness. The experience of godliness comes out of the goodness of human nature and the understanding of our need to CONNECT. But there is also the disturbed, vacant, depressed side of life, and those who relate to life in this way are just as "human" as those who share and love and grow in their belief in a God.

As we will see in Chapter Eight, regarding comparative religion, sometimes this result of openness takes place within a community of more than one person—what Buddhism calls the Sangha. In the community of shared food, experiences, or religion, we find the commonality and CONNECTION of safety and sanity. The Sangha is one of the three jewels of Buddhism (more about this in Chapter Nine); it teaches that the relationship of an individual to his community can transcend experience and that there are no longer real dichotomies. We can be led out of our depths and our fears. We need faith and reason and an experience of the real, a real more real because of our faith in the ideal (Plato).

In Chapter Ten, we begin an overview of scientific areas of investigation. I choose to express the deep appreciation for those scientists/scholars whose studies piqued my curiosity for so many years. I had a natural curiosity toward science, and my adolescent reading led to a review of cybernetics, philosophy, and astronomy, which began my urge to find unity in these areas. These writings enriched my study of how the universe integrates, and is integrated with, other areas of concern, such as the CONNECTIVITY of history and the interplay between philosophy and psychology, as discussed in other chapters. Initially my studies as an undergrad were focused on being a medical researcher. I wanted to become a virologist, to study cancer and other immune dysfunctions. Little did I predict that thirty years later I would get breast cancer myself and watch as my father died of colon cancer and my mother of an autoimmune disorder. However, in college I ultimately turned to the study of human nature and psychology. My interest came to me naturally from my parents, who were both psychologists, and this field provided a rewarding opportunity to practice my skills of integration, eventually as a licensed psychologist with real individuals with real problems beyond their medical histories.

Scientific Approaches

Heisenberg is a name familiar to many because of his "Uncertainty Principle". He states that the precise position of any particle in physics cannot be determined because momentum will be changed by the very act of one's observation or measurement. That we could explain human behavior, much less neuroscientific results, by using quantum physics, was nowhere within the theories I studied in graduate school in 1973, not even on the cutting edge. But I kept circling around to an idea I had in the back of my mind, that behavior was both the point and the wave that could explain human nature, which is just as unpredictable as Heisenberg's theory had always said it was. For instance, as described by my UFT system, it is also true that once having intervened with a patient, the therapist has forever changed the nature of his interaction with the patient, and the patient with others, in some meaningful, although unpredictable, way. We know that a "body at rest is healthy body;" even that rest is only an expression of peace of mind still existing within a chaotic Cosmos.

The most important function of all the physical sciences, for me, is the idea of statistical probability. At any point in scientific study or life experience we will come across the "Outlier", that individual/situation/crisis which defies our comfort within desired "normal curve" experiences. For instance, compulsiveness is an externalization of the mind's unrest and fear, whether in daily attempts at controlling one's environment or expressed more seriously in addictive behaviors (Chapter Sixteen). The mind attempts to control this fear by isolation and self-soothing. But in the process of control, the mind shows many intriguing components of problem-solving and even creativity. It has been my pleasure to come across mostly Outliers in my clinical practice. The wisdom about life's intricacies that they have provided me has expanded my own consciousness over the years.

I enjoy my studies of science, especially physics; I have tried to determine how such experiences as peace of mind or anxiety are quantized, because there is no doubt in my mind that they are. In a dualistic world of dark/light there always be "flow points", what Heisenberg would consider an ongoing/continual attempt at differentiation that creates a new quality.

It is Unity that Einstein sought, it is Unity that the great religions promise, it is Unity and comfort that so many patients seek in their therapy, throughout the world. I validated this belief for myself with my travels to Colombia, South America, Russia, and India. Stress and DISCONNECTION, from an inner peace and knowledge of a Self, blocks Unity and the ability to CONNECT. All this yearning for CONNECTION points to the importance of formulating a UFT for oneself, a belief system, a set of values, a way of moving through the world.

The following chapters present many ways to get a clearer view of how all paths will lead to a similar set of helpful and supportive data for developing a theory of life. What we are all looking for is equilibrium and balance. Whether it at first appears symmetrical (*Tao*) or if the asymmetry must be resolved, it will become a joy of life to understand that synthesis. For instance, I am one of those people who has always found comfort in darkness, a shaded porch or under a tree, a darkened room at dusk, or specifically what we call being a "night person". The Tibetans call it being in touch with one's night soul, and my dreams reflect that CONNECTION. It is my time of contemplation, and it gives me the ability to recognize all the ways in which I am united with my world around me.

We need to stay healthy in order for our CONNECTIVITY (microcosm + macrocosm = unicosm) to manifest. We don't need to know a lot about how our body works at a scientific level (although I will try to express that in Chapter Eleven). We just need to commit to taking care of our body, so it works at its highest potential. The growing field of psychoneuroimmunology reflects revelation that the person's interior states (emotions, psychological attitude, imagery, and intentions) are involved in the "cause and cure" of physical illnesses (Psychoneuroimmunology, *Wikipedia*, 12/4/2007). What comes first, however, the image or the manifestation? Or as Jung asked, "Who am I to whom all this happens?" (*Collected Works*, vol. 12, paragraph 152).

Gene expression involves emotional regulation and behavioral determinants, all controlled though neurotransmitter communications among individual neurons—phenotypic differences involved in brain development and function; all affected, likewise, by stress, pain, and anxiety. How did these individual patterns come about, aside from, or in addition to, genetic predispositions? Although neuroscience has been working hard to understand how we integrate information from our "reptile brains", creating a view that our brains have grown so much from information processing that we have had to create a "brain outside/beyond our brains", such as our smart phones/computers. Developmental Psychology explains how our individuality comes about. From this process, we experience receptivity. "Being is the mystical experience of CONNECTEDNESS, oneness with the Source of all life...We find life through the understanding of the creative process of living" (Catala, 1998, pp. 5, 12).

Developmental Issues

I believe it is the nature of one's childhood environments and the environmental effects that determine whether the child will operate out of a closed or open system later in life, the creative nature of an individual's personality. In Chapters Thirteen through Fifteen, I write about Developmental Psychology and its main influences. This includes the theories that could be unified, as I did when I taught, such as Attachment Theory of Mahler, Dynamic Theories of Development (Freud, Jung, Adler, Erikson), Cognitive Theories of Piaget, Moral Development Theory of Kohlberg, along with an adequate history of pre- and postnatal environmental and cultural influences. For instance, in the theory presented in *Anatomy of Reality* (1983), Salk writes of Koestler's concept of the Bisociational pattern of the creative synthesis: the sudden interlocking of two previously unrelated skills, or matrices of thought.

The child learns how to meet life from his parents, the parents from their parents, ad infinitum, demonstrating one's epigenetics and the UFT. Due to rapid technological and emotional change in our environment, the parent transferring a closed system script will tend to bias influences toward manipulation. Unfortunately, using creativity and intelligence in a manipulative manner results in an overall personality attribute where manipulation affects socialization, as we will study more about in Chapter Sixteen on addictions. It is hoped, however, that through the process of maturation and self-care, the child can grow into a balanced adult who knows the purpose of people in their life to create healthy boundaries and a meaningful life course. The basic causal determiners of personality are intelligence, motivation, and emotional stability. Together, these attributes will result in an integration of a person's sense of Self with their core beliefs.

We begin in darkness. Whether our beliefs are Biblical or cosmic, we have no expectations, no experiential biases, no bad habits to judge ourselves for. There isn't even a binary system with which we can measure or locate ourselves in space. A *Taoist* balance is waiting for the be-ingness that allows the realness to define movement, change, growth, and e-volution. This all-encompassing path to synthesis even explains how the therapeutic alliance between doctor and patient exists. When the patient first calls for an appointment, a Sangha of two or more is established. The solitude and sanctuary of the therapy office provides Maslow's sensory stage and Erikson's trust stage to be re-established in ways it may not have existed in childhood. Surrounding the dark/newness like an electron field is the energy which CONNECTS us, the balance of creative flow that bonds us, the awareness and calm mind that creates healing. It is here through which the concepts of Chapters Two through Fifteen can be shown to represent the CONNECTION of Self with Other.

Sources of Anxiety

Chapter Sixteen deals with that which is created out of imbalance. For instance, in dealing with the anxiety that underlies all addictions, rituals that were forcing negative self-injurious behaviors must now, during healing, turn into rituals that use decision, discipline and planning for positive self-care instead. We decide to confront our automatic negative responses and habits. Addicts learn to recognize that their habits have to become life-sustaining rituals even though initially there may be some resistance to a change in the habitual behavior they have developed over many years. In 12-step programs, this new set of habits are facilitated by a deep belief in a "Higher Power". The addict is also likely to segment his life into different unrelated parts which are joined only at the center by his need for self-affirmation. Also, notice that his is a closed system while the person who experiences joy and love of life generates an open moving system. This kind of love nourishes us and supports our spiritual, mental, and physical needs (Mandel, 1985). When good and evil become intertwined, instead of being opposed, one has experiences of a balanced, giving nature of a (Higher) Power which can CONNECT us all.

As this book moves into its final chapters, the reader is given a new framework and set of ways to produce a "self-analysis". Because Jungian analysts use archetypes extensively for this process, it is often called "archetypal amplification". Fragments of information are collected which ultimately enable us to formulate a unified theory, i.e., what I am trying to build with my own more general developmental unified field theory (UFT). Is there a committee meeting taking place in my head every time I must make a decision? Jung pushes us to look at the Shadow side for some of the best parts of yourself!

Creating Transformation

In the review of psychoanalytic influences, it is important to consider the path which theory took. It did not go directly from Freud to Jung to Rogers or Frankl or to the study of Individual Psychology. Theoretical side trips caused tension while studying instinctual and relational elements of people's psyche (Schwartz, J., 1999). Reflective of the individualism of American theories (e.g., William James, and Interpersonal Psychotherapy as developed by Harry Stack Sullivan), we see the influences in the mostly eclectic style of today's theories and therapists. In Britain, the theory of Melanie Klein had an influential set of ideas about how object relations develop. Each of these theories, in turn, took Psychoanalysis to a modern view of Psychology, including Psychosynthesis, one which still reflects a lot of Jung's original ideas about reaching Unity (also see Assagioli, 1980).[9]

After a review of Jung, I present a summary of the search for Self and a Higher Self in Chapters Nineteen through Twenty-One. As mentioned, this is an encyclopedic work, with an effort to synthesize everything in a great field of information, so that readers/seekers can read what appeals to them on a subject of their choice or review each subject area at will. As we see in all the following chapters, views of the world and life experiences help us gain a synthesis; the various aspects of human life are influenced by our exposure to areas such as anthropology, economics, medicine and physiology, psychology, and sociology. In no way, do I want to disregard a person's individuality and his/her developmental markers of growth. As I focus on the CONNECTIVITY, I see that in a unified theory of development, individuality remains. I want the reader to discover that our personal, social, and spiritual knowledge of our inner world directs us into having different views than those presented by the outer world, where spirituality, views on "God", and politics are man-made. We discover that we most experience our true Selves when we most feel like CONNECTING.

I refer to Buddhism, 12-step and Carl Jung extensively, especially in the second half of this book, because those three areas of philosophy are the major influences in my life and in my own process of staying on course with safe boundaries and self-knowledge. Jung was obsessed with the idea of one day writing a comprehensive account of the whole area of mythological studies. I use his work, along with my own research studies (see my thesis and dissertation in the bibliography), to facilitate an expression of creativity. I feel the most right when I am studying Self in others, and I am ready to use these areas of study to guide and inspire others.

---

[9] "Assagioli expanded Jung's idea of synthesis, stating that synthesis means a) being in touch with one's I and the Higher Self, b) working on the subpersonalities, c) being spiritually aware while on one's journey, d) being humble, accepting and able to share with others one's knowledge and experience of life, e) being able to make commitments, and f) being aware of creative forces" (Hardy, 1990, p. 61).

Chapter Two
A Philosophy of Life Influences on How We Got Here

There are many ways to learn about CONNECTION. The study of philosophy and history gives structure and contextual relevance to the other important developmental elements as they exist in a culture. I refer to philosophy as "the study of the fundamental nature of knowledge, reality, and existence" (Oxford Languages, 2021). In the next few chapters, a large amount of information will help the reader understand how the history of knowledge and philosophy is an important foundation to the rest of this book. Because of the encyclopedic nature of this chapter and the ones that follow, I present most discussions by theme rather than chronologically. If it seems like topics are randomly ordered, Greek thought then 20th century thinkers, then back to Greek thought, it is because of the CONNECTIONS I am trying to make regarding certain concepts. Also, chronologically, it may appear that one thinker/scholar influenced another; this perception may not necessarily be true, as time and location often greatly separated them.

How We Think

How can we be sure history is objective? Changes in viewpoint throughout history created shifts—beginnings and endings of "ages". The shift was also likely in response to the type of suffering that people experienced and the attitudes that resulted from experiences. We know that it is out of our suffering or our "necessity" that we have evolved.

Throughout this chapter I will refer to other chapters to CONNECT the content being addressed. For instance, in Chapter Five we will read about a long history of problematic struggles in the Middle East that are not UNCONNECTED to today's conflicts. Yet, how long can we separate the pursuit for power from "normal" levels of "familial" in-fighting in such areas (much less destruction of a whole culture). Is the need for power just the underlying "tragedy" of human lives?

As we look backward, we can see that our culture today is still reinvesting in familiar, RECONNECTING themes. There are still heroic virtues and a call for attention to the issues taught in the trivium (grammar, rhetoric, logic) during the Roman empire, and again in the Renaissance period after the Dark Ages (see Chapter Six). Our century is ready (again) for a new Renaissance built upon an understanding of scholarly pursuits, philosophy, and a coordination of the arts. Our "renaissance" is being renewed through the same belief in science, philosophy, and those heroic virtues, but there is now the addition of global consciousness and benefits of CONNECTIVITY, if we take them. Today's dwelling on negative news-worthy items has created a shaming and distant set of societal factors, and as pandemics create a withdrawal from the world, I have found in my family, friends, and patients the tendency to withdraw.

One could ask: Is the "meaning of meaning" still as important as it used to be? As we grew up, some of us had the joy of expressing meaning in our lives through music, art, meditation and even sex. These are all expansive pursuits, where the Self can be seen in the fantasy, play and rituals of these activities. To me, this brings up the "mind-body" problem, whereby we seek to differentiate soul from intuition, conscience from cognition (superego). But where are feelings? We are trained to "control;" when do we learn to "release?"[10] Our perception of "time" as a continuum allows for autonomy and commitment.

Out of fear of being too autonomous or losing successful commitments, we sometimes experience Self as distant or false; our attachments fail, and anxiety follows. We are molded negatively into depression and/or immobilization. "An age in which depression is a norm is a grim one indeed…Plato's own psychological ideal was that of an individual organized around a center (ego), using his will to control his instinct and thereby unify his psyche; reason thus becomes the essence of personality, and is characterized by distancing oneself from phenomena, maintaining one's identity" (Berman, 1981, pp. 3, 61). Thus, Plato suggested that man has many aspects, each driven by inconsistent traits and perceptions.

Philosophers in the 16th and 17th centuries also addressed these issues of meaning. Descartes believed that the essence of a human being was the faculty of thought and that thought could not be material. A man's greatest essence must be "metaphysical". He agreed with the Greeks that dualism was born out of splitting off the soul from the physical body. From the moment dualism was codified, we have grappled with how these two antithetical sides can be reunited; the process is interactional. Descartes' belief in logical sequences and classifications had proposed the possible fallacies of the mind-body split as the ultimate dualism. CONNECTING man's perception of Self and the existence of God solved many mind-body problems. "Cogito ergo sum," a thing is true if it can be thought about clearly and distinctly, including God. Descartes' mechanistic system includes the foundations for physics, geometry, and chemistry. Berkeley, we will see later, was an idealistic philosopher, who supposed a second possibility, that the interactional question is superseded by a "none-ness" (Sherwood, 1987).

The third solution was to "banish the soul from the bodily machine" altogether as the materialist philosophers demanded. Did these ideas foreshadow the central gospel of modern neuroscience, namely that mental states result from bodily events, and that there is but one substance in the universe—matter [Hobbes]? In fact, both Frances Bacon and Thomas Hobbes believed in learning through

---

[10] "The Pythagoreans attempted the first grand synthesis. After them, the Enlightenment was instead representing the newly emerging, world-centric view, with its strong belief in scientific materialism, unilinear progress, commerce, and empiricism. The result was a titanic clash of memes, which eventually unleashed at least two revolutions (American and French) …with its emphasis on the universal rights of man. This was a profound move from ethnocentric to world centric…The Enlightenment sought an ego identity free from ethnocentric bias (the universal rights of man) and based on rational and scientific inquiry. Universal rights would fight slavery, democracy would fight monarchy, the autonomous ego would fight the herd mentality, and science would fight myth" (Koestler, 1964, pp. 81–86).

observations. Bacon was a believer in new method of knowledge and set up those "idols" which man should avoid in his search for truth:

1. The total dependence of man upon his cultural viewpoint.
2. Total subjectivity.
3. Dependence upon language.
4. Total belief in ideologies.

Hobbes believed that matter-in-motion was important and that through man's relationship to this matter he can know truth. He perceived man as a social animal but thought that man had given up some of his basic goals to make social living more convenient (Haradon, 1972c). Ultimately, self-interest was man's chief motivator; certain actions might result for which man had to take responsibility. Hobbes expanded Aristotle's ideas about association, showing that our chain of ideas follows cues even when they seem triggered by an "uncontrollable" thought.

Self-disclosure enables the experience of cosmic "potentiality", states of open-mindedness, and even allows man to drift into an unconscious sense of Self-direction. It then becomes a conscious choice to use the symbolisms (feelings and imagery found in one's own inner life). Ultimately, the discovery of one's uniqueness will show one how all things are CONNECTED.

Cosmology

The last fifty years have seen a surge in the use of withdrawal to use the time for the study of spiritual pursuits; meditation and the search for serenity and peace of mind came hand in hand during a time when AA and the Self-actualization movement in psychology were growing. In either case, learning about the Self brought light out of darkness. Much of this basic sense of Self was not new and came through a cosmography from thousands of years ago, based on an understanding of the four basic elements (plus reason and faith). As astronomy became more refined, the planets were integrated into this cosmography, which also related to the Bible as: Matthew/earth, Mark/water, Luke/air, John/fire, and Jupiter/power, Mars/hostility, Venus/desire, Mercury/avarice, and Moon/moist. Cosmological studies created a stabilizing point of reference for scholarly belief in Creation/Meaning. Much of this framework was generated in Constantinople/Istanbul during the Byzantium period of religious fervor and cultural growth beyond the Greek, Egyptians, and Romans.

While Europe was in the Dark Ages, this new point of view arose in the East as a response to the need to recognize and perhaps banish oversimplified views of how culture works. Finally, the new availability of literature allowed this illumination to be shared across arbitrary cultural boundaries and for the darkness of poverty and ignorance to be breeched. Once literature took hold, in European cultures, there was no going back. Original Greek thought spread; I refer you to the standard sources of knowledge about ancient Greek literature. In presenting the following summary, I recommend a fuller review of Greek writers/coursework or a book on an Introduction to Philosophy if this is an area of particular interest to the reader.

Philosophical Writings

The earliest known Greek writings are Mycenaean, written in the Linear B syllabary on clay tablets around 770 BCE, although the epic poems of Homer and other others are the earliest full writings known to exist. Trendy fictional literature was written in verse, while scientific literature was in prose. The three poetic genres known were: epic, lyric, and drama. A preliminary list of influential Greeks writers and categories of writing includes:

POETS

Homer: *The Iliad* about the Trojan War, the Homeric dialect was an archaic language based on Ionic dialect mixed with some element of Aeolic dialect and Attic dialect, the latter due to the Athenian edition of 6th century BCE.

Hesiod: His two works were *Works and Days* and *Theogony*.

Lyric Poets: Alcaeus and Sappho for the monadic lyric and Pindar for choral lyric, Ovid, later Roman poet.

DRAMATISTS

Three tragedies and one pastoral drama performed at the festivals of the god Dionysus

Aeschylus, Sophocles and Euripides and comedies of Aristophanes (*The Birds, The Clouds, Lysistrata*).

HISTORIANS

Herodotus: The Father of History, who wrote *Histories.*
Thucydides: *The Peloponnesian War.*

PHILOSOPHERS

Socrates, Plato, and Aristotle: Aristotle was virtually without rivals among scientists and philosophers, the first sentence of his *Metaphysies* reads: "All men by nature desire to know…to have a soul to have a body organized for performing the life functions proper to a given species…Soul is nothing more than the combination of functional capacities for which the material body is organized." There are also treatises on the Soul, Rhetoric, and Poetics.

Ptolemy I: *The Museum* or Shrine to the Muses which included the famous Alexandrian library and school.

Koine Greek: Gospels and the Epistles of Saint Paul.

Plutarch: Later Greek (CE119) Philosopher and historian who wrote *Parallel Lives*, biographies of great Greek and Roman leaders, which has been read by every generation since the work was first published, plus *Moralia*, a series of essays and transcribed speeches.

Pausanias: A geographer who gave useful descriptions of Greece.

Epictetus, Plotinus (transformed Plato's philosophy into a school called Neo-Platonism) *Enneads*, which focused on the inner nature of a God within, rather than the man-like God of the Christians.

I encourage the reader to pick one or two writers, perhaps Herodotus for history and Plutarch's lives of the great leaders, as a place to start grasping this period. This background will take you far into the subsequent theories of philosophy.

Empiricism

An empiricist is one who believes that all knowledge is derived from sensory experience. Our tendency is to "define", to be "empiricists". Scientists like to categorize what is observable, to operationalize concepts by linking them to a model where all terms have been defined and thus are knowable (empirical). Scientific concepts likewise are linked to experimental procedures thereby CONNECTING every empirically significant term to observables. Philosophers are still trying to define the Mind, which over the centuries has been the subject of study and discussion. Here is a summary/list of the three areas of concern, Mind, Body, and theories which are dualistic in nature. This list will serve as a kind of backbone to the rest of our discussion about philosophical ideas.

Mind-Body Problem
What the Mind Is

Plato stated that the mind could exist both before and after its residence in the body; his idea of pre-eminence of mind came from Anaxagoras. This idea was further developed by St. Augustine.

Descartes believed that the mind and body are both substances but different; he believed in an actual mental substance or pure ego. Mind is thinking, an unextended factor. He took away the spiritualistic, teleological, and animistic features of body concept; thus, the Body was extended, unthinking.

Locke created the idea of "empirical study" (*tabula rasa*) and questioned the substance of the Mind. Later, Hume created a "Bundle theory". Mind is "nothing but a bundle or collection of different perceptions, which succeed each other with an inconceivable rapidity, and are in a perpetual flux and movement" (*Treatise of Human Nature*, I, IV, 1738). The Mind related in "bundles by resemblance, contiguity and causation."

William James presented a theory of Unity of Mind in relation to body rather than its own internal CONNECTIONS which used stream of consciousness.

Brentano's studies of the Mind determined that mental phenomena are "intentional", they have content or contain an object in themselves.

Mind's Relation to Body
Monistic Theories

Materialism—whatever exists is physical.

Berkeley—asserted that the mind and the perceptions of those minds are the only things that exist; statements about perceptions of perceivers are sensate only.

Spinoza—view of man extended so that individuals were bodily things and thinking things but neither or both exhausted the underlying substance of man at "different levels", pantheistic monism (the dynamic, unity activity also seen as the principle underlying Gestalt theory).

Hume—viewed the Body as separate from Mind and as "bundles of perceptions".

James—felt the Body enjoyed "pure experience".

Dualistic Theories

Interactionism—two substances form a single system of mutually interacting components, mentalistic and physicalist expressions differ in reference as well as meaning.

Leibnitz—parallelism was a reaction to the objection that the mental and physical are too dissimilar to be causally CONNECTED. Parallelism was guided by "pre-established" harmony in the dualism of Mind and Body CONNECTING.

Wisdom: Potential and the Ideal

The inspiration for all these theories and scholarly pursuits seems to have been a search to explain man's potential. What man potentially is, versus actually is, has been a philosophical question for thousands of years. We will start with what the ancient Chinese and early Greeks speculated about man's nature. They also had their beliefs as to what man ideally should be.

The Chinese believed that both idealism and realism were forces in man's life. His cultural and spiritual progress was dependent upon the integration of his idealistic potentialities with his realistic level of wisdom, his use of humor, and his apparent sensitivity to life. They believed that the search for one's real Self was intrinsic to knowledge of any "ideal" (Haradon, 1974a). Everyday man sought knowledge of his Self through his life work, his ability to grow old gracefully, and his striving for a harmony of mind and body. Woman, in the Chinese culture, had a specific role in terms of their additional depth of personal being, their ability to be a mother and to care for the home.

Philosophically, the Chinese believed that the individual was a manifestation of the spirit, a gentle harmony in man or woman of the *Yang* (male) and *yin* (female). Perfect harmony in an individual was the ideal. Confucius (551 BCE) proposed that one should consciously rule over one's relationship to himself and others, just as he would his relationship to the world of nature around him. This he called "reasonable naturalism" (ibid, 1974a).

Plato, and many other Greek philosophers, saw man as a mixed component of desires, emotions, and thought. The ideal human life was living together with others in harmony, with wisdom guiding the interacting parts of one's spirituality. Not until one exercised "true understanding" was the human spirit freed from the mortal body, enabling man to transcend himself and enter the world of Forms (Hardy, 1990). Plato's Forms were immutable and eternal. "We are trapped inside a cave and know the world only through the shadows it casts on the wall" (Pinker, 1997).

Today we would call Plato's ideas a reference to a "virtual" world. Man became aware of a Form because, although his body might be finite and mortal, he had an ideal transcendent nature or essence. Plato exalted courage and temperance as ideal human qualities, but the major aid to freedom of the soul from the mortal body was CONNECTIVITY to wisdom, or the mind. Self-discipline allows a synthesis of the 1) will, and 2) duality of desires and knowledge.

According to quantum physics, when a wave turns into a particle (the basic step that brings photons, electrons, and other particles into the world) we experience the "real world", that which creates "reality" out of change and chaos (the flux of the wave). According to Plato, we are trapped inside that cave, but there is still lots of virtual energy that can become tangible. As we will see in Chapter Twelve, to compensate for the properties that vanish into thin air when a single property is observed, the other properties of subatomic particles are calculated as probabilities. [think Heisenberg's theory] (Pinker, 1997; Chopra & Kafatos, 2017, p. 89). Because everything is experiential, we must remember we cannot escape our subjectivity. We will return to the underlying importance of Heisenberg's theory many times throughout this book.

Centuries after the Greeks, Hume (1711–1776) and Sartre (1905–1980) wrote about experiences that take us "outside of ourselves". Hume believed knowledge consisted of being able to analyze our own perceptions and impressions, and all mental material came from these impressions (i.e., there are no innate ideas). Causation comes from human nature and is derived from experience; it is subjective, and the idea of "regularity" influences our inferences about cause and effect.

Sartre's theory of the infinite in the finite was a dualistic one. The appearance of the phenomenon is the essence of it. Sartre further divided the experience of "being" into two different levels "being-for-itself and being-in-itself" (Sartre, 1943).[11] These sentimental positions, perhaps, took us beyond the rational levels of such philosophers as Kant (1724–1804) who believed that "whatever is can also be known" (Heschel, 1965).

Centuries after Protagoras, Kant would expand the saying "Man is the measure of all things." He took this argument to its further conclusion that "possession of a good will is the only unconditioned good," which influenced Social Contracts theory. Kant would present a similar (but his own) idea of "collective conscious". Ultimately, we are not to confuse the structure of our reality with the structure of the words we try to use to explain it. Kant had a wide range of hypothetical thinking and the use of analogies, once being able to think beyond that which was eventual only in the present. I use metaphorical processing all the time as a therapist.

---

[11] "What in me remains identical throughout the changes and transformation to which I am subject, the forms of behavior, actions, and reactions? What does my own being mean to me? What confronts me when I ponder my being here and now?" (Heschel, 1965, pp. 30, 34).
"What is implied is that the being of phenomena cannot be subject to the phenomenal condition—what is to exist only in so far as it reveals itself—and that consequently it surpasses the knowledge, which we have of it and provides the basis of such knowledge" (Sartre, 1966, p. 1).

It is important that I get my patients to use their intuition and heart space as well as reasoning only. Because my goal is to lead them to a renewal of "Renaissance thinking" about responses to triggers and eventual healthier choices. I do not encourage knee-jerk reactions. An intuitive cognition may come as a flash or epiphany, but it is also useful to sit with the new information for awhile before using it to guide us on our journey. We can anticipate our compulsive reactions, creating a feeling of being in control.

An important aid in CONNECTING the writings of classic philosophical thought to the modern age of reason, and even to scientific thought, is to remember the original position of Thales and of Socrates (in *Phaedo* as reported by Plato) that "All things are full of gods." During the last few centuries, the importance of spiritual CONNECTIVITY weighed in favor of achievement and capitalism, except for the experience of religion, and maybe not with that always either. Now with the advent and support of neuroscience we find that reasoning follows, rather than precedes, our rapid and automatic thinking. Azar (2010) states that "Philosophy lost its empirical bent sometime in the early part of the last century. We're trying to bring back that true empirical spirit by making discoveries that tie together philosophical questions with what we know about the human mind and how it influences human behavior" (ibid, 2010, pp. 40–44). Goleman (2005) has called this emotional intelligence (IQ).

The Greeks tried to bring rational thought out of the previous influences of mythology and religion. Early Greek explorers had noted these influences as they interpreted the world they were experiencing. They wanted to create a system of thought that was beyond the capricious nature of the gods that defined their previous limited understanding of science. Science was becoming the predominant course of study by Greek philosophers.

Part of the underlying principles of my unified field theory (UFT) of how we develop is that man and nature are CONNECTED by the unifying laws that control the universe. Because man is a part of nature, it logically follows that the study of the "basic material" of the world would eventually become the scientific method. Some of these early philosopher/scientists were Thales (water is essential to life), Anaximander (all things are made from the same—unnamed—stuff) whose theory is the basis of modern atomic theory, Anaximenes (the basic stuff is air), Heraclitus (the basic material is fire, and laws are fixed and nature changes according to law—you can never repeat an experience exactly [Heisenberg]), Parmenides (like is perceived by like, "Mind is a part of nature and perceives things in nature like it"), Anaxagoras (wrote the first book on Natural Science, stating that the universe is made up of a number of primary, unchangeable substances—he sought to give structure to the Universe), Democritus (created a theory actually based on atoms as the basis of the universe), Hippocrates (believed man could be freed from superstition by a medical knowledge of health and illness), Socrates (who first pointed out a later Freudian concept of the dualistic nature in man between passion (emotions) and reason (intellect), and Plato (furthered Socrates ideas that absolute knowledge is found in reason—he was the first to recognize that the sense organs, especially feelings, arose in the abdomen).

From our discussion of Plato, we move on to Aristotle's scientific ideas, including those which would become the very foundation of the study of psychology (*De Anima* or *On the Soul*—350 BC). Aristotle studied laws of association, impact of memory, sensation and perception, cause and effect (of which the final cause is reason), and the four forms of life that make up the "primary soul" (nutrition, sensation and perception, creative power, and the life of reason). He felt the unity of life and mind must not be broken.

As the study of philosophy developed beyond the Greeks, Neoplatonic hypostases (or levels of reality), "the One, the Intellect, and the Soul" became a structural foundation for describing our interaction (CONNECTION) with our environment and with each other. This CONNECTION starts with attachment through an experience because of the Soul.[12]

Wisdom

Wisdom has been defined in different ways by different cultures: the Greeks, the Christians, the Chinese and Buddhists and anthropologists. The early Greek term, *logos*, means God in every man, a kind of transcendent freedom of the spirit, an ability to use one's intellect to overcome the temporality of the environment. By this transcendence, man understands the "essence" of the universe, using the power innate within him and his innate need to feel a part of the One universe. Christians advanced this concept, creating an anthropomorphized version of God, with the figure of Jesus representing an opportunity for a direct understanding of God through "knowing" Jesus and his good works. Jesus was not only wise about his place in history, but he also demonstrated self-control and will in his own life, through sacrifices and crucifixion. He represents the concrete actualization of "ideal goodness".

The Chinese believed wisdom to be the highest kind of thinking. Wisdom was a combination of Reality + Drama + Humor. One tones down his dreams or idealism with a good sense of humor, supported by reality itself, and this outcome creates the "wise" person, the ideal character. Wisdom exercises control over foolish ambitions, and courage enables us to carry out those ambitions, which, through our wisdom, we determine to be productive and honorable.

For Buddhists, wisdom (*prajna*) was the infinite totality of things. Wisdom used intuition to recognize that which transcends all our individualistic experiences. My own belief about wisdom is like the Greeks and complimentary to that of the principles of *prajna*. A wise person comprehends his place in the universe by transcending his own consciousness and by being open to that knowledge which is available to him about the nature of others. It is not mere

---

[12] An article in the *NY Review* (11/1/2001) reminds us that through Bertrand Russell's classic history of Western Philosophy, "the dream of reason which motivates philosophical thinking seems merely a mirage. When it succeeds, it becomes science—and ceases to be called philosophy." Democritus simply made it all up and luckily turned out to be right…This seemingly scientific philosophy grew straight from the dark and incredible notions of Parmenides…A history without regard for truth is a history of ideas, not a history of philosophy, and judgments of truth can only be made from the viewpoint of the present" (*NY Review*, 11/1/2001).

coincidence that both the Chinese and Greek ideals were wisdom, truth, and harmony with oneself and nature. I believe that these are the true ideals.

I might also add the idea of "quality" to that as in making a qualitative assessment (Pirsig, 1974). Rabindranath Tagore, in *The Call of Truth* (1961), wrote that "man's inner nature not only finds success in its activity, but there it also has its joy." He insists on penetrating further and further "into the depths, from the obvious to the hidden, from the easy to the difficult, from parasitism to self-determination, from the slavery of his passions to the mastery of himself" (ibid, 1961, p. 254). Supreme values are truth, beauty, and goodness, and through the harmony of a well-balanced personality, one can act with equality to the rest of the world around him.

Self-Reflection and Natural Evolution

From a more recent Western philosophical viewpoint, Martin Buber (1945) reminds us that man can contemplate himself as part of the universe, a characteristic distinctly human in nature, and that it is this self-reflection and the freedom obtained through understanding which is ideal (Wood, 1969). [Again, very close to the Eastern and Greek ideals]. Buber believes that it is this ability for self-reflection that leads to the individuation process.

Elizabeth Borgese (1963), in the *Ascent of Woman*, maintains that the individual/collective dichotomy is represented literally by the man/woman dichotomy. Evolution proceeds through the woman, as the child-bearing agent, and therefore she is more social and more interested in the group. Borgese believes that both individualization and socialization have been important elements of natural evolution but have also caused a polarization between man and woman. Although evolution is almost always described in masculine terms, it is the feminine qualities of cooperation and need for organization that have supported the human survival of the fittest. There was finally a point in human evolution when size and strength were less important, and aggressive struggle became "dysfunctional".

Using the supplementary belief that wisdom and knowledge are the ideal human qualities proposed by every other philosophical group as well, woman would indeed have to be considered as superior. Ashley Montagu (1950) maintained that the ideal relationship is one between a man and woman in which the man appreciates the woman and shares his life with her in the same way he shares the sexual experience. Montagu, however, does not consider wisdom to be the ideal human quality. Rather, love and truth are the ideals according to him, and man is not inherently bad but inherently good. Man's survival has been based on cooperation, altruism, the ability to remember the learning of the past and the capacity to understand the importance of accumulated achievements (he calls this "inherited wisdom").

The American writer, Pearl Buck (1892–1973), writes beautifully about the relationship between a man and a woman, which when completed by a child becomes fertile for the true harmony. This balance within the "family" is Buck's ideal. She discusses the meaning of woman's new role, the new cultural equality with man, and the new sex morals. She sees the changes as a new appreciation of sex, by both the man and the woman; recognition of that moment of recognition is the unique and ideal act of sharing and balance.

The world is not just experienced as rational stimuli (far be it for me to disagree with the empiricists, but I am not alone). In graduate school, I kept a journal in which I wrote about how my study of classical philosophers influenced me. In one journal entry, I laid out the foundation of the "types" of Philosophy and how the ideas had been formulated, as my naïve Self at that time saw them.

There were four basic ideas among the early Greek philosophers. The first group were the Naturalists, led by Democritus, who believed that man is ruled by his environment and that nature is the most important factor in reality. The second group, the humanists, were led basically by the Sophists, who believed that self-identity and man's political and social action were the most important ideas. The Sophists stressed rhetoric and persuasion.

The third group were the systematic philosophers, who believed that reality could best be found through a combination of nature and self-identity. Socrates, Plato, and Aristotle led this group. The fourth group, the practical philosophers, were the Epicureans, Stoics and Skeptics. The Epicureans believed in the idea of pleasure and lived for the present and immediate future. The Stoics believed in faith in the eternal and based their system of beliefs on reason. The Skeptics maintained that knowledge can never be gained with certainty and all thought contains doubt (Haradon, 1971a).

In the Stoic tradition, thought ruled over emotions and this philosophy became the design of much of Western philosophy. As I have stated in my theory of a UFT, an integration of all psychological processes is necessary and predictable, including how thinking works with emotions to create healthy self-consciousness. Other classical philosophers influenced many of my ideas to come: the Naturalists tried to harmonize man's relation to God and Nature; the Sophists encouraged persuasion as a political and social way of life and could be later seen in the ideas of men like Machiavelli and Hobbes; Plato was an idealist, living in a dualistic world of ideas and things, whereas Aristotle believed in the reality of the one natural world. These idealists were involved in the problematic dichotomies between the establishment of their time and their ideas as inventive individuals. Their solutions were often studied during the Medieval and Renaissance period as examples of well-organized observations of reality.

Medieval Influences and the Catholic Church

Another influence upon the later philosophers was the Roman Catholic Church of the Medieval period. The church based its control during the Medieval period on certain traditions which had been passed down and which held an unquestionable position as Truth. These ideas were: (1) the idea of original sin (Garden of Eden); (2) the role of Jesus in the salvation of man; (3) the concept that man can only be free and responsible through Christ; (4) the idea that man earns grace through the sacraments and the Holy Spirit; (5) the idea of predestination; and (6) the belief that the church received authority through the Bible, church Patriarchs and oral tradition.

The Medieval church also took over education and the schools; thus, it was able to mold the culture. The triumvirate taught linguistics: grammar, rhetoric, and dialectic; the quadrivium taught the scientific aspects: arithmetic, music, geometry, and astronomy. By molding the culture of that time, the church was able to instill those ideas most important to its existence: (1) that faith should preside over reason; (2) that the church had a rightful authority over the individual; and (3) that the clergy had a duty to be placed over the laymen (which developed into a type of caste system). Scholasticism grew out of these conflicting ideas, which related the dogmas of faith to the need of the culture of the day. These ideas emphasized belief in the other world and deduction as the logical path toward truth.

Augustine's ethics (354 CE) rested on the idea of happiness and that man could achieve happiness through the four virtues of wisdom, obedience, celibacy, and justice. Augustine was exposed to other ideologies; his mother was a Christian and his father was a pagan. As described by St. Augustine, the epistemological points of discovery and metaphysical points regarding God's relevance, as described by St. Augustine, tried to prove God's existence and that God is real, known through his nature. Later, Machiavelli would demonstrate the relationship between good and evil, and Neo-Platonism would focus on mysticism and alchemy as much as upon Christian values or the Pauline principles.

The philosophers in the Medieval period questioned the right of faith to preside over reason. Anselm (1033) was an idealist who believed faith was sent by authority (*credo ut intelligenia*), while Abelard (1079) was a Rationalist who believed reason was the place to begin in searching for the truth (*Intelligo ut credium*). Finally, St. Aquinas (1225) believed the problem was on both levels; he joined faith and reason in looking for his solution. Another problem facing philosophers at the time was in the belief in Will versus the belief in Intellect. The Orthodox Catholic school believed reason and intellect to be superior, while the unorthodox mystics believed that the will was more important.

The metaphysical position dealt with the idea of universals. The realists believed that universals were eternal (*anti rem*). The Conceptualists believed that the thing conceived the idea, and the idea contained the very essence of the thing (*in rem*). The Nominalists believed that the universal has no real CONNECTION with the essence of a thing and that ideas are only names (*post rem*). The final problem was that of Grace versus Nature, or Supernatural versus Natural. One group believed natural things should be studied and truths should be realized as they occur, while an opposing group clung to the idea that knowledge comes as a special gift from God.

Epistemology and Reality

Epistemology is the study of philosophical issues regarding knowledge; it is an important concept because it CONNECTS with what the Greeks believed about reality. It is only in time and space (not tangible existence) that we understand cause and effect, only the temporal relational aspects of it (all is "relative"). Empirical knowledge is the first step to understanding, but not the totality of knowledge; it is only a small part of the foundation with which we build insight, memory, and schema. For instance, Socrates believed that clarity (truth) is more important than ultimate reality.

Existentialists of the 20th century would say that facts (raw existence) are more important than the symbols (words) we use to explain them. Beingness is in a paradox with the "transitive" ongoing-ness of the Self. Alan Watts (1915–1973) summed up the argument about reality by saying: "Man's trouble comes from identifying with something outside himself rather than with that which is within…In other words, the ego is not really a self at all; it is simply a function of that inner universe" (Watts, 1940, p. xxii).[13] Or as Van Dusen puts it: "The most profound tendency of the psyche is to represent itself" (Van Dusen, 1971, p. 4).

What was most important to me during my own studies of philosophy and my scholarly development was an awareness of how different each philosopher's point of view could be (as much as the similarity). I began to realize that only I could decide for myself what my own viewpoint ultimately would be; I would develop my own cohesive role in perpetuating my own identity in the further development of my Self (UFT). My unique and innate ideas could be related to perceptions as they were experienced.

As mentioned above, "outside of ourselves" experiences and perceptions are of two kinds and are on two levels. Perhaps, it can be compared with Sartre's "being-for-itself" and "being-in-itself;" can man ever even know his own mind? "All of man's ideas and impressions come from his perceptions…creative ideas are only results of the use of the imagination to assimilate perceptions already known" (Sartre, 1943). My own point of view is that thought not grounded in experience is possible, and this point of view will be fleshed out further below.

Man's freedom is in his ability to recognize the stimulus/response pattern and to break it—just for the hell of it. This process is where animal studies break down in relation to those using humans. Because man is rational, he can, through his own volition, act irrationally. We have an innate or pre-recognition of ideas. We know (recognize?) before we observe. How we can relate the experience to other concepts—and formulate a relational idea of what the concept is not—is imperative to recognize and eliminate differences. This process of recognition can especially be seen in the writings of William Blake.

William Blake's Philosophy

In *On Dreams and Death* (1984), Marie-Louise Von Franz wrote about Blake's "*mundus imaginealis*" (Body of God in man), a subject which was indeed the central theme of his writings and his art. Blake found his existence was one "of faculties dimmed, of possibilities denied and energies foreclosed…He never found it easy to compete with the rest of the world… [what he experienced was] nervous fear" [emphasis added] (Ackroyd, 1996, p. 21). Blake addressed the distinction that earlier philosophers had made between perception and experience, whether through actual vision or "recall" memory. He felt memory was not only an aspect of time but could be a "visionary space" as well.

---

[13] The full quote here is: "They say that if the ego can be made to look into itself, it will see that its own true nature is deeper than itself, that it derives its faculties and its consciousness from a source beyond individual personality. In other words, the ego is not really a self at all; it is simply a function of that inner universe" (Watts, 1940, p. xxii).

Ackroyd related how Blake read Bacon and Locke but mocked them by a belief in inspiration and vision. The "true soil of his genius" was that he truly believed in man's uniqueness and creativity. Blake eventually was able to fashion a mythic system of his own through his poetry and his writing.

> 'Inspiration and vision was then, and now is, and I hope will always remain my element—my eternal dwelling place'…It was an aspect of Blake's adversarial nature but it was also a part of his genius: no one could have single-handedly created such an elaborate and distinctive mythology [as he did], without a stubborn sense of uniqueness and self-certainty…Man brings all that he has or can have into the world with him. Man is born like a garden ready planted and sown. This world is too poor to produce one seed… [Blake believed in the] Protestant ethic that is inspired by the virtues of self-help and obedience, but it may equally be the first indication of his passionate desire to create a cloistered and separate identity…Blake was a synthesizer, like so many of his generation, but was his own synthesis designed to establish his own belief? (ibid, 1996, pp. 23, 59).

Blake had a bewildering range of feelings that swept over him on certain occasions; but much of his prophetic symbolism can be understood without undue difficulty. If the reader allows the experience of "a clear and simple vision," Blake may appear to be a difficult poet to read but well worth the effort. [14]

Blake's search for the divine showed up in his blending of the arts, poetry, and visuals, as well as in his CONNECTION between art, industrial economics, and what would become the "consumer societies" of modern civilization. He created an analysis that was not otherwise formulated until the present century. He gave it shape and substance. Powers of memory and the imagination create art and, in Blake's non-Newtonian universe, are not abstract forces but spiritual beings.

Blake sought "a work of no mind," a concept we will discuss at length in Chapter Four (Wilber) and Chapter Nine regarding Buddhism. He was intent upon destroying the belief that there is some distinction between conception and execution—as an artist, Blake embraced the ideals of the Greeks, the exquisite marbles, use of travertine tile (the Greeks went to Italy to get their marbles, an activity which increased the assimilation of different cultures through travel). Later, the Romans would enlarge the architectural mastery of the Greeks, bringing three-dimensional innovations to Greek two-dimensional style: arches, vaulted ceilings, and use of geometry. The Romans may have gotten their art and religion from the Greeks, but their positive influences upon Greek form grew forward into the Neo-classical period after Pompeii was discovered (1748). Obviously, Blake (1757–1827) participated in this fervor.

Man is a social animal, but his world is fragmented by his various roles, and he is not able to formulate (only) one style of life; he may be "stuck" in a value

---

[14] "'Knowledge of Ideal Beauty; is not to be acquired, it is born with us, innate ideas are in everyman born with him…man brings all that he has or can have into the world with him…he who does not know truth at sight is unworthy of her notice…the man who never in his mind and thought raveled to Heaven is no Artist'" (ibid, 1996, p. 285).

system that cannot withstand rigidity, the tendency toward fragmentation is ever-present. How is he able to hold on to an "ideal" or strive toward one goal? Can a man, whose life is made up of fragmented roles to which he must continuously adjust, find the openness of mind for true contemplation of the Real? Perhaps interrelational CONNECTION is the Real, i.e., the learning curve to subjective experience versus the absolutes: Truth, Love, Beauty, Justice, and Freedom. Does true belief always lead to understanding? I recommend, on occasion, an escape from the moving world into the world of contemplation for true understanding of the Real.

In comparing the process of conception to perception, we find that man indeed may need to escape from himself, from his desires which might block the way to true understanding, and from any irrational behavior that might cause him to falter from attainment of his goal. It is also possible to use a strong desire in the pursuit of knowledge. Does the passion that comes with contemplation also give understanding? I think that often it can. In a sensible/intelligible world the question arises, how can desire be "rational?" A book by Garth Stein, *The Art of Racing in the Rain* (2008), presented eloquently the simple idea that one is more free, flexible, and non-fragmented by sometimes letting go of the distortion in perception of the Real.

One creates one's own philosophy to react spontaneously. And not just in a life of solitude either, but the moments of mindfulness serve as a backdrop to conception. Remembering the usefulness of Plato's Forms, one can contextualize a philosophy of one's values and how one is going to "race", i.e., find a personal methodology that results in a purpose to life which results in real emotional freedom!

For me, this is the meaning of the Joseph Addison's (1672–1719) quote: "The three grand essentials to happiness in this life are: something to do, something to love, and something to hope for."

A Behavioral Viewpoint

As I did in college, I continue to take issue with a purely "behavioral" point of view. Man has needs, which I have viewed taking an unconscious or independent and preemptive effect over his behavior. For instance, decision, choice, or interpretation are all cognitive processes; although they can be reinforced to a certain degree (according to B.F. Skinner 1904–1990), they cannot really be controlled in Skinner's sense of the word. Manipulation without possible behavioral prediction he calls "Self-determination" [emphasis added]. Skinner believes that many of the same techniques used in the control of others are used in self-control. I believe, however, that there is a difference between the manipulation of public stimuli to control the behavior involved in someone else's decision-making and the manipulation of one's own behavior.

We are constantly striving to realize and actualize our uniqueness and individuality, and yet I know of no one who is not dependent on someone else for something and is not afraid of being alone. We depend on others because it is only through relationships that we can know more about ourselves…Our self 'concept' is that personality which we consciously develop because of a relationship. The level of self-stimulation produced by reinforcement cannot be measured…The failure of a response to be reinforced leads not only to operant extinction but also to a reaction commonly spoken of as frustration or rage…Skinner cannot satisfactorily explain 'understanding' any better than he has explained thought, emotion, or Self…The problem becomes apparent when Skinner tries to predict future behavior (Haradon, 1972d).

Each of us is unique. We have the potential to create, which is the result of any thought, and a complete, whole, creation is the goal of every human being. The uniqueness and potential each of us has is actualized in this creation. A finished product is important, but it is striving which gives meaning to life. Creating involves a continual growth and heightens awareness. More importantly, expression gains new dimensions when experienced again through someone else.

For some, living in the present and being real are mutually exclusive. As a fair notion of an opposing viewpoint, we can look at B.F. Skinner's representation of how all behavior can be conditioned and soul is not a valued variable. In 1970, Noam Chomsky (born 1928—), the famous linguist and philosopher, wrote a piece in the *New York Review of Books* entitled, "The Case against B.F. Skinner". In it, he refers to Skinner's position as "raciology;" to believe that what a person does is fully determined by his genetic endowment and history of reinforcement is totalitarian thinking.

Skinner imposes certain arbitrary limitations on scientific research which virtually guarantee continued failure…If indeed freedom and dignity are merely the relics of outdated mystical beliefs, then what objection can there be to narrow and effective controls instituted to ensure 'the survival of culture'…We have the physical, biological, and behavioral technologies needed 'to save ourselves;' the problem is how to get people to use them…It is a fact Skinner maintains, that 'Behavior is shaped and maintained by its consequences' and that as the consequences contingent on behavior are investigated, more and more they are taking over the explanatory functions previously assigned to personalities, states of mind, feelings, traits of character, purposes and intentions (Chomsky, 1971, pp. 1–2).

No behaviorist, and no modern-day psychologist, would argue against the fact that human behavior is a function of "conditions, environmental or genetic". The area of concern is that, even though behavior may be related to antecedent events, free choice may have been only marginally affected by the "environmental contingencies". Although Skinner would call these the "probability of response", it might be just as likely to label these responses as Outlier behavior patterns or unstable internal states. Madeo (2011) calls this asymmetrical thinking.

The libertarians and humanists whom Skinner scorned object to totalitarianism out of respect for freedom and dignity. But Skinner argues in *Beyond Freedom and Dignity* (1971) that these notions are merely the residue of traditional mystical beliefs and must be replaced by the stern scientific notions of behavioral analysis. However, there exists no behavioral science incorporating empirically supported propositions that are not trivial and that apply to human affairs or support behavioral technology (Chomsky, 1971). Autonomous man has not only the right to choose, but he also has the dignity to refuse if he has been learning about how his "Outlier" behavior fits into the greater society. His choices are more obvious when we consider the real social world, in which determinable probabilities of response are so slight as to have virtually no predictive value.

> Skinner confuses 'science' with terminology…The tendencies in our society that lead toward submission to authoritarian rule may prepare individuals for a doctrine that can be interpreted as justifying it…The problems that Skinner discusses—it would be more proper to say 'circumvents'—are often real enough. In spite of his curious belief to the contrary, his libertarian and humanist opponents do not object to 'design of a culture', that is, to creating social forms that will be more conducive to the satisfaction of human needs, though they differ conducive to the satisfaction of human needs, though they differ from Skinner in their intuitive perception of what these needs truly are. They would not, or at least should not, oppose scientific inquiry or, where possible, its applications, though they will no doubt dismiss the travesty that Skinner presents (ibid, 1971, p. 16).

Armed with such valuable points of view from such deep thinkers, we may begin to formulate our own world view. We have become aware that a balanced viewpoint requires an understanding and explanation of our mental, physical, and spiritual experiences. Attempting to CONNECT and integrate, many writers have bravely called this process the knowing of Self or "Truth". We can see, then, that the basic principles of philosophy, religion, and metaphysics may be understood in two entirely different ways. They can be seen as symbols of the undivided mind, or as expressions of the Truth that in each moment life and experience are a complete whole. "'God' is not a definition of state of experience but an exclamation about it." Secondly, however, these expressions are used as "attempts to stand outside oneself and the universe to grasp them and to rule them. The process is circular, however complex and devious" (Watts, 1951, p. 148). Historically, the *Ouroboros*, or circular snake appearing to "eat its own head," represented this process of completeness or wholeness.

Other theorists/philosophers might not go as far as declaring they had a grasp of "Truth" but would strive for the discovery of "meaning" through their studies. Even the Bible refers to the relation between healthy mind/body/spirit.

Biblical References

Proverbs 17:22 A cheerful heart does good like medicine
Proverbs 13:12 Hope deferred makes the heart sick
Proverbs 15:13 A broken heart crushes the spirit
Proverbs 17:22 A broken spirit makes one sick

The inspiration for all this "thoughtfulness" and scholarly pursuit seemed to have been a search to explain man's potential. What man is potentially versus actually has been a philosophical question for thousands of years. In the next chapter, we will see how the philosophers of the Christian Middle Ages based their beliefs as to what man ideally should be upon what the early Greeks and Asian cultures had speculated about man's nature.

Chapter Three
Revelations

"Simplicity, then, is the expression of unity; and the search for simplicity as the expression of unity in nature was a humanist idea"
– (Bronowski & Mazlish, 1960, p. 115)

An outline of contributions from the humanist period underscores a very evident finding: that we have yet to come about upon ourselves. More than gaining access to the hidden secrets of the Universe we need to "remember" what we intuitively already knew.

The Mind is Revealed

We now jump back to the 13th century and the influence of earlier Christian philosophers. St. Thomas Aquinas (1225–1274) believed that, in addressing reason, he could point the way to a type of revelation, through faith, to which people could relate. This revelation helped disclose the church's meaning for the sizable pagan population during the Dark Ages. His system of Theological Philosophy provided "proofs" based on this logical and reasoned system, incorporating the combined ethics of Aristotle and Augustine before him. Matter was real, and knowledge could be accepted as gained from the senses; man must follow God, but also his own conscience. Aquinas felt he could provide an explanation for his "way to truth", based on:

1. Eternal laws
2. Natural laws
3. Civic Laws
4. Conscience
5. The Bible

Subsequently, Aquinas included acceptance of the laws of ancient nature and that of medieval God alike. He also wrote of a view toward modern man, one that stated man must use his intellect rather than going only on authority. Aquinas stated that power is in God, potentiality is in humans.

Some say man's quest is for power and influence, not only a humanistic search for comfort. This position takes us next to Erasmus (1467), whose belief in personal piety led him to create a philosophy which stated: the imitation of Christ was more important than seeking salvation directly. Erasmus had an interest in learning the original languages, which related to the period of Biblical growth; he also encouraged learning to read in Latin and Greek by others beyond just the clergy.

With this shift in view toward an expanse of intellectual potential, a parallel objectification of individuals unfortunately resulted in a denial of human value, loss of personal freedom, and the resultant alienation that came from an individual becoming "part of" a general community's code of conduct. A spirit of competition instead of cooperation (man against man instead of man to man and man to/with himself) had been reinforced within the feudal system because it benefited both the lords and the church equally (see History as presented in Chapter Five). It was not until the period following the Great Plague (1347–1350) that individuals began to live out their own need for a sense of Self, even if that set of values was based on pure survival.

Early in the Renaissance, Hobbes (1588–1679) wrote that there was no absolute right and wrong (a new liberal attitude for that time). Hobbes' materialism implied a "doctrine of causality, ultimately developed into a rigid determinism."[15] His basic credo, "One cannot perceive anything but motion," represented his belief in objective reality, materialism, and causality (ibid, 1960).

Descartes (1596–1650) added skepticism and the need for proof (control) to the philosophical world after Hobbes. He even questioned the validity of his own writing in that "words are symbols, which cannot be used without overtones and multiple meanings" (Descartes, 1641). You see here the early influence of analysis, process, and definition over pure experience or emotional responsiveness. In the second part of Descartes' treatise (*Meditation II*), senses/concepts/God are all part of the objective (observed) and subjective (imagined) possibilities of mental experience. Descartes maintained that man is a thinking being, but he is also dependent on substance [both meanings of the word: 1—a particular kind of matter with uniform properties; 2—the quality of being important]. He thought man-made CONNECTIONS, through the pineal gland and the word "psychosomatic", grew from this idea.

In Descartes' scheme, the material universe does not consist of separate pieces: he was opposed to any atomic theory. For him, matter is continuous, has unlimited divisibility, and fills everything…Thus Descartes introduces a deep cleavage between the inward look into mind and the outward look into matter… He establishes a sharp dualism between mind and matter, in which self-consciousness is the property of mind and extension of matter (ibid, 1960, pp. 226–228).[16]

CONNECTING what one experiences with one's interests regarding external and social bonds requires a different definition of "commonality". Even during Descartes' time some felt there could be a commonality in the interest of

---

[15] "Standing alone, Hobbes' theory of causality would earn him respect. Perhaps we can summarize his accomplishment by saying that, single-handed, he translated the method and ideas of the new science of the seventeenth century into the general explanation of man and the universe" (ibid, 1960, p. 199).

[16] "My first rule was to accept nothing as true which I did not clearly recognize to be so: to accept nothing more than what was presented to my mind so clearly and distinctly that I could have no occasion to doubt it. The second rule was to divide each problem or difficulty into as many parts as possible. The third rule was to commence my reflections with objects which were the simplest and easiest to understand, and rise thence, little by little to knowledge of the most complex. The fourth rule was to make enumerations so complete, and reviews so general, that I should be certain to have omitted nothing…" (4 rules of logic—*Discourse on Method*, 1637).

individuals; "to wish to separate oneself from it is to wish to destroy oneself." Freedom and self-control were believed to be too much of a burden for some people. Church leaders used this justification to keep power from the common individuals of the broader community, with a dependence still on leaders of the church.

Following Descartes, Pascal (1623–1662) concluded that ultimately, we can understand nothing. We can understand neither the nature of the universe nor our own personality. As Pascal said: "Man is altogether incomprehensible by man…I know nothing, and of that which knows nothing of me, I am terrified…the eternal silence of those infinite spaces alarms me" (Pascal, 1973). According to Bronowski and Mazlish, Pascal had moods of despair and fear of abandonment. Those experiences of pious resignation to the will of God, the authors point out, can be just as depressing as the mood of more obvious despair. "The heart has its reasons that reason knows not…the logic of the heart was different from the logic of reason, but no less logical" (ibid, 1960, p. 236).

From a more humanistic point of view, the continental rationalists (Leibniz and Spinoza) are often linked with the kind of methodology and dogma that might be later seen in the Freudian theory I will describe in Chapter Thirteen. Leibniz (1646–1716) maintained that the Self is unique, but also is in relationship with the world as a total CONNECTION (mutual harmony).

Spinoza (1632–1677) defended liberty of thought and speech in theology and government. *Ethics* (Spinoza, 1677) presents a format closest to this concept. He stated God is the only cause of itself, therefore is a true substance. [This point of view continues into the 21st century]. Other more "finite" substances are attached to, not derived from, this substance. This Pantheistic viewpoint argues that substance becomes "a thing I know not what (it is).[17] Fulfillment directs understanding and knowledge toward relating to a God-directed and ethical way of responding. Spinoza believed that the psychology of man had two levels: man as mind or reason and man as emotion or passion driven. Every man is bound by these two factors and is caused to error and lose his freedom because of them" (ibid, 1960).

The Reformation and Enlightenment

Because of the way we gain knowledge, and reevaluation of knowledge after the Dark Ages, inevitably led to reform (which is more permanent than just temporary recovery). Luther, Calvin and other religious leaders are commonly known to have influenced the course of social and political history by their attempts to change the church's hold over the common man. Other philosophers,

---

[17] It is easy to see the Jewish influence in Spinoza's writings, in that he addresses social conventions sometimes tongue-in-check and is much more invested in love of God and respect for neighbors than in institutional religion, which he felt should be subordinated to the state. He defended an individual's right to have a private religion.

such as Montesquieu and Rousseau, also presented ideas about individualism and the humanism of the individual Self.[18]

Rousseau (1712–1778) bisected the philosophical movements of this time. His ideas may have come from his feeling of not belonging to his elite class. He perhaps attempted to justify his position by saying that man is naturally good, and that it is through institutions alone that man becomes bad. He spoke "in praise of ignorance", and about "the natural goodness of the common people". He appeared to have a greater insight into the hearts of simple people than other aristocratic philosophers. He contributed to what we call the "Romantic Movement" where men were influenced by emotions and sentiments, not logic and reason, and they were encouraged to "respond to the promptings of their heart and to the inner voice of conscience" (ibid, 1960, p. 290). His writings influenced Thomas Jefferson very much as can be seen in the Declaration of Independence.

Rousseau never lost his nostalgia for childhood. He presented his own radical view of children and the way they should be educated in an essay considered so dangerous at the time that it was initially banned throughout Europe. "Although born a man in some respects, I long remained a child and in many other respects I am one still," Rousseau confessed. The transition from child to adult, from natural man to social citizen, was one he never wished to make.[19] He truly believed that man's nature is what it is and what it is potentially. He lived as he wrote, demonstrating that the general will is the will of the whole (CONNECTION).

Rousseau's *Reveries of the Solitary Walker* (1778) had a profound effect on the educated man of the 18th century who could not only read it, and meditate upon its theses, but could use its paradigm to manifest changes in his own world. Rousseau's theory of modern man and the Hero myth was that of the Hero as a man of letters who could not only find his inner Self but could express this knowledge in a written form. His walks allowed him to gain a degree of serenity, even though it was an event, sad as it was unexpected, which had left him in a state of "total calm". He lost his respect for his society, which he felt had rejected him.

Once, for a short time, he had been able to fully engulf himself while living in harmony with someone else. However, having real periods of anxiety and isolation (usually self-imposed), his walks were meant to be successive variations of his soul, which he called "a state where the soul can find a resting place" (ibid, 1778).

---

[18] Montesquieu (1689–1755) tried to reconcile the new scientific method with the political changes taking place. "What is called unity in a political body is a very ambiguous thing; true unity is a harmonious one, through which all the parts, opposed as they may appear to us, concur in the general good of the society; like dissonances in music, they concur in the total harmony" (ibid, 1960, p. 270). If only our present politicians had read Montesquieu (sic).

[19] Perhaps it wasn't his childhood that let him down, but his adulthood, society, and politics. "Oh, if I could still enjoy some of those moments of pure and heart-felt affection, even in a little child, if I could still see in someone's eyes the joy and satisfaction of being with me, how these brief but happy effusions of the heart would compensate me for my many troubles and afflictions! No longer should I have to seek among animals the kind looks that humanity now refuses me!" (Rousseau, 1778).

A summary of his famous reveries is presented. Representations of a man's struggle with inner CONNECTIONS, they are also a mapping of the issues to be more fully addressed throughout this book.

1. [life]…incomprehensible chaos where I can make nothing out, and the more I think about my present situation, the less I can understand what has become of me, I enmeshed myself further in my attempts to be free, and constantly gave them new holds on me which they took good care not to neglect…it is easier to accept those misfortunes which befall in reality [learned helplessness] than to suffer regarding those which I fear. The threat is far worse than the blow. When they happen, I find them far less formidable than I had feared, and even in the midst of my suffering I feel a sort of relief.

Here Rousseau's attempts at freedom are contrasted with his resolve to accept his destiny much as one would see with the "turning one's will over" proposed in the 12-step model. He shows an awareness of an individual's potential to catastrophize when too internally focused.

2. Was it not for the hope of a state to which I aspire because I feel that it is mine by right, I should now live only in the past? No food left on the earth for my soul, I gradually learned to feed it on its own substance and seek all its nourishment within myself. Entirely in the present, I could remember nothing of the past; I had a distinct notion of myself as a person, not had I the last idea of what had just happened to me. I did not know who I was, or where I was; I felt neither pain, fear, nor anxiety. I felt throughout my whole being such a wonderful calm, that whenever I recall this feeling, I can find nothing to compare with it in all the pleasure that stirs our lives.

Rousseau has become more and more alienated and shows depression because of his sense of helplessness and lack of personal or social CONNECTEDNESS.

3. "Growing older, I learn all the time." Why did I not remain in that foolish yet blessed faith, which made me for so many years the prey and plaything of my vociferous friends…I would never attain the state to which my heart aspired. It was only after years of anxiety, when I finally pulled myself together and began to be myself again, that I felt the value of the resources I had made ready against adversity…And I shall be happy if by my own self-improvement I learn to leave life, not better, for that is impossible, but more virtuous than when I entered it.

Rousseau is beginning to show insight about depending upon his own resources rather than upon the external CONNECTIONS that were not useful and somewhat victimizing in his youth. His higher level of morality and self-focus demonstrates a level of meeting adversity with goodness rather than with defensiveness.

4. Oracle at Delphi: "Know thyself." Motto: "*vitam impendere vero*"—to devote one's life to the truth. Morality: I have never hardened myself against my faults; my moral sense has always been a faithful guide to me, my conscience has retained its original integrity, and even if it might be corrupted and wayed by my personal interests, how could I explain that, remaining firm and unmoved on those occasions when a man can at least excuse himself by his weakness in the face of passion, it loses its integrity precisely over those unimportant matters where vice has no excuse? Is it true that to lie is to conceal a truth which one ought to make known?

5. Even in our keenest pleasures there is scarcely a single moment of which the heart could truthfully say: "Would that this moment could last forever!" And how can we give the name of happiness to a fleeting state which leaves our hearts still empty and anxious, either regretting something that is past or desiring something that is yet to come? A sufficient, complete, and perfect happiness which leaves no emptiness to be filled in the soul. The heart must be at peace and its calm untroubled by any passion.

Rousseau is attempting to reconcile his unspent need for external passion with his internal value structure and with the belief system he has constructed to defend himself. His underrating of the state of happiness reflects his distancing himself from a pure emotional experience or sequencing of his path, which he then contradicts in Reverie #6.

6. A happy time when in following the impulses of my heart I could sometimes gladden another heart…a pleasure sweeter than any other.

7. I could find no crueller punishment as revenge on my persecutors than to be happy in spite of them. Everything that concerns my needs saddens and sours my thoughts, and I never found any real charm in the pleasures of the mind unless I was able to forget all about the interests of my body. My soul could never take wings and soar above the natural world as long as I felt it to be tied to the needs of the body…yet even so I cannot concentrate my thoughts entirely within myself, because independently of my will my expansive soul seeks to extend it feelings and its existence to other beings.

Revenge: a meal best eaten cold. Rousseau's disdain and hurt from the rejection by his social group resulted in his deep feelings of alienation and his attempts to justify his isolation through other worldliness and being "above it all".

8. The various periods of short-lived prosperity that I have enjoyed have left me with almost no agreeable memories of deep and lasting impressions: by contrast, in all the hardships of my life I was invariably full of affectionate, touching and delightful emotions which poured a healing balm over the wounds of my injured soul and seemed to change its pains into pleasures, and it is the sweet memory of these feelings that returns to me, unaccompanied by that of the adversities which I experienced at the

same time…Whatsoever our situation, it is only self-love that can make us constantly unhappy [emphasis added].

Here Rousseau speaks to a truer form of experience, that which is not materialistic nor other-focused, but rather is based on memories and a sense of self-worth. However, he contradicts his view on living the simple life, and a life without extremes in either fortune or passion, in the fantasy-oriented nature of another statement in the same reverie…

Apart from the brief moments when the object around me recalls my most painful anxieties, all the rest of the time, following the promptings of my natural affections, my heart continues to feed on the emotions for which it was created, and I enjoy them together with the imaginary beings who provoke them and share them with me, just as if those beings really existed. They exist for me, their creator, and I have no fear that they will betray or abandon me; they will last as long as my misfortunes and will suffice to make me forget them—these creatures of my heart's desire, whose presence satisfies its yearnings. Love of self alone is active in all of this, self-love has no part in it.

9. Everything has its compensations; if my pleasures are brief and few in number, it is also true that when they come, they give me a more intense enjoyment than if I were more used to them…People would laugh if they could see how my soul is affected by the slightest pleasures of this kind. Innocent joy is the only joy whose appearance delights my heart…Imagination joins forces with sensation and makes me identify myself with the sufferer, often plunging me in greater distress than he himself feels.

Rousseau has learned how to self-love, to self-instruct, and how to survive in the isolated world he created for himself. His attempts to see himself as an 'innocent' appear to be a form of denial, and yet his denial provides him happiness beyond escapism.

10. Delightful but short-lived state where love and innocence can so-exist in one heart. Ah! If only I had satisfied her heart as she satisfied mine! What peaceful and delightful days we should have spent together! We did indeed have such days, but how brief and fleeting they were, and what a fate has followed them! There is not a day when I do not remember with joy and loving emotion that one short time in my life when I was myself, completely myself, unmixed, and unimpeded, and when I can genuinely claim to have lived…Were it not for that short but precious period, I should perhaps have remained uncertain about my true nature, for throughout the rest of my life, weak and unresisting, I have been so shaken tossed and torn by the passions of others that, having remained almost passive in a life so full of storms, I should find it hard to decide what there is of my own in the conduct of my life, so unceasingly have I been opposed by harsh necessity. But during those few years, loved by a gentle

and indulgent woman, I did what I wanted, I was what I wanted, and by the use I made of my hours of leisure, helped by her teaching and example, I succeeded in imparting to my still simple and naive soul the form which best suited it and which it has retained ever since. The taste for solitude and contemplation grew up in my heart along with the expansive and tender feelings which are best able to nourish it. I need tranquility if I am to love. I needed a female friend after my own heart, and I had one. I had longed for the country, and my wish was granted. I could not bear subjection, and I was perfectly free, or better than free because I was subject only to my own affections and did only what I wanted to do. All my hours were filled with loving cares and country pursuits. I wanted nothing except that such a sweet state should never cease.

Obviously, it was love that sustained him…

Rousseau presented a view universal in its pain and dynamic in its forcefulness—of a struggle to survive even in a world seen as void of CONNECTEDNESS. To me, it is clear he had discovered the skill of attaching, but it was not to the external world, rather to the world of fantasy, memories, and inner peace at having lived a "good" and ethical life. The external world was the source of his fear; his attempts to defeat this inevitability defined his own life.

The Development of Phenomenology

When I think about knowledge, about "meaning" at its core structure, I tend to think of its use in a more metaphorical manner. For instance, it is common for me to speak to clients about their outlier behavior as a part of a greater gift, as a more complicated form of self-expression, which can mean depth and "complexity of soul" rather than only poor mental health. I often say to them, "the problem is…you're just not an ordinary person." To which I get head nodding in agreement in response. "No," I reply. "What I mean is you're extraordinary!"

The path of the Renaissance had taken philosophy into ethical individualism and away from bondage to religious necessity. Here we have the definition of right or wrong by whether it pleases us, knowledge of morals comes through custom, whether it works, and is demonstrated as effective whether revealed by God or to Self. Morality, reflected in our behavior, is created and moderated by our UFT experiences of attachment, pain and suffering, and growth.

Ultimately, however, man is a creature of free will. Political questions arise about whether anyone has a divine authority to rule. This right is given by each of us in our own consciousness. Man has a duty to preserve himself, education should look at the child becoming man and not subject matter (to God) alone. The basic theories of phenomenology come from this notion, that there is no difference between subject and object, and thus no need to take responsibility beyond an awareness of the greater good of the greater whole of life's experiences and/or self-need/protection/survival. Phenomenology is the study of experiences and consciousness "in itself" and the study of self-awareness, the Philosophy of consciousness. This process was new for scientists; they wanted constructs that were provable by hypothetical testing, or intervention variables that had operational definitions. Scientists are often frustrated when they enter the intangible world of the phenomenological awareness of consciousness, meaning, or individuation processes (see Chapter Ten on Neuroscience).

A stabilized set of core philosophical issues comes from an accumulation of the writings of many philosophers and their theories. Here is the short list of how the process/lineage proceeded:

Aquinas (1225): divine principle.
Erasmus (1467): personal piety.
Galileo (1564): dynamic world.
Locke (1632): blank slate.
Blake (1757): ideal beauty and internal truth.
Schopenhauer (1788): blind noumenal will.
Kierkegaard (1813): human reality over abstract thinking.
Brentano (1838): empiricism disputes the papacy.
Nietzsche (1844): transcendence and realism of the world.
Freud (1845): pleasure seeker (hedonist) vs. Maslow's natural man.
Adler (1870): man as victim.
Jung: (1875): archetypal individuation.
de Chardin (1881): cosmogenesis.
Reich (1897): character armor due to past experience.
Lorenz (1903): man as aggressor.
Skinner (1904): malleable man.
Bateson (1904): cybernetics.
Frankl (1905): meaning seeker.
Chomsky (1928): language gives the meaning.
Moore (1940): care of the soul.

Allport (1955) related the philosophical bases of emotional development and interpersonal CONNECTIVITY in his discussion of Brentano (at every moment the mind is active), and Wundt (creative apperceptive synthesis). These philosophers attempted to account for the molding and interpretation of input in a way that Locke and Hobbes didn't do; they addressed individuation, motivation, and interrelatedness of multidimensionality of space/time.

We learn values to understand the process of our environment (family, school, community). We categorize and predict to create structure, and even though it feels like we have free will, there is always the underlying deterministic view that tells us (phenomenologically) that we must respond to what is expected of us.[20]

This is Aristotle's "laws of association" (continuity, repetition, attention, pleasure-pain, and similarity), which were also included in Locke's (1632) theory of the blank slate. Galileo's (1564–1642) work on the dynamic view of the phenomenological world also supported these laws. Scientists call this the

---

[20] "As with the science of the seventeenth century, which represented the theorization of experience of the outer world...psychoanalysis in the twentieth century represented the theorization of experience in the inner world gained by women in human relationships in their role as the provider of emotional needs in Western families" (Swartz, 1999, p. 246).

"Observer effect", meaning that one should consider the effects of time and readiness for change from the cultural context/creation of settings.

Man continually copes with understanding not only himself, but those around him who influence his life. This result is explained by my unified field theory of environmental/genetic and developmental influences (UFT); I choose to believe in, and to be defined by, the concept of "goodness" as a force that enables my being a "part-of-everything", like Sartre's concept of being-in-itself, which has allowed me to be able to reach out to the social world. Man cannot understand the nature of Plato's Forms until he is free to contemplate his own mind and the forces at work within his soul, as they have been influenced within a context and perceptional framework.

The Idea of Soul

Many individuals relate to the idea of "soul" or spiritual practice as having the most depth or meaning. Within the wide array of philosophical concepts, the concepts regarding soul relate a dimension of being life-creating/sustaining in its most basic form. Thomas Moore (1992) wrote what I still consider the modern classic work on this subject, *Care of the Soul*. In it, he defines soul as a quality of "genuineness and depth, revealed in attachment, love and community, as well as inner communing and intimacy, [which] uses imagination to mediate between understanding and unconsciousness…it is not a thing, but a quality or a dimension of experiencing life and ourselves" (ibid, 1992, p. xi, 5).

The basic intention in any caring, physical, or psychological, is to alleviate suffering. But in relation to the symptom itself, observance means first of all listening and looking carefully at what is being revealed in the suffering. An intent to heal can get in the way of seeing. By doing less, more is accomplished…Where is the line of perversity drawn for you, where is the place where you come up against your own fear and repulsion? he asks (ibid, 1992, pp. 10, 17).

Thomas Moore takes us into a place of self-reflection, where awareness can reveal lost or banished issues. Moore encourages us to embrace contradiction and paradox, which furthers our knowledge of Self and makes suffering bearable. This is the 'goal of the soul path—to feel existence; not to overcome life's struggles and anxieties (ibid, 1992, p. 260).

Dependency is taking on an identity through another. It is the longing to protect the union; desire and self-denial work together through envy to create a characteristic sense of frustration and obsessiveness. Moore also pointed out that frequently victims have subtle control by using depression; even during bouts of melancholia (Freud) some important and creative work is probably going on internally ("brilliance in the darkness"). Of creativity Moore states: "The more deeply one's work stirs imagination and corresponds to images that lie there at the bedrock of identity and fate, the more it will have soul." By using the creative, we create our myth: "a sacred story set in a time and place outside history, describing in fictional form the fundamental truths of nature and human life."

Sometimes one must go beyond just awareness, however, to a point of acceptance. This experience comes from a type of Taoist "asymmetry", a feeling of being pulled in several directions at the same time. The secret of the release of the tension this asymmetry creates is to remember that, like in Hegel's theory, the polarity of opposites will always resolve into a synthesis of resolution if one just waits a bit for the solution to be revealed and then accepted. In the larger, societal level, these periods of social transformations are like the periods in history marked by ages (e.g., the current "Information Age"), as we will see in Chapters Five through Seven, on history.

The individual who is continually striving to discover Self just may also discover that: there is a doorway to God. There is a mutual benefit of dialogue. These discoveries are the "secrets" of the 12-step process that is open to all. Our awareness of our philosophical Nature is but a piece of the Unified Field Theory (UFT) of how we have developed as societal groups and as social, emotional, and spiritual individuals.

In practicing "spirit"-uality, Moore believes we are creating "inner religions", where we become the "curators of our own soul". I love that phrase and it reminds me of the ways in which recommending self-care is so important in the development of a treatment plan for my patients. Not only do we see "Self-help/care" areas in our local bookstores, but the concept tracks all the way back to the Greeks. Moore sees quite clearly how "care" is related to "needs", in a manner that reminds me of Adler's need hierarchy.

Love and Attachment

Although "love", in its many forms *(agape, storge, philia,* and *eros)* has long been a focal point of philosophical study, it is "devoted love", not just passion, that I would like to address next. This kind of love goes beyond boundaries, commands one to trust and demand trust from the Other, and ultimately feels like a kind of experience of spirituality itself. I am speaking of attachment, of which there is a larger discussion in Chapter Thirteen. "From 'close to himself' to close to the Other for completion [CONNECTION]…the pattern of unfolding fate will seem familiar or uncomfortable. Love finds its soul in its feelings of incompleteness, impossibility, and imperfection" [emphasis added]. When we "submit" to attachment we may be "gaining for the soul".

Philosophically, Moore discusses attachment as a function of identity development. In much of Eastern philosophy, such as in the classic Chinese text, *Tao Te Ching*, the experience of Self requires a context of emptiness first. "Maybe we could all use an emptying out of identity now and then. Considering who we are not, we may find the surprising revelation of who we are…tolerance of weakness, you might say, is a prerequisite for the discovery of power, for any exercise of strength motivated by an avoidance of weakness is not genuine power" (ibid, 1992, pp. 89, 121).

In our daily structured self-care practice, our myths, our caring and relating to others, even in our darkness and destructiveness, we can find meaning—when mind and body have been abandoned, even the Outlier can somehow still acknowledge the "dark night of the soul". What is a dream, which the Tibetans call the night soul? Integrated or not, one has meaning and one's myths appear in dreams or waking illusion, in scholarship or symbiotic fear and addiction, or in a simplistic and joyful lifetime of one day at a time. In *The Tibetan Book of the Dead* (Padmasambhava's 8th century guide for the soul), we also learn how making death an important part of "the opus of our lives" can contribute to our creativity and possible joy while growing older.

Moore quotes Leonardo da Vinci as saying:
'Why does the eye see a thing more clearly in dreams than the imagination when awake?' To the soul, memory is more important than planning, art more compelling than reason, and love more fulfilling than understanding. We know we are well on the way toward soul when we feel attachment to the world and the people around us and when we live as much from the heart as from the head (ibid, 1992, p. 303–4).

Marcus Aurelius (121–180 CE) calls surviving these difficulties of self-expression and betrayal of spirit "bearing the unbearable". He believed that one can survive the pain of betrayal as well as any other source of spiritual pain. This suffering included the emotional pain brought on by our own behavior or by being in a significant relationship with another. "The ultimate marriage of spirit and soul, animus and anima, is the wedding of heaven and earth, our highest ideals and ambitions united with our lowliest symptoms and complaints" (ibid, 1992, p. 263). Even Boswell (1740–1795) proposed: "Marriage must have its bass, tenor, treble; that is what brings it esteem, affection, passion."

Morals and Ethics

The meanings of morals and ethics overlap. Broadly speaking, morals are individual principles of right and wrong, and a system of ethics deals with sets of those principles. Both terms entered language in the Middle English period, with moral being the older form by about 100 years (c. 1300).

In many ways, my brother, 4 years older, was my first ethics teacher. Although an Outlier himself, he always managed to stay CONNECTED to his own moral compass. My brother has long been my inspiration for looking at life philosophically. When I was only ten or so, and John was fourteen, he was already being recognized for his poetry and short stories. Later, he would go on to own, and write for, a weekly newspaper in Texas, *The Washington County Journal*. As editor, he remarked on many subjects, often philosophical as well as political in nature. He also went back to school at one point, and then worked through the University of Texas with his second masters, in Public Health. One well-rounded guy. His most significant mentor at the time, Jim Summers, kept up a running dialogue with him by email for some thirty years. I usually got copied on these, receiving a blessing and usually an enlightenment from the writings of one or both.

JBH: I have spiritual beliefs, but in defense of those who do not, it is a choice. I chose my beliefs or faith. Many others were simply reared with them and so their beliefs are part of their identity. Then it is less a choice. Paul Tillich, a Christian theologian [more about him in the next chapter], argued that only those who have come out of doubt with faith really own their beliefs. The inherited belief that you own has to be a choice, not simply a culture that tells you who you are and what you believe. Those who choose not to believe in transcendent anything, can likewise choose to create the meaning that makes up their lives.

I see no difference except they must rely on a community of others who are here and now or who have gone before or will come after, as opposed to some creed or book or some presumed deities or demons ensconced in undisclosed locations. I only feel sorry for those who have not formed or joined a community of others to help them persevere in the quest for meaning. Deep faith does not seem to necessarily lead to happiness or even meaningfulness. Look at the recent revelations of the utter loneliness of Mother Teresa relative to her longing for the continuation of her relationship with her deity.

A person to whom her God spoke, who then spoke not again for decades, up until death, is a typical description of a happy person. She found meaning unto death, but she chose to do it in the face of considerable lack of what she considered evidence. As Jesus himself said, in an act of utter schizophrenia if the Trinity is to make sense, "Father, why hast thou forsaken me." The philosopher in me cannot resist asking if a whole entity can forsake itself? But these questions have nothing much, to me, to do with creation of a meaningful life [emphasis added].

The growth of the Jedi religion in Britain is just fine with me. The Jedi code is a lot like the Cowboy's.

What you are looking for is what is doing the looking. —ST. FRANCIS

8/3/2007 On morality

JBH: The looking is the Soul, not the going…we are all in fact 'prisoners' of a reality forced upon us…Jesus saying that his followers needed a lot of rules to keep them from sin, and Buddha remarked that trying to perfect one's own nature would keep almost everyone from harmful behavior toward others…fear is one root of religion, as much as the active search for any Higher Power…So to the extent that prayer teaches one how to clarify what one truly wants, it's good psychotherapy (Is there a Platonic Form for ethics?)

JS: Far be it for me to want to argue that an examined life can only be examined through your own cultural lens…You have to question your faith, sincerely doubt it, then come back to it…otherwise it is only a cultural artifact…see the context of your beliefs…constantly repeating and constantly changing motifs and motifs of meaning of generation.

JBH: The several very Christian colleagues at my work get very agitated when I point out the controversies among the early church fathers over various doctrines and how many "Christian" ideas are simply adaptations of ideas from other religions or even from pagan beliefs. Discussions about the actual logic of some of the beliefs is simply not welcome. Some of them simply refuse to hear it and will leave the room if I attempt to bring it up. Reasoned dialogue is not welcome, so clearly there is no self-examination beyond the leap of faith and stopping there.

Yet, all are aware that my understanding of the origins of their theology is deeper than their own. What is at work here is simply reduction of cognitive dissonance. …Ethics, by its very nature, is seeking a set of prescriptions and the justifications for it that transcend all cultures. The fact that no such ethical code has emerged simply suggests the difficulty of the issue. Philosophy has done no better in metaphysics or epistemology. My take is that the inquiry is what matters, the process of rational debate, i.e., reductionism creates subjectivism homeostasis and pan determinism.

SH: [I have experienced the problem with some patients over the years; when our politics don't agree I find something to discuss which is helpful].

JS: Morals and morality are about personal behavior, ethics more grandly philosophical. However, linguistic use constrains the philosophical use and helps to blur the distinction: one can have a single ethic, as in "a strong work ethic" or "an ethic of selfishness" but if we talk about a single moral, we've shifted a bit in meaning to the realm of Aesop and Uncle Remus, as in "the moral of the story". In the singular, a moral is a lesson to be learned about a single principle or right and wrong, and an ethic is a single guiding principle that effects your criteria for determining what is right and wrong. Yup. Blurry. Ethical systems often have several, such as the four cardinal virtues of courage, wisdom, justice, and temperance from Greek days.

The distinction is best illustrated by the contexts in which these terms are used. When we disparage someone's behavior, we say that person has 'low morals' we would never say that a drug dealer has 'bad ethics.' Ethics as a branch of philosophy is studied in universities and theological seminaries. We have an Office of Government Ethics and write articles about political and judicial ethics. Think of it as a hierarchy of detail: when we talk about personal ethics, we are using the primary meaning of 'a set of moral of principles.' We say that children are taught good moral principles, or morals, if they don't lie, cheat, or steal, and if they respect other people. Moral principles such as "respect others" are further broken down into rules such as "don't stick out your tongue at your sister."

Morality can be dynamic such as moral outlook (values and principles, background beliefs and theories, judgments about cases), moral pluralism (there is more than one way to view ethical values and principles and these different ways can be in conflict) and the interface of ethics and law (All written in 2007).

Wow quite an enlightened brother and friend; a lot to live up to!

Hegelian Influence

My own philosophical view of morality and scholarship has been greatly influenced by Georg Hegel (1770–1831). Hegel believed that man could obtain absolute knowledge through two methods: the dialectic mind and pure reason. It was through the combination of these methods that Hegel developed a synthesis regarding the history of man, formulated important ideas about the consciousness and Geist (Spirit) of his times, and conceived a logical process for knowing the Absolute.

The three components of the dialectical approach are thesis, antithesis, and synthesis. The main concept is that there is opposition within every idea; that is, there is truth on both sides of every debate. Formally, every idea (thesis) leads to its opposite (antithesis) because nothing is eternally static or changeless [relativity]. Einstein was also influenced by both Hegel and Kant before him (Kim, 2018). The idea of the dialectic method relates basically to the interrelationships of concepts.

These two sides, then, interact to form a higher and more complex whole (synthesis). Within the mind, thought and nature, as opposites, are united in mind and society, in man's artistic and religious products, and in the self-conscious activity. The mind struggles for power and recognition; it seeks freedom and independence. However, the reason is also practical and objective. Man's mind is controlled by his rules and institutions; these serve to form a synthesis with his freedom and independence.

Both Heraclitus (536–470 B.C.) and Plato (427–347 B.C.) used the dialectical method. It is characterized by the central role of the opposites and contradictions in human thinking. Heraclitus speaks of the struggle of metaphysics in the ontological opposites, which he considers the core of the universe. For Plato, dialectics is a necessary method of grasping ideas through the Socratic method of discussion.

Although not as subjective as Berkeley before him (1685–1753), Hegel was a philosophical idealist. He believed that only the mind is real and that it developed potentialities by embodying them in increasingly complex forms. In *Phenomenology of Mind (*1807), Hegel wrote that freedom is the fundamental feature of the mind. The mind is infinite in its freedom, but it is opposed by the self-conscious mind. He used his famous dialectic construction of thought to point out the importance of this contradiction.

Of the theorists addressed, Hegel presented the most related and succinct theory of personal development as it relates to a grander scheme and the synthetic (dualist) nature of the universe. He believed that the limitations of nature are not obstacles but are conditions for human freedom (Bronowski and Mazlish, 1960, p. 480).

The fact that the knower, and what it is to be known, generates a higher synthesis was the foundation for many more recent theorists beyond Einstein—Marxism, Gestalt psychology and therapy, Erikson's model of life span development, and current dualistic models of learning to name a few. Hegel felt that the idea of a complex synthesis was not applicable to only the abstractions of philosophy and philosophical discussions but should be applied to the concrete realities of life as well. "Every process in life calls out its contradictory process—and life takes its important steps only when it synthesizes these two into a higher form. Life is not mere being, and death is not merely nonbeing; the essential step of progress is the synthesis of the two, is becoming" (ibid, 1960, p. 482).

Hegel divides the mind into three parts. First, the subjective mind views the soul as a natural entity in the physical world, the mind's sensitive feeling essence. Secondly, the objective mind combines human will, thought, and impulse in freedom. He called this effect "actuality", or *Wirklichkeit.* Thirdly, the absolute mind controls man's artistic, religious, and philosophical nature. This idea of the absolute mind, or spirit (Geist) was a concept basic to his system.

Spirit, in this sense, comprehends all that there is and outwardly confronts the finite intelligence as an objective reality; spirit is struggling to overcome self-alienation while realizing its "ideal being". To Hegel, both man and nature were embodiments of spirit, different 'modes' in which spirit expressed its essence; the division between man as a conscious subject and the objective world that surrounds him was a division within the spirit itself.

Hegel believed that reason is part of the dialectical process, and that spirit is the realm of freedom, the realm of concrete unity, existing in-and-for itself, incorporating all opposition. It is a return of the mind to itself. Thinking, to an extent, is always dialectical, never purely linear. In fact, Hegel considered philosophy itself as that attempt to think concretely; that is, to think of experience in all its manifold relations. One of his famous statements is "The truth is the whole." From this idea also came Hegel's famous statement, "The real is rational; the rational is real."

Hegel viewed many philosophical problems in historical terms. He attempted to account for the evolution of historical man. One of his explanations of historical development compares history with the growth of the individual. There is childhood, represented by the early oriental people; there is youth, which he identifies with the period of the Greeks; there is the age of mature man, realized by the Romans; and there is old age, represented by our time—which, for Hegel, is a period not of decay, but of highest maturity. Hegel saw that even when viewed from a historical viewpoint, developments move from one extreme to another and then reach a third stage which includes, to a certain degree, the results of both preceding stages. This follows his dialectical law of thesis, antithesis, and synthesis.

The ruler alone was free in the oriental world, yet his freedom was so undisciplined that it became extremely changeable. The Greco-Roman world advanced only the limited realization that some are free since slavery was an important part of their civilization. Finally, Western Europe, under the impact of Christianity, realized that man is free. This freedom is neither changeable nor subordinate; it can arise only in an organized constitutional state, which unites through synthesis of subjective familial love and objective community interest. This synthesis can alone provide the opportunity to its citizen to develop his artistic, intellectual, and social potential—to become a true personality (Haradon, 1971b).

Essentialism also was expressed in Hegel's philosophy. By constricting Becoming as a passage from nonexistence (not-Being) to existence (Being), Hegel completed the absorption of existence into essence. Hegel tried to synthesize all the main attitudes of culture in his interpretation of that culture. He not only presented a historical survey, in which dialectical development was basic, but he also presented the idea that the coming of self-knowledge in culture was the revelation of Absolute Truth; the process was cumulative.

Modern culture held the essentials of all earlier cultures and possessed the perfected norm of human wisdom and freedom. Thus, Hegel attempted to construct an all-embracing philosophy that could illuminate art, morals, religion, politics, history, literature, and science (ibid, 1971b). Many theorists who have followed (me included) have tried to do the same. This philosophy is the reason for the subject matter covered in the following chapters.

Hegel's ethics or theory of morality contained three parts: (1) abstract right, (2) freedom to express intention, and (3) subjective will. All three of these parts took into consideration the effect upon one's ethics and general situation, the last including the family, bourgeois society, and the state. Although Hegel's "Form" continued to be idealistic, his ethics tended to have a realistic content. The entire area of right, economics, and politics was included here beside morality. In Hegel's system of morality, he differentiated between old and young. The old were those truly called to govern, because their spirit no longer thinks individually, but only "universally". The German Idealism which followed in the nineteenth century was basically Hegelian. Along the way, Hegel influenced Marx and Engels.

Notes on Symmetry

By the early 1970s, from my studies I realized that much of our awareness comes to us through 1) mirroring, 2) environmental influences and the Other, and 3) what is known best to us through Hegelian synthesis which brings meaningful sense to the dialectical process. There is also a context a type of Truth, regardless of its subjectivity. In his writings, Madeo (2006) reinterpreted Foucault's (1926–1984) ideas about Trust and the mirroring process, where "our reflections are neither subjective or objective, and in which a complex grid of historical epochs returns us to a discontinuous possibility that breaks us from preconceptions and the limits of reason" (Madeo, 2006).

Within the population of my clients, I have experienced many exceptional thinkers, mostly Outliers after all, who have set themselves up for a kind of praise and attention from the world but still demonstrate a limited range of skill set or knowledge. Are these ideas and Self-perceptions accurate? Is the apparent asymmetry of the reasoning that mismatches with the presenting/antisocial behavior make real synthesis of the dialectical in these Outliers impossible? Sometimes what is useful is a belief in favor of unreason (*deraison* in Foucault's theory). "Foucault's history of madness reveals a 'constantly shifting relationship' where madness and therefore rationality are called into question" (ibid, 2006).

Madeo asks the following questions: "Who are the self-validated sane? What does the 'common' or 'reasonable' person look and behave like? Sometimes the 'common' person appears to be nothing more than an easily brainwashed, egocentric and infantile manic?" (ibid, 2006) I would add to this a question of my own: Could the "Outliers" perhaps really be the authentic individuals in societies? What is the effect of genealogy, of one's genetic and epigenetic influences that are also part of the Unified Field Theory (UFT) of development? This concept is the core theme of this book and its focus on the multidimensional view of Personality Development Theory.

Rituals are an important part of the Hegelian process of synthesis, which is necessitated by the process of mirroring highlighted by Foucault. Rituals are based on beliefs. As an individual develops core values (based on his/her own UFT), rituals are a form of reinforcing safety, trust, and a set of tools to deal with life's difficulties. In fact, much of our strength and character has come through experiences of suffering. "Rituals can be scientifically described and scientifically executed, but they are still rituals based on beliefs, and beliefs are sometimes arbitrary, based on conditioned prejudices, and may vary considerably from one individual to the next" (ibid, 2006).

In *When Bad Things Happen to Good People,* Harold S. Kushner (1981) tells us that rituals help us understand that [God/Higher Power] has a pattern into which all our lives fit. "The purpose of suffering is to repair that which is faulty in man's personality…God does painful things to us as His way of helping us…makes us more thoughtful, more sensitive to others…purges us of pride and arrogance…tests our loyalty and strength of faith" (ibid, 1981, p. 40).

In place of chaos, if we are trying to reconcile the apparent randomness or sometimes asymmetry of our lives with the logic of science, or even the religious truths that God's world is an orderly one with predictability (sun, tides, reproduction), we must ponder these questions with an open mind that has been trained to use structured thought and ritual processing of ordered information. Kushner believes that the "image of God in us allows us to say 'no' to instinct on moral grounds. Free will does not mean following instincts, but rather when not to" [emphasis added] (ibid, 1981). Sometimes I wonder if, in the randomness of this mirroring within one's life context [Heisenberg], what we experience as "free will" is perhaps acting volitionally or really conditioned "reacting".

Morality. Suffering, and Potential

For me, the Buddhist idea of Dharma can be tied into morality as well as to suffering; to owe God your life, like Job, to hold onto self-respect, a sense of Self as a good person, with compassion, maintaining the sense that others feel pain as well. On the other hand, according to Kushner, "Job's comforters" are those who mean to help but are more concerned with their own needs and feelings than they are with those of the other person. Steven Pinker's model (1997) of morality is an excellent one and closely aligned with my own. "Without a clear moral philosophy, any cause of behavior could be taken to undermine free will and hence moral responsibility…but a random event does not fit the concept of free will any more than a lawful one does and could not serve as the long-sought locus of moral responsibility" (ibid, 1997, p. 54).

There is no "Suffering Olympics". Religion, as the most common place of spiritual experiences, likewise provides a feeling of spiritual community (what Buddhists refer to as Sangha). This is a joint experience not just to be in touch with God but to be in touch with each other; we can handle things when we don't have to face them alone. People give us courage to bear the unbearable and to remember what we have left inside rather than just what we have lost.

When we face challenges, we grow. When we face crises, this growth due to a challenge can escalate; sometimes it even radiates into an imperfect experience of our emotions and impacts those around us as well. In *A Year to Live* (1997), Stephen Levine tells us that it is not just living every day in a conscious state of mindfulness about the quality of one's experiences that counts. I believe that if we develop our own personal "philosophy" of life (UFT) as we navigate the decisions and values that the rest of our experiences require of us, we will end more balanced, whole, and happy with the results!

Levine calls this a life review.

The life review goes beneath the surface of past action to the states of mind from which these acts originated. It examines the emotional attachment to the shadows these previous actions cast over the present. Have we learned by meeting our pain with mercy instead of fear how to keep our hearts open in adversity? Our life lasts only a moment…Note these moments…from aversion to attraction…to notice this constant liking and disliking that leaves us exhausted at the end of the day. Awareness is what remains when all that is impermanent. It is the essence of life (ibid, 1997, pp. 31, 39).

Levine looks at life from a broad point of view, including that of Buddhism, when he states that it is acceptance of life's impermanence that leads to heightened awareness. As we practice awareness, we may also become more sensitive to the sources of pain or suffering around us. No one would disagree that our life is a compulsive attempt to find escape from discomfort (See Chapter Sixteen on Addictive Behaviors).

My experience of using literature, art, and music to escape outside pressures was my own personal choice. Whatever "suffering" I was experiencing at the time, from which I needed to escape, it worked for me. For others, perhaps the search for something healthy takes a longer portion of their lives? And having had experiences of growth and meaning, I know how the values of strength can infuse us with new appreciation for the changes we must accept (think Serenity Prayer in AA). We have suffered, we have grown, we have found meaning through creating an outer expressive environment. But what of our inner world and the tough questions about morality still unanswered?

Issues of Freedom

I ask myself: What is morally right? How is virtue related to knowledge? Knowledge of what is right is easily learned. As we mature, our idea of morals matures, founded on our own secure belief system. But will you consider your moral decision of today so moral tomorrow? What if your actions are contrary to another's wishes? Man has freedom of choice, but what if your security depends on someone else's approval of your actions (signs of Codependency)? Rather than trying to live by pure absolute imperatives, how are the ideas of right and self-interest related?

We are individuals and can never really be sure of anyone else's thoughts or emotions. Yet we belong to the "realm of ends", or what I would call the universal mind. All rational beings have basic beliefs and desires. Among these would be the desire to be needed, the desire to be happy, the desire to assert oneself as an individual, and the need to use one's "moral instinct" in decision-making; how can Will constrain itself? Man chooses freely and in turn the rational choice determines the disposition of the Will. Man is free from causality and yet he is a cause of himself in the sense of his Self-determinism. He is free to choose, free in his rational functioning but there it seems his freedom ends. "Man is not free to act, only free to decide" (Haradon, 1971a).

S.J. Harris (1917–1981) said: "'Freedom' is not the right to live as we wish, it is the right to learn how we ought to live to fulfill all our potentialities." The very actualization of a person's personality is the basic striving of his life. One must not be afraid to be human, to know life and himself through others. This is the heart of CONNECTING. It is through this exercising of our personalities to know others and ourselves, to realize where we fit in the schemes of life, that man is really free.

The man who does not exercise the right to know himself [through evaluating his UFT] is not truly free. He is bound to others, their security, or their opinion of him, or he is bound by his own fears and hides behind walls and shells. Fear, anxiety, and hostility may be caused by outside forces, but it depends on the freedom of the inner will to handle these emotions. Man must not be afraid to release his inner self. To stand up for one's beliefs is man's most important freedom; compromise comes only through the free decision to change one's opinion. If one is afraid of exercising freedom of his will through fear that he will be criticized or that he may hurt someone by being contrary, then he can never truly realize his total potential.

If one cannot know himself and thereby serve his wants through the available means, then he is neither free nor self-actualizing. Man must be free to express his needs and not have to be afraid of other's judgments. If I need to be alone and yet I am denying others of my company, it is still more important that I satisfy my own need for solitude before I try to share myself with others (which is different from narcissistic self-centeredness). This "aloneness", albeit even for survival, is categorically different from being self-centered, which will be discussed in Chapter Eight on addictive maladaptive behaviors.

Psychologists and philosophers ask the question: Why then does an individual often feel guilt and anxiety? Society forces us into an environment where all the norms, the ethical codes, have neatly been laid out. Then we are told we are free, rational beings and our lives are our own to determine. And yet, if we decide in our autonomy to deviate from the "norm", we may be inspected, rejected, and sent away in a neat little package. I have met many individuals, in my office seeking treatment, who have had such experiences.

Can you ever really be alone? Even when you have found your own quiet place of solitude, thoughts, memories, and emotions follow you. What is an objective decision? How can we make the "best" or "right and moral" decision in every case? [I am the only one who can judge my actions and yet with no knowledge, often, of the possible consequences]. What kind of criteria do I have to judge? Am I the first or the last to know myself? Others can put me out of their mind, but I am never alone. Even when I can put all else out of my mind, "I" am still, there, criticizing, praising, and judging my actions.

To be a part of society is to be responsible for one's behavior. Yet can one also be free in the potential dependency that comes with this CONNECTION? No wonder some individuals try so hard to escape reality (and responsibility) through alcohol and drugs. They are trying to find a level of existence from where they can understand without judging and can be free to believe without having to justify themselves to a responsible society around them!

Anxiety is conditioned through neglect and fear. As man limits himself, he becomes dogmatic, i.e., entrenched in a set of learned values. He responds according to habit rather than belief or faith. Additional knowledge can bring on a freedom from acting purely on faith. Sometimes it seems that knowing yourself and knowing God is the same and we feel a greater freedom in our faith in the unknown (Haradon, 1972c).

When I was 20, I wrote: "Man spends 1/3 of his life in bed, 1/3 of his life at work and most of the other 1/3 worrying about his work or why he can't sleep. Sexual acts take only a short time and yet most of our lives are spent worrying about how we look, and whether we are sexually satisfied. TV commercials are continually based on sexual attitudes. Man, who used to spend only few minutes a day on a satisfying biological function, now spends his whole life afraid because he is or may become impotent and he very likely will become impotent because he is afraid. What kind of a society is this? It may be sick and yet the sickness is self-perpetuating" (Haradon, 1972d).

My mother used to say: Birth is a kind of death announcement (or more positively—one is here because two people loved each other, but in the end died anyway). Our lives are constantly moving through time and space toward the end, at least in our current view of physics (See Chapter Twelve). But my soul is not in my body; my body is in my soul. My soul is all-encompassing, giving me life and allowing me to experience that which is outside my Self as really one with what is inside. And because other people are experiencing some of the same outside of themselves experiences, we can be one with each other.

It is my intention that must be moral, first, not necessarily my actions. I think man decides freely, then according to his decision he acts within the framework of his environment. Therefore, I may be conditioned but I am also free: to trust, to be autonomous, to create, to love and to CONNECT.

Summary of Philosophical Positions

The Greeks' idea of morality presented the question, "What am I to do if I am to fare well?" Plato believed that Good was transcendent, while Aristotle believed that attainment of the Good was simply a social arrangement. To both, goodness was a standard which the individual was not free to accept or reject. Man did his best to fulfill his socially established role, and somehow there was a CONNECTION between his choices and the choices that were dictated by the transcendent Forms. The Aristotelian ideal of Good was available only to the chosen few who could comprehend practical or moral wisdom as the highest good. While Aristotle proposed a life of "doing well and living well", others believed that the contemplative life should only be taken on by the political elite.

At the end of the Greek era, the ideas of independence and self-sufficiency began to appear as a basis of morality. Virtue was defined by some as the absence of desires, whereas others proclaimed that happiness came from the practice of virtue. The Stoics believed that virtue consisted in the conscious assent to the inevitable order of things. Nature was defined as the cosmic status of moral law, while convention was simply established for local observance. The Epicureans believed that morality was involved with the pursuit of pleasure. Christianity brought in the idea of God as the best moral guide. His holiness, goodness, and power gave him criteria for commanding moral goodness in terms of obedience.

Plato's dualism, the world of sense perceptions and the world of Forms, eventually became St. Augustine's world of desires and realm of divine order. The opposition between rules and desires was quickly apparent. Schopenhauer (1788–1860) believed that it was man's inner nature, his Will, which was fundamental to morality. As a "nonbeliever" he felt everything in our world of experience to be "undifferentiated". In Kierkegaard's time (1813–1855), man had begun to question the dictates of a "god" or of obedience to some categorical imperative; Kierkegaard believed that moral standards can only be chosen individually. It is the act of choice, which is fundamental, rather than acting out of the decision. He believed that man's goal is his own satisfaction, which can only be reached by allowing him freedom of choice.

Nietzsche's Will to Power

Finally, Nietzsche (1844–1900) presented the turning point in modern philosophy. He believed that power was the fundamental human goal. Christianity was the core of modern sickness in that it stifled man's thinking processes and led him to trust in dogmatic principles. Power was to be achieved by limited self-love, and Good was found to be attainable through the strivings of the free human will. Perhaps Nietzsche's "Will to Power" idea is meant to represent the ability to go beyond one's own subjective mind. Nietzsche said: "The ability in man to question himself and his life is his 'will to power.' The discharge of drives, pushes man forever toward self-realization and a closeness with existence."

Whatever is beautiful, even though it may be given to one particular person, helps the world. Thus, if we love another person with a pure love, that love goes to the root of things where all are one, and thus we help the whole. Everything that is true is released into the flow of things where it affects all life, the whole force of evolution.

We speak about 'my consciousness,' 'your consciousness,' but these are differences that we make in our ignorance. For fundamentally life is one and consciousness is one, even though it is divided, as we think, into a part that belongs to me and another that belongs to someone else. Thus, I am identified with India, with Hinduism, with my family, with the experiences of my childhood and boyhood. This consciousness identifies itself with all these things and calls itself mine.

> But suppose it can give up this identification, to detach itself from India, from Hinduism, from the traditions with which it has been connected, then it is just consciousness; then it will realize that although modified by the identifications which limit it, consciousness is fundamentally the same in all. This is a matter for personal knowledge and experience; you can know it for yourself, but first you must cease to identify yourself with so many things. From that standpoint, truth, whether given to one, to many, or to the whole world, produces the same effect (Sri Ram 1993).

Philosophical studies have broadened over the years. From Greek Sophists to 18th century British rationalists and 19th century American Theosophists, there has come a broadening menu of study from the influence of global concerns and CONNECTIONS. Third Worlds have also provided information and interest throughout this process as Eastern religions spread. A Third Force in Psychology represented the influences of Humanism in the middle of the last century (1950s to 1970s). Influences on the renewed focus on Self-actualization philosophy include:

1. Freud and the energy of the libido.
2. Jung.
3. Focus on Psychosomatic illnesses.
4. Nietzsche.
5. Discoveries in Physics.
6. Studies in Sensation and Perception/Energy from a Gestalt.
7. Theodore Reich's Work on Body Armor.
8. Karen Horney and self-analysis.
9. Theories of Conflict.
10. Scientology.
11. Maslow's Hierarchy of Needs.
12. Transactional Analysis.
13. Yoga takes hold in the West, along with Kung Fu and other martial arts.
14. Carlos Castenada brings mysticism into the 20th century.

What is freedom? How is it affected/changed by power? Why is a general social and personal philosophy important? Man's potential to discover a meaning to life gives hope and courage. Conflict between personal creativity and a need to adapt (freedom versus necessity) is how I have used the term for self-knowledge as "thing-in-itself" through intuition; "'Being' is expressed in existence, 'Thinking' is an expression of existence; Individual=whole (in-dividual) and unique" (Sartre, 1943).

What we really want is awareness without a sense of separation from it at the same time.

Alan Watts (1951) wrote that "Nothing save change itself can last" (Watts, 1951, p. 15). When all other needs seem satisfied, the "heart goes hungry" still. Sometimes it helps if our searching is within a community/Sangha: "These myths give the individual a certain sense of meaning by making him part of a vast social effort, in which he loses something of his own emptiness and loneliness…Seeing God requires a 'correction of mind' just as glasses correct our vision…Belief clings, Faith lets go" (ibid, 1951, pp. 19, 23–24). Within my psychotherapy practice, I often see the experience of the "walking dead", where individuals commit the act of "partial" suicide by cutting themselves off from the world and/or their feelings, partially due to a set of fantasy expectations in the first place. This problem is highlighted in Tolman's study of the 's-e' sequence (more about this in Chapter Thirteen). The CONNECTION between stimulus (s) and response (r) is modulated by an unmeasured expectation (e). Often these expectations can even be "substitutions for our thumb" (as we will see in Chapter Sixteen on Addictions), in that they are closely tied with attempts to allay our underlying anxiety (Edward Tolman, *Wikipedia*, 2/26/15).

Chapter Four
To Be a Hero

> The hero's will is not that of his ancestors nor of his society, but his own. This will to be oneself is heroism. Life is a desperate struggle to be in fact that which we are in design.
> – Ortega Y. Gassett

The Theosophical Society in America

I would like to now focus on an area of influence pervasive throughout each of the areas discussed in the previous chapter. Around the late 1800s, the Theosophical Society directly focused its studies on the holistic viewpoint. This scientific and psychological framework formed a two-pronged effect to create a new world view and terminology. The study of causative order looks at where we came from; the study of purposive order looks at where we are going. Ideas about consciousness and beingness sprung out of the Theosophical movement because it focused on intentionality and clarity of purpose. It was officially founded in 1875 and was based in New York; its tenets included many of the mystic or spiritualist ideas of the time, including Gnosticism, astrology, and a combining of Eastern religious practice (vegetarianism, Yoga) with Western religious beliefs.

Helena Blavatsky (1831–1891) was a self-proclaimed medium who had major influenced upon the growth and beliefs accepted early on in Theosophy. She claimed to have been trained in Tibet and knew similar mystic truths as Jesus, Buddha, and Mohammed. Regardless of the veracity of these claims, her influence continues to this day through the depth and clarity of her teachings.

Some Eastern theorists call the study of principle or moral purposiveness *Dharma.* Purposive order involves intention and action. The Theosophical Society proposed that causative order (the historical perspective) can be thought of as purely mechanical, but purposive order cannot, for it involves awareness and choice. "Every part of the universe is aware and is communicating [CONNECTING] with all other parts. We live in a world full of meaning."

> Evolution is going somewhere. It has a goal. The goal of evolution, like its systems, is threefold. Our material forms evolve toward sensitivity and refinement of nature. Our minds evolve toward an awareness and responsiveness to our environment. Our spirits evolve toward a realization of our essential oneness with all existence. We come forth from the primal unity, the Reality that is the ground of all existence, united with it, but unconscious of our unity. In the course of our existence, we develop consciousness through a sense of a separate identity (Theosophical Society, 1986).

These tenets of the Theosophical Society cross-reference quite easily to studies of Eastern religions, specifically Buddhism. We can see this CONNECTION if we look at The Three Truths of the White Lotus:

1. The human soul is immortal, and its future is the future of a thing whose growth and splendor has no limit.
2. The spirit that gives life dwells in us and around us, is undying and eternally beneficent, is not seen or heard or smelled, but is perceived by the one who desires perception.
3. We are each our own lawgiver, the dispenser of glory or gloom to ourselves, the decree of our life, our reward, our punishment.

To be enlightened is to know who we are, even though most of us experience many outer personas at times. But we have an "inner personality", which we think of as "myself". In Theosophy, this transcendent knower is called individuality. "The mind is the link between the immortal individuality and the mortal personality, for it participates in both…We think we are the inner personality behind the personas. But we are none of those. We are a pure mind individualizing the divine spirit and intuition. Live constantly by the points of Good Conduct, and especially to be motivated by Love in all our actions" (ibid, 1886). To be free is to be happy without seeking happiness, to act with a spontaneous motion which is the results from inward grace.

From the March–April 2003 issue of *The Quest*, a publication of the Theosophical Society, we find these quotes can inspire us into a thoughtful view of how we must look at the moments of our day to gain meaning and to regulate our reactivity. Humor and pleasantness toward the outcome of one's life is defined in the article as grace, which is also the result of silence and a thankful attitude as well as acts of service. Not only does this sound like the basis of all faith-based lives, be they Christian, Judaism, Islam, Hinduism, or Buddhist, but also the core value of a 12-step view of recovery model. The article tells us to "Breathe little prayers of Thanksgiving…a poem of service" (Quest, March/April 2003). Although this does not necessarily mean a life of "mystic retreat", it can't hurt to focus a bit on Self-Discovery and Social Transformation every day.

Taking a closer look at a few of these concepts, Edward Abdill wrote about the Theosophical idea that "there is no measurable time between knowing and not knowing" (Abdill, 2003). Madame Blavatsky, asserted that "Truth" was experiential and could be shared more easily than just taught "in words". "We can express our beliefs and theories in words, but we cannot cause others to experience a truth simply by telling them" (Abdill, 2003, pp. 60–64). I run into this problem frequently with my clients, and more recently experienced it with my daughter, who has a 3-year-old daughter herself. My mother, a therapist as well (as I have mentioned), used to call it the "picture in your head". When we communicate with others, we find it impossible to be precise with our descriptive language because we have been accustomed to "assuming" others will [imprecisely] figure out what we meant. I won't even tackle what it means to tell someone "I love you" or "I'm mad at you," but the example I frequently use with clients is as follows:

So, if I were to say to you, I need to go home and clean my closet (much less my garage!) you would immediately see a 'picture in your head' of what that process might entail. But it would be the picture of YOUR closet or garage and therefore that process. But let's say I'm the type to take EVERYTHING out of the closet first, making a giant mess all over my bed and bedroom, requiring the job be finished before I could go to bed that night. But perhaps you're the type to do just all the shoes first or go through the hanging clothes and remove some to Goodwill, or whatever. We would have different pictures in our head, wouldn't we?

Therefore, is it any wonder if we tell our kids, 'I'm going to the store and while I'm gone clean the living room' and when you return there's a fight because you meant vacuum and dust, and they took out the dirty dishes and trash and put the library books by the front door? We had different pictures in our heads. This is an all-to-common problem among the members of families I see for counseling.

The example from my daughter (which warmed my heart) went like this: after finding it difficult sometimes to accept the "bad" times of parenting, she called me up and said, "I figured it out! It was the picture in my head! [I can see her grandmother smiling]. I was comparing parenting with all those books and movies I'd read and seen about how perfect it is and loving and cozy and fun. Nobody warns us about the bad stuff. Then I saw a movie where the 'baby' was a hand-full and it came to me that that was what I had been doing. I feel much better now!" As her grandma smiled, so did I.

Some methods, such as Existentialism, believed the study of Self-discovery addressed the very core of philosophy, for what else could define the "study of knowledge" better than the study of knowing Self? Later, in the 19th and 20th centuries, Existentialism would try to defend human freedom from three major aggressors. First was the psychological attack that says man is drives only (Freud). The second attack was from the rationalists who said man must always have a proof for his belief (Cognitivists). The third attack troubled those existentialists who were atheists. It was the idea that every man should be God-goal oriented (Theists). Schrodinger (1887–1961) asked: "What is this 'I'? You will, on close introspection, find that what you really mean by 'I' is the ground-stuff upon which [experiences and memories] are collected...subject without object" (Schrodinger, *Seek for the Road*, 1925).

Emerson (1803–1882), a half century before Theosophy became well-known, had asked if consciousness is in the brain or in the sense organs? "Time and space are but physiological colors which the eye makes, but the Soul is light." Perceiving Self as it itself [emphasis added]. It is clear to me that we can discover the existentialist in us all. Again, Existentialism was and is the study of how one's freedom to choose affects individual existence and self-definition, the result of rational decisions made from the collection and analysis of available environmental facts and cues.

These facts and cues are the influences on the Unified Field Theory (UFT) of development discussed throughout this book. However, Existentialism is a more subjective philosophical position than pure empiricism. If judgments are made subjectively, how can we accurately evaluate ourselves? One could just as likely state that an accurate decision is improbable. And how could you be sure the feedback would be authentic, even if you had been right? This is the existential dilemma.

I sometimes see man's uniqueness turned into destructive alienation; I often see sensitivity in my patients as a reflection of their uniqueness and find it a healthier quality of temperament compared to some individuals I run across, who may not be as alone but are not emotionally Self-sufficient either. Must man compromise a bit of himself to form relationships with those around him? It often appears so. We go searching in the darkness (this reminds me of the one-half of the Tao symbol or Jung's Shadow Unconscious) to share or add to our own identity as we make CONNECTIONS with others; perhaps all we have in common is our uniqueness and our humanity. Man feels incomplete and alienated; he also learns the value of his own uniqueness.

One's choice must be free and undetermined; if an individual makes a choice, it will somehow be interrelated to his experiences. He cannot, however, rely only on his experiences. Freedom comes from losing the feeling of determinism and accepting the painful and passionate realizations concerning human value that comes from freedom. Sartre said, as we experience the anguish of our alienation from the being-for-itself and we understand the being-in-itself, we also realize that we are free and undetermined. Being is only fact and not the future. We must understand, through emotion, if necessary, that transcending process of the human condition; affective experiences are part of existentialist values. Anguish, passion, and commitment enable us to form our own theory of value.

Sartre believed that man must desire; my desire might turn into anguish and remorse, but desire can also give me an insight into the true value of that which I desire. "Man is nothing else but that which he makes of himself" (Nietzsche). I am always saddened when I see others who cannot believe in themselves. The realization of the agony of much of life must not deaden us to any emotional involvement, even with ourselves!

There is a freedom in choosing oneself; it is the reflective for-it-self which recognizes the possibilities of my "thinking" consciousness. As I understand Existentialism, there is an objective responsive part and a reflective part, which represents "a non-positional consciousness" [sort of like the idea of quanta in physics?] and which rules our reactions. The extent to which we transcend the simple objective responding toward a more reflective consciousness measures the importance it has in relation to our developing concept of Self and individuality.

Sometimes people who are uncomfortable with this internal process externalize their discomfort by reaching out to others through distracting social contact. If we verbalize what we feel, then we will remember the verbalization of the feeling instead of the true feeling ("words are just a shape to fill a lack"). People verbalize when they are unsure of what they feel or when they think they should feel something they don't. In psychotherapy this process is called hyper-verbalization.

As humans, developing our own unified field theory of development (UFT), we experience and store memories. As a viewer of ourselves, however, we transcend the storing of just memories and form judgments and methods of understanding the experience. There should be no anticipatory anxiety but rather what Sartre calls "a turning back of the future toward the present." This view of Self was prescient of today's mindfulness movement, a well-tested, successful technique for staying "in the now".

Noumenal "Realities"

Of course, there is another side to all this "inner directedness". We are constantly striving to realize and actualize our uniqueness and individuality, and yet I know of no one who is not dependent on someone else for something and is not afraid of being alone. We depend on others because it is only through relationships that we can know more about ourselves. We view our weaknesses through others and through the possible anguish of complete autonomy. Self-knowledge cannot necessarily be verbally or physically expressed. It is not innate either. It is learned and assimilated in a continual process of growth that fluctuates between conscious and unconscious perceptions and activities. Our Self-concept is that personality concept which we consciously develop because of relationships. Our Self-concept changes as our self-knowledge grows; the separation between the two concepts is one of unconscious assimilation of growth through autonomy and conscious adjustment because of dependence on others.

Madeo (2010) refers to this growth as "exactitude", by which he describes the process of how we "find value beyond the limits of mind, meaning and myth." He encourages us to go beyond exactitude by looking at the noumenal, the emotive function of mind. But problems of communication can get in the way and "our cherished ideals are unexamined structures that may unknowingly limit our scopes, our reality" (ibid, 2010, pp. v, vi, 3). Can only logic order and CONNECT our train of thought? We all have unexamined hidden motives; I have found through work with my patients that those who look most for their motives and discover their deeper values and spiritual truths come out the other side of the search both in touch with reality and in an authentic place to pursue higher truths.

Madeo examines the problem of communication by looking directly at what makes us sentient (ibid, 2010). Likewise, Pinker points out, "ethical theory requires idealizations like free, sentient, rational, equivalent agents whose behavior is uncaused" (Pinker, 1997, p. 55). Madeo gives his own description of what it means to nominalize through a discussion of Kant. Madeo asserts that communication requires us to use quantifiers, locations, states of existences and a coherence in combining of all these factors. Language embeds categorical constructs and uses "local mythogenesis" (op cit., 2010, pp. 29, 94–97). Matter leads to chaos leads to consciousness leads to noumenal or "perfect existence" (When I read this, I asked myself, "Can this be an algorithm or be indexed?" But at this time the math would be beyond me!) Madeo refers to "Absolute existence of 'pure' consciousness vs. algorithms of 'pure matter'." In describing nature, an inherently paradoxical gap develops in the circuitries of the human mind; Madeo believes that absolute existence of one universal creative power just might be within our comprehension, even though our original "label" may not equal noumenal summaries as described. We should "watch out for 'artifacts' in thought."

The material world and those who live in it (all of us) are involved in irresolvable complexities (incomplete symmetry) requiring real creativity and real art that breaks through the seemingly 'real' which ultimately, in the end, only contains metaphors or simplified images of reality. In at least one sense, nothing is exactly what it seems to be. As Kant would unequivocally agree, by definition, things-in-themselves, the really Real, are unavailable to our hopelessly anthropocentric sensibility (ibid, 2010, p. 113).

Thus, ultimately, Madeo proposes that materialism can explain how "everything knowable must originate in the senses" (made of matter in the time/space continuum) but still may not be explained, regardless of Zeno's paradoxes. What about Bertrand Russell's (1872–1970) statement that "We find [this] belief ready in ourselves as soon as we begin to reflect…an instinctive belief" (Russell, 1912, p. 11). Although Descartes had initially used doubt to point us toward certainty about our own making, it was the philosophical musings at the turn of the 20th century which concretized that there could be "something else" in matter beyond the sense-data world. Is "to know" equal to "be acquainted with", i.e., to have the sense-data, like the difference between *wissen* and *kennen* in German?

Dealing with Death

As mentioned earlier, another way of putting our knowledge in relevant terms is to think of the juxtaposition between our quest for philosophical knowledge and Self-development against how much use self-awareness might be as it leads us up to the moment of death. This question interests me and many authors have written about this issue. As Charles Tart (2008) puts it, "Death really reminds us how little we know and at the same time how important it is to try to understand." Not only must we take the process of understanding ourselves and our short lives more seriously, but Tart also discusses the relevance of using discipline in daily living. A philosophical view of Other to CONNECTS us in a way that prepares us for enriched and appreciated experiences, i.e., the *capacity* to experience. On the other hand, he points out, we must sometimes use detachment as a type of "healthy spaciousness."

Individuals learn to cherish their individuality just as they solicit membership in a group process or fellowship where they can feel validated. To maintain individual freedoms, we must "find out what theories have been conditioned into us, acquire some perspective on them, and make some adult decisions about whether to continue to automatically believe them" (ibid, 2008, p. 34). This process develops a healthy UFT and perspective toward Self as one moves toward aging and death.

Of course, some of us experience separations, whether from depression (negative) or detachment (positive), as "living death", either of which provides choices of how to deal with life and its contextual pressures "on your own terms".

In the American and European cultures, we call this behavior Self-sufficiency, rugged individualism, or narcissism (if one's addiction to their needs outweigh the common good). The result depends on the nature of the system and where the individual lies, inside or outside the source of energy driving the system/environment.

The view toward social morality, detachment, or even one's acceptance of eventual death has changed over the centuries, thus changing societal structure and culture along the way. During the last few centuries particularly, the growth of Naturalism and acceptance of women as "equal forces" has greatly influenced aspects of societal views and philosophical writings. A comparison shows:

18th century—man at his best had to be a person whose mind, attitudes and actions were controlled by culture social man

19th century—return to spiritual man, Wordsworth romanticism, man can be free from society

20th century—Two views—romantic man best viewed in his own environment, Man as realist/naturalist, however, not truly revealed in society

Long-term Influences

Over the years, my mother added her influence on my philosophy-building. As I mentioned in a review of my background in Chapter One, my mother was a philosopher, as well as therapist, and taught me a great deal; she left me quite a legacy in memories and papers from which to draw. Her comments on Adler (1870–1937), an original contemporary and brief disciple to Freud, are very telling of what is to come in this book. Parts of a longer paper are summarized here, partly out of pride and partly to share her writing, which stands on its own. My personal slant is that the Outliers found in this world should be considered as part of a whole that makes the world unified and dignified.

Below is how my mother explained it; Adler was one of the original psychologists to view the psyche as a social instinct, and he was very involved in helping the poor and less bourgeois than Freud's patients. [More about this history in Chapter Thirteen]. As a philosopher/psychologist, my mother not only used these ideas as a basis of her own interactions with patients, but she also often shared kernels of theories in daily interactions with my brother and me. She believed in the Socratic method and led always by example.

ADLER by Virginia Haradon (1970) written to complete a degree toward becoming a Licensed Clinical Social Worker (LCSW) at 57 years old.

Whereas Freud was not interested in adjusting people to society and vice versa, Adler presented ideas about interpersonal conflicts, 2400 years after Aristotle had called man a "social animal".

> Yet all human conflicts are essentially social, although the structure of our society does not facilitate the solution of interpersonal conflicts and antagonisms…all human qualities are expressions of social interaction, all human problems are of social nature. Freud's theories do not support or enrich

the principle generally accepted by social workers that the problems clients bring to social agencies are psychosocial problems. He viewed "the mental sufferings of individuals as consequences of their failure to cope with the biological urges within them, with no special importance attached to their social situation" [emphasis added] (Werner, H., 1967, pp. 11–12).

"The Desire to Belong is the prime human motivation." …Adler assumed that man is motivated primarily by social urges…he relates himself to other people, engages in cooperative social activities, places social welfare above selfish interest, and acquires a style of life which is predominantly social in orientation. Here is a list of Adler's key concepts:

- Adler's self is a highly personalized subjective system…emphasis upon the uniqueness of personality…a unique configuration of motives, traits, interests, and values; every act performed by the person bears the stamp of his own distinctive style of life.
- Adler made consciousness the center of personality…causes, powers, instincts, impulses, and the like cannot serve as explanatory principles…the great upward drive that is life itself. From birth to death, the striving for superiority carried the person from one stage of development to the next higher stage.
- Later, he subordinated this view to the more general one that stated feelings of inferiority arise from a sense of incompletion or imperfection in any sphere of life. Example: the child is motivated by his feelings of inferiority to strive for a higher level of development. When he reaches this level, he begins to feel inferior again and the upward movement is initiated once more. Adler contended that inferiority feelings are not a sign of abnormality; they are the cause of all improvement in man's lot.
- Although social interest takes in such matters as cooperation, interpersonal and social relations, identification with the group, empathy, and so forth, it is much broader than all of these. In its ultimate sense, social interest consists of the individual helping society to attain the goal of a perfect society.
- These abilities and impressions, and the way he 'experiences' them—that is to say, the interpretation he makes of these experiences—are the bricks which he uses in his own 'creative' way in building up his attitude toward life, which determines this relationship to the outside world. What Adler is conveying is that the creative self is the yeast that acts upon the facts of the world and transforms these facts into a personality that is subjective, dynamic, unified, personal, and uniquely stylized.
- Most often the individual is not aware of his goals and intentions, consciousness is also self-determined. The individual knows only what he wants or needs to know. And the need for conscious awareness is highly overrated. Most emotional, mental, psychological, and physiological

- processes take place without any awareness, which only too often has an inhibitive effect.
- Emotions seem to be our master while they are actually only our tools...Reason and emotions are tools which we use alternately as they best fit our purpose. When they seem to oppose each other, this seeming opposition serves merely as an excuse for our actions, 'explained' by our emotions...We feel guilty only if we are not willing to do what we know we should do. In this sense, guilt feelings too have an obvious social purpose.
- A feeling of belonging is essential for social and emotional well-being...The real defense mechanisms are necessary.
- The attacks of the patient, whether overt toward the therapist or via masochistic suffering for which the therapist is held responsible, come to nothing when the therapist is not involved in the duel for power and constantly, sympathetically, brings responsibility back to the patient. Encouragement is fundamental to therapy, but it must be at a level significant for the patient.

Summary

In presenting a summary of the highlights of the foregoing material, it seems pertinent to preface this with one thought that was particularly basic to social work—the idea that since the problems that clients bring are more likely to be psychosocial than ever purely individual and intrapsychic. Adler's concept that man's problems stem from group interaction and therefore must be solved through group techniques is especially significant and makes the possible appropriateness of the group approach in therapy always something to be considered. This emphasis upon the social determinants of behavior which had been overlooked or minimized by Freud and Jung was probably Adler's greatest contribution to psychological (and in many ways philosophical) theory.

One sees Adler as a forerunner of certain existentialists and gestaltists in that he felt that these experiences exist subjectively or mentally here and now as strivings or ideals which affect present behavior. Another major contribution was the concept of social interest by which he conveyed that by working for the common good, man compensates for his individual weaknesses. However, like any other natural aptitude, this innate predisposition did not appear spontaneously, but had to be brought to fruition by guidance and training (Haradon, V., 1970).

Adler realized the purposiveness of emotions. One of his most thought-provoking contributions was his concept that we create our own emotions for our own purposes although we subjectively feel driven by them. To repeat, "they seem to be our master while they are actually only our tools." Emotions are not irrational; they express our private logic, what we really think and believe.[21]

---

[21]The philosophy, (Adlerian), is difficult to explain completely, but it has these elements, among others: 1) the notion of equality of individuals in terms of human

Guilt feelings too are only pretenses, pretenses of good intentions which we do not have. They emerge only when we do not want to amend or change, but to demonstrate our good intentions. We feel guilty only if we are not willing to do what we know we should do. In this sense, guilt feelings too have an obvious social purpose. It is the movement of the individual, the goals which he has set for himself, which indicate his total personality and permit a recognition of it. Without looking at the individual phenomenologically, one cannot see him. What makes him move are not any parts operating in him, be they emotions, drives, complexes, or other phenomena in him. The force that makes him move is himself, his own determination, his pursuit in line with his goals. Neurotic symptoms also have a purpose. They safeguard the individual against failure, they permit him to withdraw or to gain special privileges and services.

Courage and Manifesting Unity

It is a Unity that Einstein sought, it a Unity that the great religions promise. It is a Unity and comfort that so many patients seek in their therapy, throughout the world, now due to stress and dis-CONNECTION from an inner peace and knowledge of a Self with which to CONNECT. All this yearning for CONNECTION points to the importance of formulating a UFT for oneself, a belief system, a set of values, a way of moving through the world. The following chapters present many ways to get a clearer view of how all paths lead to a similar set of helpful and supportive data for developing a theory of life. We are all looking for equilibrium and balance. Whether the discovery at first appears symmetrical (Tao), or asymmetrical, must be resolved. This acceptance can become the joy of life.

How does our study of the "great courses" of philosophy, literature, sciences, art, and the Renaissance great theorists help us to advance our social function and psychological concerns in this new 21st century? The key is synthesis, not just as the concept is used by Hegel, but a real combination of ideas and experiences for the creation of a union or whole new outlook on life. The survival, or even death, of a heroic character provides the writer or historian the canvas upon which to present the structure that human nature most often takes. history to symbolize the movement of purpose and morality of a culture.

From the viewpoint of philosophy, the importance of the Sangha or community, and the need for morality to become an adult, is really seen through individual challenges, or even in Outlier behavior. The hero is not regularly a 'part of' a cause or group, although he may be leading it (nicely illustrated in *The Iceman Cometh* by Eugene O'Neill). He may start out with something to prove, if only to himself.

---

rights, 2) a declaration of the importance of respect in contrast to love, 3) the value of making contracts and forcing others to keep them by letting violators suffer the natural consequences of their behavior, 4) the issue of democratic establishment of responsibilities, and 5) the point of firmness in dealing with others, being constant and consistent. Probably, all successful human relations in any group depend on the acceptance and adherence to these Adlerian principles (Corsini, R., et al. 1973, p. 6).

He experiences himself, his thoughts, and feelings, as something separated from the rest, a kind of optical delusion of his consciousness. This delusion is a kind of prison for us, restricting us to our personal desires and to affection for a few persons nearest to us. Our task must be to free ourselves from this prison by widening our circle of compassion to embrace all living creatures and the whole nature in its beauty (Einstein, 1954, p. 32).

One must be careful, however, of becoming too tolerant, even with the expression of compassion, because such behavior can turn into Codependency. The quality and rhythm of one's relationships demonstrate how much one has learned about oneself through the hero's journey to experiencing the Shadow, or even near-death, and then learning from the psychological trip. Most of all heroism will be demonstrated in the daily devotion to faith and self-care in all activities. But regardless of the restrictions, the adversity within which one finds oneself creates opportunities for success and immense growth in one's inner work. In many ways, this dynamic may all come down to an expression of courage.

Paul Tillich (1886–1965) wrote eloquently about the heroic experience in *The Courage to Be* (1952). "The ontological question of the nature of being can be asked as the ethical question of the nature of courage…The courage to be is the ethical act in which man affirms his own being in spite of those elements of his existence which conflict with his essential self-affirmation" (ibid, 1952, p. 2). Tillich's theory reflected his synthesis of the mind/body dichotomy, where reason/desire summed up one's essential nature. Thus, despite the influences that built our UFT of environmental cause and effect, Tillich believes in some "essential nature" that manifests as the resultant personality develops through the "tempering" of temperament. Tillich pointed out, for instance, how the Greek Stoics saw this process.

The Stoic courage is, in the ontological as well as the moral sense, 'courage to be.' It is based on the control of reason in man. But reason is not in either the old or the new Stoic what it is in the contemporary terminology. What conflicts with the courage of wisdom is desires and fears. The Stoics developed a profound doctrine of anxiety which also reminds us of recent analyses. They discovered that the object of fear is fear itself [emphasis added] (ibid, 1952, p. 12).

Tillich's feelings about fear, and the courage to be in the face of triggered fear and anxiety, was a "revelation of sensibility". He gave many examples of how we can reason our way out of fear, two of which are from Greek philosophers:
Seneca: "Nothing is terrible in things except fear itself." / "God is *beyond* suffering; the true Stoic is above it."
Epictetus: "For it is not death or hardship that is a fearful thing, but the fear of death and hardship."
More importantly, Tillich was a great proponent of the use of affirmations to clear one's essential being despite desires and anxieties. This process can create joy.

Holistic Viewpoint

Earlier in this chapter we discussed the studies of the Theosophical Society and its focus on purposive order and the soul as immortal. They also described the method by which we brought all this history, knowledge, ethics, morality, and symbolism into the modern world; it attempted an integration of these important foundations of civilization into what we now call the "Holistic Viewpoint", or the concept of CONNECTION.

1. In Greek philosophy, the meaning of the human point of view and holism was presented in terms of the meaning of being. In the European Renaissance, holism took the form of a humanistic and artistic educational methodology, depicting the place of the human in the natural and social world. In the 20th century, holism began to be expressed as a phenomenological and psychological rendering of human potential.
2. By researching the phenomenology of the embodiment, we can discern an anatomy of human creativity.
3. Practice is founded on the basic premise of the non-duality of subjectivity and objectivity; one capable of forging the unity of psychic and psychosomatic. This practice can lead the human consciousness to the autopoietic [self-producing] rediscovery of the natural gift of well-being (Palmirotta, 2013).

Swedenborg (1688–1772) set out to answer the question: What is the "secret" to using analysis versus science to gain understanding? He proposed it is the opening of the "gate;" the sure knowledge that nature and the material world are the vessels of eternity, the "alchemical furnace" in which the spiritual world is revealed. These concepts relate to his doctrine of "correspondences", which exhibits truth as a "threefold sense' namely, celestial, spiritual, and natural." That doctrine is why it is possible to see eternity in a grain of sand. Swedenborg also believed that the beauty of the human form is an emblem of the Supreme Being, "everything that lives is holy…every genius, every hero, is a prophet…The greater that which you can hide, the greater yourself."

Moving onto more modern philosophical views, Varela (2004) strongly advocated holistic views. He and Fritjof Capra (born 1939, *The Tao of Physics*, 1975) are two strong voices from the last century which have molded the study of knowledge, science, and ecology into an integrated and unified form. In *Autopoiesis and Cognition: The Realization of the Living* (1980), co-authored with Maturana, Varela originally referred to his concept of human cognition and consciousness as "embodied philosophy".[22]

---

[22] Likewise, Varela's concept of "neurophenomenology" stated that "the fundamental characteristic of living systems included: possessing an independent organized structure, self-maintaining and self-regenerating, which contributes to the generation of the whole system. Living systems are self-referential, they only think about their own maintenance, and all the actions which they seem to carry out toward the outside really have the aim of maintaining their own integrity with respect to environmental disturbances" (Maturana &Varela, 1980, pp. 73–76). I find this to be an exciting point

The achievements of artists, writers, statesmen, and scientists can be explained almost entirely according to the UFT. It is the environment which makes a person wise or compassionate, that provides the evidence and answers to "all these questions about purposes, feelings, knowledge. What a person 'intends to do' depends on what he has done in the past and what has then happened and so on."

Wilber's Theory of Everything

As interesting and perhaps helpful as this summary of past holistic philosophies is, more recently, philosopher, scientist, and scholar Ken Wilber wrote a book entitled *A Theory of Everything* (2000) in which he attempted to use physics, integrated with spirituality and psychological explanations, to make sense of our everyday experiences. He begins with an explanation of string theory. The first question that came to my mind was: can physics really explain everything? How about the expressiveness of poetry, for instance; would that do instead? Shakespeare seems to have done a fine job!

In 1975, just as I was finishing my dissertation, I was also becoming involved with a Science of Mind class and, while doing an assignment, I came up with the acronym—IMU—I am You, a theory describing levels of attachment based on the level of commitment, and yes, CONNECTION, we find with each other. With concentric circles, I drew a chart showing the inner core, IMU, of true attachment; the next circle out was the trust and love stages; next attachment to one's acquaintances; then work; and such continuing as the circles widened. I was amazed in reading Wilber's book to find he showed a similar schema. His theory integrated developmental stages with a theory of morality, and I will go into further detail about his point of view later in this chapter. In 1975, all I wanted to do was to simplify the explanation for why CONNECTING felt like becoming One.

Wilber's theory of what he calls the kosmos attempts to explain our dialogue with an experience of God [Unity]. His explanation is very complicated, and I choose not to replicate it here. Just read his book. But some of the ideas are supportive of my paradigm of a unified field theory of development (UFT), which I have been teaching in my Developing Psychology classes since 1985 and, subsequently, to my patients during their recovery period. I would like to think that my book presents a more practical point of view of how we CONNECT.

In Wilber's terms, there is a framework of "realms": physical, emotional, mental, and spiritual—the explanations of all create a sense of the whole.

> An integral vision—or a genuine Theory of Everything—attempts to include matter, body, mind, soul, and spirit as they appear in self, culture, and nature. A vision that attempts to be comprehensive, balanced, inclusive. A vision that therefore embraces science, art, and morals; that equally includes disciplines from physics to spirituality, biology to aesthetics, sociology to contemplative prayer; that shows up in integral politics, integral medicine, integral business,

---

of view in that it supports my own interest in how the <u>immune system</u> operates as a network as well.

integral spirituality [Note to the Reader: Wilber is working toward a consciousness Revolution where Unity in Diversity = the Integral. This word integral is "integral" (pun intended) to his entire concept] …

I sought a world philosophy—or an integral philosophy—that would believably weave together the many pluralistic contexts of science, morals, aesthetics, Eastern as well as Western philosophy, and the world's great wisdom traditions. Not on the level of details—that is finitely impossible; but on the level of orienting generalizations: a way to suggest that the world really is one, undivided, whole, and related to itself in every way: a holistic philosophy for a holistic *Kosmos,* a plausible Theory of Everything (ibid, 2000, pp. xii, 38).

I particularly agree with the developmental nature of Wilber's theory. Having based his work on G. Spencer Brown (*Laws of Form,* 1969*),* Wilber presents "growth stages" wherein "each succeeding stage incorporated its predecessors and then added some new capacity…New knowledge comes when you simply bear in mind what you need to know." I love this point of view and use it daily with individuals who need just that kind of encouragement to keep moving forward instead of fretting about the past.

Most developmental psychologists rely on determination of the sequential staging of a client's symptoms to indicate at what point in their life trauma, abandonment, or negative impressions may have taken place, i.e., the environmental factors built into my UFT of development. Wilber handles this layering effect by using color designation, as we will see below. It is also important to consider that what you were developmentally at, say 25, will affect what you become at 65; we must also consider how the UFT variables continue to change us and our "visions" of ourselves [Heisenberg].

I saw a couple who had been married for over 40 years. Among other communication issues, the husband presented unhappiness with the state of their sexual relationship. What was striking about this was that, for their ages (both over 60) and length of marriage, they had one of the best sexual relationships I'd heard of in 40 years! But I had to validate his complaints, as they were his and causing him distress. Part of the problem was he had been a "virgin" at marriage, and never having been with another woman, he consistently compared his wife, and his sexual experiences with her, to those he read in exotica and in R and X-rated movies he saw. He talked about how he remembered her as she first was and how he thought she'd be in their older sexual years after the children left home (picture in his head!). I suspected he wasn't really comparing his wife to others, or even to her younger self, but rather he was comparing the ideas in his head to himself and his own level of performance, but when confronted with this possibility he denied it.

Whether or not I was right, we continued to work on a solution. He wanted to bring other people into their sexual life; she deferred for obvious reasons, although she eventually gave in to the idea of him having a "free pass" to be with at least one other woman just "to see what it would be like one other time in his life." But even that he never took us up on. He just complained and became more distant. I began to suspect being unhappy was one of his determining personality factors and he had put all his energy into this one area of concern.

If we base our marriages on such a picture and expect our mate to act, respond and look (!) as they did 40 years before, the marriage has been heading for trouble for a long time. Feelings, motivations, ethics and values, biochemistry, degree of neurological activation, learning system, belief systems, and self-conception of mental health, all these concepts could factor into Wilber's theory of "levels". He would say that, as warm and kind as this man generally was, there was still a touch of narcissism in his view of his sexual life. "Our generation is an extraordinary mixture of greatness and narcissism…but we overestimate the importance of our Self" (ibid, 2000, p. 3)[23]. My patient was forgetting how important the mutuality of the sexual acts was supposed to be, and in his depression, he began to exhibit Outlier behavior of avoidance and living in the past.

When Huston Smith (1958) added to his prior important work on the great religions, he gave us an augmented view of religion, a mapping that summarized the world's great wisdom traditions. In *Forgotten Truth* (1976), Smith influenced Wilber's levels of Selfhood and the levels of reality, or simply the level of the subject and the level of the object. Wilber made these levels into part of his indexing system, which sometimes referred to chakra energy levels as representative of how we hold onto energy psychically.

When chakra 4 believes only chakra 1 is real, we get the rational philosophy of materialism—we get a Hobbes or a Marx. When chakra 4 believes the emotional-sexual dimension is most crucial, we get a Freud. When it puts great emphasis on chakra 3, we get an Adler, and so on…At chakra 5, you do not think about the web of life, you have a direct experience of cosmic consciousness, where you concretely experience being one with the entire gross realm of nature. At chakra 5, you do not think about Platonic archetypes, or merely pray to deity form, you are rather directly immersed in a living union with Divine Presence. At chakra 7, you are plunged into the formless unmanifest, the Abyss, Emptiness, *Urgrund, Ayn, nirvikalpa samdhi*, and so on (ibid, 2000, p. 159).

Wilber defines healthy development as a 'successive decrease in egocentrism,' decreasing narcissism and increasing consciousness. The developmental theorists mentioned in Chapter Thirteen, Piaget (cognition) and Kohlberg (moral development), tell us we strive to manifest more Other directedness with compassionate behavior (i.e. Kohlberg' theory is cumulative and shows individuals must pass through earlier conventional thinking/Piaget). Without these

---

[23] "Narcissism is not simply the overvaluing of the self and its abilities, but a concomitant undervaluing of others and their contributions. It is not simply possessing a large amount of self-esteem; it is the simultaneous devaluation of others that is crucial. The inner state of narcissism, clinicians tell us, is often that of an empty or fragmented self, attempting to fill the void with an egocentric grasping that inflates the self while deflating others. The emotional mood is, 'Nobody tells me what to do!'" [More about Narcissism in Chapter Eighteen] (ibid, 2000, p. 17).

opportunities for social skill development, we become Outliers. Wilber maintains that a "river of life" is symbolized through a "color base" and some of these bases even represent archetypes [Jung], such as:

- Red—(similar to Kohlberg Stage 2), 20% of the population
- Blue—Truth seeking behavior (similar to Kohlberg Stage 4) One and Only one right way, 40% of the population
- Orange—(similar to Kohlberg Stage 5-1), Marketplace Alliances, 30% of the population
- Green—sensitive self (Kohlberg Stage 5-2), Consensus seeking, Pluralistic Relativism, 10% of the population
- Yellow—integrative (similar to Kohlberg Stage 5-3), Flexibility, spontaneity, and functionality; facilitates knowledge and competency, 1% of the population
- Turquoise—Holistic (possibly similar to Kohlberg Stage 6, but which for Kohlberg was an idealistic position in moral development), 0.1 % of the of population (ibid, 2000, See p. 43, Figure 3-1; p. 70, Figure 4-4; p. 178, Figure 6-3 re: Chakras)

I find it interesting that the color choices of his developmental system line up with those of the Eastern theory of Chakras (see p. 178 of Wilber's book); I like to think he probably picked these colors on purpose for how his theory is indexed? Having established this color-coded ranking of how consciousness develops, Wilber goes on to build a wave system, using hierarchies (both ranking and linking) and the linguistic theory hierarchies (unranked but able to provide meaning and organization). Each wave would transcend the last.

In reading this book, I was excited about the CONNECTION I found in it to ideas I had formulated while I was teaching and practicing psychotherapy in the 1980s and 1990s. Originally, in college, I was biochemistry/biophysics major. Those who read Chapter Ten through Twelve will see these are areas that still intrigue me. That we could explain human behavior, much less neuroscientific results, with the use of quantum physic theories was nowhere, even on the cutting edge, of the theories I studied in graduate school in 1973. But I kept circling back to the idea that behavior was both the point in space and the quantum wave that could explain human nature, which was difficult and just as unpredictable as Heisenberg's theory said it was. And here was Wilber trying to put all this in words for me, but not so simply and certainly not for a general reader.

Wilber's idea was of an "integral wave", with its particle points of development, which stated "the notion of *development* allows us to recognize nested truths, not primitive superstitions" (ibid, 2000, p.112, footnote 5). My idea of how quantum development and CONNECTIONS can explain human behavior is parallel to his belief that "Integral transformative practice" would give considerable weight to the importance of relationships, community, culture, and intersubjective factors in general, not merely as a realm of application of spiritual insight, but as a means of spiritual transformation. Some the important variables in his theory also include:

- Direction of change: regressive, progressive, stationary.
- Methods of change: critical, translative, transformative.
- Types of freedom: negative, positive.
- View of nature or nurture.
- View of the Sangha as the self at every level is a self-in-relationship-with-other-selves (agency-in-communion).

To continue, Wilber refers to families as "a society of selves" with a "center of gravity that acts to bind the multiple waves, states, streams and realms into something like a unified organization [think chairman of the board]; the disruption of this organization, at any of its general stages, can result in pathology" [emphasis added] (ibid, 2000, pp. 54, 167).

At this point, Wilber's theory becomes very dense[24] about his belief that society can have a social autoimmune disease; it creates its own internal disintegration (not being integral anymore). Two examples given are his opinion that the Medieval church was blue, while Metanarratives and universals are almost always green as outlined above.

Wilber even thinks of DNA as an example of something "green" as shown in this opinion: "Development tends to proceed by differentiation and integration (e.g., a single-cell zygote differentiates into two cells, then four cells, then sixteen, then thirty-two… while at the same time these differentiated cells are integrated into coherent tissues, organs, and systems (green)" (ibid, 2000, p. 28). [Note cover art to this book, a representation of a zygote becoming two cells that is actually a picture of my grandson, Nathan!]

The intense study that Wilber requires from us can increase our knowledge, fill us with awe, and even lead us to question our prior beliefs. But ultimately the

---

[24] An example: "Both gross and subtle reductionism believe the entire world can be accounted for in third-person, it-language (i.e., they are both monological, not dialogical or trans-logical). The 'crime of the Enlightenment,' incidentally, was subtle reductionism, not gross reductionism…The 'blank slate' view of the human mind—with its correlates in psychology of behaviorism and associationism, and an epistemology of empiricism—was adopted by liberalism for many reasons, not the least of which was that it promised the 'unlimited perfectibility' of human beings through various types of objective social engineering. All innate differences, capacities, and structures were summarily rejected, and human beings, born in a state rather akin to a blob of clay, could thus be molded by exterior institutions and forces (behaviorism, associationism) into any desired state. [This perfectibility can be seen as a social engineering agenda] …By denying that the interiors themselves have realities, realms, stages, and states of their own—and by in fact reducing them to imprints of the sensorimotor world—liberal philosophy and psychology would deeply sabotage their own goals. They would, with their allegiance to merely sensory empiricism and the blank slate, be prime contributors to the worldview of scientific materialism, a flatland view of the universe that in fact acts to undermine and sometimes grossly derail genuine growth and development of the interior domains" (ibid, 2000, pp. 161–162).

outcome of any kind of "universal" study is to form a united understanding of how the mind combines imagination, language and comprehension skills, worldly experiences, and emotional reactions. We have come to the point in our studies where we can recognize, for ourselves, how the CONNECTIONS we make will enable us to move forward, never backward, toward health and transformational experiences. Even where there may be melancholy, deadness, or despair we can find solutions in "simple stoic endurance". As mentioned, I often quote Marcus Aurelius' *Meditations* (Long, 1862) as my favorite example of this Stoicism: in "bearing the unbearable" we just tighten our belt, and suffer, and don't complain, to ourselves or to others. My mother called it "soldiering on".

Hearing negative verbal feedback in our head is the worst thing for us as we are building our own internal philosophy about a healthy view of life. Buddhists call it the concept of temporality; everything is impermanent after all. "Probably commitment and engagement are the most essential [points of view], may command one to strain one's capacity to the utmost…man is always more than the sum of his parts" (Chessick, 1996b).[25] Along the way of building of our UFT we have learned that we have epistemological alternatives: religion and metaphysics can help calm us, but they must be grounded in something in the Self.

Pierre Teilhard de Chardin

I first read *The Phenomenon of Man* by Teilhard de Chardin (1959) in graduate school. It was tough going, and when I reread it, the notes I found in my own handwriting inside the front cover didn't help that much. But I feel it is imperative to include his work here as he is representative of 20th century philosophers who studied consciousness and evolution of the universe. As a trained geologist and paleontologist, he was involved in the discovery of the Peking man and in the development of a notion that human thought had its own *noosphere* or "creative energy point" in evolution. Ultimately, he believed we were moving toward an Omega Point or "maximum point of complexity". The introduction to Teilhard de Chardin's book is eloquently written by Sir Julian Huxley. In it Huxley states,

> …he [de Chardin] has effected a threefold synthesis—of the material and physical world with the world of mind and spirit; of the past with the future; and of variety with unity, the many with the one…with reference to its development in time and to its evolutionary position…human evolution and biological evolution…man to cultural evolution by defining the position of the

---

[25] "Very commonly one sees patients complaining of a great sense of deadness and wildly involving themselves in passionate adventures or the quest for excitement in order to tranquilize the sense of deadness, either physical adventures or looking for ecstatic passions or drugged states of some kind…he can only use what I call pacifiers…Modern theoretical thinking says narcissistic libido and object libido take different developmental pathways…delusions as pacifiers. Kant's Copernican revolution directed our focus onto the mind of the observer. Instead of saying there are things out there, and the mind must find out about them, he says you can only learn about 'out there' by studying the mind, because only things with certain features out there can be known by the mind (noumena)" (ibid, 1996, pp. 337–342).

individual human personality in the process of hominization (Huxley in de Chardin, 1959, p. 11–17).

Because of his vast background in the sciences, Teilhard de Cardin demonstrated the knowledge I craved at my first reading so many years ago: how the different branches of science could combine into a theory of the universe in its entirety, and which even I could understand (see Chapter Ten for my attempt to add to this process). His theoretical organization of evolution in the process of becoming, of attaining new levels of existence [potential] was seen as a new "theory of genesis". Thus, he was more evolutionary than the Vatican could accept from a Jesuit priest, and during his lifetime he was censored (although by the 1990s apparently forgiven and praised by Pope Benedict XVI).

Teilhard de Chardin (1881–1955) was influenced by reading Nietzsche, who said, "man is unfinished and must be surpassed to be completed" (Nietzsche quoted in ibid, 1959, p. 13). Teilhard de Chardin strongly felt that if man's evolution, and thus the world's, was to be understood, it had to be based on first grasping the core issue of how consciousness had evolved. Therein came his term for this process of the transforming agency, hominization: progressive psychosocial evolution. He was a great believer, as well, in "ontogeny recapitulates phylogeny", the theory by Haeckel (known as the "recapitulation theory") which states that any individual ovum, and thus fetus as it completes its development to a birthed organism, will developmentally replicate the stages and nature of its evolutionary history as a species. This theory is an undergirding of most developmental theories and one which we will return to in Chapter Thirteen. Even globally, the future of mankind will come from a "global unification of human awareness as a necessary prerequisite" (Teilhard de Chardin, 1959, p. 15).

Two other important and powerful terms used by Teilhard de Chardin to complete his developmental theory are complexification and cosmogenesis. The concept of "creating/generating" the cosmos, as opposed to it just existing there before we did, opened my mind to a greater awareness of how I could actively participate in not only my own life, but also how important it was for me to pay attention to what was going on around me and how everything really is always evolving, all the time. This concept was a great leap in my personal philosophy of life. "Cosmogenesis: the genesis of increasingly elaborate organization during cosmogenesis, as manifested in the passage from subatomic units to atoms, from atoms to inorganic and later to organic molecules, thence to the first subcellular living units or self-replicating assemblages of molecules, and then to cells, to multicellular individuals, to cephalized metazoan with brains, to primitive man, and now to civilized societies" (ibid, 1959, p. 15).

Rather than just being reactive without thought or logic, de Chardin encourages us to think in terms of alpha (start) to omega (final stages) when we analyze a situation that may be affecting us. Self-complexification may create convergent integration and more subjective mental activity, but of course with this result comes more conscious activity as well. De Chardin proposed that with full consciousness comes "the specific effect of organized complexity." Therefore, to summarize, important terminology includes:

Noogensis: evolution of mind.
Hominization: the process of becoming truly human, actualizing of potential.
Noosphere: sphere of mind, interrelations of thinking organisms.
Matter: experienced in "space-time".
Complexification: laws of evolution.
Synthesis: mind and spirit, past and future, variety and unity—he was interested in processes, human evolution and specifically the phenomenon of thought (de Chardin believes man is unfinished).
Awareness: psychosocial evolution, operations of knowing, feeling and willing, leads to higher types of organizations, patterns of cooperation, and creative products.
Soul: focal point of transformation, all energy psychic in nature.

According to de Chardin, psychic energy comes from man "taking his measure", and being aware of a whole series of senses:

- A sense of spatial immensity.
- A sense of depth.
- A sense of number.
- A sense of proportion.
- A sense of quality or of novelty, enabling us to distinguish in nature certain absolute stages of perfection and growth.
- A sense of movement.
- A sense of the organic.

These senses enable man to respond to the **cosmogenesis** around him. Teilhard de Chardin believed that "the threefold illusion of smallness, plurality and immobility" interfered with man's ability to put himself in the forefront. The "phenomenon of man" was presented as the three events—pre-life, life, and thought/noosphere—which illustrated how we got from the past and moved into the future (ibid, 1959). This collection of energy into a singular purpose is reminiscent of Wilber's green stage of development.[26] At this point in his theory, Teilhard de Chardin's ideas clearly become scientific. However, as in most

---

[26] "Energy is the measure of that which passes from one atom to another in the course of their transformations. A unifying power then, but also, because the atom appears to become enriched or exhausted in the course of the exchange, the expression of structure. Energy nowadays represents for science the most primitive form of universal 'stuff'...The history of consciousness and its place in the world remain incomprehensible to anyone who has not seen first of all that the cosmos in which man finds himself caught up constitutes, by reason of the unimpeachable wholeness of its whole, a system, a totum and a quantum: a system by its plurality, a totum by its unity, a quantum by its energy; all three within a boundless contour. [interdependence]. Although there are many contours in an attenuated environment, quantum [theory] only takes on its full significance when we try to define it with regard to a concrete natural movement—duration. All life is a process of transformation (from cosmogenesis)" [emphasis added] (op cit., 1959, p. 46).

philosophical theories since the Greeks, eventually he arrives at the belief in an unscientific dualism.

> Without the slightest doubt there is something through which material and spiritual energy hold together and are complementary. In the last analysis, somehow or other, there must be a single energy operating in the world. And the first idea that occurs to us is that the 'soul' must be as if it were a focal point of transformation at which, from all the points of nature, the forces of bodies converge, to become interiorized and sublimated in beauty and truth. Between the within and the without of things [atoms] the interdependence of energy is incontestable [emphasis added] (ibid, 1959, pp. 63–64).

It is important to know that one knows, to reflect. "There is not one instinct in nature, but a multitude of forms of instincts each corresponding to a particular solution of the problems of life" (ibid, 1959, p. 167). Steven Pinker concurs: "When all goes well, our reasoning instincts link up into complex programs for rational analysis, but that is not because we somehow commune with a realm of truth and reason. The same instincts can be seduced by sophistry, bump up against paradoxes like Zeno's beguiling demonstrations that motion is impossible, or make us dizzy as they ponder mysteries like sentience and free will" (Pinker, 1997, p. 185–186).[7]

As a psychologist, I think the interesting part of this evolutionary process is when instinct becomes intelligence; this would be the point at which a developing 'child' becomes a 'person' through the process of personalization and internalizing the influences of what I have called the elements of the UFT. But Teilhard de Chardin was careful not to "confuse individuality with personality. He was aware that in every epoch man has thought himself at a 'turning point of history.' Even in 1959, his references to 'modern man' (over sixty years ago) belied the fact that many people were not able or not interested in grasping his concepts." To this day, he still seems in many ways ahead of his time. He held a view of an "organic unity" that would be possible in society if only it was acknowledged and supported. For Teilhard de Chardin, man is the final unification.[27]

---

[27] "Knowledge for its own sake...knowledge for power...increased power for increased action...increased action for increased being...Biosphere has so far been no more than a network of divergent lines, free at their extremities...By effect of reflection and the recoils it involves, the loose ends have been tied up, and the noosphere tends to constitute a single closed system in which each element sees, feels, desires and suffers for itself the same things as all the others at the same time...only one reality seems to survive and be capable of succeeding and spanning the infinitesimal and immense: energy—that floating universal entity from which all emerges and into which all falls back as into an ocean; energy, the new spirit; the new god. So, at the world's Omega, as at its Alpha, lies the Impersonal...In the opposite direction we conceive the 'ego' to be diminishing and eliminating itself, with the trend to what is most real and most lasting in the world, namely the Collective and the Universal. Personality is seen as a specifically corpuscular and ephemeral property; a prison from which we must try to escape" (ibid, 1959, pp. 249–251, 258).

I encourage the readers to look further into Teilhard de Chardin if this subject is as interesting to them as it was to me, particularly if they have an interest in the sciences. His ideas make he wanted to define the general evolutionary process and our place and role in it. Knowledge of this process would create the higher operations of "knowing, feeling and willing."

Bateson's History of Philosophy

A summary of the history of philosophy would not be complete without a mention of *Steps to an Ecology of Mind* (1972) by Gregory Bateson (1904–1980). His writings appeal to me based on his statement that "Ecology of Mind" is a unified body of theory: areas of study of biology and behavior, interdisciplinary patterns common to many disciplines. The premises of my book are quite similar in many ways; Bateson combines so many of the issues and influences that have been my great loves, particularly anthropology (his wife was Margaret Mead). Also, he attempts to integrate behavioral sciences with physical sciences. The "cybernetics" of it all just made sense to me, and my understanding of his theories was reinforced by my studies with some of the great leaders in Systems Theory at United States International University in the 1970s. Likewise, a sensitive documentation of her life as the daughter of this famous pair, *Composing a Life* (1989), by Mary Catherine Bateson, is a powerful reflection of their influence on her.

Although not quite a contemporary of Chomsky, the simplicity of Bateson's own double bind theory can be compared to Chomsky's notations about the problems in communication, where conflicting messages create a dilemma and confusion for the listener. Because the responder will automatically be wrong regardless of response (sometimes also referred to as gaslighting), it is logical that dysfunctional relationships/families frequently demonstrate this type of manipulative communication.

Bateson also CONNECTED his theory to modern-day chaos theory in physics (see Chapter Twelve) using cybernetics and system theory. He pointed out the ways in which the interacting systemic CONNECTIONS of the double bind can actually present solutions to the original communication; however, apparent paradoxes can also look like a trap or an attempt to control the Other in the first place.

Bateson worked in tandem with many great scholars of his time, particularly in the field of psychology: Laing, Milton Erikson, Jackson, Haley and Weakland. In addition, he always gave credit to the men who had influenced his work: Lamarck, William Blake, Samuel Butler, Collingwood, and William Bateson, who all had cybernetic ideas. Ultimately, he successfully combined anthropology, psychiatry, biological evolution, and genetics with the new epistemology that came out of systems theory and studies of ecology. In addition, he was a student of Jungian theory and a practicing Buddhist. Anyone reading this book who knows me (or has read Chapter One!) will understand why he has influenced my ideas....

Although his book was called *Steps to an Ecology of Mind*, it could also have been called the ecology of "ideas". He clearly points out that his theory is a philosophical one and based on phenomenological theory built from context and meaning. "It's like life—a game whose purpose is to discover the rules, which are always changing and always undiscoverable...Knowledge is knitted together or woven like cloth...[but] in 3 or 4 dimensions" (Bateson, 1972, p. 12–13, 15, 20–21).

I wrote a paper in college, entitled "How I Plathe *Glass Bead Game*" (1973). It was based upon the premises of Herman Hesse's book by that name (1943); it was also infused with Bateson's theories of taking "ready-made ideas and shuffling the pieces" into multidimensional and phenomenological experiences that could provide enlightenment of a sort. More on this in Chapter Twenty-One.

Bateson addressed the "problem" of instinct. He surrendered to the idea that we all have a "self-preservative instinct", but he worried it was a contradiction to one's becoming self-aware.

> Is God the "explanatory principle" for instinct? Like having one big God to explain the universe and lots of little "imps" or "goblins" to explain the small things that happen. Consciousness is awareness/thought in effect...Myths and fables are made up, dreams are not as "planned" ...Dreams are mostly made of images and feelings, and if you are going to communicate in images and feelings and such, you again are governed by the fact that there is no image for "not". (The dream just leaves out the label) [emphasis added; notice this position is dualistic like the Tao, probably relates to Bateson's study of Jungian concepts?] (ibid, 1972, p. 45, 51, 55).

In this manner, an analytical system must collect all data which demonstrate aspects of Unity: "the affective, economic, chronological, and spatial, sociological/integration and disintegration of the major unit (assimilation of ideas/which)" (ibid, 1972, p. 66). It was a very early construct of Bateson's to include homogeneous versus heterogeneous variables in the development of "schemas" (Piaget, See Chapter Thirteen). This view of Unity fits nicely with that of Madeo (2006, 2010), who stated that a theory of Dynamic Equilibrium demands an explanation of both Symmetry and Asymmetry. Maybe it is its categories that are symmetrical and its relationships that are complementary? Is it that which has underlying dynamism that can differentiate and synthesize (Hegel)?

When we consider this dynamism, and the places between asymmetry and symmetry to which the "glass bead game" may bring us, the trick is to not let the paradoxes, the Catch-22, the impermanence become traps, but rather let them be guideposts along the path of Self-discovery. In 1981, Paul Dell wrote a sparse but impressive piece in the *Journal of Marital and Family Therapy* about how paradox in our lives requires us to learn the lessons of "recursiveness", meaning that whatever choices come to us, or are chosen by us, will reflect the whole and are the result of the whole before the choice. Dell takes cybernetics to a higher level when he states that meaning is never inherent. In fact:

> Self-recursiveness is cybernetic feedback wherein a statement, organism, or system alters its own behavior because its previous output feeds back to it and modifies its subsequent behavior...any and all kind (s) of feedback [creates] paradoxes...although paradox is rooted in the epistemology of the observer, its ontological foundation lies in self-recursiveness...Self-reference cannot be

conceived outside...There is, in fact, a continuing recursive evolution such that one's own personal epistemology determines what one sees, which determines what one does, which, in turn, determines what actually happens in one's world, which then helps determine one's own personal epistemology (Dell, 1981, pp. 127–130).

It is easy to see the influence of Bateson and his theories of epistemology and ontology upon Dell. In a very utilitarian manner, Dell points out how cybernetics and self-recursiveness can be used to view CONNECTIONS and untangle the confusion of a double bind situation. He points out that pride is one of the Seven Cardinal Sins (denial of recursiveness); likewise, hubris is a denial of any Unmoved Mover, untouched and untouchable, who can deal unilaterally with our world (ibid, 1981).

As we review our study of philosophy, views of reality, ethics, morals and even cosmology, we can easily see the many shifts since Socrates and Plato (2400 years ago), and yet it seems the subject matter hasn't really changed that much. The current 21st century view of philosophy has been to break its study into different approaches, such as continental philosophy versus analytical philosophy, and of course with each subgrouping is paired the group of names associated with the classifications of ideas and terms. The "continental" group is more drawn to the phenomenological point of view, embracing natural science in their foundation over the hard sciences (Rosen, 1998). The emphasis on existentialism, Gestalt theory, and direct practice (all in response to the metaphysical) has greatly influenced the growth of an "evidenced-based" practice of psychology as well.

"Analytical" philosophy is more interested in direct and immediate evidence, without regard to historical relevance. Thus, this form of study would not relate to the influences found in my Unified Field Theory of development (UFT); this set of data has been based on a lifelong set of environmental influences. Finally, the scientific method would be upheld based on less regard for evidence from unconscious or symbolic forces. Certainly, as we go into Chapter Eight, on the spiritual influences (for our soul, for our health, and for the organization of our society), we will see how the development of modern religion has had to grow beyond the simple hierarchical explanation of analytical philosophy!

Freedom and the Path of the Soul

"This is the 'goal of the soul path'—to feel existence; not to overcome life's struggles and anxieties" (Moore, 1992, p. 260).

I would consider Tenzin Gyatso, fourteenth Dalai Lama, to be a great current philosopher. He is of my generation in terms of years, although far, far removed from whatever concerns most Americans have. After more than sixty-five years in exile, he holds firmly to Truth as the path that will free Tibet from the Han Chinese of People's Republic of China, who invaded Tibet in 1949–50.

I was privileged to study with His Holiness on a 12-day retreat in 2001. Of course, his views on history and most everything is conditioned by Buddhism.[28] He was intensely educated and drilled in Buddhism, maturing with an equivalent of a doctoral degree in his religion. At age 16, he was thrown into the temporal world as administrative leader of Tibet under invasion. Throughout his life, from childhood forward, he has meditated many hours each day; the perspectives he gained allow him to view people and events on many levels, common and uncommon.

The British philosophers John Locke, David Hume, George Berkeley, David Hartley, and John Stuart Mill proposed that thought is governed by two laws that mirror many of the principles of Buddhism, as we will see in Chapter Nine. One law is continuity: ideas that are frequently experienced together get associated in the mind. Thereafter, when one is activated, the other is activated too.

The other law is resemblance: "when two ideas are similar, whatever has been associated with the first ideas is automatically associated with the second...Association by contiguity and resemblance was also thought to be the scrivener that fills the famous blank slate, Locke's metaphor for the neonate mind. The doctrine, called associationism, dominated British and American views of the mind for centuries, and to a large extent still does." Another term, used by Pinker, is that of the computational theory of mind. It is not an alternative to associationism/CONNECTIONISM, "but a variety of it, which claims that the main kind of information processing done by the mind is multivariate statistics" (Pinker, 1997, pp. 113–114).

Recent philosophical discussions consider a psychosomatic-dynamic approach, intended as a continual process which goes from the psychic dimension to the corporeal dimension, to the socio-environmental reality in a circularity of holistic-hermeneutic sphere of action. The process includes four areas:

1. A tendency to the matter's own function, or the propensity to formal configuration, stable form of all atomic and subatomic elements (principle of self-organization of matter of E. Schrodinger which inspired Watson and Crick's research on DNA)
2. Biological theories of Self-organization (Varela)
3. Ontopoiesis (moral excellence) in philosophy (Husserl)
4. Psychological tendencies, when one affirms the presence in the individual of an active will which aims at health as in Roger's Actualizing tendency and Maslow's Self-realization (Wilber, 2000)

---

[28] "Two cardinal facets of Buddhism are wisdom and compassion. Tenzin Gyatso holds tenaciously to non-violent perspectives, firmly believing that violence solves nothing. Equally firmly, he is unbowed in holding compassion for those who have so brutally decimated Tibet...Can you think of any other world figure who stands for truth more strongly than Tenzin Gyatso? He looks out to the uncommon side of realities and sees a future within which once again truth may prevail. We who appear buried by rampant untruth may also look to a brighter future" (Clark, 2007).

Ferguson writes: "Belief clings, Faith lets go." He maintains that one must learn to differentiate the difference between "I" and "me". Each cognitive concept is only a trick our mind plays on us (the illusion of memory). In truth, each "part" of us is really all of us—the combination of our memory and our nature (UFT). "It is part of our whole being, just as the head is part of the body. But if this is not realized, "I" and "me", the head and the body, will feel at odds with each other" (Ferguson, 2007, p. 42).

This dyad also exists between the weak consciousness and an all-powerful but deterministic unconscious. As our (unconscious) ego makes choices, it has a small, but important, amount of free will. Yogis believe there seems to be a special kind of consciousness within the unconscious. Karma gets expressed in unconscious ego choices, based on both traumatic and inherited patterns, which can only be decoded by a rigorous psychoanalytic process. Without this process, a psychic split will continue to cause tension, and may even be unbearable. It seems to me that man as an objective, rational creature is free to choose his role, but he will have some kind of role, often most easily revealed through an inner dialogue.

The question arises whether you are what your role defines you as. Our awareness of our philosophical Nature is but a piece of the unified field theory (UFT) of how we have developed as societal groups and as social, emotional, and spiritual individuals. In the next chapter, we delve into the influences and relevance of history and the development of culture. Our awareness of our philosophical Nature is but a piece of the Unified Field Theory (UFT) of how we have developed as societal groups and as social, emotional, and spiritual individuals. In the next chapter, we delve into the influences and relevance that history and the development of culture has had upon this process.

Shoot for perfection on your own terms, not anyone else's…Get to insight: what one wants and what reality offers. This insight can be facilitated by introspection, by conversations with friends, by therapy, by meditation, or more often by simply living (Wilber, 2000, p. 35).

Chapter Five
Social Connections
What Makes Us a Society?

Man is not in search of his origin; he is in search of his destiny—from
Who is Man?
— Abraham Heschel (1965)

The history of ideas must also be the history of the situations in which ideas have developed Bronowski & Mazlish (1960).

We now undertake a historical review of social CONNECTION and why it is that society has evolved just as it has. This review requires first wrestling with a bigger question: where shall we start and how far back shall we go to support a reasonable theoretical proposition of the CONNECTIONS within man's evolution? For instance, "historicity" is defined as the effect of past events on present relationships. I embrace the definition of "society" as "man's everyday life in community", which reflects that just as every day changes us as it moves us into the next day and new adventure or problems, society reflects a fluid (necessarily flexible) set of parameters and CONNECTIONS as well. The parts of our societal history which I have chosen to discuss further will reflect this viewpoint.

My goal for the reader is to see a flow throughout the continuum of relevant historical events and CONNECTIVITY. Ancient ideologies can be traced to more modern ideologies, to the philosophical and value bases of western civilization as it developed, and to finally the antecedents of American culture specifically.

Numerous studies of the history of civilization (Du Bois, 1903; Durant, 1968; Bronowski, 1973; Van Doren, 1991) showed forward progress in the creation of a structured (and workable) society, based on certain contributing factors. These factors seem to form a mosaic of interdependent areas of functioning and CONNECTIONS for human civilization-building. A long-held list of the factors and questions about how this process unfolds includes:

1. Organization of food production and the possibility of surplus (supply and demand creates economics and money).
2. Transportation, communication, and the impact of regional descriptors (rivers—open society vs. mountain—closed communication and CONNECTION) resulted in centralization of power during the feudal system and later a change toward the spread of ideas.
3. Political integration also led to hierarchical societal function (which was facilitated by religious structures [usually]). [Taxation was created and justified as few took care of many].

4. With religion comes the development of many forms of creative expression such as architecture, art, music, and literature based on the liturgy.
5. Eventual growth in population necessitated innovation, industrial and technological revolution (Van Doren, 1991).

More research, however, has questioned this theory of a hierarchical state, which is believed to have led to civilization "as we know it". A new theory states that "only when humans began farming food that could be stored, divvied up, traded, and taxed, did social structures begin to take shape" (Cassella, 2022). This newer theory maintains that storage also facilitated the emergence of "tax-levying elites".

The tendency toward geographic concentration, for all the developmental reasons above, contributed to an increase in CONNECTION and to societies with a united and common purpose. This concentration also caused a loss, however, of individual awareness of the purposeful intent and reasons to CONNECT in the first place. We have recently seen this loss of awareness in texting versus talking and in gaming and reality TV as virtual sustenance, which I believe creates more Outliers—We do understand that culture is a mechanism for solving problems and should be viewed as a process, a functional aid to the self-actualization of the society rather than as only a natural outcome in the struggle for survival.

As I reviewed history, one source came to the forefront as having the most CONNECTIVITY with our current time and tensions. Eugen Weber's program *Western Tradition* (1989), which was broadcast on PBS like Jacob Bronowski's *Ascent of Man* (1973), provides the most thorough review of history I could find. Many of Weber's thoughts will be woven into my own in this chapter, the first as follows: The great Hellenistic age of the Greeks had many contributions but also many of the same concerns and obstacles to wisdom on a societal level that the world is experiencing today. What follows is especially powerful considering it was also broadcast over forty years ago. Weber listed ten specific areas of comparison:

1. Psychological fragmentation.
2. Less respect and representation found in government.
3. An anti-rationalist trend in thinking and actions.
4. An overly absorbed interest in the Self.
5. An obsessive pursuit of affluence.
6. Cultism, eroticism and turning to astrology for guidance.
7. Detachment from a "home-town" feeling due to population dispersion.
8. A tendency to turn toward a questioning of place in the cosmos as a whole.
9. Social conflicts and class wars.
10. Making and keeping rules over productivity (Weber, 1989).

In on our review of history, we should understand that the fall of empires, before and long after the Greeks, are manifested through these ten issues, at least as a starting point. One last important note: In taking on a historical review, one must decide between a more classic use of BC/AD (Before Christ/Anno Domini) versus BCE/CE (Before Common Era/Common Era) in the designation of time. As I generally feel that the former refers to a more Christian-centered view of history, perhaps even with a built-in bias of those values, I will default to the second system.

Prehistory to Plato

An anthropological archaeologist (I have one in the family!) would tell me to start at the beginning, of course. We have always needed our CONNECTIONS to survive. Our primate characteristics (arborealism, being omnivores with opposable thumbs and great toes, color vision and central fovea of the retina) seem to have culminated in vertical torsos and increased relative brain size. "The tremendous increase in size and complexity of the brain in comparison with body weight… [came from] an enlarged neocortex which is the basis for awareness, imagination, and all those facilities such as speech and symbol-making which characterize human existence" (Fromm, 1968, p. 60).

Human life is probably about six million years old, although the first written records did not come, as we shall see, until about 3500 BCE. Hominoids (primates on hind legs, which made arms available) came after opposable thumbs, about 4 to 2 million years ago. There is some thought that they made stone tools—flints, which allowed them to use their teeth for gnawing less, thereby also eventually changing the shape of the face, and saving their teeth. In turn, the skull changed to make room for larger brains as the use of mentalization was more widespread and these primates became carnivores with different size and shape teeth. Something like language developed about 350,000 years ago, which helped increase communication and CONNECTIVITY. Storage of information was followed by the ancestors of language and the writing of symbols, which were more consistent and meaningful than just pictographs.

The real change in man's lineage probably occurred at least 70,000 years ago (Neanderthal man). Recent man, Homo sapiens, which literally means "man the wise", appeared around 40,000 BCE; the ongoing problem has been to determine when and how man became "wise". Obviously, the changing size of the skull, plus growth in the frontal brain region helped anthropologists to define "wise" as the ability to transmit information, the capacity for original thought, and the ability to learn. The Neanderthal man was a "residual" and specialized variety of man, having mated with the Denisovans. Siua (1988) maintains that it was around 40,000 BCE that our species, Homo sapiens, became equipped with tremendous capability to:

> fashion, manipulate, and make use of virtual presences [spiritual expression of that which is nontangible]. [They] conjured up the all-powerful virtual presences of gods, loyalty, prestige, the square root of minus one, and so on…The last of the principal qualitative evolutionary events that completed the foundation for the massive infliction of suffering began about 9000 BCE, when settlements were established at the end of the Ice Age and in those who found power through controlling others under him [emphasis added] (Siu, 1988, p. 11).

All of this, of course, was the opposite of more CONNECTIVITY because encounters with others often became a possible source of anxiety or even danger.

Likewise, archaeological digs show a beginning of "spiritual" sensibility at some point along civilization in that there is proof of temples having been built 10th millennium BCE, at least at the ruins of Gobekli Tepe in Mesopotamia (Weber, 1989).[29]

Man became nomadic, along with his animals, roughly 10,000 to 12,000 years ago. Agricultural influences increased domestication of these animals and structured society so that even walls and wells are noted in archaeological digs. As agricultural practices and food production increased, so did the need for control over animals, specifically the primitive oxen-driven plow. Surplus created patriarchal strength, trade, and an interactive (CONNECTED) society. Eventually society became less nomadic. Surplus could be traded and what we think of as a "civilization" evolved. Apparently, even the practice of the use of slaves had begun by then as well! In the Neolithic (New Stone) societies of 10,000 BCE, successful societal development reflected fertility practices, where women were seen as the "creators" and the source of specific organization of the rituals, most having to do with fears and "magic".

By the time a balance of "consumer-consumed" had been achieved (50,000 game animals to 2,500 humans because of the collection of seed, roots, insects), there was a need to congregate in food density areas and form an equilibrium level between the food and the fed. Therefore, cultural selection (through intergroup and intercultural competition) favored a certain population ceiling in each area, known as "density-dependent". This "Paleolithic human predatory efficiency" took out the smaller game, making the larger game easier to annihilate, and over 200 species are thought to have become extinct during that time due to the uniquely efficient and "noble" hunting activities of this group of primates from 12,000 to 8,000 BCE.

As part of their efficiency, people came together to create population groups. Not all crowded populations were deemed "cities;" consider the densely populated "green cities" still in existence in India, Yucatan, and West Africa. Another definition of "city" might be its relative permanence, as well as heterogeneity of population and the varied functions of the city's populace. Climate, soil, and suitable domestic animals had a lot to do with the gradual transition from solitary farmsteads to large villages of up to 20,000 or more inhabitants. Favorable conditions were also important such as elevated alluvial plains near lakes or broad, fertile valleys such as those of the Nile, Tigris, Euphrates, and the Indus (now Iraq and Iran). In these valleys crops were abundant, such as maize, white potatoes and sweet potatoes. By the 2nd century BCE, innovations such as the wheel, use of iron, and later marine transportation with better sails made the world a smaller place.

---

[29] "In 1816, a Danish archaeologist, Christian Thomsen, classified early human cultures according to the materials used for tools and weapons. The Stone Age, which he divided into Paleolithic, Mesolithic and Neolithic periods, was followed by the Bronze Age and the Iron Age. It was in the Neolithic times that agriculture and the domestication of cattle began" (Hayman, 1999, p. 287).

The yearly Nile flood represented an ongoing re-creationist story. Temples were built to commemorate the dead and represent the structure of society at the time (like Stupas in Buddhist countries and Mayan temples in the Americas). The isolation of the current day Fertile Crescent, of then Mesopotamia, being virtually an oasis, made it necessary to maintain an organization that probably became somewhat repetitive but was successful. "The Nile Valley loop is very narrow (only seven miles wide along the fertile area), which made it easily defensible" (Weber, 1989).

Eventually, the need for traders and even soldiers developed. This movement of individuals, blood lines, and their cultures created a sharing of tools, gems, arts (such as glassmaking and metalworking), and helped move civilization from the 4th century BCE (copper age) to the 3rd century BCE (bronze age) to the 2nd century BCE (iron age). By 4000 BCE, the first villages were growing in Sumer, there was irrigation and drainage, and the wheel was used for carriages, not just for spinning. However, in the Greco-Roman era, only 1% to 2% of the population census could be found within the cities, the rest were still living on farms. In fact, it took 50 to 90 farms to produce sufficient surplus to support a single artisan, merchant, priest, soldier, or ruler in the city (Davis, 1955). But urbanization was growing. This need for CONNECTION could not be overlooked.

As familial and tribal units became what we would now call "civilized", language development and oral communication helped early stories become vital to the preservation of the culture. The symbolization of male in wisdom and female in the earth led to acceptance of the ways in which the feminine was more closely related to what Jung would call the Self. Initially Egyptian myths were balanced between masculine and feminine; however, the consciousness between the two was fluid, as seen, for example, in their dress. In Egyptian myths the "creative" feminine was split off from patriarchy, which was seen as more conscious than the unconscious feminine. Gods were not immortal, as per our current definition, but rather cyclical, with sacrifices made to keep the Pharaoh healthy. Their afterlife was seen as a continuation of, and CONNECTION to, living themes, but in a different form. Myths, like the Myth of Osiris, were not "stories" per se, but were more like vignettes or were representational, like dream sequences.[30]

Although Sumerians are thought to have invented writing, by 3000 BCE what we now identify as Semites moved into this area and they created a real language with its own symbols, still used today as Hebrew. This culture was based upon a faith which separated the "Divine World" and its non-human attributes, a practice much more abstract than the realism of the Egyptians and their tombs. The "Law" was written down: "divine justice was aimed at and presented by divinely chosen leaders" (ibid, 1989). Written communication provided a unifying force that

---

[30] "A broad distinction can be made between the mythologies of the truly primitive (fishing, hunting, root-digging, and berry-picking) peoples and those of the civilizations that came into being following the development of the arts of agriculture, dairying, and herding, circa 6000 BCE. Most what we call primitive, however, is actually colonial, i.e., diffuses from some high culture center and adapted to the needs of a simpler society" (Campbell, 1949, p. 289).

underscored the successes of the evolution of civilization as it developed/CONNECTED because information could be passed down to the next generation. Land wars and "imperialism" of a sort was memorialized in stories that were repeated around nighttime fires.

Literacy has always been a key to advancement and is one of the main ways we transfer our memory and our culture. In some ways, literacy has replaced the dependence on myth so commonly found in every early culture. However, the mythological influences of our early cultures continue to arise in what Carl Jung would call the "collective unconscious", and they have the same function and purpose they have always had—to represent the deeper meaning and spiritual CONNECTION of our daily lives. By the time Greek culture predominated that region, the ideas of mythological gods to represent certain daily function were entrenched.[31]

Specific Egyptian Influences

Following the Sumerian period, the advancement of almost every important element of civilization can be seen in the "pre-history" period of Egypt (before 3000 BCE). In the period after 3000 BCE, during which the Great Pyramids at Giza were built, a legacy came down from when the Pharaohs ruled, such as Thutmose III, Ramses III, Nefertiti, and Tutankhamun.

As part man, part God, the Pharaoh owned everything, including the people. There was no codification of laws, as they might compete with the Pharaoh's whim. But by the 5th and 6th dynasties (2500 to 2300 BCE), the size of King's tombs decreased, along with his power, as the priests and nobles appear to have gained more power for themselves. On a more positive note, it was also during this period that Hammurabi's Code comes down to us. In 1755 BCE, the sixth King of Babylonia enacted a code that still exists in stone; 282 laws with punishments, an eye for an eye, tooth for a tooth, as well as descriptions of hierarchies of social status, for instance, slave versus free man versus noble.

Much of the code deals with contracts and financial issues; even then money and power were of highest concern! Around this time, a provisional calendar was developed, with weeks and months, and a common value for money was created including the use of slave time, barley, silver, copper, or gold. Interest was charged and collected. This CONNECTION to others through financial necessity was moving civilization forward in ways that could not have been predicted, even in the Fertile Crescent.

Culture became more co-mingled as trade for incense and other goods increased, and the use of slaves from other cultures increased as well. Throughout this entire period there were too many battles and shifts of power to note in a single

---

[31] The ancient Greeks gave mythic form to the importance of memory as it ruled their lives. The Goddess of Memory (Mnemosyne) was a Titan, daughter of Uranus (Heaven) and Gaea (Earth), and mother of all the nine Muses. In legend these were Epic Poetry (Calliope), History (Clio), Flute playing (Euterpe), Tragedy (Melpomene), Dancing (Terpishchore), the Lyre (Erato) Sacred Song (Polyhymnia), Astronomy (Urania), and Comedy (Thalia).

chapter, but one item of interest jumps out; we will see in many cultures as we go forward that, whether from idleness or fear, the noble classes were not the ones to "volunteer" to fight or go into service for wars. They enlisted others, or enslaved another class of people or captured peoples, to do it for them.

Egyptian society lasted 3000 years with few changes. The Egyptian attitude toward life preferred the status quo over almost any change. Tombs were built because the society was dedicated to immortality and a God "who made sure the sun rose each day" (Weber, 1989). Because this societal structure was seen as hierarchal, as most still are, Egyptian society ruled from the top down. From one occasion to another, however, some change was seen as improvement.

As recorded history passed from the Egyptians through the Assyrians (formerly the Sumerians, then known as Mesopotamia, now north Iraq, northeast Syria, and part of southeast Turkey), this area came first under the control of the Babylonians and then the Romans by the 1st to 3rd centuries CE. During the Ptolemaic period (332 BCE to 641 CE), Alexandria became the capital of Egypt, and the woman we know to be Cleopatra VII [the year the Romans sacked the city—30 BCE] became the ruler for a time as the Romans, including Hadrian and Marcus Aurelius, were likewise expanding their power.

The library at Alexandria was the center of learning, even after it was burned by Caesar in 48 BCE. Enlightened Romans such as Cicero, Seneca, and Plutarch advanced the beliefs of the Greeks Pliny and Ptolemy, including astronomical findings as related to the afterlife; it seems human consciousness has been looking for a sense of symmetry for a long time.

Aramaic emerged as a common language in speech and writing. Literacy was still a barrier, but knowledge, as such, could now be passed on orally. The Chaldeans were absorbed into Persia. The only people who consistently refused assimilation, as we will see, were the Hebrews, who were forced from the Land of Ur to Egypt, then after making it to Canaan, ultimately were broken up into the two tribes by the Babylonians in the 5th century BCE, Judah, and Israel. Persia (mostly) kept this peace for over 100 years, and its power stretched from India to the Mediterranean Sea. Only the Greeks and Phoenician cultures, becoming strong influences by 800 BCE, had escaped being conquered. But before we address the birth and influence of Greek culture, it is important that we know more about the acts in the continent of Africa which would affect the whole world, including Arabia, Islamic states, and as far away as the cultures under Christianity.

African Influences

It is written that long before any Christian influences, the queen of Sheba (500 BCE) or someone like her, perhaps a mythological figure, left Yeha to bring Sabaean/Ethiopian culture to Solomon and the Israelites. As the legend goes, she arrived with gifts, camels, spices, and gold which she presented to King Solomon. In return, according to the biblical account, he was able to answer several obscure questions put to him by Sheba and thus they wooed each other. Moreover, the exchange of culture was significant in its initiation of a trade route from that time forward.

Likewise, Ezana of Axum (an East African area which in 300 CE reached from Ethiopia to ports on the Red Sea), ruled an empire as great as the other three great empires: Rome, Persia, and China. Sailors left the kingdom of Punt and Kush to explore and trade, this being about the same time as Constantine was ruling the Byzantine empire. It is in present-day Axum (Church of our Lady Mary of Zion) that some believe the Ark of the Covenant is kept and protected. Finally, in Meroe, the last great capitol of Kush, Christianity and trade established great CONNECTIONS and the Nubians ruled for over 1000 years until the 1500s. It was the farmers, traders and nomadic tribes that defined civilization and culture during those 1000 years.

As culture also moved to Western Africa, the Maghreb tribes (Morocco, Tunisia, Algeria, Libya, and parts of the western Sahara Desert) became known as the Barbary coast, derived from the Berbers who ruled it for centuries. One Berber, Abbulah Ibn Yasina, changed the course of culture due to the literal and puritanical position he took toward the Islamic faith, known as the Almoravid movement. He established the Maliki code of worship and daily lifestyle. It continues today in the conservative Sunni sect of Islam.

Eventually Fez became the intellectual capital of Sahel, the region that forms the geopolitical division between the northern Sahara and the Sudanese Savana in the south. From Fez, a renowned writer and geographer, Leo Africannus, took that area of Africa into direct CONNECTION with rest of Europe. His travels, and contacts with such people as Pope Leo X, reached from Timbuktu to Istanbul to Crete to Mecca to Rome to Andalusian Spain, where he originally was born (Granada). Eventually, Leo changed his name to Leo Medicis and converted from Islam to Christianity.

Briefly after Leo's influence, the ruler of Mali, Monsa Musa (1312–1337) was so invested in the trade and power of that time (especially through shipments of gold), that at one point he was the richest man in the world, worth $400 billion, in today's currency. King Monsa Musa is famous for his Hadjj trip to Mecca, where along the way he stopped throughout Egypt and gave so much gold away that it affected the Egyptian economy for years afterwards.

Similarly, on the western side of Africa, during approximately the same period, the Yoruba civilization in Ile Ife (now Nigeria) contributed culture, resources, and art. Benin, still an independent state of power which lies between Togo and Nigeria, was also the source of a complex and sophisticated culture. Uba Ewuare the Great built great walls, with nine magnificent gates to protect the city's boundaries; he invested in art and showed great pride in the bronze statues and plaques (the "Benin sculptures") that were produced.

The people of Azania, mostly Cushitic, ruled the Eastern side of Africa, reaching from Kenya to the southern border edged by Mozambique; an eventual takeover by the Bantu people changed the course of that part of African. Between 1000 and 1500 BCE, the seasonal reversal of the trade winds off the horn of Africa created seacoast trading. Intermarriage and cultural trading were common here too. "Kilwa, an island off the coast of Tanzania, was the most southern of the major Swahili coast trading cities that dominated goods coming into and out of Africa, from Persia, India, and Arabia" (www.worldhistory.org, 2022).

It was through this area that Sulieman the Great reached out during his takeover and growth of the Ottoman Empire; he was the longest running Sultan of the empire from 1520 to 1566. Although he married a Christian, it was not until after his death, and a major disruption by the Portuguese, that the great transition in the Ottoman Empire happened, and its control by the Islamic Turks. Turkish rule would be maintained until after WWI, spanning more than 600 years.

Concurrently, Islamic beliefs deposed the Byzantine rule of law with their own teachings from the Koran. Through trade, the Islamic traders were able to press across Northern Africa to the Iberian coast, where Tariq ibn Ziyad, a Berber warrior leader, created Iberia as a great bridge to CONNECT Africa to Europe. The name Gibraltar (as in Rock of Gibraltar) is a Spanish derivative of his name, Mountain of Tariq. Writing, creating, law, and trade were solidified by the establishment of the University of Gondar by the Solomonic Emperors of the early 13th through 16th centuries. After Christianity was incorporated in the Ethiopian culture, the beautiful rock churches of Lalibela were carved around 1200.

The Greek Legacy

The Hellenistic Period of the Greeks left history great increases in the art of "open expressionism". It was Greek logic and philosophy that really began the type of legacy in history that I am writing about. Alexandria (founded 331 BCE) blossomed under rulers who tried to follow the lead in values and divinity of Alexander the Great, who had been a student of the great Greek philosopher Aristotle until he was 16. Aristotle said, 'the wise man brings the world into order,' and believed the cynics became the anarchists [still true today] (Weber, 1989). As noted in Chapter Two, other philosophers, such as Epicurus (find pleasure to avoid pain) and Zeno the Stoic (be in tune with the order of the universe in you that wants to be an activist) would make the CONNECTION between life as it occurs in nature and human nature as it occurs in man.

Most of the Greeks believed in some type of a moral code in this development of understanding for both sides of nature. The Hellenistic age lasted as long as it did because of a system of beliefs that inspired participation; rules that would eventually be codified by the Romans. Historically, the Pantheists and realists of the classical Greek philosophical period were just as eager to discuss process as we are today. The search for the ideal and truth drove their philosophy; "souls and the need for souls" still define the Greek thinking (ibid, 1989).

We know as much as we do about Greek history because of Herodotus (484–425 BCE). He was born in Turkey but migrated to Greece and is considered the first real Greek historian, mostly due to his organization of events systemically, particularly the Greek-Persian Wars. His prose, *The Histories,* is the first to survive and he was seen by Cicero as the "the father of history" (Sampson, 2000). Herodotus made CONNECTIONS among the relevant Greek/Ionian stories and presented many of these heroic Gods as human. *The Iliad* and *Odyssey* stories, written about a period from 1200 BCE to 800 BCE, took place during another kind of "Dark Ages", where there may or may not have been many "heroes" but there certainly was a lot of ritualistic fighting [these stories were initially orally transmitted myths and legends that were eventually written down by Homer].

Did the gruesomeness of those times support the "humanization" of the Greek gods, just as during wars of a more common era our society tries to lose itself in the TV god, or computer god? Certainly, the stories of Achilles, Athena, or Persephone continue to inspire students of Greek mythology even today. Now, as then, even in chaos if we can stay CONNECTED and aware of our limitations; these age-old examples provide us with lessons and wisdom about our own flaws and failings and our own heroic qualities. "Modern-day stories of who we are and how we fit into the universe are no longer told in the same way as the Greeks told theirs, but that does not mean that we have no such stories. The modern mind, no less than the ancient one, uses stories to reinforce its belief..." (Sampson, 2000, p.8; Campbell, 1988).

As a temporal reference, during this period Confucius was born in China (551 BCE to 479 BCE), Socrates was born in Greece (470 BCE), Hippocrates was born in Greece (460 BCE), Aristotle was born in Stagira, Macedonia (384 BCE), and Alexander the Great was born in Macedonia (356 BCE, died at 32, 323 BCE). These dates give some historical context and perspective to our timeline. Likewise, Buddha was born around 563 BCE, while Muhammad was born in Mecca around 570 CE. Although it was the middle of the Dark Ages of Europe (476–800 CE), Buddhists in India and Asia spread the eightfold path: right view, right thought, right speech, right action, right mode of living, right endeavor, right mindfulness, and right concentration. From this belief in social equality, there grew a foundation for civilization rebirth, as seen before in Egypt, Greece, and Rome and eventually to be seen during the Renaissance in Europe. In conclusion, the period of a thousand years from 550 BCE to about 550 CE, marked the high tide of classical civilization and the highest point that Western man attained until after the discovery of the New World.

Socrates and Plato Advance Philosophy

Now that we have given some perspective to the important collateral events in the pre-Greek period, it is time to look more deeply into the historical relevance of their philosophy. Known for their expertise in communications, method for studying knowledge, advances in mathematics, and revolutionary theories about matter and force (early physics), we find that the Greeks' view of ethics was also influential in the advancement of the history of philosophy in general. They made, and strongly supported, all these CONNECTIONS.

Greeks believed they must study the question: what is the "it" that does not change, that which endures. Thales (624–546 BCE) was considered the first Greek philosopher, he raised the question of whether the world was capable of being understood, and he was the first to reduce nature to a single substance. He chose water. He proposed that forms (this predated Plato) were defined by immaterial, not material, aspects of matter. His emphasis on the immaterial may have also been influenced by a lack of security after experiencing the Persian wars (600–480 BCE), during which Athens was taken and Phoenicia became Greek.

Socrates (470–399 BCE) not only added to this study of substances, but also addresses the study of "ethics;" ideas of a "common humanity" joined that of wisdom and learning as primary virtues during this time. Besides his influences upon Plato, who followed him. Socrates provided a strong foundation for much of the rest of Western philosophy. Plato presented much of what is known about Socrates through the *Dialogues*, and the so-called Socratic method is still used in education today all over the world through rhetoric and debate; a question is posed, not so much to elicit a specific answer as to spark a lively discussion which requires the use of intellectual prowess and ingenuity. During a trip to an Indian monastery in 2001, I saw thirty Tibetan monks practicing this type of spontaneous debate during their training. It was quite the sight! But more on this experience in Chapter Nine.

A student of philosophy and medicine, Hippocrates (460–370 BCE) was the first philosopher to focus Greek society away from the superstitious belief that the Gods were the source of illnesses, and rather provided clinical proofs that environmental factors were at cause. In addition, he focused on "universal education", which he believed allows the enlightened individual to distinguish between sense and nonsense. These ideas strongly advanced his procedures (some still CONNECTED to medical processes today), including diagnosis, prognosis, and awareness of the "crisis point of the disease", to enable an improved awareness of symptoms and cure (Garrison, 1966).

Plato's (427–348 BCE) advancement of history is multifaceted and has been written about in depth; it goes without saying that a limited review here is a difficult proposition. Not a Sophist as such (he took issue with their position on rhetoric), he believed that "truth" could best be gained through observation, as it reflected his famously proposed Forms, the "Immutable Ideals". Like Thales before him, his philosophical thought may also have been influenced by the war around him, in this case the Peloponnesian War with Sparta (431–404 BCE), during which important ideas caused evolutionary changes upon Greek culture.

Plato was the student of Socrates, Aristotle followed as Plato's student (although he had a much more contemplative life in Alexandria), and the three are known for their initial conceptualization of the Western tradition of philosophy in the *Academia* in Athens. A wide range of subjects are usually considered to cover the overall Trivium (grammar, logic and rhetoric) which, in addition to the Quadrivium added by Plato (arithmetic, geometry, astronomy, music), to this day makes up what we call the seven "liberal arts" curriculum of most college degrees, (as a side note, look up Durer's beautiful woodcut, 1502 CE).

The organization, and continuation of, the "finer arts" in such a way as the trivium/quadrivium had a great influence on the advancement of Greek civilization, and again throughout the Dark Ages when only small groups of literates, or those in monastic training, could claim knowledge of such subjects. Both the Trivium and the Quadrivium continued in private study and were held sacred. These studies were revived and were made available to the public during the Renaissance period of history, when medieval universities actually began the awarding of a Bachelor of Arts (BA) degree. Plato's study of ethics and the ideals also had a great deal to do with his influencing the spread of Grecian philosophy and the history of civilization.[32]

Classical artists took a previous austerity in art and produced a "timeless perfection" in calmness, but which also showed sensual movement at times (*Aphrodite* flowed, *Winged Victory* had movement as well). We call this a "classical" period for many reasons, for in looking back, its art and literature had more lifelike grace than the Romans after them, the Assyrians, or even the Egyptians before them.

Philosophically, the goal was to "be at one with the cosmic order and with oneself," to be one's own master, creating a sense of autonomy and detachment from cynicism (Weber, 1989). In a society where slavery was accepted, these values might appear hypocritical; slaves, however, could earn their freedom and were often considered valued parts of the household. Many slaves had familial rights and some even gained the right to own property.

Aristotle (384–322 BCE) was Plato's most famous student. In turn, Aristotle's most famous student was Alexander the Great, and so the lineage continued. Although a great student of philosophy in general, and ethics in particular, Aristotle was perhaps most famous for his studies of the scientific method; some of his beliefs stood until the Enlightenment period of the 18th century. He is also often thought of as the first empiricist. Aristotle's focus and method was to find the mean between extremes.

Zeno the Stoic (490–439 BCE) predated the Greek philosophers mentioned above but was not well known until Aristotle wrote about him, specifically in his attempt to refute Zeno's nine surviving famous "paradoxes". Some current theoreticians look at these paradoxes as simply mathematical problems, but in the long view of history, I believe they were meant to point out ethical dilemmas in the philosophical thought processes of the Greek mind.[33] Others believe that the paradoxes can even be seen as metaphysical dilemmas, causing us to "conform the will to the Divine reason…A man is happy if he fully accepts what is and does not desire what cannot be." Ultimately, I can see that giving in to the nature of these paradoxes is like being able to "forgive yourself for being human…" (ibid, 1991, p. 71).

---

[32] "A civilization is bound up with one way of experiencing life." What is the "civilization" that composes each of our own lives, our truths about the influence of needs and failed attachments, successes and missed adventures that is summarized in the roles we enact so unconsciously and yet so intricately that they are like the individual threads of a spider's web, fragile yet strong enough to bind others to us or us to others? (Bronowski, 2011, p. 41).

[33] Centuries later, Karl Marx would write his dissertation on "The Difference between the Democritean and Epicurean Philosophy of Nature," a work which foreshadowed his later work in socialism and the opposites of his dialectical beliefs. "The glorification of the heaven body is a cult which all Greek philosophers celebrate…It is the intellectual solar system. Hence the Greek philosophers, in worshipping the heavenly bodies, worshipped their own mind" (Marx quoted in Boorstin, 1985, p. 616).

Alexander the Great (356–323 BCE) was the next in line to be taught through the Athens Academia lineage. The son of Philip II of Macedon, Alexander was a direct student of Aristotle until the age of 16 and became a king at the age of 20. It took him only ten years to create the empire which reached from Greece to the entire Persian peninsula throughout Asia Minor. He was only turned back when he tried to invade India. Although taught the sensitivities of the Trivium, one cannot overlook the cruelty of these wars, during many of which he slaughtered his enemy rather than take any prisoners. During this time, his life was equated to that of a God, or at least a Philosopher-King. His military exploits and successes are the model for many military studies until this day.

Because of the wide-ranging nature of Alexander the Great's empire, he is perhaps best known for the acculturation of his society into those he conquered, and the collection of cultural writings into the great library in Alexandria. His absorption of, and CONNECTION to, Greek, Byzantine, and Egyptian cultures greatly influenced the ongoing nature of the Near and Middle East up until the 20th Century. It is no wonder that to many citizens of the world, particularly the Greeks, Alexander the Great was raised to near god-like status, with even a rumor of having Zeus as his father! Although he died of a fever at only 33, after his death the fusion of the Greek scholars with the Persian nobles, and their thought, resulted in a great empire which did not necessarily last intact but did create a Hellenistic "Age" that lasted until the great rule of Cleopatra from the Egyptian south (51 to 30 BCE).

Romans Imitate the Greek Model

Knowledge of these first philosopher/historians, and the historical background which CONNECTED them, will help us move smoothly through each relevant epoch. For instance, Cicero (106–44 BCE) became supplier of history in the Roman empire during the last turn of a millennium. Yet, the virtues of openness, honesty, and fairness (which he strongly supported) were, nevertheless, somewhat hard to come by. He was protective of human nature and man's individualism; as one of history's greatest orators, he wanted to provide a path of study by which men could communicate/CONNECT with each other. He is chiefly credited with keeping the Greek art of humanistic studies alive in the manner which it would ultimately continue through the Dark Ages into the Renaissance period. He wanted moderation even in religion; for example, to turn away from worship of the Isis type gods with charms and soothsayers and to instead turn to Stoicism. He believed in *salve*, or health of the soul (Weber, 1989).

In considering the individual, his nature, and the natural law, Cicero wrote: "Their humanness gives them the right to be treated with respect" (Van Doren, 1991, p. 74). In addition to his success as an orator, his political influence was wide-reaching; throughout the last century of the BCE period, Cicero supported the Greek's Republican method of politics. He was a great champion of Julius Caesar, but unfortunately his lack of fondness for Mark Antony resulted in Cicero's assassination in 44 BCE by the hands Mark Antony's soldiers when he attempted an escape from Italy. One only needs to look at the legacy of Cicero's life to see how Greek democracy and Roman oligarchy varied.

Ultimately, a compromise evolved and by the time the Common Era period arrived, society was ruled by parts of both cultures. "Like so many Roman adaptations of Greek ideas, it was a pragmatic and very successful compromise" (ibid, 1991, p. 62). Although Greek ideas were preferred to Roman ones, after a while Roman strength took over. It was not until the 6th century, under Justinian I (527–565 CE), that Justinian law or a new codified set of laws was written down.

There is a myth that Roman power arose from their gods. The truth, however, is that Rome is situated in a good geographic position, in a fertile plain over the Tiber River and 15 miles from the sea (Weber, 1989). This CONNECTION between city-state and sea came to be known as the Appian Way, and its stones are still visible to this day. Initially piety, virtue, and responsibility were values taken over by the Romans from the Greeks. The Romans held the notion of exercising power to obtain control and "salvation" for others.

For instance, Julius Caesar used unrest to advance his own career, but he was subsequently murdered in 44 BCE for it. Before him, Augustus had reformed much of Roman society, his ruling period (27 BCE to 14 CE) was the first to really provide a sense of cultural safety and stability in Rome under his will. This period is referred to as "Pax Romana". Imperialism, likewise, Romanized the Christian church; the "Church of Rome", became somewhat of a bureaucracy. Augustus had a way of organizing, centralizing, and thinking about human nature. Later, Tiberius (14 to 37 CE) took up the cause of the poor but was also murdered, probably because of being too popular!

My personal favorite philosopher of this period was Marcus Aurelius, the Stoic (born 141 CE, who became emperor as well, 161 to 180 CE). He introduced influences from the East, where self-mastery, temperance and courage created a solid mind-soul CONNECTION. He counseled equanimity in the face of conflict (the Buddhist influence). Unfortunately, there was also a shift to anxiety and uncertainty during his time, due to the Marcomannic Wars against the Sarmatians.

The Roman "Reconstruction Period" lasted from 284–305 CE, after which "conspicuous consumption", decadence, showing of wealth, Coliseum fights, squandering, and recklessness, were followed by a period of Roman decline. Aside from the period of Christ's crucifixion, this is the Rome in movies and books which most of us think of when considering Roman history. Nero fiddled while Rome burned, so that in 476 CE the Visigoth Barbarians, led by Alaric, who had initially laid siege in 408 CE, were able to sack Rome in only 3 days. Alaric surrounded the city of 800,000 and forced it into starvation, and perhaps even cannibalism, before Rome was sacked. He took with him the surviving residual wealth of the city.

Romans Transition History

Even as Greek culture declined and Roman culture became dominant, there was an awareness that the Greeks had developed something special, contributing to civilization in politics, philosophy, and education. From then to now, these contributions are demonstrated through their myths and legends (perhaps historical, perhaps not so much so). These stories were passed on, just as stories have been by indigenous peoples before the Greeks and will be by future civilizations. In our labeling of that Grecian period as "classical", the Romans recreated it magnificently in some areas (think of Pompeii), but it was never quite as refined or completed with the same quality and quantity of raw materials.

During the Neo-classical period of the 18th and 19th centuries, the attempts in European culture, particularly in France, to recreate frescoes and internal home décor ala Grecian classical ways was extensive. Pompeii and Herculaneum were uncovered, lost to all since volcanic ash from Mt. Vesuvius had covered these active seats of Roman culture in 79 CE. These cities were added to the "Grand Tour" of Europe by 18th century aristocracy and historians. But of all the gifts passed on to us by the Greeks and then the Romans, their studies of the mind were the most valuable and lasting. I see this bounty even in my patients with significant mental health issues, where the Roman concept of "soldiering on" (Marcus Aurelius) is their primary psychological function.

Greeks lived by two famous mottos: "Moderation in all things" and "Know thyself." Although the Roman world was anything but moderate at times (think Caligula or Nero for opulence or lechery), their cultural sensitivity did advance a historical perspective of viable societal structure. This influence (and CONNECTION) is especially valid when it was taken westward into settled/expanded Britain or pushed up against the residual pre-Judeo-Christian paganistic traditions that influenced future folklore.

Formulation of an organized Christian church structure, first under Paul's followers and then the papal legacies, could not match the Celtic heritage in presentation of a CONNECTIVITY myth. When one studies genealogy, as I do, the tracing of one's family back to the Magna Carta or the Celtic Kings provides one a sense of lineage that CONNECTS to, and sometimes helps to combat, the true historical facts of that time.

Christ, the Redeemer

Augustus ruled from 27 BCE to 14 CE, carrying the Roman empire through the early Christian period. He tried to reestablish traditional ideals toward marriage, the idea of service, and moral virtues, which in many ways was carried forth through the seventeen successive emperors until the fall of Rome in 410 CE. For instance, during the time of Marcus Aurelius (161–180 CE, the Stoic felt as if he carried the weight of the world on his shoulders. He tried to create a nation of philosophers, who would base their conduct on the conformity of moral beliefs. He CONNECTED his ruling principles to the universal humanitarian ideals. The Roman Senate became more individualized, however, with less acceptance of variant and creative behaviors as seen under Augustus. Finally, a sense of security from the societal structure collapsed; people were looking for a "divine intervention" and the salvation that they ultimately found in Christ.

As we enter the Anno Domini or Common Era, we find a complex society— philosophically, psychologically, and spiritually. All societies seemed to have a complex behavioral system at that time: values, beliefs, philosophies, morals, religions, and even a world view. There was ongoing worship of Isis (in Egypt) and Mithra (in Persia), still available at most overnight traveler stops, along with other "Earth" cult religions and fertility rites, where wine flowed, and the change of seasons were celebrated. Into the view of the Sun and its planets, lay the mystery cults. Into emotionality, internality, and concerns for the Soul, lay a concept of

"Man's Ideal". Into this societal structure of Hebrews, Earth cults and Stoicism came a Savior, a Human Redeemer/Christos, Jesus of Nazareth.

The influence of Christianity will be discussed at length in Chapter Eight on religion. However, as Weber notes (1989) there are three main influences that can be used to understand how Christianity fits into/CONNECTS with history. First is the contextual influence, for along with Orientalism and the Gnostics, the early Christian practice could be skeptical yet tolerant, materialistic yet protective, all simultaneously, forcing many cultural choices upon the individuals who became early Christians.
Secondly, the Jewish influence must be considered; many early "Christians" still considered themselves Hebrews, with the caveat that only they were the ones with a real identity, acknowledging that the Messiah had come as foretold in the Torah. There was no need for separateness (as such) until Paul (Saul) wrote Epistles that CONNECTED Rome and the rest of the Mediterranean together through the Greek language. The Hebrews, and "Judeo-Christians", especially the Gnostics, resisted assimilation and the influences of the Pharisees (who at that time reinterpreted Moses' laws), preferring to live by the message of the Sermon on the Mount. Jesus taught Judaism to the Jews but with reformed ideas, which fulfilled his Messiah prophesy.
Hebrews kept their identity and their ideas of a unique relationship with their God. Finally, many other shifts in culture also took place between 100 and 400 CE, and the interdependency between one's "religious faith" and the "abject condition on earth" created the need for belief in some sort of salvation, whether from the earthly emperor or the heavenly God (ibid, 1989). After all, it was felt that Jesus' sacrifice showed "God's faith". As the Hellenistic point of view was rejected, there was a release sought from the skeptical, materialistic, but also overly tolerant society which took the Roman empire to its demise.
Religion varied as idealized versions of the Divine, and of the denial of the Self from coming closer to God (See Origen the Theologian, 253 CE for more on the ascetic life of those times). Although the idea of monastic life was not new, and taking retreat in a monastery was a satisfactory result of the scholarly and mystical need to follow the teachings of Christianity, it also turned out to be a safer alternative to town-dwelling during the Dark Ages as we shall see. Having the written Bible to bear out stories helped balance the ongoing influences of paganism. Whether one was a Christian, a Barbarian, or a tax collector, life during the 3rd century was complex.

The Fall of Darkness

As much as the Egyptians and Sumerians brought light to civilization through writing, the Greeks through philosophy and mathematics, and the Romans through politics and law, the world was soon to become "dark", a term to me representing a lack of "light" from knowledge and the lack of integral structure within society. What really caused the Dark Ages? Although the Romans had invaded many countries and cultures as far away as Britain, the Fall of Rome (410 CE) began even before the Visigoth Barbarians invaded each Roman territory in turn. As noted above, when they finally stormed the walls of Rome, they were sorely disappointed to find their blockade had worked a little too well; the city was in ruins. Did Rome fall in only three days? Well, sort of, but the ruin of its social and agricultural infrastructure had been coming for some time.

In the 3rd and 4th centuries, there were 65 million people living from the Tyne River in England to the Euphrates in Egypt. What we consider the "Middle East" did not become Islamic culture until the 7th century. This was also the period when one gang of Barbarians at a time conquered the fortified towns that had sprung up. Likewise, there had been an increase in peasant soldiers and nationalism in the outer provinces; these areas had become "militaristic" empires on their own.

In some ways, these areas accepted the coming of the Barbarians because it was almost a relief from the increasing taxes of the prior ruling class. The Barbarians were the army by 378 CE, and they were also being influenced by the Christianity they encountered. Many of the great European cities well known to this day started out as army camps. Byzantium became Constantinople. Constantine reunited many peasant states through his conversion and Christian hierarchy into the power of the church at that time.

The Eastern empire was more "compact" and easier to control than the decentralized Western empire. As a Christian since the age of seven, Constantine referred to the area under his power as the Holy Roman Empire. During the time he was emperor, from 306 to 337 CE, it stretched from Hadrian's Wall in England to the Adriatic Sea. As a Christian city, Constantinople copied much of how Rome had operated before it fell into destruction. Eventually, the practice of Christianity in this area also followed the papal rulings (Holy Roman Catholic church). Constantinople continued at its height of culture and military strength from the 8th century to the 12th century when it was impacted by destruction from the Crusades. After that, it was smaller but more compact and therefore more defensible.

The Roman Rule of Law became less influential the further into the country one got. Whether peasant or noble or scholar one was "anointed by the Lord" and one's independence served just as well as the autocratic powers, who often murdered each other. "Diplomacy was cheaper than war" (Weber, 1989). Sad to say, even some of the bishops had slaves and concubines; others were touted as saints after becoming interveners who created refuges for the suffering of the time. Decline began when simple raids became full invasions (alliances and political intrigue abounded); the societal format failed to evolve or adjust socially and economically. Vandals (Germans or Goths) took control over everything from Hadrian's Wall in Britain to the Adriatic Sea; it was known as the Holy Roman Empire. The Huns were even more brutal under Attila, and many "citizens" looked forward to death. Shortened lives and an increase in suffering created the "darkness" of the Dark Ages especially where in addition there were harsh climates. Eventually, existence in the world of the Dark Ages was so horrible that the suffering of the faithful turned them to the eternal afterlife.

Weber (1989) lists five reasons the fall of Rome came as easily as it did. First, as an agricultural society, disease, poverty, and malnutrition had taken its toll. There was a high level of mosquito-borne malaria, the soil was exhausted, and the people were burdened with taxes. Second, there was more consumption than production. Third, focus had turned to pleasure and entertainment over productivity. Fourth, the overall economy had taken a downward spiral because of inflation and bad planning. Finally, the "empire" was too spread out for effective government to operate and protect its own interests.

Overall, there was a lack of confidence in leadership, and there had been a growth of Stoicism, which was drawn to nature and humanism but not to effective governance. I think it is of profound importance to emphasize how the Romans' increased interest in art, the Soul, and Self took influence away from interest in realism and self-reliance (Weber, 1989). On the other hand, Christianity was able to survive the Dark Ages because of the Hellenistic influences around it, the strong Hebrew core within its teachings, and finally, its ability to stay flexible and adapt within the contemporary world regardless of changes to power or belief systems (contextual influences).

We are still influenced by many of the cultural factors passed through the Barbarian period. As bloody as this period was (murder, incest, violence, and corruption), there was also a reorganization of political powers, and more land fell under control of the Roman Catholic church. New areas of delineated cultures include the Anglo-Saxons in Britain, the Franks and Burgundians in France, the Lombards in Italy, and the Arabs in Spain. Cultural assimilation of peoples continued, but often without a historical context or mythological basis.

Now independent from the fallen Roman empire, formerly acquired lands had no protection for its citizens. The walled structures of most townships were closed off due to a need to fortify and protect themselves. It was a bloody, dreary life; the aristocrats moved to the country in protected "villas". These rich villas were like "little kingdoms". Many farms were deserted, and the economy was very disrupted; each small area of countryside had its own local ruler; the feudal system was born. For instance, the British began to use Danish and German (Anglo-Saxon) mercenaries to protect them. In return, the British gave them land, mostly in the area now known as Kent (Hinds, 2002).

The *King Arthur* legend was probably written about the Britons against the Anglo-Saxons. By 600 CE, however, the former "Britons" had only held onto the North (Scotland) and the West (Wales); the rest became known as "Angle Land". Thus began the source of a thousand years of battling for land and power in the "British Isles".

In the Asian continent, the Great Wall of China, begun in the 7th century BCE, was finished in 1344. Huns turned west and began to organize themselves, pushing the Vandals and Goths further west into the Balkans, Italy, and Germany. Back in the Roman area, the fall of the empire (410 CE) attracted these Huns, Goths and Vandals and they were able to invade, almost at will. Yes, there had been more focus on baths and entertainment than in churches, libraries, or defense. On the other hand, Jesus of Nazareth had made his influence known, causing the BCE to CE shift in our calendar and our thinking about the historical continuum. "Where wealth had been the measure of a Roman, now poverty became the measure of a Christian. The central premise was to be content with what you have, not what you want; if wanting comes first, you will never be content. If contentment comes first, it does not matter how much you have [or what you lack]" (Van Doren, 1991, p. 96).

The Rise of the Papacy

The early papacy originated from St. Peter himself and grew through the appointed bishops until the fall of Rome. Most of these popes died in the same martyrdom as the rest of the early Christians. The first "named" popes (after 384 CE) were appointed out of the college of bishops, much as St. Peter had come from the college of Apostles (Dulles, 1985, p.140). During and after the reign of Constantine (306–337 CE), it was the landed heads of churches that consolidated their holdings into papal "states" within and around Italy. Much confusion, however, lies around this heritage. As noted above, Constantine's conversion (313 CE) and the Edict of Milan stipulated that there would be "tolerance" for Christianity in his empire.

In simple terms, he "legalized" it. He convened the first council of Nicaea (325 CE), which also seemed to create an ecumenical nod toward the papacy, and it is rumored that he passed his crown directly to the papacy, having already built his own Constantinian Basilica, now called St. Peter's Basilica and housing the Pope's main residence (Gibbon, 1776). This behavior was in direct opposition to the already stated support of the Eastern-held beliefs and construction of a mother church in Constantinople, which was meant to work with the Bishop of Rome, not in conflict with him. The disagreement led to the first East-West Schism (381 CE) and the founding of the Eastern (Greek) Orthodox Church, which combined the original churches established by early Apostles in the Balkans with those in the Middle East.

As heads of a church as well as the head of a family, powerful individuals began to rule great portions of land and to make sovereign claims to power within their territorial areas. The one central power that did continue was the influence of theology, and specifically that of Christianity, by the 5th century strongly centered in the papacy. Finally, St. Jerome became the *Pontiff* (379–382)—of the bridge—and the first Italian pope in 100 years. By the 5th century, when there was no emperor to rule (although the Pope took on this "head of state" status in many areas), it was as if Jesus and his legacy functioned as an in-absentia emperor of all (Weber, 1989).

In 498 CE, Clovis (King of the Franks) was converted. He won over Gaul from the Romans and controlled political turmoil by using Christianity as a common thread which offered peace. The empire split into smaller powers versus the previous "papal areas", and the Christian religion survived through a long period of assassinations, violence, and corruption.

Weber provides two ideas about how religious practice outlasted barbarianism. The warlike behaviors created a sense of military "honor" in the men who fought and when they returned, in triumph or as failures, they sought peace in their faith and their priests. Likewise, because life was full of fear and death, an ongoing awe of God's wrath and His protection created a sense of seeking refuge whenever possible. Remember, this was before a written liturgy was available to the illiterate masses; religion was assimilated through "manifested deeds and actions which led to the sense of true conversion" (ibid, 1989).

History Is About Power

With the regaining of power over Rome by Emperor Justinian in 529–565 CE, once again there was an emperor not only stronger than the Pope, but one who installed a Pope of his own choice, Pope Vigilius (537–555 CE). This practice of "selected" popes was to return for several hundred years. Unfortunately, Justinian faced many historical factors to deal with, not the least of which was a plague which killed between one-third or more of the known world's population at the time. This was not the Plague of 1347–1351, which began in Mongolia and by its end three years later had spread as far as England. The "First" Plague killed at least 100 million and represented the terrors of the "Dark Ages", a repetitive series of plagues, war, and withdrawal of trade and industry due to fear and mistrust between towns, city-states, and countries.

Although many of the people who still lived off the countryside found solace in their practice of pagan religions, they also had a healthy respect for the practice of the monks, cloistered now as they were behind monastery walls for their own safety. Monasteries were the center of action, monks were the "guardians of culture" and science. St. Augustine (354–430 CE) and his Benedictine followers were a prime example of this outcome as they experienced the struggle between religion and science. Ultimately, it was decided that "it is the will of God that shapes the Universe" (Boorstin, 1985, p. 24).

After winning the Battle of Tours, 732 CE, most of the territories of the old Roman empire were unified under Charles Martel, Charlemagne's grandfather (who practiced Christianity) as the Holy Roman Empire. This period is known as the Middle Ages. The term Middle Ages was not coined until the Renaissance period, when in hindsight the "Middle Ages" was seen as a clear dividing period between the Dark Ages and the Renaissance.

The Catholic church came to claim its next emperor under the rule of Charlemagne (742–814), King of the Franks. After Charlemagne became the king, he was able to drive back the Barbarians in Europe and bring order and structure. He also gave legitimacy to the theology of the papacy and was crowned Holy Roman Emperor on Christmas Day (800 CE) by Pope Leo III. His empire was called a "Roman empire", but it was not as organized as the real Romans had been with trade or schools. Nevertheless, this power base continued through the next emperors, crowned by the popes (themselves selected from the surrounding power-based "papal states") through the Medieval and Middle Ages until almost the Reformation.[34]

---

[34] Throughout Europe a sense of "darkness" and isolation continued even during the uniting reign of Charlemagne and the Franks (770 to 814 CE). But other good things were happening, not the least of which was that Charlemagne was a "devotee of the written word." "The shadowy textbook figure who was crowned Holy Roman emperor on Christmas Day, 800, comes to life as the sponsor of bookish culture, reformer of the Latin language and the Roman alphabet" (Boorstin, 1985, p. 494). The vernacular word CONNECTED many and "provincialized" what reading was available. Eventually, the King James Bible became the accepted English version, in a much more vernacular form that the Catholic Latin Missal. The importance of genealogy for legal and inheritance issues also influenced "record-keeping."

Charlemagne's system became an enduring one; the return of strong aristocracies reflected the agro-military economy. From Spain to Bohemia, he broke power down to trusted territorial areas, naming dukes, counts, and marquis so that surplus crops and goods could be gathered and accounted for. This new method of accounting was to underscore his authority by "yoking his power to the historical Roman 'empire'" (Weber, 1989). Land that had been given as a retainer became hereditary property; the structure was built on revenue and land in return for being defended professionally. He built abbeys and palaces that contained Christian signs and symbols to validate his beliefs and to underscore again his power over other's beliefs. During his reign, there was a great increase in the work at monasteries, and the Illuminated Bibles were created. Unfortunately, after his death in 814 CE, much of Europe regressed again, with the Hungarians taking power back for over a hundred years.

In England, in 793 CE, the Vikings took England's wealth like pirates, the ease of which was somewhat due to overpopulation, famine, and economic instability (its own kind of DISCONNECT). Normans from Scandinavia also overran much of England, conquered by Ivar the Boneless. Of the survivors, Alfred the Great ascended to the throne of Wessex and was able to create another army, and many men were knighted for their warring efforts. These "knights" were almost like what the twentieth century would have called "thugs", angry young men looking for a fight. Another image might be that of the Wild West Texas Rangers, created out of the jobless and wandering men once the Civil War was over.

Thus, in Medieval England the men had a mercenary spirit, but it was not until the beginnings of the Crusades that these men had a cause worth fighting for. Included in this system were also the beginnings of the idea of "courtly" love, another factor worth fighting for. It started in the 12th century in France and was a variation of homage to one's lord. Two hundred years later, this segment of society emerged from the feudal system, and "knights" again traveled to the East to serve the Pope. The future's middle class was also formed. Guilds and the revival of towns where artisans lived became market cities at crossroads and bridges. Not only were more people literate, but most had some form of mobility as well.

Tired of constant fighting, in 886 CE Alfred finally gave the Vikings land in York, but in 917 CE, his son fought to get it back. And in 1016 a Dane, King Canute, took the throne briefly; this history may have been where Shakespeare got his idea to create the play, *Hamlet*. Edward the Confessor (great-great-great-great-grandson of Alfred the Great) picked his brother-in-law, Harold Godwinson, to succeed him and to fight off the Norwegian invasion. Weakened, Harold then had to fight his cousin, William the Conqueror of Normandy, at the Battle of Hastings (1066). As king, William was the first to really organize and survey the

---

During this time, innovative individuals came up with the rotary plow to ease farming, along with the idea of allowing land to lie fallow at times for improved crop production and use of animals. Manure was used for fertilization. The wheel was used for crank and waterpower; more wheat and meat became available, at least to the middle class and above groups. By the 9th century, iron became available, both for weapons and household uses (ibid, 1989).

landowners, but (on his own behalf) he may have taken land from them as well (Hinds, 2002).

From there the succession is Henry I, to Matilda, to Henry II (with wife Eleanor of Aquitaine) [who can forget Katherine Hepburn in *Lion in Winter*], to Richard I (Richard the Lion-Hearted) who went off to the Third Crusade. Richard's brother John was the infamous king of the *Robin Hood* story, who also in reality also lost the French lands and was forced to sign the Magna Carta in 1215.

In 1295, England established its first model Parliament. Henry III failed to win back the French lands, and Edward I and Edward II failed to win back Scotland after it was lost in battles with William Bruce (*Braveheart*). And after more than 500 years of warring, the kings of England were still trapped on their island under the Pope's religious control.

Crusades Increase a Growing Schism

As mentioned, by 1059 in the old Roman area new popes were being selected by the college of Cardinals. At least in theory, many popes, such as Pope Urban II (1095), used their power for war and called for a Christian army to defeat the Turks and recapture the Holy Sepulcher from the Muslims. Overall, several hundred thousand Roman Catholic Crusaders responded to this call from the pope. In 1095, the Council of Clermont reinforced this powerful motive, which resulted in the First Crusade. For both William the Conqueror and Pope Urban II, the issue was to develop systemic control over growing populations and the pilgrims who yearned to travel to the Holy Land.

Plunders by another name can be called "Holy Wars". The First Crusade was successful in that on July 15, 1099, Jerusalem fell and became Palestine. The Muslims declared a holy war (Jihad) which in some ways has never ended (Think about what a mess the Middle East still is!) Failures to hold onto land and riches gained during the Second Crusade led, in turn, to the sack of Constantinople in 1204 during the Fourth Crusade.

It wasn't until 1291, after a series of other Crusades, that the Crusaders were finally driven out of Palestine and Syria (It could not have made the Muslims very happy when they returned with T.E. "Lawrence of Arabia" with the promise of defeating the Turks in 1916–1918, during the First World War). But similarly, to what you see in the movie by the same name, just as the English helped unite the Arabs in 1918, the Crusaders came into their lands during the 12th century, and for a while Pope Innocent 1198–1216 was the closest thing to a unified theocracy of prestige and power that the Muslims had.

Part of the Crusaders' motivation was to escape the poverty of the Middle Ages, and part was the indulgences promised to all who went to regain the territory in the church's name (Riley-Smith, J., 2005). It was not until the Middle East fell from Muslim's rule to the Ottoman Empire in 1187 that Turks allowed more travel across borders. They even allowed visits to the Church of the Holy Sepulcher in Jerusalem.

The Crusades were a great equalizer. Nobles and farmers rode out alike, across Europe to Constantinople, once also a seat of Christianity. These men were promised absolution from sin and eternal blessings in heaven, whether they died immediately on the battlefield or in old age! They were joined, at times, by the Armenian Christians, who came at the command of the Byzantine emperor. The Western Crusaders initiated the Third Crusade to collect the enormous money that had been promised to them by the Byzantines (ibid, 2005). After 1261, when the Byzantines regained the city of Constantinople, the Muslims prevailed. The Christians retreated, taking with them new knowledge, language and books, artwork, foods, and spices, as well as an improved trade route. Even the growth in literature was a type of inner pilgrimage for "ideas" unknown until shared and spread along the route (Boorstin, 1985). Supply lines were opened; new and improved roads were created. The Medieval awakening had begun!

In the mid-13th century, there was a schism again, when eastern and western conflict resulted in basically three papal claims, not resolved until 1417 at the Council of Constance and the appointment of Pope Martin V. Finally, during the Renaissance period, the papacy as we know it, with a strong leadership, patronage of the arts and accumulation of wealth, came to present its religious and political presence. Yet this power was not to last for long, as Martin Luther (1483–1546) and the other clergy of the Reformation were waiting on just the other side of the end of the Dark Ages (500–1500). However, the Dark Ages held one more dramatic and final touch of destruction and darkness, the Plague (1347–1350), during which nearly one-half (½) of the world's known population would die in just three years!

Within the Dark, a Glimmer Still Shines

What really happened between Roman rule and the Renaissance? This period is one of my favorites to look deeper into because in many ways the 13th century was like the 20th. Both had to recover from war and disaster with what Cantor (1991) calls "sensibility, imagination and faith" (ibid, 1991, p. 18). Also, 90% of the wealth was held by 10% of the population, the other 90% were still peasants. Yes, we have been discussing the "dark" and DISCONNECTED parts of the 1000 years between the fall of the Roman empire, and we will be adding the death and destruction of the upcoming plague of 1347–1350.

But before we move on to this part of our history, it is important to point out that all was not negative during this period during Medieval times (1066–1485). After all, this was also the time of Charlemagne, St. Frances, and Chaucer. In general, it was only the monks (mostly) who were literate but beginning with the future saints Augustine of Hippo (354–430 CE) through Thomas Aquinas (1225–1274 CE), the influence of these Christian theologians and philosophers on Western civilization is immeasurable. "Faith is a higher guide to truth than knowledge is" (St. Aquinas).

Augustine is known for his maxim "Truth is found within," and he helped develop an overall worldview that not only included the Catholic church as an organized "City of God", but also included a view of salvation and grace that is accepted by most Protestant churches (TeSelle, 1970). He and one of his congregations established the first Benedictine order of monks in England at Canterbury in 597 CE, which followed the Rule of St. Benedict, and was therefore named after him, although it was not started specifically by him. Anselm (1033–

1109) was the Archbishop of Canterbury and, because of his scholasticism, was able to bring an ontological argument to the discussion of the existence of God.

The Italian monk Frances of Assisi (1181–1226) was one of the most venerated monks in history; he has been followed by many believers outside of the Catholic church proper because he decided to give up a worldly life for the way of a simple monk and committed himself to helping others. His order (the Franciscans) was authorized by Pope Innocent III in 1210 and since that time has drawn large numbers of supplicants.

Thomas Aquinas (1224–1274) was viewed as a "natural theologian" in that his view of philosophy of life included ethics, natural law, politics, and metaphysics, all of which made him a well-rounded monk, one who was referred to as "a model teacher for those studying for the priesthood" (Butler, 1866). As a Dominican monk, he was seen as having a "modern" and socially invested CONNECTION to the poor. Likewise, Franciscans thoroughly devoted their life, through their own poverty, to the poor and ill, while Dominicans were more disregarding of the poor, instead focusing on education, austerity, and conforming. It was Dominican monks who became the Inquisitors of the 12th century, focusing on what they, and the Catholic church of Rome, felt were acts of heresy.

Throughout this period, it was not just the prayer and philosophy of life that the monks were maintaining. Although monasteries were often founded as centers of prayer, knowledge, and protection of the souls of the common people, or even the nobles, it was also the splendor and magnificence of the liturgy and manuscripts they created. These illuminated manuscripts are now considered great museum pieces beyond being historical works of religious art. The manuscripts had decorated borders and initial letters, generally with gold, silver, and primary colors, and were created painstakingly by the monks as their way of adding emphasis (Putnam, 1962).[35] Beyond bibles and psalters in many languages, the monks translated Greek literature, Far Eastern and Islamic manuscripts, and other important documents which were links to the literary past. As, generally, the only literate people living without a province or territory, the monks provided a vastly important conservation service, advancing Christianity and saving souls.

Beyond the preservations by the monks, and the writings found in monastery life, there were a few other "lights" of non-liturgical literature. Although most of the new literature was created by anonymous writers, often allegorical in nature like *Beowulf*, some authors such as Chaucer (*The Canterbury Tales*), Dante (*La divina commedia*) or the writings of females such as Heloise (*The Letters of Abelard and Heloise*) or Catherine of Siena (*The Dialogue*) are better known even to the non-historical reader. Of course, writing was also taking place in other languages, such as the Irish and Nordic languages, French (*The Quest of the Holy Grail, Le Morte d'Arthur*), Spanish (*Poem of the Cid*), as well as Armenian and

---

[35] "Had it not been for the monastic scribes of Late Antiquity, most literature of Greece and Rome would have perished in Europe, as it was, the patterns of textual survivals were shaped by their usefulness to the severely constricted literate group of Christians. Illumination of manuscripts, as a way of aggrandizing ancient documents, aided their preservation and informative value in an era when new ruling classes were no longer literate. Papyrus, vellum, leather, or paper could have been used" (ibid, 1962).

German. Even Marco Polo (1254–1324) is known for having written down his adventures (*Il milione*).

These classic writings have provided mankind not only sources of wisdom, but also a structure of how to view the world as the writers of that time experienced it. They portrayed a struggle between man and his view of himself as protagonist, between his higher and lower impulses. These writers of the Middle Ages were focused on the concept of destiny, what writers in the 20th century called the "quest". The writings showed a spirit of confidence and inquiry which could be compared to writings about the glory of Greek and Roman civilization.

If not for the monks' transcriptions, we wouldn't have the works of Cicero, Vergil, and Horace (Van Doren, 1991). The scholars who studied the classical writings were focused on portraying the beauty in their quest and in Nature, particularly as it supported their worship of God. More written material survives from this period than from the entire period before it, but unfortunately not all of it was saved; some of it was used as kindling!

William of Ockham (1300–1349) tells us "Reason, the light of the natural intellect, is a kind of intruder in the realm of mystical communion between God and man." Ockham is best known for his philosophical presentation of "efficient reasoning", or the concept that best explanation of something is usually that which can be given with the fewest "causes, factors or variables." Later known as "ontological parsimony", his philosophy was used as the grounding for thinking about man's place in theology, as well as a theory of knowledge. This thought reflects the beginning of a shift in ideas which were greatly promoted after the devastation and rebooting of society and economics by the plague years. Ockham died in 1347, the year the plague began (Baird, F. and Kaufmann, W., 2008).

Dante (1300) noted, "Be free from wrong and misguided impulses, concealment leads to shame and slavery." These ideas of "man's place in the universe" are deeply rooted in the archetypal values of our society, as well as in our art and drama. Fourteenth century art showed man as glorified yet also afflicted with the limitations of the Dark Ages.

As noted above, the Dark Ages were called that not only because social, financial and infrastructure systems failed after the fall of the Roman empire, but also because individuals on a personal level were unaware and unwilling to trust those outside a very small social/familial world, which became inner-directed and survival oriented. An overview of the period looks almost like [societal] borderline personality disorder to me as a psychologist; no internal "sense of (societal) Self" was really developed but rather all decision-making, sense of security, boundaries, and modulations of emotional regulation was lacking [think aggression, treachery and even wars during this period].

There were outliers of each type: the strong survivors with narcissistic instincts took power and claimed positions of nobility, the weak or ill were easily controlled. Bravery and treachery were equally rewarded. It was only the monastic life that seemed to maintain the moderate and rewarding focus on literacy and individual achievement, albeit in God's service.

The Darkest Plague

Much has been written about the years leading up to and during the Plague. By 1300, there had been three or four centuries of settled times, although the feudal system continued to abuse the lower classes. After Charlemagne's warrior family split prior communities into "principalities", growth in each area gave power to the church and "kingships". It remained a patrimonial, nucleated society (Cantor, 1991). The kings and church established a workable method of shifting power, although there were often small outbreaks of violence between warring factions.

During this period, gunpowder became known in the Western hemisphere, and battles became much more brutal than the previous hand-to-hand combat. "About the middle of the thirteenth century…battles were transformed by bigger guns, emergence of infantry and portability of firearms, which royalized warfare and helped the prince to establish a monopoly on the use of organized force within his territory" [Spain was known at this time to have spent two-thirds of their revenue on weapons to fight in Europe and the Americas] (ibid, 1991, p. 15). And into this atmosphere, where almost unceasing warfare had made existence more fearful and real, came the most exacting experiences of death ever known, the Plague.

The Plague probably started in the Far East and traveled through Mongolia because of the trade route. But initially there was a slow transmission, and thus some of the epidemic was contained by usual methods of the time. The rapid epidemic death rate was secondarily the result of flea-infested rats arriving from the Far East by way of trade ships from Caffa to Messina, Sicily. From there, it was quickly transmitted to the Italian shores and into the main routes around Europe. Ships took it to Marseilles and then to Barcelona, quickly spreading its flea/rat host to every culture of the time.

Another theory, however, is that the plague, which had come from the East to Crimea, was caused by a besieged commander from Kipchak, who left a corpse in Genoa on purpose, and someone transported it when they sailed to Sicily, killing half the population of Messina. From there, it spread in all directions throughout Europe. A newer theory believes it was a human-to-human transmission due to the high level of lice in many communities. Regardless of method, within a period of only three years, from 1347 to 1350, almost half of the known world was wiped out, and death estimates as high as two-thirds can be found in the European region.

The social and psychological ramifications were horrifying and far-reaching. Mysticism and the representation of a fear of Death could be seen within all the arts, writing to painting. Some of the shifts in religious outlook came from the effect of fear of contamination during the Plague, when even priests would not attend to the last rites of their parishioners. Therefore, people began to hear the last rites of each other, foretelling the reformational nature of European religion a century later. They did not find the church's teachings particularly comforting at that time either. The parishioners began to question the religious hierarchy in a manner that was different from their previous blind faith and willingness to pay for indulgences, a system which was not saving them anymore.

Religion even became "privatized", to some degree. The rich could afford their own chaplains who were known not to be carriers. There were even those who felt the Plague overall was a punishment from God for unknown sins or was

Apocalyptic. These individuals prepared themselves accordingly through penitent lives or flagellation. Finally, a scapegoat was sought, and as was common throughout history, many turned to looking at the Jews and "Christ-killers" as somehow to blame. Many Christians thought the Plague was the result of a Jewish plot, where the symptoms were the result of the water having been poisoned. Jews were driven out of Europe by the thousands and into Poland (where they were relatively safe until Hitler found them [sic]), or into Spain, where they suffered under the Inquisition, and again when Franco came to power in 1936.

A positive outcome of the Plague years were discoveries in clinical medicine, as well as an equalization in supply and demand for food and other goods. Because these had not been famine years, one's diet improved. However, things worsened for the ruling class because a huge portion of their serfs had died. There had to be an increase in labor-saving inventions, particularly in producing cloth and milling. Another good result was that all possessions which had been someone's who died without heirs now became consolidated into use by the general population, and there was a prosperity into the last quarter of the 14th century. "The Plague consolidated money into the hands of the survivors; great spending sprees resulted in consumerism and appreciation for availability of books" (ibid, 1991).

Around 1340, during the period of the Plague in Britain and France, a larger outbreak of armed conflict began that would turn into the 100 Years War. In England, Edward III was respected but his involvement in the war was again an attempt to win back France, whose king (his uncle) had died without leaving any known children. Succession to the crown went to the French, but the ruling parties left the countryside in ruins. The cost and resources of abandoned citizens during the war resulted in an ongoing feudal order; in some areas the system lasted well into the 20th century.

These two countries, England and France, continued to intermarry and share or, through intrigue, demand European power, during which time Edward IV aka the "Black Prince" (because of the black armor he always wore) finally won a great battle that shifted power to the English crown again. But Edward IV did not live to become king, following his father, Edward III. I am proud to say that my genealogy goes back in a direct line to his brother John of Gaunt, third son of Edward III and head of the government at that time!

Upon his death, Edward IV's son Richard II became king instead. He was only ten at the time and is sometimes seen as a "bad" king, as much for being manipulated by others as for actual "bad" leadership on his part. The rule of baronies also came from that period. Likewise, having claimed power, Pope Clement VI moved the seat of his power from Rome to Avignon, France, where Richard II kept court.

The peasants rebelled against Richard II because of war taxes he had demanded, and instead accepted a series of Henrys: Richard's cousin Henry IV, Henry V (who lost to Joan of Arc in 1429), and finally Henry VI, the first Tudor, who was seen as kind and religious, although his actions did contribute to England entering the War of the Roses in 1455. The claim of Richard, Duke of the Yorkists, and direct descendant of Edward III, set himself up to rule as Edward IV (a different one from the Black Prince).

Rather than being a success, however, his brother Richard III, sent him to the tower for life, had his sons killed, and took control. As destiny would have it, Richard III died in battle, in 1485, the last king of York and of the Plantagenet's' rule. Henry Tudor became Henry VII and married Edward IV's daughter, uniting the two sides finally, and all was well. So went the English soap opera of the 15th century!

The outcome of these two long wars, the constant shift of power in England and Europe, changes in religious viewpoint, as well as loss of control of the feudal system, all contributed to a major yearning for stability. The limitation of resources (human and agricultural) required a shift in the hierarchical process and available innovation. In summary:

Milling and printing…were all invented in response to the need for more efficient use of resources, for instance the use of rag paper over parchment. Consumerism had been born and all this agitated activity presented fertile ground for someone like Gutenberg to arrive with his printing press. It changed everything, including the fact that knowledge would now be disseminated to the masses. It was a remarkable conjunction of events—the new availability of rag paper, the invention of printing with movable metal type, and the sudden appearance of a large number of excellent manuscripts crying out for publication—that propagated the Renaissance (Van Doren, 1991, p. 155).

In its sense of "coming out of the darkness", the Middle Ages also created recovery because both Germany and the area around Rome had less of an economic slump, and the countryside became a base of society and stability. Although the feudal system was designed to support collaborative goals, a tug of war for power continued. These areas had been less ruined by Barbarian times, and what influence remained was easily assimilated so that the less disciplined and individualized Barbarian nature became part of the strong, survivalist nature of the Middle Age European citizen.

The clergy had their own type of value, a sense of what eternal presence could provide into one's dreary existence. Thus came the rivalry for architecture of the greatest value and glory, to God versus government, churches versus palaces. Yes, the Dark Ages may have stood for hard times, but "Medieval" also still stands historically for art and cathedrals. From 1050 CE to 1350 CE, in France alone there were 80 cathedrals and 500 churches constructed, resulting in one church per 200 people. It was during the 12th century that we had the construction of Strasbourg, Notre Dame, and Chartres, to name a few. Likewise, towers were raised in Pisa, Florence, Sienna, and San Gimignano. These edifices were forms of expression of creativity and civic pride.

Obviously, these edifices took up a great deal of space in every town, and later town halls and trade centers also solidified centers of powers with architecture. Regardless of the stated religious "humility" (to work is to pray said the Benedictines), it was as if the edifice would represent what "clerics thought about public matters." This revival of town life, combined with a fierce local patriotism, resulted in "competition between piety and the success of the town" (ibid, 1989). Merchants were more interested in making money than in feudal "politics".

As much as the Crusades had been an economic stimulus and an increase in quantity and qualitative of roads from west to east, the Middle Ages were heralded by a continuation in banking, shipping, and protecting the diversity of investments for both popes and Kings. The Medici family, for instance, achieved great honor when Lorenzo's son, Giovanni, was made a cardinal at the age of 14. Giovanni later became Pope and took the name Leo X, who was the mentor to Michelangelo. Like his father, Leo was a great patron of all arts (Médicis themselves gave us four popes and two French queens in the 16th century alone).

It was a time of many transitions. Of the citizens of most areas, ninety percent were peasants, and the nobles were still rich and powerful, but the social order was breaking down. The Middle Ages stood for a larger middle class, villages with more production and surplus, some luxury due to artisans/burghers and the demand for their services. As we discussed, knights created an entire culture and financial enterprise out of the Crusades, a fight for religious justice and cultural beliefs (not unlike what has been going on since the end of the 20th century). If it wasn't for this violence and the outbreak of the Spanish and Italian Inquisition in the 12th century, things would have been judged as taking a real turn for the better.

Holding the "crown" became important during a period when cities were flourishing, and trade was extensive because of relative "peace" in the Eastern Turkish Ottoman empire as well as the founding of "city-states" in Italy, the seat of Western papacy. During this period people began to use surnames, literacy increased, and commoners could move up through military service or financial gains, even into knighthood regardless of having been born into the middle class. Finally, the Dominican idea of severity in worship, some of which had been reflected in the ideals of the Inquisition, began to give way to the Franciscan attempt to reconcile "reason and faith". Leading up to the Renaissance period, a "community of man" was formulated. It would eventually come to be known as Humanism.

Chapter Six
The Renaissance
A New Historical Framework Begins

> Experience does not ever err; it is only your judgment that errs in promising itself results which are not caused by your experiments.
> – Leonardo da Vinci (c. 1510)

Although some scholars date the Renaissance period as overlapping the Middle Ages, starting as early as the 14th century and continuing until the 16th century, Bronowski and Mazlish (1960) note that some historians date the Renaissance from "the fall of Constantinople to the Turks in 1493, on the grounds that this drove Greek scholars westward into Mediterranean Europe; others hold that the Renaissance was really set in motion by the rapid printing of books from movable type, which was introduced about 1451 and became common fifty years later" (ibid, 1960, p. 3). This period may even be viewed as the renewal point of everything that makes up our modern age, refined from the Greeks, including the influences from the birth of hypothetical science, the view of man as having his own soul and consciousness separate from God, and the secularization of the state. These forms of progress define for us the deeper meaning of the Renaissance as "rebirth". There was an increase in wealth and leisure, culture, and passion for Neoclassicism, and a revival of classical Latin and Greek. "The history of the Renaissance is the history of the attainment of self-conscious freedom by the human spirit manifested in the European races...The force then generated still continues in the spirit of the modern world" (Ralph, 1973, p. 2).[36]

My view of modern outcomes, from the Renaissance period and the CONNECTIONS of man, is based on several indicators. First, there was a clear reiteration of classical philosophical ideas during the Renaissance. Secondly, Plato believed we come into the world furnished with a view of it which we simply "rediscover". We also note the church prior to the major Renaissance period had a strong hold upon the spirits and the minds of the individuals living then. An acceptance of reason (what would a "reasonable" person do?) was shown through progress, optimism, and enlightened self-interest (common good). The opposition

---

[36] "These scholars exalted reason [as did Freud], defining it as a uniquely human faculty—inferior to the divine intelligence, but like that intelligence, a motive force enabling man to direct his own destiny. Although set in the framework of a mystical and hierarchical world view which would reduce the individual to a mere peripheral object, Renaissance Neoplatonism actually magnified man's importance. It assigned him to the middle rung of the cosmic ladder, endowed him with the ability to move upward or downward according to his own volition, and hailed him as the CONNECTING link between God and the world" [emphasis added] (ibid, 1973, p. 169).

against religious control is sometimes referred to as Humanism, the attainment of "the good life", in addition to duty to society resulting in human values.[37]

> To each species of creatures has been allotted a peculiar and instinctive gift. To horses galloping, to birds flying comes naturally. To man only is given the desire to learn…for learning and training in virtue are peculiar to man; therefore, our forefathers called them *humanitas*, the pursuit of activities proper to mankind…By 'literature,' humanists meant Greek and Roman literature; by 'learning.' classical learning; by 'virtue,' conduct modeled on the precepts of ancient moral philosophy. 'Humanism' (a useful and legitimate word in spite of the fact that Germans coined it in the early nineteenth century) thus denotes something quite specific: an educational and cultural program based on the study of the classics and colored by the notion of human dignity implicit in humanity (ibid, 1991, p. 67).

To combat the types of power portrayed by men like Machiavelli, individualism was the underlying and evolutionary force in the fourteenth and fifteenth centuries. Burkhardt's Italy showed "an emergence of a secular concept of the state; a stress on the development of the individual; a discovery of the world based partly on the new voyages of exploration and partly on the new work in natural science; and a discovery of man, involving a new psychology and a new concept of humanity" (op cit., 1973, p. 4).

The Renaissance is seen as standing not only for renewal, but also for resilience and for the opportunity to "reset" from where the modern culture of that time found itself. The first printings by Gutenberg were all Latin and Greek works, previously available only in manuscripts. After the initials Gutenberg printings in 1445, [by 1500] 15 million books had been printed, and publishing continued for the "simple" readers, especially about chivalry, piety and adventures. Out of this birth of new literary availability, and new knowledge, grew what would come to be known as the philosophy of theology, philosophy of mind, metaphysics, and a shift in the study of ethics and logic. With the use of the printing press came the flourishing of art, music, and literature, as well as the Neo-classical period in philosophical areas overall; the very DNA of the Renaissance period created change.

Let us return to papal Italy. By the year 1300, the little city of Florence had become the "banker" of Europe. Its coin, the florin, became the first international currency.

---

[37] "In one sense, humanism was a pagan movement. The doctrine of the medieval church was original sin—the belief that the soul and the body are sharply divided and that, because man cannot express his soul except through his body, he carries an unavoidable sin. The doctrine of humanism was original goodness—the Greek belief that the soul and the body are one, and that the actions of the body naturally and fittingly express the humanity of the soul…Humanism was not only literary but also an intellectual movement, a shifting of values and a new self-consciousness of the human spirit" (Bronowski & Mazlish, 1960. P. 62).

But Florence was more than just a business corporation. Its citizens also sought a kind of glory not dreamed of since fifth-century Athens; a splendor of art and architecture belonging to all the people that would make their city the envy of people everywhere and would produce in the hearts of Florentines a satisfaction and civic pride unknown for centuries (Van Doren, 1991, p. 156).

This "nobly guided" society provided a fertile ground for the Renaissance and later the Reformation. As can be seen from European art, architecture, and religious and societal structure, Italy continued as the technical and cultural pupil of Greco-Roman antiquity.

A secular spirit also arose during this period in a manner equal to the rise of the spiritual "soul" during the Medieval period. By the time of the Renaissance, a virtuous life was still important, but simple things like indoor chimneys, spinning wheels, compasses, and sailing charts CONNECTED people in ways impossible during Medieval times when life was tougher. There was more free will and with the idea of a "classical curriculum" the professional scholar was reborn. The works of Aquinas and St. Francis ushered in a foundation of rational thinking upon which Erasmus, Machiavelli, Botticelli, and Michelangelo represented that "man isn't perfect, but he can still be great" (Weber, 1989). Erasmus, in particular, taught morals and culture from the point of view of Christian values. "Before 1500, Europe imported ideas and techniques; after 1500, Europeans were cultural creditors."

It was truly the age of discovery on many levels. From 1487 on, the explorers also added their influence on history: Diaz, Columbus, Balboa, Magellan, Pizzaro. It is utterly amazing to look at a timeline that shows us the following: in a period of forty years, Columbus and other explorers sailed west, Machiavelli wrote *The Prince* (1513), Luther became prominent and started a Reformation, Rafael and da Vinci died, and Michelangelo finished the Sistine Chapel. We currently think of our society changing so rapidly with the advent of computers, mass CONNECTIONS and a global economy, but changes must have been just as exciting for people of that era! By 1500, recovery from 200 years of war and plague began the eventual breakdown of the feudal system.

The original feudal system included three estates: fiefs, vassals, and reeves. Chaucer wrote about these in his *Canterbury Tales,* a satirical but accurate view of the system at the time, which he represented in his Knight, Parson, and Plowman. If an individual had a "court" issue, fines were paid to the vassal. In time, he could become a lord and those below him could buy their freedom or gain dependence through military service as well. Towns sprung up as part of the convenience of collection of fines and taxes and to provide the services necessary to keep the system going. English Common Law had been enacted under Henry II after his brother, King John, signed the Magna Carta in 1215. The Magna Carta created the 63 original estates (lords); a council, or Parliament, of these lords was declared in 1236 and continues today as the House of Lords. In 1265, de Montfort led a group of representatives from some of the lower estates to form the Commons or current House of Commons.

The bourgeois class sprung up in many skilled arts, and apprentices from four to twelve years old could find a way out of poverty. In practice, however, bourgeois virtue rarely resisted the attraction of aristocratic status; the ambition of most merchants was to exchange the social ambiguities of trade for the universally recognized prestige of nobility... "simply by living 'nobly' the bourgeois family displaced or merged with the older nobility" (ibid, 1991, p. 58). This loss of the middle "working" class changed European social structure for hundreds of years to come.

Even though Oxford University had been formed in the 1100s, and Cambridge in 1209, this pervasive respect for knowledge didn't help the lower classes for many centuries to come. For instance, in Britain, it was the CONNECTIVITY through a common language that influenced changes. Celtic (Welsh), Briton (Latin), Anglo-Saxon (Old English/German), and influences from the Bible (Hebrew and Greek) all contributed to a language cemented into what we how call the "English language". Growth in personal awareness and shifts in social dependencies also changed the structure of communal life; people lived much closer to each other, knew each other's families and daily activities, and there was a need for protection that communal life could provide. It was as though there was a recapitulation of the Greek concept of the city-state.

Regardless of the strong influences of the religious structure of the church during this period, there was a dichotomy between the renewal of superstitions (the "witch hunting" of the Inquisition starting in 1229, run by the Dominicans in Rome), versus a rise in Alchemy and belief in magic. Likewise, there was a recurrence of wonder about the natural world, a recovery of Greek ideals of reason and beauty, and an empowerment of women by increasing their status through involvement in village life and daily survival.

Awakenings: How We CONNECTED

If we look at individual versus communal evolutionary patterns, it was the joining together into towns that created the greatest shift in CONNECTIVITY. Reading provided not only distraction, entertainment, and empowerment, but also an opportunity for individuation. As Frances Bacon (1561–1626) would later write:

> "Reading maketh a full man; Conference a ready man; and Writing an exact man. And 'therefore, if a man Write little, he had need have a great memory; if he Conferre little, he had need have a present wit; and if he Reade little, he had need have much cunning, to seeme to know that he doth not. Histories make men wise; Poets witty; the Mathematicks subtill; Natural Philosophy deepe; Morall grave; Logick and Rhetorick able to contend. *Abeunt studia in mores"* (Frances Bacon, 1605).

Education and Humanism not only began to grow as attributes of the developmental hierarchy, but the Trivium (grammar, rhetoric, and logic) and the Quadrium (arithmetic, geometry, astronomy, and music) also regained importance. As mentioned earlier, if we add languages, literature, philosophy, and history, we now call this course of study "liberal arts". The point is, most dramatically, that the "common" man had time for these pursuits because of the efficiencies that were being invented.[38]

Unlike Da Vinci, not everybody can be a Renaissance-type "expert" in all areas. The new Renaissance style in painting showed realism and vitality. The idea of a "renaissance man", however, did not just start with that period. Humanism in art had started as far back as the St. Francis period (1334); by 1435, a hundred years later, Van Eyck had added a total new realism of the secular times. Fifty years later, Botticelli (1485) painted the *Birth of Venus*, showing the sensuality that came to define that period and was so much a part of Michelangelo's work on the Sistine Chapel (*Last Judgment* in 1541). This artistic view demonstrates how the Renaissance "supplanted" the Middle Ages, with the additional assistance of the courage and excitement of the Explorers of the time. It was a period of "singularity of impulses" (Weber, 1989).

As Van Doren proposes, science + education = competence; it is important to distinguish between science and nonsense if the "searcher/researcher" is to find answers (Van Doren, 1991, p. 135). Weber calls this process a "universal education" and such concepts, begun long ago with the Platonists, were continued during da Vinci's time. As mentioned, Bacon preferred inductive over deductive reasoning, the exception rather than the specific, but in the kind of studies I will be discussing in later chapters (neuroscience and spiritual/metaphysical), we often now combine both perspectives in the scientific method and in a sort of "omi-cosmic" study of the world.

Truth became defined as a belief in the impeccable and unimpeachable; it was also available to scientific method. From Ptolemy and Pythagoras to Copernicus, to Bacon and other Neoplatonists, all wanted to discover a purity beyond just the

---

[38] "Life was changing…Modern ways of understanding the universe date, not from the Medieval point of view, but from the Renaissance. Believing himself capable not merely of experiencing but of doing… [he wanted] to control his environment. Man still viewed himself as located in the center of the universe, but it was now a universe he was capable of understanding and fashioning for his own purposes. Nature was viewed not as symbol but as reality; life was no longer a vestibule to eternity but a place of wonder and joy and fulfillment which God wanted man to experience before he attained Heaven (St. Francis of Assisi, for example, felt one reached God by enjoying Nature); the leader on earth was not the priest but the prince; and man achieved a new identity in the great chain of being—he was no longer an insignificant speck in the universe but a unique creation, lower than angels but higher than animals, endowed with the divine faculty of reason, 'What a piece of work is a man,' says Hamlet, reflecting the Renaissance view, 'How noble in reason! How infinite in faculty!'

This new sense of order can be seen in all aspects of the Renaissance—in politics and the sense of history, in philosophy and religion, in art, in science—and it helps make clear why the Renaissance is the threshold to today's world…via means rather its ends. The Renaissance focus derived ultimately from the Greek notion of man as the measure of all things: No better illustration of this humanistic theme can be found than in the visual arts, particularly in Italy, where there appeared a parade of such artistic geniuses as the Western World has not seen again" (Isaacson, 2017).

senses (Boorstin, 1985). The contributors during the Renaissance gave imagination, artistic value, and romanticism to their works, and for some they gave even more influence upon values and beliefs.[39]

Leonardo da Vinci was known for both his study of painting and science, in other words, that of natural phenomena and the investigation of what is. He was curious about art, as well as the human body and its anatomical functioning. He was also just as excited about understanding the mechanical world. Living in a time when illegitimate individuals (which he was) could not join the guilds, he believed in experiences and experiment above what books could tell him, or others' authority on any subject.

Before we discuss de Vinci at length, let me note that Ficino (1433–1499) was one of the greatest of the Renaissance Neoplatonists. Leonardo da Vinci came to know him while visiting the home of the Medici. At the Academy of the Medici, Ficino proposed renewed contact with the many cultures of antiquity, and not just the Greeks and Romans. He made serious contact for the first time with the Aztecs and the Incas, the East Indians, and the Chinese, encouraging sixteenth-century Europeans to increase trade and knowledge for a new freedom from temporal provincialism and a more self-conscious understanding of their own society (Van Doren, 1991).

The Eastern World (Muslim, Chinese) seemed "more complacent about navigation and trade; they just let others come to them and in that way reaped rewards. This complacency may have been due to the basic tenets of Hinduism, Buddhism and Confucianism—to be more concerned with the inner world than with the outer world" (Boorstin, 1985, p. 201). All these factors found a confluence, then as now, and it is in those experiences which transcend the cultural and environmental influences which form our personalities, which contribute to

---

[39] Do theoretical treatises impact man's actual behavior? Or even his production of artistic works (a form of Self)? Renaissance scholars were having to keep up with the changing reality of experiences at a very fast pace, e.g., changes in geographical findings from explorers' discoveries. Even though he was illegitimate, Leonardo was at least literate, and he made the best of it, having at his disposal some of the great literature of the world. "The Ottoman Turks were about to capture Constantinople, unleashing on Italy a migration of fleeing scholars with bundles of manuscripts containing the ancient wisdom of Euclid, Ptolemy, Plato, and Aristotle. Born within a year of Leonardo were Christopher Columbus and Amerigo Vespucci, who would lead an area of exploration. And Florence, with its booming merchant class of status-seeking patrons, had become the cradle of Renaissance art and humanism. Fully a third of Florence's population was literate, the highest rate in Europe…A collector of ancient manuscripts who had been schooled in Greek and Roman literature, Cosimo de Medici supported the rebirth of interest in antiquity that was at the core of Renaissance humanism" (Isaacson, 2017, pp.18, 26–27). But Leonardo did not just integrate the knowledge coming from rediscovered books of antiquity, he created pathways of knowledge from his own experiences and keen observations. "Thus, Leonardo became a disciple of both experience and received wisdom. More important he came to see that the progress of science came from a dialogue between the two. That in turn helped him realize that knowledge also came from a related dialogue: that between experiment and theory" (ibid, 2017, p. 173).

what I am calling the unified field theory (UFT) of how we CONNECT, and which is the core concept of this book.

Art and Love

As much as Leonardo da Vinci (1452–1519) is considered the quintessential "Renaissance Man", always looking for a synthesis, he did not always bring things to fruition. Looking at the things he started, but never finished, he probably had ADD or some other kind of processing deficit. Some researchers conjecture his mental health may have also been driven by periods of mania; some refer in veiled innuendoes to his homosexuality. What we do know is that he was often pulled in many ways by the nobility and royalty to whom he owned his income. We might just as well have owed such things as "flying machines" and solar power to da Vinci if he had ever published his ideas.

But instead, most of his notebooks lay fallow and were later inherited by his great "friend" Count Melzi. It was mostly his painting that those in power wanted. He painted for friends and popes alike during his long life. He was more driven by "restlessness than stasis", possibly a reflection of his own nature as compared to that of some famous Greek philosophers like the Stoics or epistemologists, such as Aristotle. Those scholars gave themselves restive periods to think and write. Regardless, it was after these great thinkers that da Vinci sometimes wished to model himself. "Man is the measure of all things" can also show up as a reflection of how an Outlier sees things; we all view the world through our own lenses!

Leonardo was a great one for using analogy and seeing patterns in nature. In fact, Leonardo developed his own precursor to Galileo's principle of relativity (which also preceded Einstein's!). "The effect of moving air on a stationary object is as great as it is when the object is moving, and the air is stationary." He understood a bit of wave theory that would become quantum physics, (that light and sound traveled in waves), and "with his gift for analogy and ability to notice movement, he even viewed emotions as traveling in waves" (ibid, 1985, p. 435).

This finding pleased me as I attempted unifying so many theories as well (UFT). He understood sensory input and a bit about how the brain processes this perceptual input. "His fascination with the CONNECTION between the mind and the body became a key component of his artistic genius: showing how inner emotions are manifest in outward gestures" [emphasis added] (Isaacson, 2017, p. 185, 219). Leonardo da Vinci grew up among the Medici and studied art with Verrocchio, student himself of Donatello, and his contemporaries were Michelangelo and Botticelli. Not too bad for the child of a middle-class notary and a peasant woman, born out of wedlock.

Just as there were changes in attitudes and methods toward the larger life aspects of art, methods of gathering data, and obtaining knowledge, there was another cultural shift during this period in the view of love as attainable versus the previous view of spiritual or Platonic and/or unattainable love. Plato had originally presented these ideas of reaching out to "other" as a Trinity: essence of life, intelligence, and the power of comprehension. Many of us have heard of the concept of a "Platonic" relationship. But what did he say about love?

He who loves, dies; for his consciousness, oblivious of himself, is devoted exclusively to the loved one, and a man who is not conscious *of* himself is certainly not conscious *in* himself. Therefore, a soul that is so affected does not function in itself, because the primary function of the soul is consciousness…The one and same Truth given to us all by God, acquires the names of various virtues according to its various powers. According as it shows divine things, it is called Wisdom, which Plato asked of God above all else. According as it shows natural things, it is called Knowledge; as human things, Prudence; as it makes men equal, Justice; as it makes them unconquered, Courage; and as tranquil, Temperance (Van Doren, 1991, pp. 308, 318).

Later theories redesigned this trinity into Passion, Communication, and Intimacy, and added Commitment.

Because "romantic love" was becoming a more widespread practice, Shakespeare also addressed these issues, feeling love was the "best representation of human life" (ibid, 1991). Dante and Petrarch performed the magic of bringing love into literature for Italian readers, as did Cervantes for Spanish, Lessing, and Goethe for German. The quote, "We are such stuff as dreams are made of" (Shakespeare, *The Tempest, Act 4)*, may help us remember that the "stuff" is our illusionary view (perhaps) of our life, the life that will get us eventually to the true reality "afterlife".

The Prince

After the death of one-third (minimum estimate) of the population from the Plague of 1348, community resources were consolidated and financial concerns (always the source of wars and intrigue) became prioritized, possibly because of papal financial influences in Italy. Why was so much happening in Italy?[40] Much of this process is explained in Machiavelli's *The Prince.*

Machiavelli's *The Prince* was written as a vivid representation of the egoism of the general population and the rules that rulers felt necessary and justifiable. "*The Prince* reflects a startlingly pessimistic view of human nature…In Machiavelli's view, the rules must be not only intelligent and forceful but also a master of the arts of deceit. Understanding what men are really like, the prince 'must know well how to use both the beast and the man'" (ibid, 1985, p. 25). Cesare Borgia, often felt to be the model for Machiavelli's prince, was the illegitimate son of Pope Alexander VI.

---

[40] "Simultaneously there was the rise of the Papal States; in Florence, only a small minority even of those men who lived within the city's walls were citizens and participated actively in political life. The rise of the Medici principate in the fifteenth century and its re-embodiment in the grand duchy of Tuscany in the sixteenth century resulted in the suppression of the civic liberty of a people, but of the privileged position of an oligarchy; while beyond the walls stretched the political hinterland of the Tuscan territories, ruled by and in the interests of the citizens of Florence and their prince" (ibid, 1985, p. 580).

Born at the end of the fifteenth century in Italy, he was killed in 1507 at the age of thirty-two and the hopes of his family died with him, as did the dream of the historian Niccolò Machiavelli (1469–1527), who had seen in Borgia the unique combination of a powerful [future] pope and a brilliant young commander who proposed the prospect of an Italy free of foreign control (Boorstin, 1991). Up until the 15th century, this established paradigm of the "warring" Feudal Period had been famously adapted, for power and control, by greedy landowners, power-hungry members of the clergy, and members of the monarchy.[41]

How did the appearance of so many new monarchies change Europe? In France, Louie XI tried to control the previous high levels of violence, while in England Henry VIII wanted to stimulate an exchange of goods. Fernand of Spain, who sent out so many of the times' explorers, was in the pursuit of a patriotic identity. Indeed, much of the growth and change was built on power and money, the exchange of goods and loans at the highest levels. It wasn't until Henry III of France allied himself with Phillip II of Spain in the 1580s that the importance of one's religious life, and whether one was Catholic or not, also weighed in so heavily (Weber, 1989). Kings often thought it was their divine right to rule, and this included power over the church as well. The kings of France, for instance, wanted to be worshipped but also struggled to keep a civil peace. Ultimately a "code of behavior" evolved.

By the time of Louie XIV, those who ruled from Versailles had a disciplined set of roles and rules to follow. It seemed there was a "struggle between passion and duty." Much of this interplay is seen in the Shakespearean plays of the time, where Roman law had strengthened the power of the Pope but heroic deeds in battle had also given many Royal figures authority as well. Ultimately, everyone's culture was served by more law and order and the idea of representation grew from England onto the continent and became the birth of Rationalism. General assemblies could be found in France and Holland; civil service was a reputable job in many provinces. Marriages, deaths, and the general collection of indulgences needed to be recorded for the benefit of the Pope's coffers. As we will further see, this type of pressure finally led to the call for reform by Martin Luther in 1517 (Martin Luther, *Wikipedia*, 3/29/2015).

---

[41] "Machiavelli had been hoping for change as well. Although his book was seen as shocking and controversial, it is still read as a portrait of societal corruption. *The Prince*'s methods can also be seen as a necessity in any pursuit of control and gaining power. Then, as now, it is the opening of the closed off nature of society (or of the Self) that creates change and light out of Dark, for example, destructive pre-recovery addictive behaviors I see in people who are about to enter AA, OA, NA and so on. The Renaissance period shifted societal norms because of revival of trade and the growth of towns, which in turn created the rise of a middle class of manufacturers, traders, and bankers. This dynamic change in structure, combined with a redistribution of wealth after the mass death during the Plague, "all tended to promote a greater social mobility and threated the supremacy of feudal magnates…The towns and their inhabitants could not fit comfortably into the feudal scheme of things, and as commerce expanded, even the larger and better governed feudal territories were inadequate to provide the protection and facilities that merchants required" (Van Doren, 1991, p. 251).

One thing that can be said about the structure given by rules, whether now or in the Middle Ages, is that they facilitate a unity and balance within the individual and society. Dualisms of mind/soul and body/emotions could resonate more closely together and not at crossed purposes.

Challenging Religious Basics

The period of the Reformation covers the "reign" of twenty popes, starting with Pope Julius II and ending with Pope Innocent X following the Thirty Years War (1618–1648), which devastated much of Germany (where Martin Luther lived). In 1510, Pope Julius was pushing Michelangelo and Raphael for new art, without regard to the financial and political effect it would have on Italy and the Roman Catholic church in general. The Pope had been a de Medici and had already faced opposition by Michelangelo and Leonardo da Vinci when Leo followed Julius as pope. Henry the VIII took Pope Julius II to task for his fiscal and political instability (1503). Henry focused on reforming the clergy, even though he really wanted a divorce and to save for himself the English riches regularly taken by the English monasteries and Rome.

In 1517, Martin Luther (1483–1546) wrote his ninety-five theses against Roman Catholic church's practice of purchasing freedom from sin with indulgences (money); Pope Leo X's version of salvation, which Rome stated had to be earned by the sacrificial behaviors and intervention by a priest. In 1520, Luther was excommunicated for his straightforward point of view. The German princes ultimately backed Luther's version of reform at the Diet of Worms in 1521, with Emperor Charles V presiding, but it was no secret that they also joined Henry VIII in wanting independence from the financial and political pressures put on them by Rome.

> He [Luther] believed the justice of God was completed, for man, in the gift of faith, that man was therefore justified by faith, and faith alone. Thus, there was less need for the vast infrastructure of the church, which seemed to him to be an obstacle, rather than an avenue, between man and God…Reform became both an end in itself and a rationale for other purposes. And there were many other secular forces at work as well (ibid, 1991, pp. 163–164).

Luther added his own form of fighting against the Catholic church's control by his basic belief that it is neither safe nor honest to act against one's own conscience. In 1525, Luther wrote *On Bondage of the Will*, thought to be written in response to *On Free Will* by Erasmus. Faith was a "gift from God", and salvation came from God's grace and because God allowed free will, this freedom enabled man to act out of choice and to earn merit. Jesus had died for our sins; that was enough according to him. Because Luther believed that man was saved by faith alone, "God is not only just, but also merciful."

In Luther's eyes, the Roman Catholic church's sacraments—baptism, confirmation, the Eucharist, penance, ordination, marriage, and extreme unction— were all methods of gaining authority over the parishioners and to teach them that they could not "cooperate in their own salvation;" in other words, they needed to pay the indulgences. Luther's ideas followed from the existing social and religious motives and political unrest. Luther also helped focus the church more on women in the church's history, for instance St. Anne and the Virgin Mary, and away from worshipping only relics and indulgences as sources of spiritual expression. This approach appealed to women parishioners as well (Weber, 1989). The bourgeois' view of the Reformation was that it provided "reality in a hard world". Scholars had already begun to take practicality from ancient points of view, by the practice of Neoclassicism and Humanism. Into this period came another reformer, even more practical than Martin Luther—John Calvin, a real authoritarian.

John Calvin (1509–1564), who broke with the Roman Catholic church in 1530, is most famous for his writing *"Institutes of the Christian Religion,"* a document designed to be a complete account of Christian teaching. In it is presented a synthesis of sixteenth-century Protestant thought as it was developing (including that of Melanchthon and Bullinger). These tenets have been highly influential on Protestant development and thought ever since.

When studying these first two great reformers, however, their country of origin may well explain a difference in the type of influence they had. Whereas Luther was German, Calvin was born in France and his ideas of predestination and absolute "sovereignty" of God's will reminds us of the longstanding influences of many French monarchs. So much so, he ultimately fled to Basel and is usually associated with being Swiss instead.

To this day when we speak of "Protestant ethics", we are probably talking about the philosophy as presented by Calvin. Although we can think of the Reformation as a revolt against theology which condescends, Calvin's view of dogma stated that people could relate directly with God, a concept even further away from Rome than Luther's ideas. Work and activity to God's glory was what counted (the Puritan way). Having grown tired of religious and political wars, the people's struggle was between indivisible truth and salvation versus tolerance (keep peace for the state).

As a psychologist (who once wrote a paper comparing Freud, Gandhi, and Martin Luther King Jr.), I need to point out something similar and interesting in the histories of these reformers. Both Luther and Calvin were raised by strong fathers who influenced their pursuit of higher education, both men went ultimately into the study of law, both men had a "conversion experience", and both men also suffered from periods of anguish which I would currently only call depression. The one strong difference in the CONNECTIONS between these men, however, was that Calvin was never an ordained priest. Rather he started as a humanist/reformer, and if anything, became more conservative as he aged, whereas Luther was ordained for 12 years (15 years until he was excommunicated) and his crisis of faith grew out of his studies and his clarity of philosophical thinking.

Therefore, the Lutherans were soberer German bourgeois while other Protestants were more "people of the Book" and less ceremonial (Weber, 1989). On the other hand, the most important thing they had in common was the emphasis they put on faith. Luther's influences started many other societal effects, not the least of which was the predictable reaction by the Catholic church. At the Council of Trent, a Counter-Reformation act changed the catechism and areas of the Vulgate version of the Bible to Loyola's Jesuit outline.

Luther's acts of religious reformation provided steps toward a more complex, and usually just, society. Evangelical ideas gave the listeners the opportunity to "think for themselves" and, for once in their lives, these ideas were less contradictory to the everyday reality they faced. The worshipper's choices could hold weight and their God might listen to them without having to go through an authoritarian intermediary first.

It is reasonably easy to understand what the victim of religious persecution died for. He died for the truth of an individual interpretation of Scripture, and to maintain the integrity of his own conscience. Luther stated at the Diet of Worms: 'I am bound by the Scriptures I have quoted, and my conscience is captive to the word of God. I cannot and will not recant anything, since it is neither safe nor right to go against conscience' (Van Doren, 1991, p. 150).

Having reviewed societal influences and CONNECTIONS that resulted from the Reformation, let us revisit the effect of politics and an argument about whether the "church" had ruined the real study of philosophy before we move on to review the growth of science during the Renaissance. As detailed above, the ongoing organization of the church appeared to use punitive actions as its chosen form of correction, for instance torture in response to the behaviors of superstition. The Early Inquisition Tribunals, established by Pope Gregory IX, (at their height during the 12th century, and used particularly in northern Italy and southern France), thought this torture the best method to control heresy.

During the Renaissance, there was a renewal of this practice of using an inquisitional council to question reformational believers and "heretics". This "new" Inquisition had a broader European basis, including Spain and Portugal and Inquisition panels of the Counter-Reformation of the Catholic church were even held into the New World once the expansion of the church into the Americas began. Bishops in the Inquisition period believed that the heretic was a danger to society but also "to him/herself".

The humanistic period of calm, and the willingness to believe that the structure of the city-state and relative benevolence of the nobility could regain and continue into a period of Reason or Re-Naissance (rebirth) of the classical virtues, was disrupted by the upheaval in religious beliefs and practices against the monopoly of the Roman Catholic church. While new scholars, church leaders, artists, scientists, and community leaders arose, in certain areas the "dark ages" continued. What the strong had most in common was a sense of continuity and lack of division. Someone like da Vinci virtually represents the overall ability and sensibility in all these areas. In fact, to this day, the term "Renaissance Man (or woman)" designates a person of such attributes.

The one possible variance in this concept of a "unified position" about the Renaissance may have been the slowly developing myth that theology and science could not be reconciled as both rational and spiritually based. Discoveries in science, as well as by explorers around the globe, were like a new crusade, and were also seen as a chance to spread Christianity once again. The exploring mind encouraged seeing travel as an adventure as well as an aspect of fame. Likewise, the scientific method was seen as another form of "adventure", promoting a comparative approach and the ability to "judge for yourself". Objectivity was the great liberator.

Da Vinci demonstrated that people could experience and experiment through their own scientific observations. Theses would be created and then revised or disproved, even about the shape of the world. The study of other cultures found by the explorers, and then traders, influenced the relativism later found in the Enlightenment period.

As mentioned, Leonardo may be just as famous for what he didn't finish as for what he did. Isaacson (2017) explains that this may be, in part, because of the state of flux that the world was in. Da Vinci wrote about how no one moment was self-contained, and that life was like a flowing river. These explanations sounded so much like Heisenberg's theory of uncertainty and incorporated many of the ideas I have been trying to convey—that all our knowledge is just points on a wave called our life experience and that what seems momentarily important, or even distressful, will pass into the next "something" that will come along.

Although he was better at conception than completion, "what made Leonardo a genius, what set him apart from people who are merely extraordinarily smart, was creativity, the ability to apply imagination to intellect. His facility for combining observation with fantasy allowed him, like other creative geniuses, to make unexpected leaps that related things seen to things unseen" (Isaacson, 2017, p. 518). Da Vinci, for instance, believed in the fundamental "identity between the microcosm of man and the macrocosm of nature…his mind leaped to the concrete and the particular… 'Nature speaks to us in detail, and that only through the detail can we find her grand design.' Leonardo proclaimed" (Bronowski and Mazlish, 1960, p. 17–18).

Do we want our myths exposed? Science sometimes attempts to do that, familial life tries to protect myths, and even the Bible infers an Accommodation Theory. In psychology, this theory of accepting and "accommodating" to the "parental" figure most seen as having the authority or of whose love one is most afraid of losing (for instance during a custody battle, or perhaps because of religious pressure?). Accommodation is commonly presented as the explanation for why individuals/children do not always make a decision that might best represent their needs, values or even conscience. We necessarily adjust to those with whom we are communicating and CONNECTING.

We certainly can see changes in the course of history due to the influences of accommodation on the ways in which 1) acceptance affected whether powers settled with each other, through intermarriage and an exchange of land or riches, or 2) took control through warfare. When the discoveries of science came along, or at least became more known through the dissemination of knowledge because of the printing press and more literacy, myths and fears that were so great during the Darkness began to fall apart in the Light. I am not sure that this change was the real focus of Luther, Calvin, Zwingli and the others, but I do know that as men of knowledge they were also leaders in "reasonable thought" and were CONNECTED in their opposition to specific dogma. They would have embraced the kind of thinking that came along with John Locke a century later.

In. 1689, John Locke (1632–1704) presented what may be his most well-known work, *Two Treatises of Government*. This position on political philosophy proposed the idea of a "social contract" that was so powerful it helped justify the act of overthrowing the government of James II of England in 1688. "It is to avoid the state of war that often occurs in nature, and to protect their private property, that men enter into civil or political society, thus the state or society. It is also the state that men return to upon dissolution of government, i.e., under tyranny" (John Locke, 1689). This action, plus his well-known concept of *tabula rasa* [man is a blank slate upon birth, ready to be written on solely by sensory experiences], provided him a legacy within the History of Philosophy.

Locke's view of liberalism can also be seen as a foundation of man's need for individual freedoms; it would lead to writers like Emerson, who presented ideas about self-reliance, but not for another 150 years. We can see this point of view in opposition to the previous societal state of mind where peasants turned their responsibility over to noble "surrogates". Even though the general population may have opposed Roman rule, it took them some time to become more responsible for a healthy Self even when, during the Dark Ages, it was clear that society had fallen into a destructive mode.

Scientific Method

Although it is true that formal "Scientific Method" began with the Greeks, and scientists within our own century have made literally countless discoveries that have advanced our understanding of neurophysiology, medicine, computer science, physics, and other sciences, it is difficult to comprehend the growth in knowledge. But every period of investigation is contextual, and I truly believe that the discoveries of the 14th to 16th centuries must have felt just as powerful to those who lived in that European culture. What Humanism brought to science was the ability to look outside of religion and Self, to the physical world which was not there just to provide food and a place to abide. Aristotle had called this a fifth state, beyond the four states with which we are familiar. "Quintessence' is the pure state. Water/Air/Earth/Fire were others…things in a state of imbalance are seeking a place of balance."

What does quintessence have to do with the advancement of science? It helped dispel the myth that only a higher authority (the Pope) could decide what was "real" in terms of the natural experiences that individuals were having, and in bringing back the Greek ideas, certain writers were stirring up the possibility that individuals could experience the natural world directly, and they could understand how it worked!

For instance, although Copernicus (1473–1543) made many discoveries that he waited to disclose until he was near death, it was clear that his real motive was to allow the "common man" to have the experiences he had had and to know what he knew. His true passion was to pursue the discipline of critical thinking; for instance, he presented a summary based on a comparison between the conclusions of Aristotle and those of Ptolemy (90–168 AD). This is of note, because before the Crusaders brought back the Greek writings and Gutenberg's press made them easy to distribute, it is highly likely that Copernicus would not even have had these manuscripts available to him, nor made the CONNECTIONS he did. And it was his observational skills that led to making his interests in the heavens into astronomical history.

It is fair to start our review of the explosion in scientific investigation during the Renaissance by continuing our focus on Copernicus (*De Revoluntonus*, [Revolutions of the Heavenly Spheres], 1543). In 1500, he was lecturing in Rome on mathematics and astronomy, where year-time was taking on a new importance. He asserted the universe was heliocentric, which won him the scorn he felt it would because of its complexity and "novelty". He had shown his work to some of his friends and the word got out. Even in the end, he tried to smooth things over by dedicating his book to Pope Paul III.

In addition to the many areas of classical scholarship to which Copernicus contributed, it was his scientific methodology which also created a shift in the classical view of scientific study. His use of logic in procedures (both inductive and deductive) was joined with experimental methods and precise measurement. Later, Da Vinci would take these methods even further. Before Copernicus, scientific generalizations and conclusions had come from direct sensory experience; after Copernicus, methods from that time on had to be tested quantitatively, and although qualitative and phenomenological data was not completely overlooked, it was often overruled arbitrarily based on more important measurable "facts".

Kepler's (1571–1630) studies of planetary motions followed the slowly revealed observations and discoveries of Copernicus after his death. "Kepler's Laws", as they are known now, grew out of his belief in a solar-centric planetary system, which he called "celestial physics". The laws include: the law of ellipses, the law of equal areas, and the law of harmonies. These laws led directly, in many ways, to Newton's discoveries about motion.

It was Galileo's physics that gave birth to Newton's math. Kepler's Laws had, of course, preceded Galileo's (1564–1642) major improvements in observational astronomy. Because of Galileo's improvements to the telescope of his time, he was able to confirm such discoveries as the phases of Venus, the satellites of Jupiter, and to observe sunspots. In fact, he is often called the "father of modern science".

Galileo was an early crusader for the "paradoxes of science against the tyranny of common sense. There is only one Truth [he said], but it is communicated in two forms—the language of the Bible and the language of Nature" (Boorstin, 1985, pp. 316, 322). Much of his methodology came at the price of a fight with Pope Urban VIII and the Roman Catholic church. Galileo was sent before the Inquisition in 1615. When he refused to back down again and was placed under house arrest for 9 years, he used this time to write his greatest work, *Two New Sciences*. Galileo designed his own "Theory of Relativity", a fact of major influence centuries before Einstein.

Galileo put forward the basic principle of relativity, that the laws of physics are the same in any system that is moving at a constant speed in a straight line, regardless of its speed or direction. Hence, he claimed, there is no absolute motion or absolute rest. This principle provided the basic framework for Newton's laws of motion and is central to Einstein's special theory of relativity (Einstein, 1954). Galileo also demonstrated the principle of falling bodies (remember the leaning Tower of Pisa story?). It would not be until 1741 that the Vatican lifted its ban against Galileo and a complete copy of his writings was accepted for publication under their authorization.

It is common knowledge from our time in high school science classes that much of the "scientific method" first conceptualized by the Greeks was reformulated and expanded during Galileo's century. In the scientific method, we ask: how specific does the knowledge have to be? Is it predictive? Can it be a hunch or intuitive, as it often starts out?[42]

In many ways, "science" itself was the major discovery, or invention, of the seventeenth century. However, society and individual souls were still strongly held in check by the church and its views as well. Political and financial power demanded control if nothing less. With the adoption of scientific methodology and a belief in the truth it presented, "Scriptures [often] conflicted with scientific truth, [and] the Scriptures had to be interpreted allegorically, to avoid 'the terrible detriment for souls if people found themselves convinced by proof of something that it was made then a sin to believe'" (ibid, 1991, p. 202).

To summarize, many historians believe that the beginning of the end of the church's control over society was Galileo's invention and use of the telescope. His censure by the church was a specific reflection of the church's attempt to keep limited the common man's experience and knowledge of the community much less the universe. Many of the scientists of that age (Copernicus, Kepler, and Galileo) had the faith that "nature moves in a regular and harmonious fashion in spite of the bewildering variety of appearances…Man's task, therefore, was to understand the nature or structure of things and to adjust himself harmoniously to the necessary results of this structure" (Bronowski & Mazlish, 1960, p. 353). Scientific findings could be understood and CONNECTED to everyday experiences. Galileo's discoveries contributed to the dissolution of the bonds to the church and allowed knowledge to factor into one's natural state.

Descartes (1596–1650) came upon an originally unique way to insulate himself against the church's views pursuing him: he proposed to doubt everything to prove it. "He proved the existence of God mathematically and at the same time showed how God had created a world that would run forever without his assistance, like a huge, complex, and ornate clock. And he managed to do all of this in twenty-five pages" (ibid, 1991, p. 204). And yet, beyond this logical approach to proof, Descartes did believe in God's hand in the act of creation. It was just invaluable at that time in his philosophical formulation to maintain Rationalism. In *The Discourse on Method* ("*cognito ergo sum*," [I think, therefore I am]), he presents the foundation of his ideas, later further advanced by Pascal

---

[42] "Both art and science enlighten us…Science deals almost exclusively with things, not ideas or feelings; and with the external world and its workings, not inner states and their workings, despite the effort of some psychologists to be or seem scientific. The human body is considered to be a part of the external world; the soul is not…Ex: The external world of scientists contains some things, like quanta, quarks, and quasars that are as mysterious as angels and normally as invisible. But this does not trouble scientists as they believe they can deal effectively with the elementary particles that they cannot see and according to the uncertainty principle never can see, but not with angels, which will probably never appear to scientists because scientists do not believe in them" (Van Doren, 1991, p. 187–188).

and Spinoza, who each had a comment on this attempt to reduce theology to a scientific geometric form.

Considered a "natural philosopher", Isaac Newton (1642–1726) was curious about almost everything and his influence upon science in the 17th century ranged into mathematics, mechanics, optics and physics (Westfall, 2007). His passion for understanding gravitational attraction, and how far the celestial influences might be, was influenced by seeing an apple falling from a tree. Along with Leibniz, he is given credit for inventing differential and integral calculus (as well as Laws of Mechanics). Most of us are at least aware of his laws of uniform motion and universal gravitation: change of motion is proportional to the force impressed upon the body; for every action there is an equal reaction, i.e., effects come from causes.

In a review of the *Principa* (1687), Thayer presents Newton's four rules of reasoning, and warns us of unguarded hypothesizing without quantitative data from an experiment to back up the findings. Explanations must be directly supported by experiments; this is the definition of the scientific method as it has been practiced since Newton's time and as it is still practiced today, for the most part (Thayer, 1953).

As the story goes, Einstein was looking for one unified theory that would explain all the forces of the universe as he understood them in the early 20th century. In the early 17th century, the Enlightenment philosopher/scientists were trying to use the concept of "Nature and Natural Law" to explain most ideas in science of that time. Newton's findings were a dynamic piece of the foundation for this way of thinking; his "truths" were so relevant that much which had been calculated before was often discarded. Even social and economic theorists fit their ideals into his methodology at the time.

Naturally, therefore, it was not long before the religious elements of the time had to likewise come to terms with his influence upon the world within which they found themselves. His teachings helped do away with some of the residual "metaphysical" elements that still lingered into the 17th century following the prior practice of pantheism, particularly in rural areas. On the other hand, he was consistently interested in alchemy and finding a "philosopher's stone" which would address some of the unresolved issues of what we today might refer to as "chemistry".

Copernicus and Kepler were both practitioners of their faith and Galileo was a member in good standing as well. Therefore, science did not have to be incompatible with religion (e.g., Descartes was a Catholic who moved to Protestant Belgium). Spinoza was Jewish but was excommunicated because he tried to "bring some reason back" to the state of beliefs about the universe. The point is that all these men of science had a faith of some kind which CONNECTED them and yet they wanted to understand more than just what rational dogma told them; they had reasonable minds and their faiths, which could co-exist, could still wonder, search, and find new answers.

How Enlightenment Reformed

The rise of science affected how many aspects of religious and biblical influences were re-evaluated, not the least of which was the whole "de-deification of creation". The debate between the Socratic method and the Masonic belief in a religion of reason led to a whole new view of "deism". There had been a long period of allowing dominion by the church over personal beliefs and behavior, over ownership of property, and even an avoidance of using a "reasonable" point of view toward personal ethics. Trust in God and maintaining one's faith to explain the laws governing the world had been the way of life for a long time. What led us toward technology?

The counterpoint to the thoughtfulness and inner directedness of humanistic thought had been the previous structure and the hierarchical background to the concept of "sin". The seven sins were: anger, greed, pride, sloth, envy, lust, and gluttony. I think of the list as representing public versus private crimes. The common and often poverty-ridden Man had not previously spent that much time in self-review. In the Middle Ages, God's presence and God's rules made the possibility of a transgression even more possible. Moral Failure was a failure of character, disobedience, and willfulness. There may have been a sort of ruthlessness in the undercurrent of higher level of society of that time; sinning was not forgiven in God's common people. To sin meant to hurt someone else; but often the social structure dictated that nobles were intrinsically full of grace and forgiveness.

> The law and the church were so sure of themselves and so fixed on the position that all behavior is conscious and voluntary (unless accidental), that when scientists began to assert themselves about involuntary and unconsciously motivated behavior, some of them simply carried their thesis too far. Their absolutism is just as offensive and misleading as that of their opponents...all evildoing in which we become involved to any degree tends to evoke guilt feelings and depression...The wages of some sins are death, without doubt; and the wages of lesser sins, while less than death, are substantial, including reparation, restitution and atonement...Guilt feelings give rise to a need for self-justification. It is aggressive, it is pleasure giving, it is attention getting, it is problem-solving, it is self-injuring and destroying [emphasis added] (Thayer, 1952, p. 48–49).

The need for expression in many individuals may have been sublimated into hard work, which stifled their guilt. The nobles or clerical hierarchy controlled and/or funneled into daily artifacts the emotions of the peasants' life. Expression became slowly stimulated, however, by the appearance of tradesman, availability of other cultural artifacts, and the inspiration of imagination through reading stories of the travel and travails of such renown as Aladdin, Marco Polo or the King Arthur's Knights. Likewise, a revitalization of the "Greek way" helped appeal to the Renaissance's spirit and formed an order while still rewarding creative expression, if not for Self, then for the glorification of God. "The Greek notion that man could give form and order to the world appealed to the Renaissance creative spirit. The painter, sculptor and architect were concerned with natural form; the musician with the expression of human emotions; and the writer with actual rather than ideal behavior" (ibid, 1952).

The Middle Ages were aptly named in that the problems of that period represented transition between focus on God and Nature, during the Dark Ages, to the focus on Man and Art and Science of the Renaissance and Reformation. "Faith turned to rationalism, control of will became use of intellect, mysteries of life to truth through ideas. There was an increase in tolerance, growing self-confidence, and self-assertion. The character of the age, and the apparent intentionality, showed that the changes in personal and social goals created space for deeper thought and imagination" (Ralph, 1973, p.14).

Although it was a time of great creativity and social change, the most important actual shift was in the type of ideals and moral values that came out of the prior greed of some nobles and the poor treatment of the peasants. Spirituality as a guiding principle now became available to those beyond the walls of the monasteries. Relativism grew, in literature, in the view of other cultures, and from an increase in travels.[43] "The humanists did not view their intellectual problem as a conflict between reason and faith, between the secular wisdom of the pagans and the spiritual wisdom of Christians revelation. They were more interested in using Man's highest potentialities; he was allowed to manifest a metaphorical justification of his own self" (ibid, 1973, p. 126).

Scientific development gave man a place to find God tangibly (i.e., Koestler's theory of "bisociation" as a model of CONNECTIONS: science/chemistry, past/present, male/female, etc.). Many in our time manifest a belief in a tangible God through the simple affirmations of faith most noted through practicing the 12-steps of AA, where they develop their own personal view of a Higher Power. Luther's religion, for instance, was based on the inner experience of the communion of the soul with God. This concept has been combined in a new age of experience with a greater dualistic recognition of freedom of conscience needing to be balanced with a renewed Augustinian doctrine of predestination. One of the unique aspects of the Renaissance was the combinations of self-expression, religiosity, and social responsibility in a way that the worlds of art/literature/economics/politics were balanced.

This vacillation between a backward respect for the Greek view of philosophy and science was therefore blended with new discoveries and a forward-looking view which the giants of the Renaissance used to propel the structure of the 17th century into the more flexible view of Enlightenment period of the 18th and 19th

---

[43] "The Renaissance became interested in the world per se, in nature, in the discovery of man's environment. And a newly ordered concept of the earth slowly emerged. Ironically, even as man displaced himself from the center of the universe, his mastery of that universe became strengthened…If we live today in a world forgotten by God where our choice seems to be between the absurd and a return to faith, between earthly as opposed to divine goals, perhaps we have here, too, to thank the Renaissance.

What this period in history asked, we are still asking, but perhaps our answers will only come with a complete understanding of that time when man first turned to the here and now for his place in the universe—the Renaissance (Van Doren, 1991, pp. 29–30).

centuries. Although the art, music, and literature of this period is magnificent, perhaps only in Philosophy did some continuity of study help continue the belief in the usefulness of the classical method. This method would carry Humanism into the 20th century, seen most recently in the Third Force movement of the 1960s study of psychology.

Colonialism: Yearning and Freedom from Other/Self

The voyages of exploration and European expansion, and the idea of colonization, caused political and economic changes for both entities, colony and colonizer alike. Although much of the effort to explore and colonize was driven by a desire for power and financial rewards, there was always the influence of the church, Catholic or Protestant alike, lying somewhere in the background. Just as Europe had experienced its own cultural patterns, now these individuals and their "imperialism" had created a vast effort to impose these patterns on the whole globe.

Much of what is written about the East India Company (established December 31, 1600), for instance, is how it created outposts in British Malaya, Burma, Ceylon, Hong Kong and Singapore. As much economic and social growth as this action created, the need for commodities also contributed to an increase in piracy. Although privateers also already existed in the 17th century, they previously operated their ships most frequently in the Caribbean.

There was a downside to these historical events involving the company—monasteries were destroyed in Tibet and the Opium Wars promoted opium struggling; the cultural involvement because of trade also led to the destruction of regional patterns of the indigenous peoples. Over time, the company began to experience less and less popularity and its nefarious reputation influenced negative feelings toward England and Europeans overall. Its position had become particularly tenuous during the time when Oliver Cromwell took over "ruling" England from Charles I in the 1650s, which coincided with the renewal of the company's second charter. Following a successful realignment of both government influences and managerial methods, the ultimate outcome and establishment of what we would now call a "monopoly" on trading in the East was to be a future business model for centuries.

New cultural awareness of other lands also added to the depth and breadth of British society, culture, comforts, and education. Because the desire for goods continued, 15% of British imports were from India by 1720, almost all passing through the company. Thirty years later, the Seven Years' War, (1756–1763), created a need which boosted the company's income by sustaining the troops and the economy during the war(s). England began to see itself as having created the one world it sought. During this period, there was an intensification of the competition between England and France as well; competition created a fear of change, regulations, and the authority of power. In my mind, it was a type of dysfunctional family trying to compete with the outside world but also to maintain the level of bickering within its own boundaries.

Although there was a type of "calm after the storm" because of the Renaissance and Reformation, everyone seemed on guard against too much change during the 18th century. Adam Smith (1723–1790) was a Scottish, Oxford-educated, writer who combined the rational and empirical into one scientific method; first, he introduced the historical method into economic discussion, and secondly, in his economics, he gave a central place to the value of profit and to the division of labor. He wrote of the need for mercantilism (economic liberalism) and strong free enterprise; social consciousness took the form of social contracts, where harmony of self-interest could provide a "peaceful contest within a peaceful context." Everywhere, the concept of "free" abounded: free trade, free enterprise, free navigation, and freedom to practice one's religion. The philosophy of the day was "humanitarian reform and democratic rights" (ibid, 1989).

In addition, Benjamin Franklin and Adam Smith both believed that punishment should fit the crime and that government, to be a just ruler, had to provide the same penalty for all social classes. It is said that Franklin, who was a frequent visitor of the French court prior to both American and French revolutions, attempted to reconcile his well-known love of the common man and the protection of rights with his own amorality. Although some modern 20th century writers (D.H. Lawrence, for one) felt that Franklin discovered the rules which lead to success and turned them into a religion, Bronowski and Mazlish (1960) feel this belief is false. There are some implications, however, regarding Franklin's ongoing phrases for which he is so famous, such as "well done is better than well said," found in his *Poor Richard's Almanack.* He also came up with the term "self-evident" in the Declaration of Independence.

Obviously, some of these issues served as the foundation of the French Revolution (1789–1799), where the American model of self-interest and freedom turned into reasons for a "revolution", a much more ideological and glorified concept, where a new distribution of wealth and thus power was called for. Napoleon himself was a very philosophical man, who despite his lust for power and success, was "filled with the spirit of endless striving toward an unreachable goal" (ibid, 1960, p. 413). The French Enlightenment presented new values and progress in the arts and sciences. Voltaire (1694–1778) believed that "progress was counteracting 'ignorance, superstition, fanaticism, oppression and barbarism" (Hayman, 1999, p. 308).

It was Voltaire who brought these ideas into public opinion, where he depended upon common sense. Rousseau, on the other hand, "blamed civilization and its institutions for destroying the simplicity and spontaneity that were natural to man, corrupting the life of natural justice" (ibid, 1999). Rousseau expanded this idea that virtue and nobility could result in one's happiness through a return to nature and the heart. This search for happiness also had a utilitarian purpose; it showed up in transformation of vocabulary, personal usefulness, medical advances and a "reliance on the heart" [Rousseau]. Anti-materialism formed a basis of a kind of "counter-culture" of that time.

During 1700s, these theories had parents bringing up their own children and looking for useful, reasonable, and other-directed lives. Robert Owen (1771–1858) was not only a great believer in rights and individualism, but he was one of the first philosophers of this modern age to write of the rights of the child as well.[44]

---

[44] Owen ultimately began a commune in Indiana (New Harmony) and initiated the Cooperative Movement. "Human character is formed in early childhood and is formed

This period of 18th century colonial friction, and then 19th century revolution in France (which to a lesser degree caused the Napoleonic Wars with Prussia and Russia), led to the idea of overthrowing rulers which had never happened before. Weber (1989) proposes that three ideas steered this period: 1) men could strive for perfection independent of another's control, thus 2) sovereignty should be a sovereignty "of the people", and 3) all men were equal. These ideas had obviously become slogans to CONNECT revolutions for all time to come.

Even Karl Marx (CONNECTED to the Russian Revolution and Communism) and Freud (advent of modern psychology) were influenced by Rousseau's ideas. Marx, for instance, did more than propose the abolition of the private party and property. He passed on the influences gleaned from Nietzsche to Freud (Boorstin, 1985). "The proletarians have nothing to lose but their chains" (Marx, *Communist Manifesto*, 1848, p. 33). Marx believed that the need for centralizing communication of needs can either lead to more enlightenment about how to make society work better and/or cause the middle class to become more conservative. He added: "Revolution is rupture with traditional ideas, with the result that the outcome is Truth" (op. cit., p. 91). Was Marx advocating some Messianic idea, or did he believe in a Utopian dream?

Regardless, he took the influences of the Romantic Age and tried to point out how the common man was being exploited and that these class distinctions led to class struggles. To quote Weber again, "reason can lead to intolerance," and "dogmatic rationalists went to war against [even] priests in the name of reason…Liberty and equality became victims of an evolution that was carried out in their name!" (Weber, 1989). Perhaps it is best to consider the historical conditions and pre-existing cultural struggles of any time of major change, even that, for instance, which we saw during the pandemic of 2020.

If the "common man" was looking for freedom and happiness, then why did absolute governments rise again, especially in France, where Louie XVI (executed 1793) had presided over Versailles with court rituals and discipline? It was as if "affairs of the heart" had abandoned "affairs of the head". So many changes in the hierarchy of culture, and a type of "aimless quiescence" that it caused, may have created a need for law and order, ultimately looking for a father image such as Napoleon, who is almost mythological and who could cement group process.

This outcome paralleled the famous argument between Hobbes and Locke which was discussed at length in Chapter Two on Philosophy. Hobbes, who believed in Charles I, stated that the monarchy was needed to control man's

---

entirely by environment…attach either praise or blame to what people do in life…In order to avoid their being criminals in later life, one must take hold of people in early childhood and see that they lead good lives. Thus, society has a responsibility—to itself and to the individual—to educate and to provide decent living conditions for all. The lessons Owen gave as to the formation of man's character made it 'evident to the understanding that by far the greater part of the misery with which man is encircled may be easily dissipated and removed,' and that with mathematical precision he may be surrounded with those circumstances which must gradually increase his happiness" (Boorstin, 1985, p. 470).

outlandish nature, whereas Locke believed that liberty led to anarchy but that that was a positive prerequisite determining his true nature, given that he was born *a priori*, a blank slate. Individuals had a right to rebel. There should been no infringement on liberties, and tyrants should be removed (Weber, 1989). This philosophical viewpoint, held by 18th and 19th century philosophers such as Newton, Hume, Voltaire, and eventually Emerson, became the rationalists and free thinkers of the Age of Enlightenment (although the peasants throughout Europe fared no better for centuries to come).

The influence of these writers was so great that their writings changed the point of view of Princes, Kings, and Parliament (Voltaire: Frederick the Great/Prussia; Deudereaux: Katherine the Great/Russia). Because Germany had fewer ports and had to depend on the great Rhine River for trade and transportation, along with Russia, it often fell behind England and France in culture and building, although they copied their churches, palaces, and theaters.

One hundred years or more before mad King George III took on two failed wars on the American soil, with the death of Elizabeth I in England, power transferred through James VI of Scotland/to become James I of England to Charles I, who then had trouble with Parliament over taxation that created a seven-year civil war (see more if interested re: Cromwell). The Stuart line was restored under Charles II and William II of Orange was victorious in the Glorious Revolution of 1688.

Chapter Seven
Growth of American Idealism

Birth of a Revolutionary Spirit

"Rugged individualism" had been a standard of the nobleman and knight throughout recorded history, and especially in the lore about such figures as Robin Locksley, King Arthur's Knights, some of the conqueror kings, Joan of Arc, Columbus and the other explorers, and the rebellious standard bearers such as Martin Luther, Copernicus, Galileo, John Locke, and John Calvin; all were viewed as "Outliers" of their time. Writing about the new American spirit, Emerson said impulsivity, as part of pre-American personality, was a reward in itself (Emerson, 2010).

When the first brave souls arrived at Jamestown and Plymouth Rock, when Daniel Boone took a group of men descended from Welsh Quakers who traveled to America with William Penn (settling in Pennsylvania, and then going south to Kentucky), when the Revolutionary War was fought by men who after all were settlers and could have been hung for treason even if not killed in the War, all these stories demonstrate a remarkable urge/yearning for freedom from another's control, and for the rights of the individual.

Although political dependence on Britain was highlighted for the 50 years of the 1700s preceding the Revolutionary War, a goal of political independence started almost immediately after the founding father arrived in America; much of their struggle was legalistic. There was the trouble of "ruling an empire" that was too far away with which King George III concerned himself; it was easier to turn decisions over to the Commanders of the British Army in residence. However, by the time Britain tried to get control back, it was too late. The colonists' demands for equal rights included how they were to be treated—as humans, not just as Englishmen.

It is a paradox that these colonists were so worried about their own rights, considering how they had treated the Native Peoples they found inhabiting Northern America a brief period before, a fact which often went unnoticed. There were no less than 55 independent tribes at the time, and as many as 12 to 15 more if Canada and Alaska were included in the count. The fact that there was little unity among the tribes contributed to the ease with which the early settlers gained control over the land they crossed. "Conquistadors" were greedy and usually cruel, and up to 90% of tribes succumbed in very short periods of time. This self-centered point of view shows the parallel selfishness with all individualism and subsequent isolationism, as we shall see repeatedly, CONNECTING what eventually became policy in the United States.

Just as the early settlers (as immigrants) depended upon farming and domestication of animals, it is believed that the earliest Americans came as "immigrants" across the Bering Strait or other land masses from Siberia. It is also possible that long boats took the waterways down to Central America 9000 years earlier, and there was some migration northward from there. These earlier Americans learned over time to cultivate mostly beans and corn, and they made pottery to store it in. They adapted culturally, and eventually they found that they were happier and safer in CONNECTED, town-oriented, social groups such as the Anasazi (Pueblo) peoples in Chaco Canyon and Mesa Verde in New Mexico.

On the contrary, the "mound people" lived as the Mississippian peoples near St. Louis, Missouri. Both tribes were probably still living like Stone Age groups when the Spaniards showed up in the 16th century. It is estimated that in 1520 there were 25 million indigenous people, but by the early 17th century there were only 1.3 million indigenous individuals in North America due to death from uprisings and, more specifically, diseases introduced by the European settlers from which the indigenous people had no immunity. As "agents of God's purpose", men like Columbus and De Soto, with their "crusading mentality", won out (Miller, 2000).

After the defeat of the Spanish Armada in 1588, the seas were clearer for exploration. Given the problems Jamestown experienced, however, a second colonial group, the Pilgrims, decided to land farther north in New England. These immigrants were Separatists, both in religion and ideology. They founded their new culture in a much more rigid and organized form, a Commonwealth, than Jamestown had and they survived much better.

In Jamestown, all but 38 had died 9 months after arrival (this is the famous story of John Smith and how Pocahontas helped feed the settlers). Corn kept them alive, along with the Mattaponi tribe's attempt at peace (ibid, 2000). By 1620, the English monarchy
 had taken control of running the colony of Virginia, specifically because of the income to be had from the tobacco product. This colony was the first to have land grants, a House of Burgesses, and the first to import slaves, due to an abundance of land but a shortage of free laborers. Plantation owners grabbed the best land and used either slaves or indentured servants, who suddenly found themselves CONNECTED in more than one way.

We tend to create myths about the early settlement of America, but of course these early times were very "European" in culture, style, and social behaviors. Religious, legal, ethical and literary influences tended to be socially influenced by the affluent; immigrants in the lower classes or even indentured servants were not considered "citizens" as yet but did have an influence in their own way as well. Much of the early CONNECTIVITY was found through their work. The difference was that once freed from their servitude, there were "too many free wild men on the loose" (ibid, 2000). These now "free" men and their families wanted land for themselves, and their stories of survival represent the "rugged individualists" upon which the country would be founded.

Meanwhile the slave trade just kept on growing. In 1650, there were only 400 blacks in Virginia. By 1675, the use of slaves and indentured servants was strongly supported as a way of life up and down the Eastern seaboard. Britain profited from the sale of iron, rum, and other goods to the rulers of West African nations; these sales allowed the sale of "slaves" captured by the African rulers themselves; this "triangle" of trade then moved to the West Indies and Florida, where ships brought back molasses to New England to be made into more rum. Therefore, a process of trade imbalance was rectified and navigation, shipbuilding, and creation of firearms all improved and created a profitable commerce. By 1700, there was a well-developed slave system, and spread-out plantations depended on these unfree laborers. It was not until 1808 that Congress began to look at an Abolitionist bill. The issue of slavery will be covered in more detail below during a discussion of the Civil War.

Contrary to the experience in Virginia, by 1630 Winthrop had created a well-prepared self-governing colony with the Puritans in Massachusetts Bay. Its communal structure generally came down from John Calvin's belief in Self-determinism. Calvin added his own special form of control and rededication to the Humanism movement. "Puritans had a special devotion to the truth as they saw it for themselves, and a grave indifference to the authority of the past, both of which are still summarized in the word 'nonconformist'" (Bronowski and Mazlish, 1960, p. 182). They were also the model of Christian charity, and thus Boston had focal units of government; the "commonwealth" concept grew out of CONNECTED common ideals and economic forces. Towns were tightly knit, and "church and state acted together with orthodoxy, high literacy, and high moral standards" (op cit., 2000). Hard work and self-denial were the foundation of the society.

It took several years, with the success of the tobacco crop and influx of the first slaves, until Jamestown approached Plymouth's level in survival or success. I am making an issue of citing Miller's hosted show, *A Biography of America*, because I think the point is well-taken; not only did the difference between the colonial histories of Boston and Virginia lead to a civil war in the United States two hundred years later, I believe that the cultural differences in the ways that the towns were laid out and how the merchants structured their supply systems continue to this day and explain the DISCONNECTED political system of North versus South, now almost four hundred years later.

Much of the settlement of America resulted from the search for religious tolerance. As we have also seen previously in this review of history, the pursuit of individual rights soon translated into a need for group cohesion as well to CONNECT. We can see example after example of this throughout the history of the colonization, revolution, expansion west, 'gold fever,' and railroads CONNECTING this country, which ultimately facilitated the Industrial Revolution.

This period in history was the beginning of a new hierarchal set of "American" rules for the achievement of power and accumulation of wealth. Because classism continued differently than the nobility of England, we see the haves being threatened by Outliers who didn't CONNECT in the same way. They were the rugged individualists who wanted to strike out on their own—Rebels were compared to Conservatives. Ultimately, once the societal boundaries of everyday life were established, hereditary inheritance and the hierarchy of privilege recreated some of the same inequality and tensions that had existed before the Revolutionists fought so hard for their "freedom". There was little to no social mobility until the Industrial Revolution.

Into this confusion and attempts to dominate through dysfunctional power shifts came the Transcendentalists and their ideas of scholarship and romanticism; they expanded on the ideas of "freedom of spirit and discovery" as a definition of one's rights within a democracy. As Michael Polanyi said, "Our believing is conditioned at its source by our belonging…Human freedom includes the freedom to believe." Emerson's ideas of a stoic English character (*Self-Reliance,* 1841, *English Traits*, 1853) versus American use of wit may seem at times contradictory. In brief, Emerson felt that the internalizing personality of the English "temperament" was more ideational, reflective, and responsive to internal cues than external ones.

In contrast, Americans, who had forged ahead in a New World, tended to respond with more externalizing behaviors and were extremely sensitive to input from outside cues because of natural instincts for inventiveness, success, and adventure. I like to say that in England it was "She who must be obeyed," with English men being polite and orderly within their family structure (Mortimer's *Rumpole of the Old Bailey*), whereas Americans seemed to shift toward "He who must be obeyed," putting work and productivity first. Humanism encourages us to think about ourselves which, after all, is not always an easy task.[45]

After writing in the last chapter about how Luther's influence on European Reformation culminated in its influences on Henry VIII's reform of England, as well as its influence on the new American colonists, in this chapter we now move on to review culturally specific Anglo-American issues. It is not that such historical concepts as the development of philosophy, economics or science are not globally generalizable to the rest of Europe or even Africa and Asia, but it is important at this point to build a case for the American "narcissistic" or as Emerson saw it, the "self-reliant" personality, where "Outliers" become Outliers because the norm is revered and glorified. Or to see it as a more binary function of internalizer versus externalizer (explained above); there is a consistent teeter-totter between each because of need for control through dominance or control through weakness.

Pre-Revolutionary Influences

William Penn was given land because Charles II owed his father money, but it was freedom to practice the Quaker faith Penn was seeking. Men and women were to be treated equally; the Quakers were looking for a peaceful place to experience the "inward light" and to practice pacificism. Not only did they believe in religious tolerance and political freedom, but in Pennsylvania the rights of all citizens and persecuted sects, including Indians, were protected. Unfortunately, after Penn's death in 1718, this structure fell apart and citizens began to grab Indian lands. Inequality increased due to political agitation, and there was even a return to England of large numbers of Quaker citizens.

---

[45] Montaigne was aware of how difficult it is. "To some extent, everyone refuses to know himself, which means admitting to himself that he is no more or no better than he really is. All of us sometimes, and most of us always, are steeped in a brew of illusions…To compose our character is our duty, not to compose books, and to win, not battles and provinces, but order and tranquility in our conduct. Our great and glorious masterpiece is to live appropriately" (Montaigne quoted by Van Doren, 1991, p. 144–145).

Likewise, the early piety of the Puritans turned into attacks upon the "ungodly" because of feelings of religious superiority (which they previously had fled from). All these problems with the second-generation colonists could probably have been predicted, if so much time was not being taken up with survival and keeping an eye on England's control over them. Some people do not know that in the late 1600s there was a short-lived "Dominion of New England", which was King James II's unsuccessful attempt to reverse decades of lax oversight (Hudgins, 2020). Massachusetts, Rhode Island and Providence Plantations, Connecticut, and the Province of New Hampshire and Plymouth were joined by New Jersey and New York after England secured them from the Dutch in 1688.

There were also non-Puritans living in the region, who were often prosperous, although they could not vote, hold office, or worship freely. The desire for change was growing and some believed that a "Dominion" could provide protections and freedoms not previously existing. Town meetings and the exercise of both executive and legislative powers provided balance. However, in December 1686, a new governor of the Dominion, Edmund Andros, arrived and began to bring the powers of the Dominion under his control (and England's), alone.

Limitations became even more strict after the "Glorious Revolution" of 1689, when James II abdicated in favor of William and Mary, who refused to return control to the members of the Dominion. Colonies were considered "royal", even though some of English control was lost during the distraction of the French and Indian War. When the crown and Parliament again tried to tighten control was when they lost America altogether.

Half of Americans had not even been born in England by 1700 (Miller, 2000) and cultural ambivalence grew. "Could America truly be great without England?" In 1700, there were 250,000 nonindigenous people in America; in 1775, there were 2,500,000 people. Most of the growth before 1700 had been because of the large families of the primarily English population, but after that time it was mostly because of immigration (and the large families) of the Germans, Scots, Dutch, some Irish (the potato famine had not happened yet), and of course Africans. These "immigrants" were mostly slaves or indentured servants, as mentioned above.

Of those who could read, people generally only had the *Bible* and Franklin's *Poor Richard's Almanac*, making Franklin easily the most famous man in American even before the Revolutionary War. What little middle class existed were the farmers. Regardless, it was an orderly society without even much of a government or police force. Tyranny would soon be experienced from [mad] King George in the form of taxes that no one wanted.

Much is known about the "shot heard round the world" as the tensions between the British government and colonists were at a fevered pitch. After a previous colonial legislature was dismissed by General Thomas Gage, bitter colonists began to stockpile weapons and provisions. Upon finding out about these arms and supplies, General Gage ordered them destroyed. On the night of April 18, 1775, more than 700 British soldiers marched from Boston to destroy what was stored in Concord. The leaders of the "Sons of Liberty", Samuel Adams and John Hancock, were also sought.

Two alarm riders, Paul Revere and William Dawes, sounded the alarm with a lantern in Boston's North Church, as Samuel Prescott traveled alone to Concord to notify others. I am proud to report that my genealogy includes several colonists who "answered the call" on that night and rode with the Sons of Liberty. The colonists were able to repel the onslaught in Lexington and later forced a retreat near the Old North Bridge in Concord. This retreat, however, culminated in the siege of Boston and the outbreak of war.

When Thomas Paine declared, "O! ye that love mankind! Ye that dare oppose not only the tyranny but the tyrant, stand forth!" he spoke for a nation growing into a democracy. "When people think of America's Founding Fathers, they usually recall George Washington, Thomas Jefferson, or Benjamin Franklin. These were all rich and powerful men. In contrast, Tom Paine was the founding father closest to the common people" (Johnson, 2002, p. 41).

Paine's pursuit was for moral and political happiness. He made the CONNECTIONS necessary, not only in our revolution, but by writing in defense of the French Revolution as well. Paine immortalized himself by claiming, "These are the times that try men's souls;" he put into one phrase the very symbol of all conflict, where the idea of freedom must overrule one's main fear of authority to gain a country's independence from sovereign power and destruction. Paine had wanted his countrymen to control their own affairs; this concept drove men to fight for thousands of years and would continue to drive men to embrace their destiny into our present century.

An American Conscience

Are Americans really more democratic, freer, wealthier and moral than other people? (ibid, 2002, p. 26). President Reagan certainly thought so in 1988 when he made the speech about the "shining city on the hill". Perhaps, in the beginning, when American ideals were still shiny and new, there was that possibility. The American Revolution certainly inspired the French Revolution through many acts and writings of the time. The way these CONNECTIONS changed the course of history is without argument. Even today, the United States inspires the beginnings of democracies, no matter how flawed (think Arab "Spring" that started in December 2010 and played out until May 2014).

Our own revolution lasted six years, if you start from the Boston Tea Party (1773) to April 30, 1779, the day George Washington became the first President of the "United" States at the Federal Hall, New York City. Before the Revolution, in 1763, the Peace of Paris had been signed, giving more land to King George III from the French holdings in America. Unfortunately, these lands were not as rewarding, financially, as King George had hoped. Within the next 13 short years until 1776, Indian uprisings tapped out his coffers (most of which was pay for his British army in America), necessitating tax increases imposed through a Stamp Act.

The lack of representation ("taxation without representation") angered so many that The Sons of Liberty was formed, an import boycott organized, and rebellion was coming to a head. The Boston Tea Party took place (on December 16, 1773), after King George had the nerve to levy a tax on imported tea through the East India Company, and, as they say, the rest is history.

Once Boston came under military rule, one-fifth of the colonies' citizens who had been loyalists (mostly Tories and Scots) found themselves in a difficult position. Many fled to Canada. A little-known fact is that as many as one-third of the citizens of the original 13 colonies stayed "neutral". Of note is that the First Continental Congress actually asked King George for mercy, but it was he, not them, that declared they were in a "state of rebellion" and washed his hands of it, so to speak, turning what he thought would be an easy transition over to his generals in residence. It should have been, and almost was. It was the Second Continental Congress that declared a state of "independence" and thus war. So why did the early Americans win? The militia was called up on their own turf and these patriots were fighting to save their own farms; they were fighting for survival, not just for "king and country" as were the British soldiers. They were truly driven to claim democracy.

The first "American" government was strong on states' rights, which resulted in a weak central government due to a lack of the necessary political CONNECTIONS for the tax collection necessary to help citizens and pay soldiers. The Continental Congress also owed bills to other governments, who had helped fund the American side of the war. The country had to find new economic markets, as its major trade had been with England; they had to start their own patent offices, and so forth. "We liked individual enterprise in this country, but we still needed government…We'll rule ourselves (Republic) and if it doesn't work then we can turn to a Caesar to return us to order (Federalism)" (Miller, 2000). If you look at this theory, it coincides so strongly with the 2016 election, I can hardly mention any of my own opinions here…

It wasn't until the Constitutional Convention, with Washington presiding under the Federalists, that the influences of Hamilton and Madison created a tighter central government. The Constitution became the strong guardian of our Federalist Republic. Much of the eventual Constitution was Federalist oriented, focusing on a balance of powers to appease the Congress in session; in response, it was the Anti-Federalists that pushed for the Bill of Rights to be added as an almost immediate amendment.

Ultimately, the dispute was between Jefferson and Adams versus Hamilton. Weber (1989) talks of this period as being of "men of principles versus men of property". For instance, Jefferson represented his "life, liberty and the pursuit of happiness" through his own belief in man's need for dignity and freedom to obtain self-knowledge and individualism. Jefferson, who had written the Bill of Rights in addition to the Declaration of Independence, continued to fight for rights, as opposed to Hamilton, who more strongly upheld a strict interpretation of the Constitution. In this manner, Jefferson followed the principles of Locke, fearing tyranny and corruption of power, whereas Hamilton feared the corruptions of human nature and thought government should "save man from himself," ala Hobbes (ibid, 1989).

In many ways, the Colonial Revolution became a World Revolution because of its effect not only on France but, ultimately, on aristocracies throughout the world. Nations and their people still strive for democracy to this day. But only the northern American states dismantled the use of slavery, a major obstacle to true democracy; the idea of equality and breaking away from the tyranny of King George apparently did not reach into the backyards of the Southern plantation owners of the time. The legend prevails that the "south" (parts of Maryland and Virginia) got to have the U.S. Capitol, Washington, D.C., because of negotiations over slavery. [Have you seen the show *Hamilton*?]. The Continental Congress, Hamilton in particular, was trying to appease the southern states, who feared a capital in New York or Philadelphia would be too vulnerable to northern abolitionists' viewpoints. The variance in opinion about slavery only grew after the Louisiana Purchase doubled the size of the country and brought about another focus on slavery when the new state of Missouri wanted to be a "slave state".

Growth of the American Territory

The 80 years of U.S. history following the Revolutionary War is often defined by the growth of settlement, innovation, and industry in this country. During this period, Jefferson called the United States the "Empire of Liberty" (Miller, 2000). For instance, even before the second war with England in 1812, we had doubled U.S. land mass with the Louisiana Purchase (1803), and Fulton had invented the steam engine (1807). As president himself, Jefferson was at the ready with Lewis and Clark to explore the newly acquired areas. Growth in Kentucky and Tennessee had already been tremendous. In Kentucky alone, the population grew from 10,000 in 1780 to 110,000 in 1790 and the population was "itching" to move West.

In *A Biography of America*, Miller discusses how much we forget that America at the time (pre-railroad or even steamboat) was really a country of bodies of water interrupted by land; this fact made travel and settling further West difficult, but the early settlers were not to be deterred. It was finally the canals that created progress in settlements, the first to be the Erie Canal, which would connect New York to the Great Lakes (and therefore Chicago), and ultimately by canals all the way down the Mississippi River to New Orleans. Fulton's steam engine and Whitney's cotton gin would bust open commerce all the way across the country from that time forward. Suddenly the prior view toward slavery, even in the South which had become somewhat more pro-Abolitionist, turned back to keeping slavery because of the need for labor to produce the abundance of cotton. Existing racism was not about to end any time soon.

The second war with England (1812) came from escalated tensions after Britain continued to seize U.S. ships and keep sailors captive, partly as a "side-war" from their initial hostilities against Napoleon Bonaparte. In some ways, we can be thankful for that initial fighting, because it was to finance his wars that Napoleon sold off the lands in the Louisiana Purchase in the first place. By 1812, the British troops left to fight in America were limited, but America only had 8000 troops at ready itself, most of whom were either very old (Revolutionary) or very young (new recruits).

After an embargo failed, President James Madison declared war. After many campaigns and even some victories at sea against the largest navy in the world (often using what were called "privateers"), victory finally came, even though the White House was partially destroyed and had to be rebuilt. [My six-times removed Uncle Jonathan Haraden was a privateer, to such great acclaim that he has had not one, but two, U.S. warships named after him!]

As usual, war is good economics due to the many financial CONNECTIONS that are made and maintained. Post-war growth in mills, factories and railroads increased the employment rate for immigrants, and even some women (mostly Irish) began to work outside the home (Weber, 1989). Although there was a rise in capitalism, and the United States became the leading industrial nation on earth at the time (passing England), much of life for the average person in poverty was one of misery, with many children having to work as well. Apparently, there had been a growth in production with a limited supply of workers. In 1801, there were 5 million people in the U.S.; in 1901 there were 77 million, with at least 30 nationalities (op cit., 2000). The United States had truly become a "melting pot".

How did the government deal with this growth? Adam Smith (1723–1790) and others wrote at the time about the effect of economics on "unrestrained competition;" *laisse faire* economics theory believed that what served self-interest would ultimately be best for the greater good, with good being "reasonable and intuitively right". However, it did not always trickle down economically to the poor masses. Jefferson did not want America to be like the terrible slums of Manchester, England, and tried to speak against developing the country too quickly. de Tocqueville (1840) called this process "industrial slavery".

By the end of the 19th century, there were some social reforms in place: pension allotments for old age, illness and even unemployment. There was a spirit of empathy and charity, (or guilt?) especially in larger cities. Temperance and Abolition opinions grew out of a great re-awakening of Christianity at the time as well. A meeting at Seneca Falls in 1848 CONNECTED women to continue a movement for their social and civil rights. *The Declaration of Sentiments* was written and signed by 68 women and 32 men at what is viewed as the first woman's convention.

The changed view about had suffrage started in the 1820s when all men finally got to vote (well white men that is) regardless of social standing or financial situation. People began to feel they could fight back when they felt the need. Social instigation created events that would start a larger process in CONNECTED American thinking about revolt for freedom from slavery (like the book *Uncle Tom's Cabin* in 1851 and John Brown's raid on Harper's Ferry [1859] in protest of the Fugitive Slave Act). Many women joined this fight for freedom of rights, realizing they had a lot in common with the slaves.

de Tocqueville (1840) wrote about his experiences visiting America, coining the phrase "American's Individualism." His experiences impressed upon him how America's reformism (for instance of the penal system) and the development of its own class values had contributed to a middle class. His concern, however, was whether this social and moral order was also contributing to a sense of cultural isolationism (Miller, 2000). It was true that individual free will and free moral agency grew out of an objection to the prior stringency of Calvinistic doctrine of predestination. Emerson's writings entered this philosophical venue during the 1840s and there was a dovetailing of the abolitionists feelings with Emerson's concepts of "the triumph of principles and the Self" (ibid, 2000).

Slavery Fuels Dissent

Although it would be impossible within the limited space of this chapter to cover the events of the civil war, of note is the DISCONNECTION which led to it; the slavery issue was not the only "growing pains" experienced in the United States. Immigration had increased the country's population to one million by the 1850s, and then another six-fold during the 1860s due to the immigration of Irish after the potato plight in Ireland. Between 1800 and 1820 over one-fourth of the population had moved west of the Mississippi River, easing some of the urban crowding. In 1850, the United States had just gained Texas, California, Washington, Nevada, Utah, and most of New Mexico and Colorado as states (the rest to come after the war with Mexico that year).

The major question on the minds of citizens and representatives alike was: What should the role of government in these new states be? Two main political parties emerged. Andrew Jackson's Democrats consisted of members mostly outside of the original thirteen states, who believed in the need for territorial expansion ala Jefferson and Madison's Manifest Destiny. The Whigs focused mostly on industrial development and the use of Federal Authority, and were represented by the ideas of Clay, Webster, and even Lincoln in the beginning of his career. Their position resulted in the relocation of most of the Indian tribes east of the Mississippi River (see the Trail of Tears History).

The idea of "Manifest Destiny", whereby it was inevitable that settlers should move West or in whatever direction necessary to complete occupation of the North American continent, complicated the slavery question, as the need for "menial" workers continued. Of this new population in the West, for instance, 1.5% were black slaves. As I write this, I think of how this country continues to "need" menial workers in some areas, and always will; these necessary jobs are often taken up by immigrant workers. How can I justify any type of behavior but that which is honorable and spiritually fit to accomplish those needs? Need and respect can fit together and in many other cultures than the United States they do.

The status of slavery was such a major point of contention, specifically in Missouri and some of the other new states, that it was addressed through the Missouri Compromise of 1820 and Fugitive Slave Act later that year. However, rather than resolve the slavery issue, these laws only facilitated bounty hunters coming into northern states to grab free Negroes who were not even escapees or pursued by any owner in the South.

Some individuals, including President Lincoln himself, supported an idea to return the slaves to Africa by creating a new colony specifically for them, which was named Liberia, and which still exists to this day. Newspaper editor Lloyd Garrison, of *The Liberator*, wrote extensively that slaveholding was indeed a sin, (which increased both the cause of Abolitionism and his readership). These actions only instigated the break off of the Southern states from the "Union".

Another factor that led to the civil war was the difference between the attitude and cultures of the Northern and Southern states. The North was industrial, mechanically prepared, and had 12 of the 20 largest cities in the country at the time. Therefore, its citizens wanted tariffs, improved transportation, and didn't mind immigration or the attitude of abolitionists.

The South may have had a cause but had fewer people (33% of the total U.S. population), and about a third of these were slaves. From another point of view, 11 million people lived in the South by then, and 4 million of them were slaves, but only one-third of the white men owned all these slaves, and most had fewer than 50 slaves at any one time. Thus, only a very few men, with very large plantations, owned most of the slaves; they eventually had the power to start the war and to create a new Southern government.

New Orleans was the only Southern city with over 100,000 people, whereas New York had over 700,000 at the time. The South, as an agrarian society founded on cash crops for sale and export, did not want tariffs. There was a very small middle class, but a large elitist culture that owned the plantations which had slaves or poor sharecroppers working under them. Cotton was half of the total of all U.S. exports at the time, and worth fighting for.

"Why didn't the Southern slave owners see the humanity of the slaves they owned?" they were asked by the North. They answered back that not only did the North mistreat their own "wage" laborers just as much, but that capitalists were "moral cannibals" (ibid, 2000). In addition, the South felt controlled by the government in Washington, D.C., which was geographically "Southern" but very "Northern" in culture. Some Southern congressmen tried to present bills to reflect their views but were voted down in the House of Representatives; the Republican party broke off from the pre-Whigs to underscore its stance against slavery. In February 1861, the South wrote a new constitution which protected slavery and avowed that states should have sovereignty.

CONNECTEDNESS was unraveling (much as it did after the divide of the 2016 election). It appeared to be Northern "guilt" versus Southern "shame", and no one was about to give in. Each side felt some kind of "unity of spirit" for only their own point of view. But was it enough to prepare them for what was about to come? The Nat Turner uprising (1831), in which slave owners and even their families were killed, made everyone nervous in the South. By the 1850s, there was also bloodshed in Kansas. By the time Lincoln was sworn in, in March 1861, seven states had already seceded, but Lincoln did not start the war. He tried to buy time in any way he could, even though Southerners were taking over government buildings. After the skirmish at Fort Sumter (April 1861), which was under siege and surrounded, Lincoln called in some militia; this action only angered the South more. Lincoln responded: "A nation cannot exist divided against itself." With two weeks, four more states had seceded, making Washington, D.C. itself very vulnerable.

The Civil War

Considering these background influences allows many causative pieces of a puzzle to fit together. In the beginning, circumstantially, the South was more motivated to win the war, but its weak central government was a real detriment to mounting a long-term successful campaign (Anderson, 2004). The North had more resources, twice as many people, five times as many factories, and 1½ times more gold! Many families had brothers or other family members fighting on opposite sides of the war, and even Mrs. Lincoln openly rooted for the South because that was where four of her brothers lived and fought. Robert E. Lee himself started out as a Union general until Virginia seceded.

The civil war created total devastation, killing 620,000 people. Over 1.5 million casualties occurred if the wounded and non-combatants are included in the count. Only 640,000 people had died in all the other U.S. wars together up until that time. What kept the war going seemed to be the perpetuation of action that, once started, was focused only on the outcome.

I've been reading a book about the Viet Nam War these last few weeks and the parallel is undeniable: A man is killed; they send in a rescue helicopter, it crashes, six more men are wounded or killed; they send in another helicopter, and perhaps that one crashes as well. At some point, they get out as many dead bodies and wounded as possible (for their loved ones) and consider it a job well done. Literally, congratulate themselves and have a beer. Or so the book said. And sometimes they did not even recover the original body they went in for. It seems to be important that they tried, and the success was in the trying.

As I was reading, I thought of how much of this strategy could describe the Civil War. They had strategies: to blockade New Orleans, Richmond, or Washington; to capture or kill the "enemy;" and ultimately to gain more territory and in the Union's case, to get the enemy to surrender to their will, an acceptance of the Emancipation Proclamation and a change in the Southern way of life (however briefly). Which is exactly what ultimately happened.

Each war has its own new military technology; in the Civil War it was gunboats, more modern cannons, and individual rifled muskets with bullets that would spin and travel much farther, up to 400 yards (Miller, 2000). [Once, while visiting Fredericksburg, Virginia, the guide showed us how "effective" these new guns were: "A man stood here, behind these battlements, and killed men all the way over there," he bragged, a tree about 300 yards away]. Disease was a great additional killer because many of the men, Southerners in particular, had been isolated on farms before enlisting, with no medication or exposure/inoculation. They just arrived with their guns, and some with their horse and/or slave.

Although there was fighting throughout the South, most of it was concentrated in Virginia, around Richmond, and near Vicksburg, and in New Orleans along the Mississippi River. Initially, Union General George McClellan wanted to protect the Southern way of life, the plantations, and slaves, and he created a strategy to try to keep the war short. He felt the Union soldiers could win quickly and the South might still maintain its dignity. After several Union losses under his command, however, he was relieved of duty, and U.S. Grant took his place. The triangulated history of Grant's winning the battle of Vicksburg, the horrible losses at the battle of Gettysburg and Chancellorsville, and Lincoln signing the Emancipation Proclamation was set in action.

After the Emancipation Proclamation went into effect (January 1, 1863), the focus of the war shifted even more to the racial issue so that the North felt it was fighting to "free people, not just to defend the Union." This period is when the destruction of the property of the Southern towns really began, the burning of plantations and acts of racial violence by both whites and blacks. Eventually, as elegant as the Emancipation Proclamation was meant to be, it really did not create any useful action.

Nothing changed in the North, nothing changed in the border states, and as new states were declared, like California, each took its own position on whether the Negro was to be free or not and whether they had the rights that had been fought for. Both the North and South wanted new states included during the war. GOLD! had been discovered in Colorado and California just days before Mexico finally ceded the land to the United States in the Treaty of Guadalupe Hidalgo. The population also suddenly grew from 17.1 million to 23.2 million, not counting all the immigrants, mostly from Mexico and Asia, who came to work alongside the miners and new homesteaders.

Post-War Identity Issues

After the Civil War, the compromise, CONNECTION, and unity within the country, for which Lincoln had yearned, was undone by the administration of Andrew Johnson (1865–1869). Johnson was a white supremacist. Many of Johnson's presidential choices led to his impeachment, which was the first for any standing American President. After the Civil War, the (Northern) Congress asserted that Southern state readmission depended on acceptance of the 13th, 14th, and 15th amendments. Johnson himself fought this ruling and ultimately was impeached for his remarks and behaviors. Republicans controlled the Congress at the time, their wish for revenge and justice was sometimes also led by the abolitionists.

Until things cooled off in the South, a military occupation continued. The conflict of conscience about slavery had led to the Civil War, and then created post-war reconstruction attitudes. Although post-war growth provided an opportunity for individual successes and a boom economy for some states, the capitalism that developed also created further discrepancies between social classes. By 1877, the "reunited" government had all but abandoned its black citizens again. National focus was on the economy and post-war productivity.

Not to say that the spirit of dissent did not continue. A national railroad strike in 1877 severely impacted the economy after previous slowdowns. The "panic" of 1873 forced many companies to cut wages; racism was again woven into national/economic issues. Some white families protected blacks, at least as they still needed the labor to work for them as "sharecroppers", but these same men, in the light of the day, were the "scalawags" and carpetbaggers who disenfranchised the blacks. Thus, it was almost a period of "second slavery" (ibid, 2000).

After Andrew Johnson was impeached, his successor Ulysses S. Grant tried to gain some type of control over wrongdoings in the South, but much of Grant's focus was taken up with catering to the powerful Northern businessmen. "White supremacy" gained a foothold in the South for another century and a half, at least. The KKK was born. Racism continued as a national, not just a regional, issue.

In the South blacks were now "free" to move. "The Great Migration" to the cities of the time took place, (Chicago, Detroit, New York and Washington, D.C.), whereas some of the poorer Southerners joined Northerners in the land rush to Oklahoma (Homesteads), Nebraska (Beef), Ohio (Land), Colorado (Silver), and California (Gold).

Are there any social or political CONNECTIONS to gain from studying the horror that was the Civil War? Families fought hard to stay together, and the ideal of individual freedom resurfaced, symbolized in "40 acres and a mule", as well as in workers gaining the vote. Land was what the United States, united again, had the most of to give to its poor and war-ravaged citizens. By 1869, the movement West was aided by the growth of the railroad and availability of lines all the way to California.

Things were tough for these transplanted farmers, with the Homestead Act and the Farmer's Alliance attempting to aid those on the move (St. Louis, 1892). For the urban worker, there was some improvement in working conditions and higher incomes, at least in the North. It took six weeks or more to get to California on the Oregon Trail. Along the way, "boom" towns sprung up that are now well known to us, settled by pioneers and immigrant railroad workers alike. Unfortunately, any Indian tribes that got in the way suffered. Most people have heard of Little Big Horn (1876), battles with Geronimo (1886), and Wounded Knee (1890). Finally, the Dawes Act (1887) officially authorized the U.S. to "break up tribal lands" (ibid, 2000).

Societal Upheaval Between Wars

Between the 1880s and 1914, when World War I started, the "common man" gained some advancements in quality of life and some even achieved what we now call a "middle class" status. Scientific ideas of the 19th century, such as Darwin and his ideas of evolution, also influenced a view of social and economic shifts in society, its own "survival of the fittest". This viewpoint not only appealed to agnostic viewpoints, but it also negatively affected ideas and behaviors toward the "unfit". DISCONNECTION became more prominent, in both families with mental health issues, and in corporate worlds.

Although places like the meat packing plants in Chicago (Armor, Swift) used the latest methods in automation to supply the demand for fresh meat, (production and distribution methods became CONNECTED), treatment of the workers was often inhumane, even when it was the humans that were the CONNECTING parts of the system that made it all work. Survivors were neither treated well nor given that credit for quite some time. Titans of industry (Carnegie, DuPont, Ford, and Rockefeller) all used the rallying call "No waste".

Efficiency might have been at an all-time high, but "workers were like industrial slaves" (ibid, 2000). Those who developed mental health issues due to inhuman working conditions were also not treated well. Asylums were available, but treatment was rare except for alcoholism, which was rampant.

Weber (1989) gives his own impressions on societal influence, and on what improvements were gained, a list which could be used as a measure for any period of societal upheaval:

1. Literacy and education, even an increase in college and upper-class education.
2. National pride and a common identity.
3. Increase in people with the vote and understanding of representation.

4. Industrial Revolution changes transportation, communication, and agriculture [People could get goods to market, fill out forms, read papers, keep accounts, and send children to school. All were forms of increasing CONNECTIONS].
5. Increase in patriotism and willingness to go to war.
6. Organization, self-help, and unionization.
7. Capitalization, supply and demand, more consumerism.
8. More leisure time and the idea of "entertainment" (Weber, 1989).

Job satisfaction shifted from pride in one's work (even if unskilled labor) to what you could buy with the money you made. Workmen began to believe they could participate in their culture and be better producers, even if their jobs were brutal and unfulfilling. "Holy" days became "holi-days;" hotels and the travel industry were born. Workers had more free time for outside activities. "Ball" games, organized educational systems, and social clubs and teas created leisure but also provided structure to productivity and CONNECTIVITY. In 1896, there was even a revival of the Greek games from Olympus. All these changes in commerce, health, and social influences created a type of UFT for how social growth occurred.

Turn of the Century

The 1900s are sometimes called "The American Century" (ibid, 2000). The Industrial Revolution of the 1800s had created a new class of millionaires and, by 1900, one-third of the world's manufacturing output came from the U.S.; bigger corporations gobbled up the little guys (just like the early 2000s) (Van Doren, 1991, p. 107). Capitalism and big corporations seemed to run everything. Not only did inventors like Edison, Westinghouse, and Tesla advance U.S. productivity and ingenuity, but during this time millionaire magnates like the Rockefellers, Vanderbilts, and Carnegies also set a new standard for philanthropy and social consciousness toward ongoing poverty. Some men, like J.P. Morgan, made the CONNECTION that one was able to make money (and give money to others) by making nothing at all except more money in the banking and stocks business. Trusts were established by companies like Rockefeller's Standard Oil, and Carnegie's U.S. Steel, as well as by coal and mining companies. "At the time, it seemed for a while that politicians didn't run America, big business did" (op cit., 2000).

At the turn of the 20th century, some of these issues were addressed in the presidential election between W.J. Bryan and W. McKinley. By 1892, the new Populist Party had won some Congressional seats and, in 1896 McKinley's administration controlled workers and farmers' income, which gained more profits for business. McKinley was killed six months into his second term, making his vice-president Theodore Roosevelt Jr. the 26th President of the United States from 1901 to 1909. He was the right president to take America into the 20th century.

What did the 20th century represent? In the beginning, at least, it represented airplanes, cars, Roosevelts, Depression and Wars, unions, and lots of reform because of the "Progressives". Consumerism boomed with the advent of electricity, the use of the telephone (even for long distances) as well as other conveniences, such as the radio and the washing machine. Eventually, many of the enlightened asked the question: "How big should government be?"

Journalism took on a more important position in society and helped keep corruption under control, or so it thought. Roosevelt, the environmentalist, started the process of protecting national land by creating the National Park system. However, did a growing sense of "national pride" also lead to World War I?

While every American male had had the vote, blacks included, since 1867, women did not have the right to vote until 1919. Many individuals showed interest in social libertarianism (Comte's ideas, 1798–1857), a theory that grew out of the Positivism of the 19th century (Weber, 1989). Although a great amount of building (Eiffel Tower and Suez Canal) had been accomplished, and social liberations begun (Simon Bolivar in Latin America, the Greeks rising against the Turks), it was still the problems of the working class that interested people like Karl Marx and the Nationalists in Germany.

England/France and then England/Germany helped each other put down small revolutions; leaders like Queen Victoria, Emperor Napoleon III, and Prince Bismarck of Prussia tried to win leadership through reform, not war (ibid, 1989). The war in the Crimea/Balkans was fought after Imperialism had increased the power of these countries in response to English colonialism, trade, investments, and settlement of land.

As a genealogist, the legal and hereditary CONNECTIONS between the major players are particularly interesting to me. Wilhelm II, the last Emperor of Prussia, hated England even though his mother was sister to King George's father. The Tsar of Russia and King George were cousins through their mothers, who were sisters, and they tried to remain allies. Indeed, Queen Victoria was the grandmother to all the royal cousins, and before her death she had tried to keep them all from going to war (Hamilton, 2003). She failed.

In 1912, back in the U.S. there were four men running for election for President: Woodrow Wilson, Theodore Roosevelt, William Howard Taft, and Eugene Debs. Wilson won as a "Progressive" Democrat who ran on a platform of staying out of the war. But he took the U.S. into WW I anyway, first in Mexico in 1914 (there had been secret U-boats off the coast of Texas!) and then in Europe after his re-election.

For one thing, World War I diverted focus from the unresolved issues of Wilson's administration. There were many treaties in place at the time, some secret, some public. Many of these CONNECTIONS may have started as early as the Franco-Prussian War (1870–1871), which ended French domination under Napoleon III. The longstanding adversarial relations with Russia began. In 1905, Russia lost the Russo-Japanese War (1904–1905) and tensions continued through the unrest in Russia (remember Lenin and Trotsky?), while events were leading up to the first Balkan War in 1912. The French and English tried to protect their coastlines together but were still drawn into the second Balkan War in 1913. These events culminated in Gavrilo Princip shooting the Archduke on June 28,1914 in Sarajevo.

Finally, the Russo-Japanese War was a precursor to the eventual tensions over a balance of power in Asia that contributed to WW I; it would become truly a second "Thirty Years War" (1914–1945). The U.S. entrance into WWI was the first war on foreign soil in almost 100 years; it established a pattern of almost constant foreign wars for another 100 years (World War I, World War II, Korea, Viet Nam, and conflicts in the Middle East).

Princip was part of a secret society in Sarajevo known as the "Black Hand", whose goal was to crush the power base and the CONNECTIONS that intermarriages and alliances/treaties had created, especially after Bosnia-Herzegovina had been added to the Prussian empire, with Sarajevo as the capital. The Black Hand society believed that the Austrian-Hungarian Emperor's power base made it impossible for the common Slavic people to have any rights. It was the third conflict in three years. Does any of this sound familiar (think Isis 2014)? I would say that Princip's assassination of the Archduke not only broke up some of the power structures, but it also broke up the world structures for the rest of time to come. Between June 12th and August 18th of 1914, there were declarations of war between many countries; Japan joined in on August 23rd, Turkey was drawn in by November 2nd, and Italy declared war on Austria-Hungary on May 23, 1915. There truly was a world war.

The World at War

In the beginning of WWI, Germany thought it would have to fight just France and Russia; it didn't consider when it invaded Belgium (to get to France—which had a secret treaty with England), that Belgium would enter the war as well. England especially chose to go to war to protect its expanding colonial empire (Dell, 2014). Initially, the Germans seemed to be on a road to success, winning the Battle of Tannenberg, 8/26–8/30, 1914, but it was the last real German success of the entire war. By September, trench warfare, with its air raids and poison gas, had closed in on the soldiers; by 1915, there were 475 miles of trenches running throughout Europe.

On May 7, 1915, the English war effort was hampered by the sinking of the Lusitania, which was carrying munitions. Previously, Germany had no real luck at sea, but eventually their U-boats, which had been used to sink the Lusitania, became highly successful. Also in 1915, the terrible Armenian tragedy took place, in which Turkish forces "slaughtered" between 800,000 and 2 million Armenians in response to accusations of Armenians having helped the Russians. The act is now historically declared an act of genocide.

The year 1916 saw the two Battles of Verdun (the second of which was still in deadlock after 700,000 were killed) and the Battle of the Somme, which lasted four months. Global visions of the war were growing ever more complicated as the Russians experienced their own revolution in March of 1917 and set up a provisional government in Petrograd. Lenin then created the "second" revolution, in October of that year, to take control of his own organization, the Bolsheviks (Communists).

The Russian civil war, between the White (Pro Tsar) and Red (Bolshevik) armies created during this Second Revolution, also caused a brief lag in the war with Germany, during which Germany turned back toward its European offenses.

By July, the Tsar and his entire family were executed after a year of house arrest at Yekaterinburg.

U.S. voters struggled with the news they heard about the "war in Europe" and, by February 24, 1917, they declared their wish to join the war effort. On April 6, 1917, the U.S. declared war on Germany; by May, conscription began, and some troops were ready to go overseas. However, the first real offensive was not until 1918, with a strong U.S./Allied showing at the second Battle of Marne. The Austria-Hungarian empire began to break up according to ethnic nationality (the Slavs and Czechs became Austria and Yugoslavia respectively). The Battle of the Argonne was another success for the Allies; the Central Powers were collapsing.

In September 1918, T.E. Lawrence ("Lawrence of Arabia") completed his push into the Ottoman Empire, and thus the English had influence over the Middle East for another fifty years. After an initial plea for armistice on October 4th, and the abdication of Wilhelm II on November 9th, Armistice Day was finally declared on 11/11/1918. Fifteen million soldiers were dead and 21 million more were wounded. Soon after, twenty to fifty million more people would die worldwide of the Spanish Flu. There was no immunization available as there was with the plague-like COVID pandemic 100 years later in 2020.

The Roaring Twenties Led to the Great Depression

Of course, this "war to end all wars", didn't. What was the result? In some ways, the First World War caused the second. By the end of the conflict, Europe no longer was the center of the world. Monarchs had fallen in Germany and Russia, and Germany had to pay $33 billion in restitution, a debt which crushed their economy and spirit; the Fascist party came into power, created by Mussolini and harnessed by Hitler. Megalomania would lead to a second world war only twenty years later. However, it wasn't as clearly good versus evil. There was also new CONNECTIVITY and new borders, particularly because there had not been much large-scale warfare since Napoleon fought on the continent in the early 1800s. How did the CONNECTIVITY shift European politics? Trade issues and lust for military power had pushed these countries into conflict, so nationalism and general DISCONNECT grew. Individual European states then claimed "self-defense" (Hamilton, 2003).

After WWI, there was new independence for some citizens, particularly women in the U.S., who finally gained the right to vote in 1919. By the time the U.S. got to Europe in 1918, the war was over in 9 months; of the millions who died, 110,000 of them were Americans, many of illnesses. Unfortunately, economic hardships and rationing continued so many women and children had been left alone with little sources of income, both in Europe and the U.S. In addition, many soldiers came home but as broken men, physically and/or psychologically. In Britain, eight out of ten men would return after being wounded, but one-third of them eventually died, mostly of the infections that set in (Hunter, 2014). Some, like Hemingway who lived to write about it, had volunteered and/or went over on their own, especially to work in the field hospitals. Many of those who survived the war came home to die of the Influenza of 1918, as mentioned.

Blacks fought in this war with new hopes of adding to their social standing and career paths, but there was little fruition from that plan. In some cases, their attempts at inserting themselves into society upon return from the war instigated an increase in riots or lynching. By 1924, the Klu Klux Klan had 3 million members and had infiltrated the governments of Colorado and Idaho (ibid, 2014, pp. 138, 144).

After World War I, the whole world, and the U.S. in particular, was in a state of self-alienation and fear.[46] The U.S. became more isolationist. Although Wilson had tried to form the League of Nations, the United States itself did not vote to join it; broken-hearted Wilson suffered a stroke that wrecked his body throughout the rest of his presidency. In Europe, borders had been broken. Even though WWI had been fought to gain stability, skirmishes continued, a good example of which was the Russian Revolution. It really took the sad and devastating equalizing force of World Wars again to bring the U.S. back from two Depressions (1900s and 1930s) and to create renewed opportunities for a struggling middle class.

There is a relationship between the losers of WWI and the growth for other countries during the next decade, the "Roaring Twenties". Mass consumption was the rule, and regular citizens were afraid to "rock the boat" (Van Doren, 1991). They were satisfied to enjoy themselves as much as possible after the atrocities of the last five years. It was as if society wanted the best of the new while clinging to the old. America especially was moving fast, with its cars, mass production and automation for most new items. The ideas of the economist Adam Smith (1776) had been built right into the system of division of labor in plants all over the United States. General Motors introduced credit buying and was the first to build obsolescence into their product. Because of the growth of the auto market, highways had to be built. Automobiles were the new "prairie schooners". Soon, mass transit was born (Miller, 2000).

There was an exception to this frivolity. In European countries such as France, many were over 60 years old (the rest having died) and were fearful. In Britain, there was high unemployment and so much pressure on colonization in "third-world countries" that the economy was affected. This fear of financial difficulties was growing worldwide and finally culminated on October 19, 1929.

---

[46] WWI created fissures in every national government through which pressures for change along class, sexual and colonial lines erupted. The individual national crises are well known. Put together they describe a world system in a state of collapse: the 1916 Easter rebellion in Ireland, the 1917 Russian revolution, the declaration of a workers' republic in Finland in 1918, Red Clyde in Scotland, the first social democratic governments in Scandinavia, female suffrage in Britain, the 1919 Hungarian Soviet Republic, the 1919 French general strike and revolt of the fleet, the 1919 Austrian social democratic government (which introduced unemployment benefits, the eight-hour day, statutory vacations, and in the Army a right to trade union organization and elected governing bodies for soldiers), the 1920 general strikes and factory occupations throughout Italy, the 1926 general strike in Britain, and the 1929 stock market crash in the U.S.

The Stock Market crashed due to a lack of regulation, which was soon corrected, but not until many Americans were ruined financially and most Americans were thrown into the financial "depression". After Franklin Roosevelt was elected in 1933, the FDIC was created to protect bank deposits. The New Deal gave much needed assistance: the employed gained Unemployment Insurance through one's employment; the 25% unemployed, and without any benefits, were also now guaranteed income. These unemployed finally had a sense of CONNECTIVITY among themselves. Was this, at least in part, Socialism?

The process certainly stressed the importance of equality and not Fascism, which was seen as also denying one's freedom. The 300,000 farmers who were devastated early in the 1930s were not worrying about politics. During the Roosevelt years, the movement West from the Dustbowl did little to really improve the plight of those who were without adequate food (still needing soup kitchens) or even had resorted to picking crops or becoming "hobos". I can testify to these facts, because my father was one of those transient people for many years, before World War II gave him a chance at redemption. "Suffering was the word of the day" (Miller, 2000).

Of course, there were some who still had lots of money, as the movies at the time tried to show us, meant to represent that times could get better. The incongruity of it all, in spite of some availability of money at the Federal level, resulted in Roosevelt's New Deal. Construction and new infrastructure all over the country (Works Progress Administration, Civil Conservation Corps, Tennessee Valley Authority, Federal Security Agency, Federal Housing Administration and so forth) provided jobs for millions.

The CCC alone employed 2.9 million 18- to 25-year-old men over a nine-year period. One-fifth of all homes were saved from foreclosure and farms could be more easily refinanced. Individuals were pleased and comforted to find out that the Social Security Act would provide for them, if disabled and/or after retirement. Eventually, one out of six citizens were getting some type of assistance, at least temporarily. The country began to feel a positive CONNECTION again, with itself and between its citizens.

But this renewed sense of security was cold comfort for the racial issues which had been building after WWI and during the Depression. Even more people of color were out of work than whites, and whites resented any non-white man taking a job they might have had. Although the military was "integrated" during and after WWII, blacks continued to find life back at home (North, South, East, or West) as difficult as it had been before WWII, and tensions were coming to a head.

War Looms Again

As mentioned earlier, the second world war was really a result of how much Germany was hurt by the Treaty of Versailles and wanted its territory back. Hitler initially became influential after he founded the *Sturmabteilung* (SA) in 1921; later known by the Brown Shirts they wore, his power increased as he drew more members from former anti-leftists and prior military soldiers. He eventually called part of this group of troublemakers the Nazi Party. Many theories exist about Hitler's mental health; possibly he had bipolar disorder along with his obvious psychopathology and probable drug use. He was able to claim even more credibility, however, by successful political campaigns until finally, in January of 1933, he was voted in as Chancellor of Germany (partly by "awing" his listeners into submission) (Nicholson, 2005).

By 1938, he was able to take control of enough military power to invade Austria on March 22nd. His hatred of all but a "pure" race is well known (the history of which would fill a whole chapter). His hatred of and authority over Jews culminated in *Krystallnacht* in Poland, on November 7, 1938, the name meaning "breaking glass". Hitler annexed Poland in September 1939.

In Germany, membership in the *Jungvolk* represented perfection and Aryan attributes. On the other end of the spectrum, readers are aware of the Holocaust, where 6 million Jews died in pogroms and concentration camps, and many thousands of other ethnicities and 60,000 gays were also killed. One of the most famous concentration camps, *Dachau,* had been opened as early as 1933. Eventually, there would be as many as 1000 small to larger of these camps, which were run exclusively by the SS. "Disobedient" prisoners were treated with draconian measures, including death, especially the fate of most Jews.

The German people did not have it so easy either. With all of Hitler's energy and resources pointed toward a military build-up before and during the war, the regular citizens often starved. I once had a German national as a client, who had been born in Germany in 1939. She recounted her memories of having only the gruel of two potatoes per week to eat, and that had to be enough to feed four people.

Many other factors, in many other countries, contributed to the build-up of tensions during the late 1930s. Hitler called other leaders "worms", but [ha!] the worms finally turned on him. Where WWI was a war of trenches, WWII was a war of movement. To keep up, the U.S. created a giant war movement of munitions, with a jeep built every two minutes! At one point, we were fighting in North Africa, or Italy, or Normandy, France [my father served in all three of these countries], then in the Battle of the Bulge and the Pacific Islands, and so forth. Finally, it all came to an end with President Truman's decision to use the newly developed atom bomb on Hiroshima and Nagasaki, Japan. It is said that by shortening the war, he killed 225,000 residents of Japan to save 30 million people worldwide.

Initially there was a kind of "phony" war (ibid, 2005). The opposition between German Fascism and Russian Communism was superficial; in August 1939 a non-aggression pact was signed between Germany and Russia. As mentioned, in September 1939, after *Krystalnacht*, Poland was invaded by a *blitzkrieg*, with *stuka* bombers, tanks, artillery and infantry. England and France declared war in response but did not initially attack.

Then Hitler also went after Denmark and Norway (April and June 1940) and one month later invaded the Netherlands, Belgium, and Luxembourg. What followed was the Battle of Dunkirk, a brutal start to the war, when Germany held the upper hand, mostly due to its superiority with U-boats that sunk everything including supply ships. On June 14, 1940, Paris was invaded, and the *Vichy* government was established; the French could not regain a foothold to fight against Hitler's forces. By July, the *Luftwaffe* was bombing across the English Channel and the Battle of Britain had begun.

Hitler's military superiority continued for quite a long time. Initially Stalin was his ally, but full of the lust for power, Hitler turned on him as well, gobbling up other Eastern European countries that he had promised Stalin. In June 1941, Germany broke the pact with Russia to keep Poland for itself and moved against Russia for more "space". After fighting in Russia for two brutal winters, Hitler began to realize the error of his decision to fight on two fronts. Apparently, he had never studied Napoleon's similar failure (sic). The Americans realized that it was time to do something, especially after the bombing of Pearl Harbor by an Axis member, the Japanese, on December 7, 1941.

U.S. Enters the War

Why did Japan bomb Pearl Harbor? Franklin Roosevelt had tried to avoid direct involvement in the war for several years, although he did send aid and armaments, setting up the war factories as noted above. Finally, in 1940, Japan invaded China, and the U.S. sent a fleet to the Pacific, creating a type of embargo (as we do today when we are establishing sanctions against a state power in the Middle East, for example). Like freezing foreign assets in U.S. banks, Roosevelt felt he could contain U.S. actions to another type of "non-war".

The Japanese response, however, was more direct! Previously allies during WWI, Japan and the U.S. had experienced mounting tensions for a decade over oil. It is commonly believed that Japan wanted to draw the U.S. into WWII, expecting that their then alliance with Hitler and Germany would pave the way for obtaining all the outcomes Japan had been trying to achieve—oil and rights to the Philippines and other Pacific islands.

The bombing of Pearl Harbor, in Oahu, Hawaii, knocked out one-half of the total U.S. Navy in one day. Not only did this well-planned assault bring us into the pre-existing European War, with Japan as Germany's ally, but our involvement brought home to the U.S. a whole different type of war. Armament factories tried to keep up with the increase in air power and military tactics. The result was civilians all over occupied countries were now bombed and killed on a level never seen in warfare. During its time in the war, the U.S. bombed more than 50 cities in Germany and Japan. The death toll was hard to phantom. Altogether, on both sides, more than 50 million people died during WWII, plus the 6 million or more Jews, homosexuals, and blacks murdered in the Holocaust.

Of this large number dead, "only" 400,000 Americans died, and the U.S. seemed to be the only country to grow "fatter;" industrial complexes went wild trying to keep up with the need for armaments. This growth helped bring on the end of the Depression as mentioned (Miller, 2000). The high-quality production started out having to use unskilled labor (most men were serving in the war) or even women. Fifteen million Americans changed their address and crossed the country to gain work. By the end of the war, these individuals were highly employable with new, desirable skills in the ever-growing economy. Some women went back home with their returning husbands, or new husbands, to then create families which would become the "Baby Boomer" generation.

Although we had already entered the war, most people are aware of D-Day, June 6, 1944, when 175,000 troops entered Europe. Another million more (British,

American, and Canadian) would come in the next month. This group represents the "Greatest Generation", of which my father was one individual, going on the beach at Normandy on DD +6 days. The two main objectives of the Allies' plan were to engage German troops in Northern France and then to surge south and east from Normandy into Paris.

Successfully Paris was liberated on August 25, 1944. But in the following eight months, there were many losses in such actions as the Battle of the Bulge at Ardennes in Belgium, and Bastogne, December 20, 1944, where Patton led a brilliant attack, backed up by the 761st Tank Battalion (Black Panthers). Hitler lost up to 200,000 men there, plus he was still fighting the Resistance everywhere else. After Eisenhower took over the Allied Forces of Europe, the final hours of the war were clearly approaching. In May 1945, a street fight to gain access to what was believed to be Hitler's bunker revealed that he was already dead, reportedly by suicide on April 30th.

As the end of the war neared, the U.S. played its part, as far as contributing to the devastation. In 1944, we wanted to activate plans for B-29s to reach Japan and took Saipan to make sure we could implement this plan; air raids on Tokyo in March 1945 were "effective", with 2000 tons of bombs dropped. The first atomic bombs were dropped on August 6th (Hiroshima) and August 9th (Nagasaki). Victory in Japan Day (August 15, 1945) was a foregone conclusion. The Japanese had no choice but to formally surrender on 2 September 1945. We justified, we worried about the outcome after we saw it, but in the end, we told ourselves that the Japanese were so fanatical it had become the only choice we had; they would have fought on and on.

Conspicuous Consumption but also Civil Unrest

This "modern" war may have created fearsome weapons, but there were positive outcomes as well, ones which showed new global CONNECTIONS. Improved and accessible communication came as an outcome of how the war boosted consumer interest in creating efficiency at home. At first, women had "Victory gardens", but then suddenly many "instant" foods became available (e.g. sliced bread, potato flakes, and factory processed and packed foods).[47] Other influential changes through communication included mass utilization (for pleasure) of television, the "advent" of rock and roll music (Elvis!), transistor radios, and the effect the teenage culture had on the rest of the U.S. and the world.

But not all was growth and productivity. Although the United States became a dominant world power during World War II, leading the way for the United Nations to be housed in New York, the "cold war" would continue for at least 40 years (and perhaps if you ask the CIA or someone in Russia, where I have visited,

---

[47] I have often used this paradigm of "instant foods" to illustrate the therapeutic problem the Baby Boomers have with a need for instant gratification, with which they were brought up. It leads to many psychological problems, not the least of which is substance abuse (alcohol and/or drugs). Until an adult individual can recognize the toddler-level indicators of impulsivity shown through such craving (substitutions for their thumb as shown in Chapter Sixteen), it is very difficult to implement therapeutic and familial change.

it has never ended—look over your shoulder and there's the KGB). The Truman Doctrine of giving support to any country threatened by Communism led the way for the United States to enter both the Korean and Viet Nam Wars. Tensions also continued in post-war Europe, where NATO (established in 1949) finally became more inclusive and accepted Germany in 1955.

The Marshall Plan was moderately successful, using economic growth to help fight poverty and hunger, to hold off Communism, and to create an increase in industrial output worldwide. The consumerism and consumption of the 1950s created a generally positive attitude (Miller, 2000). By the end of World War II, women had more than the vote to look forward to; many of them wanted to continue in some form the work they had started while their husbands were away on the European front.

Politically, President Eisenhower's obsession with keeping America safe from Communism made it easy for McCarthyism and other clear evidence of the Communist threat to take hold. It was a time of "disagreement and dissent" (Kerouac, Rachel Carson's *Silent Spring*, Ralph Nader, Betty Friedan, and Birth Control) (ibid, 2000). It seemed like the roots of several revolutions soon to come (Black Power, Feminism, Liberalism) were all being set down in the complacency of the late 1950s, even though there were some benefits like the GI bill and more prosperity for most middle-class homes.[48] Savings bonds, initiated during the war, created an atmosphere of fiscal awareness. Suburbs grew, as did unions, college loans, and the size of the middle class and its Baby Boomer families.

However, U.S. contentment and containment finally burst into multiple "revolutions". The lower classes, many of them men and women of color [including the 761st Tank Battalion mentioned above], came back from World War II to pretty much the same unacceptable conditions, if not worse, especially when they compared themselves to those around them. The unrest that ensued came from a fertile ground prepared for the following social, political, and legal changes: Brown vs. Board of Education (1954); Rosa Parks (1955); the rise in notoriety of Martin Luther King, Jr (1958) and the NAACP; the Civil Rights Act (1964); and the rest of the actions presented by President Lyndon Johnson[49] under his Great Society program, such as Head Start and Medicare.

---

[48] "Dissent (defiance) is the native activity of the scientist…and it has got him into a good deal of trouble in the last ten years. No society has ever died of dissent, but many may have died of conformity…Dissent is not itself an end; it is the surface mark of a deeper value. Dissent is the mark of freedom, as originality is the mark of independence…Democracy is a constant tension between dissent and respect; between independence from the view of others, and tolerance for them…Respect for others must be founded in self-respect" (Bronowski, 2011, pp. 61–63).

[49] During the Johnson presidency, I would have been 12- to 17-years old, my father was working on a military facility, in Texas no less, and our usual fishing spot turned out to be right across the river from President Johnson's Texas ranch. Now, you cannot trespass on a river, so we continued to go to the same spot and could clearly see the Secret Service men placed along the opposite side of the riverbank. Often, we could also see his helicopter landing. It was exciting stuff for a teenager, and for my father as well, I think.

As the next president, John Kennedy was probably more worried about Communism than segregation. The episode of the Bay of Pigs was a result of Castro and his forces overthrowing Baptista and expropriating U.S. assets in Cuba. Kennedy's focus on keeping Communism out of Cuba and South Viet Nam by standing up to Communist forces also led to the Viet Nam War becoming a terrible distraction for twenty long years (starting in 1964). The war, however, did not completely detract from a women's movement during the same years, following Betty Friedan's impressive, but controversial, book, *The Feminine Mystique*, in 1963. The women's movement paralleled the Civil Rights Movement and the example set by the freedom riders. "Feminism", a relatively new term, created a National Organization for Women (NOW) and an Equal Rights Amendment (ERA) for women, which set the stage to pass Roe versus Wade for abortion rights in 1973.

However, the ERA has yet to pass on its own virtues after twenty attempts. Gay rights also grew during this time and became more public after the AIDS crisis of the 1980s. Unfortunately, several of these gains in social rights have fallen under right-wing dispute, with Roe versus Wade being rescinded in 2022.

A positive distraction during the 1960s was the U.S. goal to put a man on the moon. Practically anyone over six alive on that day in June 1969 remembers it. This challenge to our nation was highly involved in, if not directly responsible for, the growth of the computer industry (think Apple computers 1976 compared to now). But the memories of those years may surround many with shades of negativity because of assassinations, riots, demonstrations, and finally the deaths of four students at Kent State. Some political analysts feel it was the unrest of the 60s, culminating in the gas crisis, and conflict in the Middle East, that led the U.S. into a period of more conservatism and environmentalism.

Finally, the "Moral Majority", as it came to be called, was born out of an attempt to grasp a higher ground and a survivalist mentality. President Nixon, for instance, was probably able to sweep political control away from Democrats (especially after the deaths of Robert F. Kennedy and Martin Luther King, Jr.) through an appeal to morality and centrism. The terrible events of September 11, 2001, which led to the Patriot Act, also returned the U.S. to a similar type of political point of view as President Johnson previously faced.

Currently, there remains a split decision in this country about gun control in view of the hidden "terrorist enemy" which has been a confounding part of the world's giant push toward globalization. Our more recent terrorist issue here at home and political partisanship only adds evidence to the growth of fear as part of the U.S. identity, even within the Christian right. The violent turn in some of our youth and almost daily school/public shootings speaks to our country's failure to handle this huge issue.

Throughout the 1990s and until the present, the United States has had to deal with a vacillating cultural identity which is influenced by growing technological desire and seizing its opportunity to truly be number one in the world. Rapid ideological changes came with the fall of the Berlin Wall (1989) and the break-up of the Soviet Union in 1991, sober times such as the loss of face over the Iranian hostage incident (1979–1981), nuclear accidents, ignoring AIDS, poor sustainability by greed, corporate accidents and oil spills (Exxon Valdez hitting Prince William Sound's Bligh Reef, March 24, 1989), and changes in perspective about abortion. If the U.S. were a company, run by a real CEO, could the leaders of this country give our clear mission statement, beyond "to protect and defend?" I am not sure.

We Become Therapized

As a logical outcropping of the religious revolutions of the 17th century, the flourishing of philosophical studies of the Self provided an impetus in the 19th century, through CONNECTIONS we gained, not only a framework of how the world can be understood beyond pure scientific reasonings, but also a structure for one's inner world and self-reflection. Publications were available to the public; Rousseau, Emerson and Thoreau, (among others), were widely read. The Theosophical Society (founded 1875) was well-attended by many of these writers of the 19th century; as naturalists, their goal was to find their "place in the universe". This point of view is an attempt to reconcile/CONNECT macrocosmic/microcosmic theoretical differences (think Platonists).

The shift here by these writers/philosophers was to a belief that an individual could "heal thyself", as well as achieve self-reflection. A healthier lifestyle should be the norm, not the Outlier exception. Eventually, there was an actual attempt to synthesize these pursuits, and "religions" such as "Science of Mind" (Church of Religious Science) were born, which featured the writings of Emmett Fox in the early 20th century.

Neurologist Freud, and spiritualist son of a pastor, Carl Jung, brought science and religion to the study of the human mind, and the field of psychotherapy was born. Consciousness was a "divine spark in each of us, and the Self as soul" (Pinker, 1997, p. 560). Scientists may ask "why does the universe have consciousness?" But I am satisfied to add consciousness to other scientific terms such as space, time, gravity, and electromagnetism, all as part of a CONNECTED UFT theory of the understanding of Self.

Although therapeutic issues and therapy as a science will be addressed more fully in future chapters, it should be pointed out here that it did not take long for Western Euro-American culture to see self-analysis as an antithesis to its tendency toward impulsivity, narcissism, and projection of guilt onto others. Where Greek and Romans had their gods, wars and survival consumed the mentality of the Middle Ages, Catholics were able to resolve conflictual inner moral dilemmas through confession, and early American society had puritanical and ritualistic mentality.[50] Often the focus was on the presenting problem, sometimes on the underlying anxiety (neurosis). But the goal of self-reflection was to find a core

---

[50] "Freud's interest in archaeology expressed his quest for our whole unacknowledged inheritance from the past. When in his forties he turned from the world of neurology to the world of culture and history, he committed himself to the archaeology of the soul, the 'psyche.' 'The unexamined strata of experience, both of society and of the individual, were his digging ground" (Boorstin, 1985, p. 613).

experience that could lead one more directly to an attachment to a "Higher Power" as it became known—something "Other" which is part of what we will be calling the "uni-cosmic" view (Van Doren, 1991).

Transitional Issues

Was it something about this new tendency for global self-reflection that freed our psyches on a cultural level as well? Feminism and the 20th century had vacillating sexual influences (20s, 40s, 60s, 80s), which certainly contributed to a strong and permanent shift across all levels of societal functioning. In a post-Freudian world, many involved in psychotherapy feared society had become too clinical. Decision-makers were motivated by finances, values shifted from "both-and" to "either-or", which is a major concept we will return to in this book over and over.

For instance, rather than continue institutional care for the extremely mentally ill, in the 1970s the belief in Mental Health Outpatient treatment led to the release of many psychiatric inpatients to non-existent community services, a result I strongly disagreed with; this error shifted the homeless/Outlier population once again to the margins of society. Self-help groups did "help" to a point; thankfully there were groups like those of the 24-7 available 12-step program system or others modeled after it, which have saved many lives.

A rebirth of the humanistic view called a "Third Wave" presented the ability of some therapists to use more empathy. Treating others in such a manner, whether in a therapeutic model or not, has encouraged our society through several financial/social/moral crises in the last five decades. We are all in this together, it seems, and CONNECTIVITY continues to prove itself as the default survival mechanism, because impulsivity, albeit "rugged" individualism, hasn't quite pulled us through.

And what about what we used to call "The Third World?" Under-industrialized countries' ideological influences and "Western ways" have been evolving. They want our culture, and we want their products (which might have often led to our meddling in their culture). Since the year 2000, China, Japan, and many other Asian countries, along with much of the Middle East and some of Latin America (think of Brazil) took on large roles in a global society and economy.

"The subject of this natural history of society would be culture, redefined as 'that complex whole which includes knowledge, belief, art, morals, law, custom, and any other capabilities and habits acquired by man as a member of society'" (ibid, 1985, p. 647). To stabilize world culture, there has been a need to accept more of global ideas about labor, property, and "tribal life" than might have seemed possible in 1950 when my aunt traveled in these countries consulting for the Rockefeller Foundation.

The truth is that more can and did happen in two generations than had changed in the last 500 years, leading to "insecurities of change" on both sides (Weber, 1989). The internet and immediacy of technological news brings us knowledge of warfare and imbalances due to differences almost immediately. Likewise, the colonial system obviously could not be sustained where literacy and yearning for democracy continued to grow. "Political decisions command material possibilities" (ibid, 1989). Do we want cultural uniformity? No. Does nationalism tend to come in repeating cycles? Yes. Are we afraid of overt nationalism? Probably.

Modern technology has also brought positive changes worldwide. Not only do we have an "easier life" but there have been revolutionary gains from advances in medicine, such as: new medicines and inoculations, the eradication of many global diseases, and new technology such as MRIs (which surpass X-rays). Conditions like cancer and heart disease are not as daunting as they once were, and people in many countries are living longer. But not all, not as long as the cost of pandemics, wars, and self-destructive societies keep bringing down the average life expectancy, which before the 1990s was raised by the reduction of fetal death and death from disease.

Why as a leading Western culture do we have a mortality rate 2X higher than the rest of the Western world, Australia and Japan? Even the terrible disaster of the diseases of AIDS and SARS-type immune dysfunctions helped lead the way to find new serums and antibiotics. The terrible COVID-19 pandemic of 2019 is still not under control as I write this; history will show the long-term effects after this book is completed.

Weber summarized the *Western Tradition* (1989) with the statement that all the outcomes that have brought us to our current level of "comfort" have necessarily contained, if not resolved, the dialectic:

1. Authoritarianism and individualism.
2. Personal initiative and centralization.
3. Obedience and revolt.
4. Faith and questioning.
5. Inertia and enterprise.
6. Conflict and reconciliation (Weber, 1989)

It is the two sides of the constant dilemma, between curiosity and ambition, which result in an evolving society.

The study of the development of CONNECTIONS in history predicts patterns of continuities. Why are there continuities? Bronowski's (1973) major life goal was to investigate the underlying matrix of cultural patterns that went beyond the pale of social ramification but were, by their nature, integrative across fields of human study. Once the Self is released from the search, Bronowski believed that the intellectual approach acts and is dependent upon an individual's understanding and taking pleasure in manifesting his own skill. "Discovery is a double relation of analysis and synthesis together. As an analysis, it probes for what is there; but then, as a synthesis, it puts the parts together in a form by which the creative mind transcends the bare limits, the bare skeleton, that nature provides" (ibid, 1973, p.115).[51] This synthesis is the power of the dialectic we saw from Hegel,

---

[51] We find that "the study of history incites to virtue and discourages vice. It trains future statesmen in politics and war. It is the mother of experience and the grandmother of wisdom. Old men are said to be wise because their judgment rests on the accumulated experience of a lifetime; a right reading of history builds a vicarious experience that also makes men wise" (Van Doren, 1991, p. 72).

Nietzsche, and Marx, and which we will study again with Erikson in Chapter Thirteen.

Hopes for the Future

In the early 21st century, certain transitional issues, starting with September 11, 2001, presented our society with an opportunity to struggle, much as it did at the last turn of a century in 1900s with WWI, the Spanish Flu, and the "Roaring 20s". These struggles always move us toward resolution of opposing forces for a synergistic path. As Sartre believed, a new humanism can transcend our loneliness by providing us self-determination, even if it arises from despair. How often in history has society regrouped and arisen from despair?

Throughout the last three chapters, I presented too many examples to count. Whether we want to refer to these changes as Humanism or Existentialism, leadership examples such as Martin Luther, Gandhi, and M.L. King, Jr. have shown us how to take care of others while we provide an excellent example/mentoring to those who really chose us. What did the death of these famous people really represent to us? Certainly, in death there is a loss of CONNECTIVITY, of someone or something representing our memories. We search for a manner of facing mortality which will also enhance the meaning of our omni-cosmic presence. We face our understanding of the purpose of survival and then death in the first place. For instance, the Tibetans study the Book of the Dead, which provides a path for healthy living, of which death is only an end goal.[52]

In the next chapter, we look at how spirituality has evolved its presence in our lives during the last 25 centuries—this pursuit includes the use of computers and attempts to verify the sources of man's "neurological" will and passion. If man's inner world and spirituality have not really changed that much, then the practice of understanding how the outer societal forces have changed freedom of expression is our next focus. St. Augustine is quoted as saying, "It is the will of God that shapes the Universe and Science." This belief has a lot of truth because all true works of art, as well as scientific insight, have this same origin.

---

[52] "The men who made the weapons and the men who made the paintings were doing the same thing—anticipating a future as only man can do, inferring what is to come from what is here. There are many gifts that are unique in man; but at the center of them all, the root from which all knowledge grows, lies the ability to draw conclusions from what we see to what we do not see, to move our path on the steps to the present" (Bronowski, 1973, p. 56).

Chapter Eight
The Spirit and the Self How Connections Provide Us with Pathways to Comfort

As seen in the previous chapters, the structure of philosophy, education, science, and religious belief have guided civilization through the last 6000 years or more. Signs of religious activity have been documented as far back as 100,000 years. Religious beliefs were viewed as a by-product of the growth of our brains, our cognitive tendencies to see signs and patterns, and our drive to create order from chaos. Therefore, our current level of understanding of the universe, cultural continuity, each other, and ourselves evolved/CONNECTED on an interpersonal level within the context and relevant dynamics of history. "Religion has survived because it helped us form increasingly larger social groups, held together by common beliefs" (Azar, 2010, p. 53). To look at spiritual changes specifically, both within and outside "organized" religion, we will compare the common elements found in most religions and how these elements are guideposts for us.

The Concept of God

First, organized religions generally refer to a belief in one (G)od, although there may be a subtext of beliefs that God has a dual nature (Taoist), is a Trinity (Christian), has ten dimensions (Judaic/Kabbalah), or is polymorphous in terms of demons or *dakinis*/angels (also many Eastern religions, such as Hinduism and Buddhism, are often taught or practiced only as a "philosophy").

To expand further, the *Yin* and *Yang* of Taoism (550 BCE) presents students with perfect paradoxes, which ultimately provide an opportunity to synthesize thoughts about the unknowable. *Yin* has been referred to as passive, feminine or even more negative energy, whereas *Yang* is positive, male energy. The *Yin* and *Yang* are opposing qualities and yet are also parts of a mutual whole, transforming each other into a balanced equilibrium. This quality of energy (also sometimes known as Higher Power) is known as the *qi*, or the embodiment of the *Yin* and the *Yang* as balanced and not diluted.

A self-existent and omnipresent archetype, called God, has been held up for worship as long ago as the existence of the supernaturalism of the ancient world and certainly in India by the concept of Brahma (6,000 BC or earlier). Pre-existing naturalistic myths are usually found in civilizing cultures. In turn, there is a more intentional group practice of belief in an intelligent universe of some type. With cultural advances, the worship of anthropomorphized gods developed more archetypal and symbolic beliefs. "Religion, in a sense, outsources social monitoring to a supernatural agent" (Azar, 2010, p. 56). Eventually, some sense of conscious intent in the choice of worshipful behaviors became self-evident; an inner sense of these processes showed in spirituality and self-reflection.

The concept of Tao or wholeness as "unity in duality" is a concept which arises as well in many other faiths and philosophies, predating even Buddhism. We find the idea in such philosophies as that of the Greeks, for instance in the writings of Heraclitus (535 BCE). The Greeks humanized their gods; gods such as Athena and Persephone took on characterizations and unresolved mysteries of Greek life. The Greek Protagoras (490 BCE) said "Of all things the measure is Man, of the things that are, that they are, and of the things that are not, that they are not." Here is a perfect example of how the Greeks needed their gods to represent a contextualized version of their own problems, just as later the early Christians would find solace in the fact that Jesus claimed to have allowed his death for their sins.

Judaic Studies and the Kabbalah

From a different point of view, the Jewish Kabbalah formed the basis of much of early Judaic studies and thus influenced later Christian ideology. The Kabbalah strives to describe God's "being" as monistic, but also as pantheistic because of the 10 ways He can reveal His will. Judaic study of the "truth of God's being" dates from the Bronze Age, more than 3000 years ago, or as some might say, from the "Garden of Eden" period. An organized form of the study of its mystical aspects finally appeared in the 12th century in Southern Europe, where many Sephardic Jews resided.

Mystical teachings were transmitted from teacher to student directly. [This is still a major practice in Tibetan Buddhism. I took an oral transmission of Tantric Buddhism directly from the Dalai Lama in 2001]. Kabbalistic teachings, therefore, tended to be abstract, impossible to understand without guidance, and very difficult to learn without the interpretations required (Rabbi David Cooper, 1997).

In many ways, early Judaic study resembled meditation, in that insights best came from this altered state. On the other hand, there is a second type of Kabbalah studies that does not always require a guiding teacher, for the student is his own channel to God's message of creation. The *Zohar*, as it is referred to, is a commentary on the Torah and other symbolism in Jewish beliefs and it is still studied today. Supposedly, its writings referred to "ancient texts" that were a collection of esoteric Hebrew writing, given to the world about 1305 by a learned Spanish Jew, Moses de Leon. These writings were supposed to be drawn from the hidden wisdom of Moses, having been "pondered by him during his forty years in the wilderness."

Special instructions contained in the writings ultimately became the first four books of the Pentateuch, from which can be "extracted by a proper understanding and manipulation of the mystical number-values of the Hebrew alphabet," the lore and the techniques for rediscovering the Kabbalah (Campbell, 1949, p. 268). The Kabbalah and *Zohar's* fullest development probably came in the 16th century when Isaac Luria (1534–1572) and his disciple Hayyim Vital (1542–1620) reinterpreted many Kabbalistic ideas. "The Kabbalists of Safed understood that every event in the created universe, indeed the very act of creation itself was a mere introduction to, or preparation for, *Tikkun ha-Olam* (Restoration from Chaos)" (Drob, 2010, p. 102).

Hasidic Judaism took the study of the mystery of the Kabbalah for its own in the 18th century. There is also a "Christian" Kabbalah, first translated into Latin, which included many sayings of the Zohar, and which supposedly was relied upon greatly by the psychiatrist Carl Jung (Chapter Eighteen) in his studies of alchemy.

"We should also note that the Kabbalah has important affinities to many of the themes in Plato and Neo-Platonism, and Christian mysticism" (ibid, 2010, p. 11).

The Kabbalah is based on two primary aspects: 1) God himself is unknowable; and 2) the revealed aspect of God which created the universe, preserves the universe, and interacts with mankind. God is all that really exists; all else is completely undifferentiated. Therefore, the Kabbalistic view might be defined as monistic pantheism; however, parts of its theoretical basis sound a lot like concepts of the Tao as well, especially in its attempts at integration of unbalanced aspects of the Universe (Dennis, 2007).

The primary symbols of the Kabbalah can be found in the chart below, but this limited list and description can in no way cover the detailed meaning behind the labels and CONNECTIONS to the processes in other philosophies. Study of the Jewish Talmud and Zohar can help one understand Judaic traditions, but it is not inclusive.

Ein-Sof (Pleroma of the Gnostics): Infinite God/Unknowable prior to its Manifestation.
Tzimtzum: Divine Contraction/Creating and Concealing.
Adam Kadmon Primordial Man/The Divine Light of *Reshimu* (the residue).
Sefirot Divine Archetypes/10 *Sefirah* (See below) 22 *Otujot* Lettersnumerology.
Shevirot ha-Kelim: Breaking the Vessels.
Kellipot: Shells, Husks/Separation, and Individuation of The King (male) and Queen (female).
Tikkun ha-Olam: Restoration/from Chaos becomes Order.
Partzufim: Divine Face/Visages.

The ten Emanations through which God reveals His will include:

1. *Keter*: will
2. *Chochmah*: wisdom
3. *Binah*: understanding
4. *Chesed*: loving kindness
5. *Din*: judgment
6. *Tiferet*: harmony (as in Unity of Self)
7. *Netzach*: victory
8. *Hod*: glory
9. *Yesod*: foundation
10. *Malchut*: sovereignty

"*Tiferet* [the Self], *Sephirot* [the Emanations], and *Gevurah* [restraint, control] form the triad of the Divine Soul. *Yesod* [foundation] is the I, which is directly in touch with the Self, and with the active principle of *Nezah* [eternity] and the passive principle of *Hod* [submission]" (Hardy, 1990).

There are also important concepts that help us compare Kabbalah to Christianity and Buddhism; for instance, the attribute *Sephirot* provides a view of ten "agencies" through which God created the world (wisdom, insight, cognition, strength, power, inexorableness, justice, right, love, and mercy). As mentioned, *Sefirot* is the process of ethics which confirms how, by being a "righteous" human, ethical qualities lead us to God's blessings, and *Emunah* defines the "faith" by which we can use and show compassionate actions. Ultimately, it is also necessary to show compassion toward oneself to share compassion toward others. This basic concept of compassion crosses all religious lines and provides the developmental basis for all human activity, evolution, civilization, and CONNECTION.

Kabbalah also believes Collective Unconscious exists as a necessary aspect of the creation of God to give man free choice. Free choice reflects the inner moral combat within mankind between the dictates of morality and the surrender to one's basic instincts. In the study of these concepts, the mystical can be found in the "white spaces" between the letters of the nominal, a concept mirrored in many other religious beliefs about the Infinite, the Invisible (think Trinity), and the indeterminate ether of classical philosophers. This intellective portion of spiritual study is often based on mystical elements. Drob's excellent summary and integration of the Kabbalistic view shows how it is based on a dialectical process of its own and is also believed to have influenced Jung's work in psychology (Chapter Eighteen).[53]

Regardless of labels or divisions, we all take this journey of Self-discovery in some manner during our lifetime. This image of an active God, and structured ideals for us to follow, provides a way for looking at one's inner "potentialities" that we will further evaluate in Chapter Nineteen. Despite how many parts God may manifest; it is 'His' spiritual emergence that counts.

Egyptian Worship

Early Egyptians handled beliefs about the soul very concretely. The *Ka* was the Egyptian concept of vital essence (somewhat like Taoist *qi*), the *Akh* was the idea of intellect, not as mind but as a living entity, the *Ba* was the person's uniqueness/personality, and the *Jb* was heart, the seat of one's emotions and one's will and intention. In addition, one's *Sheut* (shadow) contained the representations of oneself seen in statues or after death; found in the tombs, one's *Ka* had the

---

[53] "According to the kabbalists of Safed, if *Tikkun* is to be achieved, the sparks of divine light (*netzotzim*), which had been alienated from their source in God by the Breaking of the Vessels, must be liberated from the Husks (*Kellipot*) that entrap them in the dark world of the "Other Side" [Jung's Shadow]. The extraction of the divine light, referred to in the Kabbalah as the act of "*birur*," is, metaphysically speaking, the very process of *Tikkun ha-Olam*, and the very essence of "the good" as it can be achieved by humankind. It should, however, be apparent that because the *Kellipot* (which are sustained by the sparks of divine light which they contain) are the source and substance of both matter and evil, the process of extraction (and thus the very process of *Tikkun*) requires a sojourn in the realm of evil, the realm of *Sitra Achra,* the "Other Side." *Tikkun,* the "raising of the sparks," proceeds as it were, out of the *Sitra Achra* and as such there is no goodness, i.e., no liberated light, except that which issues forth out of the evil realm. 'The perfection of all things,' the Zohar tells us, 'Is attained when good and evil are first of all commingled and then become all good, for there is no good so perfect as that which issues out of evil'" (Drob, 2010, p. 106).

function of carrying forth the soul into death, where the *Jb* was weighed by *Anubis* (God of mummification) for judgment of one's character.

Finally, one's *Ren*, or name, was a representation of one's soul in that if one's name was spoken, he would live on, which explains the need for pyramids and tombs to guarantee surviving worship. This worship took place through the many gods, but it was not until Ramses II (1213 BCE) when beliefs changed; he believed that, as Pharoah, he could join himself with *Ra*, the sun god creating a more monistic point of view. With each dusk to dawn after his death, his own return would guarantee the life of his subjects by the return of the sun itself. *Ra* is associated with Horus, often represented as falcon or hawk, who was worshipped for millennia until long after Jesus' birth.

Other beliefs throughout the centuries suggest the multitude of visual forms that God can creatively take on (such as in Paleolithic and other figures, Earth Mother, and in Mithras, an Indo-Iranian God of light, mentioned in the Vedic texts). Many religious practices involved this union with God through some type of initiation (Osiris, Dionysus, Messiah, Christus, and even Gnostics); Man plus God heralded the *Adam Kadmon* of the Kabbalah's "Perfect" first Man.

Adonis, for instance, was adopted by Semitics, Greeks, and Romans. These archetypal ideals ultimately led to a liturgical idea of soul and worship that would be befitting man's need for such an essence. For centuries, there was an ongoing worship of many previous Gods/Goddesses and religions concurrent to that of Jewish life or Christianity practices: Osiris/Isis, Mithras, Attis, Zeus, and so forth. Pantheism still recognized the "earth" religions of fertility, wine, seasons, Sun, and planets. All these multiple views did not detract from a belief in *Yahweh* or a Redeemer/Christus the Savior; they continued to underscore the strength of a human ideal. All the mystery cults, Judaic studies, and Gnostic influences focused to some degree on emotional substance, and most importantly, belief in a soul. "It is only by coming to understand the true nature of reality, through gnosis, that we can find our way home" (Hardy, 1990, p. 127).

Transcendence and Healing

Another common concept of religious experience is that of transcendence, or the act of experiencing beyond the limits of material existence. Transcendent experiences require a belief in that which is above/beyond/more than—a something that protects, and which has been universally experienced as providing both in-the-world grounding and an out-of-this-world sense of hopefulness and peace. Part of this grounding takes place within the community, the actual experiences of the religious meeting place/fellowship, the next common denominator of many religions. Most religions have a detailed explanation of how tribe/community life/fellowship contributes to the overall quality, CONNECTION, and "variety of the religious experience" (William James, 1902). In Buddhism, for instance, the Sangha (community spirit) is one of the three Jewels of practice, and its importance will be discussed more fully in Chapter Nine.

This inclusion in a group consciousness often facilitates a place for mind and/or body healing to take place. Comfort and trust go together, and over the centuries pre- and post-civilized societies often turned to spiritual practitioners for remedy and repair long before consistent and respectable medical care existed. A troubled soul could clearly lead to health issues, for where does the mind reside after all? The term psychosomatic was originally descriptive, then pejorative, and now obviously an underlying key concept to all of Psychoneuroimmunology (see Chapter Ten). On the other hand, enhancement of senses and involvement of mental faculties is often brought on by heightened sound, colors, or intensity of experience during religious practice, such as through music, repetitive chanting, colorful artwork, vestments, other special clothing, or even through the inner work of meditation because of the absence of such stimulation.

Science of Spirituality

Many different points of view described the feeling of oneness with any type of transpersonal power, including shamanistic ritual, Christian prayer, and Buddhist meditation. All tap, however, into the same underlying universal energy (quanta, God?). Whether it is through general reading, lifelong religious practice, a History of Religion class, a Psychology of Philosophy class, or a Sensation and Perception Psychology class,[54] any of a variety of source materials allow us to understand, in structured terms, what we have already experienced in personal ways. Humanity and Spirituality can be viewed as parts of the same unity.

When my daughter was in the fourth grade, I volunteered to give her class a speech on how the human brain works. In summary, I explained how the brain is a three-part organ, the triune according to MacLean (1990). There is the primitive "reptile brain", mainly the brain stem and basal ganglia, which reacts in the same way in us as it has in reptiles for millions of years, stimulating our instinctual responses. There is the overlying mammalian "doggy brain", which includes limbic emotive and hippocampal memory centers, which we share in evolutionary sequence with all other mammals. And finally, there is the neocortex, or "monkey/frontal brain", the most developed outer part of the cerebrum, which mediates higher functions such as cognition and conscience, and which we believe that we alone as a species possess.

My lecture presentation was meant to be a platform for discussion: could they understand that their emotions (reptile brains) might be driving their fourth-grade drives and aggressions, and thus behavioral impulses, but that their higher (primate/people) brain could use judgment and take responsibility and control? I was amazed at how many of these 10-year-old children not only understood my examples, but then asked thoughtful questions. If only more adults were willing to take responsibility for their actions!

---

[54] "This all has to do with how we contact the world. We understand the world through our senses: sight, sound, smell, taste, touch and, in the Buddhist world, mind. Our entire relationship to the world comes from our senses. Oddly, we spend little time training our senses, but the senses are basically our instrument, whether we are working as a painter, musician, poet, dancer, textile designer, or someone who simply appreciates those things" (Schneider, 2002, pp. 18–22).

Now we come to the question: where is God experienced? Many neuroscientists in the past would have supported the view that the frontal brain defined our spiritual experiences for us. Yet I, along with others, prefer the artistic/romantic view that God lives strongly through our emotions (more realistically contained in the midbrain/amygdala). Is this spiritual experience [God] consciousness? Is it more than just "ethical" behavior? Perhaps God is all the above.[55]

We all experience a constant toggle back and forth between all the areas of our brain, driven by systems and neurotransmitters further described in Chapter Ten. Even if we are willing to accept our experience of "God" as an ethical, moral encoded conscience, along with higher-learned behavior driven by a belief system, what is the subconscious and how is it explained? Are experiences of intuition just internal messages re-signaling us from parts of the midbrain/hippocampus? The Greeks coined the word *cryptomnesia*, which was the retention of unconscious memory of information that had been learned through normal channels. Neuroscientists now know that previously learned information, which is consciously forgotten, may be stored indefinitely within the "subconscious", and these scientists are beginning to find that area in the brain anatomically.

Furthermore, psychiatrist Carl C. Jung claimed *cryptomnesia* was not only a normal mental process but a necessary one as well. If it were not for this process the human mind would always be cluttered or overloaded with random information. In his study of archetypes, one of the symbols Jung was drawn to was the *Ouroboros,* symbolized by a snake encircled and "eating" or swallowing its own tail (see more on Jung in Chapter Eighteen). The *Ouroboros* is meant to represent that "All is One" (God, Tao), and symbolizes the cyclical nature of the Universe. Our experience of our impulses, whether conscious, unconscious, or on the border between the intuitive memory of either, is all part of this experiential world of One.

Even as we think we have started to get a handle on this world of how our brains work, and how that activity might interface with how we manage our spiritual experiences, we now have also externalized our brains into the world of computers and social networks. Beyond how computers make our lives more expedient, our lives, our memories, and our consciences have become overflowing; the need for batching (clearing our head of information while we sleep) creates even more dependence on an "external brain" and *cryptomnesia.*

Computers and Transitional Objects

Many years ago, two things were happening in my life simultaneously. First, I was married to a computer techie who worked at National Cash Register (NCR)

---

[55] "God as perceived in the concrete world is attributed to the workings of our reptilian brain, whereas God felt as nurturer, an object of affection and love, reflects the emotive system of the mammalian brain, and God as the Word, Logos, is a New Testament portrayal of the divine which is affirmed through the advanced neocortex. Religion in modern culture seeks properly to attribute spiritual meaning to the experience of the physical world, whereas science lays no claim to meaning; it is always agnostic" (McLean, 1990).

and who trouble-shot hardware problems because he'd had some training in hardware systems while in the Navy. Then he learned software programming because his mother finally (under threat) paid for him as an adult to "finish college".

Not really a hardware engineer and not really a software designer, he quickly learned, as he jumped from one start-up company to another, that he could help these two disparate parts of any computer company, particularly a fledgling one, talk (sort of) to each other. Now a full-time trouble-shooter, negotiator, facilitator, inside salesmanship(er), he quickly rose through the ranks of one after another of these many start-up companies in California. My education, as his wife, became one of understanding the complexities of how software works with hardware, and we were "the first family on the block", so to speak, to have a PC in our home.

My interest was less technical than spiritual; what I mean is that even then I could see how computers were becoming an externalization of our brains. I discussed how computers might eventually take over this externalized role in our lives, such as any other similar "spiritual leader/guru". Simultaneously, in addition to my private practice as a psychotherapist, I was working within the foster care system. In my work, I constantly saw signs of how the longstanding developmental theory of transitional objects (think pacifiers, comfort blankets, beers, or any other "substitutes for one's thumb") needed to be updated for needy "children" of every age.

Individuals were now finding satisfaction, distraction, and attachment through visits to video game parlors (this was 1980s, 40 years ago after all!). Soon individuals could play in their home with Game Boys and X boxes bought for children, taken over by their parents, and ultimately available on phones and the computer itself. The perfect format for escapism, computers soon became prayerfully such a source of Higher Power and attachment for many, many people that Apple and other game stores were like sanctuaries where Sanghas of people formed a community of the similarly minded.

In my reading, I came across the most remarkable passage by the author Jane Smiley. In her fictional story, "Moo", one of the characters, Marly's father, gives the following representation of computers in just the kind of description I am trying to convey.

> Computers, he told her, had been designed specifically to forward the progress of secular humanism—"Christians had to count one thing at a time, so they went slow. The secular humanists weren't going to stand for that, no siree. The computer is the atom bomb of secular humanism. You ever seen a computer that acknowledges the Lord? The computer is the greatest false prophet there ever was. I wouldn't touch a computer with a fork" (Smiley, 1995, p. 25).

But by the end of the novel, another character, Tim, has formed and expresses a different opinion about why and how spirituality is experienced and should be expressed.

> The body, the mind, and the spirit don't form a pyramid, they form a circle. Each of them runs into the other two. The body isn't below the mind and the spirit; from one point of view, it's between them. If you reside too much in the

mind, then you get too abstract and cut off from the world. You long for the spiritual life, but you can't get to it, and you fall into despair. The exercise of the senses frees you from abstraction and opens the way to transcendence (ibid, 1995, p. 251).

As much as transcendence may be the action of moving apart from material existence, the use of the computer, even as an "object of attachment", can facilitate the achievement of just such a goal. I support the idea that it is an authentic and acceptable process, if, in whatever way, it aids one in finding the source of their spiritual experience.

CONNECTING is Communicating

How often have we noted that our liturgy has been written in the verse of poetry and hymns, or that great literature strikes a spiritual chord in us regardless of whether references are made to Biblical/religious history or not? Those who feel the spiritual need for expression of their CONNECTION to a God or Higher Power have discovered that the very acts of reading or writing, in other words creative expressions and CONNECTIONS to inner joy, provide the opportunity for inward/outward work on Self-esteem and serenity. In *Kingfishers Catching Fire: Seeing with Poetry's Eyes,* Jane Hirshfield (2000) writes in detail about the passion and perceptual clarity that writing, particularly poetry, can provide the writer.

> We feel something stir, shiver, swim its way into the world when a good poem opens its eyes...to make by words the possibility of a new perceiving...poets "come back to the realm of things for test and confirmation" ...poetry, itself, is an organ of perception, the heat of CONNECTION is in us...Another way to put it: a poem is not the outer event or phenomenon it ostensibly describes, nor is it the feeling or realization it apparently reveals or evokes. A poem is, more complexly, a living fabrication of meaning. A poem's core happiness, then is not its "message" or "meaning", nor is it any simple recording of something outside its own essence. Poetry's particular wisdom and pleasure is its own indwelling experience of an embedded and intertwining being-in-the-world.
>
> Includes the communicative elements of content and craft...writing poems is fundamentally a contemplative practice. Poetry's seeing takes place in the border realm where inner and outer, actual and possible, literal and imaginable, meet. In a poem, everything travels both inward and outward...the mind catches light enabled in the net of things...Consider these three words: apprehend, comprehend, prehensile...to understand is to grasp...A true poem plucks into voice the INTERCONNECTEDNESS of being. In his *Rhetoric,* Aristotle praises what he calls "active metaphor" for the quickening it brings to the reader's mind [emphasis added] (ibid, 2000, p. 9–12).

Art and Spirituality can become an adventure when artistic and spiritual expression is the "Goal-in-Itself", such as journaling, poetry writing, painting, and so forth. Some call this type of spiritual expression pure love. The Diarist—now called euphemistically "blogging"—has always been a pure form of "goal in itself". Samuel Johnson (1709–1784) considered diaries and autobiography the most important form of literature and his works, especially his *Diary* (1765–1784) and *The Vanity of Human Wishes* (1749), have been quoted more than any work other than Shakespeare. He believed in contemplative language, and his use of clear, descriptive imagery created a whole new genre in expressive writing. He believed that a spiritual life was achieved through virtuous action, political soundness, and Christian ethics.

I enjoy *Heron Dance,* a newsletter/diary type of format, visual and written. This labor of love, by Roderick MacIver, was published quarterly online and in print as a combination of philosophical musings, interviews, color-wash arts by his partner Ann O'Shaughnessy, and overall inspirational journalism. Its ongoing print version closed in 2013, but my review of what I received and online blogs still inspire me to go to my own "deeper layer of creativity" almost every time I pick up these issues and blogs, which I'm glad I've saved.

Heron Dance Issue 51 (2007)
Removing the Veil: Exposing your Creative Spirit by Ann E. O'Shaughnessy

Asking these questions enough times, opening myself to the possibility that I was indeed creative, that I did have a gift, led me to a tiny slice of an answer. "Just move one step in the direction of your soul's longing. Do not worry about where it leads. Don't try to imagine the specific form of what you will eventually create; it will come."

(Rod MacIver) "…The gift is your essence revealed. It is just you—the you that is usually obscured by the personality—the ego mind…"

"There is the love pile and the hate pile, the way I look at it, and we've got to try and put as much stuff as we can in the love pile, however we can do that." (Greg Brown, folksinger)

Art becomes an adventure!

Morality, Liturgy, and Religion

We now move onto another example of how the influence of different religious practice, or at least of spiritual influence—forgiveness—provides us a guidepost. Whether through direct actions and words, or through the structured process of liturgy and holding up the examples of the Bible, we have already spent an extensive discussion on morality in Chapter Two (Philosophy).

In the King James Version of the Bible, it states: "And forgive us our debts, as we forgive our debtors." Forgiveness leads to deeper letting go, another gift that we can give one another, an opportunity to let go of the mistakes that tie us to others in negative ways. If we embrace emptiness with every mindful breath, we can reach deeper into the nature of "debt". Therefore, "debts" as used in this terminology can be seen as offenses hiding past failures or mistakes, toward others or toward us. Releasing must be done consistently and regularly to clear our relationships and to become whole and stable again. This process is the very core of the 12-step process and will be detailed in Chapter Sixteen.

Spirituality, of course, has been a fundamental component in the theoretical development of psychology and moral concepts since Plato and Aristotle. Rucker's (1969) Value Continuum theory (see Chapters Fifteen and Twenty-One also) was an attempt to clarify and thus build a schema based on man's search for meaning through his relationship with Self and Other as an expression of his ethics and his experience of Spirituality/God. Much of Rucker's work is grounded in Adler's theory of "man's" basic needs (to belong, to be social, and so forth).

Kohlberg's *Essays on Moral Development* (1981) based most of his study on men and their specific development of reasoning; he neglected to include the type of relational processing at which women excel. Later, Carol Gilligan's work, *In a Different Voice* (1982), also presented something highly significant as it differentiated moral development as girls turn into women from that previously studied primarily in men. It appeared to Gilligan that men focused on their own needs first, commonly using "I" in sentences, whereas women were inclusive and responsive in their communication style and moral development. Women's morals had to do with "needing" others, and "needing" accomplishments to reflect a CONNECTION and community of spirit.

Speaking of needs, as I have mentioned before in Chapter Four, as a therapist herself, my mother wrote her master's thesis on Adler's theory of needs and the view of moral/social implications in society of these needs, somewhat reminiscent of Huxley's earlier theory in *Tomorrow and Tomorrow and Tomorrow* (1952) [see more on Adler in Chapter Thirteen]. In her papers, I found this list of "needs", which I know she often shared with clients, as a way of determining a baseline of their spiritual fitness or character deficits. I would encourage everyone to be aware of whether they are getting these needs met:

- Love
- Aesthetic
- Intellectual
- Practical
- Psychological
- Spiritual
- Humor/fun
- Leadership
- Compassion
- Weightless
- Understanding
- Grace—Animal grace
- Survival—pleasure
- Power for good and evil
- Appreciation—cooperation—energy
- Chemistry effects (intellect/emotions and therefore decisions)

The satisfaction of all these needs might be based on our decisiveness; 12-step programs, certainly, would view the ability to remain sober depends on decisiveness and discipline! The trick to work toward real spiritual growth may be to figure out how to inspire our change process. Once surrender of will and access to Higher Power takes place, then the next step in spiritual fitness may be the decision about how to accept and when to change. Most religions, including the New Age/Alternative types, believe that if one releases ego into life's "flow", a "synchronization of will/imagination/body" will be accomplished, and this process can be helped along by starting with Self-compassion. No act of love toward an Other, no act of *Dharma* or compassion toward an Other, or within a Sangha, can be as strong as the act of Self-compassion first. This belief comes directly from the teachings of all major religions. Then all loving will be relational.

I can now honestly tell the story of my mother's "favorite client". I believe this to be true, not just because she spent the most time with him in her later years as she neared retirement, but as a daughter/colleague, she began to share with me his story as a learning process and for her own support as she was very worried about him. He was depressed and suicidal. He had had several bad marriages and his adult children did not approve of his current wife, whom my mother felt might be inciting these bad feelings for the sake of "bad blood" at the time of inheritance. One son even believed she wanted his father dead, although nothing really pointed to it.

As my mother grew older, and I was lucky to give her two granddaughters, she came to visit my house several thousand miles away from her home in San Antonio, Texas. She and this client continued contact through letters. This letter was in her own effects at death. It is so poignant, particularly given the nature of his depression and lack of spiritual comfort for himself at the time. I choose to include it here.

Friday, 4 October

Dear Harry,
I love quotes on human nature. We humans are a bunch of queer ducks, at the same time such remarkably wonderful ducks, that I never cease to stand in awe of…the least and the most of us! I guess that's why I've always loved my work.

AA certainly knew what they were doing, making the seeking of forgiveness a part of their 12-steps. I hope each day is better than the one before. Even though there may be little mood dips along the way, the direction is up!

My best,
Virginia

When I found this brief note, it particularly touched me because "Harry" did eventually die, apparently by a suicide, albeit a suspicious one. We never really knew what happened; it grieved my mother until the day of her own death. But she had her own deep spiritual life, and she used her faith, even with his loss, to help herself and then go on to help others. One of my mother's favorite sayings was,

"If you tell a man there are 300 billion stars in the universe, he'll believe you. But if you tell him a bench has just been painted, he must touch it to be sure."

It is human nature to test, and even to be oppositional at times. We may look, during those times, as if we are unable to accept responsibility for how our behavior may affect others, and what it is that has been internalized about the whole experience. However, individuals do feel and know, even Narcissists. Perhaps, even Narcissists feel the most deeply.

Foundational Aspects of the Bible

In the 21st century, many individuals rely on some kind of spiritual experience; much evidence exists regarding the evolution of religious practice. But first, I want to back up my survey of the more recent religions by reviewing the cultural lore and religious history in the Bible itself. The first five books of the Old Testament were written specifically to provide Jews history and law. The Hebrew book of *Tanakh* contains: The Holy Scriptures for the Hebrews, including the five books of Moses (*Torah*), the books of the Prophets (*Nev'im*), and the writings (*Ketuvim*). These books were probably handed down verbally, then the subsequent books of the Old Testament were written down in Hebrew, all sometime before 282 BCE. First, they were being translated into Aramaic, and then eventually into Greek, during Ptolemy II (283–246 BCE).

The *Septuagint* was the Greek translation, named for the five books of Moses in the Hebrew Bible that were supposedly translated by 70 different scholars, who all came up with relatively the same meanings. This translation became the original Greek Old Testament, still used today by the Greek Orthodox Church; the Greek Orthodox Church separated from the Holy Roman Catholic church after the Schism of 381 CE. The *Apocrypha* (books written originally in the first four centuries CE and eventually placed between the Old and New Testament) did not form part of the accepted canon after the 6th century CE. They were finally included as an intertestamental book by Martin Luther in his Bible in 1534.

New Testament books were added to the Hebrew, Greek, and Aramaic versions of the origin *Tanakh* (Hebrew Bible) to document the teachings of Jesus and Paul. As mentioned, the original *Tanakh* had been written in Hebrew and eventually translated to Greek during the classical period when there was a high level of literacy. During the time of Constantine, who converted to Christianity in 312 CE, Jerome (382 CE) first used the original codices to translate the whole Bible as it existed at that time, from Greek into Latin, known as the Vulgate (for the common or Vulgar language), even though some felt Jerome "lacked Divine authority". This translation was used to make the beautiful bound books of the Illuminated Period.

Finally, in 1455, Gutenberg perfected easier printing; the demand for Bibles created a wish for translations (into German and for William Tyndale's 1535 well-done translation of the Bible into English). Henry VIII formed his own Anglican Church of England in 1536 after his fight with the Pope in Rome (he wanted a divorce). His daughter Elizabeth I brought about a review of the existing Greek and Latin versions, and finally the existing versions were replaced by James I of England (James VI of Scotland), the King James version (KJV) of the Bible. This translation was the accepted version for study and prayer after 1604 and took Christians well into the 20th century.

Although many of the Apocryphal books have been of doubtful authenticity, they included tales of history and Jewish life, wisdom, and reflections on religious faith and Proverb-like sayings about good behavior and common sense (Davis, 1998). One of the morality tales included was that of the Maccabees battle, the legend upon which the Jewish holiday of Hanukkah is based.

I find two of these Apocryphal books particularly interesting: Esdras (1 and 2), including the Zoroastrian parables from Persia, was rooted in the common Indo-European system that was carried out of the Aral-Caspian steppes into India and Iran, as well as into Europe. "Persian belief was reorganized by the prophet Zoroaster according to a strict dualism of good and evil principles, light and dark, angels and devils. This crisis profoundly affected not only the Persian, but also the subject Hebrew beliefs, and thereby (centuries later) Christianity" (Campbell, 1949, p. 348). These prophesies speak of the "coming of a Messiah".

After Jesus died, many historical events heralded in the Dark Ages as was seen in Chapter Six. Divisions within the early Christian sects, reinforced by both widespread crucifixions and the need for secrecy, influenced the development of one group, known as the Gnostics (180 CE) (Davis, 1998, p. 345). The work of Elaine Pagels (*The Gnostic Gospels*, 1979) suggests that there was a relationship between the texts and Buddhist sources, supporting the belief of some scholars that Jesus may have been influenced by Hindu or Buddhist traditions during his early years and travels. Gnostic texts, known as the *Nag Hammadi*, were found near that city in 1945. Their discovery in an earthenware jar is often confused with the Dead Sea Scrolls found near Qumran (1946–1956). These seven scrolls contained re-copied documents from 200 BCE-68 CE, hidden from the Romans by the Essenes, another Jewish sect. The Scrolls show just how accurate the Old Testament had been (ibid, 1998).

The Gnostic writings were believed to have been written much later than the original Aramaic Bible, at least 2nd century CE. Blended with Eastern spiritual beliefs, as well as Greek and Roman philosophy, in the Book of Thomas, for instance, there is a verification of continued Christian life through the eyes of "a living Jesus". Thomas writes, "the Kingdom of God is inside of you, and it is outside of you. It is, then, a state of transformed consciousness" (Pagels, 1982). Regardless of being excluded from the Bible, as is now accepted, these books have long been seen as holding "secret wisdom" or knowledge about the nature of God, Jesus and even evil. More recent groups, such as the Theosophists of the 19th century, as well as practitioners of Jungian psychology, have found that Gnostic ideology aids in a focus on the question: what was "God's word" really? In the New Testament, God and Jesus were more nurturing than the God of the Old Testament.

Even female leaders were represented and supported. It appears that the Gnostics believed in, and were waiting for, a final battle at Judgment Day, between good and evil, dark and light, and thus had sequestered themselves and the Gnostics writings at Nag Hammadi.

As shown in the review of the history of this period (Chapter Six), there was much enculturation, with influences from lands as far away as China and African empires such as Ethiopia, where Christianity was accepted as early in the 1st century. Some of the early Bible stories were probably "borrowed" from other cultures; Babylon and Egyptian cultures influenced the Exodus story and Proverbs.[56] The authors of many chapters were not just great historical men such as Moses or Solomon; many books of the Bible had more than one author and perhaps as many as five (Davis, 1998). Exchange of trade, behaviors, and the boundaries of personal nationalist ideology were all affected. Because writing it down didn't start until 1000 BCE (David and Solomon period), many biblical stories could have been influenced by the writers up until 400 BCE, when most common copies are dated. The New Testament amendments continued until 90 CE or later.

How does the Bible, or the myths that contributed to its stories, lead to man's attachment to a God that seemed more human or anthropomorphized? "We convey largely unconscious human knowledge by myths and fairy tales, by religious or sacred symbols, by depictions of forms of good and evil" (Hardy, 1990). In addition to the many myths regarding floods, hell, and Gilgamesh, many stories related tangible societal development necessitated by survival: the wheel (6500 BCE), domestication of cattle, and congregation in towns/cities (5000 BCE). By 4500 BCE, animals were put to plows to irrigate, and 3500 BCE was the beginning of the Bronze Age (during which an alphabet and counting arose). The seven-stage pyramid in Babel Tower is dated at 1900 BCE, although there is no mention of pyramids in the Bible. Likewise, Passover is a representation of how the Hebrews were led out of Egypt, but it also originally coincided with barley festival time. The exodus of the Babylonians included up to a million plus people.

For perspective, the Sphinx in Egypt is believed to date from 2550 BCE, while the story of Joseph going to Egypt is believed to be around 1700 BCE. Could Moses have lived during the time of Queen Hatshepsut or even King Tut? But as the movies tell us, if it was Ramses I, we know that it had to be before 1309 BCE because Seti's rule was from 1308–1291 BCE. Ramses II, on the other hand, is known to have built a lot of burial sites (those poor slaves!). His conquests ranged

---

[56]Archeological activity in the land of Canaan has shown just how much Canaan was a bridge between Africa, Asia, and Europe (op cit., 1998, p. 24). The first settlements were as old as 10,000 to 8,000 years ago. As a community with social CONNECTIONS, the Stone Age peoples (the Natufians), practiced burials and other meaningful worship activities. The discovery of "Jericho" reveals it to be older than the Pyramids. The early cultures had originated many Gods, but their religions focused on one group of beliefs with the supreme creator called EL (as later in IsraEL and BethEL). Even after the Hebrews focused these beliefs on EL, the worship of the pantheistic gods continued. Archeology finds altars to Egyptian Goddess *Isis, Astarte/Ishtar* (fertility and war Goddess), and *Ashereh* (consort of *Yahweh*). *Baal*, originating in Syria, probably another "incarnation" of Jupiter, were often included with the seven "deities," *Helios, Seline, Athena, Hermes, Zeus, Hera* and *Genneios*. Remember when Moses came down from Mt. Sinai with the 10 commandments (Exodus 34:28) and found the Hebrews afraid and abandoned; how they had reverted to worshipping the God *Baal* with a Golden calf?

through the territory of Canaan, almost to Turkey. Getting to the Red Sea would not have been that far of a trip.

After reaching Canaan, the Hebrews co-existed with Philistines from 1200–1000 BCE. David won many battles and, as King, passed his power to his son Solomon. David was quite the hero, like Jason of the Gold Fleece or Perseus and Medusa the Gorgon (Davis, 1998). He was a Campbellian (1949) hero, who had to overcome his own *hamartia* to find his true purpose and use his faith in God and in himself. He was the first to pick Jerusalem as "home" and David's son Solomon built a temple there (9th century BCE) during a reunited Judah and Israel. The "Holy of Holies", it supposedly held the Ark of the Covenant, which contained the Commandments.

But after Solomon died, civil war split Canaan into Israel and Judah again, and the ten tribes broke away. Eventually the Assyrians won over northern Israel and "ethnically cleansed" the area by sending many tribes to the Euphrates River area. These "lost tribes of Israel" now lived in Syria and Iraq. One hundred years later, Judah was conquered by Chaldeans as well. During this dispersal, but needing to maintain culture and customs, it is believed that the Jewish book, the *Talmud*, was written for such guidance.

This period is often called the original *Diaspora*. By 587 BCE, looting of the temple and periods of exile to Babylon may have resulted in the Ark of the Covenant being moved when Jerusalem was destroyed by King Nebuchadnezzar II (Some insist it is in the protection of the Ethiopian Christians now). The Aramaic language was more common than Hebrew, but then Greek became the unifying language as the classical Hellenistic period influenced the area.

The Books of the Chronicles I and II are the "Reader's Digest" versions of long periods of biblical history (ibid, 1998), not only of begats and the development of rituals, but also of the concept of the synagogue life, development of Talmudic Scriptures, and Messianic predictions. Much of Jesus' later teachings were written down earlier in these books of the "Law", such as Josiah and Isiah. These admonishments and warnings were important as the *Diaspora* grew, for once in Babylon, many Jews assimilated, and many Jews did not want to return to Israel even if they could, although a second temple was completed there in 516 BCE, during the beginning of the Hellenistic era (330 BCE).

Even those who know little about the Old Testament beyond the first five books of the Jewish *Torah* (Genesis, Exodus, Leviticus, Numbers and Deuteronomy) have probably heard of the Book of Job. While it is generally believed that this book is about how even the righteous must suffer, a more straightforward question might be: Could a faithful person still "believe" if left with nothing? In recent times, books like *When Bad Things Happen to Good People* (Kushner, 1981) challenge this question in depth, but it seems to be the basic notion of CONNECTION in the first place that keeps faith fulfilling. Since we can never fully comprehend God's power and purpose (or the Cosmos), making an amends (repentance/12 steps) is not weakness but strength; it takes surrender and sacrifice to embrace the simplicity of one's original faith and the goals that were created by that primary CONNECTION to one's God or Higher Power.

"An ancient sage is said to have rejoiced at the world's injustice, saying 'Now I can do God's will out of love for Him and not out of self-interest'" (ibid, 1981, p. 40). I can understand that Job's misery came from the fact that we live in an unjust world, from which we cannot expect fairness. There is a God, but He is free of the limitations of justice and righteousness. The answer is that our misfortunes are none of His doing, and so we can turn to Him for help. Our question will not be Job's question "God, why are you doing this to me?" but rather "God, see what is happening to me. Can You help me?" We will turn to God, not to be judged or forgiven, not to be rewarded or punished, but to be strengthened and comforted. There is a moment in lifelong CONNECTING when innocence will be lost, even God's.

Many worshippers believe that in addition to works of the New Testament, the Psalms and Proverbs, found in the Old Testament, are their most important literary adjuncts to faith. Luther called these two books, Psalms and Proverbs, "A Bible in miniature." Most of the books of the New Testament were written between 60 and 110 CE, although, as we discussed earlier, the *Apocrypha*, Gnostic Gospels, Dead Sea Scrolls, and other collection of books have been found which were not previously included in the Gutenberg and King James versions of the Bible.

The immediacy of this chronicling, so soon after Christ's death, was probably based on the high literacy skills of the Roman empire and previous Greek influences. The New Testament was accepted as is by Augustine 400 CE (Athanasius Canon 382 AD). As this version was conceived, the two concepts of a Jesus—the one we follow by "faith" versus a historical Jesus—seemed to sort itself out. This outcome included, for instance, Christmas (Christ's Mass) developing into his birth day holiday out of *Saturnalia* at the time of the Winter's Solstice. In fact, the Jews and Christians did believe in the same "God" for a long time.

No better spiritual summation can be found than in the Sermon on the Mount, (Matthew 5:1 and 5:17). In these Beatitudes in particular, Jesus is quoted as speaking more about a "reward" for righteousness than ever before. This reference to a "heavenly place" was new to the New Testament and not a Hebrew practice as such; righteousness, to the Jews, was its own reward. Jesus gave tools for working toward a better life, reframing Josiah, Psalms and perhaps even a little Buddhism. "The Light of the World cannot be had [Enlightenment], put it on a light stand for others to see; Let your Light Shine [Step 12]."

Right-mindedness and correct vision keep us on a straight course, but making amends helps us to lower worry and regret, God cares for us. "Today's trouble is enough for today. I know what I need to know for this moment" (Matthew 6:34—sounds like mindfulness to me!) "But small is the gate and narrow the road that leads to Life, and only a few find it" (Matthew 7:14). Yes, we should live! Live! Live! to quote Auntie Mame! Finally, Jesus is well known for his use of parables, most of which show that "God desires mercy more than sacrifice" (Davis, 1998, p. 389). Some of the most famous are Parable of the Sower, Parable of the Weeds, Parable of the Mustard Seed, and Parable of the Pearl.

After Jesus' death, several factors influenced the disciples' split in their faith over his teachings. What we could loosely call "Jews for Jesus" continued to maintain their heritage but added his teachings as a belief in his Messianic message. He was a Messiah who had won over a generation with love not war.

Other groups also included gentiles and even Roman citizens who went out on missionary works as far as Alexandria (Book of Acts), where documentation of precious pre-civilization wisdom was held in its great library. It was to these communities that the converted tax collector Paul (nee Saul) sent his famous Epistles. By 64 CE, however, the strength of the new "religion" scared Nero and he began the martyring of Christians in the Coliseum.

It was not until the growth of Imperialism in the Roman empire (Caesar Augustus' way of thinking, organizing, and centralizing) that a romance with the idea of the Christian church began. Gradually the development of a "Church of Rome" turned into the papacy. The development of many sects would grow: those dependent on good deeds and indulgences to serve saints and the Pope (Catholicism), faith over good works (Lutheranism), Spiritualism, Baptism, and even a focus on Revelation and the Second Coming (Baptists). However, what level God was viewed as an authoritarian-type parent figure versus faith-based on an inner personal experience was the most factor important in discriminating among these sects.

Christianity and Islam Expand the CONNECTIONS Between Europe, Africa, and the Middle East

By the time the Byzantine empire came to power (2nd century CE), the acceptance of Christianity was a foregone conclusion under the Roman rule. Another type of dispute among Christian worshippers arose at that time, that of the nature of Jesus. As mentioned, some felt his message had shown his persona to be that of two natures (human and divine), others only accepted one, united, individual existence and nature. Some scholars still see this argument as the core disagreement in modern religion. Just as Buddhists had followed the "Way of Buddha", most Christians followed the "Way of Jesus" regardless of how much of this way was built on myth.

In his book, *The Hero with a Thousand Faces* (1949), Joseph Campbell presented an excellent summary. "Jesus the guide, the way, the vision, and the companion of the return had his disciples as his initiates, not themselves masters of the mystery, yet introduced to the full experience of the paradox of the two worlds in one" (ibid, 1949, p. 230).

The variances in religion became more complicated; in the 7th century CE the teachings of Muhammad, which came to be known as Islam, were spreading quickly. As an Arab religious, social, and political leader, he was seen as prophet and reformer. Not only did his teachings have a united and cohesive nature, but Muhammad preached a worship of, and prayer to, all the prophets that had come before, including Hebrew Patriarchs and Jesus.

However, he added, belief in one God and belief in one Prophet (him) was the best and last basic virtue, even taking precedence over the teachings of Jesus; worship of the one true God would bring true believers to Heaven. In Islam, God is called Allah. Some Islamic rituals, like those formerly proposed by the Jews, made a monotheistic God more accessible (without the complications that would later come within Christianity). Particularly, the pure believers would go straight to heaven if they died in battle for the Cause of Allah. Given the longstanding stresses between the Palestinians and the Judeo-Christians, this teaching only made the pressures more obvious as recently seen in the conflicts of Fall, 2023.

Islam presented a strong set of beliefs, and in the short thirty-eight years from 632 to 670 CE, it spread from Arabia to India to Spain; the Islamic world began to have international influences as well, much as the Greeks and Romans had previously. Islamic believers created changes in medicine, language, numerals and algebra, and paper. By 732 CE, their influence was felt all the way into Gaul (England) but was driven out in the Battle of Tours. This Frankish win, however, can also be seen as somewhat of a loss of cultural opportunity; explaining why, during the Dark Ages, Constantinople was much more cosmopolitan than London!

During the Medieval period, there was 1000 years of papal control over much of Europe and beyond; it would be another 400 years of edicts and demands for payment of "indulgences" before Martin Luther demanded a change in the church's influence on the poverty of the worshippers. The greed of the church powers was proof of Luther's point that a Re-formation was needed, and the Protestants emerged.

By the time of Luther, Europe was ready for a reformation, which was "a revolt against condescension" (Weber, 1989). Luther believed that theology was too distanced from the common man. The Bible could now be read and understood by any literate person—printed in "new" Vulgate versions (not Latin), first in German (Gutenberg Bible) and then even in English. Faith did not have to depend on dogma; Luther called for a change in the manner of the relationship between the priesthood and the parish as well. People could and should relate directly with their God, not only through the priest as intermediary. One's work and daily activity was to God's glory (as underscored later by Calvin's Puritans). Although initially German Lutherans were sober bourgeois (businessmen), overall Protestants were "people of the Book" because now they could read the Bible themselves and felt less ceremonial about the practice of their faith.

Alternative Beliefs

In a previous chapter I discussed the philosophical influence of the Theosophical Movement on many aspects of psychological and holistic movements in the late 1800s. As a theoretical, philosophical and/or spiritual practice, the movement encompassed a full spectrum of attributes on a continuum meant to support alternative religious beliefs. The Theosophical Society was founded, in New York City, by H.P. Blavatsky, Colonel Olcott, William Judge and others, in 1875, in order "to seek Truth". Many of the founders' methods came through spiritualism, study of the occult, and the Kabbalah. There was also interest in Eastern religions, and for some years Blavatsky and Olcott lived in India. The group of followers was further extended to India in 1886.

From their studies, these founders hoped to form a non-sectarian, universal, "brotherhood" of humanity to study religion, philosophy, and science. The three aims of the Theosophical Society were: "a) to be the nucleus of a universal brotherhood, b) to promote the study of Aryan and other Eastern literatures, religions, and sciences; and c) to investigate the unexplained laws of nature and the psychical powers latent in man" (Hardy, 1990, p. 165). Likewise, the "psychosynthesis" (Assagioli, 1980) of concepts such as transcendence (God being experienced as the 'Other') and immanence ('the God within') paralleled those elements found in all mystical religions, where "emphasis on transcendence and dualism (the differentiation of spirit and matter)" become the goal of the aspiring person (Weber, 1989).

A CONNECTION between division and unity within the person would unite lower and higher selves. As such, the Theosophists felt they had to account for the incidence of chaos theory affecting one's life, a concept we will further discuss in Chapter Twelve. Theosophical "principles" are found primarily through a review of the *Mahatma Letters* to A.P. Sinnett, interpreted by Madame Blavatsky and catalogued by A.T. Barker.

Letter 5 outlined a moral dimension of life and the belief in Karma. Karma is the law of cause and effect, the law of reward and punishment, the law of opportunity and the principle of balance, harmony and, as Emerson called it, "compensation". We will return to a discussion of Karma in Chapter Nine when we discuss Buddhism further. Letter 5 explains that the way we think brings on all our actions. We can also change them by our present choices, as well as make the sort of world we want, which is viewed as the power to shape the future. "Karma is limitless potential...Karma is what maintains harmony and balance in all of nature, a point of equilibrium" (Barker, 1886, Letter 5).

The Hindis believed Karma (the law of cause and effect) is the "hand that is dealt" from birth, a fixed destiny, whereas *Dharma* (one's true nature) is more about the moral duty to live out one's Karma as best as possible. This process is a manifestation of their belief about the three "planes of consciousness:" the "subconscious (instinctive and affective thought); the conscious (ideological and reflexive thought); and the superconscious (intuitive thought and the higher truth)" (Hardy, 1990, p. 66). In Letter 5, it is easy to see influences on the psychology of the time (Freud, Jung, Adler, Assagioli). In this Theosophical writing, likewise Theosophists believe in a tension theory, between *Karma* and *Dharma*, as their explanation of CONNECTION: Out of the interplay of those opposite forces—action and reaction, cause and effect—comes a still point, a balance and a harmony in our lives.

The principal ideas of the "Secret Doctrine of God" are spelled out in Letter 10 of the Series written from 1881–1883, that is, the God of theologians as compared to Nothingness and/or Universal Mind. "Humanity's evolution on Earth is part of the overall cosmic evolution, overseen by a hidden spiritual hierarchy, which includes advanced spiritual beings at its highest levels." Blavatsky referred to these "spiritual beings" as Mahatmas. Touches of this theory can be found in the Science Fiction classic, *Stranger in a Strange Land* by R. Heinlein (1961), for those who have either read it or heard of it.

The causes of evil in human behavior and thought are also addressed in Letter 10, as are the words of Buddha on the Four Noble Truths and mankind's suffering. The Way of the Buddha is primarily that of preserving and cultivating "purity of heart", virtue and sincerity. Blavatsky said, as told to Barker, that she had five principal points to make regarding the Secret Doctrine, *Isis Unveiled* (1877).

The ideas in the book are not her invention; on the contrary, they are the accumulated Wisdom of the ages, and all she did was to write them down as she had learned them. They are as follows:

1. The fundamental concept in this Wisdom Tradition is that, underlying all manifestation, there is a single root cause—an absolute Reality, from which matter, consciousness, energy, and law all derive. It is the Unified Field of all existence. [emphasis added]
2. Universes manifest periodically out of that one ultimate Reality. The universe has no original beginning and no imaginable end, but only cyclical comings-into and goings-out-of being.
3. In comparison with the absolute Reality, all manifest universes are 'Maya,' that is, illusions in the sense they are not what they seem to be. All manifestation is temporary, changing, and relative. Only the Source is absolute.
4. Everything in the universe, down to the smallest particle of matter, is conscious. All things are not, of course, conscious in the same way or to the same degree, but everything has some form of consciousness in it.
5. The universe is not an artifact created by a personal maker. Rather it is a complex of matter-energy-consciousness emanated from the ground of all being, the absolute Reality. The whole universe and all things in it are evolving toward a higher state of being (Barker, 1886).

The Science of Mind movement followed shortly thereafter, in 1926, when Emmet Fox (1887–1960) took Theosophy's major tenets and created the practice of "Religious Science". Along with Mary Baker Eddy (founder of The Church of Christ, Scientist), Fox is thought to be one of the greatest influences on religious philosophy in the last one hundred years. He combined his take on "The Sermon on the Mount" with a belief in connecting our Higher Spirit or a Higher Power (HP) as it were, like the Unity Church but different in its specific metaphysical tenets. One of the church's core beliefs is in the power of the mind and its use as an energetic source for change. Science of Mind was seen as something that could be practiced on an individual basis as well as in an organized religious setting.

Alternative Spiritual Practices

It is highly likely that upon reading this heading most individuals thought "New Wave" Spiritualism, Dreamwork or even the practice of Magic, I will discuss those areas and perhaps dispel some of the reader's concerns. New Wave Spirituality is not only an experiential form outside of traditional religion; it is also often associated with Holistic Healing. Herbs, Acupuncture, Yoga or Meditative states are often combined with one's religious practice to produce the spiritual experience, or at least the hope of a healing experience. The priest/guru/mentor effect is often quite strong and a change in lifestyle choices may accompany inclusion in a basic practice group. Diet and nutrition, choice of medical treatment, or even relational situations are often addressed by many of the "alternative" spiritual-based lifestyles.

A more dramatic extension (or attraction) of this initial alternative practice choice may combine spiritual practice with educational classes in such things as dreamwork, alchemic studies, or the awareness of comparative religious studies to broaden the possibility for serenity, hope, and healing. The belief in magic may seem far-fetched even within this context, but the finding of some use of 'magical thinking' in these group members may not be unusual. The causal CONNECTIONS between healthier behavior choices and a renewed belief in oneself can keep one "coming back" when no other use of logic would do. Some may call this superstition, or even a compulsion, but it makes sense to me to fight a negative compulsion with a new, healthier, compulsion, so whatever works is just fine with this therapist!

Probably the most studied type of alternative spirituality is dreamwork. In my extensive studies, the best summary of how to use dream analysis came during a lecture series at First Unitarian Universalist Church of San Diego. On 3/4/11, Jeremy Taylor discussed "Dreams: The Magic Mirror that Never Lies." The major premise of his talk was that all dreams come in the service of health and wholeness, and that if we learn to listen to, and work with, our dreams, we will greatly enhance our view into our inner Selves and strengthen our approach to daily living. On the other hand, nightmares are the way our unconscious tells us to "Wake Up! This is important!"

If we do pay attention, we can interpret the meaning of the archetypal symbol that appears. The symbol is trying to show us a threat and will give us a clue to some survival meanings. Taylor refers to "Darwinian listening" to another's dream, which is a type of interpretation where there is a "picture in my head and my relative understanding is premised upon it. We all project," Taylor maintains, "but just because we project doesn't mean it isn't true." His point is that, even in a group setting, we can listen to others' dreams and get something out of the symbolism; previously unconscious material of another can "clearly be seen for a solution to our own problem." Growth is the reversal of both the projection and over-simplifying the problem. Taylor concludes, "Take responsibility and lose *Maya*. If it were not in me, I wouldn't even notice it in you."

Taylor also referred to others' studies of dreams. Ferenczi (1873–1933) was a member of Freud's inner circle and believed that a dream asks us, "Who it is we are becoming?" Taylor recommends Scott Cunningham for a reading resource about how the divine can come through to us in our *Sacred Sleep* (1992). He calls this "dream incubation," and he points out many questions about how our emotional life is further clarified in our dreams; self-deception may take more energy than one has available; he feels that this experience is the definition of depression. Aging (which is just another name for changing) can bring up feelings of abandonment and betrayal due to unexpected or unwanted differences in prior projections that can also be played out in dream themes. Thus, dreamwork is an all-important source of spiritual information for each of us. All things are sacred: introspective, developmental, and integrative.

A more mainstream form of spirituality expressed in Western countries may be an incorporation of such Eastern religious practices of Yoga/Tai Chi, mindfulness, awareness of *Dharma-Karma*, and most importantly, the function of appropriate breathing for overall well-being.[57] Although originally a secret Yogic

---

[57] In 4-count breathing one find any rectangular object in a room (if you start to notice, there have always been scores of them!) As you look from corner (or side) to corner,

practice related as much to breathing as to certain body positions, yoga has certainly taken off in this country, even if only for the general benefit it has for health because of daily stretching, without the emphasis on the concomitant spiritual practice.

Concepts such as *Dharma* and *Karma* have dovetailed with American values of moral behavior and ethics to create a pseudo-religious fervor for kindheartedness and responsibility toward others throughout our society. Healthy 4-count breathing has become part of the American psyche whether in Yoga centers, delivery rooms or corporate boardrooms.

But of all these "alternative" viewpoints, perhaps it is the three activities of study, meditation and service that best CONNECT these various points of view. Whether it is in practice of 12-Steps, private reflective meditative states, or a collective practice of Buddhism in a Sangha of 300 people—if all three of the components above are not part of one's spiritual actions, then it is likely that the results will be less than fulfilling or grounding. We will continue as willful and unfulfilled as when we started.

Numbing Out is not Inner Work

The 1960s brought the proverbial drug experience; but most people ended up disappointed and moved on. Those who continued beyond recreational use destroyed their ability to CONNECT to anything else (see Chapter Sixteen on addictions). Some turned inward to search for Heaven and a Higher Power.

Although associated with recovering addicts (Alcohol, Drugs, OA, Gambling, SA, and so forth) the concept and methodology of 12-step programs have long since permeated the vernacular of our society—concepts like "HP, Serenity Prayer, One Day at a Time, Let Go, Let God," just to mention a few—give daily solace and a framework for living to almost everyone who has struggled emotionally at one time or another. It is my opinion that the idea of sponsorship greatly influenced the boom in the field of "Coaching" that enabled unlicensed counseling to take place in many specific goal-oriented fields, particularly real estate, sports psychology, and weight loss.

Much of 12-step work is not only about the morality of "giving up" self-destructive behavior (admit powerlessness); it is focused on living a more prayerful life (spiritual fitness) under God's direction (as one has come to understand God on their own personal level of experience). It is also about the real and deep spiritual work, in which one is looking for a way to reach, re-parent, or nurture one's original Self/Inner child. This work, done through inventories and daily meditation, is not that different from other religious practices we have discussed (Catechism and Buddhism comes to mind).

A power-giving tool is often recommended, like daily meditation reading. Food for thought as it were, which is often meant also to stimulate deeper

---

one breathes: 1. Takes in a deep breathe; 2. Holds it for a few seconds; 3. Let it go; and 4. Rests. The fourth step is the most important, for many of us think mindful breathing is more like a three count; breathe in, hold, exhale. It is those few resting seconds between exhaling and re-inhaling that will make all the difference in dealing with fight/flight/freeze or any other causes of stress.

exploration through journaling. Entries in one's journal can be shared with a sponsor or for personal use only, but the idea of finding oneself, being kind to oneself, and forgiving oneself is pervasive. Here is an example:

Meditation on Loving Kindness

Feel yourself surrounded by warmth and patience.
Allow any anger you feel to dissolve into warmth and patience.
With each breath, breathe in warmth.
Feel the warmth nourishing you,
Breathe in patience. Feel the spaciousness that patience creates within.
Allow your warmth and patience to give rise to forgiveness.

The power of forgiveness is so great.
Release yourself from any tension and stiffness you may feel inside, that is caused by resentment.
Let go of the pride that holds onto resentment.
Allow the pain of old hurts to dissipate.

Reflect on someone who has caused you pain—intentionally or unintentionally—and send them forgiveness.
Forgive them as best you can.
Allow the forgiveness to grow.
Allow the resentment to dissipate.

For those whom you have caused pain, ask for their forgiveness.
Let go of the judgments on yourself and on others and allow understanding to replace it.

Forgive yourself for any pain and suffering you have contributed to.
Gently open your heart.
Give yourself time.
Wish yourself well.
Let your heart fill with loving kindness.

To yourself:
May I be healed.
May I be at peace.
May I be happy.
May I be free from suffering, pain, and anger—free from fear—hiding and doubt.
May I be filled with love and with joy.

Then toward someone for whom you feel great love:
May you be free from suffering.
May you be free of anger—jealousy, tension, and fear.
May the painfulness in your heart fall away.
May you be happy.

May your joy increase.
May you be at peace.

Again, to yourself:
Let your love expand.
Let your loving kindness radiate out to all beings.
Feel the light of this love.

May all beings be happy.
May all beings know peace.
May all beings be free of pain, suffering and fear.
May we all have joy in our hearts.
May all our hearts be open.
May we all be healed by the power of love and caring for ourselves and for each other.

Take a step with me that we may all know peace.
Take a step with me that we may all be healed by the power of love.
Take a step with me that we may all be free from suffering.

– Anonymous

An AA practice only? Sound like a Buddhist meditational prompt? No, this was given to me, listed as being by "Anonymous", as a Jewish prayer, but yes could easily have been taken as a Buddhist one if a person didn't know the difference (note references to suffering). All three practices (12-step, Judaic Studies, and Buddhism) are focused on present-mindedness and self-care, healthy psychological concepts.

Resolve to find thyself; and to know that he who finds himself, loses his misery.
—Matthew Arnold (from September 10th—12 step *Just for Today* AA daily meditation book)

Once access to Higher Power and surrender of Will takes place, then the next step in spiritual experience may be the decision when to accept and when to change. Most religions, including the New Age/Alternative types, believe that if one releases life's "flow", a "synchronization [CONNECTION] of will/imagination/body" will be accomplished, and this process can be helped along by starting with self-compassion. No act of love toward an Other, no act of *Dharma* or compassion toward an Other, or within a Sangha, can be as strong as the act of self-compassion first.[58] This belief comes directly from the teachings of

---

[58] When Leonardo da Vinci was working on his painting "The Last Supper," he became angry at a certain man. Losing his temper, he lashed the other fellow with bitter words and threats. Returning to his canvas he attempted to work on the face of Jesus but was unable to do so. He was so upset he could not compose himself for the painstaking work. Finally, he put down his tools and sought out the man and asked his forgiveness.

all major religions. Then all loving will be relational and CONNECTED. The question is: How do we treat the world on each side of our skin, which we falsely see as a boundary? I can be no more loving to Other than I have been to my Self.

How we develop our character attributes has the eventual outcome of affecting the psychodynamic process of how we function in our families and other groups. Simple rules we grow up with affect those early skeletons of morality and ego development, the principal ideas of the "Secret Doctrine of God" spelled out. Mom/parent use such concepts to create a moral baseline in her child, we can see in full detail how each fundamental building block is added to the development of a whole, hopefully healthy, functioning ego (one' UFT). Whether it is from our original parenting, a therapeutic process, or Self-analysis at home, it is through an understanding of our flaws as well as our dreams, our needs as well as our wants, that we are better able to find a *New Design for Living* (Holmes, 1959).

As mentioned early in this chapter, the *Yin* and *Yang* of life presents us a binary breakdown of each choice, each influence in our life, and each experience of underlying instinctual urge. Tibetans believe that in the balance of the *Yin* and *Yang* of Taoism, revealing what was obscured and obscuring what was revealed, it will provide the continuity for us to experience initial quiescence or emptiness, the ultimate experience in Buddhist meditation. We advance in self-understanding through this balanced approach to life's challenges. As shown more fully in the next chapter, many influenced by Buddhism believe that the secret to success and happiness comes from doing things "a little at a time", step by step. Balanced with giving to others rather than yearning for love for Self only, Buddhist practice can only improve outcomes for everyone all the way around. A deeper understanding of these processes will come from searching through specific Eastern philosophies and patterns.

The man accepted his apology and Leonardo was able to return to his workshop and finish painting the face of Jesus (as quoted by V. Haradon).

Chapter Nine
Buddhism and the Practice of Mindfulness

"The Sun Still Shines Behind the Clouds."
– Buddhist saying

"Upon finding the boat of human now, cross the great river of suffering. O fool, there is no time for sleep, for this boat is hard to catch again."
– Shantideva, quoted by Jones, 2003

Attachment blocks our growth and flames our fear. Each of us has an "It"—that which brings us sorrow, suffering or creates an obstacle to that which we believe we must have, as in "I have to..." Eastern religions vary in approach and admittedly I will be discussing Buddhism (Zen or Tibetan) and Taoism, more than Hinduism or Confucianism. However, the principle of dealing with our "have to's" is the same as the desire and need which results in the attachment to an "It". To release our "It" through surrender, and to find inner serenity and outer CONNECTIONS, we need to figure out how the "It" controls us, soothes us, or allows us to hide. Then we can release "It" through surrender and find inner serenity and healthy outer CONNECTIONS. Buddhism and Taoism use healthy philosophical and spiritual methods to reach that goal.

We often use a dualistic view to look at the Self and other parts of our personality. We ask ourselves: Does a dualistic view create a separate Self? Does this view split off part of the original Self, or does it allow an inner dialogue with existing Self? "Obstacles are really roadmaps to making something meaningful out of one's suffering…Karma, concepts, and emotional patterns are only temporarily preventing our consciousness from unfolding its enlightened state" (Tulku Thubten, 2006, p. 99). If we look at the dualism within an experience of suffering (one of the Four Noble Truths of Buddhism), then the dialogue between anger and calm or between confusion and understanding can be balanced. We can be guided on our journey to gain the understanding needed, which our unconscious may have already known but has blocked.

One may have heard that Buddhists "practice" a lot.[59] Whether it is in a three-year retreat, organized prayers with their community (sangha), a three-minute morning meditation, or compassionate kindness toward another, a practicing Buddhist has no "goal" other than an immediate and authentic experience. Even Charles Darwin believed that humans are uniquely dependent on "kindness" for survival.

---

[59] "True, real, and sincere human beings result from 'practice;' to produce a harvest, for the sake of the process itself (spiritual maturing/'steadfast cultivation of the total self—somatic, psychological and spiritual—striving, questioning, and ultimately becoming attuned to the working of the Buddha') …overcome wavering motivation, loss of confidence, increase in doubt and fear of failure" (Taitetus Unno, 2002, p. 5).

The Buddhist tradition, and in the language within which it was developed, had its own terms, important concepts, and processes. Those most familiar to Westerners probably are *Karma*, *Dharma*, *sangha*, and perhaps *satori* (awakening). I will be using some terms new to readers in this chapter but will limit new vocabulary to those words which add depth and meaning to my discussion. One of those, for instance, is the word "*metta*", which describes the opening of the heart and developing the qualities of "loving kindness and compassion" toward all living beings. Beginner's mind is "open, flexible and kind" according to Pema Chodron, who goes on to explain that the more we practice being open and mindful, the more we can become "softer" and more kind, which ultimately leads to healing and obtaining *bodhichitta* transformation.

As we become more compassionate, with ourselves and with others, we learn how to better shield ourselves from pain and open ourselves to love. This way of being allows us to alleviate some of the suffering common to all. "*Siddha*" is the skillful means or creative practices to reach enlightenment, and "*Samadhi*" refers to the training in meditation, mindfulness and awareness which assist in one's daily practice. "*Sila*" shows us an honest, ethical, and honest life path, and finally "*prajna*" is our deep intuitive insight, nonconceptual knowledge of things as they are. Chodron says we should "train as warriors" in the practices of "meditation, loving kindness, compassion, joy and equanimity" (Chodron, 2001, p. 6).

During meditation practice, "heart-essence" remains the same—the goal is to awaken to your own true nature and to manifest wisdom and compassion toward the world (authentically). We must practice through "agreeable and unagreeable" situations; this is the way of really accepting the meaning of impermanence. "Always practice on that which provokes resentment" (ibid, 2001, p. 32). We cannot run away from insecurity; rather we embrace it as part of our imperfect selves and then we learn to detach from it.

Although many of the terms and practices that I will refer to in this chapter are based on Tibetan Buddhism, another approach is Zen Buddhism, most often found in the Pacific Rim (China first, then Japan, Korea, and Vietnam). Zen Buddhism uses a different system: sangha practice is in silence—*Zazen*—but the meditation is specifically directed. Zen Buddhist practices I have attended have had brief discussions by a lama or leader, presenting an idea or "*koan*" upon which to meditate throughout the rest of the hour.

Koan study is considered a form of religious study, whereas not all Buddhist studies are looked at in that way. The *zazen* meditational form has as its aim the bringing of the student to "direct, intuitive realization of Reality" using the *koan's* meditation on "words or concepts". Proficiency in *zazen* is the basic ground of *koan* study, experienced during the meditational period, where a state of enlightened consciousness is achieved, that which has been the goal of the *koan* to illuminate all along. *Koans* do not represent private opinions (Koan, *Wikipedia*, 3/6/2015).

In Zen Buddhism, this form of meditational revelation is passed down from master to student. Zen wisdom is not founded on Scripture; it is concerned with the Absolute Mind. Historically, masters told students statements of formulas which would bring a deeper understanding of their *koan;* there was a criterion of attainment and examination for mastery of knowledge. Some students of Zen Buddhism believe *zazen* without *koan* study leads to passivity and lifelessness. Practice alone cannot be a true dynamic experience of *satori*, or awakening (ibid, 2006).

The Zen Buddhist way, therefore, is to use practice to achieve "*kensho*"— seeing into one's own nature, looking at one's own mind to find Buddha. The three essential requirements for the study of Zen Buddhism include: 1) A great root of faith; 2) A great ball of doubt; and 3) A great tenacity of purpose. The path of the Four Noble Truths teaches followers of Buddhism and Taoism that reason, an ultimate and absolute principle, can help with daily practice and obtaining *kensho* (the first *satori*), but it is surrendering to the path of suffering and uncertainty (Heisenberg again!) that allows, in Tibetan Buddhism, a feeling of release from daily struggles.

In addition to having a group, or sangha, it is important to practice with a good teacher. Once a new practitioner becomes centered in spiritual maturing and cultivation of an understood Self, there may be a regressive sense of loneliness because of being without the "I" that one is used to, especially if there has been a long period of grandiosity. This shift in focus influences somatic, psychological, and spiritual growth, affecting both motivation and confidence simultaneously. These fears are exactly where a CONNECTION to the sangha and a good teacher comes in.

In psychology, we refer to the need that comes from the "I" as attachment. It is a healthy need that begins in very early childhood. However, one of the basic tenets of Buddhism is "non-attachment". If one's attachment to a sangha and a guru is important to practice than how do we define "non-attachment?" Is it being completely unbounded in the now or having such good personal identity and inner boundaries (my favorite word!) that the flow toward non-attachment comes easier?

Sometimes living in the now comes from a radical experience of losing the now or taking away meaning altogether. A patient of mine, who was suicidal for years and had several minor attempts of his own, was called as a rescuer to the scene of a serious suicide attempt of someone very dear to him. She had gotten drunk (strike one), taken a multitude of pills (strike two), and then gotten into a warm tub and slit her wrists (strike three). Setting aside for a moment the always interesting question of why, if she was so serious, did she make a 'goodbye' phone call--my own reflection and learning process was greatest from his retelling of the story the next day in therapy and the effect on him of finding her with literally 30 minutes to live (according later to the ER doctor). He talked about the externalized visual of her near-death as like looking at himself and what it would have been like if someone had found him.

The shock of the experience and her re-embracing life was gratifying to everyone, and of course he was the hero of the day, but it took him several months to completely get over the recognition that he had tried suicide himself before and had nearly given up his own life so many times. We spent a lot of time in therapy discussing how clear it now was, because he was alive, just what being alive meant, what he had in each day that could appear meaningless but really wasn't.

Yes, life was impermanent, he had faced that straight on; he was ultimately in charge of every day and the decision to stay alive.

Most importantly, what really mattered was that his death, and the drama of it, was not a focus anymore. His focus became making a life that could matter. This indeed is a lesson in experiential enlightenment. "Let us learn to part with things gladly; the good side of parting is that it loosens the mind's hold on transient objects and makes one aware of the illusion of possession" (*Bhagavad Gita*).

I like to think that he learned each moment needs to be followed, looking ahead to a constant challenge but also a constant miracle of change. In Buddhism, *prajna* is the wisdom of no self, no subjectivity, no grasping; therefore, one can appreciate each lesson learned. Wisdom is the joyful result of finding out how uncomplicated our minds really are. Seeing clearly does not have to be complicated. It's not so much good versus bad, virtue versus non-virtue, it's about the grasping. "Why am I like this now" (*Sheng Yen*, 2006, p. 16).

Referred to also as the "prismatic display", I work with my clients on seeing many sides of themselves rather than getting caught up in self-demeaning practices by an obsession about just one aspect or character defect. The most important life skill I can teach them is learning to be kind to themselves.

In December 2001, I spent a month in India studying with the Dalai Lama. When not in initiation sessions or practicing, I often ventured outside of the monastery into the southern Indian countryside and several small nearby villages/towns. One day I was approached by a Tibetan girl, who subsequently befriended me for life. Gakey Dolma taught me many lessons, the greatest of which was to slow down. She initially asked me if I needed a guide/translator, and I thought it might not only be a good idea but an interesting cultural experience (perhaps I envisioned myself as Phileas Fogg with a Cantinflas at my side?). Anyway, off we went quite often on adventures I would never have had on my own.

As a middle-aged American woman, I would try to control each day in my inevitable Western compulsive way: "the bus isn't here yet (really just a golf cart), how will we get to town and back by lunch?"; "Yes, I want to buy the *sari* (Indian wrap dress), but how do I know how much I should really pay and should it be less if I get more than one as presents for other people?"; and on and on. To each of these situations she replied, "Step by step…Step by step."

And gradually she taught me, rather than the Ph.D., bright and happy American, teaching her anything. She taught me to just slow down, and it will all turn out OK. Step by step…if one were to consciously think of each step as difficult or an obstacle, life would be even more daunting—(is this how depressed people feel?) whereas if you "just hit the ball" (as golfers practice), you can just move on. This is the action of the Self of compassion and wisdom. Gakey taught me if you think you must hurry, it is probably better to wait anyway, have a cup of tea and see what might happen instead, and if you slip, try again. Overall, Buddhists call this having a position of "attitude over action".[60]

---

[60] "According to Dzongar Ganyand Khyantse, consequence is karma, gathered by consciousness…Any so-called good action that is not based on these four views (motivation, action, love tolerance and a wish for others to be happy) is merely

Suffering, and the relief from suffering, is a major tenet of Buddhism. With an attitude of non-attachment—"emptiness"—one can turn toward other sources of happiness and stay away from the sources of suffering. Some people call this "flow", moving within the energy, the social demands, and the familial structure around them. Many symbols are designed to represent something re-creating itself, an example of which is the *Ouroboros* (snake head to tail—a circle or endless cycle). I want to highlight the importance of such an interdependence and CONNECTION in the Tao circle figure as well, which represents more than dualistically shown.

Buddhist Concepts

The term *Karma* is used to describe the "consequence" of actions. Such terms have many viewpoints and may indeed be meant to be nebulous in definition to further the conscious study and pursuit of inner acceptance. "*Karma* [and other such concepts] is only temporarily preventing our consciousness from unfolding its enlightened state" (Tulku Thubten, 2006, p. 99).

One of the most basic concepts in Buddhism is that of "taking refuge". Like turning over our will in Step 3 of AA, turning over our will and taking this opportunity for peace and sanctuary through the practice of Buddhism will enable a centered focus for our prior chaotic and "unmanageable" lives and point us toward the life of a *boddhisattva*. The process also highlights another important set of Buddhist concepts, that of the three Jewels.

Taking refuge in Buddha is the first jewel; the second jewel is following the *Dharma*, the inner truth from taking refuge which leads to selflessness and "suchness;" and inclusion in and solace with the Sangha is the third jewel (community/CONNECTIVITY to the principles and practice).[61] Healthy CONNECTIONS are part of the eightfold path, which supports the validity of maintaining values regardless of the human condition, including a recognition that suffering and even greed can be overcome.

---

righteousness, designed to feed and support the ego…Your constant need to <u>solve</u> problems becomes like an addiction. How many problems have you solved only to watch others arise? If you are happy with this cycle, then you have no reason to complain. But when you see that you will never come to the end of problems solving, that is the beginning of the search for inner truth…As we begin to understand the four views, we don't necessarily discard things; we begin instead to change our attitude toward them, thereby changing their value. <u>Freedom</u> is what we call wisdom…Through contemplation, we begin to apply awareness to every situation and moment" [emphasis added] (Jones, 2003, p. 35).

[61] I ask myself: Holding on equals to suffer, but does thought always equal clinging? "*Sangha* is a community of individuals who come together to…know what to accept and what to reject in order to go forward on [a] path…cultivate the qualities to take us forward…[rather than] reacting with aggression, confusion or attachment (3 poisons)…We're so busy trying to avoid what we don't want, and to ignore our suffering that we don't even know what we're doing…we begin to see how we use anger to maintain the solidarity of 'me', even if it means hurting others" (if I get angry I get what I want) (Sakyong Miphram Ripoche 2002, p. 15).

This practice of taking refuge is reinforced by an understanding of the Four Noble Truths and study of certain Sutras. The First Noble Truth is that suffering comes from living, the logical process of birth, aging, and death. The Second Noble Truth is that the source of the suffering is craving (attachment), a very narrow perspective after all. It is also ignorance of the true nature of things. The Third Noble Truth is that the cessation of suffering is possible. The Fourth Noble Truth lays out the path of practice to obtaining that cessation.

These practices represent what the Buddha stated in his teachings as the core unifying principles, which have lasted for 2500 years, and which are set out in the Sutras, as mentioned. For instance, according to Nyogen Senzaki (1876–1958), the Diamond Sutra "teaches us egoless-ness, formlessness, non-dwelling and non-attainment." It teaches us about release of attachment and attainment, as well as liberating self from reaction and resentment to perception.

The Sutras

How did the Diamond Sutra get its name? The Buddha is quoted as calling this teaching "The Diamond of Transcendent Wisdom, [because] its teaching will cut like a diamond blade through world illusion to illuminate what is real and everlasting" (Chodron, 1999). Jewel imagery features strongly in Buddhism. At the center of the faith are the three jewels, or triple-jewel as mentioned: the Buddha (taking refuge), his teaching (the Dharma), and the spiritual community (the Sangha). "The six transcendent actions, or paramitas, are: generosity, discipline, patience, exertion, meditation, and *prajna* or the wisdom that cuts through suffering…The key is to relax and see things as they are" (ibid, 1999, p. 100).

In another, The Heart Sutra, the chant is:
Gone, gone, gone over (Gate, gate, paragate)
Gone beyond (Parasamgate)
Awakened Mind (Bodhi)
Homage! (Svaha)

This sutra is ultimately about awareness, then release, then non-attachment regarding outcomes.

This entire process dilutes suffering, which can remediate the endless cycle of suffering, also providing the "knowing" (wisdom) that can serve as "the antidote to the distress, anger and suffering we find in ourselves and the world around us."

The goal is to "nurture the confidence, courage, and compassion so needed." Compassion is "the path of cultivating human bravery and kindheartedness" (Chodron, 1996, p. 15). Awareness of the cycle of our suffering is inevitable but can be turned toward the action of detachment.[62] There are always triggers for

---

[62] "We don't realize that if we try to gain something, we had better be ready to lose it. A simple truth: all the pleasure the world can offer eventually turns to pain. And trying to hold on to pleasure only causes more pain. Our existence is marked by impermanence, selflessness, and suffering. When we contemplate this insight in our morning meditation, we're letting the truth about existence penetrate our

panic, but if we learn to slow down and live with acceptance of discouraging moments, and the thoughts that arise in our minds at those times, we can protect ourselves from the alternative, often seen in addictive behaviors.

Current practitioners of Buddhism, such as Ezra Bayda (2003), teach the method of meditational breathing, three breaths at a time, to remind us that it is easier to "go with" an experience than to always resist it. I use this method with my patients who may have addictive issues as well as underlying anxiety. This pause for self-awareness is very helpful to focus on the solution more than every detail of the initial experience.

Some readers might be now wondering how the practice of Buddhism is any different from the rational use of scientific data and logical conclusions about daily experience? Even Einstein taught us everything is relative! However, where science has founded itself in mathematics, Eastern philosophers remain grounded in the additional original formats of logic, rhetoric, debate, and contextual reasoning. In this way, this spiritual practice of acceptance is not unlike that of Heisenberg's theory of uncertainty.

Because we live in a non-scientific world, our daily experiences become our truth through the relative personal and emotional influences we encounter. This internalizing process is dependent upon paying attention, using consciousness wisely what Buddhists call "being awake". What does it mean to be awake? How would your life change if you genuinely accepted yourself? To be genuine is the real challenge. When we look at ourselves, others, and the world, we do not actually see these things as they are, but rather through the lens of our individual hopes, fear, and dreams.

As described psychologically by the theory of Karen Horney (1937), the coming from within "toward" the Other balances with the "moving away" from the Other in a set of "paired opposites" (Tao) between the human need for attachment and need for freedom (non-attachment).

In summary, meditation requires turning over of the will and a use of logic and guided practice based on philosophical reasoning, which provides the practitioner a sense of CONNECTEDNESS and comfort, even if not total *nirvana*. The basic concepts, Three Jewels, Four Noble Truths, and using the Sutras in practice, sustains the goal of clarity through non-thought and blessings through actions toward others.

An Attempt at Synthesis

Because we can practice spirituality with or without complete understanding, we need at least a bit of peace and serenity in our larger continuum of stress and responsibility. How can we relate this spirituality to our real world? Marcus Aurelius spoke of "bearing the unbearable" as the state of forbearance and

---

being…Competition doesn't enable us to accomplish what we want. It just adds the grind of trying to gain by outdoing somebody else…We are only as good as we are and forcing another person down doesn't make us any better. Be self-victorious over ignorance, desire, and self-infatuation. Be mindful of what you practice" (Sakyong Mipham Ripoche, 2005, pp. 13–14).

mindfulness, which gives us a "knowing" calmness even toward ourselves out of the stillness of reflection and a resultant compassion when life is confrontive and irrational.

Once I was experiencing a great sorrow over the loss of a loved man. Although I had sent him away because it was "the right thing to do", part of me, of course, wished for him to pursue me or at least check up on me. When I didn't hear from him for three weeks, I was bemoaning the situation to my brother, a wise philosopher/scholar who has greatly mentored me over the years. My brother clarified with me that I had in effect sent him away, for his own good and with a specific "no contact" boundary for a certain amount of time. "Has that time passed?" he asked.
"No, but I'm miserable!"
"Well," he replied, "seems like he's actually the kind of man I'd be proud to have for my sister."
"Why!" I wailed, "he hasn't called!"
"Exactly. Purity of Intent. You don't see much of that anymore…" They were both leading me toward a very specific truth: to heal oneself one has already recognized what is needed to be healed in the other, and in the CONNECTION, to provide a unity in spirit, purpose, and purity. Staying "right there" or "in the now" requires quite a lot of trust because one is no longer holding on to something wished for—doing that is often the source of most anxiety.

Of course, it may seem counterintuitive to make a case for anxiety being the result of letting go rather than the more common view of its source being "holding on, or a need for control", such as in OCD, hoarding, and needy and possessive relationships. It is more likely that the source of anxiety-created addictions, obsessions, attachments to loved ones, or all the above, are grounded in the developmentally unresolved need for a secure bond. Common everyday experiences of anxious abandonment or phobic responses, comes frequently from the common vigilance of the highly sensitive person (HSP), experienced as acute sensitivity in responses to mental, physical, or emotional responses to external stimuli.

Descartes ("I think, therefore I am") wanted us to believe that our "truth" can only be defined and guided by our experiences. This paradigm may not shift far from the original tenets of Buddhism that the mind is reality. Regardless of which methodology one accepts, scientific or spiritual, reality will be disclosed through the discovery of what inspires you (fills you with the urge to be creative or with the "breath of spirit")!

Aspiration is positioning ourselves to do something. Before we do something, there's a thought process involved: Most of the time we're trying to figure out a problem based on our attachment…Our mother who gives us unconditional love. She nurtures and supports us and takes care of us when we are weak…Even the person who's got our number has done something good for us—maybe just by passing the salt… every encounter becomes an opportunity for us to practice repaying their kindness. Mahayana school [of Buddhism] calls this the 'great activity,' this attitude is so vast it's difficult to imagine. If we had this attitude even for a moment, we'd begin to see that everyone we meet has helped us, directly or indirectly, and we would want to repay his or her kindness. By taking this attitude in working with others, we could experience our lives in a completely different way (Sakyong Mipham Rinpoche, 2007, p. 15).

Sylvia Boorstein (2009) calls this experience temporality: It does not need to be sad; it is just true. "You are making it sad by your commentary about it." We are all running a constant commentary or "crawl" in our head, trying to control our emotions and our reactions rather than gain the "gratitude blessing" of just experiencing that temporality described by Sakyong Mipham Rinpoche in the quote above. It is true that often when we give up control things may fall apart or feel unbearable, but if we practice letting go (non-attachment), we will be able to also experience a new sense of clarity (Chodron, 1996). Sylvia Boorstein says we should wake up each day with "a Thanksgiving for having been kept alive and sustained until this moment" (Boorstein, 2009).

In psychotherapy, we also call this practice the "attitude of gratitude" and sometimes a therapist gives some homework "assignment" of writing one's gratitude list daily to help ground one in the experience of temporality. Unfortunately, some of us take the act of soothing our anxiety to another extreme—denial and avoidance. The Shadow side of our Tao follows a binary system (good/bad, which can lead to splitting) where the Bisociation point can also result in a type of mourning for the loss of our better selves (Koestler, 1964). Lorraine Filipek writes beautifully about an experience of that Bisociation point:

> As I and others embarked on our careers and life paths, we entered the first stage of mourning for our loss-numbness and emotional denial. We lived without thought or feeling for that half of us that we had given up (or else we compartmentalized the two halves so that they wouldn't interfere with each other) …We entered the second stage of mourning—emotional awareness. This stage brought with it anxiety, anger, protect, guilt, a very upset gut…Because it lacked something, either choice brought with it a strong desire to convince others—and especially ourselves—that ours was the right choice (Filipek, 2003, pp. 24–27).

At the Bisociation point of pain and suffering versus self-care and gratitude, we also come to realize how much we are fighting basic biological impulses. We are not genetically conditioned to be "happy;" the better term might be "safe". The concept of "fight/flight/freeze" will be discussed at length in Chapter Ten, however it is important with this discussion of suffering to remember that we humans are conditioned to seek pleasure and to avoid pain, no matter how inevitable pain might be. Over half of our brain (frontal lobe) is taken up with inhibitory CONNECTIONS (Moss, 2020).

When one begins to practice meditation, or even mindfulness during every day ordinary experiences, being one with our experience, it is usually the initial need for concentration that one finds the hardest to achieve. One does not control experiences, but rather learns how to be with them. This skill leads to the all-important achievement of acceptance, of experience, of concentrating on the moment, of accepting life on life's terms. If "mindfulness is the ground, refraining is the path" (Chodron, 1999, p. 33).

Of course, there are many ways in which to meditate, including: *Metta*, which focuses on an attitude of compassion and cultivation of benevolence toward others; *Tonglen*, which focuses on the specific suffering of others during the period of meditation, and *Anapanasati*, which focuses specifically on the breathing technique and the effects of mindfulness throughout the body. In my practice, most clients come in looking for symptom relief, not for a radical reordering of their consciousness, but I am frequently able to teach these techniques to clients as a "gateway to symptom reduction" (Siegel, 2011).

Conditioning the Mind

Changes in our evolving nature may come from the unfortunate as well as from the pleasant. It is all enlightening. Because of the scientific way in which the mind works (input/output), as noted earlier, we respond through our perceptions, experiences, values, historical references, and spiritual "humanity" (UFT). We are conditioned mammals after all. Traleg Kyabgon Rinpoche (2003) wrote about the "conditioned nature of mind" and the stirrings of Buddha nature, stating that unfortunately that which we must heed and respond to may come from misfortune, grief, disquiet, or unhappiness.

During grief, for instance, we practice acceptance and contentment by avoiding unnecessary activity, quelling desire, and not seeking out disruptive or agitating interactions with others simply for the purpose of distraction. In using these Buddhist practices to condition the mind, one decides to use wholesome and virtuous dispositional properties instead of unwholesome states of mind and habit patterns.

How do we relate these Buddhist concepts, centuries old, to more recent findings about how the brain evolved? Dan Siegel's work on the "Wise Heart and the Mindful Brain" (2007), as well as "Relational Meditation" by Bruce Crapuchettes and Francine Crapuchettes Beuvoir (2011), reveals findings about how we as humans interact with each other, even while still trying to maintain our own core centers of calm or serenity.

> The human brain evolved as an "anticipation machine", constantly scanning the environment for threats in order to increase the probability of survival. Early humans were able to relax only when the environment looked and felt extremely safe. The challenge for many of us in our 21st century lifestyles is that we've forgotten—or never learned—how to turn off this dangerous scanning process. Mindfulness practice can provide a way of doing just that. When you focus on the breath coming in, you can safely anticipate that the next breath will go out, which will be followed by "in", and the "out". Breathing is predictable, so life at that moment becomes predictable and safe....
>
> Turning away from the "outside" world and focusing "in-close" on breathing calms the limbic system, the brain's alarm center, creating a sense of sanctuary

in the middle of the storm...This area is critical to the kind of emotional states and behaviors that all therapists strive to evoke with their clients: attuned communication, emotional balance, fear modulation, response flexibility, insight, empathy, body regulation, moral judgment, and intuition (Siegel, D., 2007, p. 44).

Siegel referred to these integrative states of mind as "The Magic Nine". An example of one brain mechanism that appears central to experiencing The Magic Nine is the firing of the much-celebrated mirror neurons, which can make us "intuit" what other people are about to do. More about these experiences in the next chapter.

At this point one might be thinking of the therapeutic process as an example of "mental conditioning". Therapy's most valuable asset may be the therapeutic nature of unconditional support, but it is really the listening, the ability to mirror and validate that heals. One specific conceptual framework newly on the scene is "Imago Relationship Therapy". It nicely combines the tenets of historical relational-based psychotherapy with meditational concepts. Instead of a couple focusing on the in-and-out of their own breath, however, they concentrate on each other's breath and, during the dialogue, while engaged in a formalized process of mutually mirroring each other, they are creating safety by engaging in predictable behaviors: mirror, validate, and empathize.

The goal of the process is to shift a couple from an angry, mutually reactive stance to a calm, accepting, listening one. Being the receiver, learning to mirror (to feel safer) what the other is saying in a neutral and accepting manner, and learning to validate ("I follow what you said. Your perspective is important and valuable to me, and you make sense") and emphasize possibly activates the same areas of the brain, the prefrontal cortex, as mindful meditation does [emphasis added] (Crapuchettes and Crapuchettes, 2011, p. 45).

Generally known as the empathetic response, Buddhism also includes this common process of mirroring in its definition of compassion. Interestingly, we now know that empathy and mirroring are measured on brain scans as activating the same areas of the brain as mindful meditation, in the prefrontal cortex. Unfortunately, this area also allows us humans to process, and sometimes thinking can get in the way!

The Process of Buddhist Practice

The focus of this chapter up until now has been on the theory and descriptors of how Buddhism can guide and influence our daily lives. Now it is time to move on to the how of daily practice. I practice what is called Awareness Practice = Now Practice. I point out to my patients that those who are depressed are generally focused on, or even stuck in, the past. Those who are anxious, vigilant, and needing to control themselves and others are generally focused on, or stuck in, thinking about the future. Therefore, for a path to serenity, the logical conclusion is to focus on the immediate present through meditation/mindful awareness practice.

"Spilling something and making a mess can be a signal that we are too concerned about time and all the things we [feel we] have to do. Developing the skill to recognize that we are distracted and to return the mind to awareness of the present moment enables us to appreciate our self in all activities" (Bell, T., 2011, p. 70).

When we rest in "presence awareness", we embody a kind of poise of being in which we are present to our inter-CONNECTEDNESS with all of life, and our consciousness can rest in its own pristine and unobscured nature. This experience is truly "mindfulness" at its best, showing us how spirituality in the Buddhist tradition allows us to experience insights on many levels. I also practice *Qigong,* a traditional Chinese practice, which uses the "field awareness" of an energetic centerline, CONNECTING the three dynamic centers of the body—head, heart, and Hara (belly)—to open the "spinal pulse;" the results are like the way acupuncture opens the flow of blood in the meridians of the body.

So why don't we all meditate or pray or at least have a non-addictive way to dispel anxiety?

Quite apart from the semi-magical (but true) explanation that one's ego is threatened by meditation and therefore puts up resistance to doing it, there is the feeling, known to all who try it, that one does not meditate very well. The actual experience of it does not compare well to one's imagination of what meditation is supposed to be, nor to descriptions—meant to be supportive—that one might read in a book…One feels a failure at it, and who needs more failure? To continue for years to practice, and to glean the undeniable benefits of meditation—among them mindfulness, empathy, self-knowledge, insight, flexibility, and humility, as well as the occasional entrance into refined absorptions—one needs to come to terms with the feeling of failing (Baker, 2011, pp. 79–81).

The statement above addresses what someone called, "dharma combat"; and what Baker calls the "sticky balance of gratitude and arrogance and irritation and pride" (ibid, 2011). Speaking of ego, perhaps it is inevitable that once the Self is made aware of itself, at 16–18 months of age, (noted experientially), the development of ego and ego defenses are soon to follow. This developmental stage becomes "my this" and "my that" as anyone with a 2-year-old knows.

Integration

"Whatever is beautiful, even though it may be given to one particular person, helps the world. Thus, if we love another person with pure love, that love goes to the root of things where all are one, and thus we help the whole. Everything that is true is released into the flow of things where it affects all life, the whole force of evolution." This statement is how the Theosophical Society describes Western philosophy as it blends with Eastern religion to help create a more powerful point of view.[63]

---

[63] "The test of being a religious person lies in the widening of goodwill and love for others—irrespective of religious affiliations—and a diminution of the individual self

Dialectical Behavioral Therapy (DBT), a newer and very useful form of therapy for dealing with boundary and personality issues, explains that there are essentially three states of mind/consciousness. Perhaps this Westernized version of a classic Buddhist concept is easier to grasp: Reasonable Mind (cool, rationally, and intellectually evaluating evidence/facts in a situation); Emotional Mind (hot, reactive, and impulsive state of consciousness); and Wise Mind (which balances these two).

The Buddhist world addresses these states of mind, for instance, Francisco Varela, in a *Shambhala Sun* article (September 2004) entitled "Intimate Distances". He breaks down the selves into two types: "The 'Experience Self,' which is continuous identity (congruency), and 'Grounded Self' which is just the world as visited by immunologists." Varela continues: "Our feeling of existence is doubly rooted: in the basic sentience of our bodies and in the lived dimension of our experience." The factor which defines being alive is the activity of being a part of: "He was part of, not separate from, what he could live with, not just control" (Varela, 2004, pp. 42, 50).

Buddhism teaches us to avoid symptoms of clinging to Self and ego, whether through body or mind, and to displace destructive emotions with a different focus. Ego is just our opinions, nothing more permanent than that. Buddhists view existence on the following three levels: physical existence (outer), perceptual existence (inner), and selflessness (core). We achieve, through daily practice, a CONNECTION with the root of emotion (mindfulness of the body) which leads to attachment, as well as a state of calmness which is *shamatha*, and awareness through emptiness which is *shunyata* or basic openness (Jones, 2003). "Resonating", that is a unity of the biophysical with the spiritual, reflects how much the body is experiencing in the now.

Jones reminds us to ask the following meditation questions: "What is the worst thing of the whole problem? What is the situation wanting now? What is in the way of everything being fine?" [in other words, focusing is waiting for the answers] (ibid, 2004, p. 61).

---

and its narrow preoccupations. 'Of all the arts that exist, living demands the highest quality of intelligence and is the most exacting. The experience of living is ultimately the experience of a nature in ourselves, which shows itself as beauty, as love, as truth.' We speak about 'my consciousness,' 'your consciousness,' but these are differences that we make in our ignorance. For fundamentally life is one and consciousness is one, even though it is divided, as we think, into a part that belongs to me and anther that belongs to someone else. Thus, I am identified with India, with Hinduism, with my family, with the experiences of my childhood and boyhood. This consciousness identifies itself with all these things and calls itself mine. But suppose it is able to give up this identification, to detach itself from India, from Hinduism, from the traditions with which it has been CONNECTED, then it is just consciousness; then it will realize that although modified by the identifications which limit it, consciousness is fundamentally the same in all. This is a matter for personal knowledge and experience; you can know it for yourself, but first you have to cease to identify yourself with so many things. From that standpoint, truth, whether given to one, to many, or to the whole world, produces the same effect" [emphasis added] (Theosophical Society in America pamphlet).

Let us take a moment to synthesize/summarize. We are moving toward a state of non-duality, a unified theory and CONNECTION (think of the Tao as One). An experiential response to an original need state, a drive to understand "cognitively" the unexplainable, to know what cannot be verbalized, such as the unraveling of a *koan* or the AHA! moment of intuition, can contribute to our sense of actualization. Therefore, I believe the universe, uni-cosm exists, where a quantum point of I/Thou experience meets and passes into a wave I/Me experience which can be embraced. In this state of non-duality, one realizes in two senses: by cognitively understanding the *koan* and by making actual becoming an instance of non-duality oneself.

The moment [point] of asking the question is eternal. The movement [wave] into embodiment happens as this realization informs how you go about answering your life question [using quantum terms] (Hori, 2003, p. 65). Within the "cognitive" system by which we judge our environment and ourselves, there continues to be the need to explain how emotions lie beyond logic yet sometimes show up in the cross-sectioning of any "logical" argument. Some might call this experience God, feeling the experience needs an explanation/name.

Beingness Without a Head

A jewel beyond all price—it's the *vajra* sword cuts out the 'head' to make 'no head.'

– *On Having No Head,* (Harding, 2002)

Douglas Harding has written this excellent, if a bit obscure, book about having realization through separation from the experience and ownership of one's body as "the center of one's universe", so to speak. OK, so are we unified yet? (No little one, we're not there yet, for there is no there, there). In fact, if we read Harding (2002) carefully, we may be convinced we even have no head! I am going to give a detailed summary here, asking forgiveness for the inadequacy of my skill in comparison with the brilliance of the author, but if the title of the book puts one off, a bit of it resides here in the next few pages, and more importantly may prompt the reader to pursue further study of the original source.

Because our bodies are "the meeting place [unification] of psychology, physical science, philosophy and religion, it creates in us an awareness beyond words. Often, insight derives from images more than it does from reasoning" [emphasis added] (Harding. 2002, p. 14). Harding bases much of his premise on the concept of *Anatta*: no self (no permanent, individual self). He quotes Meister Eckhart (1260–1327): "The less of self there is, the more there is of Self," as well as Ludwig Wittgenstein (1890–1951): "To one who knows nothing, it is clearly revealed."

Harding goes on to propose a methodology by which one can see into one's true Nature. To see one's "headlessness" is to experience an upsurge of creativity, rising energy and confidence, a new and childlike spontaneity and playfulness, and above all a lightness (as if one were not so much gone with the wind as the wind itself). "The aspects of things that are most important for us are hidden because of their simplicity and familiarity" (ibid, 2002, p. 15).

Right speech, for instance, requires us to ask three questions: "Is it true, Is it kind? Is it helpful?" Having achieved this skill, the purpose of "headlessness" is to encourage true self-reliance, which Emerson (1803–1882) also pointed out. When Harding writes directly about his self-taught experience, it is amazing and inspiring to discover how deep and profound the outcome can be. What I believe Harding has portrayed here is the idea of Self-CONNECTION, in the first-person singular, present tense, that which we have been traveling toward in building our developmental UFT.

> I was utterly free of 'me,' unstained by any observer…Look who's here instead of imagine who's here, instead of take everybody else's word for who's here. As a very young child I didn't recognize myself in the glass, and neither do I now, when for a moment I regain my lost innocence…my real Self here…ageless, measureless, lucid and altogether immaculate Void…wildly paradoxical, affront to science, common sense tidied up somewhat…It is only when this terminus is reached, and the molecules and atoms and particles of these brain cells are affected, that I see you or anything else [emphasis added] (Harding, 2002, p. 38).

We may now ask about how such a concept would work within the world of the Other. For Harding, the experience of the Other is simply an opportunity to know another piece of extended Self. Therefore, the question that one can ask, when mirrored by another's experience of them is: "What is it really like where I am, now?"

Unification of Internal and External – The Archetypal Way

Although we will talk more at length about archetypes and the symbols they represent in the chapter on Jung (Chapter Eighteen), the influence of such concepts is clear throughout the reading of Harding's little book. For the author, perception does not necessarily make something real. Everything "there", no matter how large or small, is equal, especially as it comes to show him "that I am nothing here".

Of course, such a belief system would provide one the freedom from limitations and the stresses of judgment. "How much the Void currently includes and excludes is unimportant, for I see that it remains infinitely empty and infinitely big regardless of the scope or importance of the finite objects it's taking care of. It makes no real difference whether it's dissolving my head (as when I look down) or my human body (as when I look out) or my Earth-body (as when, out-of-doors, I look up) or my Universe body (as when I close my eyes)" (ibid, 2002, p. 57). [I think this was my favorite passage from the whole book.] Whereas in psychopathology, disappearance/abandonment means annihilation, under the concept of No-Head, absence of CONNECTION means no fear. Harding has an opinion on fear as well.

It seems that, from an early age, our learned view of ourselves, from outside, begins to overshadow, to superimpose itself upon, and eventually to blot out, our original view of ourselves from inside. Greedy, resentful, alienated, frightened, defeated, tired, solemn, phony, uncreative, unloving, crazy ("delusion-based suffering")—these are strong but familiar words in our description of dealing with daily life. Use of them results in a creation of egocentrism as well. Harding believes the antidote is "in-seeing", or as he also calls it "zero-centricity", without a central point of ego function. Ego in this case meaning false selfhood, limited ends, and an attempt at power over others.

The process of Harding's awareness practice, of knowing one's "head" versus "no head", becomes its own meditational process. This practice becomes a form of stress reduction, particularly for the face (eyes, mouth, and neck), but can it also change one's center of gravity, according to Hardy, lowering it and centering and shifting breathing to a deeper place, both physical and metaphysically. From this process often comes an increase in creativity, spontaneity, and "childlike lightness".

Pursuit of Well-Being

One's concept of Self can also be viewed collaboratively whereby both philosophical and psychological theories enable a path to spiritual enlightenment even if we do not reach all the way to "losing our heads". Perhaps we are best convinced of the progress in our quest when it brings us pleasure. But is it a pursuit of pleasure or the search for release from suffering? Mental suffering is often catalyzed by environmental and social influences, and presumably always has neural correlates (Ryff, C.D., and Singer, 1998).

On the other hand, positive psychology (Seligman, 1975) and other theories maintain that "Satisfaction is less a matter of getting what you want than wanting what you have (Wallace and Shapiro, 2006, p. 691). Happiness that has "vanished" is/was merely "on loan" anyway. As we go through maturational stages, satisfaction comes from developing signature strengths of our own (Seligman, 2004). Although we may at times feel isolated and confused, we do not need to change; in our training to be more balanced, we may not always find joy, but we find contentment."

Considered both a philosophical and psychological theory, the collaborative work of B. Allan Wallace was the bridge between religious studies and psychology. He brought to the forefront the realization of spiritual liberation and enlightenment found in Buddhism; he shared with us his view of its goal: mental well-being. Even the 14th Dalai Lama himself has stated in *The Art of Happiness* (1998), "The very motion of our life is toward happiness." He would also agree that "grasping objective things and events," believed to be the true sources of happiness, produces a wide range of psychological problems. On the contrary, Buddhism believes that freeing the mind of afflictive tendencies and obscuration can result in realizing one's fullest potential in terms of wisdom, compassion, and creativity.

People may derive enjoyment from sensual pleasures, such as attractive visual images, sounds, aromas, tastes, and tactile sensations, but as soon as they lose touch with these stimuli, the resultant pleasure fades. The acquisition of material goods, financial security, power, and fame may lead to happiness, but it too is transient. All such pleasures are contingent on stimuli, either from the environment, from interactions with other people, or from various kinds of physical and mental activity. But when those stimuli cease, the associated pleasure wanes (Ricard, 2007).

Tolman (1951) called this "latent learning", in that stimulus-response reinforcement could take place without the overt behavioral reinforcement factors, but rather as influenced by the expectations of the recipient, sometimes referred to as the "little e", found between a stimulus and response. Tolman's proof was strongly based on Gestalt psychology and the theories that autonomic responses could be triggered solely by the environment (UFT training), rather than only when reinforced by specific and planned behavioral factors. We frequently call these factors "triggers;" focus on holistic ideas also contributed to the humanistic movement in psychology during the 1960s.

The Buddha and his Affirmations

The history of Buddhist thought starts with the life and teachings of Siddhartha Gautama, an Indian prince (560–480 BCE), who found enlightenment while in retreat from his world of privilege by sitting under a Bodhi tree until all that seemed contradictory and confusing became clear and simplified to him (we call this process enlightenment). Trust me, I've sat under that tree, chanting with Tibetan monks, and it does seem like things are simpler and more clarified the longer one stays there.

Buddhism practice spread to China and Japan, assimilating its basic tenets with those of their cultural beliefs. Zen Buddhism, particular to Japan, focuses on the use of mindfulness while meditating, which had been an original tenet of the Tibetan Theravada Buddhist tradition. During the 1960s, the writings of Fromm, Watts, and Suzuki brought these Eastern beliefs and practices to the West.

In her book, *The Wise Woman Who Talked Back to God* (2005), Bonnie Myotai Treace comments, "All of me is dancing in spite of myself!" [emphasis added] This comment reflects her enthusiasm about how she experiences the outcome of her life choices and the influences of the other women around her. She is deeply aware of what she has "inherited;" that is, "in spite" of herself, she finds herself as a spiritual, loving and trusting person. But trust for others starts first with trust for ourselves and it is the use of Buddhist practice that has allowed her to reach a state of mind which can also function without support of others if necessary.

Intimacy comes from finding your own assurance and your own joy first. In *The Little Prince* (Antoine de Saint-Exupery, 1943), we find that the ability to love so largely and to take care of others comes from the realization that giving is intimacy, found both through mysticism and courage. "You become responsible, forever, for what you have tamed." I strongly recommend that one finds his/her own personal reminders of absolute sufficiency or independence of character; therefore, the "purity of intent" I discussed earlier.

Of course, purity of intent is not just about sitting or waiting. In American culture, it may have to be also about effort or self-discipline. Right action, right thought, right morals…these are all concepts readily expected in a practice where each moment also counts for something. Suzuki Roshi (1904–1971) is quoted as telling this story: "He was asked 'Roshi, what's the most important thing?' And he answered, 'to find out what's the most important thing.'"

From these experiences we are free to develop compassion. For instance, Wayne Dyer's philosophy (*10 Secrets for Success and Inner Peace*, 2001) is based on Buddhist and Vedantic concepts. Dyer presents these concepts in more contemporary terms. If we worry, we could also tell ourselves, as Dyer maintains, that basically, "no one knows enough to be a pessimist." Therefore, we consider everything with an open mind, and without judgment. Dyer's version of Buddhist non-attachment is to point out the "in no way can this really be…" kind of thinking and to block the "If I can't do/have, then…" thinking.

Instead, Dyer believes we should put "I can be happy regardless…" thinking in place, which creates an affirmation despite my fear or other's opinions. Affirmations help me thrive because I am focusing on my own core beliefs, in the moment. From there the Self learns to grow and can give itself esteem. Because you cannot give away what you don't have, the law of attraction would teach one to focus on what you must give—therefore, "take the inventory of what you have to give."

Dyer addresses how we can tap into universal creativity. We all need to listen to our creative Selves. One way that we can access our creative Selves is through taking the time, often through silence or even meditative periods, to find the inner core of originality. Dyer calls this finding the One (*Tao*) that is indivisible. I call it Bisociation, following Salk's lead (1983). In other words, black and white thinking—where we have fused the dichotomies, resulting in a silence that cannot be divided. Another example would be Thoreau and Emerson's transcendentalism, where they believed in embracing the indivisible. Here are some of Dyer's mottos:

You cannot solve a problem with the same problem that created it [I love this]. "Rewrite your agreement with reality." Take your own inventory and admit that you are wrong. It just did not work.

Treat yourself as if you already were what you'd like to become.

Treasure your divinity, don't dismiss your own thoughts and moments of genius. It's from there the Self learns to grow and can give itself esteem which can become your own—to be connected to your source.

Wisdom is avoiding all thoughts which weaken you—Shame shifts disempowering thoughts—neutral thoughts are more empowering—love and spiritual consciousness is the most empowering (Dyer, 2001).

CONNECTING the Inner and Outer Experiences

There are more than just the outer-related issues in the life changes that Buddhism brings; for instance, what of the inner-driven life and the search for an essence at our very core? Like Harding, Blake Bazel talks about a pervasive need many of us feel to "plan" much of our lives. Much of our low-level dis-CONNECT with Self is really lack of understanding of Self, of having neglected our Selves, and/or our not having taken the time for solitude, which is needed to "know" us better. From this ongoing adventure of self-knowledge comes both authenticity and an awareness of our "core essence".

Buddhists talk about *nirvana*, which is neither a place nor a mental state. It is the experience of no afflictions, destruction of desire and ignorance (Dyer, 2001). Of course, the problem of low Self-esteem is huge in our society. When I first studied Buddhism, we were taught to practice compassion for Self. This practice was the normal beginning from which we changed our behavior toward others.

A question arises, however: Does compassion for others, and especially for Self, really result in Self-esteem? When the Dalai Lama first heard of the Western concept of Self-esteem, he had to have it translated for him several times before he understood the idea that people, especially in America, had such problems with self-loathing. There is not even a word for that concept in Tibetan. He does not believe that one should use comforts to subdue mental suffering, but rather look to a compassionate attitude, toward Self and others, to lead to being content and to practicing self-discipline (Dalai Lama, 2001).

Spending all your time and energy pursuing material comforts means you will eventually continue to suffer anyway; instead pursue devotion, compassion, and the ability to forgive. These attributes help us to develop care and a sense of purpose. The Dalai Lama's goal for humanity is that we continue to grow until death so we can develop our minds infinitely and there will be no limitation. Ultimately, "it is better to forgive than to spoil your peace of mind with ill feelings" (ibid, 2001).

Compassion Internalized and Self-Esteem

A well-known expert in the field of compassion research is Kristin Neff (2011) at the University of Texas. Her concepts and findings are quoted by many other researchers, including those "hardcore" scientists who are just beginning to see a relationship between mindfulness and other types of human behavior. Neff recognized that there was a relationship between problems of Self-esteem and the absence of self-compassion (ibid, 2011). Her definition of self-compassion has three parts: understanding, shared experience, and awareness or mindfulness. Her theory is found through her Compassion practices—8-week Mindful Self-Compassion course. It includes an awareness of how much the mind creates suffering for itself.

Neff writes that individuals are trapped in "self-critical patter", and that using her techniques with psychological clients takes finesse because it is "counterproductive to push clients too quickly into uncomfortable, destabilizing waters; [the helper must] establish safety before either uncovering repressed memories or moving toward disavowed feelings. [On the other hand] …loving kindness and self-compassion practices can help move people toward safety." In my practice, I have found that most new clients initially seek symptom relief and acceptance, even if they are having a hard time accepting themselves and their underlying shame experiences. Neff's system is a great way to teach these techniques to clients as a "gateway to symptom reduction" (ibid, 2011, pp. 27, 49).

Neff also writes about the individual's need for an inner-directed voice. "Most people's internal dialogue is actually quite harsh…The self-kindness part requires reframing your dialogue so that you are kind and supportive...The second component involves framing your personal experience in light of a shared human experience. When something goes awry—a common emotional reaction is 'Why me?'" Without external grounding or an inner-directed sense of Self, individuals will become isolated, anxious, and depressed, especially when things in their life are going badly.

The opposite of that victim mentality is recognizing that we all experience imperfection and suffering. When you're compassionate toward yourself, it is the beginning of an ability to feel. Something more positive. This awareness is at the root of the Buddhist practice of *Tonglen*, as I have mentioned, which is taking on the suffering of others for the overall good and relief of their suffering. It is sending and receiving wishes for healing from a "noble heart" with the goal of using compassion to achieve healing. "Love may be happiness alone, but it is far greater if one can rejoice in the happiness of many. For spiritual love becomes greater in the individual if it is common to all. It does not decrease when it is shared, for its fruit is to be found unique and undivided in every individual" (Hannah, 1981, p. 121).

The third element of self-compassion centers on awareness/mindfulness. One is able to curb self-criticism because mindfulness requires that you see things as they truly are rather than being a victim who manifests unhealthy self-pity (Weir, 2011b). More about Neff's concepts and organization can be found at www.self-compassion.org.

Another author who works with Self-esteem, Laurie Meyers (2007), defines mindfulness as "being aware of whatever is most salient and dominant in your field of awareness, your thoughts, feelings and sensations in the present moment" (ibid, 2007, p. 32).[64] Meyers position is that for people who choose psychotherapy to aid their mindfulness practice and to increase self-esteem, the therapist should not focus on what the patient is not accepting. Treatment needs to shift from decreasing anxiety toward increasing acceptance.

Spiritual guidance is part of the sanctuary and refuge needed to begin the hard work of facing Self and the possible shame of past traumas. Ultimately Buddhism proposes that one accept this concept: that freedom and understanding are innate in each of us but take a bit of practice to achieve. Development of the simultaneous qualities of relaxation, attentional stability, and vividness affects mental and physical health.[65]

---

[64] "Let us begin again with a clear definition of mindfulness. Mindfulness is sustained, voluntary attention continuously focused on a familiar object, without forgetfulness or distraction. Meta-attention: the ability to monitor the state of the mind, swiftly recognizing whether one's attention has succumbed to either excitation or laxity..." (Wallace and Shapiro, 2006, pp. 695–701).

[65] Sometimes mindfulness is seen as being at odds with current cognitive theories. The goal of mindful practice is to change one's relationship to thoughts rather than changing the content of the thoughts themselves, whereas cognitive therapy emphasizes the latter. The meditator, therefore, develops a metacognitive state of

Outcomes and Benefits

Once a sense of selflessness is gained and kept in balance through practices of compassion and good self-care/esteem, what new insights are available to us about our spirituality? Speaking about how meditation can help us deal with inexactitude or the afflictions of our daily experience, Richard Schwartz (2011) discusses whether one should approach and accept pain as an illustration of Dharma? Fear and/or pain can be seen as an opportunity to focus on what we need to change in our lives. Sometimes we can access answers, and those mediate a whole host of long-term influences on our attitudes and behavior.

> A personal quandary in psychotherapy, as well as in spirituality, is whether the goal is to help people come to accept the inevitable pain of the human condition with more equanimity or to actually transform and heal the pain, shame, or terror, so that it's no longer a problem. Are we seeking acceptance or transformation, passive observation or engaged action, a stronger connection to the here and now or an understanding of the past? (ibid, 2011, p. 35).

In my work with clients, I often engage their awareness of the "voices inside their head", which are the residual representations of parts of their original family system. From this perspective it somehow seems easier to observe the Self—to acknowledge that one may have abandoned or sought to improve one's initial Self is more difficult. I added another method to my previous view of dealing with "our many selves" (O'Connor, 1971), using the ideas from Internal Family Systems (IFS). Schwartz designed his own type of psychotherapy whereby all the "voices" are structured into a literal "internal" system of dialogue with those early childhood feelings which have been "exiled".

Talking to the "family"/people inside your head could be productive or destructive; for instance, could suicidality be a part of some "internal" voice trying to help or hurt them? Other therapists have referred to this process as dealing with the "demons", "inner work", or "transformational work", IFS' exiles. We will define more of these systems in Chapter Sixteen. The point is that, as therapist/listener, I am trying to access the information in any way I can, whether the inner voices are felt to be friend or foe, and to respond to the "voice" with compassion, following that moment up with lessons in self-compassion. "It's possible to go beyond simply witnessing our inner world to actually entering it, in this mindful state, and interacting with the parts of our psyches with the same kind of loving attunements that create secure attachments between parents and children, or between therapists and clients" (op cit., 2011, p. 37).

Tim Desmond (2012) presented an excellent example of using the Buddhist approach of "*metta*" meditation, one that cultivates compassion and love. In the process of psychotherapy with one client, he was able to reach the Self-critical part, the one with low Self-esteem, by first creating an image that inspired a feeling

---

detached awareness of thoughts prior to engaging in any evaluation or intent to change their content.

of "love, compassion and warmth" (the client's one-year-old niece), which could then be internalized to comfort the critical self-talk. Starting with "May you be happy. May you be healthy. May you be safe"—the experience of unselfish love was transferred internally to "May I be happy, May I be healthy, May I be safe."

This process created a feeling of "acceptance and support", which offered the internal critic a purpose that was not all negative but instead was perhaps purposeful and/or even protective. The client was able to find out how his inner critic (exile) was trying to help him. This discovery could not have been made if it were not for the initial process of using compassion and acceptance of whatever outcome the questioning and listening process might bring to the forefront during the meditation period. Thus, acceptance leads to compassion, and modern psychotherapeutic treatments have become adept at including these skills. Mindfulness as a concept has been found to be useful to treatment as it has become popular and integrated into current psychological training.

Communication Through Mindfulness

Some of us love to communicate. We organize our day or even our careers around the idea of it. Others of us are shy and would prefer almost any other human activity to a prolonged or detailed act of verbal communication with another. Most of these differences are hard-wired and are defined as a reflection of your temperament, yours uniquely from birth. Your temperament is then reinforced through the development-sequencing of parent-child interactions and other environmental cues (UFT's mutuality).

Compassion practice makes us less egocentric and easier to live with. First, we have practiced compassion for ourselves, then we have mirrored the skill of using compassion toward others. In her review of a book by former astronaut Edgar Mitchell (*The Way of an Explorer,* 1996), Dora Lora wrote about Joseph Campbell's two types of acts of relating to others, seen by him as perhaps even "heroic acts".

> Joseph Campbell, in *The Hero's Journey*, describes two types of heroic acts—a physical act in which the individual gives his or her life in sacrifice for others, and a spiritual act, in which the hero returns to share an extraordinary experience, and thus deeply benefits the community. The moral objective is the same: "saving or redeeming" others with an act or idea. The result of all heroic acts, notes Campbell, is 'transformation of consciousness' (Lora, 2003, p. 19).

Buddhists say the solution is to "reflect like clear water" because energy is precious and is not to be wasted on angry actions. When I discuss an expression of anger with my clients, they frequently admit the initial experience only lasts a few seconds, and yet they continue to feel shame and to avoid any kind of acceptance that their anger is a natural human emotion. I think that what lasts longer is our ego-driven memory of the factors involved and our investment in the outcome (attachment).

This investment can make the experience of anger last longer and certainly "the fight" can continue long into the night, as many of us know! Some of us experience what is called "Achilles" anger or "sustained rage". Aristotle said, "he who cannot be angry when he should at whom he should, and how much he should, is a dolt." Buddhist practitioners may experience shame or anger, but they are on a path to the Bodhidharma Self-nature that is inconceivably wondrous.

In addition to different kinds of anger, there are the different things we do with anger. Some of us suppress it, some of us act it out, and some of us disguise it as something else. We have exiled these feelings/memories of traumas. "Some of us get very angry, even at ourselves, and some of us haven't the vaguest idea that we are even angry" (Schwartz, 2011, p. 79). I believe, however, that underneath the emotion which drives the expression of anger, is the emotion of fear, of which there are many types, including fear of annihilation, fear of being rejected, fear of shame of our anger, need to deny our fear because it does not fit our image. We can still hope, however, that we will rise above these binding experiences.

Rather than becoming frustrated by our inability to rid ourselves of these shortcomings, we can notice that our interdependence with all life also brings us kindness and joy, unconditionally. If we chant, *'Namu Amida Butsu'* (I am one with Infinite Light and Life), it leads us to admission into the Pure Land because of the steadfastness of our faith (wisdom and compassion). We can release a life force of negativity simply by letting go of our shame and denial. The question remains: can there be anger that does not come from an ego-driven Self, anger that is not defensive or based on the activity/delusion of separation?

I have noticed something more and more obvious, and therefore curious to me over my years attending Buddhist functions. As in any group, when one analyzes group process, there seems to be an assortment of "types". For instance, there are the serious practitioners of Buddhism itself, reverent, serene, and almost distant in their depth of spiritual security to an egoless experience. There are also many people who appear sincere and earnest to learn, to serve the guru and to advance for the sake of the religious/spiritual principles or even "rules" if you will.

Obviously, there are the newbies and/or people who only come a few times or intermittently (for holidays) and their interest seems pretty much experiential. But it is a final group that most bears further discussion in their clear presentation of distress, displaced need for attachment, and a real sense of using the spiritual practice as a form of psychological treatment.

If this type of individual were interviewed, they would probably present enough symptoms of Depression, Anxiety, PTSD, or all the above to benefit from Mindfulness training. That fact isn't my concern. It is the experience of people whose boundaries are insufficient for age-appropriate functioning with whom I'm concerned. Because they are having trouble letting go in their personal lives or do not have sufficient boundaries to protect their ego needs, expecting the experience of Buddhist practice or the strength of the bonds/attachment to the Sangha to aid in their Self-discovery can be an "iffy" proposition. Still, they may be more resistant than they know or want to acknowledge.

All this effort on their part can still be disrupted by stress, illness, fear, or holding on versus the awareness of impermanence that Buddhism teaches, which may bring them some solace. Once impermanence becomes part of our awareness, compassion and courage in our actions follow. We learn that abundant life is natural and that we don't need an intermediary to find peace.

The most important question Buddhist practitioners can ask themselves is: what am I going to do about___ (fill in the blank), not "why did this happen?" Buddhism teaches healthy coping skills in a perhaps less threatening environment than a therapy office and can be a starting point for healing. Contrary to the potential negativity stated in the above section, practice of Buddhism can encourage use of the right brain and creative skills for going beyond the ego.

When anxious individuals put their inner turmoil "out there", they are using what is called "projective identification" to lighten their own load and to find something outside of themselves to identify with and CONNECT to. I suggest we make it our mission to differentiate between projective identification and our experience of the world as it really is. This is the true work of the "warrior!" A Navy Seal friend of mine always says, "Strong mental!" but I believe life is also about tough mind and tender heart. It is the Ego which labels the "I's" in our communication, it is the Self which experiences and responds out of emotional/learned schemas and cares for the needs of the "me". Learning to differentiate between these two types of responses can help teach focused awareness.

Suffering

The first of the Four Noble Truths is that we all suffer—therefore neither guru nor therapist promises "relief" per se. Rather, the healer presents a method to adapt to the present trauma and the future uncertainty that is coming, including facing one's own mortality.[66] Pema Chodron (1996) often writes about suffering. "You can't get away from suffering. That's the good news. For at the core of your most painful experiences you will find the seeds of your awakening… Step by Step, toward a full realization of your true strength—the strength that can come only through embracing the reality of your own experience" [emphasis added] (Chodron, 1996, p. 40).

The stories we tell ourselves to defend against pain often turn into bad habit triggers (conditioned responses); Pema Chodron recommends we turn away from this self-soothing and use Self-seeking instead. "Find your 'Inner Treasure.' Breathing, body attunement, and transforming anger into seeds of kindness, can relieve deep-rooted inhibitions and fears, find freedom from harmful habits in waking life (enhance problem-solving and creativity)" (ibid, 1996, p.132).

---

[66] Compounding this litany of ways we make ourselves feel bad is our terrible prognosis: we're all going to get sick and die, and on the way, we're likely to decline. No wonder we're so often upset. When trying to focus on mindfulness, our propensity to dwell in painful thoughts by redirecting attention out of the thought stream toward awareness of sensory experience. Most practices begin by developing concentration…Instead of trying to control experience, it helps us learn how to be with experience and accept it. Acceptance modulates our stress response…By practicing acceptance of changing body sensations during meditation, we learn to ride the waves of unpleasant emotional responses (Siegel, R., 2011, p. 25).

Tender Heart, Tough Mind: As the Spiritual Self, so too the Brain

> Which Self do you want to enhance, the one that is going to die, or the one that will survive/transform? Death is like a mirror in which the true meaning of life is reflected.
>
> – Pema Chodron

Suggesting Mindfulness (2011), by Michael Yapko, compares the ongoing state of mindfulness to the induced state of hypnosis. As someone who learned the art of self-hypnosis from Harold Greenwald himself back in 1974, I would have to agree that the two states of consciousness seem similar. Over time I have come to experience the "underappreciated healing mechanisms of hypnotic suggestion" (Siegel and Yapko, 2012). Yapko informs us about the use of self-regulation strategies, such as how to use our breath and employ guided imagery. His purpose is to help us to shift attention and to experience the deep power of accepting what is unchangeable or inevitable.

Many forms of psychopathology are disorders of non-acceptance. When we try *not* to feel anxious, we become phobic and avoidant, perhaps even agoraphobic. When we try *not* to feel sad, we shut down and become depressed. When we try *not* to feel some other dysphoria, we start drinking and have substance abuse problems, and on, and on. Acceptance is often a key factor in resolving most psychological disorders (ibid, 2012, p. 45).

Self-regulation strategies, whether through prayer, creative activity, or sharing relationally with another human, are all viable forms of communication and CONNECTION that help us heal. Yapko calls this "Believed-in-Imagination". In his article co-written with Ron Siegel, he emphasizes that as a culture we have put too much emphasis on "thinking" and not enough on this process of imagining "good stuff" instead of obsessing about the "bad stuff" that can happen to us.

Yapko believes that one must detach oneself from experience to transform it and, even if this state is experienced by the self as dissociative, it can be relabeled as positive. Yapko recommends that success comes from allowing feelings to surface but to not letting them overwhelm you. Ultimately, we are more than our experiences, we are more than our thoughts, more than our behaviors, and certainly more than our history (UFTs).

Summary

Having learned to "bear the unbearable", we stay in our present-mindedness selves, showing trust, with purity of intent, willing to heal ourselves. We become calm and compassionate, we let go of anxiety and discover what inspires us. Not only does the work require an internal locus of control at times, but it also requires effort to work through the painful past, which is why psychotherapy alone does not just work through simple techniques. One must be "willing to open up to unpleasant experience—whether it is anxiety or restlessness that draws us toward intimate encounters with previously split off emotions, including sadness, anger, loneliness, and vulnerability…" (Siegel, R., 2011, p. 25).

As noted above, in *A 'Dyadic' Model of Reality,* Dora Lora (2003) asserts that energy is the basis of everything. Experientially, we often begin to CONNECT energy to that around us which is creative. In other words, energy and information can be a dyad. Awareness and intention (another dyad) are also aspects of the evolutionary process leading to consciousness. "Awareness and intention (postulated components of informational energy patterns) are the roots or seeds of self-reflective consciousness" (ibid, 2003, pp. 19–23).

There has always been a deep engagement between philosophical studies and meditative experiences, particularly when reflective of a group consciousness. Many modern authors have studied the frequent tendency of consciousness to return to a collective state. If one were able to truly operate "as if" what they experience, their "knowing" during states of mindfulness, was their true consciousness, then a usefulness about unresolved infantile longings to return to a state of oceanic oneness (as proposed by Freud) could radically transform the mind.

C.S. Lewis said: "Fear is the absence of faith." Even if we call it suspending disbelief, the act of healing requires this focused mind we have been discussing. Therefore, we must be able to explain the inter-CONNECTED relationships between time, space, energy, and matter to begin to answer the questions of Faith and Meaning. But before we directly investigate the methodology of the mind, we must first understand the physical structure of the world within which our brains reside.

"Deep knowing requires an exchange of information with this universal archive of information—and that is precisely what prayer, meditation, and the rituals of mystics are designed to accomplish" (Edgar Mitchell, former astronaut).

Chapter Ten
The Neurological Universe

"Our mind is a set of operations carried out by our brain. The same principle of unity applies to mental disorders."
– *Gray Matter* Eric H. Kandel, Nobel Laurette

"If Copernicus pointed out that the earth is not the center of the universe and Galileo saw stars and planets but not angels in the sky, if Darwin showed that man is related to all other living organisms, if Einstein introduced new notions of time and space and of mass and energy, if Watson and Crick showed that biological inheritance can be explained in physical and chemical terms, then in this sequence of eliminations of the supernatural the main thing science seems to be left with is the brain, and whether or not it is something more than a machine of vast and magnificent complexity" (*The Brain* D. Hubel, 1984, p. 10)

Cosmological Constants: Can Science Explain Everything?

As with our overall physical development, our psychosocial development, and our moral development, our neurological development is sequential from childhood to elder years. We now know that an infant has twice as many cells as are necessary, and then cells begin to die off after one year due to the plasticity of the brain. Current research has enabled us to be more specific in localizing certain functions (although we know the brain is also interactive and systemic). Because the entire focus of this book is on the UFT of function, such an interactive theory will also help explain change, especially as the understanding of change is modulated by the brain.

Our main concern in this chapter is with how the brain and immune system function and deal with attention, memory, and decision-making, as well as any negative effects of neurodegenerative disease. Patterns of overall brain activity are based on the patterns of CONNECTIONS between the activity in the individual neurons. Thus, the brain must be viewed as a heterogeneous structure with many specialized parts (Pinker, 1997).

Steven Pinker has done an excellent job of reviewing past research at leading institutions, (such as NIH, Harvard, UCSD, University of Texas and Stanford). He believes that the study of neuropsychology can explain our behavior. Part of the brain's job is to repair damage from stress as it occurs, such as resilience to changing environmental cues stressful to our immune system throughout the lifespan.[67]

---

[67] "Although it is now well established that repeated psychological stress can cause permanent physiological injury, the mechanisms remain unclear and are under active investigation today" (van der Kolk, 1987).

In this scientific age, "to understand" means to try to explain behavior as a complex interaction among (1) the genes, (2) the anatomy of the brain, (3) its biochemical state, (4) the person's family upbringing, (5) the way society has treated him or her, and (6) the stimuli that impinge upon the person (Pinker, 1997, p. 53).

In other words, Pinker's thoughts parallel those defined within my unified field theory of individual development (UFT). When I taught developmental classes, I focused specifically on types of information such as: behavior at different ages, changes with age, environmental events, and variations within individuals.

Here is a detailed list of some of the areas that will be covered in this chapter.

1. Brain function, neurotransmitters, and the effects of disrupted brain functioning on the rest of our behavior. Current foci of research include pharmacology, psychiatric illnesses, and the causes and cures of dementia.

2. Early studies in Sensation and Perception, as well as Cognition (Piaget, Beck), which provided the foundation for more current advances in the neurosciences, especially at UCSD (Squire), Harvard (Benowitz, Chapham, Rosenberg, and Walsh) and University of Wisconsin-Madison (Davidson).

3. The triune brain: As humans, we use our (pre)frontal cortex to process information, and to process executive functions, which is the "go" and "stop" part of the brain per se. The executive process is something we experience as the Self, the will, the "I". Cognitive processes in this part of the brain are also connected to "reward" centers (the "go" messages in the limbic center) in such a way that immediate pleasures can often be delayed (the "stop" messages) in the interest of long-term benefits. In other words, the executive function "learns" to manage and forego implicit/impulsive functions, at least for short periods of time. Higher processes lead to "coping efficacy", such as problem-solving, managing negative thoughts, and obtaining support. All this mastery, even in the face of trauma, allows for resilient brain functions (Bandura, 1997).

The simplest way to explain brain function might be to break it down into the functions of reptile brain, doggy brain, and monkey brain as noted in my story about teaching this material for fourth graders in Chapter Eight. In 1990, Paul MacLean took the original Greek idea of the Triune or Trinity and used it in the design of a theory of a triune brain, which contained three layers. Although not as acclaimed by up-to-date neuroscientists going into the 21st century, the simplicity of MacLean's theory is a good way for me to start this explanation of brain function.

First, there was the basal ganglia or Reptilian Brain, seat of the primitive emotions or instincts like eating, fighting, and sexual drive (reptile brain). Second, there was the primitive Mammalian Brain wherein lies the limbic system (which MacLean is given credit for naming in 1952) and the beginning of social emotions (doggy brain). Finally, there is the neocortex, which contains all of primate evolution and houses human intellect (language, abstraction, planning, and perception) and which started out in higher mammalian development (monkey brain). In these areas, messages are sent from the autonomic nervous system (ANS) which we barely recognize, but which controls the same fight/flight/freeze reaction that other animals experience.

How does the brain CONNECT with peripheral processes? The ANS is composed of sympathetic and parasympathetic branches which affect organs such as the stomach, the heart and immune systems (thymus, bone marrow, spleen and lymph nodes) (Maier, Watkins and Fleshner, 1994). One question to ask is: how much are residue effects there from each of the lower areas of the triune as it moves up from an instinctual area to areas of newer and higher functioning? The answer explains how anger and stress hold our bodies "hostage". However, a more positive "moral" sense may have developed, through evolution, to control these lower instinctual parts of us from creating havoc (Pinker, 1997).

Another way to look at the triune brain is developmentally. Individuals can be observed, starting with the developing infant. Right from birth, we observe the infant's instincts, need for social contact, and eventual information-gathering and processing skills are observed right from birth. Pinker points out an example of all three parts of the triune brain at work: "Since every parent should evolve to recognize sham crying, the baby's most effective tactic might be to feel genuinely miserable, even when there is no biological need. Self-deception may begin early" (ibid, 1997, pp. 445–447). On the other hand, a child's instinctual actions may run a bit too much for early or young parents and "just as parents often act against a child's interests, they may try to train the child to act against its own interests."

4. Neuro-immunology is the brain's reaction to changes/stimuli by the thymus and enzymes, which are created by amino acids. Among the major steroidal hormones in a human are the glucocorticoids called cortisol and corticosterone, which regulate the metabolism of glucose. This metabolic response is controlled by the "releasing factors" from the two master organs: the pituitary and the hypothalamus. Why would there be "receptor sites" for any drug, for instance valium, if there wasn't a receptor site already there? This "natural" receptor site is most likely for cortisol. Cortisol facilitates the uptake and conversion of the protein of amino acids into sugars (as measured by an A1C glucose test). Adrenocorticotropic, ACTH, is a peptide that acts as an endorphin to increase a sense of reward and satisfaction. It is produced by the adrenal gland—sub-rosa to the pituitary system overall, and in severe cases a toxic metabolite is created. The other major peptide hormone is insulin.

The thymus also controls negative reactions to stress, through high levels of cortisol, on the hypothalamus, amygdala, and adrenals. In the past, "psychosomatic" was a negative diagnostic description of self-focused hypochondriasis, but we now know that we all have psychosomatic interacting symptoms (psych=mind, brain; soma=body). Thus, most of us understand how our hormones run our body, and that thyroid stimulating hormone (TSH), cortisol stimulating hormone (CSH), and follicle stimulating hormone (FSH) are all related at a higher level of systemic function in the adrenal/hypothalamic system. These hormones are affected by stress and are glucocorticoids. These concepts will be expanded further below.

Neurotransmitters signal the response patterns of the "lower" part of the brain; cognition includes ideas, thoughts, concepts, and categorization, all of which the frontal cortex processes; neurotransmitters signal the response patterns of the "lower" part of the brain. Conscious perceptions as well as preconscious intuition are experienced in these areas. As neuroscience research has expanded, newer paradigms show how the synaptic view of cognition explains "networks and quality control" (to use a metaphor from construction) by controlling an underlying awareness of factors defined by Heisenberg's Uncertainty Principle (Livingston, 1986, personal communication).

Dr. Livingston explained that the term "mind" should not be a noun, but rather a verb; thus, the concept is better understood by using the term "minding", which will help describe the self-organizing nature of the systems and how they become coherent. Livingstone proposed that the term "adapting" could also be used to represent this self-reflecting, even within the cognitive structure at the cellular level. Unconscious responses can be seen in ANS muscle tension, duration, selective attention, and neuroplasticity.[68]

Cognitive schemas, as described by Piaget (1962) and Siegel (2012), generally represent images and conceptual metaphors in the prefrontal cortex; they facilitate the CONNECTIONS between areas of the brain that contribute to the pattern of response, whether physical or verbal. Somewhere in these CONNECTIONS is where self-awareness and Will lie. These factors influence behavioral outcomes.

5. Memory patterns in the hippocampus and amygdala affect individual reactions through language, behavioral patterns, and emotional content in the response patterns. The amygdala is an almond-shaped organ buried in each temporal lobe, which directly affects our emotional response patterns. Its position in the temporal lobe facilitates the processing of the simple signals it receives from lower areas of the brain, as well as more complex ones from higher areas. "The amygdala in turn sends signals to virtually every other part of the brain, including the decision-making circuitry of the frontal lobes" (ibid, 1997, p. 372).

Do we embody our brain signals, or rather do we allow environmental factors to filter our neurological functioning? Nature versus Nurture is an age-old question. Of course, probably both theories are true. The percentage of influence focused on each area by science shifts from time to time as scientists provide us with new data. Perhaps this instinctual awareness of patterns over thousands of

---

[68] "Are the immune changes 'directly' conditioned or is something else conditioned (e.g., fear, anxiety, aversion, glucocorticoid release) that is then responsible for the immune alterations? [A second finding] involves the potential practical implications of conditioned immunomodulation. Could conditioned immune responses occur in real-life settings and influence disease processes, and could conditioning procedures be used in clinical settings?" (Maier, Watkins and Fleshner, 1994, p. 1007).

years, as well as psychoneuroimmunological influences, has created the human use of, and need for, metaphysical communication for CONNECTION.

How do we "know" we know? Margaret Wilson (2002) provides schemas to explain cognition as a system:

Six Views of Embodied Cognition:

1. Cognition is situated.
2. Cognition is time pressured.
3. We offload cognitive work onto the environment.
4. The environment is part of the cognitive system.
5. Cognition is for action…situation-appropriate behavior…our vision is encoded into our minds as 'what' and 'where' concept…renaming the structure and placement of an object. This idea goes back to what we are used to and what we have been exposed to [nurture]. Our perception of what we see comes from our experience and exposure of it. Memory in this case doesn't necessarily mean memorizing something. Rather, it means remembering it in a relevant point of view instead of as it really is. We remember how relevant it is to us and decide if it's worth remembering.
6. Off-line cognition is body-based. Children utilize skills and abilities they were born with, such as sucking, grasping, and listening, to learn more about the environment [nature].

The skills are broken down into five main categories that combine sensory with motor skills, sensorimotor functions. The five main skills are:

- Mental imagery—visualizing something based on your perception of it when it is not there or is not present.
- Working memory—short-term memory.
- Episodic memory—long-term memory.
- Implicit memory—means by which we learn certain skills until they become automatic for us.
- Reasoning and problem-solving—having a mental model of something will increase problem-solving approaches (ibid, 2002, pp. 625–636).

As developing individuals, we need to balance the phenomenal/metaphorical functioning of our cognition with the logical part in the neocortex, which is available for use as we discriminate, decide, remember facts, and pass IQ tests! The Myers-Briggs Test (1962), or the updated version, Kiersey (1984) using Jungian constructs, does an excellent scientific job of developing a measurement of cognitive "type" as it affects personality development. A simplistic paradigm for our current discussion might be that presented by Jean Millay (2001). In terms of "thinking about thinking", Millay wrote an article about how we learn to think, use logic, learn to discriminate, and learn to enhance our natural intelligence. For instance, "working memory" accounts for a large extent of the variation in fluid intelligence among individuals (Weir, 2014). Millay provided the following outline with thought-provoking questions.

1) How do you think? Ask yourself, what verbal or perceptual systems dominate your cognitive style? Words? Images? Feelings? Smells? Can you translate what you feel into words? Can you find words to describe your images? Are your words, images, and feelings in harmony, or are they in conflict over which will be used to express your personality?
2) What do you think about: Two subjects dominate: a. our personal relationships, b. our special areas of interest, such as jobs, sports, or our own field of study?
3) What do you think about those things that you choose to perceive? Our ability to perceive all that is going on around us is limited. We must focus on something or allow our attention to be scattered. We choose by habit. What aspect of your mind becomes the chooser? Are you conscious of choosing your perceptions? You may have been indoctrinated into a particular belief system (for instance, religious or ethnic). Whether you accepted or rejected that indoctrination, those early habits of perception may still determine your logic, since logic follows belief [emphasis added].
4) Every thought, feeling and emotion is accompanied by chemical activity in the brain (Millay, 2001).

Of course, the collection and storage of information is of massive importance in the above process. It takes a "correlation between two things", assessing and evaluating in the mind (Livingstone's "minding"). This correlation does not occur by chance, but rather is the reflection of the logic that can be mathematically measured. "Without goals, the very concept of intelligence is meaningless…[and] the emotions are mechanisms that set the brain's highest-level goals, which then trigger a cascade of subgoals and sub-subgoals that we call thinking and acting…no sharp line divides thinking from feeling" (Pinker, 1997, pp. 372–373).

Adaptation and the Limbic System

One of the primary contributing factors to my unified field theory (UFT) of CONNECTIVITY is the concept of adaptation to inner and outer world. As an early neurological system found in all species, the limbic system exists in even such primitive animals as crocodiles. Located in the middle of the brain, the limbic system is a complex set of structures which include the hypothalamus and the amygdala, along with several other smaller structures. One of its main functions is to provide homeostasis to the body, maintaining a "set point" that the body can return to, even after fight/flight/freeze—something like a stretched and released rubber band. It also regulates other survival mechanisms like hunger, thirst, response to pain, levels of pleasure, sexual satisfaction, anger, and aggressive behavior.

The limbic system takes its cues from within; it is an area excessively vulnerable to stress. Stress also affects other parts of the brain, of course, particularly the prefrontal cortex, the decision-making part of the brain.[69] "This primitive brain that can neither read nor write, provides us with the feeling of what is real, true, and important. And this disturbs me, because this inarticulate brain sits like a jury and tells this glorified computer up there, the neocortex, 'Yes, you can believe this'" (McLean, 1978, p. 49).

Some regions of our brains interact with the outside world and others interact with the inside world, connecting sensory input with our bodies and our organs through an extensive system of "wiring". "Information is transmitted along these pathways via the action of neurotransmitters [at least 50 different ones]. Each neuron produces tiny quantities of a specific neurotransmitter, which is released into the microscopic space that exists between neurons (called a synapse), stimulating the next cell in the pathway—and no others" (Silver, 2007, p. 29).[70]

Developmentally, we have a better chance of survival if we can/could control our neuroplasticity. This skill most likely begins in childhood as the orbital frontal cortex creates healthful levels of dopamine, endorphins, and serotonin (Siegel, 2012). "Chromatin regulation", or methylation, affects gene expression and resulting modifications of epigenetic formation. We will discuss more about methylation in Chapter Eleven. Overall, the process of methylation supports my unified field theory of development (UFT), where one's personal paradigm is a collection of each person's knowledge, experiences, attitudes, beliefs, values, and convictions; this is the epigenetic layer.

One's ultimate "personality" represents aspects of consciousness. "Changes aren't permanent, but change is." Pinker (1997) associates consciousness with short-term memory, just as he does free will with the executive subroutine in the anterior cingulate sulcus. "Our minds evolved by natural selection to solve problems that were life-and-death matters to our ancestors, not to commune with correctness or to answer any question we are capable of asking" (ibid, 1997, p. 561). Can we reduce consciousness to structures this simply?

Sentience is defined as having the power of sensation or perception, and for me this also includes meanings of the word "feeling". Sentience is important to our conversation here because it is not just reflected in free will. Although Pinker

---

[69] Your accumulated thoughts and actions weave your neurons into the unique tapestry of your mind. "Virtually all the cells in an amphibian or reptile brain directly process sensory information (input) or control movement (output), but in humans a great gray area—about three-fourths of the cortex—lies between sensory input and motor output, called the association areas. These include the frontal lobes and parts of the temporal, parietal, and occipital lobes" (ibid, 1978, p. 50).

[70] For instance, this structural explanation describes the alleviation of pain. "The coincidence of the location of encephalin pathways and opiate receptors supports the hypothesis that the encephalin neurotransmitters act as opiates and can be related to methylation or how the enkephalins and some endorphins suppress the perception of pain" (Snyder, 1985, p. 29). Medications work by blocking the biosynthesis of peptide neurotransmitters, allowing precise control over a patient's neurochemistry. Do we/can we consciously control our elemental particles? Is this also what meditation can do/be?

is bound to his "computational" theory of the mind, ultimately, he does believe in free will and a "Selfness" that can represent an "I" which culminates over time in some kind of unity of experience.

Consciousness, self, will and knowledge all create paradoxical questions, but we enjoy the search for the answers, nonetheless. In an attempt to summarize these concepts, Pinker tells us

> the computational aspect of consciousness (what information is available to which processes), the neurological aspect (what neurons in the brain correlate with consciousness), and the evolutionary aspect (when and why did the neurocomputational aspect emerge?) are perfectly tractable, and I see no reason that we should not have decades of progress and eventually a complete understanding [UFT] (ibid, 1997, p. 563).

Can the brain understand itself? Can it understand its own complexity? Can a brain be both a machine and a Self? Bronowski (2011) says "yes", in that Nature creates the machinery and individual experience fashions a Self. For him, the brain is a Darwinian "machine". Although we have viewed experience mostly as dualistic to this point, there is also the monist point of view, whereas in many theories of identity the idea is that mental (psychological, spiritual) events and brain (physio-chemical events) are one and the same. Instead of two separate sorts of "stuff", mind and matter, there is only one substance. This is the central dogma of current neuroscience. Physical, electromagnetic, and chemical processes can be seen as equivalent (Teresi, 1986).

I would now like to present a definition of change as a dynamic shift between stillness and movement (duality of up-down, wave-particle, Yin-Yang of the *Tao*). It is also the balance plus the undefinable more of adaptation, and yet in this dualism we can find a sense of sameness/constancy regardless. It is a basic tenet of philosophy that "all our desires, problems, issues, and searching for answers" comes from the feeling of separateness or incompleteness we feel. The question is whether every completeness will come to us as a symmetry, or if some answers result in an asymmetrical feeling of incompleteness or uncertainty? If we come across a value/paradigm that makes us feel "better", we think that if the belief works so well for us, we want it to work for everyone else. This belief can lead to an attempt to control, to project, and even to war.

When I was a teenager, the Robert Heinlein book, *Stranger in a Strange Land* (1961) had an immense influence on my emerging adult brain, as it had for many of my generation. Its basic premises taught me that things will continue to change and that I could be open to an inner world beyond that which I have learned and accepted in my Protestant upbringing. It opened my mind to certain possibilities that later resulted in my study in college of Comparative Religion and Buddhism, and ultimately to my current philosophy of life and research in Developmental Psychology. That philosophy is the basis of this book, whereby a dualistic view of the universe as "parts and pieces" versus unified potential and inter-CONNECTEDNESS creates change.

Plasticity of the Brain

Because the entire focus of this book is on a UFT of interactional function that will also help explain change, the reader should constantly keep in mind the theory of Uncertainty as set forth by Heisenberg (1930): based on the finding that any individual electron appears to have no definite position or velocity, as soon as we choose to focus on a system, we influence the probability of its measurement/perception/response set. Einstein grappled with integrating this theory into his theory of relativity; there is no "now", there is no "absolute" in motion or time, even in the brain.

Although the theory of relativity was eventually going to collide with newer ideas about the rules of quantum theory, the basic ideas of the relativity effect is also found in medicine, healthcare, psychology, and education, where findings must be reflective of the point of reference being compared to, such as normal temperature or weight, normal or deficited learning styles. In looking at the functioning of the brain, it is important to understand how on/off switches work. As I said, we could break down the brain as a "system" by looking at the "parts and pieces" or focus instead on the interconnectedness of systemic functioning overall.

As noted, our theory of CONNECTIONS is a developmental one. Daniel Siegel (2012) writes about the early development of neuroplasticity in children. It is known that brain cells are determined by what kind of cells they start out as, where they are in the brain, and "what patterns of triggering input they get during critical periods in development" (Pinker, 1997, p. 36). If the child has been well cared for, with low stress and healthy attachment patterns, then there will be the appropriate levels of bonding and trust between parents and child, which helps facilitate brain development in the frontal cortex and its secretion of dopamine, endorphins, and serotonin. The chemicals found to influence CONNECTION are referred to as neuro-affiliative and include oxytocin and testosterone. Experiences of care and compassion have been found to increase levels of immunoglobulin.

On the other hand, immune levels are lowered overall by sustained negative states such as anger. "Every healthy baby is born with [either] potential...Testosterone is a very reactive hormone. It fluctuates throughout the day and over the course of a lifetime." This is a very interesting finding and may go far in explaining the difference in levels of empathic nurturing between men and women.

Not only do I believe that women perceive the world differently than men, but I have run across many examples of women's health and hormones being unjustifiably ignored. Take clinical trials for instance. Medical research, drug companies, and health providers are starting to be more responsible about clinical trials using both men and women, taking into consideration hormonal levels, size, weight, and life experiences. On the other hand, women are not always included in mental health studies because their hormones would interfere with the results. Studies have shown that there is a difference in a woman's level of cortisol, estrogen, and dopamine; results show a woman to be more reactive to equal experiences of stress than those when given to a man.

We are aware of the terms "fight, flight, or freeze," but these concepts can also be termed "tend or befriend versus run" because of the influences of the hormones on our tendency to either face our fears, nurture ourselves, or run away. Therefore, compassion acts almost as the opposite of fight-or-flight responses. Likewise, in many ways the changes that occur during meditative states are the opposite of the changes that occur in the body during stress. The time-space concept is also very similar to that of impermanence (lack of determinism) as presented in the study of Buddhism.

We must be vigilant regarding our influences, however, because over-identification with ourselves as a variable can also interrupt openness to change; dependent variables, as science would call them, are always highly sensitive to the "uncertainty" factor. Research in the field of neuroscience, which I will describe in further detail below, has presented new and exciting evidence that the brain does have plasticity and, in addition, we can act to encourage an openness to change. These factors are just some of the influences on human neuroplasticity.

Individuals with mental health or psychological issues often suffer because of long-term childhood abuse/stress which impacted the stability of neurotransmitters. A common diagnosis of "dysregulation", both in brain function and behavior, is meant to reflect this finding. In addition, the neurobiology factors revealed may have de-volved because of the childhood psychosocial history and allostasis, which is the inherently unstable nature of the brain's system, sometimes leading to pathological results (Koob, 2013).

The brain is expected to use allostasis to maintain stability, which is necessary for survival; however, often environmental cues can create quite a state of chaos, or the individual may even seek out that state of hyperarousal because an "unstable" brain is generating the production of more neurotransmitters to achieve allostasis as a part of an addictive cycle. Of course, we must define whether the stresses in our life experience are self-caused or inadvertent, trauma being an extreme example. Koob (2013) mentions some stresses that can lead to dysfunction in the brain: anxiety disorders, depression, pain and stress, memory problems, sleep disturbances, and autoimmune disorders. The emotions influence the glands via the hypothalamus—a discovery with enormous implication for psychosomatic medicine.

The hypothalamus also regulates the "internal milieu:" blood pressure, body temperature, and appetite control. Sapolsky (1997) refers to the term senescence, our ability to survive "environmental insults" or our resilience, as a powerful measure of how much we as individuals have succumbed (or not) to being vulnerable or surviving emotional and physiological insults. In addition, a lack of sleep can create immune dysregulation, inflammation and poor health, the result of larger cytokine spikes following stress and/or depression. The pineal gland controls our internal clock and biological cycles set by light and dark cycles of the outside world (Sherwood, 1987).

Sleep is a "multidimensional biobehavioral process including components such as sleep duration, continuity, architecture, timing, rhythmicity, regularity, and satisfaction" (Hall, Brindle and Buysse, 2018, p. 995). Sleep deprivation, which can cause high blood pressure, arterial stiffness, and inflammation (elevations in interleukin-6/IL-6) has also previously been shown to impair high-level executive thinking.

These factors can be determined by an fMRI, whose data reveals less activity in the prefrontal cortex after sleep deprivation. Surprisingly, however, parietal lobe activity increases, perhaps becoming a factor in cognitive and somatic hyperarousal in the fatigued. Metabolic dysfunction has also been shown in some studies (ibid, 2018, p. 998). Finally, "activity in the left temporal lobe"—a class language-processing area—has been shown to decrease during sleep deprivation. Insomnia has been connected to so many possible other health issues it is becoming a number one concern of health providers.

If there is anything sacred about a human being it is surely his brain—especially, perhaps, the frontal lobes (Sherwood, 1987, p. 41). I once had a client who fell off a second-story roof, right onto the left side of the top of his head, but without another scratch on him. He went into a coma, which lasted for 5 weeks. I continued to sense somehow that "he" was still in there and encouraged his mother not to "pull the plug" [but that's another story]. When he did wake up, he was immediately alert and hungry! But many of his left-brain functions were obviously skewed [somewhat the same symptoms that manifest after a left side stroke]; he had trouble verbalizing and was over-sexualized (the nurses suffered more than he did!) It was an amazing example of Sherwood's point above and changed my feelings about comas forever.

The Brain's Power Plant

The brain CONNECTS to itself, as well as to that which is "outside". The brain does an excellent job of providing, through complex forms, the effects of chemical, anatomical, physiological, embryological, and psychological causes on behavior (Crick, 1984). Crick proposed a general theory of the brain which divided it into four broad areas or "constraints". The first constraint, based on the nature of the physical world and the concrete perceptual space within which we live, consists of objects of size and shape, and consists of that to which we react.

The second constraint, the one "imposed by biochemistry, genetics and embryology", consists of the neurons made of specialized cells. Sodium and potassium are extremely important factors in the functioning of brain cells and the maintenance of healthy transmission of neurotransmitters. The third constraint, provided by probability theory, is how cells communicate with each other or mutate or miscommunicate, all mathematically relevant. Finally, the last constraint, that of evolution itself, wherein structure and function, and the role they play in the cellular presentation, should never be forgotten.

According to Crick, when new functional areas of the brain arise in evolution, it is a good bet that they will arise in pairs! Therefore, we address ourselves to the nature of the dualistic CONNECTIONS and the orderly nature of the brain, which made perfect sense to Crick. The strength of the CONNECTIONS is adjusted 'by experience' based on certain well-defined rules, usually so that pathways that are often activated together are strengthened in some way [emphasis added] (Crick, 1984, p. 19).

As an example of Crick's constraints, your brain is affected by electromagnetic forces like the rest of the universe; your brain is full of "electricity", even though it is basically invisible except on a fMRI (functional magnetic resonance imaging). Because the neurobiological structures and functions operate off the tiny electrical impulses created by the field that influences its own activity, we call this process "neural feedback".

An article by Ferris Jabr in the November/December (2010) copy of *Scientific American Mind* describes this activity. The article summarized a study published in *Neuron* (July 2010) which suggested that the brain's electric field was not a passive by-product of its neural activity, as scientists once thought.

> The field may actively help regulate how the brain functions, especially during deep sleep. Although scientists have long known that external sources of electricity (such as electroshock therapy) can alter brain function, this is the first direct evidence that the brain's native electric field changes the way the brain behaves…it is a feedback loop…Although researchers knew that periods of highly synchronized neural activity (such as that of deep sleep) are crucial for maintaining normal brain function, exactly how these stable phases are coordinated—and why they go awry in disorders such as epilepsy—was never clear.
>
> The new study indicates scientists may find some answers in the surprisingly active role of the brain's electric field…Frohlich sees therapeutic applications as well, particularly in improving a promising technique called transcranial direct-current stimulation (tDCS), which applies weak electric fields to the scalp to treat, for example, depression and chronic pain. Traditionally, tDCS uses standard electric fields that do not change much, as opposed to the dynamic electric fields used in the new study to mimic a living brain [Author's note: since the time I initially wrote this section, tDCS has become a frequent treatment for depression in my area of California] (Jabr, 2010, p. 10).

The idea of tDCS is certainly exciting as a possibility for adjunct treatment of long-term unrelenting depressive patients who have not responded to typical psychotherapy, with or without psychotropic medication regimens. However, I once had a patient with chronic, intractable pain from a genetic disorder. He had tried everything for pain management, with only limited success. He found drinking alcohol worked better than anything. But he heard about tDCS and found a local doctor who provided this treatment for people who had the kind of pain he did and the subsequent depression that went with it. I believe he had three treatments. Regardless, at least for him, it did not quell any of his symptoms. He finally settled all his affairs, started a fight with his wife to make leaving her easier for them both, and drank himself to death.

A terrible loss for all of us who knew him, but I can't say I didn't understand. I am not being insensitive. The nerve pain he experienced, somewhat explained in the reference above, can be some of the worst pain anyone can experience, perhaps except for being burned, for which I have also had to give auxiliary treatment. Each of us experiences hopelessness in our own way, and finding a solution, or escape, is sometimes the only thing on which we can focus.

Overall, understanding neural feedback loops and how neural activity is synchronized within the brain provides us information about a "normal" brain;

from these findings we can hypothesize about the disordered brain, whether because of epilepsy, MS, closed head injury, Alzheimer's disease, or depression. Helen Mayberg, a professor of psychiatry and neurology at Emory University, has been studying one specific region of the brain, Brodmann area 25, which is overactive in depressed individuals. She believes that Broadmann area 25 is a "junction box" that interacts with other areas of the brain that are integral for the functioning of emotional and cognitive health (Mayberg, 2005). Our brains are more malleable than once thought;[71] if selective serotonin reuptake inhibitors (SSRIs) can affect the neurotransmitters regulating our emotions (depression and anxiety) or increase our concentration, then it is quite acceptable to also consider how we could also best control and regulate such neural activity through the CONNECTIONS made with long-term Cognitive Behavioral Treatment (CBT).

Management of Neuronal Damage

Robert Sapolsky, a professor at Stanford University, has been studying glucocorticoid hormones and neuronal damage in seizure and stroke patients. The focus of his research for over 35 years has been the physiological effects of stress. He does an excellent job of summarizing how medication can help chronic stress and depression.

> What happens to the neurotransmitter molecule after it has done its job and floats off the receptor? In some cases, it is recycled—taken up by the axon terminal of the first neuron and repackaged for future use. Or it can be degraded in the synapse and the debris flushed out to sea (the cerebrospinal fluid, then to the blood, and the urine). If these processes of clearing neurotransmitters out of the way fail (reuptake ceases or degradation stops or both), suddenly a lot more neurotransmitters remain in the synapse, giving a stronger signal to the second neuron than usual. Thus, the proper disposal of these powerful messengers is integral to normal neuronal communication…
>
> One class of antidepressants, called tricyclics, (a reference to their biochemical structure), stops the recycling, or reuptake, or norepinephrine into the axon terminals; another class of drugs, called MAO inhibitors, blocks the degradation of norepinephrine in the "synapse" by inhibiting the action of a crucial enzyme, monoamine oxidase (MAO). The result, again, is that more of the messenger remains in the synapse to stimulate the dendrite of the receiving neuron…Not only do dendrites contain receptors for neurotransmitters, but it turns out that on the axon terminals of the 'sending' neuron, as well, there are

---

[71] Beck (1967), one of the founders of CBT, believes depression to be a disorder of thought rather than emotion. People who are depressed are fighting against the hopeless, aggressive, and negative thoughts in response to stress hormones that come about no differently that someone engaged in battle or any other emotional sense of threat. In a simplistic way, your brain manages to convince you that a negative "thought" is as real as any other physical stressor. In this way, chronic depression occurs because of the cyclical nature of this hyperarousal between the thought processes and the stress hormones reacting to it.

receptors for the very neurotransmitters being released by that neuron (Sapolsky, 1994, pp. 204–208).

As a therapist, my way of explaining this process to clients is as follows: just like the paper towel commercials, you need the right amount of paper towel absorbency to clean up a spill. On one hand is the amount of spill (over-production of neurotransmitter receptors), and on the other hand is the right amount of towel (medication). When there is a balance, the "mess" is cleaned up and the patient feels better! In summary, the process results from an action potential depolarizing the presynaptic membrane, so that dopamine is released into the synaptic cleft, which then diffuses across to postsynaptic receptors. This complex set of events is determined by whether the biochemical composition of the neurotransmitter creates an excitatory or inhibitory stimulus. Whether a given synapse is excitatory or inhibitory depends on what chemical transmitter the presynaptic cell makes and on the chemistry of the postsynaptic cell's membrane (Hubel, 1984).

> The entire neuron—the cell body, its long axon and its branching dendrites—is polarized so that the inside is about 70 millivolts negative with respect to the outside. Two properties of the cell membrane are responsible for this 'resting potential.' First, the membrane actively transports ions, extruding positively charged sodium ions from the cell and bringing in positively charged potassium ions, so that the concentrations of the two kinds of ion are quite different inside the cell and outside it. Second, the ease with which the ions flow through the membrane is quite different for sodium and potassium. It is changes in the resulting outside-to-inside resting potential that constitute the electrical signals of nerves (ibid, 1984, p. 6).

In summary, your brain sends electrical impulses through the neurons to communicate/CONNECT with other cells throughout the body, maintaining balance and control of smooth muscle reactions. This process may also more simply be known as electrolyte function. The axons have "voltage-gated" potassium channels that help to terminate the nerve impulse (desired or not) by letting potassium ions flow out of the axon, thereby counteracting the inward flow of the sodium ions. As constant as this may be, cell bodies themselves change their impulses to reflect the intensity of the stimulus. The stronger the impulse, the faster the rate of firing will be.

The duration of the action of the neurotransmitter is also dependent on the presence of other agents and enzymes, a further discussion of which is beyond the scope of this chapter. Its importance reflects just how many ways neuronal health, or dysregulation of neurotransmitters, can quickly change homeostasis of the cells and thus our experience of pain, depression or generally feeling unwell (like eating too much Chinese food with MSG or after our Thanksgiving meal!). This is not a random process; functionally related systems in the brain have common neurotransmitters. Because it is important for the neurons involved to work together, it must be pointed out that other drugs (or alcohol) and neurotoxins may alter behavior by altering this natural process.

During the last decade, many researchers and theorists (for instance, Adam Anderson, et. al., at Cornell, Joseph LeDoux, et. al, at the Nathan Kline Institute, and Nikolaus Kriegeskorte at the University of Cambridge) have approached the study of the brain and neurology with the larger goal of understanding how we regulate our emotions and whether we have any choice in the matter. Also, can we impact the size of our cognitive capacity or delay the loss of cognitive processing through dementia with daily "exercises" or health-oriented behaviors? Alan Wallace (2011) believes we should have a "long-term strategy for motivating the heart and mind to fully draw forth the beneficial capacities of the human mind" (ibid, 2011, p. 690–701).

Additionally, Ellis (1994) believed that painful emotions spring more from people's beliefs than from reality itself. Thoughts alone can lead to anguish, challenge beliefs, or test new possibilities. I believe one should learn to identify with whatever emotions one is having (a valuable source of information), as well as with the art of training oneself to become skilled in recognizing other states of mind such as concentration, kindness, and happiness. With practice, developing these skills and states of mind allows one to have a "benevolent" source of improved mental health (Ellison, 2006).

In fact, the Positive Psychology movement has grown significantly since its inception and creation by Martin Seligman in the 1990s (see Chapter Twenty). I witnessed his keynote speech at the APA convention in 1999 and I will never forget that moving experience. One considers the concept of *eudaimonia*, the Greek ideal of happiness as a virtue, as the highest of human good and as a source of living an ethical life. This ideal creates "in a ragged line" from Aristotle to Buddhism to Maslow to Sartre to Seligman, and so it is not hard to see how the Positive Psychology trend would re-enter and CONNECT our world of scientific inquiry at this point in history.

One obvious factor would be that "happiness" facilitates Darwinian survival of the fittest; feeling comfortable, safe, and loved all contribute to that concept. Joseph Addison said that the secret to happiness is "something to do, something to love and something to hope for (look forward to)." It has been my experience that people rarely define themselves as "happy", although they may strive to be, they would settle for something more like "contented".

Although I work closely with my patients to identify and accept the suffering that comes naturally to their lives by being part of humanity, this experience doesn't have to be "our default mode;" we can learn to relax and cope with stress, relinquishing bad mental habits, all of which can result from improving our Self-monitoring skills (Chapter Thirteen).

Sapolsky (1994) generally believes that plasticity in the brain is not only involved in learning and memory but is also critically involved in maintaining the immune system. The stress response is the body's attempt to restore homeostatic balance.

> This consists of the secretion of certain hormones, the inhibition of others, the activation of particular parts of the nervous system and other physiological changes…We worry ourselves sick, which knocks out the homeostasis…One of the hallmarks of the stress response is the rapid mobilization of energy from

storage sites and the inhibition of further storage. Glucose and the simplest forms of proteins and fats come pouring out of your fat cells, liver, and muscles, all to stoke whichever muscles are struggling to save your neck (Sapolsky, 1994, p. 11).

Because allostasis changes the "set point" of the previous stable homeostasis/equilibrium (Koob, 2013), Sapolsky differentiates between adaptive and maladaptive responses. Adaptive responses, generally seen in fight/flight/freeze situations, include increased energy, cardiac output, and alertness, with a decrease in digestive and immune functions. Many of the maladaptive responses fall under the dis-ease category, such as myopathy and hypertension, colitis, loss of libido, increased disease risk overall, and other "stress-related" conditions.

The human body has the amazing capacity to heal itself that is [normally] automatic. In an aligned, balanced state, our self-healing is maximized. Our body constantly attempts to protect us from external threats. Symptoms are a sign that balance has been lost and inner resistance is less than outer stress. Pain and illness are warning signs that we need to withdraw our attention and energy from outside involvement and allow our body to use as many resources as possible to deal with internal challenges.

Dis-ease is a manifestation of a deeper challenge that involves the whole person and how we have dealt with stress—past and present (ibid, 2013). YoYo Ma, the renowned cellist, told an interviewer about how much he enjoys working with young musicians and being mutually exposed to their musicality because the "energy" has such a deep capacity to change, heal, and make him evolve himself.

Sapolsky coined the term glucocorticoid "neuro-endangerment", whereby stress and glucocorticoids not only can damage neurons but can also impair the capacity of such neurons to survive such insults (Sapolsky & Pulsinelli, 1985, pp. 300–305). In our study of CONNECTION, it is most important to recognize how the internal systems (CRF FSH, and TSH, known as the Hypothalamic Pituitary Adrenal (HPA) axis) are directly CONNECTED to the external systems, such as work, family, environmental toxins, and prior history.

"Development may be giving with one hand—conferring developmental advantage through blunting of the HPA axis to protect the brain from iatrogenic effects of prolonged cortisol elevations—while taking away with the other—the blunting of the cortisol response leading to longer term health costs" (Blair and Raver, 2012, p. 313). We have control over some of these factors, like blood glucose, heart rate, blood pressure and nutrition; other factors (such as other people!) we do not. As a therapist who sees patients with chronic diseases, I am particularly concerned that both my clients and I keep an up-to-date awareness of how these factors affect their condition, especially as to why stress hormones can be immunosuppressive. The autonomic nervous system has everything to do with one's response to stress.

Sapolsky also defines something he calls the "cascade effect;" it is the effect of the glucocorticoids on the immune system, including both the sympathetic and parasympathetic nervous systems. Energy is the "measure of that which passes from one atom to another in the course of their transformations" (de Chardin, 1959, p. 42). It is a unifying power, but the atom appears to become enriched or exhausted during the exchange as well. In a stressful emergency, however, energy comes from the liver and fat cells, not the immune system and only the parts of the immune system essential under those circumstances are activated. That difference is possibly why long-term stress is felt to diminish the effectiveness of the immune system's production of the T cells needed to fight off cancer cells. [72]

In 1987, Richard Sobel conducted his doctoral research on the role of emotional expression and personality factors in the development of varying diseases in which immunosuppression was a factor. He found significant differences between the arthritis subjects, the heart disease subjects, and the cancer subjects. A "control group" of healthy subjects was also included.

There were preliminary indications that the healthy subjects were more time-competent, self-actualizing, sensitive to their own needs and feelings, free to express feelings behaviorally, and were more comfortable with intimate contact than the three disease group subjects. Conclusions derived from the results indicated that early experience, emotional style, and personality factors do play etiological roles in the development of the three diseases studied. Additionally, the author of the study concluded that there is some evidence to support theories which propose the existence of immunosuppression-prone, coronary prone, and hardy healthy personality types (ibid, 1987, doctoral dissertation).

We have since discovered that cortisol created higher levels of inflammation all the time as a symptom of this chronic stress in people who felt unhealthy; depression and many medical findings are critically linked. Depression is now seen as a risk factor for death from all causes in coronary patients.

Metacognition and Pain Management

These findings bring us to a discussion about "Metacognition." Although technically this word means "knowing about knowing," in our context we consider the connotation of how knowledge gives us strategies of problem solving and survival under stress.

Whether we are discussing controlling emotions, pain, addictions, understanding our dreams, or achieving serenity through meditation, researchers and practitioners such as Beck (1967), Sapolsky (1994), Ellis (1994) and Siegel (2012) have all pointed us back to core principles of metacognition. How the brain

---

[72] "One half of this system is activated in response to stress, one half is suppressed…the part turned on is called the sympathetic nervous system. It helps mediate vigilance, arousal, activation, mobilization, the nerve endings of this system release adrenaline…epinephrine is secreted by the sympathetic nerve endings in your adrenal glands, norepinephrine is secreted by all of the other sympathetic nerve endings throughout the body (neurotransmitter role/hormones)…the parasympathetic component mediates calm, vegetative activities…The autonomic nervous system sends nerves into the tissues that form or   by the pituitary under the control of the brain…'conditioned immunosuppression'" (Sapolsky, 1994, p. 24, 132).

learns, how memory works, how the immune system protects us, and how our overall belief systems (as an end-product of psycho-social and biological development throughout all of the above) have given us a way to escape the suffering of our bodily of psyche's pain; a method to control our thoughts that either contribute to healing or need to be challenged as self-destructive.

Memory is created when the sensory-motor cortex, facilitated by proteins, send signals down a synapse to a new pathway CONNECTING and consolidating new experiences. These memories are "saved" and "resaved" as necessary, going in and out of the "hard drive" of our brain. In this way, the brain is self-organizing, a reflection of behavioral sentiments and the recursive nature of our reactions to environmental stimuli. We have perception, then choice and action. Both functions also enhance the efficiency of habit formation and developing executive memory.[73]

When we are suffering (physically and/or emotionally), we seldom feel in control of our environment or the outcomes of our responses to pain. However, we do have choices. If we practice wellness behaviors throughout our life, these practices will serve us during the tough times. If we view ourselves as limited, we will act disabled; if we view ourselves as supported, capable of fighting against adversity, and willing to challenge ourselves to obtain success, then we will have much better outcomes during periods of pain. As discussed, these thoughts and actions are shown to affect certain parts of the brain that are especially important in neuroendocrinological responses. If our bodies release the right pain management neurotransmitters at the right time, if our brains recognize the need for positive Self-talk during a depression, we can become the champions of our own recovery. More on these behaviors and patterns in Chapters Thirteen through Sixteen.

Because these chapters are focused on psychological constructs and the development of psychotherapeutic techniques, the core issues of risk assessment, Self-awareness, and historical influences (UFT) are strongly presented. But it is not just psychological influences that can repair broken hearts or bring recovery to someone deep in addiction. One's own belief system has a powerful impact on all kinds of chronic conditions. The concept of "psychosomatic" influences used to be considered a part of neurosis or personality disorders. We now know that the

---

[73] "Metacognition is considered to have two general categories of function: awareness and executive. Awareness functions are those metal activities that permit us to have knowledge of at least some of our thoughts, memories, self-monitoring, and knowledge about knowledge. Executive functions are those mental activities that allow us to alter and direct our cognitions voluntarily. They include functions like self-regulation, problem-solving and control processes. This system is responsible for deciding which items are to be rehearsed in short-term memory and transferred to long-term memory. This system illustrates how executive processes are 'above' the flow of environmental input to control its processing [think about parenting!]. In this sense, the cybernetic system appears to create and execute its own programs...This is a system which [then exists and] behaves for the manifestation of its own goals" (Ravn, 1988, p. 123).

psychological (psycho) part of our neurological system is deeply CONNECTED to the way our bodies function (somatic). These insights have shifted most, if not all, of the manner in which modern medicine responds to suffering.

For fifteen years I was honored to facilitate a class at the UCSan Diego Medical School. It was focused on Behavioral Science issues in medicine, and I thought of it as the "bedside manner" class. First year students came from all over the country (Yale, Berkeley, NYU, University of Chicago) with undergraduate degrees in Biochemistry, Biometrics, Neurolinguistics and more. They were the brightest students, used to being the best of the best in their cohort. And then they arrived at UCSan Diego and suddenly everyone else around them were the best of their group as well and the competition was high. Expectations were also high; the day of our class they had Neurobiochemistry at 8 am, our class as 10, lunch and then Pediatrics and hospital externships in the afternoon.

Our class taught them all aspects of dealing with the developmental and psychological symptoms of disease: dealing with the aging patient, telling someone their disease was terminal, adolescent medicine, discussions of sexual issues, and the psychosomatic components that lie within every patient's view of themselves when ill. Many of the students were still trying to decide what specialty they would choose; I am proud to report that, after taking the class, over the years many chose the specialty of Psychiatry or Pediatrics. What is most important here is that the students' sensitivity always seemed to increase from their initial starting hyper-focused academic attitude of "teach me and let me get a good grade." They got what we were trying to teach them beyond the facts and symptoms of a condition, they understood the necessity for empathy and relational treatment.

What we think about how we feel, therefore, is a multifaceted experience. Our processing or cognitive functioning is usually based strongly on our UFT, what we have been exposed to in the behavioral processes of those around us and our experiences of trust with those who raise us. Our feelings, however, are ours alone. Feelings begin early; watch any one-year-old and his expressions of inner life on his face, even though he does not have verbal skills yet. Our feelings are reinforced by the same neurotransmitters that will stay with us throughout our whole life and external experiences of our UFT only influence whether we express or hide our deeper emotions.

Cognitive Behavior Therapy (See Chapter Fourteen) is based on the awareness and integration of what one is thinking (cognition), feeling, and acting (behavioral) on one's impulses and intellect. In the treatment of certain symptoms, whether medical or psychological, the more we recognize the input of each of these three factors into one's "suffering," the more we can understand and mitigate our reactions, whether impulsive, angry, or open and supportive to Self-care. Our view of our suffering is recursive (repeating itself infinitely) --the more we think we can help ourselves, the more our brain/mind comes up with helpful solutions and is open to support from others, the more we think that our situation is hopeless, the more our brain/mind sends negative concepts and pain-enhancing neurotransmitters, particularly when the pain is caused by nerve damage or an addictive reaction in the brain.

Most behavioral programs set up to treat pain and provide pain management require 10 to 12 visits with a Cognitive Behavioral program before pain management will be administered (Kaiser is famous for this procedure). One must demonstrate a knowledge of and willingness to practice Self-assessment and practice of behavioral techniques, such as relaxation/ meditation, increased cardiovascular capacity, increased positive Self-talk and willingness to reach out for support and help from others when experiencing a diminished capacity to function due to pain. Once there are positive indicators of some successful control of pain episodes, then a practitioner will collaborate with the patient to provide the best option for medicinal relief as an adjunct to the behavioral techniques. Research shows that it is the result of both of these options, Self-care supporting and potentiating medicinal treatment, which show the best outcomes in pain management.

Given the requirements stated above for pain management, the criteria do change a bit for elders. Elderly patients not only are fearful about what is happening to them, but they are also less likely to change daily routines and behavioral patterns they have had for their whole life. And given the fear and discomfort that comes with pain, a natural inclination to feel like giving up is not unusual. It is sometimes couterintuitive to explain to an elderly person that even though they can barely walk they need to get up at least stand/stretch once an hour. I try to CONNECT this pattern of behavior with the commercial between TV programs or the chapters read in a book. The sense of accomplishment by doing this is also a form of metacognition for the elder.

In metacognition, insight and perspective are gained from intuitive awareness. While under stress, strategies that enhance Self-care are usually also vicariously helpful with pain-management and other positive outcomes of meditation (serenity). Practitioners in both cognitive science (Sapolsky) as well as cognitive therapy (Beck, Siegel), have all focused on metacognition as a helpful illustration of how the brain/mind works. Metacognition is particularly important in synthesizing the areas of the UFT, the influencing factors of our life that culminate in personality as well as behavioral patterns. If we survey our thoughts, we will uncover our influences on Self, positive and negative. Our belief system will reflect all the above influences, and also the metacognition aspects of our intuitive sights and ongoing choices to enhance or deter the choice of healthy behaviors. Problem-solving and dealing with stress becomes part of the everyday flow.

Again, it is the proteins used in the process of formulating memories, which create a new pathway to CONNECT memory of experiences. Because the brain is self-organizing, and tends toward compartmentalization, we save memories through the perception of sameness to some previous memory. Likeness and CONNECTION in executive memory determine where the behavioral reactions and emotionality fit; these functions are interactive and studied by neuroscientists and behaviorists. We still know little about some brain functions. But we can measure reactive shifts in neurotransmitters (flooding) and changes in brain function in response to stimuli using MRIs and CT scans.

Oxytocin and Emotional Intelligence

The basic feelings of attachment and empathy are experienced through release of neurotransmitters. Oxytocin is a naturally occurring hormone which stimulates feelings of bonding and trust and can reduce fear and anxiety. It is one of the neurotransmitters most important to our discussion of how a UFT of our physical biology, neurological, and spiritual elements would lead us to recognize a sense of Self, "of an Us-ness that gives us meaning, value and purpose" (Hartshorne, 2009, p. 19). Even during a therapy session, the release of oxytocin can bring about a psycho-physiological change.

Joshua Hartshorne writes that in the activation of the vagal nerve, oxytocin is associated with feelings of caretaking and ethical intuition. He presented some examples of this neurological response to social function, from deep within the hypothalamus:

- Experiences of reverence in nature or of being around those who are morally inspiring improve people's sense of connection to one another and their sense of purpose.

- Meditating on a compassionate approach to others shifts resting brain activation to the left hemisphere, a region associated with happiness, and boosts immune functions.

- Talking about what we are thankful for boosts happiness, social well-being, and health.

- Devoting resources to others, rather than indulging a materialist desire, brings about lasting well-being [12-step behavior] (ibid, 2009, pp. 18–19).

The ability to focus on others could be said to "shift the neurochemical responses from fight-or-flight response of cortisol to the calm-and-CONNECT response that oxytocin primes in the brain to alter the ways neural networks process emotions, thoughts memories, and feelings" (Graham, 2009, pp. 23–24). In today's language of psychology, we need to learn the wisdom of emotional intelligence (Goleman, 2005), which enables us to build respect and trust for ourselves and others. Many of these skills are first developed as consciousness develops. Prenatal studies have concluded that many of the circuit elements necessary for consciousness are in place by the third trimester.

Gallese and Goldman (1998) described how we develop our ability to infer (beliefs and desires) from "reading" other people, as well as how we eventually learn through reinforced experiences which eventually become our behaviors. Thus, a Self (UFT) is experientially and phenomenologically the sum of interior interpretation (prefrontal cortex) of experiences, social and interactional, storing patterns of behavior sequences while simultaneously modulating physiological [genetic and epigenetic] encoding through these cultural determinants (Marks-Tarlow, 1999). A "theory of mind" refers to our inferences about others' mental states (beliefs and desires) which we determine based on observation of their behavior and emotional responses.

It is important to ask about the "subjective" experience in all these neural pathways—where is imagination, volition, and the precursors of emotional "choice?" In a way, the mind records (or "time stamps") its memories or experiences into a memory center in the hippocampus, but the concept of "individual" or "Self" cannot be found in the neural network. An individual may have a specific temperament, morality, or role identity, but does such patterning dispute the output of the intellect? Even the new studies of metacognition, mindfulness and meditation using PET scans cannot completely answer this question. As much as the brain is often compared to a computer, or the other way around, a computer must remain strictly dependent on its binary codes to communicate and for data storage [although note that there is a quantum computer in development that does not use binary functioning!]; the human brain is often less precise; it can become "bugged" or toxic, not to mention confused. "Creativity and confusion travel together" (Anderson, 2014).

Neurotransmitters and PTSD

We have discussed how the limbic system is the source of most of our hormones and neurotransmitters. The limbic system contains the pathways for well-being, resolution, and enjoyment, as well as eating and sexual pleasure. A whole host of altruistic attitudes and behaviors are also believed to be reinforced there. Perhaps this is the mind? Note quote that begins the chapter! It would seem reasonable, therefore, to acknowledge that disruptions in this system may lead to fear and other negative emotions. For instance, post-partum depression is believed to reflect negative emotions and "maladaptive traits" tagged onto to adaptive ones because of stress (Hartshorne, 2009). One specific example of this type of anxiety or panic response is Post-Traumatic Stress Disorder (PTSD).

> The essential feature of Post-Traumatic Stress Disorder is the development of characteristic symptoms following exposure to an extreme traumatic stressor involving direct personal experience of an event that involves actual or threatened death or serious injury or other threat to one's physical integrity; or witnessing an event that involves death, injury, or a threat to the physical integrity of another person; or learning about unexpected or violent death, serious harm, or threat of death or injury experienced by a family member or other close associate. The person's response to the event must involve intense fear, helplessness, or horror.
>
> The characteristic symptoms resulting from the exposure to the extreme trauma include persistent re-experiencing of the traumatic event, persistent avoidance of stimuli associated with the trauma, and numbing of general responsiveness, and persistent symptoms of increased arousal. The full symptom picture must be present for more than 1 month, and the disturbance must cause clinically significant distress or impairment in social, occupation, or important areas of functioning (APA, 2000, p. 463).

As noted, many different neurological functions participate in the PTSD responses of hypervigilance, startle, sleep disorder, emotional numbing, and heightened arousal, including Sympathetic Nervous System (SNS) and Parasympathetic Nervous System (PNS) circuitry in the amygdala, hippocampus, thalamus, sensory-cortex, anterior cingulate cortex, and prefrontal cortex. "Many of the normal pathways that allow extinction of fear memories have become impaired" (Koob, 2013, personal communication). Cushioned by the neurochemical systems, the brain pathways become flooded, and the person may experience learned helplessness, "that you have little control over your circumstances," which in turn is experienced as depression. The more learned helplessness, the less sense of belonging and self-worth one will experience.

A question often arises in therapy with traumatized patients: is there a direct correlation between failing immune symptoms and the fear responses of high levels of stress? It seems to me that, of all the neurological factors common to both elements of human experience, the one most likely suspect in this scenario is the hypothalamus because it is here that most hormonal and life-sustaining functions are signaled. It is also here that the brain activates the "fight, flight or freeze" response.

There are some scientists who use the theory of quantum mechanics to understand the brain, proposing that "atomic events" [one particle of activity at a time, one event at a time] is the best way to describe how primal feelings, stress, or fear can activate the chemical reactions of fight, flight, or freeze (Williams, as quoted in Madeo, 2010, p. 81). As Teilhard de Chardin pointed out: "From the real evolutionary standpoint, something is finally burned during every synthesis to pay for that synthesis. The more the energy-quantum of the world comes into play, the more it is consumed" (de Chardin, 1959, p. 51).

How do we experience fear? "Fear is sensed through the thalamus (the brain's receiver), analyzed with the cortex (the seat of reasoning), and remembered via the hippocampus (the memory-input device). It takes only 12 milliseconds for the thalamus to process sensory input and to signal the amygdala" (Siegel, M., 2005, p. 4). The thalamus is at the base of the cerebrum and is its waystation. The cerebrum also allows a synchronization of neural firing by a looping process through the cortex to the thalamus and back, a process that facilitates planning in the frontal lobes (Pinker, 1997).

Of course, we could also try to explain our felt experience of emotions through our knowledge of the fight, flight or freeze response. What this complex system of reactivity really means is that we have very little time or control over our reactivity to a fear response. And yet it is possible to retrain ourselves to deal with fear and/or anger under unusual circumstances and stresses (think a warzone, childbirth, chronic pain, and so forth). How do we accomplish that? I believe it is because we are CONNECTED in an even deeper, quicker, and more profound way to the internal functioning of our brains and our immune systems.

To best ensure that our brains and immune systems function at their highest capacity, it is important to choose and control the ingredients of the food we ingest. Food is our fuel. We know that, but from an early age we are reinforced to think of food in so many other ways: as nurturing, as a reward for good behavior, as a social function, to 'stuff' down negative feelings, and as a necessary inconvenience if we're tired and/or busy with other things. But ultimately, the 'fuel' our body needs are based on carbohydrates, proteins, and fats. It is the fats and oils that most affect the functioning of our brain.

Food and the Brain/Inflammatory Diseases

Healthy brain function depends on several factors. Circulation is important, and clogged arteries can have a negative effect on the brain. Blood must transport nutrients and oxygen into the brain fluids by crossing the "blood-brain barrier". Nutrients are then transformed, by adrenal function from available insulin, into neurotransmitters; these neurotransmitters send thoughts and other information across the space (synapse) between neurons. Hormones play a key role in brain health as well, and an imbalance in hormones in one area of the body will affect all other hormones, so balance is the key. "Basically, the brain doesn't quite trust that the pancreas won't still secrete a little insulin. So, a second step occurs—during stress, glucocorticoids act on fat cells throughout the body to make them less sensitive to insulin just in case there's some still floating around" (Sapolsky, 1994 p. 67). Food can help mediate the stress response after the initial shutting down in digestion.

As mentioned above, when we experience physical, mental, or emotional stress, we produce the stress hormone called cortisol. Ongoing high cortisol levels have a negative impact on many body systems, including the brain. Candida (yeast) overgrowth, food sensitivities, intestinal toxemia, tension and stress, or chronic pain and illness all affect cell reactivity (We often develop sensitivities to the foods we eat most and crave most!). When the good bacteria are killed off, the yeast gets hungry, attaches to our intestinal lining, and starts to grow there, becoming a parasite. Symptoms such as skin rashes, extreme fatigue, brain fog, digestive upset, and immune system disorders can develop. When this happens a successful diagnosis of the cause can be achieved by a change in diet. As certain foods are eliminated, one by one, the individual can often determine the direct source of the allergy or food sensitivity.

It is recommended that the diet first be changed to eliminate simple sugars and processed carbohydrates like ground flour, gluten, dairy, alcohol, and coffee, whatever is the most liked or common food source taken in daily. This high intake frequency could have caused a food allergy (Hall, nutritional consultant, pamphlet). What a tall order, I know. But if one is suffering from the symptoms listed above and wants to find relief (often within 3 weeks or less), it is well worth it.

Inflammation in the body is a response to tissue injury, infection, or other irritants. "The purpose of the inflammatory response is to limit damage caused by injury to a local site. In the case of a pathogen, inflammation limits its spread and kills and removes the pathogen…In addition, inflammation involves the initiation of repair processes designed to fix tissue damage though proliferation of CONNECTIVE tissues…" (Maier, Watkins, and Fleshner, 1994, p. 1012). Because the level of inflammation directly correlates with adrenal changes, stress responses and rises in glucocorticoids cause an increase in glucose factors in the liver and changes in the effect of amino acids on protein breakdown.

Good and Bad Fats

There are even more reasons why we should pay particular attention to what we eat and the potential our intake has for affecting our inflammatory response. The worst ingredient, especially for the immune system, is called trans-fat (hydrogenated oil)—which is hard to process and creates inflammation throughout the body. This is an extremely toxic fat. It is one of the main causative factors of disease, memory impairment, and mood disorders in our country. In addition, for years, fast food restaurants have reused oil in frying food, which makes cholesterol oxidize and is thought to be carcinogenic. Luckily, some restaurants have begun to change their policy about this usage.

The "good" fats include those from olive oil, seeds and nuts, avocados, and eggs. Omega 3 essential fatty acids (EFAs) fight inflammation in all body tissues and create healthy cell walls. Ground flaxseed is a great vegetarian source of Omega 3s along with fiber to remove toxins. What we call Omega 3s can be found in over-the-counter supplements as well. Essential fatty acids have been found to be helpful with depression, anxiety, aggression, emotional outbursts, memory, attention, and focus.

We also know that sugar and flour products are depressing foods, and they increase inflammation and accelerate the aging process. "Sugar's effect on your mood actually comes from your brain's chemicals (neurotransmitters) that operate in your neural brain…Your pancreas produces insulin to metabolize sugar and the insulin then makes available to your brain an amino acid called tryptophan, which converts to serotonin, a major neurotransmitter" (Hall, nutritional pamphlet). High fructose corn syrup used in processed foods causes a blood sugar spike in the body, generating weight gain and setting the stage for diabetes (not only a long-term immune disorder, but also one which can have chronic and immeasurable effects on the brain as well).

As noted by Sapolsky, immune system responses sometimes cause the rest of the body's "economy" to collapse. "If you constantly mobilize energy at the cost of energy storage, you will never store any surplus energy. You will fatigue more rapidly, and your risk of developing a form of diabetes will even increase" (Sapolsky, 1994, p. 14). Stimulants such as coffee and caffeinated tea make our brains release serotonin, the major "feel good" neurotransmitter, only to leave us depleted and drained of this crucial component of brain health. Drink decaffeinated green tea and water instead.; ultimately, to make this easy, my recommendation is keep processed, nutritionally dead food out of your diet!

Considering the immune system and brain function, protein is also very balancing for the blood sugar: fish, eggs, chicken, and turkey. An anti-inflammatory, brain nourishing diet would have lots of fish, vegetables, seeds, and nuts. Of course, nutritionists will tell us that the best recommendations for health also include exercise; walking, yoga, *tai chi* and breath work are the best choices to relieve stress, anxiety, mood, and insomnia. If you are just starting yoga, for instance, it's OK to back off if the stretches become too difficult. Keep practicing every day and you will find you can do at least what you did the day before. Your body will wisely tell you how much you can handle. If you compare your body to a simple machine, you see that it has many similarities:

- Moving parts designed for locomotion (for instance, joints, muscles, and ligaments).
- A fuel-distribution system providing energy to the moving parts (circulation and digestion).
- An on-board computer to regulate all these systems (brain).
- An electrical system to CONNECT the computer to the rest of the body (nervous system).

When everything works properly, your human "machine" can be considered healthy. This health will be seen in age-appropriate body mobility, balance, stability, strength and flexibility.

- Movement is essential to life. Without it, your blood would not circulate, your digestion would stop, and you would find it impossible to breathe.
- Balance also results from appropriate range of motion and good joint health.
- Strength and flexibility come from active use and resilience of the muscles around the joints (for instance, ball-and-socket joint of the hip).

Often our bodies become unhealthy, often noticed in inflammation. Medications are available, but inflammation can also be helped by rest and nutrition. These choices can reverse the process of "oxidation" that comes from stress which damages cells, tissues, and organs. Food high in antioxidants include:

- Fruits: blueberries, strawberries, cherries, and red grapes.
- Vegetables: brightly colored and dark green leafy vegetables.
- Nuts: Pecans, walnuts, and hazelnuts.
- Legumes: Black beans, pinto beans, and red kidney beans.
- Green tea
- Olive oil

(Brican Systems Corporation)

Finally, another important predictor of health, just as important as diet and exercise, is that of belonging to a social group or network. It enhances our resilience, enables us to cope, and demonstrates just how inter-CONNECTED everything really is. Studies show that there is significantly less memory loss in those who were more socially integrated and active. "It's best not to have all your eggs (social identities) in one basket in case misfortune strikes. Recognizing the importance of social identity opens new thinking, not only in psychology but also in sociology, economics, medicine, and neuroscience" (Jetten, et. al. 2009, p. 26–33).

Research shows that if you belong to no groups but decide to join one, you cut your risk of dying over the next year in half. And if you get bad medical news, I suggest you try to focus on the positive, not the negative. Problem-solving immediately after a medical disaster is not constructive without social support, and often the last thing a person needs is detailed information about how bad reality is or advice to "get control". Rather, my recommendation as a breast cancer survivor of twenty years is to work on a sense of resiliency, of being loved and supported. One needs to develop a flexible plan that includes a method of picking one's battles slowly and with informed caution. Designate a support team by giving an assignment to each person for whom it is best suited. It was a no-brainer to have my friends in the insurance business file my disability claims and my unemployed friends drive me to chemotherapy. It wouldn't have made sense to plan it the other way around!

> Those who cope with stress successfully tend to seek control in the face of stressors but do not try to control in the present things that have already come to pass. They do not try to control future events that are uncontrollable and do not try to fix things that are not broken or that are broken beyond repair. When faced with the large wall of a stressor, one should not assume there will be a breakthrough, one single, controlling solution that will make the wall disappear. Assume instead that the wall can be scaled by a series of footholds of control. Each one small but still capable of giving support (Sapolsky, 1994, p. 279).

Chapter Eleven
How We Connect to Our Physical Bodies

The Universe of Cells and Genes

Next, we turn to a brief discussion and model of the biological sciences. To understand what forms the primary CONNECTING sequence of life, it is first necessary to look at the function of cells. Terms like nucleus, neutrons, protons, and electrons, which rotate around the perimeter of cellular function, teach us how cells CONNECT through valence bonding to form molecules, collectively called chemical bonds. "The outermost skin of electrons is an atom's major source of contact with its surroundings. Through such contacts, individual atoms join in any number of ways to form fairly permanent combinations which are called molecules (relationships)" (Sherwood, 1974, p. 42).

Molecules are the scientific names for everyday substances (for instance, Sodium/Na+Chloride/Cl=salt). H2O is another example of electron bonding forming a molecule (like Codependency in a human relationship). Oxygen (O-) will be attracted to the hydrogen (H+) atoms, and if an atom is an electron acceptor, as hydrogen is, the molecule is formed. In short, a bond is formed between two atoms when each have a "half-filled atomic orbital", the unpaired electrons form the structure called the "valence bond". Carbon (C+6), Hydrogen (H+1), and Nitrogen (N+2) are the frequent valence bond formers in the universe.[74]

Although it has only been a hundred years since G.N. Lewis first proposed how a chemical bond forms (by shared bonding electrons), the amazing advances in science since 1916 have helped prove such subsequent scientific findings as: 1) the concept of covalent bonding, 2) Schrodinger's wave equation, and 3) quantum mechanical considerations to support the concept of covalent bonding.[75]

> The dissolution of the indestructible solid atom would come from two sources, one familiar, the other quite novel—from the study of light and the discovery

---

[74] Not all possible combinations happen. "If a compound is formed, it is because the process is energetically favored—the same reason a ball runs down a hill from top to bottom. Energy is given away in the process and energy loss, in general, means stability again" (ibid, 1974, p.42). An orbital quantity only represents the probability of its position about the nucleus, its readiness to bond. (Similarly, a relational encounter requires knowing who you are!).

[75] According to Charles Coulson, author of the noted 1952 book *Valence*, this period marks the start of "modern valence bond theory," as contrasted with older valence bond theories, which are essentially electronic theories of valence couched in pre-wave-mechanical terms. Faraday had already tried to find a "unity and coherence of God's creations...[Lewis] showed that his 'lines of force' were not polar (directed to the nearest pole) as the old Newtonian theories would have suggested but were continuous curves. His crucial conclusion, the axiom of modern 'field' theory in physics, was that the energy of the magnet was not in the magnet itself but in the magnetic field" (Valence bond theory, *Wikipedia*, 8/25/2014).

of electricity. Einstein himself described this historic movement as the decline of a 'mechanical' view and the rise of a 'field' view of the physical world which helped put him on his own path to relativity, to new explanations and new mysteries (Boorstin, 1985, pp. 679, 682–683).

DNA and Epigenetics

Most of my readers will be aware of how we became created through a DNA sequence of 23 pairs of encoded messages for life, called hereditary factors; the mothers' 23 chromosomes and the fathers' 23 chromosomes combine into pairs. It may be more surprising to learn that we, as animals, share up to 99 percent of our genes with many other mammals, for instance 85% with dogs. In addition to what we know about genetic expression in growth, health, and behavior, the new field of epi-genetics has shown that environmental factors play a significant role in determining which genes get expressed in any individual. This study of epigenetic factors (the changes in genetic expression modified by environmental influences) is the area where behavioral and neurodevelopmental disorders are created and gene expression is found to overlap (therefore a link between hereditary genes and environmental and epigenetic behavior, as in drug and alcohol abuse) (Epigenetics, *Wikipedia*, 5/30/2008).

Another important messenger gene is RNA, called the replicator because it is able not only to make copies and carry messages but to make copies of itself. In a 2007 article in *Scientific American*, Robert Shapiro described how in *The Selfish Gene,* Dawkins (1976) provided an expanded discussion of the discovery that the replicator gene had the extraordinary property of being able to create copies of itself. [76] (This process proved useful in the development of a vaccine for COVID-19 during the pandemic of 2020).

It may be unfortunate that Dawkins used the word "selfish" in his title. It was indeed a loaded concept to refer to RNA in such a way, as biased and subjective as it was. He also presented the concept of "memes": ideas, stories or other representations that spread from brain to brain and, during this transmission, gain

---

[76] "In carrying out its various duties, RNA can take the form of a double helix that resembles DNA or of a folded single strand, much like a protein. "In the early 1980s, scientists discovered ribozymes, enzyme-like substances made of RNA…life began with the appearance of the first self-copying RNA molecule…appeared before proteins and DNA in the evolution of life. For example, many small molecules, called "co-factors," play a role in enzyme-catalyzed reactions. These co-factors often carry an attached RNA nucleotide with no obvious function. Such structures have been considered 'molecular fossils,' relics descended from the time when RNA alone, without DNA or proteins, ruled the biochemical world…RNA's building blocks, nucleotides, are complex substances as organic molecules go. Each contains a sugar, a phosphate and one of four nitrogen-containing bases as 'sub-subunits.' Thus, each RNA nucleotide contains nine or 10 carbon atoms, numerous nitrogen and oxygen atoms, and the phosphate group, all connected in a precise three-dimensional pattern…Amino acids are far less complex than nucleotides. Their defining features are an amino group (a nitrogen and two hydrogen molecules) and a carboxylic acid group (carbon, two oxygens and a hydrogen), both attached to the same carbon" (Pinker, 1997, p. 44).

their own features through a form of evolution to become better adapted to spreading themselves. Dawkins used this analogy to describe how natural selection explains replication of genes, and at least one of its definitions indicated that perhaps genes are selfish, in the use of the word to mean altruistic toward the self, since their activity leads to our survival (Madeo, 2010, p. 95).

In his 2007 article, Shapiro also outlined possible theories about the origin of life. According to Shapiro, origin of life proposals contains these five common requirements:

1) A boundary is needed to separate life from nonlife. Life is distinguished by its great degree of organization, yet the second law of thermodynamics requires that the universe moves in a direction in which disorder, or entropy, increases. A loophole, however, allows entropy to decrease in a limited area, provided that a greater increase occurs outside the area. When living cells grow and multiply, they convert chemical energy or radiation to heat. The released heat increases the entropy of the environment, compensating for the decrease in living systems. The boundary maintains this division of the world into pockets of life and the nonliving environment in which they must sustain themselves (lipids do this job now).
2) An energy source is needed to drive the organization process, for instance, redox reactions. They entail the transfer of electrons from an electron-rich (or reduced) substance to an electron-poor (or oxidized) one (valence shift).
3) A coupling mechanism must link the release of energy to the organization process that produces and sustains life. A mechanical CONNECTION, or coupling, is required (ATP). The energy released by this reaction serves to drive processes necessary for our biochemistry that would otherwise proceed too slowly or not at all. One assumption of the small-molecule approach is that coupled reactions and primitive catalysts are sufficient to get life started to exist in nature (or in all CONNECTIONS).
4) A chemical network must be formed to permit adaptation and evolution. "A driver reaction," serves as the engine that mobilizes the organization process.
5) The network must grow and reproduce. A compositional genome is one where heredity is stored in small molecules, rather than as a list such as DNA or RNA…The small-molecule approach to the origin of life makes several demands on nature (a compartment, an external energy supply, a driver reaction coupled to that supply, a chemical network that includes that reaction, and a simple mechanism of reproduction) [emphasis added] (Shapiro, 2007, p. 47).

Thus, in the building blocks of life, the replicator RNA is felt to be older than DNA. As a "sub-subunit", RNA distinguishes the need for enzyme reactions, an important factor in hormonal responses and pain management as we will discuss further on in this chapter. Methylation, the process of replacing a hydrogen molecule, can also affect protein function in gene expression. DNA methylation studies have had positive effects on understanding aging and environmental signals. "DNA methylation frequently occurs in repeated sequences and may help to suppress junk DNA...Epigenetic changes of this type have the potential to direct increased frequencies of permanent genetic mutation" (Tajerian, et. al. 2011, p. 68).

DNA methylation patterns are known to be established and modified in response to epigenetic influences—the "larger forces that shape gene expression." As will be discussed further in Chapter Sixteen, epigenetic factors from repeated trauma during developmental years, as well as causes of addiction, can shape how DNA has learned gene expression and experienced the process of methylation. New technology has enabled researchers to study the epigenome phenomena thought to be linked to autism and ADHD.

Let us define epigenetics further. According to research, epigenetic influences can include any aspect other than DNA sequence that influences the development of an organism, including those environmental and social influences described by theorists such as Erik Erikson (1950). I am making epigenetics an important variable in developing our UFT because so much of our behavior, our mental health, and even our spirituality may be co-factored by these influences. The epigenetic code is used to describe the set of epigenetic features that create different phenotypes in different cells (phenotypes are the genetic characteristics resulting from interactions of the individual genotype with the environment). Phenotypes are also affected by experiences—in other words, cell memory, a theory of how nongenetic material can be passed from parent to offspring.

Our Immune Systems

Medically, differences between everyday "cytotoxicity" (that which is toxic to cells) and causes of cancer, as an actual disease, influence long-term physical and emotional health. To understand disease processes, remediation, and possible prevention, let us first expand the discussion in Chapter Ten about the immune system. Robert Sapolsky (1997) describes the immunological effect of toxins in this way, "Standard dogma: DNA codes for RNA which codes for proteins. Standard virus contains DNA, inserts it into the DNA of your own cells, takes over the replicative machinery, starts making more viruses, messes up your cell in the process" (ibid, 1997, workshop). "Retroviruses" work in an even more complicated way, taking over your DNA and becoming "protein viruses—prion viruses", but that is a more complex story. For now, it is important to recognize that all kinds of viruses exist which require individual responses for protection.

When we talk about "pathogenesis" (even in referring to depression, for instance), we are referring to cell modulation by inflammation, oxidation within the cell, and the effects of stress. To reverse these effects, we usually promote physical activity and its positive effects on "neuroplasticity stimulation", cognitive functioning, and even sleep patterns. Simply put, an increase in activity can improve overall health, control for the underlying factors of the immune system's failure to protect against cancer, and even decrease depressive symptoms.

As defined by Norman Staines, Jonathan Brostoff, and Keith James in *Introducing Immunology* (1993), the immune system is a "collection of tissues, cells and molecules whose function is to maintain the internal environment of the body by destroying infectious organisms" (ibid, 1993, p. 5).

When I read this passage, I also thought about the function of the epigenetic features of DNA and our genetic makeup. Or even the defensive structures of consciousness. Such ideas come to mind because I am always thinking about CONNECTIONS, how in our universe everything is interactive; explanations need to take into account these parallel features between systemic functions as well. No biophysical system works in isolation; it is all multi-systemic, mind/body, holistic, "psychosomatic"—pick a conceptual framework. So, a question: is it that the immune system is multi-systemic, or is it all one physiological system, constantly working for us—individuals who would not naturally think to consider themselves vigilant about their immune systems really should be? We will see as we pursue this area of study.

The concept of acquiring immunity, again, can cross-reference developmentally into other areas of adaptation.[77] For instance, what factors of "natural" child development can cross-reference to acquiring "behavioral" skills that can mediate social adaptation. "Acquired" cognitive/emotional immunity creates memory and specificity for appropriate cognitive/social behaviors through the repetition response sequence. The most well-known sequence is the assimilation/accommodation sequence as defined by Piaget (1962), who believed that the infant is a constructionist, and that his growth as a child is dependent on his developmental experiences.

Organization and adaptation (use of schemas or action patterns as a "basic cognitive structure") are permanent aspects of functioning. Piaget broke down adaptation into three parts: assimilation (event fitted into the already existing cognitive structure), accommodation (cognitive structure must change for the new event to be learned), and reciprocal assimilation (equilibrium of assimilation and accommodation) (see Chapter Thirteen).

Psychoneuroimmunology studies the interaction between psychological processes and the nervous and immune systems of the body (Irwin, 2005). Of interest particularly to our discussion of a developmental UFT is that autoimmune diseases, often exacerbated by stress, fall under the study of psychoneuroimmunology. Any changes in emotional state, such as in the experience of fight/flight/freeze, will show up in changes in the immune function. The response system is very effective due to its "bidirectional communication pathways". "Although antigens do initiate immune responses and cytokines do regulate immune processes, recent research demonstrates that there are

---

[77] We see an example of this metaphoric "accommodation" pattern in the immune system through the development of how immune cells "defend" us. "As the cells divide, they progressively become committed to a particular path of development, in other words, their daughter cells differentiate to produce the various types of cells in the blood…molecular mediators that modify the function of other cells or the cells that made them in the first place. Cells responsive to a particular cytokine have receptors on their cell-membranes for that cytokine" (ibid, 1993, p. 22). In what is referred to as "thymus education" or the Goldilocks factor, not "just right" cells are eliminated. Daughter cells either die after a few weeks or do not make antibodies to any great extent but recirculate in the body and may persist for many years as memory cells.

bidirectional communication pathways between the immune system and central nervous system (CNS), with each providing important regulatory control over the other" (Maier, Watkins & Fleshner, 1994, p. 1004).

The authors concluded that any psychological event that potentially alters both the neural and hormonal factors can alter immunity. Such mood states as anxiety and depression are often the result of "dysregulation of the pituitary-adrenal system". Likewise, the immune system seems to have a high degree of "redundancy" and ability to alter steps in between the beginning of the system's reaction and its endpoint. We will see many effects like this as we study biology, physics, psychology and human behavior, factors of Heisenberg's Uncertainty Principle throughout systemic functioning.

Inflammation in the body is a response to tissue injury, infection, or other irritants. "The purpose of the inflammatory response is to limit damage caused by injury to a local site. In the case of a pathogen, inflammation limits the pathogen's spread and kills and removes it. In addition, inflammation involves the initiation of repair processes designed to fix tissue damage though proliferation of CONNECTIVE tissues..." (ibid, 1994, p. 1012). Because the level of inflammation directly correlates with adrenal changes, stress responses and changes in glucocorticoids may cause increases in glucose factors in the liver as well as changes in the effect of amino acids on protein breakdown.

Thus, we should pay particular attention to what we eat and the potential our intake has for affecting our inflammatory response. Negative systemic changes or effects usually show up first in the stomach, with nausea, cramping or other stomach distress. Since it is known that all cells in the body have a particular life span, it is no surprise that the stomach cells, with the shortest life span of about 4 hours, would have the first reaction to toxins such as food poisoning, medications, or chemotherapy.

It has been discovered more recently that there really is a second brain of sorts, in the "gut" (what does your gut tell you?), that is also processing input with neurotransmitters, hormones, and neuropeptides. The "gut" brain may in fact react as quickly, if not first, to such effects and particularly to stressful situations just as cells and transmitters do in the walls of the brain and in the immune system.

Early researchers studying immune function, such as Cannon (1911), Selye (1956) and Solomon (1964), contributed to findings in the biological functioning of the glucocorticoids that signal the nervous system, which then affects the immune function. "The immune and endocrine systems are modulated not only by the brain but by the central nervous system itself" (Muscatell, 2020, pp. 1–3). The main effect is on the inflammatory response, or the "itis-schmitis" as I have heard it called, meaning many things that end in "itis" have a common immunological source, often autoimmune.

Although we have already gone into the effects of stress in detail in Chapter Ten, it is important to further underscore the influences of cytokines and cortisol here. Because glucocorticoids suppress the synthesis of proinflammatory cytokines, and inflammatory cytokines making adrenocorticotropic hormones (ACTH) stimulate cortisol secretion, glucocorticoids thus disrupt the homeostasis of a healthy body.

But our bodies also use the inflammatory response to save us! Complex interactions exist between cytokines, inflammation, and the adaptive responses in maintaining homeostasis. Like the stress response, the inflammatory reaction is crucial for survival.[78] Systemic inflammatory reaction results in stimulation of four major programs:

- The acute-phase reaction.
- The sickness syndrome.
- The pain program.
- The stress response.

Our goal is to maintain cognitive and affective health by recognizing that sympathetic nervous system (SNS) and endocrine changes, which are signs of possible immune function damage, may have been taking place over a long period of time, influenced by our own personal UFT. Because stress often manifests in just this type of pattern, physiological changes during and after a trauma or stress should be noted or treated with medication and mindful relaxation techniques. On the other hand, positive self-care experiences over a long period may have boosted the ongoing immune function in an individual.

Self-regulation

In psychology, "self-regulation" is another term for self-control or willpower, but it signifies much more. Self-regulation demonstrates that we have learned strategies to control and improve our emotional stability in the face of negative or anxiety-producing stimuli. However, as I have seen with clients during a therapy session, sustaining attention toward one activity of self-regulation often distracts from another. Often the client has been self-reinforced by the experience of focusing on one (insignificant) problem, by which they can distract themselves from another (core) issue. Self-regulation can have a positive effect, however, when it allows us to distract ourselves from disturbing negative experiences or physical pain sensations. Training in self-regulation is often an intrinsic part of behavioral psychotherapy.

I have CONNECTED this description of the response in cells to that of chaining of memories that takes place in learning sequences (Piaget). As a corollary, individuals learn through the accumulation of experiences and self-awareness, having built up our own UFT data base, how to protect and "suppress" the effects (whether social, emotional, or spiritual) upon our inner or outer-directed reactivity and CONNECTION to the world around us. We speak of "immunity" on several levels, therefore, not the least of which is our physical health.

---

[78] "Recent studies show that pro-inflammatory cytokine processes take place during depression, mania, and bipolar disease, in addition to autoimmune hypersensitivity and chronic infections. Chronic secretion of stress hormones can also lead to the dysregulation of neurohormones in the adrenoreceptors and the functional activity of different lymphoid cells. Behavioral parameters, such as 'hyperactivity' and 'systemic anti-inflammatory feedback,' may contribute to the pathogenesis of disease" (ibid, 2020, pp. 1–3).

Is there a self-regulation gene that affects the levels of serotonin and potential anxiety? The "anxiety gene" has been found to be very common, especially in more than half of the Caucasian population who has inherited it from at least one parent (Canli, 2008, p. 53). However, this author also noted that the risk of increased depression or felt anxiety was also directly correlated to the contextual cues from "difficult life circumstances". Some subjects could maintain a "resting state" when cued to negative stimuli, while others seemed to be in a "chronic arousal" state and were the subjects most likely to experience "anxiety, fearfulness and, possibly, a predisposition to mood disorders such as depression" [and rumination] (ibid, 2008, p. 55).

How can we measure the functioning of our immune system? The balance of healthy with unhealthy daily choices can be compared to how much has been conditioned by the past impact of child developmental issues (UFT). These issues and/or choices may have caused adaptive immune responses for many years, with subsequent changes to originally healthy neuroendocrine and mental health systems.[79] Some of the factors that lead the list of potential assaults to the immune system are:

1. Prenatal factors
2. Pre-permanency/postnatal babies are born autoreactive until mother's antibodies are absorbed through thymus—lymphoid tissue, where "T cell repertoire" is learned.
3. Child abuse
4. Medication

T cells do not make antibodies or secrete special antigen receptor molecules, but rather, after activation, differentiate into cytokines (accessory molecules on their cell surface). T cells help B cells make antibody responses by synthesizing and secreting cytokines that promote activation, growth, and differentiation of B cells. They are locally produced in the hypothalamus, resulting in some behavioral effects as well.

There is also a nonspecific immune response, "the body's rapid new take on psychoneuroimmunology" (Azar, 2001). This "sickness" response also copies the stress response, releasing stress hormones such as cortisol because of the energy needed to fight the possibility of infection. Also, the signals from the hypothalamus trigger behavioral signals in the brain. The interesting question is

---

[79] "A description of the difference between B cells and T cells is helpful here. In your immune system, any cells that lack your distinctive cellular signature are attacked. Moreover, when your immune system does encounter a novel invader, it can even form an immunologic memory of what the infectious agent looks like, to better prepare for its next invasion—a process which is exploited when you are vaccinated—immune defenses are brought about by a complex array of circulating cells called lymphocytes and monocytes, T cells and B cells. Both originate in the bone marrow, but T cells migrate to mature in the thymus, while B cells mature in the bone marrow. B cells principally produce antibodies, but there are several kinds of T cells (T helper and T suppressor cells, cytotoxic killer cells, and so on)" (Sapolsky, 1994, p. 134).

how the signals are transferred so quickly; the answer seems to be an involvement of the vagus nerve in the "gut", where there are pockets of neurotransmitters called paraganglia. The exciting part of the finding of the paraganglia neurotransmitter is how it completes a "bidirectional" immune-to-brain circuit.

How do viruses affect us, and how is this different in Autoimmune Deficiency Syndrome (AIDS)? Viruses can only replicate intracellularly, so special forms of immune reaction are needed to eliminate them. "We need two kinds of immune reaction to the virus; first an antibody response which affects the virus outside cells and in the circulation, and secondly a true cell-mediated response to reach the intracellular virus" (Staines, et. al, 1993, p. 74). Genetic "deficiencies" that lead to a failure of the "pairing" [CONNECTING] between components that require complements may lead to severe diseases, such as chronic infections and immune disorders.

Human Immunodeficiency Virus (HIV), the precursor to autoimmune deficiency syndrome (AIDS), is measured by the CD4:CD8 T cell ratio. Detection of either antigen or antibody RNA in the virus is copied as DNA and then becomes integrated into the DNA of the infected cell. We see the effects of this damage in skin lesions, lung disease or brain disease.[80]

Immunity and Our Emotions

It is our T cells we had better protect when we tell ourselves we "don't need stress" in our lives, and which are most affected by the adrenal axis fight/flight/freeze reaction. This concept is further discussed below as related to pain and emotional management. On the other hand, we can also experience the healing effect from care and compassion by an increase in immunoglobulin, which lasts for several hours after the actual experience is over. "It is well known that any heightened emotional state boosts our immune defenses via a short-term spike in immunoglobulin. While positive emotions, such as compassion, sustain long-term immune-boosting effects, negative emotional states, such as anger, are soon followed by a drop in immunity" [emphasis added] (Azar, 2011, p. 41).

Indeed, on a biological level, compassion acts as almost the opposite of the fight-or-flight response.[81] Compassion may be self-perpetuating as well.

---

[80] "The intensity of a hypersensitivity reaction often increases with repeated exposure to the stimulating agent. The thyroid is one of the tissues most often affected by autoantibodies, which are directed against cells and molecules on and in the gland itself (organ-specific autoimmunity) …little of the normal structure survives, the thyroid being almost entirely replaced by inflammatory cells which may become organized in lymphoid follicles…immune damage to the endocrine tissue upsets the hormonal balance of the body" (Staines, et al., 1993, p. 88).

[81] "In addition to bestowing us with innate tendencies toward empathy, compassion, altruism, trust, and cooperation, evolutionary forces have equipped us to take advantage of that fact, even if we're only now beginning to come to terms with what it can mean for our future. Within the medial septum, there is a 'synchronizing system' which organizes the effects of oxytocin" (Azar, 2011, p. 42).

Oxytocin is the "mammalian hormone that also acts as a neurotransmitter in the brain, released into the blood from the posterior lobe of the pituitary gland." This hormone is a peptide of nine amino acids (a nonapeptide). Oxytocin neurons make other peptides which act locally, along with "a modulation of hypothalamic pituitary adrenal (HPA) axis activity" (Hartshorne, 2009).

Understanding the importance of oxytocin receptors becomes relevant when we recognize how many parts of the brain and spinal cord, including the amygdala, ventromedial hypothalamus, septum, and brainstem, are receptor sites for oxytocin. Reception of oxytocin results in the monogamous pair bond/CONNECTIONS that we have been discussing. There are a variety of other functions that oxytocin also provides, including the inhibition of tolerance to various addictive drugs (opiates, cocaine, alcohol). Oxytocin also helps reduce withdrawal symptoms. For an addict in withdrawal, compassionate listening or even physical contact can be a lifesaver.

Chronic Pain

We now turn to the long-term effects of pain, something that we may all experience at one time or another. We have shown in the previous chapter that chronic pain, and its effects, have a highly significant impact on neurological functioning. We need to understand that nociceptors (peripheral nerves) create a pathway that can become pathologically damaged. Allodynia, pain that is caused by a stimulus which does not normally produce pain, is common in individuals with long periods of chronic pain. Foot neuropathy could be an example of allodynia.

> Pain produced under these conditions reflects pathological changes in pain pathways and represents a disease in and of itself. Altered neurons unleash exaggerated reactions to tissue damaging input. Hormones or inflammatory molecules that the body produces in response to injury may sensitize nociceptors, making them more impulsive, a change that could instigate the development of chronic pain and abnormal sensitivity to mild stimuli (Porreca and Price, 2009, p. 34–41).

Understanding the chronicity of the pain is of paramount importance if we are to help ourselves or our patients manage the pain. We refer to the reaction of the wounded nerve as "hyper-excitability". The continuation of pain is often caused by a reaction of the wounded nerve, along with healthy nerves nearby, even after the original injury is gone or healed. It is also difficult to differentiate whether the level of pain is due to hyper-excitability, or not, especially if the individual is masking his/her healing process by a continuation of medication use beyond the necessary period even though the injured nerves have regenerated. External factors such as high sodium intake, diabetes, cancer treatment, and alcohol/drug use may stimulate changes in voltage-gated sodium channels, which play an important role in how sensitive or excitable a neuron is (ibid, 2009). This chronic excitability creates a process called long-term potentiation (LTP).[82]

Chronic pain then sends these messages from the spinal cord or the brain stem to the anterior cingulate cortex (ACC), felt by some to be "the seat of the will" and the region responsible for emotional responses to pain (also found in the amygdala part of the limbic system) (Pinker, 1997). We then have an individual in physical pain who is also catastrophizing psychologically, which engages the ACC. "This is a common occurrence where there is chronic pain in patients who also manifest conditions such as depression and PTSD" (ibid, 2009, pp. 34–41).

I have put the emphasis on the footnote above but, along with the nutritional advice at the end of the last chapter, we know we can have some control over our pain experience by controlling what we eat. For instance, monosodium glutamate (MSG) affects sodium channel blockers that affect inhibitors of enzymes such as nitric oxide synthase that yield active neurotransmitters. The way in which MSG (such as in Chinese food) affects so many people is that it opens the channel, causing a rise in blood pressure. This process may well be part of the development of inflammatory proteins or nerve growth factors that are thought to boost the excitability of these pain-transmitting neurons.

Sapolsky explains this process simply by stating that glutamate causes more excitation in the postsynaptic neuron than any other type of neurotransmitter. The binding of glutamate to its receptors "causes those receptors to open channels which allow torrents of excitatory ions (such as sodium and calcium). If lots of calcium floods in, relatively permanent structural changes occur in that synapse so that it works better forever after" (Sapolsky, 1997, workshop).

As discussed above, long-term stress can disrupt long-term potentiation. For example, high levels of glucocorticoids released from the adrenal function can result in memory loss, glutamate/calcium cascade of degeneration, queasiness, tiredness, and even stroke or seizure. Whether glutamate is effective, or toxic, is seen in cellular survival, synaptic behavior of cells, and the balance in the right concentrations. "The signaling effect of glutamate is not dependent on the chemical nature of glutamate, but on how cells respond when exposed" (Vaskovic, 2021).

Ronald Melzack and Patrick Wall (1965) developed the "gate control theory" to explain the complex interplay between the central nervous system (CNS) and

---

[82] "A hyperactive pain axis not only increases pain intensity but also augments the aversive qualities of the experience. Chronic pain may thus reflect a switch from a bottom-up condition in which painful sensory information dominates to a top-down state in which emotional and cognitive assessments control pain behavior…No one knows for sure how chronic pain could lead to neurodegeneration, but the increased neuronal excitability that we now know characterizes chronic pain may provide a clue. Such excitability often leads to excessive release of the neurotransmitter glutamate, [as in Chinese food?] and glutamate is known to be toxic to neurons in large quantities. At this point, however, the glutamate explanation is purely speculative, and researchers are actively investigating various possible molecular causes of this neurodegeneration" [emphasis added] (ibid, 2009, pp. 34–41).

the peripheral nervous system (PNS). The CNS includes the spinal cord and brain whereas the PNS includes the nerves outside of the brain and spinal cord. After an injury, the damaged nerves (depending upon their location) will send a message through the spinal cord to the brain, where it then is registered. The gate theory of pain management states that how much of the nerve pain, as an electrical message, gets through is determined by whether the "gates" between the brain and location of the pain site are "open" or "closed".

Gate factors which can close the pain channels to decrease the experience of pain include successful surgery, medication, improved diet and hydration, behavioral changes (better chair, rest, relaxation, fun, distracting activities), and positive and self-affirming thoughts and emotions. Gate factors which open the pain channels to increase the experience of pain include: failed surgery, recurring trauma to pain site, inappropriate medication use, poor diet, nicotine use, behaviors which increase stress (trying to do too much, long periods of inactivity, poor sleep patterns, worry, concerns about disability, family problems), and negative or depressive patterns of thoughts and emotions which focus on the pain instead of focus away from it.

This balance between the CNS and local processes (such as the production of T cells in the lymph nodes) is based on the CNS having an ability to "receive information about events in the body and the status of the immune process". The immune system serves as a diffuse sensory organ to provide the brain with a variety of inputs. "The immune system controls neural function, and the CNS controls the immune system…there is a pathway by which psychological factors could impact immunity [as well]" (Maier, Watkins, and Fleshner, 1994, p. 1005). The balance maintained by these systems is all arranged by the "functional significance" of the body's needs.

As mentioned above, Sapolsky (1994) discusses the relationship between the autonomic nervous system and how the hypothalamus secretes CRF, which triggers glucocorticoid in the adrenals. All this adrenal function could have similar pathways as that of endorphins and opiate receptor sites which are stimulated during chronic stress. The question arises: Can chronic stress make you an endogenous (self-perpetuating) opioid addict? One way to answer this question is the reverse engineering of how we can treat the anxiety and risk caused by opioid use. To mitigate the anxiety, providers try to identify the sources of anxious feelings so that a "taper" off the drugs will be manageable. The message a provider tries to send is "We need to get you off opioids because they're doing more harm than good" (Lembke, 2018).

We explain that the very "high" the drug once gave them is now causing epinephrine, glucocorticoids, prolactin, and other substances to be secreted, all of which model the process which happens during stress. Rather than repairing our stress reaction, the hormones are secreted to the same extent regardless of the intensity of the stressor (all-or-nothing responsiveness). It turns out that not only can the body sense when something stressful (or painful) is happening, but it is amazingly accurate at "measuring just how far and how fast that stressor is throwing the body out of homeostatic balance" (ibid, 1994, p. 179).

In clinical terms, the level of addiction can be measured be by Lembke's four C's: Control (as in how out of control the addict is), Compulsion (mental preoccupation regardless of conscious desire to quit the drug), Craving (physiologic and/or mental state), and continued use despite consequences (Lembke, 2018, p. 18). For instance, patients who started an opioid for genuine pain will begin to "hoard" their drugs for use when they need a change in mood and energy rather than to treat the pain (which may have physiologically healed anyway). I once had a client "addicted" to Klonopin (a Valium-type drug for anxiety). She was taking 4x the normal dose. The common form of weaning her off the drug did not work; without it she barely slept.

So rather than reduce her dose 1 mg every other day or so, we had to reduce her dose ¼ mg every four or five days. It took her 6 months to completely abstain from her cravings and side effects. The lesson here is that regardless of "medical recommendations", treating severe drug abuse is a very personal issue; we all have different drug chemistries to start with! Resetting the "pain threshold" requires knowledge of the effects of the drug of addiction, including opioids originally used for pain management, as well as an assessment of the psychological issues of the patient. Tolerance for high levels of the drug will not only have to do with levels of dopamine being released, but an addictive response is also dependent on whether the pain increases as a form of drug tolerance.

Pain and Addictions (Drug, Alcohol, Food, et.al.)

We have reviewed some of the causes of pain, and how pain is experienced neurobiologically. How do psychological interpretations of pain vary between individuals? What role can pain play in the development of a whole host of addictions not limited to drugs and/or alcohol?

First, we will consider how verbalizing helps us to control or delay reactions to felt pain. Cognitive Behavioral Therapy (CBT) is used in Kaiser Permanente's pain management classes. Regardless of suffering (physical or the result of mental health problems), one must learn positive responses to life's travails, and it is likely that in the mesolimbic area (midbrain) messages allow us to self-stimulate survival patterns. This response comes from the same pathway that is the source of eating and sexual instincts. These instinctual pathways tell us to "act anyway!" Someday neuroscientists may even be able to prove that altruistic attitudes and behaviors arise from the same area: generosity, compassion, forgiveness, listening, nurturing, courage, creativity, and celebration. We can teach ourselves to use these more positive attitudes when dealing with our own experiences, even suffering.

Functional magnetic resonance imaging (fMRI) shows that when an area of the brain works particularly hard, it needs more oxygen than adjacent regions and is therefore more heavily perfused with blood. Research has also found that verbalizing an emotion may activate the right ventral lateral prefrontal cortex (VLPC), which then suppresses the areas of the brain that produce emotional pain (amygdala and VLPC). Therefore, one of the techniques recommended in pain management involves self-talk, journaling, group, or individual psychotherapy. Any technique which helps one find other similar ways to express one's feelings about the management of chronic pain will likely be effective. These behaviors are not just distractions; they are important parts of the whole healing cycle.

The prevalent state of anxiety can make pain worse. Although there is a hope that opioid receptors along the pain pathway will produce their analgesic effects (naloxone), expectations of a reward (food or drugs) can profoundly affect pain intensity as well because reward and pain relief have a partially shared neural basis. "When a person anticipates a reward such as a delicious dinner, the body releases endorphins, activating the receptors along the descending pain-control pathway and controlling pain signals as they enter the central nervous system" (Fields, 2009, p. 46).

This type of anticipatory reaction is referred to as "the effect" in 12-step programs because this release of endorphins is exactly the effect sought by the "using" behavior of the addict. Because our HPA (hypothalamus-pituitary-adrenal) axis regulates our relief from stress, we have some control over how, and how often, we want it to reward us. We can make ourselves the rats in the experiment of life, and this rewarding process is referred to by psychology as "Self-medicating".

George Koob (2013) differentiates between the positive hedonic (pleasurable) effects of drugs of abuse (dopamine, opioid peptides, serotonin, and GABA) and the negative hedonic effects of withdrawal (dopamine-dysphoria, opioid peptides-pain, serotonin-dysphoria and GABA-anxiety, panic attacks). As we will cover in Chapter Sixteen, the addiction cycle starts with preoccupations and then moves to dependence, then to binging and actual physical and psychological addiction, with withdrawal symptoms on removal of the substance.

Koob summarizes this cycle as follows: repeated reward-seeking despite negative consequences, craving for reward, loss of control in limiting intake, normalized behavior even when under the influence and higher tolerance, withdrawal when abstaining with negative emotional states, and craving and relapse triggered by environmental cues and stressors. For the purposes of our discussion, it is the paradox of the addiction/CONNECTION/need for the drug, "chasing relief with a response that maintains the 'distress'," which illustrates the negative paradigm of some Outlier behavior. "Outlier" behavior, a more and more commonly used term in non-scientific areas, is a reference to the scientific boundary of probability beyond a .05 or .01 percent statistical finding that something or someone is not within a "normal" curve or expected set of circumstances because they "scored" (their quantifiable behavior) lower than the "norm".

Outliers are those individuals who either do not fit in socially because of social or life experience, or may indeed fit an external criterion, but they themselves feel they don't fit in. Life becomes unmanageable and, because they are unable to "fit in", the urge to escape pulls them further and further away from healthier CONNECTIONS and into a powerless need for isolation and the use of substances to control stress and anxiety. In this case, the quantum events of anxiety don't just exist one particle at a time; experienced as waves, they persist![83]

---

[83] In Outlier analysis, although outside the normal curve by one standard deviation or more, an Outlier can have a highly significant impact on the total outcome and statistical average of the overall measurement. In a likewise manner, a social outlier can easily affect the outcome of any social or family situation by his or her behaviors or lack of attachments.

We have mentioned the positive consequences of a healthy diet. As Koob details, there are many addictive features in "comfort" foods. Beyond the development of compulsive eating-in-itself, there is food dependence and a failure to recognize hunger signals, overstimulation of reward neurotransmitters, and development of a negative cycle of eating to relieve negative feelings from chronic compulsive overeating! If the "drug of choice" is food there can even be a result of "acquired dopamine deficiency," or "repeated exposure to drugs of abuse or fatty foods which leads to down regulation of dopamine receptors," where the food is sought out despite obvious negative consequences (ibid, 2013).

The twist of this scenario is that transmitter-stimulating effects of compulsive behaviors, as we have seen, often cause stress and anxiety reactions, especially upon withdrawal. Therefore, withdrawal from food as one's "drug of choice" can be the most difficult type of abstinence because, when the stress and anxiety come, there may no longer be that neurotransmitter stimulating effect, or there may even be negativity about feeling deeper emotions for the first time in years.

Of course, there is always a "cost benefit analysis" inside the brain, particularly within the pain-control circuit, to determine whether tolerating the pain to reach some kind of goal or other is worth it (addicts in recovery sometimes refer to this as "turning it over"). Sometimes the distraction of the attempt to reach the goal will be exactly the positive effect sought. The term "placebo effect" is used to describe how the analgesic properties of anticipated rewards can sometimes take place. On the other hand, a bad mood may increase pain; we know that catastrophizing, somatization, or depression all magnify pain. In addition, feeling isolated and abandoned are an ultimate source of stress to the endocrine system.

Up until now I have been discussing the processes and effects of stress and addiction on the HPA and specifically the limbic system. However, for the purposes of understanding how these states are manifested in behavior which may result eventually in habits, we must look at the prefrontal cortex, where decision-making and executive function reside.[84] Of course, not every addict is plagued by poor impulse control and poor executive functioning/decision-making, but there certainly may be an assumed correlation between these two factors. Therefore, we speak of "dysregulation" (as a general term) as affecting all neurological systems: limbic, motor, cognitive, and attentional.

The variance between positions in the prefrontal cortex (PFC) for the function of two important systems explains a lot about our issues with control. The "go system" is in the dorsal lateral (dlPFC) and the "stop system" is in the ventral medial (vmPFC). Because their neurological pathways are not directly CONNECTED, behavioral patterns require constant monitoring to achieve

---

[84] "The hippocampus and connected structures, which put our memories into long-term storage, and the frontal lobes, which house the circuitry for decision making, are not directly connected to the brain areas that process raw sensory input (the mosaic of edges and colors and the ribbon of changing pitches). Instead, most of their input fibers carry what neuroscientists call 'highly processed' input coming from regions one or more stops downstream from the first sensory areas. The input consists of codes for objects, words, and other complex concepts" (Pinker, 2000, p. 90).

"appropriate or effective outcomes", especially resilience to reflective or instinctual response patterns.

Without brakes, the limbic system (amygdala) will fall out of homeostasis, and the hippocampus cannot consolidate or, in the case of PTSD, may stimulate flashbacks or hypervigilance. "In a panic disorder [PTSD], this part of the brain misinterprets incoming information and executes an inappropriate emotional response" (Teresi, 1986, p. 126). With increased CRF or serotonin production, there may be a reversal, wherein the "go system" may slow down and the "stop system" may be agitated or stop functioning altogether (Koob, 2013).

We also know that there is a "bidirectional" communication system between the brain and stomach ("gut"), where microbiota colonization modulates much of brain function and neural processing of sensory information in the hypothalamic pituitary adrenal (HPA) stress response. The serotonin produced there is correlated with much of neurophysiological behavior. Again, a leaky blood-brain barrier (i.e., leaky gut syndrome) can affect proteins that influence appetite, executive functions, and decision-making, all factors in obesity! (Davidson, T.L. et al, 2013).

Antibiotics, infections, poor nutrition, and stress can throw off the systemic balance that is so important to keeping the central nervous system functioning in the healthiest manner possible. This need for a "stable gut" explains the growth in use of probiotics in this country. Probiotics lower inflammatory cytokines and can decrease the oxidation caused by stress. How do we repair or learn emotional regulation without depending on external self-medication?

The critical area is the stop center in the ventral medial Prefrontal Cortex (vmPFC) as mentioned above, which not only interprets stimuli, but can also modulate amygdala response patterns, particularly to fear (Koob, 2013). Control over the stress response cannot only eliminate the immediate effects on an individual, the opposite outcome is found in individuals suffering from PTSD, where this region is apparently not activated as effectively.

Memory and Mirroring

Memory keeps what is essential and lets the rest go. That effect is why we sometimes have memory lapses when our functioning is impeded by other stresses. In terms of the extinction of affect-laden (emotional) memories, the memory is not really extinguished, just replaced with time and space limitations. But then, of course, a doughnut works temporarily too (OK, no sugar humor allowed...). We know that stress impairs neurogenesis, while exercise and medications can impair it as well. The trick is to rename stress triggers as circumstances beyond your control (powerlessness), as circumstances within your control (it's no big deal), none of your business or something we can detach from altogether (let's hear it for the Buddhists!). Then our preplanning or strategizing may (or may not) still protect us, but overall, we hope to feel as if we no longer are under threat.

Researchers Banks and Jordan (2007) have found that brains are hard-wired to CONNECT. For instance, what we refer to as mirror neurons fire in response to the firing of another person's neurons in the first person's proximity. The process of mirror neuron firing is believed to be the explanation for imitation and language acquisition as well as other skills, where a whole network of neurons ("neuronal assembly") is activated when an action is observed. For instance, when watching someone else's action, a person's eyes are also likely to anticipate what the other person will do. Research has observed this behavior in toddlers before 12 months of age, a process which may help human infants understand other people's actions.

Whether mirror neurons create specific mind skills versus language abilities is still being argued. Regardless, mirror neurons are a clear biological function of how we CONNECT while we are processing information from others in our environment. Electron quanta are to waves as words are to sentences—to communicate, or make an effective impact, elements which are discontinuous by nature must join in a combined and similar destination. Both are necessary means to describe reality (ibid, 2007).

Scientists have discovered that the mirror neurons discussed can also be a type of empathy neuron.

A large number of experiments using functional magnetic resonance imaging (fMRI), electroencephalography (EEG), and magnetoencephalography (MEG) have shown that certain brain regions (in particular the anterior insula, anterior cingulate cortex, and inferior frontal cortex) are active when a person experiences an emotion (disgust, happiness, pain, etc.) and when he sees another person experiencing emotion… providing more direct support to the idea that the mirror system is linked to empathy [emphasis added] (Mirror neurons, *Wikipedia*, 12/9/2008).

Similarly, humans show the source of acute emotional sensitivity through these mirror neurons. This CONNECTION between empathy for others and the maternal bond suggests that the impulse to respond to others in need, like attachment to the parent, is wired into our most primal structures of care and CONNECTION. Social support networks create positive biomedical effects through the level of attachment patterns available to us. "We now know that we need CONNECTION to grow, and that isolation actually damages our neurobiology…" [emphasis added] (op cit., 2007). I refer also to *The Neuroscience of Human Relationships* by Louis Cozolino (2006), which gives an excellent review of neurobiology in relational context. How these CONNECTIONS will continue or change in the future is left for our children and their children to discover.

Alternate Views of Neurophenomenology

Before we move from our genetics, our brains, and our immune systems to the functioning of the rest of our bodies, some metacognition or meta-neurological experiences cannot be overlooked. How does the mature mind sort through the stimuli presented by the living world? We are constantly presented with the "stuff" of philosophy, morality, and even spirituality.

For instance, one could ask: what are dreams? Orloff (2008) writes they can be:

- Statements to yourself that convey information.
- Neutral segments that evoke or convey no emotion.
- A detached feeling, like you're a witness watching a scene.
- A voice or person counseling you, as if you're taking dictation from an outside source.
- Conversation with people you never met before who give instructions.

Regardless of the explanation, there is a common experience that is intuitive and feels like a tiny fragment that is remembered and then it is believed to reflect something bigger about the whole psyche. Dreams may also give clues to the underlying self-similar repetitions of the personality which are built into a repertoire of memory (hippocampus) and experience of Self (prefrontal cortex). These patterns are referred to as "self-referential loops" or sometimes just as "consciousness" (Marks-Tarlow, 2002). Dreams, like other forms of metacognition, provide us with an opportunity to really look at certain [mental] goals: "to tolerate ambiguity, to hold opposites without succumbing to the tension of reducing one side to the other, and to understand ambivalence" (ibid, 2002, pp. 311–345).

The perception of other people, a social function psychologically needed for social functioning and survival, facilitates perception of Self. As mentioned above, "mirror neurons" function as a form of actual CONNECTIVITY of consciousness between people. A misalignment of this neurofeedback can be seen in Narcissistic Injury, a psychotherapy term sometimes used in other relational fields of study. Narcissistic injury to a child is defined as the toddler becoming confused by the mother's failure to CONNECT and to protect during this period of defenselessness, thus giving confusing attachment signals early in the bonding period.

As a result, the child mistrusts either her own internal signals and neediness or will not trust the mother herself, which in turn generalizes to other authority figures in their future. Other symptoms of a narcissistic injury include:

- Mother emotionally insecure and depressed, depending on the child responding in a certain way.
- Insecurity hidden behind an authoritarian façade.
- Child learns "to perceive and respond intuitively to the needs of the mother."
- Child learns to accommodate his mother's needs to the detriment of his own needs out of fear of loss of love.
- Prevented from living his emotions, the child cannot develop and differentiate his true Self (Taken from my teachings notes, 1987).

By integrating neuroscience and physics theory (with the idea of fractal borders representing "inner and outer") with the psychological concept of "boundaries", we see that understanding the oscillation between the subjective feeling state of "engulfment" versus that of "abandonment" can help understand our initial experiences of shame, guilt, and rage. We come to an understanding of how to resolve confusion of the boundary between Self and Other, especially that which may have been confused by early time and space-dimensional factors and/or disappointments.

As seen in comments earlier in this chapter, brain imagery (MRI) has revealed information that helps us format our ideas about Self versus Other. As the frontal area of the brain (concerned with identity) helps us maintain a sense of Self through executive functions, the temporal area can "clue us into Others' feelings", and the limbic system (seat of emotions) serves to facilitate the boundary between the two (Rockman, 2017).

Neurophenomena

Meta-awareness and mysticism are neurophenomena. This "practice" can be achieved, whether supported through meditation, Tai Chi, or just a general state of mindfulness. Harold Bloomfield (1976) has long been held as an expert in this field. He has more recently been joined in the research of mindfulness by such cognitive scientists as Davidson at University of Wisconsin, and Flaxman and Flook at UCLA.

The depth of the meditative state can be measured by oxygen consumption, one of many metabolic activities that drop about 16% during the transcendental meditation (TM) technique. There will also be a decrease in blood lactate levels. Although scientists measure such things as O2 and blood lactate levels, changes in consciousness may still be subjective experiences.[85]

Another form of metacognition is inner directedness. On Everett Shostrom's Personal Orientation Inventory (POI) (1964), a self-report measure of personality factors, a high score on inner directedness demonstrates an ability to express feelings during a spontaneous action, as well as the acceptance of one's aggression and his overall capacity for intimate contact. These individuals are more open to their own and to others' deep experiences of their feelings. Whether pain patients or addicts in recovery, for the purpose of our discussion, the measure of inner directedness correlates with an improvement in their ability to concentrate and a decrease in tension, anxiety, and nervousness during stress experiences.

High outer directedness, also called "field-dependent" by some researchers, include anxiety or hypervigilance responses, which are the common denominator of almost all mental disorders.

---

[85] During the TM technique, oxygen consumption sharply decreases, heart rate and cardiac output decrease, muscles relax, blood lactate diminishes, skin resistance increases markedly, the brain achieves greater synchrony, and the meditator experiences a refreshing state of restful alertness. "The comprehensive and integrated hypometabolic state produced by the TM technique appears to be the opposite of a maladaptive anxiety attack...Despite this rapid decrease, the TM technique does not produce any respiratory abnormalities, and will return to its normal resting level, indicating a return to a metabolic level suitable for initiating activity. Generally deep meditation goes to a fourth major state of consciousness and has other positive results: an overall rise in alertness, energy, perceptual acuity, and efficiency, with an overall decrease in anxiety" (Bloomfield, 1976).

Neurosis is characterized by excessive anxiety which arises when there is no manifest danger, or which continues long after danger has passed. It interferes with the individual's pursuit of a normal life. Sometimes anxiety becomes part of the individual's identity or defense structure. Fear of illness or of social situations is a response to feelings of anxiety as well. Alcoholism and drug abuse are some of the destructive habits that are attempts to relieve anxiety. We now know that mindfulness and meditative practice can alter functioning of the nervous system such that energy is no longer wasted by anxiety, anger or worry. Humor is also an area of neurological investigation. Movies, comedies on TV or in books, lightness, and laughter can decrease our stress and increase the neurotransmitters in the reward areas of our brain, including the auditory association areas (the ability for detection), and in the amygdala and prefrontal cortex (the ability for appreciation).

What results are we looking for? We need to find ways to eliminate stress and go beyond it; loss of Self-esteem is more common in our current society than any other feeling we might experience daily. Stress leads us to a decrease in self-worth. TM/mindfulness programs foster self-reliance and greater autonomy, encouraging acceptance of life in a more relaxed and less controlling fashion. "Life on life's terms" (AA, *Big Book*, 1939/2001). Individuals in recovery are taught to let their thoughts go, and skills are given for a greater identification with others, so that there is an experience of unboundedness. Resentment can be released and improved cognitive skills counteract the chronic anxiety that frequently precedes major depressive episodes.

More commonly thought of as Mindfulness Training as it is currently used in psychotherapy, TM techniques encourage the resolution of emotional conflicts and allow for previously unacceptable aspects of the Self to become integrated into the personality. Without this level of mindfulness and cognitive skills, the anxiety-ridden individual will lose the ability to improve Self-regard, decrease anxiety and/or improve the Self-reliance that Bloomfield discusses.

Issues in the Study of Alzheimer's Disease

Perhaps the area of neurological research of most interest to the general reader is the study of memory, dementia, and Alzheimer's disease. For researchers to study the function of memory, and the probable causes of memory disorders, it was first important to understand how the homeostasis function of the brain worked and in what ways a stress reaction impacted that function. Obviously, the most noticeable patient-experienced symptom (from stress) is that of memory damage, which for many first appears in difficulty during multi-tasking. Training in the skill of multi-tasking abilities again, however, can lead to benefits in other areas of attention and cognition.

I am drawn to using the word plasticity here, negative neuroplasticity being the influences or sharing of negative impacts of environments and medications, such as we find in pain management. On the other hand, homeostasis in our brain is represented by the ability to maintain physiological equilibrium, with a normal and stable range of neurochemical reactions and no measurable pathology as evidenced in blood chemistry or memory loss.

At some point, with the onset of aging, most of us have experienced the common effect in an older individual, whose "parts are wearing out", of not remembering something that happened five minutes ago, but who are having vivid and/or detailed memories of their history. Recent brain research has shown that although the hippocampus is primary in memory function, as an individual ages the participation of the hippocampus changes. Areas in the frontal, temporal, and parietal lobes display increasing activity for recalled events. This process is referred to as "consolidation".

The parietal-limbic-reticular loop reflects a combination/overlap of the parietal cortex with the cingulate gyrus. The limbic system within the frontal lobes combines with the reticular formation in the midbrain, which is the center of alertness and orienting of attention. A deficit in any of these areas can significantly impact either learning or memory. "Problems with encoding and consolidating long-term memories characterize the memory deficits of individuals who have brain injury and many dementias, especially Alzheimer's disease" (Howard, 2013).

While being stabilized, a memory takes a long journey from the hippocampus to the neocortex, where it is "interpreted".[86] It may only bear a faint resemblance to its original form, and this transition explains the source of revisionist history, our retelling of stories from our past. As Freud asserted, it is our interpretation of our memories that makes them meaningful to us.

Another factor affecting dementia or Alzheimer's is the thinning of the anterior cingulate gyrus, part of the limbic system. This loss of brain health has not been entirely tracked down but, according to Sapolsky (1997), the inflammatory component of Alzheimer's damage shows up not only in a change in personality, affect, and motivation, but eventually there are obvious early signs of neurological shifts in a type of declarative memory (consolidating new memories and retrieving old ones).

This symptom is distinguished from other forms of dementia, wherein the symptom of memory losses can be much more dramatic with facts disappearing suddenly and forever. Sapolsky feels this "cellular neuropathology" is the result of both amyloid plaque build-up and neurocilliary tangles, the "twisted mess" which results from the tau proteins becoming disconnected and then re-clumped together. These neurons obviously don't last very long once they get all "clumped" or "twisted around" together. It is not clear whether the clumping is because the

---

[86] Initially a memory resides in the hippocampus and in some areas the structure CONNECTS to the neocortex, the outer part of the cerebral cortex. "Over the first few hours, a memory can become more stable, resistant to interference from competing memories. But over longer periods, the brain seems to decide what is important to remember and what is not—and a detailed memory evolves into something more like a story….as we sleep, the brain might even be dissecting our memories and retaining only the most salient details…changes in synaptic strength arise from a molecular process known as long-term potentiation, which strengthens the CONNECTIONS between pairs of neutrons that fire at the same time" [emphasis added] (Stickgold and Ellenbogen, 2008, p. 28).

subject is at risk for developing the disease or whether many people can live a long time with these proteins in their bodies.

"In fact, scientists still aren't entirely sure whether the amyloid plaques cause Alzheimer's disease or are merely side effects of the condition." The basic point to absorb here is that Sapolsky feels Alzheimer's is an inflammatory and autoimmune disease, and his belief certainly speaks to the point I am trying to make about CONNECTING with and protecting our immune systems! Current studies show that while aging is the single biggest risk factor for age-associated memory impairment (AAMI, 1998), aging is only 20% of the variance in causation. Other proven associations, presented by Matthew Howard (2013), are:

- Cardiovascular disease with atherosclerosis and high blood pressure.
- High levels of blood lipids like total cholesterol, LDL, and triglycerides.
- Low environmental stimulation and new learning brain activity and lack of exercise.
- A diet high in calories, refined carbs & sat/trans-fat.
- A diet low in antioxidants, micronutrients, and Omega-3 PUFAs.
- Chronic physical and psychological stress.
- High levels of oxygen free radicals.
- Obesity, high blood sugar, insulin resistance, and diabetes.
- Excess inflammatory markers.
- Smoking, toxins, high alcohol, and drug intake.
- Sleep deprivation, chronic anxiety, and chronic depression.

In other words, the risk for age-associated memory impairment can be reduced by adhering to a healthful lifestyle.

Nutritional factors are known to strongly affect brain health. Obesity, whether in young or aging populations, links to changes in the production of certain hormones, such as leptin. Reduced leptin, when reduced, is associated with a 4 times higher risk of Alzheimer's disease. Enlarged abdominal adipocytes and high levels of inflammatory cytokines (proteins important in cell signaling and found in high levels of stress) are also linked to higher levels of circulating free radicals, which damage the brain (ibid, 2013).

Another example of tissue damage is when a glucose molecule does the same thing in a person with diabetes, causing cataracts due to protein "filminess". Rather than strong T cells cleaning up this cellular "junk", "oxygen radicals can damage DNA, and DNA repair abilities decline with age in cells" (ibid, 1997, p. 75). This oxidation is particularly true in those cells with high metabolic rates, such as bladder cells, or those where the neurons have stopped being replaced, such as in the brain.

Thus, free radical factors enhance the vascular system damage and effects of oxygen deficits in obesity, diabetes, or other related health conditions. This outcome is why so many diabetes patients end up on kidney dialysis. For some, there is a confusion between the terms dementia and Alzheimer's disease. However, for the purposes of this discussion, Alzheimer's is viewed as a type of dementia. According to the publication *Diagnosis, Management, and Treatment of Dementia* (2019) by the AMA, dementia is described by the following guidelines.

- Dependent on others for activities of daily living.
- Complains of memory loss only when asked with no details.
- Close family members are more concerned about memory.
- Recent memory for events/conversations noticeably impaired.
- Difficulty in conversations and finding words.
- Pauses in speech and word substitutions.
- Gets lost walking or driving; may take hours to get home.
- Can't operate common appliances; unable to learn new ones.
- Loses interest in social activities; socially inappropriate.
- Abnormal mental status performance for age, education, culture.

To clarify, dementias are classified as secondary and reversible (effects of alcohol use, acute brain inflammation, anxiety and depression, drug effects or interactions, respiratory problems or oxygen deprivation, metabolic diseases, sleep problems, chronic stress, dietary deficiencies, effects of anesthesia) or primary irreversible and neurodegenerative (Alzheimer's disease, Parkinson's disease, Huntington's disease, Lewy-body dementia, Vascular Dementia & Stroke and a host of other more rare conditions). Most individuals who develop Alzheimer's disease have mixed dementias, most with accompanying vascular dementia or Lewy-body dementia (Howard, 2012). According to Howard, the most common periods found in Alzheimer's disease, which is progressive, are as follows:

- Stage 1 (confusional stage) 2–7 years, difficulties are slight and easily concealed.
- Stage 2 (mild to moderate impairment) 2 years, ADLs may need assistance, social withdrawal begins
- Stage 3 (moderate impairment) 18 months, at this point cannot live independently.
- Stage 4 (severe impairment) 2 ½ years, unaware of present and recent experiences and the memory for personal history is impaired.
- Stage 5 (very severe impairment) 1 to 2 ½ years, person requires 24-hour assistance.

The following list presents the classic signs to watch for when diagnosing this type of dementia.

10 Warning Signs of Alzheimer's Disease

1. Recent memory loss affects job performance. Everyone forgets things and then recalls them later. Alzheimer's patients forget often, never recall, and repeatedly ask the same question, forgetting the earlier answer.
2. Difficulty performing familiar tasks. "People with Alzheimer's disease could prepare a meal, forget to serve it and even forget they made it."

3. Problems with language. A person with Alzheimer's may forget simple words or use inappropriate words, making speech incomprehensible.
4. Disorientation of time and place. People with Alzheimer's may get lost on their own street and forget how they got there or how to get home.
5. Poor or weaker judgment. Even a normal person might get distracted and fail to watch a child. "A person with Alzheimer's disease could entirely forget the child under their care and leave the house."
6. Problems with abstract thinking. Anybody can have trouble balancing a checkbook; a person with Alzheimer's "could forget completely what the numbers are and what needs to be done with them."
7. Misplacing things. "A person with Alzheimer's disease may put things in inappropriate places—an iron in the freezer or a wristwatch in the sugar bowl—and not be able to retrieve them."
8. Changes in mood or behavior. Everyone has occasional moods, but people with Alzheimer's can have rapid mood swings—from calm to tears to anger—within a few minutes.
9. Personality changes. A person with Alzheimer's may change drastically and inappropriately, becoming irritable, suspicious, or fearful.
10. Loss of initiative. People with Alzheimer's may become passive and reluctant to get involved in activities (Alzheimer's Association, 2017).

Although I have spoken of brain health and nutrition for healthy aging, no one really knows what causes Alzheimer's disease. Both Sapolsky and Howard present theories of this process and the research continues. As mentioned, some ideas include beta-amyloid plaques in arteries, altered neurotransmitter balances, decreased metabolic levels of cells, oxidative damage to mitochondria and cells, glutamate factors, breakdown of the blood-brain barrier, low insulin and high blood sugar, low omega-3 fatty acids and myelin sheath decline, and inflammatory diseases.

Newer research being conducted at Lund University in Sweden has shown that an increase in unwanted "intracellular beta-amyloid" occurring early on in Alzheimer's disease (in mice) is caused by a loss of normal function to secrete beta-amyloid. "When the synapses can no longer hold the increasing amounts of this toxin, researchers say, the membrane breaks, releasing the waste outside the cells and leading to the formation of plaques, the long-time hallmark biomarker of the disease" (Novotney, 2012, pp. 60–66).

Any of these factors, or a combination of them, could be at fault. As we age, we can do something to make sure we, and our brains, are as healthy as possible, by paying attention to our nutrition and our metabolism. Regardless of the growth of our knowledge, however, the ultimate outcome of the aging process will be death.

Dealing with Death

The Tibetan culture views death as something to be understood and embraced as a guide to living and healing as a lead up to death. Some of these approaches have been discussed in Chapter Five. Western cultures tend to view death from an approach of general avoidance. The concept of death is frightening, as are all experiences of the unknown, and being out of control presents too many variables of unmanageability (Step 1 of AA, "Our lives had become unmanageable"). Although we often would like to view ourselves, and our views about death, as 'rational' individuals, being in full control of our reasoning, we think we have been endowed with the capacity to reason and use logic which allows one to be "of sound mind".

But there is another view about death. As a science of consciousness, noetics (the study of metaphysical philosophy concerned with mind and intellect and, particularly, Divine Intellect) considers how we experience, internalize, intuit, externalize, and attempt to release our need to control elements of our neurological functioning for enhanced perception, conscious awareness, and acceptance of passing through the death experience by heightened consciousness and spirituality (Noetics, *Wikipedia*, 9/11/2013).

The discoveries of evolutionary "convergence, participation, and directionality", and the influence of mirror neurons are felt to provide individuals with the source of acute emotional sensitivity. The more we share and CONNECT our authentic Selves, the more unified the bounds of our experience. Unified goals always produce greater results than those which isolated individuals can experience. This discussion gives us an excellent conceptual place to start our next section on how our cells truly represent a microcosm of evolution: the birth, growth, and death of humans as complex organisms.

Focus on Survival

As mammals, we exist as the result of reinforced behaviors (+ or -) through a long developmental history of physical, psychosocial, and spiritual experiences. However, how do we explain the ongoing spontaneity and flux in the world? Our "parts" communicate mutually, to create the CONNECTIVITY used to move together as a system toward change for good, and for survival. These parts also move contextually and systemically to create useful and universal shifts, whether in business, education, or consciousness. The quality of the focus toward the "Other" creates the context.

Disordered, dysregulated, inner-directed souls usually do not do well with a larger outer-directed system. However, these individuals often need the outer-directed type of support and the ability it provides to comprehend their own evolving new design for effective living. How can the structured and systemic functioning of community units communicate with an individual suffering soul? As we have previously discussed, mirror neurons work for more than processing information and language; they provide input for emotion, empathy, and compassion. This "hard-wired" function is as much a part of our CONNECTIVITY and survival as our other basic DNA functions.

The psychologist and researcher, B.F. Skinner (See Chapter Fourteen) believed that we are only conditioned creatures; I disagree in that our highly developed consciousness does influence the outcome of our daily lives. But I am also open to ideas about how our cosmological world impacts the development of this consciousness. The concept of "Purity of Intent" is one's belief and expectation that intentions toward me, or any random "Other", has an objective, cognitively ethical plan of action.

This point of view would mean intentionality automatically earns and deserves our trust and respect. Obviously, in building our UFT we want our variables to be descriptive, but such unmeasurable mysteries of reality as empathy and other phenomena may take even higher levels of science to be understood.

I recently had the pleasant opportunity to lunch with the head of Informatics at Vanderbilt University in Nashville, TN, William Stead, M.D. Our meeting was arranged to discuss issues regarding my last book, *Care from the Heart*—the memoirs of Thelma Ingles, R.N., who was instrumental in creating the idea of Physician Assistant with Dr. Stead's father, Eugene Stead, M.D., during the 1950s. They were both professors at Duke University and had obtained a Rockefeller Foundation grant for the project. However, I soon found myself swept up in interrogating him about his work and ideas behind having founded the Department of Informatics at Vanderbilt University.[87]

Informatics, in his context, is the study of how collecting biological data describes normal cellular activities, which can further affect disease states. The data gathered is studied statistically, as would be any other data collection, probably with the use of AI [and the newly designed quantum computers?], but in this case such things as protein structures and amino acid activities take precedence over bits of straight computer data sets. Wow! We have come a long way, and hopefully our studies will lead us toward cures for some of the deadlier chronic diseases. One pragmatic use of Informatics is demonstrated in the tracking of neurogenesis. Neurogenesis is often seen as the "glue that binds neurons together" (Krauss, 2012).

During reverse engineering in the last 20 years, researchers have come to discover that emotions adapt "in harmony with the intellect [and] are indispensable to the functioning of the whole mind" (Pinker, 1997, p. 370). According to Stickgold and Ellenbogen (2008) emotions are traced to glial cells, which are nutritive cells in the brain and facilitate maintaining a meditative state. "The neuroglial cells gradually 'learn' to retain their meditative state activation even while the neural brain is busy processing all your input" (Abravanel & King, 1990, p. 223).

Likewise, Gould (1996) stated that it was a "use it or lose it" situation. "If new cells are not put to work, they will die more rapidly than if they have a purpose." Gould was interested in the effects that social subordination or fear, i.e., adverse effects, can have once anxiety is produced by exposure to a negative stimulus. What he found was that fear affected the production of new neurons, which quickly fell away, dropping below normal. Does this experience explain the affective outcome of ultimate control? Is this what happens to us, at 5 years old or 35 years

---

[87] "Informatics is the development of new algorithms (mathematical formulas) and statistics with which to assess relationships among members of large data sets, such as methods to locate a gene within a sequence, predict protein structure and/or function, and cluster protein sequences into families of related sequences [provide] pattern recognition, visualization, [and awareness of] so-called junk DNA" (Informatics, *Wikipedia*, 12/20/2021).

old, when presented with an undue level of stress? Researchers are beginning to think that the production of new neurons, through neurogenesis, would definitely slow down during stress. But a bigger question is: "How could you program cells in the brain so that they develop normally when other cells start to fail?"

I now ask myself: why do we need biosystems and even physics to explain everything for us? For some, it serves to provide disconcerting proof that free will is an illusion. But in this age of "re-enlightenment", it is important to understand how the true nature of the universe is not only self-organizing and functional, but also fluid and beautiful in its inherent cooperation (Zohar, 2008). I am also not quite ready to shift from "God made me do it" to "my genes made me do it"; perhaps it should not be either/or. Our deeper meanings, purposes, and values need to be investigated and revealed through all layers of science and metaphysics.

Time to go back to what we do know about the physical world, that which has been confirmed by historic scientists in physics, including Einstein, Planck, and Heisenberg.

Chapter Twelve
The Universe of Physics
The Ultimate Cosmos?

"Complexity is woven in both space and time."
– From *Composing a Life* Mary Catherine Bateson

We have seen in the previous chapter how the cell is the CONNECTION of the two worlds of physics and biology: the evolutionary line between past and future. The cell merges quantitatively and qualitatively with the world of chemical structures. From another point of view, the laws of physics are also real and apply to us. And yet, they don't always seem to explain all known phenomena. Mostly, physics describes the symmetry that allows humans to exist. We also must explain, which unfortunately disturbed Einstein, the ways in which sometimes the world is asymmetrical. Having contrived "naming", with our left frontal lobe verbal functions, to sustain awareness of the world around us, we use words to CONNECT to our physical experiences.

Basic Concepts

Teleology is defined as the difference between description and explanation. Laws, according to Wittgenstein (1889–1951), are descriptions but not really explanations. If we stay with the centuries' old belief in the use of cause and effect to keep us honest, then how could we possibly control all the dependent variables in the physical universe, so different from the social or psychological sciences? Just because a thing (or infinite number of things) could affect an event, how do we know the ultimate cause (Gilbert, 2006)?[88] Therefore, we ask what basic concepts of the physical world can we understand?

Up until this point, in Chapters Ten and Eleven, we have been discussing ways to describe and perhaps understand how to structure our perception of and interaction with the natural world. Do we depend on our biological and

---

[88] "Space and time are organically combined in a dimensional milieu which is the only way we have found to explain the distribution around us of animate and inanimate substances...the distribution of objects and forms at any given moment can only be explained by a process whose duration in times varies directly with the spatial (or morphological) dispersion of the objects in question.

"Only one reality seems to survive and capable of succeeding and spanning the infinitesimal and the immense: energy—that floating, universal entity from which all emerges and into which all falls back as into an ocean; energy, the new spirit; the new god...In the opposite direction we conceive the 'ego' to be diminishing and eliminating itself, with the trend to what is most real and lasting in the world, namely the Collective and the Universal" (de Chardin, 1959, pp. 83, 258).
For more on origins of life and the Big Bang Theory, Charles Pelligrino (2005).

neurological sensations and programming to respond? Do we only use mathematics and the rigidly proscribed methodology of science to test hypothetical questions about the universe? Or finally, do we go with the gut and create a spiritually meaningful explanation that provides a roadmap, one which perhaps would provide resolution of one's sense of powerlessness, and which could also allow understanding and meaning in life to emerge? In his time, Albert Einstein engaged in all three of these processes for explaining "reality". But let us start at the beginning.

The scientific path to understanding how Einstein explained reality starts with the Greeks (Moring, 2000). From the Greek understanding of atoms and energy, the giants of physics (Galileo, Copernicus, Newton, Volta, Faraday, Lorentz, Planck, Maxwell, and Bohr) prepared the way for Einstein's two great theoretical systems which changed the course of science: 1) relativity, dealing with space, time, and the structure of the universe as a whole; and 2) quantum theory, dealing with the fundamental units of matter and energy, undulating charges of electrical energy in spherical electron paths. Theories about the atom were amended to a system of superimposed waves. And at best, those waves, according to Schrodinger, were only "waves of probability".

The theory of relativity (or position and motions) added complexity to the probability function as well—the Theory of Uncertainty, the necessary restriction on the accuracy of simultaneous measurement of position and momentum (Heisenberg, 1930).[89] Time was not only personal, but subjective. There are no absolutes in nature's laws; they are uniformly harmonious and inconsistent (CONNECTED, but also consistent in their predictable unpredictability).

One researcher (Barbour, 2020) goes as far as to assert that time is a measurement of the disorder of the universe, of the complexity and "order of a system of particles". Because size, along with all other measurements, is relative, it is also relative to a measure of distance which is internal to the system and based on ratios. He also comments on change as a function of proportion and uncertainty. "In reality, the change only exists for those who argue as if space were absolute" (Poincare quoted by Barbour, 2020, p. 3). Because we can never see space and time, "but only things and the way they change, in themselves and relative to each other."

Barbour suggests that we describe the evolution "exclusively as the change of its shape, rather than of its size" which, after all, is only measured as relative to something else that has changed its size, but its separation from another object can be measured as increased. It is a basic tenet of geometry that size is always a ratio (think of triangles). "The measure of intrinsic size as well as the measure of complexity, is directly related to Newton's theory of universal gravitation." A

---

[89] "For relativity tells us that there is no such thing as a fixed interval of time independent of the system to which it is referred. There is indeed no such thing as simultaneity, there is no such things as 'now' independent of a system of reference...Concepts of space and time take on physical significance only when the relations between events and systems are defined. These are known as the laws of transformation" (Barrett, 1948, p. 48).

general conclusion that can be drawn is that "whereas the increase of entropy in confined systems corresponds to an increase of disorder [Newton], the increase of complexity corresponds to an increase of order" (ibid, 2020, pp. 9, 14). Finally, Barbour concludes with the conjecture that "the complexity not only defines the direction of time but could be time itself."

The Search to Define Reality

Einstein's broadest view of the universe was that "reality" is found in the "big picture". It continued to drive his search for a unified theory of physics and cosmology until the end of his life. He spent twenty years looking for a law which would explain our whole cosmos, from the big to the small, from infinite space down to the smallest atom. The infinite is where his theory of relativity was descriptive; the infinitesimal is where he used quantum mechanics. This broad view was a commonly held position of many Greek scholars. We have already reviewed the historical relevance of Greek influence on philosophy and science in Chapter Two, but for this discussion their view is particularly important.

For instance, a brief historical review shows that Anaximander (610 to 546 BC) was an early dualist and believed that the world was composed of interacting, aggressive opposites (hot/cold, light/dark). This view expanded the explanation of oneness and wholeness to one which explained the metaphysical, as well as the physical world. Most of us are familiar with Socrates' famous dicta, "Know thyself," "The unexamined life is not worth living," and "The wise man is the man who knows that he knows nothing." It is sometimes difficult to remember that the complex Greek society and its philosophical bases of belief was 2500 years ago because this philosophy has followed us into the very core of our societal, scientific, and metaphysical development right up until current time.

Plato (428 to 348 B.C.) and Aristotle (384 to 322 B.C.) brought scientific concerns into the study of philosophy. Plato wrote that we are cognitively trapped inside a cave and, through the shadows cast upon the wall, we create our set of beliefs about the world. These idealized shadows are our first mental representations. As a precursor to Heisenberg's theory of uncertainty, Plato also believed that the perfect nature of heavenly motion is distorted by human perception.

Aristotle was responsible for differentiating between Dynamics (how things move or evolve in time) and Mechanics (why things move or evolve in time).

> Aristotle believed that the laws governing the motion of the heavens were a different set of laws than those that governed motion on the earth. As we have seen, Galileo's concept of inertia was quite contrary to Aristotle's ideas of motion…Thus, the groundwork was laid by Galileo (and to a lesser extent by others like Kepler and Copernicus) to overthrow the physics of Aristotle, in addition to his astronomy. It fell to Isaac Newton to bring these threads together and to demonstrate that the laws that governed the heavens were the same laws that governed motion on the surface of the Earth (The Physics of Aristotle, *Wikipedia*, 8/29/2021).

Aristotle's Superposition principle may have been a foundation for Galileo's theory of Relativity and subsequently Einstein's famous equation, e=mc2. The Superposition principle explains complex motion that is a combination of both horizontal uniform motion and vertical uniform accelerated motion, whereas Galileo's theory of Relativity added the importance of a reference point.[90] The famous example of this is Einstein's thought experiment that if you were in a moving car with covered windows motion might not be detected (Moring, 2000).

As a student of dynamics and mechanics, Einstein understood the problem [of the moving car] and knew from the beginning the importance of CONNECTION and time as his breakthrough variables. To get from the historical relevance of Galileo's relativity to Einstein's relativity and description of quanta takes us through 400 years of scientific study of energy, gravity, and electromagnetism.

Although Lorentz (1858–1928) is called the "father" of theoretical physics, Newton's work (1642–1727) in gravity, mass, force, and motion obviously laid the foundation of all modern physics up until Einstein's thought experiments. Newton discovered that electrical force can be attractive or repulsive, while gravitational force is only attractive. Therefore, gravitation is the direct result of a mass distorting space, but it has no duality. We will come back to this "problem" below.

Newton, with his classical three laws of motion, demonstrated his belief that all causes led to effects, as forces acted directly on objects, but he did have trouble with containing his measurements of absolute time. He had taken from Galileo a "relativity" principle to build a better system of inductive versus deductive logic. But whereas Newton used primarily inductive logic, analyzing data, and looking for patterns, Einstein was drawn to his thought experiments in which he would come up with a general idea or grand theory and then "deduce" all possible outcomes or solutions from there. For Newton, force was equal to mass times acceleration (f=ma) but as mass approaches the speed of light, acceleration decreases. Einstein considered acceleration and gravity as the same thing. Reconciling his findings with those of Newton led Einstein to e=mc2 because he proved that mass and energy are different manifestations of the same thing.

In a way, we are all intuitive physicists, psychologists, biologists, and mathematicians; we make assumptions and from those assumptions make predictions and inferences about our daily perceptions. These outcomes have to do with instinctual temperaments and inborn talents, demonstrated in each person's developmental UFT, which has been constructed and supports and embellishes experiences throughout the maturational sequence.

A quantifier is a symbol that can express what Pinker calls mentalese. For instance, as we will see in the next section, parts of quantum physics and string

---

[90] "Galileo wrote that the book of nature is written in the 'language of mathematics; without its help it is impossible to comprehend a single word of it.' Galileo's dictum applies not only to equation-filled blackboards in the physics department but to elementary truths we take for granted…Our understanding of the physical world is more sophisticated than children's because we have merged our intuitions about objects with our intuitions about number" (Pinker, 1997, p. 359).

theory were developed to explain such events as quantum entanglements and nonlocality, "interconnected particles that are separated by a vast distance will respond identically and simultaneously." Einstein never gave up his search for the UFT of the physical world because he continued to reject major parts of quantum mechanics, even though he had originally named quanta himself in 1905. Quanta was defined as self-perpetuating pulsating parts of the universe that were consistent binary fluctuations, undulating in wave-like patterns of on and off.

However, Einstein fiercely believed in locality, that S was always separate from S-1 and one cannot affect the other. He believed that there was a built-in paradox between Heisenberg's Uncertainty Principle and the simultaneous action of entanglements (Bohr). Heisenberg felt the act of measurement was itself a type of entanglement in that the very act of observation may cause the wave function to collapse (Isaacson 2007, pp. 452, 455). We will be discussing many of these theories in more depth in this chapter, mostly as they have to do with CONNECTION.

The other major force to be described was electromagnetism. An ampere was defined as the magnetic field at a given point in space that was proportional to the current and inversely proportional to the distance. This is important to understand because a description of the interaction of electrical and magnetic "fields", called electromagnetic induction, not only explained properties of light but evidently led to (quantum) wave theories and thus the foundation of modern theoretical physics. Faraday (1791–1867) was one of the first theorists to focus on "field theory". "Faraday ended up doing for electromagnetism what Einstein would do for gravity" (Moring, 2000 p. 82).

A field theory, per se, uses mathematical quantities to describe a point or force in space and the way it can affect another field, such as gravitational "field" or magnetic "field". Maxwell (1831–1879) expanded these findings into the coupling of the two fields, electric field with magnetic field, naming light as the electromagnetic "wave" for the first time.

Thus, to understand the underlying forces of creation and cosmos we must understand the basic CONNECTIONS of science: gravity, electromagnetism, and quantum mechanics. In the past, there was a need for a timeless constant. Previously there were ideas about ether as the invisible (and unmeasurable) factor, which seemed to be the unifying "stuff" of any energetic reaction. Currently, some go as far as claiming this as a "God constant". In 1900, Planck (1858–1947) wanted to understand the use of a constant to explain gravity, as well as how atoms react the same regardless of environment, size, or shape (Planck's constant).

In addition, Planck explained that the curve of radiation wavelengths at each temperature created "energy packages", showing that all energy is quantized. "Particular sized packets of energies (quanta) are required to affect the stretching and rotation of molecules, which means that particular types of energy are preferentially absorbed by different molecules. The differential absorption of various energy sources can be used to characterize molecules" (Sherwood, 1974, p. 69). We are like free-floating points in space where only local time applies. This concept really was the forerunner of Einstein's 1905 famous paper on "Special Relativity". Einstein wanted to answer the question of how rotating electrons

CONNECT in a magnetic field and so he described these "energy packages" as "quanta" waves and, as they say, the rest is history.

Einstein's Contributions

So far, we have reviewed the relevant history and principles of basic physics. Einstein wanted to use these factors as a unified theory to understand our own experience of reality and physics.

> Out of the supercharged German-speaking intellectual world, in which physics and mathematics and philosophy intertwined, three jarring theories of the twentieth century emerged: Einstein's relativity, Heisenberg's uncertainty, and Godel's incompleteness. The surface similarity of the three words, all of which conjure up a cosmos that is tentative and subjective, oversimplifies the theories and CONNECTIONS between them [emphasis added] (Isaacson, 2007, p. 510).

In his entire life, Einstein's most prolific period was probably during the four-month period from March to June 1905. Still working as a patent office clerk, he had the time and clarity of thought to write not one, but three papers. Perhaps reading the incoming patents helped spur on his creative and inductive juices as well? Some writers have joked that it was because his work at the patent office was so boring it left his mind free to think about his own ideas. Regardless, in trying to decide whether the Greeks had been right, and the world was made of atoms and particles, or Maxwell was right, and light (and thus energy) really was made of electromagnetic fields/waves, Einstein formulated the basic ideas of his theory.

In his first paper, Einstein began a debate which would intrigue and ultimately plague him for the rest of his life. He wrote to a friend, "I have now found in a most simple way the relation between the size of elementary quantum of matter and the wavelengths of radiation" (Einstein quoted in Isaacson, 2007, p. 97). Quanta is what he called particles of light; this formulation, however, led to a quantum theory without causality and certainty with which he ultimately did not agree. Einstein demanded his theories maintain "invariants, certainties, and absolutes", which could provide a "harmonious reality" (ibid, 2007). For Einstein, the best explanation of reality was always that which put forth the simplest set of factors, particularly as they could be put in mathematical terms.

In his next paper, even better known, Einstein created his own concept of "relativity" (remember Galileo had already addressed this), defining it as a "relatively" simple idea (sorry couldn't help myself!). Einstein wanted to prove that the fundamental laws of physics are the same whatever one's state of motion. Relativity had to explain time, space (with no directions, no boundaries), motion, position, and the resistance to change manifested in mass under force.

Whereas Descartes proposed that the mere separation of bodies by distance proved the existence of a medium between them, Einstein was convinced that man could define reality as only that which he perceived through the screen of his senses (Barrett, 1948) (See Chapter Two for more on epistemology). Thus, from the beginning, Einstein showed the importance of "unifying" the many factors that make up reality.

Electromagnetism creates a single cohesive force, that binds particles of matter and causes them to maintain their shape. Seems obvious now, but at the time it challenged not only years of common experience in the "real" world but Newton's laws themselves. His thought experiments proved to be true, and he became, well, Einstein of fame.

It is now important to explain how time figures into our explanation. "Time" is considered a linear event because of the way information is processed in our brains. If our brains worked differently, we would experience time differently. As mentioned above, Newton struggled with the concept of time. For instance, Newton always expressed distance in relation to time. "Time dilation" (the difference in time as measured by two clocks) has been described as time intervals that become larger as time slows down. "As you approach the speed of light, the intervals between moments become slower and slower, until all of a sudden you're in the present moment forever" (Moring, 2000, p. 172).

Therefore, Einstein's theory of relativity came from questioning Newton's "fictitious" frame of reference, which used "empty space" as an anchor (Pinker, 1997). Einstein's theory of general relativity had described gravity as a force, in terms of three-dimensional geometry. He had done his thought experiment and "seen" the stronger or weaker gravitational effects as something that he could graph as curvature in space. The more mass and energy involved, the greater the curvature (Chopra & Kafatos, 2017).

Einstein also took that which came before him to focus on the electrodynamics of moving bodies. As he proceeded, Einstein still had not explained inconstant motion and gravity at a distance; he would be left to explain relativity as applied to accelerated motion instead. These factors were important because he wanted to support Newton's theories. But Einstein couldn't do so, especially when he was measuring the weak states field, a problem which he never solved.

Other properties of physics that Einstein had to fit into his UFT included: Frequency Threshold or the finding that each metal has a certain frequency of light beyond which it would release its electrons; Brownian motion or the motion caused by the thermal motion of the water molecules; (Stress) Energy or the limitation on molecules so that they are no longer free to move around and mix with other molecules—all they can manage to do is vibrate; and finally, how entropy in a closed system always increases—loss of heat lowers efficiency (which is entropy in action).

The rebellious part of Einstein's nature, which had driven his early career, seemed to diminish with fame, and he became more conservative in his spiritual, political, and scientific points of view. As he aged, he tended to cling to his long-held views which were associated with "classical" science, particularly those associated with "field" theories. He wanted to deal in "invariances", not Heisenberg's Uncertainty probabilities, and he felt strongly about the principle of separability (particles with different locations in space have independent and unrelated experiences and measurements). Both he and de Broglie (1892–1987) wanted to save "reality" if possible and supported the "double solution" for the particle/wave "problem", even though they knew it was a problem of probability.

Much can be said in review of Einstein's personal life and personality, all of which contributed both to his view of the world and his science. Many authors have written about his eventual stubbornness when it came to finding a solution to his unified theory, one in which he chose to include his view of reality over the revelations contained in quantum theory as it was evolving.

Because Einstein found freedom from underlying personal problems in the creativity of his work, he could be humble, outgoing at times and generally not aloof regardless of his "caricature;" he had a great sense of humor. Although humble and curious, these traits competed with the fact that he did not like authority. The withdrawn or aloof nature of his character may have been part of a protective persona he had developed so he could do his work, rather than reflecting on the politics of some of the academic situations within which he found himself. More than taking pride in his intelligence, he felt he had moments of "illumination" (Isaacson, 2007, p. 549).

He had a passion for science, but also a passion for life. Ultimately, he felt it would be "glorious" to find the underling unity in any seemingly separate or unrelated phenomena. Unfortunately, his views kept his ideas anchored in the physics of the past and thus made any shot at unification even more complex.

Einstein was able to continually convince those individuals important in the world of physics, both in Europe and America, to give him support and academic positions within which to do his research. When he finally found a home at the Institute for Advanced Studies, Princeton, in 1933, he was intrinsically left to work out equations, intermittently believing he had found the answer.

Not only was he the great synthesizer, but Einstein was also the great empathizer and his published comments on philosophy, religion, and social problems of the time are generally better known and understood than his scientific theory, regardless of how simple he tried to make them. Einstein left us spiritual and philosophical writings, greatly influenced by Spinoza and Hume. Although he did not believe in a personal God, he agreed with Spinoza that God was a unified entity based on a 'causal dependence of all phenomena' (Einstein quoted in Isaacson, 2007, p. 334).

This type of belief in determinism led him to follow Hume's skepticism about 'mental' constructs and thus to always question whether his theoretical formulas were simple enough for a universal mind to have produced their outcome.

Try and penetrate with our limited means the secrets of nature and you will find that, behind all the discernible laws and CONNECTIONS, there remains something subtle, intangible, and inexplicable. Veneration for this force beyond anything that we can comprehend is my religion…The fairest thing we can experience is the mysterious. It is the fundamental emotion which stands at the cradle of true science. He who knows it not and can no longer wonder, no longer feel amazement, is as good as dead [emphasis added] (ibid, pp. 384–385).

This view was shared by other great scientists—Niels Bohr, Max Planck, and Werner Heisenberg. Moving beyond Einstein's theories, Bohr, Heisenberg, and others proposed theories which tried to explain the Big Bang, string theory, dark matter, and other ideas in advanced theoretical physics. Bohr, a friend and yet nemesis of sorts to Einstein, studied angular momentum, which is the momentum when moving in a circle (like a ball attached to a string). Bohr's electrons (and similarly the planets in the solar systems) were traveling in an orbit around the nucleus (sun), exhibiting angular momentum. When an electron moved from one orbit to the next, it was a "quantum leap".

"The faster you swing the ball, the greater its angular momentum is …and then the electron jumps! [And you never knew when it would happen]. A binding force would be discovered, which was neither electrical nor gravitational in nature, would also be discovered. Einstein combined Bohr's model of the atom with Max Planck's theory of the quanta" (Isaacson, 2007. p. 323).

Einstein believed in imagination and in mystery, and he was constantly trying to reconcile natural law and ethical freedom. Although he was a rebel early on, and an idealist in his ability to do thought experiments and to challenge conventional science, he had a deep-seated belief system and sense of morality, especially when he looked at post-WWI Europe, and pre-WWII Europe and America with realistic rather than idealistic perspectives. In many ways, he was a "citizen of the world."

Niels Bohr's Principle of Complementarity

Heisenberg's Uncertainty Principle (the position and velocity of an object cannot be measured properly; cause and effect break down) and Bohr's principle of complementarity (that the acceptance of two apparently contrasting theories can explain more in a unified way than either could have when taken separately) can also be applied to natural phenomena. Interdependence or "life-in-common" (such as symbiotic cells) illustrated Bohr's concepts of functional complementariness between two factors, and ultimately what de Chardin called the "cohesive whole" (de Chardin, 1959). Because of the dual nature of quanta (particle and wave), we ask how these two opposite behaviors exist together. "Quantum phenomena are neither waves nor particles but are intrinsically undefined until the moment they are measured…As the philosopher Berkeley said, 'To be is to be perceived'" (Chopra & Kafatos, 2017, p. 135–137).

I relate this experiential finding to my own work with relational attachment between individuals, where there is a high "valient bonding" through emotional commitment/love; then an expression of the energy causes a "jump" in oxytocin and behavioral changes during the experience; then bonding can take place and there may be commitment made through physical and legal attachment (Brown, Brown & Preston, 2012).

Of course, all this theoretical belief in quantum "leaps", whether electrons we can't see or emotions we can feel, challenged Newton's mechanics, because there was only the "probability" of the occurrence with no way to predict exactly when the emission of the photon would take place (or, in my example, the expression of trust). This finding is what pushed quantum mechanics truly into a four-dimensional world.

These multiple explanations and views of forces, which had to be discovered and explained over the last 400 years, are another way of relating these theories to our idea of CONNECTIONS. The principle of complementarity not only requires consideration of references to opposites (dualities such as *Taoism*, and the dual nature of wave and particle theory) but may also require consideration of the Codependency of these dualities. Of course, many readers see the word and may think of it in a psychological frame of reference. But in the "Principle of Complementarity", you can't define the nature of one thing without reference to its complementary opposite. Can we use this type of theory to explain the dual nature of Bohr's wave and particle theory as well as Beattie's (1986) theory of Codependency?

Einstein believed that mass and energy were equivalent, not complementary, but as later physicists came to believe in what is called "mass-energy" (the mass of a body also regards its kinetic and potential energy), he chose to adapt his thoughts on this matter. This debate lasted until his death in 1955.

Louis de Broglie (1892–1987) was one of the first physicists to propose that energy had wave properties, also showing that the momentum of the photon was equal to Planck's constant divided by the photon's wavelength. As the wavelength of light decreases, its momentum (mass + velocity) increases. Standing waves are not equivalent, just really slow! Going back to my idea of valient bonding being equivalent to attachment between individuals, maybe this awareness of wave theory is one way to explain the behavior and lack of bonding within Outliers, especially the human type. They may not be responding, or even appear to want to be responsive, to an attachment pattern coming from a significant Other. Of course, they are responding in their own internal manner, just really slowly…well, now that I write this, of course they are; no one doesn't respond, do they?

Perhaps, as Maxwell and Lorentz showed in their study of electromagnetism, electronically charged particles (ions/the need for attachment) create forces, even at rest. When they move, it is these forces which create the magnetic field. Because the law of conservation of charge requires the total amount of electric charge to remain constant, the moving charge creates an electric current between the particles; in other words, the hyper-aroused sense of "Other" between individuals. The angles of deflection of alpha ray contact (during radiation deterioration) is greater as you get closer to the nucleus where the mass is greater; the Outlier may try to deflect but creates a mass deficit in doing so (loneliness, depression, anger, or addiction).

In a quantum state of ionization requiring/attracting positive energy, there will be an opposite negative energy of the binding effect. It is a synthesis of the opposites; the variance in binding energy due to changes in the kinetic energy/potential energy ratio will result in quanta excitation (and perhaps relationship-building!). Heisenberg's Uncertainty Principle basically summarizes this potentiality by showing how the changes in position and momentum can never be accurately measured, just like trying to predict another person's behavior.

An important question in theoretical physics/cosmology emerged from this debate between Einstein and de Broglie and those who followed them: What allows the electron to radiate away its excess energy as light? Schrodinger (1887–1961) proposed that light was produced, or energy was emitted, because of a harmony between the upper and lower vibrations of the electron waves, whereas Bohr maintained that a wave was not made of a real particle but was just a probability in space for finding an electron (Isaacson, 2007, p. 230). Our perception was a probability function; it was used to describe the distribution of likely occurrences.

From these ideas, we see the beginnings of Heisenberg's Uncertainty Principle being developed. Because "when you observe something, you see either one fact or its opposite, but not at once," it was easiest to describe that process of quantum mechanics (especially for us laypeople) by stating that "quantum particles travel like waves, but arrive as particles" (ibid, 2007, p. 219). As mentioned above, we have accepted our four-dimensional view of the world as a place in which we will never know exactly when a particle will arrive, that is, of it becoming a wave; we can also say we will not know the precise position of a particle or potentially "leaping" electron. Position is a property of a particle, but momentum is a property of a wave.

Uncertainty, complementarity, probability, and the collapse of a wave function combine into something called the "Copenhagen interpretation". This discussion of the theories of both Bohr and Heisenberg, as a useful description of the behavior of energy, was one of the earliest explanations of the theory of quantum mechanics, explaining the importance of dealing only with probabilities when observing or measuring quanta rather than expecting "exact" outcomes of either a particle or a wave. There are still a lot of variances in the meaning and findings of these discussions.

Those who follow Heisenberg believe it is meaningless to ask what atoms and particles are doing when we aren't looking at them. We will relate this to personality and interpersonal dynamics more as we proceed, particularly in Chapters Thirteen and Sixteen. Like human relations, social functioning, and the brain's utilization of our memory and neurotransmitters, there is still the obvious fact of our uncertainty, fallibility, or "incompleteness".

Understanding Wave Theory

Physicists know that validity of a theory lies in measurement. However, we now accept that the statistical probability of quantum mechanics indicates that it is "incomplete". Measurements of a certain property done on two identical systems can give different answers. Particles, and their "hidden waves" that guide their motions, point to a view of the world that is more interactional than one would have originally thought.

The collection of particles each function according to Schrodinger's Equation (density conforms to the magnitude of the wave function). Also known as the "Pilot Wave Theory", "nonlocality" and "non-relativistic" formulations apply. The finding is a "hidden variable theory" which can have realistic independence from the observer and is also deterministic of the positions and momenta of the particles. According to this theory the point and matter waves are both real and distinct physical entities, both guiding the duality.[91]

This paradigm often reminds me of the research concept of "dependent" variables. Any system has dependent variables that affect outcomes, for instance: position and momentum; in the workplace (product development); individuals within a relationship; in the development of a medical or addiction recovery plan; whatever. Another way of putting this is perhaps quantum potential may not be as mysterious as we thought if we are willing to acknowledge the power and potential of nonlocality and duality. Another view of duality in wave function is the theoretical belief of an "empty" wave function, which Einstein called "ghost waves". But that goes far beyond the scope of this chapter. Just a cool thought to consider, isn't it?

I believe that a case can be made for subatomic matter (and its attributes of Nonlocality, Quantum entanglement, and Coherence). Entanglement is caused by partner photons being sent off in different directions yet remaining capable of instantaneously "CONNECTING and communicating" across vast spaces—an action which is also a reflection of nonlocality. These recent discoveries have taken quantum information theory from the subatomic level to macro-scale functioning—an entirely new direction within physics research. We can now postulate theories about the behavior between two distant objects, but more importantly to this discussion of CONNECTIONS, we can look at the way in which entanglement and nonlocality might impact relational behaviors and policies between humans.

String Theory and the Big Bang

By the 1920s, there was a belief that not only could a generalized cosmological theory be hypothesized, but also that the hypothesis had been generally accepted in the physics community. Labeled "The Big Bang Theory", the history of its development goes as follows: beginning in 1924, Edwin Hubble worked at the Mount Wilson Observatory in Pasadena, California, and discovered first Andromeda nebula (later known to be a whole other galaxy) and then dozens of even more distant galaxies. In a more dramatic discovery, he found that by measuring the "red shift" in the stars' spectra, it could be proven that the galaxies were moving away from us.

---

[91]"Wave packet: an envelope or packet containing an arbitrary number of wave forms…'probability wave' describing the probability that a particle or particles in a particular state will be measured to have a given position and momentum…This trade-off between spread in position and spread in momentum is one example of the Heisenberg Uncertainty Principle…The energy of light is a discrete function of frequency E=nhf …an integer, n, multiple of Planck's constant, h, and frequency, f….This particle-like nature of the world was significantly confirmed by experiment, while the wave-like phenomena could be characterized as consequences of the wave packet nature of particles….One theory hypothesizes that the origin of the observable universe occurred when two parallel branes collided. [A brane is a physical object that elevates a point particle to a higher dimension and is part of M-theory, also known as string theory]" (Abers and Pearson, 2004).

There were at least two possible explanations for the fact that distant stars in all directions seemed to be flying away from us: (1) because we are the center of the universe, something that since the time of Copernicus only our teenage children believe; or (2) because the entire metric of the universe was expanding, which meant that everything was stretching out in all directions (Isaacson, 2007, pp. 353–354).[92]

This second finding eventually led to proof, as well, of Einstein's theoretical cosmological constant. The term cosmological constant was a new term for an old concept, going back to the Greeks and beyond (in Latin "quinta-essential") most frequently referred to as "ether". Often seen as a "repulsive force" of some kind, it needed to be explained if it was to be controlled for by way of a stabilizing tensor, which Einstein designated with the Greek letter lambda. This complexity was referred to as his "transformational" problem, partly because it was determined that space-time can need ten independent components making the mathematics complex for most of his equations. But even if a rotation was "relative" [pun intended], Einstein could not find a workable equation for the transformation that took place, so he ultimately went back to the importance of gravitation.

He never solved this complexity, however, even though (at barely 36 years old) he had presented the theory of general relativity which began an integration of space, time, matter, and energy. This theory, then, was labeled a macro to micro theory of mechanical laws because of the addition of "space-time". Einstein's constant is also now known as the vacuum energy density, which he initially discarded in 1931. It was a foundational idea which came and went throughout his long career; Einstein's philosophy of life was to keep moving forward, to never give up the search for answers, especially as long as the answers could do better than harm.

Recently, theorists studying string theory have attempted to reconcile the concepts of order and chaos, the defining force most studied being gravitational. Newton had attacked the problem of gravity, seeing it as an elegant combination of answers to macrocosmic and microcosmic questions. Einstein, however, felt it became a question of force versus energy and changed force into a measure of mass and energy [f]e equaled mc^2. "The general theory of relativity was very useful in explaining reality on a large scale, the macrocosm; quantum mechanics was very useful at explaining reality on a very small scale, the microcosm" (Pinker, 1997, p. 280).

---

[92] "While the universe was expanding and cooling in the first few minutes, nuclear reactions were occurring that built up complex nuclei [RNA replicators we spoke of in the last chapter] from the primordial protons and neutrons, but because the density of matter was relatively low, these reactions could occur only sequentially. Protons + neutrons = hydrogen, then combining deuterons with protons or neutrons or other deuterons to make heavier nuclei like helium...During this time, neutrons were changing into protons, just as free neutrons do in our labs today. Sometimes what we think is a fundamental law of nature is just an accident" (Moring, 2000, pp. 315).

Another example of string theory—vibrational power—has its own distinct characteristics. The similarity to musical constructs is noteworthy in that "subatomic harmonies" build up to create specific particles like quarks, protons, and gravitons and, ultimately, complex structures [like chords] (Chopra & Kafatos, 2017).

The four forces in nature which can describe movement or change are:

1. Gravity: an attractive force that binds together the solar system.
2. Electromagnetism: holds together the atom, determines the structure of the orbits of the electrons, and governs the laws of chemistry. 'When the atom is disturbed, the motion of the electrons around the nucleus becomes irregular and they emit light and other forms of radiation. This is the purest form of electromagnetic radiation.'
3. Strong force: responsible for binding together the protons and neutrons in the nucleus. Highest radioactivity: beyond one hundred protons in the nucleus, even the strong nuclear force has difficulty containing the repulsive electric force between these protons.
4. Weak force: when breaking apart comes, radioactivity in these elements make the nucleus unstable and it disintegrates. Therefore, another weaker force must be at work, one that governs radioactivity, and which is responsible for the disintegration of very heavy nuclei (Kaku and Trainer, 1987, p. 7).

As the theory proposes, after the Big Bang quanta were created because nature always prefers to be in the lowest energy state. "As the universe cooled, one by one the symmetry holding together the four forces began to break down" (ibid, 1987, p. 126). Gravity breaks off first, then strong force, then weak force, leaving only electromagnetic force unbroken.

It is important to also have an explanation for the irregular or asymmetrical behavior of the statistical or social Outlier. We will set aside that question as it relates to humans for the time being and come back to it in Chapter Sixteen. As Freudian theories of analysis opened us to viewing processes in an inductive manner, so has science begun more and more to use reverse engineering to come up with logical explanations. Whether derived by choice or driven by outside forces beyond one's own control, a problem is often resolved best by simplicity and a straightforward sense of a goal.

Einstein was often driven to use Newton's laws to find his unified theory. He was also driven by a deep belief that the God and Nature of his understanding could not be some complicated set of laws as represented by quantum mechanics and especially by string theory. He wanted simple mathematics behind the equations he had to produce to prove his theoretical "thought equation;" it just never worked out that way (Moring, 2000).

Physics and the "Mind"

What do the neurons, whether functioning as particles or waves, tell us about where the "mind" is? Is it just reflexes and neurochemical reactions, or images translated through special prefrontal cortex symbolic coding and meaningful presentation, traveling along as quanta? Research has shown that infant growth is cephalocaudal and proximodistal, and the same head-to-toe progression is reflected in the control and complexity of movement and motor ability.

Once cortical activity takes over, what was once a reflex must be relearned as a skill. In higher organisms, reflexes or instincts begin to get associated with rewards and eventually can be "freed from bodily drives and physical stimuli and responses and can associate ideas directly to each other" (Pinker, 1997, p. 180). Recent researchers have shown that beyond Pavlov's experiments and Skinner's operant conditioning, there is learning by association and other such types of multivariate responses in the brain. Is the mind in the brain, or conditioned by the heart (think emotional choices, probably driven by oxytocin and adrenal function)?

"Nothing happens in the mind that is not prefigured in the brain. Everything you think and feel has its neuronal precursor or progenitor; and since neurons are made of molecules, the mind is fundamentally a molecular machine—it consists of molecules in action" (McGinn, 2013). I personally try to live by "strong mental, tender heart". Is it true the soul is in the atoms of the neurochemistry of the mind/brain as well? I still believe we should talk about Self-awareness as a subjective quality which is intimately linked to your beliefs about yourself, about others, and about the world. However, I also accept that this sense is modulated by neurochemical impulses which travel by the actions of wave theory.

Carl Jung (1875–1961) took this idea of inner structures of the mind even further (see also Chapter Eighteen). He believed that we lose our divine nature during our lives on Earth and may despair of ever regaining it, but we can do so if we desire it enough to weather the trials and tribulations that come our way, never losing sight of our goal. Today the word psyche means the whole Self, all the emotional, intellectual, and spiritual aspects that make up a human being. "Jung realized that the unconscious is a world that can only be viewed indirectly, through its byproducts and relationships" (Moring, 2000, p. 246).

Jung's premise is very similar to the world of quantum mechanics, where physicists study subatomic particles that can only be viewed indirectly through their probable and uncertain relationships with other particles. This statement brings together many of the factors that form the basis of my own developmental UFT, which I first began to teach and write about 30 years ago. The Uncertainty Principle makes it meaningless to worry about what is happening when we "aren't looking;" but joyfully, Einstein did point out certain concepts about the nature of reality as we experience it, and not just "theoretically".

> The true value of a human being is determined primarily by the measure and the sense in which he has obtained liberation from the self…Surprisingly, because the role of the observer plays an important part in the study of the quantum world, there may be a close relationship between the dynamic

structure of the quantum universe and the nature of unconscious (Einstein quoted by Moring, 2000, p. 247).

It is no accident that much of the clarity of our thought about Self and consciousness comes from those who studied science as well as the mind. We see this throughout the scientific world, from the Renaissance period up through the interests of the Dalai Lama, who has been studying neuroscience, or neurosciences and psychiatry, as these disciplines involve meaningfulness. When I took a 12-day initiation with His Holiness at Ganden Monastery in Southern India, December 2001, a friend was called into his private quarters to demonstrate how solar panels could improve the monastery in Dharamsala, and the report came back that His Holiness was much taken with all kinds of new (at the time) scientific and electronic gadgets!

Enlightenment

For me, the most powerful way to cross-reference physics and particle theory to psychological constructs and human experience is by thinking about light. Enlightenment: the act of using new knowledge and understanding to find insight and wisdom about Self and that within which one finds oneself. Jung proposed that personalities differ in at least four major ways: "whether a person is sociable or retiring (extroversion-introversion); whether a person worries constantly or is calm and self-satisfied (neuroticism-stability); whether a person is careful or careless (conscientiousness-undirectedness); and whether a person is daring or conforming (openness—non-openness)" (Pinker, 1997, p. 448). These traits are about 50% genetic, and only about 5% from home influences. But where does the other 45% come from—the events in one's life influenced by iatrogenic factors and unique experiences (or traumas) that have shaped each of us individually (UFT)?

A recent development in cosmology—a new elementary particle found at CERN (site of the large hadron collider) called the Higgs particle—is also an explanation of our nature. Could this particle bridge biological science with physical explanations of the cosmos? Scientists have been looking for the Higgs particle for almost 50 years, and its discovery is at the heart of our current best theory of nature. How can this new information bring us closer to a simple unified idea of ourselves, our universe, and how we become "enlightened?"

The concept, which the Higgs particle influenced, was advanced more recently by Andrei Linde after his verification of "chaotic inflation", a polarization of the cosmic microwave background (Andrei Linde, *Wikipedia*, 3/21/2014). In 2004, he received the Gruber Cosmology Prize for the development of inflationary cosmology/phase transitions: Linde maintained, contrary to prior belief, there was not much difference between weak, strong, and electromagnetic interactions in the very early universe. They became different from each other only gradually after the cosmological phase transitions, while the universe expanded and cooled down.[93]

Whether called the "God particle", Einstein's cosmological constant, or even Higher Power, human consciousness has the capacity to experience more than one level of reality at the same time. "All life is a cycle. The Force [*Tao*] views the universe as a system of energy rather than as a system of material forms" (Moring, 2000, p. 342). If the energy/force communicates, impacts, affects, CONNECTS us, then perhaps we need to explain the intermediary field which modulates the results of spontaneous symmetry, breaking what physicists call "weak force". Is the field predictable in its symmetry or does it fall under the probability issues of the Uncertainty Principle because of asymmetry?

Tesla's View of Energy

Nicola Tesla (1856–1943) is a name associated with the study of energy, before quantum physics and even before Einstein's first publications. Tesla was an inventor, a physicist, and a mechanical and electrical engineer. But he is best known, perhaps, for not being given credit for all that he discovered, and which has influenced us scientifically up to this day. These inventions and discoveries include some of the electrical current ideas and inventions for which Edison was given credit, as well as much of the basis of our modern wireless communication, which Tesla first demonstrated in 1893. Because of his eccentric personality and sometimes "mad scientist" type claims about his work, he was ostracized within the scientific community and his work was never lucrative. During this time, around 1891, he was influenced by the Vedic philosophy teachings of the Swami Vivekananda, which may have also created his isolative behavior (Nikola Tesla, *Wikipedia*, 8/29/2014).

Tesla was interested in harvesting the energy that is present throughout space. "Ere many generations pass, our machinery will be driven by a power obtainable at any point in the universe" (Tesla, *Experiments With Alternate Currents of High Potential and High Frequency*, February 1892).[94] In 1897, Tesla researched

---

[93] At this point all elementary particles and matter emerged after the end of inflation in a process called "reheating." Linde also confirmed (in 1974) that the energy density of scalar fields (tensor field of order zero) breaks symmetry during polarization between different interactions ("waterfall" instability). Thus, it can play the role of the vacuum energy density (Einstein cosmological constant). He was able to propose a more unified theory than the then existing "old" and "new" inflationary theories, which he called "chaotic inflation." Of course, a self-reproducing inflationary universe, according to Linde, could ultimately become a "multiverse."

[94] "Tesla began to theorize about electricity and magnetism's power to warp, or rather change, space and time and the procedure by which man could forcibly control this power. Near the end of his life, Tesla was fascinated with the idea of light as both a particle and a wave, a fundamental proposition already incorporated into quantum physics. This field of inquiry led to the idea of creating a 'wall of light' by manipulating electromagnetic waves in a certain pattern. This mysterious wall of light would enable time, space, gravity, and matter to be altered at will, and engendered an array of Tesla proposals. When he was eighty-one, Tesla stated he had completed a

radiation, which led to setting up the basic formulation of cosmic rays, and in 1898 he proposed radio-controlled objects, one being a torpedo (an idea which remained a novelty until the 1960s). He was the first to develop the "Art of Tel automatics", a form of robotics.

Aside from these advancements by Tesla, most of which were not accepted in his lifetime, who's to say if perhaps they did influence Einstein's eventual theories; some other influences were also suggested specifically by Michelson and Morley in 1887. These scientists certainly led Bohr and others to an accepted bilateral explanation (particle and wave) of energy and light. Likewise, the study of quantum physics also leads to the idea of quintessence or a hypothetical form of dark energy.

> We can't always predict the weather, but we know pretty well how weather works...There has been speculations about a vacuum energy (sometimes called 'dark energy') since Einstein first turned his attention to cosmology...Einstein, in 1917, introduced a modification in the equations of his 1915 General Theory of Relativity known as a Cosmological Constant, which was completely equivalent to attributing to empty space as energy per volume, that is always the same everywhere and (Weinberg, Quiescence, *Wikipedia*, 11/2001).

Einstein had concluded that light, like any material object, travels in a curve when passing through the gravitational field of a massive body. He suggested that "the greater the concentration of matter, the greater the resulting curvature of space-time. The total effect is an overall curvature of the whole space-time continuum: the combined distortions produced by all the incomputable masses of matter in the universe cause the continuum to bend back on itself in a great closed cosmic curve" (Barrett, 1948, p. 96). Thus, Einstein predicted black holes, stating "space has no borders because gravity bends it back on itself...finite, yet has no limits."[95] These are the "repulsive forces" mentioned above that contributed to his formulation of his theory of a cosmological constant.

---

dynamic theory of gravity, that it was 'worked out in all details;' and that he hoped to soon give it to the world. The theory was never published. At the time of his announcement, it was considered by the scientific establishment to exceed the bounds of reason. [Rather] some believe that Tesla never fully developed his own unified field theory. He died alone of heart failure in the New Yorker hotel in 1943" (O'Neill, 2007).

[95] "In some modern theories there is an additional vacuum energy that evolves with the universe; this is sometimes known as the 'event horizon.' Black holes are made of nuclear particles and electrons, just like ordinary stars, but a black hole is so compact that its gravitational field stops light from escaping from its surface, while any light that escapes from just outside its surface is slowed so much that, to an outside observer, time on the surface of the black hole seems to have stopped. From the point of view of an observer falling into a black hole, nuclear particles will seem to be decaying with the same half-life that we will observe on earth [or hope we will], but from far outside they seem to live much, much longer. Therefore, in any galaxy beyond a certain

Subsequently, black holes have been found to be gigantic atomic furnaces that release the energy stored in the strong force, "energy created by the strong force tends to be explosive, and the gravitational force, tends to be implosive" (Kaku and Trainer, 1987, p. 150). There is a distortion of space-time because of the intense gravitational force. Time slows down as you near the center of the black hole. Here Heisenberg's Uncertainty Principle explains that there is no "accurate" description of a particle without writing it down as describing the probability function that goes with every quality of being. "It is a possibility of being or tendency for being" [emphasis added] (ibid, 1987, p. 70).

The mind has the developing process built in, like a Kodak camera, and this epistemological view has lasted through attacks even by Kant and Hegel. But once Einstein's relativity physics and Heisenberg's Uncertainty Principle led to new scientific views, the observer's part in nature had to be included in the view that no formulation could be determined without including the effect of the observer on the process. Our view of ourselves, and our inner depth crises (suffering, hopelessness, or de-evolving) is no easier to explain than similar concepts in a macrocosm world. For we are only observers of ourselves, like scientists who oversee the universe, the cellular world or the workings of the mind and its neurotransmitters. We do not understand those dark feelings much more than we currently do the cosmological questions about dark energy, but we continue the search.

Nature of Dark Energy

The exact nature of dark energy is a matter of speculation. It is known to be very homogeneous, not very dense. Two leading models—quintessence and Einstein's cosmological constant—really did describe what we now consider "dark energy". Both models include the common characteristic that dark energy must have negative pressure: "Independently from its actual nature, dark energy would need to have a strong negative pressure in order to explain the observed acceleration in the expansion rate of the universe" (Wang, 2016, pp. 503–508).[96]

Asymmetry/Divergency (as in divergent thinking) is referred to as Phantom Energy in physics. As most of us have been brought up in a dualistic philosophy of thought, where being able to relate to and use divergent perspectives is important for understanding and controlling asymmetrical outcomes. Physicists have long had to face the idea that phantom energy causes divergent expansion. The equilibrium we are used to is unstable; if the universe expands slightly, then the expansion releases vacuum energy, which causes yet more expansion. [Think how dense dark matter is, as discussed above.] "With Einstein's famous moving train thought experiment example, he really started the thinking that there is no

---

distance, the 'event horizon' would be forever unobservable" (Weinberg, *Wikipedia*, 11/2001).

[96] "In the standard model of cosmology, dark energy currently accounts for 74% of the total mass-energy of the universe...In general relativity, the evolution of the expansion rate is parameterized by the cosmological equation of state. Measuring the equation of state of dark energy is one of the biggest efforts in observational cosmology today.

way to prove that two events can happen simultaneously, i.e., twin paradox or 'time dilation'" (ibid, 2016, p. 130).[97]

How could the right and left hand of the universe work so independently of each other? Superstring theory maintains that both quantum mechanics and relativity are necessary to make a basic quantum theory of gravity work; for instance, changing the "electric field" creates a "magnetic field". Likewise, psychological personal space or even avoidance (of the field) is seen in the psychological concepts of splitting ideation or deprivation behavior/learned helplessness, a parallel construct to that of physics above. Richard Feynman redefined the charge and mass of the electron to absorb or cancel out the infinities. Could we do this absorbing? The theory of particles was standardized in the 1970s and consists of 17 fundamental particles which make up most of the known universe. There are two main types of particles: fermions (the "stuff" of matter, including six types of "leptons", including electrons, and six particles called "quarks") and bosons (the forces moving that stuff around) (Wells, 2022). Within the theories that use this particle theory, we find new views of gravity, dark matter, Higgs boson, and even unification [CONNECTION] of forces.[98] "Only electrons can be classed as a fundamental lepton particle, and protons and neutrons are instead represented by their respective quarks" (ibid, 2022, p. 2).

Discontinuous events (atomicity) and continuous events (continuity) have a boundary between them, and a study of this difference may soon lead us to a question: is this finding a form of Hegelian thesis and antithesis? "The whole precedes reality of the parts" and the creative function by necessity results in projective aspects of the mind so that we may be able to see the inner world of "Other". How can that not be measurable? (Madeo, 2010, p. 74).

---

[97] Kaku and Trainer note that the world is also full of examples of symmetry being hidden because it is "broken." "The universe would be a rather dull place if symmetry were never broken. Humans could not exist (because there would be no atoms), life would not be possible and chemistry itself would collapse. Everything would be perfectly homogeneous and dull. It is symmetry's breaking, therefore, that makes the universe so interesting" (Kaku and Trainer, 1987, p. 121).
One scientific goal is to reconcile small quanta to be consistent with large quanta (such as described in the theory of relativity). Einstein's theory of general relativity had described gravity as a force in terms of three-dimensional geometry. He had done his thought experiment and "seen" the stronger or weaker gravitational effects as something that he could graph as curvature in space. Simple concept, complex solution. Dark Energy is the most popular way to explain these observations, that the universe appears to be expanding at an accelerating rate.
[98] A form of Dialectical Materialism is noted in the supersymmetry described by the forces of particle theory: "each layer of physical reality is created by the interaction of two poles [thesis/antithesis]. Quarks obey the rules of symmetry as subnuclear particles; therefore, the quark can turn into [synthesis] an electron by emitting another particle" (ibid, 1987, p. 79).

Mandelbrot Set: The Study of Boundaries and Self-sameness

As a researcher for IBM, Benoit Mandelbrot (11/20/1924–10/14/2010) first named the self-perpetuating clustering of disjointed figures, which he discovered were found everywhere in nature. Because of his access to computers and his ability to create graphics, he was able to display fractal geometric images, which led to the phenomenon called "the Madelbrot set".[99]

The failure of the universe to act "normally" was found to reflect the geometric influences of triangulation (also found in Dark energy); Self-similarity was represented in fractal dynamics. Known mostly as the study of patterns, Madelbrot's set c, c2+c, (c2+c) 2, ... is also seen in personality organization by observation of the repetitive nature of human behavior. And it is not only the pattern but only the "'dimensionality and scaling' of the personality-driven behavior that presents in significant patterns" (Marks-Tarlow, 1999). In fact, the paradox of quantum theory is that continuous and Self-sameness does not equal real. Many examples of Mandelbrot's patterns have been given, such as the complex, yet simple, repeating pattern of a rocky coastline and the internal patterning of a halved cauliflower.

Mandelbrot applied his theory to such scientific fields as information theory, economics, and fluid dynamics. Capra has famously written about some of these findings in *The Tao of Physics* (1975). Including these new ideas in physics with Capra's work shows even more dramatically that the territory outside the fractal is out of control, the edge between these two realms (as is the dividing line in the *Tao* figure) is the delicate interface between unbounded and bounded areas. "It neither flies out of control nor comes to rest. Instead, it self-organizes into an infinitely deep border zone that moves dynamically along" [emphasis added] (Marks-Tarlow, 1999, pp. 311–345). This border is a "paradox of the non-linear kind", and because of having a non-linear nature it represents "irregularity, discontinuity, evolution and change." We learn to notice and accept asymmetry within a consciousness of balance.

One example given by Marks-Tarlow, from psychotherapeutic casework, includes the differentiation between a borderline patient, who shows high complexity of symptoms with a low level of involuted consciousness, as compared with an enlightened individual, who demonstrates low complexity of behavior but with a high level of consciousness. Obviously, these are opposite ends of a

---

[99] "The shape—it looks a bit like a warty snowman or beetle—came to represent the newly fashionable science of chaos…Time and again he found simplicity and even beauty where others saw irredeemable messiness." By his use of computers, Mandelbrot was able "to show how visual complexity can be created from simple rules," and he was able to "unfreeze" the difficulties mathematics was having visualizing the complexities of chaos theory. "They were there, even though nobody had seen them before. It's marvelous, a very simple formula explains all these very complicated things. Frequently, the goal of science is starting with a mess, and explaining it with a simple formula, a kind of dream of science" (Wolfram, 2012).

continuum, but the discrepancy between the two personality types presents a baseline of understanding about how their therapy can be designed out of the Self-same set of behavioral indicators.

Likewise, Prigogine and Stengers (1984) believed that Self-similar dynamics can exist at multiple levels within the human body. They studied how fractals are involved with communication and transformation of energy, matter, and information between the various systems within the body. They wrote about how complexity could operate effectively in conditions that were far from being "in equilibrium". As mentioned above, we most often experience balance when asymmetry is resolved.

A Locus of Control

When we use a Gestalt therapy model, we can define areas (or loci) of control. Inner-directed focus, or an inner locus of control, has firmer boundaries and "feels" in control although emotionally it may not be. Outer-directed focus, or an outer locus of control, creates more possibility of being out of control due to environmental factors and makes one more susceptible to PTSD. The edge between the two now becomes our therapeutic focus, the boundary of ego defenses if you would, between bounded and unbounded. Thus, we end up with situational and diagnostic influences on how we (as humans) or the Universe (as Light and Dark energy) splits and reflects boundaries. "Shall we examine the real possibility that most of nature is non-linear? Can an asymmetrical universe be explained?" (Madeo, 2010, p. 36).

In psychology we also use the term triangulation to refer to the possible (unhealthy) relationship between any three people or parts of an organization where gamesmanship (victim, blamer, rescuer) can play out (Haley, 1973; Satir, 1976). In causing unhealthy outcomes, the triangulated (geometric) boundary is broken by at least one of the parties refusing the bond and denying further participation. In other words, the triangulation is broken by some party stepping out of the Codependent and predictable systemic pattern. In physics, the laws of gravity have been unified (so far) with those of quantum mechanics through causal dynamical triangulation (CDT) (a similar pattern to the psychological construct above), resulting in "loop quantum gravity".

This process keeps the "attachment" or CONNECTION in place and determines the overall geometry by "summing the probabilities of all the possible configurations of simplexes" (Alpert, 2007). Four-dimensional space-time allows us to merge dynamically the basic ingredients of experience into a smooth set of findings by using fractals of life experience, but on a small scale.

We are CONNECTED to Nature and to the Universe itself. We stay "tuned up" by a healthy lifestyle and relationships. Being "out of tune" with ourselves, our environment and specifically our CONNECTION with others leads to a type of disconnected and invalidated experience of the world. In the next chapter, we will explore further how, during the original "narcissistic injury", a toddler is side-tracked from normal developmental tasks—a preliminary example of "boundaries gone wrong". As discussed earlier, narcissistic injury to a child is defined as the toddler becoming confused by mother's failure to CONNECT and confusing attachment signals early in the (valient) bonding period. As a result, the child will mistrust either her own internal signals or the mother, a loss which, in turn, will generalize to other authority figures in her future. Triangulation self-perpetuates and asymmetry prevails.

As noted by Marks-Tarlow above (1999), long-term violation of boundaries results in chaos, and boundaries can be easier violated if one isn't clear about how to manage the ongoing negotiations of the fractal border of inner and outer; borderline personalities tend to oscillate between subjective poles of engulfment and abandonment, often harboring central issues of rage and shame. They repeatedly express confusion between self and other. "At times, interpersonal confusion reaches a crescendo, to the point of denying psychological existence altogether. That is, the borderline personality may claim that she has no self, to assert in essence that 'I don't exist'" (ibid, 1999, p. 340). [I have a patient who often says just that...]

We refer to this loss of Self, one without boundaries, as "chaotic logic". On the other hand, one of the goals of good parenting is to teach our child to "tolerate ambiguity, to hold opposites without succumbing to tension of reducing one side to the other and to understand ambivalence" (ibid, 1999, p. 339). I had a therapist once, while I was in training, who told me "Ambivalence is the best form of defense; it allows you to know you're just not ready to make a decision yet!" The relationship between constructs in physics such as boundaries, chaos theory, symmetry and asymmetry and similar concepts in psychology seems straightforward.

Summary

Now we know, or at least we think we do, how it all began. The Earth evolved from an initial state where it was rich in the primary elements of life, carbon, hydrogen, oxygen, and nitrogen. These formed an atmosphere containing carbon dioxide (CO_2), nitrogen (N_2), and water (H_2O). The volcanic gasses (hydrothermal vents) from the Earth's interior added to the molecular formations (Deamer, 2012).

RNA began a spontaneous self-replicating cycle ("catalytic activity"), possibly due to an environment rich in water, carbon, and energy. This process is called "self-assembly;" complex molecules are created out of simple ones. The ribozymes, strands of RNA with catalytic sites resembling those of enzymes, create the potential to "act both as catalysts and carriers of genetic information [mRNA]; they have been proposed as the primeval genetic material" (ibid, 2012, p. 15). Hydrocarbons, amino acids, and simple sugars, needed to create life as we know it, became available. And it has been proven that most of these compounds were initially "impermanent" (due to bilayer permeability or defects), a concept which is not only asymmetrical, but also core to the Four Noble Truths of Buddhism which include impermanence.

Of course, there were also potentially other compounds brought to the Earth through the impact of meteorites and "stardust". Astrobiology (the investigation of life in the universe) tells us that "organic compounds composed of carbon and the other biogenic elements are not limited to the Earth and its neighboring planets in our solar system but are present wherever stardust gathers into interstellar clouds" (ibid, 2012, p. 3). The image of "stardust" gathering is a spiritual one for me, the universe providing an opportunity for creation and beauty at the same time.

Where will the future of science take us from here? We have questions about the things we haven't accomplished yet. These questions include concerns not only about how the brain functions for axonal firing, dendritic synchrony, and the effect of drugs on our neurotransmitters, but also about how our "minds" take in subjective information and analyze it differently from objective experience.

How does "personality" show up in the brain, affect the mind, and will we be able to someday see it on an MRI or PET scan? (Spoiler alert: some of that work is already being done on narcissists and their lack of empathy!) How will other changes in technology affect our Self-awareness, Self-sufficiency, and Self-control? How do we see ourselves as part of cosmological explanations for macrocosmic and microcosmic Self-sameness? And finally, how does the science of consciousness fit into all of this, differentiating inner experience from outer influences, meditative states from addictive influences?

Thus far I have attempted to use a review of scientific concepts to create a unified theory (UFT) or at least a practical understanding of how the constructs of (1) neurological, (2) biological, (3) physical, and (4) the science of consciousness is all interrelated. From my experience, this interrelationship not only shows how our inner and outer systems work, but also how we CONNECT to function, how we survive, and how we are constantly evolving through technology and higher consciousness.

The connection between consciousness and quantum events seems to be much more intimate than simply agreeing upon what we all see…Human consciousness has the capacity to experience more than one level of reality at the same time…One of the reasons there has been a lot of interest in drawing analogies between quantum interpretations and consciousness is that the two are so fundamentally linked at the quantum level (Moring, 2000, p, 338–339).

Chapter Thirteen
Theories of Attachment and Personality Unified Field Theory of Development Comes to Life

For fifteen years, I taught a class in Developmental Psychology. Although I can honestly say over 500 people took and were influenced by those classes, the most important result was the individual responses I got from their study of themselves. They reported how they developed, were "supposed to develop", and perhaps got off track or were ill-equipped for life (one of my favorite therapeutic phrases) by what had happened to them during childhood. These students were mostly masters level students or beyond who were planning on becoming Special Education teachers, school counselors, drug counselors in training, or psychiatrists (some of these classes were part of the UCSD Medical School). They knew theories, they had degrees in psychology, sociology, English, chemistry, philosophy or whatever. However, they did not have a degree in themselves, in understanding the developmental process that had created who they were. This process is the being, doing, thinking, and becoming skillful that supports the identity with which they think of themselves.

By the end of the class, students often came to me and stated, by way of a thank you, "This should be a class in high school!" "Why didn't I learn this stuff before?" "You should write all this down!" So here it is, abbreviated but generally intact. I hope after plowing through it, you will feel the same way as those students.

The second important result of this class was, of course, the effect that teaching the material had on me. While fifteen years or more passed, I had gone through nearly every adult developmental stage myself—from early marriage, pregnancy, raising two children while still working and being a full-time wife and housekeeper, to taking on a post-graduate course in Public Health, to considering a second career after my first child went to college, but then getting cancer and having to watch my life slow down. How much I learned! How much did I change my verbal presentations and how much did what I taught to each class change? Probably quite a bit, at least as influenced by my experiences and opinions. It would be something to compare the notes of someone in a 1986 class to someone's notes from a class in 2000.

So how do we get to adulthood? What are the universals that motivate how we act? It is obvious that we are influenced by psychological, sociological, literary, and philosophical pursuits, language development, creative and economic opportunities, as well as political and synchronic influences. These are the areas/units that make up the Unified Field Theory (UFT) of development so frequently referred to in this book. How we get to feeling "unified", however, is probably more influenced by acts of intimacy, community, and CONNECTION than anything else.

As adults, we are supposed to have learned to live in harmony, to find dimensions in each other that provide us companionship and safety, and we will move through our lives more successfully if we feel our own personalized definition of hope. We all find our "Middle Way" differently, based on the self-evident truths to which we have been exposed. There are no real dichotomies in this growth; we need both faith and reason, the ideal and the real, the indefinite and the finite, the asymmetrical and the symmetrical to provide us with a context within which we can discover a vision of ourselves as our developmental process becomes meaningful.

As we discussed in the previous chapter, my descriptions are like a crossroads between faith and science, spirituality, and physics/neuroscience. As perhaps a definition of CONNECTION, I propose that the finite ego (particles) strives to establish points of contact (quanta) with the infinite (GOD) within us (waves). Previously, concepts about this intersection were mostly theoretical as noted by theologians and scientists alike. Now we have real quantum mechanics theories, and physicists would agree we are the engineers of our own development, even given Heisenberg's Uncertainty Principle. Yet we do not independently experience life alone in our own force field; we interact with others' fields of consciousness as well, and if we have a basic need, it is for interaction and love (Adler, 1907).

Creation of the Vessel: How We Attach

Ernst Haeckel (1834–1919) is most known for his statement, "ontogeny recapitulates phylogeny." He was attempting to describe man's nature through an analogy to embryonic development; "the movement from potency to action, the leap of faith in the integral CONNECTIONS that are known, not seen, used, not possessed" (Koestler, 1964, p. 230).[100]

There are whole books written just about the many theories of childhood development and how we attach. If interested, I encourage you to seek further resources. However, for the purposes of this presentation, the use of the five main developmental theories (Freud, Erikson, Adler, Mahler, and Bowlby) will allow us to document the course of growth and development.

The reader will note a return to the same themes over and over. Aside from these five theorists that I am discussing at this time, it is important to point out that there have also been four major schools of psychotherapy in the last 150 years: behaviorist psychology, using reinforcement and aversion techniques; psychoanalysis itself, the work of the Freudians, including Karen Horney, Erich Fromm, Melanie Klein, and Gertrude and Rubin Blanck; the humanistic movement in psychotherapy, known as the "Third Force", including the work of

---

[100] This quote is frequently reported to be by Darwin who reinvested the idea in his theses regarding adaptation and survival of the fittest and the process of biological development. Gregory Bateson gave his own spin to the phrase when he said, "the evolution of ideas is a tale of ever-repeated differentiation, specialization and re-integrations on a higher level; a progression from primordial unity through variety to more complex patterns of unity-in-variety" (Bateson, 1972).

Maslow, May, Rogers and the Gestalt theories; and transpersonal psychotherapy, which follows Jung, Assagioli, and Frankl in their focus on the Soul (Hardy, 1990).

We begin with Sigmund Freud, for however archaic he may seem, including that he did not appear to know much about the variance of development in women, he did get some things right. His five classic stages (oral, anal, phallic, latency, and genital) allow us to categorize development, infancy through adolescence, in many of the classic areas important to psychological investigation and treatment as in the newer Freudian influences, for instance Blanck and Blanck (1974).

Looking at one's experience during each of these developmental stages is an excellent start to collecting data about who the Self might have come to be. I use the Blanck and Blanck developmental chart frequently in the creation of a treatment plan for my patients. It includes assessment for relational issues and what sort of counseling approach might work best, especially taking into consideration personal history and any issues which need cultural resonance.

According to Freud, man's deepest sense of Self comes from his instincts, his vital drives of food, sex, and power, and the successful development of the mental attributes that will create satisfaction. This bondage to instinct is seen as the basis of fight/flight/freeze responses. Freud's studies of human central nervous systems created a belief that in man, as in any hydraulic system, pressures (drives) build up and required "discharging". But as Jung would say, "after satisfaction, what?" When the loop of instincts-satisfaction-instinct is complete, then what does man do with his need to manifest his Selfness, the "fullness of his existence" (Heschel, 1965, p. 57).

Erikson (1950) built his own developmental lifecycle theory based on Freud's theory, but he broke away from Freud's dependence on natural philosophy and a belief in instinctual man. Freud was influenced by his Jewish Talmudic background, medical traditions, social reform of his age, and the post-Machiavellianism of making money/being successful. For Erikson, his theory was based on the post-Industrial Revolution era, where time for Self-analysis was more common. Compared with Freud's five stages of psyche development, Erikson wanted to study the "whole lifecycle", including old age and death. His stages were created out of dichotomies (for instance, Trust versus Mistrust), that were not meant to indicate catastrophic difference between the positive and negative side of the dichotomy, but rather a dialectic turning point, where overcoming the crisis at hand created a stronger individual going into the next stage.

Erikson divided development into seven stages: Trust versus Mistrust, Autonomy versus Doubt and Shame, Initiative versus Guilt, Industry versus Inferiority, Identity versus Role Confusion, Intimacy versus Isolation, and Ego Integrity versus Despair. In his clinical-psychotherapeutic methods, he used a Hegelian dialectical system where the synthesis of opposites was the necessary balancing of developmental forces to provide health and progress to the next stage (very *Taoist* of him!). Each stage hopefully created an opportunity for mastery, for developing the level of social relationship appropriate for the age (for instance, 3 to 6, or 18 to 35).[101]

Erikson's model was also a foundation to the subsequent therapeutic process known as Transactional Analysis because it was the transaction between therapist and patient that could represent all underlying trauma and history. Structural analysis is concerned with the segregation and analysis of ego states (Parent/judgmental in an imitative way seeking to enforce a set of borrowed standards, usually from own parents, Adult/information processing, Child/pre-logical thinking or still under parental influence).[102]

Transactional Analysis is concerned with the transactions between people, for instance parent to child, adult to parent, and so forth. Within the development of personality and the Self, a Parent ego state can also work on one's own Child ego state, causing guilt or oppositionalism. For example: In working with smaller children, I used to explain to them (and to their parents!) that a healthy passage to the next stage was not based on the child learning, for instance, that there were individuals that they could trust (GOOD) and others that they could not trust (BAD) (Stage One). This viewpoint leads to what Freudians call "splitting". It is much better for the Adult ego state to mediate, integrating the flow of energy from the libido for the development of ego boundaries.

Erikson saw the "ego" as a function of strength which had the job of reconciling variant discontinuities between cognition and behavior. Further, the identity formed from "the unconscious striving for continuity and sameness of experience [like electron balancing in chemistry]. [The ego/Adult state] was responsible for testing, selecting, and integrating the 'self-representations derived from the psychosocial crises of childhood." Finally, "ego-strength" was "a sense of being at one with oneself as one grows and develops. It depends on the 'support first of familial and then of social models'" (Roazen, 1976, pp. 25, 36).

For Erikson, trust in the caretaker by the infant reflects the capacity for hope and faith (later the child will also discover his spiritual Higher Power). A synthesis of the dialectic that some people can be trusted most of the time but perhaps not always, and that bad people are not always bad, was a better synthesis of how the real world works and would be experienced by the child as they grew older. Otherwise, this failure to integrate would leave the former/younger child, represented through symptoms and dysfunctional adult actions, with inappropriate

---

[101] Erikson tried to work out a schedule of "unifying strengths" as they are called forth by a developing life cycle. "Each of these new strengths are the task of resolving a crisis in growth, and very resolution involves both psychological and social dimensions, and therefore presents 'a chart of psychosocial gains which are the result of the ego's successful mediation between physical stages and social institutions'" (Roazen, 1976, p. 110).

[102] It is particularly important that a child not be made to feel that his right to existence comes from living up to the parents' expectations. "Measuring up to their standards or ambitions for him, enhancing their prestige, giving them blind devotion; in other words, he may be prevented from realizing that he is an individual with his own rights and his own responsibilities (Horney, 2013, p. 44).

expectations and the potential for experiencing lots of loss in the future. The child had not built a communal sense of trust activation in Erikson's first stage, Trust vs. Mistrust (infancy to 3 years old).

> Trust is the premise of a child, a necessity for survival in a position of dependency. Children need to believe in the good will of parents, even when they are neglected or beaten. Often, they become convinced that they deserve their sufferings because it is easier to embrace a sense of diffuse guilt and unworthiness than to believe in the malevolence of all-powerful beings... Every loss recapitulates earlier losses, but every affirmation of identity echoes earlier moments of clarity (Bateson, MC, 1989, pp. 189, 222).

Erikson's theory lays out healthy, coherent, understanding and response patterns while hoping the child internalizes the dynamics of each stage. The child develops his or her own "adaptive" pattern, which is later conceptualized as the identity of the person. This process starts during the Autonomy versus Doubt/Shame stage (3 to 5 years old), where self-control is learned and neither a too strong nor too weak "will" is helpful. During the next stages, Erikson (1950) wrote of the importance of achievement during elementary school years, showing that the developmental task at that time (Industry versus Inferiority, 7 to 11 years old) could overcome residual doubts from Freud's Oedipal issues developed during Initiative versus Guilt (5 to 7 years old).

During this time, triangulation often develops with increased peer relationships and the development of "heroes" outside of one's immediate family. The sense of competence that comes with industriousness provides insulation against the opposite feelings of unworthiness/danger if the child has an overwhelming experience of inadequacy during this fourth stage. Developing one's strength and health leads to a strong identity during the next stage during adolescence (Identity versus Role Confusion, 11 years old to end of adolescence). Good self-esteem comes from positive appraisals (from Self and others); bad self-esteem develops from negative appraisals from others which leads to a sense of inadequacy and inferiority, discouraging the child from healthy identifications with the world in general.[103] Identity issues also require experiencing "relativity" in relationships and managing one's "secondary narcissism" during adolescence, as we will shortly discuss in reviewing Mahler's theory (1973).

Next there is a shift from developing a big "ego", when the identity of "myself as a thing" becomes the identity of "I" during adolescence. "I" refers to the now strongly developed Self, as Fromm writes "the category of being and not just of having" (Fromm, 1968, p.83). Intimacy versus Isolation (early adulthood) is the stage where Self-absorption of adolescence evolves instead into a search for the "Other", along with affiliative behavior. Love and feeling CONNECTED usually culminates in marriage or selecting a life-partner.

---

[103] "Self-determination is vital to the ego's survival: many sick or desperate late adolescents, if faced with continuing conflict, would rather be nobody or somebody totally bad, or indeed, dead—and this by free choice—than to be not-quite-somebody" (Roazen, 1976, p. 101).

When we find love, we discover a peace that comes from joining with another's world, their fears, their boundaries, their joy. It is a recognition of one's identity as mirroring in the Other. The second half of adulthood is noteworthy for its parameters of Generativity versus Stagnation; the danger of stagnation can prompt a midlife crisis which occurs when a man stops to realize what he has to originate in others rather than experience for himself (becoming a mentor), and women have trouble dealing with the "empty nest" or being left, which seems to be the most basic feminine fear.

Often these feelings are also set off by the graduation or leaving home of the adolescent; the father (sometimes mother) compares himself to this 18-year-old and feels like the last 20 to 30 years have just sped by without any occasion for him to think about or realize his own dreams. Now his child is beginning the adventure, whereas he is left behind to wonder where his dreams have gone. In extreme cases, the parent will try to recapture this lost youth and early adulthood by "acting out", a kind of tertiary narcissism, with affairs, new cars, overspending.

During the last stage, Ego Integrity versus Despair (70 and older), a healthy resolution of life experiences comes from an integration of one's personal lifetime "aspirations, achievements, and failures" (Butler, 1969). Fear of transformation and tertiary issues during the second half of life highlights the differences between the seeking of new or the fearing continuance of old, which arouses anxiety and the "dragon of death". Renewal and healthy integration of changes in lifestyle and health parameters creates dignity. Wisdom is experienced and accepted as the memories of one's previous life are seen as being a "little place for genuine regret, atonement or remorse, for [one] holds that frustration of wisdom in despair." The individual needs to accept the integrity of experience and learn to "mourn" his youth (Roazen, 1976, p.115).

Many of the early theories of adult development, and thoughts about the formulation of "identity", did not differentiate between male and female issues. It was assumed that the male psyche's development was the prominent force in society, and that as men lead with example, so women would follow. Maturational issues such as menstruation, childbirth, and menopause were all variants for which women had developed their own methodology. On the contrary, Erikson thought the process was different for men and for women. He had to veer away from only using the formulation of an occupation as a defining moment for adulthood (a factor found predominantly in males but not in women during Erikson's time). Even by the 1950s, Daniel Levinson (*Seasons of a Man's Life*, 1978) and Vaillant (*Adaptations to Life*, 1977) used only male subjects in their important theoretical work about development (not to mention that the subjects were predominantly white!)

It was not until Gail Sheehy wrote *Passages,* (1976), as a popular book specifically for women to come to terms with their own developmental rites of passage, did theories likewise begin to follow suit with serious and research-oriented studies that included women. Role definitions, from daughter to wife to mother, were still considered important focuses of study, but the age ranges with which such changes took place were broadening, and family support for choosing a career as well as motherhood (or instead) were acknowledged.

However, as Erikson highlighted, the issue of "separation" from mother as the primary caretaker was as significant for women as it was for men, living not only in their mother's image but in their overall concept of "home" as well. Independence was now studied by Erikson, and those who followed him, as an overall trait of adult development. Over the subsequent years, the "bipolar" theory of development (men: aggressive, independent, active; women: soft, dependent, nurturing, passive) was proven to be arbitrary; however, attributes such as women being more cooperative, affiliative, and so forth had to be accepted because of the research that proved them to be true.

Thus, what has finally developed is both a "role-transcendent" model and a "relational" model. These two models are not exclusive of each other, but rather form a complementary and unifying point of view of how women can be like men in their developmental process, and yet oftentimes different as well (Lewittes, 1982). This position is also supported by the multidimensional theory of how personality traits develop studied by Thomas and Chess in the late 1970s.

This book attempts to simplify in some cases, and expand in others, aspects of an individual as developing and CONNECTING organism:

- Needs of drives, figures, objects, or circumstances.
- Significant conflicts.
- Nature of anxieties: physical harm or punishment, disapproval, lack or loss of love, illness or injury, being deserted, deprived, or overpowered.
- Main defenses.
- Drive control: evasive, vulnerable, nature of drives.
- Thought processes (association/orientation to reality).
- Communication skills.
- Interpersonal: withdrawn, self-confidence, submissive, distancing, dependency.
- Nature of affect.
- Strengths and coping mechanisms.

If indeed there is a binding force which drives us to manifest our systemic bipolarity, as electron theory would have us believe, then we have no choice about the sequence in the unfolding of our life. "A choice is free when it can be made with a minimum of denial and of guilt and with a maximum of insight and conviction" (Roazen, 1976, p. 162). Some sequences become significant, for instance the seemingly simple, monotonous sequence of DNA, while other paths apparently are complicated by wealth, fame, or catastrophe; these paths may wander without meaning. What makes the outcome significant is the level of the resonance in CONNECTIONS with others.

Because Erikson's model was a phenomenological/experiential one, the child is viewed as striving toward the need to redefine the Self at each developmental period. What Erikson considered developmental "acting out" might be seen as "age-specific action" (Schlein, 1994). The therapist's goal to "rebuild the foundation of identity" uses possible regressions as opportunities for building trust and reintegration of the client's identity at a higher level. Therefore, the search for wholeness and mutuality requires the therapeutic alliance to stay as present and actualized as possible. Mutuality is seen in relationships where the partners depend on each other for development and support of their "respective strengths".

Although I use elements of Erikson's theory almost every day, I do not call myself a psychoanalytic or "psychodynamic" therapist because I have not had the formal training through a Psychoanalytic Institute. When I was in my late twenties, however, I shared offices with three psychoanalysts and what I learned from them was to focus on emotions in my attempt to find the core causes of distress.

By doing this, I was able to identify patterns and to connect "old history" in childhood with the concurrent triggers happening in the present. Most individuals arrive, in theory, with what they perceive are interpersonal problems, but it has been my experience that the primary intrapersonal relationship with Self is the core source of emotional pain and usually the most fruitful source when the therapeutic relationship becomes a mirror for their issues.

The Child in Development

Bowlby (1960) and his colleague Ainsworth (1978) inspired many years and thousands of research studies on the process of attachment, whether it be secure, insecure (anxious or ambivalent), or avoidant. If the child maintains flexible attention so that she or he can explore the world and master developmental tasks she or he has a secure attachment. This security creates emotional and behavioral regulation, a coherent sense of Self in relation to others, and personal identity (from evocative memory of care that is integrated).

An insecure attachment is characterized by rigid attention and inhibited ability to explore the world, inadequate development along many developmental lines, and a faulty sense of Self and personal identity [The dictionary defines identity as: 1) the state or fact of being the same, and 2) a. the state of being a specific person or thing; individuality, or b. the state of being as described]. An avoidant attachment is seen in children (and adults) as isolative and exhibiting defensive behavior when confronted with the need for help or to CONNECT.

Soon after Erikson and Bowlby, and theorist Margaret Mahler (1973) viewed childhood development as a direct reflection of the initial health of the attachment process. Her theory delved deeply into the psychodynamic processes of the development of attachment, using a more Freudian viewpoint. Her developmental phases, including the stages of symbiosis, differentiation, narcissism, rapprochement, separation/individuation, and full individuation are now classic terms embedded into our vocabulary. These stages are repeated in adolescence (secondary differentiation, secondary narcissism, and secondary rapprochement), and even for a third time in adulthood, often coinciding with midlife transition/crisis.

Mahler focused heavily on initial symbiosis during attachment and the three phases of development leading finally to the separation-individuation process. This process never means physical separation but refers to the child's psychological awareness of his separateness, although a mother may welcome too wholeheartedly her toddler's increasing independence as freeing her from caretaking duties as well. Attachment theory provides a bridge among evolutionary biology, developmental theory, ethology, and cognitive science, and among psychodynamic cognitive behavioral schools of thought, "…the relationship between psychotherapist and patient is where both biology and biography can be modified and/or ameliorated" (Judd, 2003).

Robert Hinde (1997) looked at the dialectical nature of how biological and psychological processes reinforce the "little e (e)" function, which operates continuously, even when the "behavior" is switched off. He used Tolman's theory describing the "expectation" (e) that lies between every biological/instinctual stimulus and a result/response. Insightful learning through expectations was one of the most influential influences on the psychological studies of Tolman's time (1951). In my opinion, expectational influences form the basis of how humans attach. My mother started teaching me to watch for the "little e" (e) in others' behavior when I was still quite young. More of her writings later in this chapter.

John Bowlby (1960) initially wrote about how he saw the infant's responses to maternal attachment behaviors and expectations (e) as comprising a group of fixed action patterns (crying, smiling, crawling, walking, talking). Each new behavior pattern was elicited under appropriate circumstances but with little inherent organization (goal-correcting system). He became part of a study group on the psychobiology of the child convened by the World Health Organization, which also included such noted scientists as Piaget, Lorenz, Margaret Mead, Julian Huxley, and Erik Erikson (Ainsworth & Bowlby, 1991).

Ultimately his graduate student then colleague Mary Ainsworth expanded Bowlby's original theory, based on an extended theoretical concept of "detachment". When there is a fear of abandonment, the pattern of anxiety found in infants or adults follows a sequence of: 1) active protest/distress, 2) depression, 3) detachment takes place. Crying (or adult disruptive behaviors when anxious) is followed by an appearance of sadness, pouting or withdrawal. Finally, if no desired effect is forthcoming from the Other, the infant/adult shows detachment behaviors, such as refusing nurturing or bottle, discomfort when provided normal blanket or toys, or even appearing happier with a different person/stranger than the normal object of attachment.

Thus, the abandoned child first experienced fear, then depression, and finally showed behaviors indicating detachment or a subsequent failure to attach when given the opportunity. Ainsworth shifted the theoretical concept from Bowlby's detachment to one of how children attach in the first place. Her new studies showed, through actual situational observation, how the affectional bond with the parent served to create stability over time, for the infant to seek proximity and contact with a specific figure. If successful, this CONNECTION reinforced the attachment.

Ainsworth joined the research team studying attachment (including Anna Freud) at the Tavistock Clinic in London. She remained there for 4 years, and then, newly married, went with her husband to Uganda to continue to develop a cross-cultural confirmation of their theories. Together, Bowlby's and Ainsworth's theories described how secure infants seek proximity and contact (if mothers are sensitive and responsive to their babies), insecurely attached infants are not readily comforted and ambivalent toward caregiving, and finally infants who are avoidant can be solitary and/or fiercely independent as they get older; they rejected their mother, had aversion to bodily contact, controlled anger and were generally compulsive.

Infant attachment classifications were also derived through studies based on Mary Ainsworth's Strange Situation Procedure (SSP), a research method which used coding and classification based on observations of how infants and toddlers react to separation from their mother.[104] She built upon Mahler's and Melanie Klein's work on annihilation anxiety. Klein had pioneered the technique of play analysis—and observation of the child's inner world shown through their play—which created a basis for formulation of theories about the level of anxiety, lack of attachment, or depression that the child might be experiencing (Schwartz, J., 1999). The idea of separation anxiety was intrinsic to Ainsworth's subsequent research.

Not only are these patterns of attachment apparently fixed, (and the theory has been proven in cross-cultural research for over fifty years), but the initial pattern seems to remain until adulthood and is found to even affect attempts by adults to attach. Lack or loss of adequate attachment figures in childhood can result in anxious adult bonding behaviors and disruptions during bereavement, especially when triggered by human expectational (little e) behavior (Bowlby 1980). More importantly the research began to show a relationship between the development of a secure base and self-reliance as the child matured.

---

[104] It is important that attachment researchers do not talk about the "strength" of attachment.

"Attachment is ubiquitous. The emphasis is placed on the organization of attachment behaviors and the form they take to ensure proximity to the attachment figure… Securely attached children have highly organized and predictable approaches for maintaining proximity to the mother…Children with insecure/avoidant attachment also have a highly organized approach to maintain proximity. They maintain a focus on the toys in the room. They do not cry on separation and appear overly involved in play as mother leaves and returns to the room. They act as if they are not attached and it does not matter whether other is present or not…Children with an insecure resistant/ambivalent attachment are preoccupied, i.e., rigidly fixed on the parent throughout the procedure. When the mother returns to the room the child may seem angry and alternately seek and resist the parent's attempts to comfort him.
The child is unable to settle down and return to play. They appear to maintain behavioral organization through a hyper focus upon the parent to the exclusion of exploration of the room and toys. This pattern develops in response to maternal insensitivity specifically with unpredictable responsiveness. The parent either overwhelms and intrudes on the child or withdraws and neglects. The child learns that the most effective method for obtaining and maintaining parental care is through displays of continuous distress. However, this method diverts the child away from other important developmental tasks" (Judd, 2003).

Summary of Attachment Theories

1. Attachment includes the use of the mother as a base from which to explore: protest and despair result from her disappearance (Bowlby 1960 and Ainsworth 1978).
2. Kaufman (1973) suggests that the protest-despair sequence in separation is but one example of a fight-flight reaction followed by conservation of energy and withdrawal that is seen in many stressful situations.
3. The despair phase is explicable in terms of learned helplessness, but the initial protest must be regarded as a response to loss of freedom and control (Brehm, 1976). Sometimes learned helplessness comes as the result of attempts at "social sameness;" for instance, self-deception and evasion while in social situations becomes a negative trigger because of previous negative input over ADD behavior or shyness. When children can adapt to underlying feelings of "active tension" (William James), then they can experience the feeling of being most deeply and intensely active and alive (Roazen, 1976). They can continue the search for "the real me".
4. For a person to know that an attachment figure is available and responsive gives him a strong and pervasive feeling of security, and so encourages him to value and continue the relationship. This is particularly true during periods of crisis or emergency throughout the lifecycle. This potential is called learned helplessness, out of the drive for protection (Seligmann, 1975), and may be viewed as the logical explanation for the Child Accommodation Syndrome. This is a legal term sometimes used in custody situations. where an abused (particularly molested) child will not reveal the abuse. Indeed, they will protect the perpetrator, who after all, is providing consistency in attachment and attention, whether negative or destructive.

When the original attachment during childhood becomes anxious, ambivalent, or avoidant, the child may grow up to have bonding issues with their own children or partners. I sometimes refer to this with clients as the "motherless mother" effect. Not meant as a slam on "mothers" specifically, rather it is meant to reflect a comment on the nurturing function. Likewise, when the transference function appears during therapy (putting upon the therapist feelings and functions as though the therapist was the actual original parent), the type of attachment style becomes readily apparent. If there was a secure base, clients perceive a therapist as a protective and supportive figure, facilitating an attachment.

The mental health and standards of the parent also affects the type of parenting used. I addressed these factors in a paper, "The Dynamics of Maternal/Infant interaction in a Substance-Abusing Mother," written when I was a consult to a Neonatal Unit in San Diego, Ca. In short, acute intoxication in a neonatal drug-exposed infant is not only the result of the long effects of drug use on the developing fetus; it is particularly notable during the first two years of life, when attachment and social interactive behavior is crucial to survival and parent-infant long-term bonding. In fact, the whole course of one's life, and the development of one's personality, may be seen as an act of survival.

Some of the fluidity in attachment theory might be dependent upon the newborn's APGAR score, five areas of postnatal functioning arranged into an acronym: Appearance (pink or blue color of body, hands, and feet); Pulse rate; Grimace (the crying or grimacing response to suction), Activity (muscular vigor); and Respiration. The earliest attachment process results in appropriate exchange of signals between mother and infant: this is a cybernetic process.

Because it appears that up to 20% of newborns will suffer the majority of measured and reported illnesses and disorders through their life (compared to the other 80% of the population), these initial signs of differences in dealing with adversity or psychosocial trauma can provide us with enough information to predict the long-term nature of attachment style. The other 80% may show similar life events, but because they did not have the original susceptibility, due to prenatal teratogens like drugs or alcohol, they likely will show less vulnerability and more resilience.

Mothers who had an anxiety-ambivalent attachment style themselves as children may grow up to be perpetually anxious lest husband or boyfriend desert them and may expect little or nothing in the way of love or support from anyone. In fact, these parents may invert the relationship, eventually expecting care and attention from their own children.[105]

Ultimately, we are looking for healthy developmental observations in the following areas: physical (brain development), motor (quickening during pregnancy and subsequent postnatal behaviors), cognitive (thumb-sucking and other purposeful behavior) and emotional (early breathing, temperature regulation and feeding receive structured parental responses). After the postnatal period, holding and feeding behaviors will reinforce the attachment but must also show an understanding of the child's particular temperament, which is biologically determined and shows the early "personality" traits to come. Any "bad fit" between parent attachment style and the child's temperamental needs can create real problems later. This includes the father's reaction, which may not be as fixed and responsive due to his own primary concerns or past attachment difficulties as well.

---

[105] "Among features reported as especially frequent among abusive mothers we find the following: prone to periods of intense anxiety punctuated by outbursts of violent anger, they are said to be impulsive and 'immature'. Although their 'dependence needs' are described as exceptionally strong, they are extremely distrustful and consequently unable or unwilling to make close relationships…the responses showed, in addition, that while these women yearned for care, all they expected was rejection. Indeed, repeated threats to abandon are as pathogenic as actual separations and probably more so…Thus, whilst constantly yearning for the love and care she has never had, she has no confidence she will ever receive it; and she will mistrust any offer she may receive. Small wonder, therefore, if when a woman with this background becomes a mother, that there are times when, instead of being ready to mother her child, she looks to her child to mother her. Small wonder too if when her child fails to oblige and starts crying, demanding care and attention, that she gets impatient and angry with it" (Bowlby, 1973, p. 85–86).

Along with the impetus for attachment (oral needs, safety, security) comes the famous "transitional object" (security blanket being one example), and thus begins the projection of our need to soothe ourselves onto an external, cognitive representation of bits and pieces, moments of safe times and warm "memories" reignited in the hippocampus by a so-called fantasy and its stimulus—the toy. In 1986, Stefan Kanfer wrote an article in *Time* magazine called, "In All Seasons, Toys are Us", in which he discusses how most toys are "in fact manifestations of ancient lore, the oral and written history of the human race at its most impressionable" (Kanfer, 1986).

Based on a "firm and ancient foundation", study of these symbols and attachments can also explain the nature of many historical fairy tales, which take on the exciting/soothing effect that the toy previously did. Bruno Bettelheim (1976) is famous for his study of fairy tales as an external projection of our attachment needs, fears of abandonment, or need for control—in other words, "seeing in the external world an unacknowledgeable part of yourself" (Hardy, 1990). Kanfer continues:

> Bettelheim observes, "more can be learned from [fairytales] about the inner problems of human beings, and of the right solutions to their predicaments in any society, than from any other type of story within a child's comprehension."…W.H. Auden believed that the fairy tale is "a dramatic projection in symbolic images of the life of the psyche, and it can travel from one country to another, one culture to another culture, reaching back to the little votive objects of ancient Egypt, Greece and Rome, as well as the crèche miniatures of Europe in the Middle Ages. [Jung called these consistencies in symbol the Collective Unconscious] …The old myths still animate these toys, but with an unfortunate difference: designers and promoters are interested more in what children like than in what they are like…The imagination is, after all, the foundation of the moral sense" [emphasis added] (ibid, 1976).

Adler, Jung and Freud

Freud 's treatment was coined "the talking cure", but other theorists came along to emphasis it really is "the listening cure". Jung said the shaping is done by awareness of primordial patterns, and Adler believed the personality is primarily shaped by social instinct. With study, we find that the search for how to bring disparate findings into a coherent and healing methodology took different courses for each theorist. All three theories, Freud's psychoanalytic, Jung's archetypal, and Adler's (and his followers) interpersonal, are based pragmatically upon how the analytic hour is conducted, using concentrated listening to inform an understanding about the source of the individual's suffering.

I previously quoted from some of my mother's thesis on Adler's theory in Chapter Two (Haradon, V, 1970). In that chapter, we discussed Adler's concept that philosophically man's problems stem from group interaction and therefore must be solved through group techniques. "This emphasis upon the social determinants of behavior, which had been overlooked or minimized by Freud and Jung, was probably Adler's greatest contribution to psychological (and in many ways philosophical) theory" (ibid, 1970).

Man becomes anxious because of the conditions around him and his unique reaction to them. In these cases, the external world has been given up due to "unbearable anxiety". Psychoanalyst Harry Stack Sullivan (1953) refers to this anxiety as the etiologic cause of a "not-me" experience.

> Each person in any two-person relationship is involved as a portion of an interpersonal field, rather than as a separate entity, in processes which affect and affected by the field. [emphasis added] The not-me is literally the organization of experience with significant people that has been subject to such intense anxiety, and anxiety so suddenly precipitated that it was impossible for the then rudimentary person to make any sense of, to develop any true grasp on the particular circumstances which dictated the experience of this intense anxiety (Sullivan, 1953, pp. xiv, 314).[106]

Although Freud is often considered the founder of psychodynamic theory, Adler and Jung were equally great contributors; they helped to mold psychotherapy into the discipline it is now. Therapists combine an understanding of a person's personality (Freud) with signs and symbols of the patient's inner world (Jung's Shadow), along with his interpersonal manifestations and strengths (Adler).

The first major contribution to Adler's theory, based on man's social interest and a striving for superiority, led it to be referred to as Individual Psychology. Adler's second major contribution to personality theory was his concept of the creative Self, that Self which searches for experiences which will aid in fulfilling the person's unique style of life; if these experiences are not to be found in the world, the Self creates them. In essence the doctrine of a creative Self asserts that man makes his own personality. The creative Self gives meaning to life; it creates the goal, as well as the means to the goal. A third major contribution was Adler's concept that the way in which man satisfies his sexual needs is determined by his style of life and not vice versa.

Fourthly, Adler made a giant leap ahead from classical psychoanalysis when he propounded the idea that man is motivated more by his expectations of the future than he is by experiences of the past. One sees Adler as a forerunner of certain existentialists and gestaltists in that he felt that these experiences exist

---

[106] "Dreams, unconscious motivations, anxiety states, phobias, mental distress and human subjective experience are real things…Freud's style was to look for unifying threads in the array of symptoms located under the headings of hysteria, anxiety, obsessions and melancholia…Jung criticized Freud's neurotic inability to acknowledge religions and spiritual feelings. Adler argued that Freud's emphasis on the fundamental role of sexuality in the etiology of the neuroses was a product of Freud's own personal experience (and a failure to accept man's own agency in his actions). There will always be those who find their psychology in Adler's insistence on the human capacity for autonomous action, or with fundamental conflicts represented by Freud's drive theory, or by Jung's evocation of symbol and myth and the intriguing question of the collective unconscious. The task for future theorists of the analytic hour is to restore the common ground of psychoanalytic exploration" (ibid, 1953, pp. 62, 64, 92, 129).

subjectively or mentally here and now as strivings or ideals which affect present behavior. Fifthly, Adler was a possible trailblazer, who influenced Goldstein and his principle of self-actualization by way of the concept of "striving for superiority", or, terms I prefer, striving for perfect completion, or the great upward drive.

A sixth major contribution was Adler's concept of inferiority feelings and compensation. This idea is tied in closely with the foregoing striving for superiority since his concept was that feelings of inferiority arise from a sense of incompletion or imperfection. He felt that inferiority feelings are the cause of all improvement in man's lot, because he is pushed by need to overcome his inferiority and pulled by the desire to be superior. A seventh major contribution was the concept of social interest by which he conveyed that by working for the common good, man compensates for his individual weaknesses. However, like any other natural aptitude, this innate predisposition does not appear spontaneously, but must be brought to fruition by guidance and training (Haradon, V., 1970)

Fromm (1968) continues that man has five needs: relatedness, transcendence, rootedness, identity, and frame of reference. The subjectivity of one's sense of "well-being" reminds man that he has choices in his pursuit of these deeper experiences.[107] We will see more about Fromm later in this chapter.

Adler realized the purposiveness of emotions. One of his most thought-provoking contributions was his concept that we create our own emotions for our own purposes while we subjectively feel driven by them. They seem to be our master while they are only our tools. Emotions are not irrational; they express our private logic – what we really think and believe. Any conscious opposition to our emotional impulses is a false pretense. Guilt feelings too are only pretenses, pretenses of good intentions which we do not have. They emerge only when we do not want to amend or change, but to demonstrate our good intentions. We feel guilty only if we are not willing to do what we know we should do.

In this sense, guilt feelings too have an obvious social purpose. It is the movement of the individual, the goals which he has set for himself, which indicate his total personality and permit a recognition of it. Without looking at the individual phenomenologically, one cannot see him. What makes him move are not any parts operating in him, be they emotions, drives, complexes, or other phenomena within him. Assagioli (1980) developed a therapeutic model based on these concepts called "Psychosynthesis". The important aspect is growth, to learn from viewing the gestalt of everyday experience, as we relate to the world as figure in the background.

---

[107] A possible clue to the phenomena of self, so far as psychology is concerned, lies in a statement made by Alfred Adler, 'What is frequently labeled 'the ego,' he writes, 'is nothing more than the style of the individual.' Lifestyle, to Adler, has a deep and important meaning. He is saying that if psychology could give us a full and complete account of lifestyle it would automatically include all phenomena now referred somewhat vaguely to a self or an ego. I will define "ego" as something whose original is empty, and "self" as man's real identity, "a concrete reality that has to be sought out to be known. It has absolutely nothing to do with individuality or personality" (Bronowski, 2011).

Growth is defined as developmental processes in time. On every level, biological, emotional, social, and educational, growth can be impeded simply by the lack of integrity, motivation, or commitment by those whose support is required for the maturational processes to be completed. The processes themselves are complex and often need to be individually determined, an expensive if not tedious job for a society that is often more focused on its immediate goals than on the long-term outcome of its participants. Time also is a major and unbending factor, for so much of what is crucial in a child's development is biologically and emotionally programmed.

"Missing the window", as we colloquially say now in a computerized society, is not just inconvenient, it is devastating to the developing organism. Success of the strengthening needed will be built on the authenticity of the process and the efficacy within the developmental sequence. We can only become well and stay well when we come to know ourselves through self-disclosure to another person.

Developmental psychologists are aware of when Self-concept is stabilized (a child will recognize himself/herself with rouge on their nose in the mirror). We are less sure about how this happens. It is quite likely a part of all the other bits of cognitive development during this period. Study of the different aspects of cognition (abstraction, generalization, and learning) are still held in esteem; as its primary theorist, Piaget (1962) is often taught even into the medical school level of academics.

Because there are many aspects of personality that make for an inward unity, these aspects create a multidimensional experience, with many resultant "selves". These "subpersonalities" are often driven by fear and sensitivity and are defended by withdrawal or defensiveness. But more positive subpersonalities could be creative, fulfilling and interested in growth. It was as if there was a "board meeting" going on all the time inside one's head and the dominant subpersonality for the situation would make the final decision (O'Connor, 1971) (As indicated in O'Connor's book, *Our Many Selves*, I often ask a client "who's showing up at the conference table [in your head] right now?") Let me reinforce that this concept is not a function of the diagnosis "multiple personalities".

This factor of subpersonalities is common to all of us, healthy and mentally distressed alike. It is simply that all formulative experiences have reinforced certain views and reactions toward the world in a unifying center. There is an obvious tension between what is and what could be, which makes the meaning of the word "dialectic" perfectly clear in describing the way children develop their own personality and their own boundaries.

Cognitive Development

I believe the very act of CONNECTING is a cognitive process. However, there is a separation in psychological theory between cognition and its subsequent behavior. Overall, the differences between cognitive psychology and behaviorism are very definite. Cognitive psychology, as a perceptual model, deals with differential conscious experience (knowing, meaning, understanding). Behaviorists ignore conscious states and reduce cognition to mediational processes of implicit (Stimulus-Response) behavior. Cognitive psychology proposes very complex theories while behaviorists have proposed parsimonious constructs about cognitive processes.

Instead of stimulus-response connections, cognitivists focus on discovering psychological principles of organization and functioning governing the different states of consciousness and important cognitive processes (abstraction, generalization, and learning). For this discussion, I will focus mostly on cognitive issues over behavioral influences.

Pinker (1997) presents a very succinct summary of how Piaget's theory (1962) explains the importance of attachment and cognitive development. "[Piaget] claimed that infants were sensorimotor creatures, unaware that objects cohere and persist, and that the world works by external laws rather than the infants' actions". The observer was able to denote a qualitative shift within the developing child, along with the quantitative changes one would expect. "The concept of an object is useful because bits of matter that are attached to one another usually move together [mirroring]" (Pinker, 1997, p. 316–317).

Piaget outlines six basic stages of the primary level of his sensorimotor theory: reflex actions, habit formation, instrumental learning, search for new schemas/supportive behavioral patterns, and combination of external and internal. Forms of the schemata can be rhythmic and reflexive, reversible, and include different affective stages as well. There is often an intermediate reaction of discomfort, anxiety, and other reactions to strangeness and growing complexity of behavior; these shifts, and subsequent adaptations, also lead to the formation of the Self. Once there is a Self, the child can begin to form social attachments to the Others around him. The Other has obtained some permanence for the child, perception changes so that external constancy of form, size, and figure-ground become more apparent.

As the child moves from sensorimotor level to the next level of constancy, there are motivational indicators, such as symbolic function. The child will demonstrate an ability to use imitation, symbolic play, drawing, and other more advanced indicators of intelligence. We begin to see habit formation. In fact, mental images are internalized imitation. With the use of language around two years old, the child is transitioning to mental representation which requires sensorimotor-type constructive processes and shows an "instrumental" effect, as in its utilitarian quality. "Language does not constitute the source of logic, but is, on the contrary, structured by it" (Piaget, 1962, p. 94).

Although I am not going to go into detail about language development, another important form of communication and CONNECTION is not only how language development usually comes out of left-brain dominancy, but also the specific effects of brain structure on word fluency. Dominancy is a sign of brain asymmetry; language develops in predictable stages due to the impact of experiences on the wiring in the brain. In addition to these localizations, experience can change the cortex at any age and gender will have a predictable effect on differences as well.

As the child moves into the third stage of affective development, object relations are noted: "There is a double formation of Self differentiated from other people and other people becoming objects of affectivity" (ibid, 1962, p. 26). The four cognitive processes which are most important during the conventional stage of development are: mental representation, the ability to represent sequences of events; conservation; class inclusion, that parts and wholes are logically related; and serialization, that objects can be arranged according to some quantifiable dimension.

The last stage is that of Formal Operations. It is in the stage of formal operational thinking that the child displays three new qualities. His analysis of a problem is systematic, his thought is self-consciously logical, and his thought organizes operations into more complicated, higher-order structures that enable him to solve major classes of problems. Thus, the now adolescent individual is capable of thinking about ideas and propositions that may even violate his understanding of reality.

Whether we are concerned with what type of attachment a child, then adult, will develop, how their CONNECTIONS will provide consistency, or with possible underlying anxiety, the external Object becomes more important than the initial experiences with cognitive images. Sensorimotor experiences imprint the child with either trust or a lack of trust and security. By seven years old, the child sees rules as absolutes. Rules are external absolutes; the young child feels his parents and other adults are all-knowing, perfect, and sacred.

By ten years old or so, Piaget believed that intellectual growth and experiences of role-taking in the peer group naturally transform perceptions of rules from external authoritarian commands to internal principles (development of Morality- see Kohlberg below). Piaget defines intelligence as the "construction of a complex system of action-schemas (the structure or organization of actions as they are transferred or generalized for repetition in similar or analogous circumstances)."

Malerstin & Ahern (1982) are the most explicitly Piagetian in their approach. They discern three types of character structure, named after and taking form from three intellectual stages defined by Piaget, the symbolic (ages 2–4), the intuitive (ages 5–7), and the concrete operational (ages 8–11). "The symbolic type needs attachment to other people to have a secure identity; the intuitive needs other people for narcissistic supplies; the operational is achievement oriented and has more mature relationships. Everyone falls into one of those types" (quoted in Loevinger & Knoll, 1983, p. 216).

In addition, there is the factor that at some point we put "God in charge", which sometimes facilitates the "us versus them" mentality of our moral kinship model. We build upon our innate moral cognitive functioning (found in the frontal cortex and anterior cingulate cortex) until our "moral reasoning" of adulthood seems intuitive and unflinching. Pinker calls this developmental process "moral realism".

The internalization of a standard implies a capacity to make judgments maintaining the standard for oneself and with others. This judgmental side of moral development has formed the focus of recent work and theory inspired by the earlier studies of Piaget (1962). Moral character has generally retained its common sense meaning as the total of a set of virtues. Virtues or character-traits are conceived of as "those traits of personality which are subject to the moral sanctions of society."

They are assessed from actions, rather than from judgments and feelings. This level of self-awareness provides an internal structure, but what about the external need for CONNECTING and attachment? In the Buddhist teaching this outcome or set of beliefs is referred to as "*dharma*", evidenced through high integrity and right action. If one is aware of one's own main concerns and can overcome "symptoms" of discontent, goals can be achieved. The meaning and path to achieving the goal is viewed as more valuable than "feelings" about the concern (Gersten, 2013).

Cognitive Behavioral Therapy (CBT) presents more useful and generic theories about cognition. CBT is a treatment model developed by Ellis (1961), Beck (1967), Young (1994), and others to overcome skill deficits in the developmentally "ill-equipped" who have trouble overcoming feelings in the way of right action or successful outcomes. The theory is focused on an individual's thinking patterns, ergo the cognitive element. This theory creates the shifts in behavioral outcomes as a new learning curve is implemented with the therapist's help. In *A Guide to Rational Living* (1961), Ellis discusses ways to recognize the antecedents (A) to eventual bad outcomes, or consequences (C) and to recognize and take responsibility for one's irrational beliefs and measurable behaviors (B) in between. The of use his ABC methods to prevent getting into difficult patterns with other people is the basis for many other cognitive behavioral therapies developed after him. Ellis presents ten specific "irrational" ideas that can lead to "bad" feelings.

1. It is a dire necessity for an adult to be love or approved of by almost everyone for virtually everything he does.
2. One should be thoroughly competent, adequate, and achieving.
3. Certain people are, wicked, and should be blamed and punished for their wrong mindedness.
4. It is terrible, horrible, catastrophic when things are not going the way one would like them to go.
5. Human unhappiness is externally caused, and people have little or no ability to control their sorrows or rid themselves of their negative feelings.
6. If something is or may be dangerous or fearsome, one should be terribly occupied and upset over it.
7. It is easier to avoid facing many life difficulties and self-responsibilities than to undertake more rewarding forms of self-discipline.
8. The past is all-important and because something once strongly affected one's life, it should indefinitely do so.
9. People and things should be different from the way they are and it is catastrophic if perfect solutions to the realities of life are not immediately found.
10. Maximum human happiness can be achieved by inertia and inaction or by passively and uncommittedly "enjoying oneself".

Patients focus on triggers and then use new skills in four specific areas: thoughts, emotions, social and/or personal behaviors, and physical awareness.

Ellis outlines five techniques that can be used to show the client how he is reinforcing his own negative thinking.

1. Reveal the underlying philosophy of the patient.
2. Attack irrational ideas.
3. Strive for disclosure of attitudes instead of drive or feelings.
4. Teach the patient how to change the internalized sentences.
5. Re-educate the patient in the problematic activity.

Ellis labeled his theoretical ideas "behavior therapy", not only because it changed patterns and raised frustration tolerance, but also because he strongly believed in giving homework for ongoing practice in the taught skills. He encouraged assessing the client's basic philosophy of life as quickly as possible, and he stated he had discovered that the clients he saw were "inevitably self-defeating". "They want to prove themselves instead of be themselves." They were usually too stuck on words like "should, ought, must" and had tendencies to denigrate themselves (Ellis, 2005, p.13).

I often point out to clients, and teach them about, how not only are they fallible, but that it is only human to be so, to be perfectly imperfect (which appeals to the perfectionists, which these individuals usually are!) "Oh, so you've discovered you're flawed like the rest of us!" This technique draws them away from the feelings of self-pity, hopelessness, rage, and depression which usually defines them when they come into initial sessions. Feelings of wholeness become substituted for their yearning for perfection.

The cognitive theorist Aaron Beck selected the term "reframing" to reflect a need for individuals to reassess and reorient their way of looking at their decision-making processes. If the patient could be reoriented and remotivated to correct the cognitive distortions, then improved behavioral patterns would naturally follow. "Reappraisal" is defined as "using cognitive strategies to actively 'spin' a new interpretation of a previously aversive cue" and takes place in the ventral medial Prefrontal Cortex (vmPFC) or ventral lateral Prefrontal Cortex (vlPFC). Beck's method of treatment has been embraced by both clinicians and insurance companies alike because it has measurable goals and outcomes and is usually time limited. "CBT focuses on the present and future with historical exploration as needed (only) and patients leave with new skills to prevent relapse" (Koob, 2013).

CBT has a prominent lineage: Siegel (1999) took Beck's work (1975), based on Piaget's original work (1962), and as a neurobiologist found the "schemas" (Piaget's original concept) that could represent the "script" of someone's story, seen as his or her "permanent record card" of experiences (UFT). The new coping behaviors learned through CBT replaced self-defeating patterns and could teach the individual to pay attention to self-talk (reality testing as Freud would call it), also referred to as temperament.

The developing child's temperament has been found to be stable and somewhat predictable, starting as early as 12 weeks. Thomas and Chess (1977) provided research documenting the nine stable areas of temperament to be: activity level, rhythmicity, approach/withdrawal, adaptability, intensity of reaction, quality of mood, persistence, distractibility, and threshold of responsiveness.

These areas showed a "goodness of fit" when matched with the attachment style of the mother/parent, based on the mother's own temperament, social, and emotional development, rhythm, reaction, and frustration styles. As Siegel (1999) and Young (1994) used the word, schemas include: beliefs, cognitions, visceral emotional sensations, temperament/nature/nurture, temperament/environment, and Self-acceptance. On the other hand, the release of stress hormones when negative schemas are triggered can short-circuit the executive areas of the brain [push my buttons!], creating uncomfortable physical sensations and biased thoughts so that the person engages in self-defeating behaviors. The following is a comprehensive list of schemas as compiled by Jeffrey Young, Ph.D.

Schemas

- Abandonment/instability.
- Mistrust/abuse.
- Emotional deprivation: of nurturance, of empathy, of protection.
- Defectiveness/shame: hypersensitive to criticism, rejection and blame.
- Social isolation/alienation: not part of a group.
- Dependence/incompetence: helplessness.
- Vulnerability to harm or illness.
- Enmeshment/undeveloped self.
- Failure.
- Entitlement/grandiosity.
- Insufficient self-control/self-discipline.
- Subjugation: of needs, of emotions (can be passive-aggressive).
- Self-sacrifice (doesn't avoid others' needs, acute sensitivity to the pain of others.
- Approval-seeking/recognition-seeking ("fits in" rather than having a secure self).
- Negativity/pessimism.
- Emotional inhibition.
- Unrelenting standards/hyper-criticalness (perfectionism, rigid rules and "should", preoccupation with time and efficiency).
- Punitiveness.

Typical Schemas that Trigger Narcissists

- Self-sacrifice
- Subjugation
- Abandonment/instability
- Defectiveness/shame
- Emotional inhibition
- Emotional deprivation
- Mistrust/abuse
- Unrelenting standards

Typical Schemas Associated with Narcissistic Thought/Behavior

(For example, could even be triggered by entering a room of strangers)

- Emotional deprivation
- Mistrust/abuse
- Defectiveness/shame
- Subjugation
- Unrelenting standards (perfectionist)
- Entitlement/grandiosity (avenging bully)
- Insufficient self-control
- Approval-seeking (competitive braggart)

Finally, Young arranged the schemas identified above into domains for assistance in determining patterns and the strength of influence of each type of schema and its script.

Disconnection and Rejection

1. Abandonment/Instability
2. Mistrust/Abuse
3. Emotional deprivation
4. Defectiveness/Shame
5. Social isolation/Alienation

Impaired Autonomy and Performance

1. Dependence/Incompetence
2. Vulnerability to harm or illness
3. Enmeshment/Undeveloped self
4. Failure

Impaired Limits

1. Entitlement/Grandiosity
2. Insufficient Self-control/Self-discipline

Other-Directedness

1. Subjugation
2. Self-sacrifice
3. Approval-seeking/Recognition-seeking

Over-vigilance and Inhibition

1. Negativity/Pessimism
2. Emotional inhibition
3. Unrelenting standards/Hyper-criticalness
4. Punitiveness

The length of this list only serves to highlight how vulnerable individuals (and their schemas) really can be (Young, J. 1994).

Moral Development

Lawrence Kohlberg (1964, 1981) expanded the concepts of moral development and schemas. Building on Piaget's theories of cognitive development, he believed man could be no more morally developed than he was cognitively developed (although the opposite may not be true). He believed all humans are born without an innate moral framework, but develop one through six distinct stages, from simply avoiding punishment to internalizing moral social standards to developing and acting on a personal set of moral principles (Weir, 2016). For Kohlberg, the most important idea is that of sequentiality; each stage must be conquered in order. Each group of two stages are of a grouped typology based on Piaget description of how cognition develops.

Under Pre-Conventional ideology 1) Punishment orientation involves deference in fear of physical consequences, and then 2) Instrumental orientation reflects a desire for reward as the benefit. Under Conventional ideology, conformity demonstrates identification with the group. 3) Interpersonal concordance now allows a judgment of behavior by orientation of "goodness", and empathy and affection begin to appear. It is important that the child can anticipate disapproval of others. 4) Law and order orientation reflects concerns about respect and authority. The ideas of "honor" and sacredness of life appear.

Under Post-Conventional ideology 5) Social contracts are made with legalistic orientation, standards are critically examined and the idea of relativity of personal values appears. Finally, 6) Universal values and ethics show the importance of principles such as Justice, Reciprocity, Equality and Dignity. There is respect for the ideal of the Individual. That is why Kohlberg's 6th and highest level of moral development was that of Self-recognition and demonstration of these universals.

In the process of moral socialization, it is not necessarily the fixed values that are important, but rather the stimulation and reaction of the child's restructuring his experiences so that logical consequences can be applied at each level. There must also be an awareness of how the child's developing moral awareness is integrated with the pre-existing attachment style as per Bowlby and Mahler described above.

In essence, Piaget viewed internal moral norms as logical principles of justice. Pinker uses the term "moralization" in that the rules it invokes are felt to be universal (although he concludes that the choices are very much affected by lifestyle choices). He notes that the "universal" aspect has been verified in studies, where cross-culturally many of these universals were found: "distinction between right and wrong; empathy; fairness; admiration of generosity; rights and obligations; proscription of murder, rape and other forms of violence; redress of wrongs; sanctions for wrongs against the community; shame; and taboos" (ibid, 2008, p. 4). Thus, socialization (attunement to rules), empathy (social sensitivity) and ethics (conscience) seems to be the developmental order necessary for the creation of useful moral knowledge (Loevinger & Knoll, 1983). A good "short list" would be "Do no harm, play fairly, be loyal to your group, respect authority and live purely" (Azar, 2010, p. 56). These values start early and ultimately turn into rituals that help unite people in cooperative behaviors.

Sebes and Ford (1984) took Kohlberg's original writing (1958) and pointed out how a theory of moral development could be integrated with other stage theories. They highlighted shared values and rules, personal self-regulation, and interpersonal monitoring skills. However, they disagreed with Kohlberg's "sequential" perspective, stating that "a wider variety of form and content of moral reasoning may be potentially available at much younger ages than the Kohlberg model suggests, [that there is] situational variability in the study of moral behavior versus moral thinking…[they believed in] establishing specific relations between cognition and conduct…" (Sebes and Ford, 1984, pp. 379–381). The overall goal is to tolerate ambiguity and uncertainty, which according to Heisenberg, and ancient Buddhism, can never capture, or allow us to adjust to, the limits of our experience. We must simply use acceptance of our life parameters and the limitations about how we make life choices.

Moral character has generally retained its common sense meaning as the total of a set of virtues. Virtues or character-traits are conceived of as "those traits of personality which are subject to the moral sanctions of society." They are assessed from actions, rather than from judgments and feelings. This level of self-awareness provides an internal structure, but what about the external need for CONNECTING and attachment? "Obviously a person's character and pattern of behavior is to a large extent dependent on the nature of that higher entity of which he feels himself to be a part" (Koestler, 1964, p. 259).

We can look more often to children for a sense of our natural gifts: the availability to each other through nonverbal cues, modulations in voice, and the opportunity to use physical contact given by nonverbal cues to both stimulate and symbolize psychological availability. As adults we sometimes call this "metacommunication", as if we had made a great discovery that children knew all along, i.e., qualities of speed, tone, inflection, intensity, emotional coloring, and nonverbal cues (eye contact, bodily stance, facial expressions, and gestures) all help us interpret and classify the information available to us.

Abraham Maslow (1968) specifically uses signs of metacommunication as an indicator of "transcendence", of one's knowledge of one's own identity through the instincts we had as children. Self-actualization is the highest need to be satisfied on Maslow's needs hierarchy. This hierarchical need for gratification runs parallel to the degree of psychological health achieved (For more above Maslow, see also Chapter Twenty). Maslow describes the experience of self-actualization as a "peak experience".

"A peak experience" is what you feel and perhaps 'know' when you gain authentic elevation as a human being. A peak experience is a coming into the realization that what 'ought to be is, in a way that requires no longing, suggests no straining to make it so. It is individuality free of isolation [emphasis added] (ibid, 1968, p. xvi). The peak experience or the ability to transcend superficial relationships and to experience core-to-core relationships with another or oneself is one of the main aspects of a self-actualizing person. We desire synergy (one person's advantage is the other's advantage).

> This Good Person can equally be called the self-evolving person, the responsible-for-himself-and-his-own-evolution person, the fully illuminated or awakened or perspicuous man, the fully human person, the self-actualizing person. Maslow came to emphasize our innate emotional and spiritual capacities. First, however, he embraced the far more fashionable social science doctrine of cultural relativism (ibid, 1968, pp. 19, 81).

The Development of Character: Values Clarification Theory

My favorite definition of "character" is one that takes into consideration one's good habits, conscience, ability to maintain stable focused attention and to control defects of unsocialized impulses or failures in ego development. Generally, the aggregate of these forces is best seen in what W. Ray Rucker (1969) calls one's "values". I was grateful to sit in two of his classes while in graduate school (1974), during and after the development of his now widely accepted Values Clarification Theory (see more in Chapter Twenty-One). He maintained that one's ability to achieve good Self-esteem and find satisfaction with his/her environment was based upon both "decision-making capacities and fixed behavior traits." Personality constructs of dependency, sexual needs, aggression, and competence are "all located and explained" within Rucker's system.

Likewise, it appears Rucker was influenced by Kohlberg before him. Many scientists now know that what we consider "traits" (the pattern of habits and emotional tendencies) may even be the results of specific brain circuitry. Moments of awareness and shifting periods of the child's use of energy will assimilate into tendencies of indifference or hate toward others, as well as love or core-to-core relationships. As Harlow et. al. (1965, 1971) showed in his work with monkeys, learning to love at the early stages of development later generalizes to others, and to self-love, and to feelings of competence. As a great influence upon my own developing UFT, this concept of integrating experiences with traits (nature and nurture) came to epitomize the foundation of my own core beliefs and teaching curriculum.

> The average level of moral conformity is the same in early childhood as in later life [which] suggests that the basic forces of moral character develop very early...At younger ages, 'moral' conduct may be based primarily on fear, on lack, or on arousal to transgress (for example, to win by cheating), while at older ages it may be based more on moral beliefs, guilt, and ego factors.

Parental warmth, trust, and firmness or consistency are necessary factors in the production of mature moral character (Rucker, 1969, pp. 392 394).

Having expanded Kohlberg's theories, Rucker's Value Continuum Scale showed what man tended to value. When one took his measure, they rated themselves on a 6-point scale (12 attributes for each value), such as affection, respect, skill, understanding, power and influence, economic well-being, well-being, and responsibility. Rucker developed a continuum ranging from Dehumanization (Low synergy) to Humanization (High synergy), with all levels dynamically interacting.

As noted in previous chapters, my own mother, a License Clinical Social Worker (LCSW), was the other pervasive influence upon my developing view as a theoretical clinician. She took Tolman's original ideas about expectations (which also influenced other behaviorists such as Beck) and developed her own impressions about a "Basic Needs" concept (the theme of her master's thesis, Haradon, 1970). Basic Needs equal Power, Affordability, and Compatibility.[108] Likewise, with simplicity and concern, Charlotte Towle presented a theory of "Common Human Needs". Descriptions of her theory include stages of life, basic human motivations, needs and desires…and how to assist clients in meeting those needs (Towle, 1987).

Here Rucker's Value Continuum comes into play as well. A man is emotionally stable or unstable, not in a vacuum but by reference to the specific values which his culture prescribes [UFT!].

As formal frames of reference, what we mean by intelligence is the probability of success in reaching goals; by motivation, probability of persistence in striving toward goals; and by emotional stability, probable tendencies not to exhibit unacceptable deviations in the pursuance of such goals. [Therefore] intelligence is tendency to succeed, motivation is tendency to persist, and emotional stability is tendency not to exhibit unacceptable deviations [emphasis added] (op cit., 1970, p. 230).

---

[108] We reflect on the expectancy (little e) that Behaviorists now acknowledge influence the response pattern. As noted above, in 1945, (*Science* 2/16/1945) Edward Chace Tolman first wrote about "A Stimulus-Expectancy Need-Cathexis Psychology" as his primary outlook upon behavior. Although he believed behavior was a reflection of the biological drives (appetites and metabolic conditions) when combined with aversions caused by fear experienced in the limbic system; it took the social context to influence the outcome, which he referred to as being "enmeshed." "There are certain basic laws and principles which can still be studied more conveniently and with just as much validity in rats as in men…basically, these are merely the realization that every adequate description and every quantified rating of any aspect of human behavior must always involve and refer to a particular cultural milieu" (Haradon, V., 1970, p. 229)

A Jungian Perspective

Now that we understand physical, cognitive, and moral development, including how attachment and parenting adds to the general formula of a UFT, we can look into a human's personal development. We learn the grammar of human relations just as we learned our spoken language, and as Jung (1934) teaches us, there is also the influence of the Collective Unconscious, that part of our "unconscious" mind influenced by impulses, dreams, and expectations (little e), which he believed was a cross-cultural phenomenon. I have referred to Jung several times earlier in this chapter, specifically as he compared himself to the other pioneers in the field of psychology. Jung is discussed at length in Chapters Seventeen and Eighteen.

A few brief words about his contribution to understanding personality development are called for here, however. He is particularly noted for his extension of developmental theories into the period of older age, which Erikson placed in the seventh of his developmental stages. It was here that both Erikson and Jung felt an individual had to finally give up all illusion of youth and, instead, gravitate toward becoming a mentor and example to others.

Bair's excellent biography of Jung (2003) summarizes my points of interest about Jung. Some of the major elements of Jung's theory include: 1) extraversion (first discussed by Freud), an openness or vulnerability to outside influences on "thinking, feeling, and acting"; 2) introversion (recognized also by Adler), interest in the internal processes such as personal "concerns, aims, feelings, and thought processes"; 3) complex (detached fragments of personality), which maintained an independent, autonomous function within the unconscious, and "from which they (one or more complexes) were capable of exerting an influence upon the conscious mind"; 4) ego-complex (one's ego-contents, feeling of "subjectivity or 'I-ness', neurotic (control issues), exhibited in someone who "can never have things as he would like them in the present, and who can therefore never enjoy the past either"; 5) intuitive, heightened abilities of perception, personal unconscious, (intentional repressions of ego defense), painful thoughts and feelings; and 6) "archetypes (see also Plato), metaphysical ideas/which comes first, (picture in the head)/apprehension, or an impulse to act (defend)" (Bair, 2003. pp. 7, 14, 66).

A follower of Jung, Assagioli (1989) believed that only through a "psychosynethesis" of the fragmented parts could the patient feel "put back together again". The parts usually contained "creativity and will, joy and wisdom, as well as the impulses and drives" (Assagioli, as quoted by Hardy, 1990). Jung's motto was "Know thyself, possess thyself—transform thyself," a saying he probably took from the early Gnostics.

Ego psychology also trains therapists to look for how the ego uses reality testing to find qualities that help maintain ego-strength and shows the therapist elements of the overall prognosis of the patient. For instance, one's IQ is not just a measure of cognitive development but is also an indicator of being able to make qualitative assessments. Rumination and struggle may be the only way to get high cognitive functioning. Individuals may have also taken pragmatic stances toward their own growth processes. The goal here is to make subjective decisions based on one's inner world, objective decisions based on one's outer world (causality and nature of how things work), and normative information about how things should be consistent and apply equally to everyone.

For religion to survive, it must be personalized. Victor Frankl (1948) spoke of the three virtues: objectivity, courage, and sense of responsibility; likewise, as what we give to life, what we take, and the stand we take to express our meaning to life. "Man has the possibility of holding himself above the influence of his environment when he finds the meaning of his life through is activities, his works, his experiences, his roles, his pleasures, his annoyances, his successes, and his failures" (Haradon, 1972b).

Existence is essentially unconscious and can never be fully reflected upon and thus cannot be fully aware of itself; "the self does not yield to total self-reflection; however, human existence exists in action rather than reflection" (Frankl, 1948, p. 28). A man's identity is available through responsibility and through fulfillment of meaning, characterized by his search for meaning rather than only search for himself. Lack of meaning and purpose is indicative of emotional maladjustment (Haradon, 1972b, 1975). Identity is the best in you. Frankl agreed with Freud in at least one way, that there is a constant transition between conscious and unconscious results, a major factor in agreement with Koestler's theory of "Bisociation" (Koestler, 1964).

Frankl's writings focused on more than just awareness of a Higher Power and acceptance of death. He also wrote eloquently of love. "In love, the self is not driven by the id, but rather the self chooses the Thou" [emphasis added] (Frankl, 1948). More will be discussed about this part of his theory in Chapter Twenty when we address achieving a sense of "well-being". Frankl also felt that "human existence is essentially Self-transcendence, rather than [only directed toward] Self-actualization. Self-actualization is not a possible aim at all, for the simple reason that the more a man would strive for it the more he would miss it" (Frankl class notes, 1974).[109] He maintained that using paradoxical intention as a therapeutic tool helps work through the anticipatory anxiety the therapy causes. Milton Erickson is the modern family therapist who is best known for this technique.

What comes to consciousness in existential analysis is not drive or instincts alone, as Freud would contend, but Self. "It is not ego that becomes conscious of the id but rather the Self that becomes conscious of itself—it meets itself" (ibid, 1948). Once one is centered around the existential part of a person, his or her spiritual core, the human being is not only individualized but also integrated. The self-actualizing person is one who "increasingly develops his talents and capabilities, functions relatively autonomously, has a positive and realistic self-image, uses his time effectively, and tends to live in the present" (Maslow, 1962). We are hoping for positive integrity and expression of our deeper emotions.

---

[109] Frankl's concept of a "will to meaning" was developed alongside Adler's "will to power", motivational theory (Murray), and Freud's concept of the "will to pleasure" or pleasure principle. A will to meaning comes from the exercise of a "freedom of will", or meaning available to each one of us, encompassing aspects of self-transcendence. (Frankl, 1948)

Chapter Fourteen
Personal Growth
Emotions, Personality and
Self-Actualization

Emotional Development

Considering all the variables that make up our temperament, as well as our values and environmental experiences/expectations, how do we explain these emotional systems in a dynamic, interacting, developing human individual? Do we use a Freudian model and consider levels of anxiety or defense? Do we use Mahler/Bowlby/Ainsworth and describe the outcomes of having or not having a secure attachment? Or do we watch behavioral cues, defaulting into labeling and diagnostic categories, which give us a familiar and comfortable recognition of "symptoms" and possible places to start interacting with this person? (For instance, I believe you to be "bipolar" therefore your behavior indicates you have certain underlying "emotional problems" that I can predict and watch out for?). These are all valid questions; a general knowledge may help us understand as we add psycho-emotional issues to the development of our UFT.

Freud's theory became known as "psychodynamic" because it was meant to represent the active interpersonal and intrapersonal causes and outcomes of human development, especially given biological and parental influences. His primary goal was to make the unconscious conscious, as most people and their behavior were more influenced by unknown motivations (and even values!) than they were aware of.

The psychodynamic prototype emphasized unstructured, open-ended dialogue (e.g., discussion of fantasies and dreams); identifying recurring themes in the patient's experience; linking the patient's feelings and perceptions to past experiences; drawing attention to feelings regarded by the patient as unacceptable (e.g., anger, envy, excitement); pointing out defensive maneuvers; interpreting warded-off or unconscious wishes, feelings or ideas; focusing on the therapy relationship as a topic of discussion; and drawing CONNECTIONS between the therapy relationship and other relationship [emphasis added] (Shedler, 2010, pp. 104–105).

Adding to its psychodynamic point of view, the initial tenets and practice of psychotherapy influenced the eventual development of the cognitive behavioral school of psychology/therapy as well.

Developing Authentic Self-Awareness

It has been my experience that the primary motive behind human behavior is to maintain an attachment and sense of safety as discussed earlier. It is much harder to know ourselves as easily as we know others. Beyond an "ideal" of emotional development (whether using psychodynamic or CBT influences) is an individual's actual functioning and development of an authentic personality and view of Self, which includes memory, imagination, intuition, learning and logical thinking. What does a therapist do with this information; what could more people do with Self-knowledge if it was readily available? Since we are all "primed to avoid pain", a relevant question is often "what am I avoiding?" Avoidance may be a valid defense in many circumstances, but it doesn't facilitate Self-knowledge or intimacy with others.

Sometimes we have been manipulated and, to recognize the need for withdrawal or Self-protection, we must look at the backdrop/context of how the Other has manipulated us. We try to use historical continuity (UFT) to make sense of our transference onto another. That information then can best serve us in disengaging or becoming aware of why those around us may be able to manipulate us, or even worse, cause us to turn to avoidant or addictive behavior. Most importantly, we begin to learn the boundaries of the Self.

In childhood, many individuals did not receive information about how to interact with others, how to have a relationship, or how to deduce warning signs from an Other's behavior. They lacked "parental interest, guidance, affection, concern, and safe physical contact… [Instead, they experienced] emotional distance or enmeshment for a number of reasons—parental influence, chemical dependence, high stress, unmet needs, or inability to protect oneself" (Katherine, 1991, p. 71). Katherine adds that marriages may be the last chance some individuals have to determine how their interest in a relationship/attachment might CONNECT them with another—shared interests, similar values, kindred goals, comparable backgrounds, roughly equal intelligence, and a somewhat parallel way of looking at things.

In addition, there is an intrinsic need for relationships to be viewed within the context of the times, whether it be the feminist movement of the 1960s and 1970s, the addiction treatment models of the 1980s and 1990s, or the scary loss of financial well-being and the pandemic of the early 21st century. Underlying all these societal influences was a growing understanding that resultant mental health issues, and depression, could be viewed from the point of neuroscience and whether one should be treated with psychopharmacology. [I will share here that although I support the use of medication for clients who start seeing me and report they have found it helpful or are clearly demonstrating an Affective Disorder such as bipolar symptoms, I generally focus more upon the social, cultural, and traumatic forces in their history]. Depressive symptoms are often the result of these social skills creating "learned helplessness", a chronic aversive reaction, and lower norepinephrine in the brain.

I once had a client whose presenting complaint was about depression. She reported a long history and had seen several other therapists before me over a period of twenty-five years or so. The interesting corollary to this story was that she had been married for over 30 years to a very supportive, if not long-suffering, man, who eventually came in to see me for collateral contact. I often find such meetings with a spouse or other significant family members very useful in providing information about behavior at home or within the community. His theory was that perhaps her longstanding emotional difficulties had been exacerbated by menopause.

When I asked him how he dealt with the depressive episodes, he told me of cautiously caring for her so as not to present any more stress. Then I asked him the relevant question, "So therefore, she seems to have more power in the relationship when she's depressed than when she's not and when you expect 'normal' behavior from her she feels she's getting less attention, is that right?" He seemed completely shocked. He just never had thought about how much he might have been reinforcing her symptoms all those years. I'm not saying there wasn't a core of some natural endogenous depression in her makeup. What I'm saying is that she had determined, early on in their relationship, how to maintain control in the relationship. There is also something is this story which speaks to the overall dynamic common in world politics, the "poor me" attitude that often sparks either defensiveness or a position of weakness so other countries will fix the underprivileged countries underlying complaints.

Many a client who presents and shares their "diagnosis" with me haven't ever even delved into the possibility of prior traumas, and subsequent PTSD, causing daily triggers that manifest as anxiety and/or depression. The idea of trying to understand the possible neuroscience of some presenting symptom, much less trying to explain it to a client, is just too daunting for some therapists. The one time I genuinely find it useful to try to do so, besides an explanation of the causes of PTSD triggers, is when I work with clients who suffer from self-damaging, addictive, or other forms of Compulsive Disorder. Their understanding that they are probably "under the influence" of neurobiological circumstances beyond their control is an aid, not a hazard, to their treatment.

Relationships between individuals require an even more fine-tuned view of how a CONNECTION is manifesting within a biochemical, contextual, and cultural framework, creating corrective action for mind, body, and spirit. Sometimes we find we have both attachment and trauma in a marriage, as eloquently described by Anne Perry in one of her Charlotte and Thomas Pitt mysteries. Here we have Charlotte and Tryphena discussing love…

> I think if somebody loved you, they would want you to be the best you possibly could. Isn't that what love is, wanting someone to fulfill all the best in themselves? But then you would want the same for him, wouldn't you? And be prepared to give something that might cost you quite a lot, to the end? If you love, you stay, even when it isn't convenient, or fun, or easy. If you leave the moment, you no longer feel like staying, isn't that simply selfishness? You are talking about freedom to please yourself, freedom from hurt or boredom or duty. Life is about giving and being vulnerable, which is precisely why it needs both courage and self-discipline (Perry, 1980, p. 203).

Additionally, in *The Authentic Heart* (2001), Amodeo points out that satisfying relationships don't just happen, they reflect the culmination of commitment to a certain "path of growth", of a willingness to be vulnerable, while also looking for equality and respect. Rather than timidly hoping for the dream of love fulfilled, a relationship will be healthier if you bring your truest self to it, able to do your own "self-soothing" instead of expecting the Other to do it, i.e., Self-CONNECTION facilitates a healthy relationship. Amodeo summarizes her viewpoint by asking us to answer the following questions:

1. What's really important in life?
2. Do I need new priorities?
3. What's getting in the way of the deeper CONNECTIONS I want with people?
4. Am I doing something that's pushing people away?
5. Are my expectations too high in some ways and too low in others?
6. What can relationships provide for me, and what do I need to do for myself? [emphasis added] (ibid, 2001)

These are very psychodynamic questions. By noticing recurrent themes, we can discover that there is much benefit in self-awareness.

Manipulation and the Unstable Ego

Manipulators can make us feel and do things we wouldn't normally do. Even in my own life it took me many years to learn to accept the Elwood P. Dodd School of self-care (from the movie *Harvey*, with Jimmy Stewart): "In this world you can be oh so smart or oh so pleasant; I recommend pleasant." People may act like they want you to care for them and be smart and willing do anything to avoid rejection but what they are really doing is setting you up for being manipulated. Being pleasant allows you a totally different set of boundaries. It is smiling and nodding a lot, yes. But it's also protecting oneself by graciously [indeed] being able to say, "No thank you!" when necessary. A lot of individuals reach this point of Self-care through healing and recovery by way of a 12-step program and call the guidance and boundary-help they get their "Higher Power".

This process is not as easy as it sounds because as much as we want to believe change is possible, and we want to be forgiving of those who have harmed or manipulated us, much of the early change process can just be our own projective need to be believed. But little change may be forthcoming from the Other. They may have an alternate means of relating, sometimes called "drama", in the vernacular, which also kind of goes back to the old Transactional Analysis Model of the Blamer-Victim-Rescuer triangle (Virginia Satir, 1976).

The family member who is most often a Manipulator/Blamer may not recognize this behavior in himself, even to the point of shifting to the Victim position when "blamed" for problems in the marriage or in his children. Or another more precise example would be the military guy (think *The Great Santini* movie) who has ultimate power and controls everything when on duty but then can't make the adaptation to be an appropriate and nurturing parent when he's home and obviously not in control of most things. This character is an extreme example of Piaget's concept of failure of adaptation.

As discussed by Margaret Mahler (1973), symbiosis is not intimacy. Anne Katherine, author of *Where You End and I Begin* (1991), asks: "What do we hope to find in marriage?" She further elaborates with a list of what many of us are looking for: support, understanding, companionship, affection, loyalty, financial balance, security, the opportunity for self-expression, and sexual passion and fidelity. "…. heart to heart, not heart to mind" (Katherine, 1991, p. 160).

My own list of the characteristics of a satisfying marriage includes:

- Respect of qualities in each other.
- Tolerance of failings and vulnerabilities.
- Ability to maximize assets and minimize liabilities.
- Work on communication skills to achieve quid pro quos.
- Common goals.
- Non-static relationship.
- Willingness to change.
- Not threatened by a good old-fashioned fight.

On the other hand, destructive marriages are the result of:

- One element has contaminated the entire system (job, child, etc.).
- There is an avoidance of self-disclosure by partner's constant attacks.

(I am thinking here about the law of physics, where for every action there is an equal but opposite reaction, in marriage this shows up as victim/victimizer)

- There is a constant lack of decisions from the incomplete transactions.
- Each tends to make and act out of assumptions.
- One wants to earn attention/control by being a "benevolent dictator".
- There is cross-complaining as a form of disarmament.

Daniel Siegel (2007) encourages parents to use "contingent communication" to help us set up better boundaries with our children and with each other. If the attaching behaviors feel safe, collaborative, and appropriately "contingent" on contextual cues, then the bond will be trusting and successful. This outcome can be seen in adult relationships as well and is very behavioral in nature. We become attuned with better listening skills and the ability for "genuine self-expression within the context of a conscious, here-and-now state of mind."[110] Dan Siegel

---

[110] A technique I often use in therapy sessions can be found in Anne Katherine's book about boundaries (1991) where one imagines the Manipulator's (Narcissist's) experience from his point of view:
"His painful feelings, his sense of defectiveness and shame, his loneliness and emotional emptiness, the impossible but inescapable conditions he had to meet to gain

(2007) states that when we send out a signal, our brains are receptive to the responses of others to that signal [mirroring]. Ralph Waldo Emerson said, "it is one of the most beautiful compensations of life that no man can sincerely try to help another without helping himself." This significant thought is also an expression of most religions and even the 12th step of the 12-steps of AA.

Katherine gives us useful techniques because they take us "beyond fight, flight, or freeze," and into an internal emotional state of CONNECTEDNESS with our own Self-affirmation and mindfulness. We especially need to practice safe boundaries when dealing with a Narcissist; the best response is one of Self-advocacy. It is important to approach the Narcissist's need to gain status, as seen through his tendency to ignore the rules and to expect special attention from others.

One can address his behavior with "time-outs", by acknowledging his need to be heard, and by building into CONNECTIONS the time for him to de-escalate. In conclusion, whether a therapist, partner or parent, a basic skill list for dealing with a manipulator is to slow down (pace yourself), don't react, and ultimately preplan for the type of situations that are predictable with "dramatic" people. Disable the drama by non-responsiveness, not displaying a reaction you do feel inside regardless. Better to be "oh so pleasant" and perhaps underneath a little "oh so smart" as well! Be aware that problem-solving most situations will fall on your shoulders.

Communication

One of the most useful theories of communication was developed in the 1980s, that of Nonviolent Communication. I was blessed to work with a protégé of the founder Marshall Rosenberg for 20 years and she willingly shared her knowledge. Nonviolent Communication, as a process, has four steps: observing what is happening in each situation; identifying what one is feeling; identifying what one is needing; and then making a request for what one would like to see occur (Connor & Killian, 2012). The internal focus of how one initiates communication with another often comes from a position, therefore, of what one needs or feels one deserves.

For instance, my need for communication is driven by my intuition. Since I was a child, perhaps four or five, I have been aware of noticing other's needs and picking up intuitively on stresses and anxiety around me. As an empath, I experienced early in life an amazing source of information about others with which to CONNECT, be creative and have fun. As I grew older, I came to realize that

---

attention, love or approval…Limited reparenting includes empathy and setting limits, experiences the narcissist didn't have as a child, modeling ways that he can nurture and care for this part of himself…It isn't your fault that you feel upset. It's just a feeling. However, it is your responsibility to figure out how to express those feelings without blaming me or putting me down. To do otherwise is simply unacceptable. This behavior is hurtful to me and to our marriage…in order for the narcissist to feel comfortable and connected in relationships, he must learn what he never learned as a child: that he is fine for who he is underneath the bulky layers of glitz and gloss" (ibid, 1991, pp 115–122).

other people didn't always feel comfortable with my ability to pick up on their emotions, unsolicited, and could be unkind about my feedback, as if in giving my intuitions about them I was crossing some boundary or other they had set up to protect themselves. For, of course, they had been taught by their parents and families to do so. So, I then became more hypervigilant about being so intuitive, probably by 12 years old or so, although I could always relate well with adults, which in turn adultified me early on.

The exception to this social difficulty was one friend I managed to make. In the eighth grade, one day out on the asphalt during recess, I was befriended by another 13-year-old girl, who recognized my powers of perception and asked if I could use them for (her) good. She wanted to know if I could figure out what made a particular boy (Mike) tick so that she could better attract his attention. Having had no attraction to this boy myself (again I was drawn to the older boys, friends of my 17-year-old brother, but that's another story), I was able to make an objective assessment of his moods and interests in the matter of a few days, upon which she did eventually draw his attention. Her comment to me was, "Wow, that was like being a Magic Lady."

From that point on, my nickname by her became Magic Lady or ML for short and subsequently it was used by all significant Others. For it was a measure of their intimacy with me if I was able to let down the fear of ostracism and, being less guarded, be my true spiritual and creative self. This is a Self, to this day, which can be loving and compassionate to myself, to CONNECT in so many more ways than a conventional Self ever would be able to. By the way, that eighth-grade friend, Janice, and I are still friends to this day, 60 years later.

Where does intuition come from? People's intuition derives from a desire to find patterns and CONNECTIONS in—and to figure out how to act within—an otherwise random universe (Greer, 2005). However, sometimes our intuition can be overly inclusive or sensitive to "wrong" information. I think the solution is to gain a more grounded sense of Self through practice of awareness, mindfulness, and acceptance. From this state of psychological health, it is easier to differentiate one's true intuition from possible projections or defensiveness.

Among the many types of communication, some are spiritual as well as nonverbal. Often when we first become attached, when trust grows (whether as a newborn infant with mother or a newly born sober addict with sponsor), the yearning for security and sense of guidance that comes with this experience nourishes us on a spiritual plane. What I am describing is communication and CONNECTION that is beyond language alone.

The Search for an Ideal

The search for an ideal, whether through identity or through a specific purpose, can be tracked from Plato to Blake and William James. We can be aware of how we can CONNECT, from one person's Self to another person's Self, finding comfort in shared values, symbols, and goals. It has only been recently through a renewal of renaissance spirit,[111] that an intersection of these pursuits and cultural

---

[111] Jacob Bronowski felt that the Renaissance spirit will inspire men with a feeling that there is a "picture of man, the essential man, to which they themselves

values have focused as well on a deep engagement to intersect philosophical and contemplative inquiry with modern science and philosophy.

What lies "beyond language?" Much of Buddhist practice focuses on getting beyond the "traps of language", instead focusing on the freedom that can come from communicating through images, thoughts; beyond words unless they also convey symbols and pictures (Fischer, Z, 2011). The Eightfold Path of Buddhism (see Chapter Nine) points us to communication which can be a hefty part of our spiritual experience: right view, right intention, and right speech as described by Socrates (Platonic dialogues). Buddha pointed out the trap of getting caught up in language and he noted there were four ways of answering questions: "categorically, analytically (clarifying definitions and trying to determine what was being said); by deconstructing it (usually under analysis the question proved meaningless); posing a counter question; and to put the question aside (not beating your head against a wall, walk around the wall)."

> …what makes us miserable,
> what causes us to be in conflict with one another,
> is our insistence on our particular view of things:
> our view of what we deserve or want,
> our view of right and wrong,
> our view of self, our view of other,
> our view of life, our view of death.
> But views are just views. They are not ultimate truth (Fischer, 2011).

Gertrude Stein once commented, "There is no there, there." And although she was specifically speaking of Los Angeles at the time, one could speculate, yes, where are we when there is no there, there? C.S. Lewis says it is the place "where there is no we," which I would interpret as the space where there is no ego [emphasis added] (1955). Perhaps the absence of language-driven behavior can help us stay out of this zone of "thereness".

---

aspired…emphasis on the full development of the human personality…his creative powers are seen as the core of his being. This vision of the freely developing man, happy in the unfolding of his own gifts, fulfilling the special gifts with which a man is endowed…embracing his own self-fulfillment…For if men cannot develop, and have nothing in them which is personal and creative, there is no point in giving them freedom…Freedom for each man to grow in his own direction…Behind the minds are men; ideas are made, are held, and are fought for by men" (Bronowski & Malisch. 1960, 498–502).

The Personality Develops a Self

Personality can be defined as an enduring pattern of recurrent events which affect one's ongoing life. The resulting "Good me" is the result of a successful action of rewards, "Bad me" the result of experienced anxiety, and the "Not-me" the result of obliterative experiences, resulting in sudden and severe anxiety. Of the many schools of psychology, that followed the original theoretical formulations of such pioneers such as Freud, Adler, Jung, Erikson, Watson, Mahler and Bowlby, the ones I personally found the most useful as an active clinician were those that focused on the development of the Self.

The Self is the system-product of interpersonal experience (arising from anxiety and growth encountered in psychosocial development). Such theorists as Karen Horney, Kurt Goldstein, Erich Fromm, Gardner Murphy, Abraham Maslow, and Gordon Allport all contributed to the psychodynamic literature when it came to conceptualizing how the personality develops and how different types of character defects arise.

The individual's experience of social, emotional, or intuitive situations is processed with his personality. He has various backgrounds or "fields" (Gestalt) from which to pick meaningful solutions and within which learning, and assimilation take place. Most psychologists agree that the original experiences in the first two- and three-years ingrain most of the potentialities in the individual. These potentialities become possibilities from which to choose in deciding his values. These experiences also operationally define how the person will act out his values behaviorally as he matures, how he will choose to spend his time interacting with others.

For example, the child may have become masochistic because any attempt at a love attachment from the very beginning was dehumanizing and indifferent. The point is that either type of interaction takes the same weight when assimilated; the moments of awareness and the child's use of energy will assimilate indifference or hate as well as love or core-to-core relationships.[112] As Harlow (1965) showed, learning to love at the early stage of development later generalizes to others, and to Self-love and feelings of competence. Harlow believed the mother was the secondary reinforcer for primary drives.

I maintain that drives emanate from the energy source in the Self core. Likewise, Maslow (1968) writes of the process of infantile differentiation. He states that "the child's own impulses toward growth and self-actualization mean there should be a greater stress on spontaneity and autonomy rather than on

---

[112] *In The Third Force* (1970), Goble investigates the relationships that parental love will or will not have on later behavior. "A child prefers consistency, fairness, and a certain amount of routine. When these elements are absent, the child becomes anxious and insecure…Parents must avoid over protection and overindulgence [as well] to the extent that the child's every need is provided for without any effort on his part. Such a child is unable to develop strength and self-reliance [I think of this as a bit of inoculation for later.] It may produce a person who tends to use other people, rather than respect them. Such indulgence shows a lack of respect for the child and his potential to develop…If they are loved and respected, they will show far less destructive and aggressive behavior [emphasis added] (ibid, 1970, pp. 39, 66–67).

prediction and external control in the first few years of experience…the need for self-worth, to feel worthwhile, is intimately related to the concept of love" (Maslow quoted in Goble, 1970, p. 14, 157).

Karen Horney (1885–1952) was known as a proponent of the Sociological School, which maintained that personality characteristics were generated by cultural conditions rather than individual experiences. In *The Neurotic Personality of Our Time* (1937), Horney presented the idea that neuroticism can be deduced in others through an awareness of a certain kind of philosophy of life toward Self and others. "Neurotic" individuals showed a compulsion for affection, power, or modesty which tainted the way in which they related to world. According to Horney, over time this pattern would manifest in one of three possible ways:

* Moving toward people: compliant aggressive and detached compulsive, general Dependence
* Moving against people: everyone else is viewed as hostile expedient, control over others excel, success, planning, and foresight
* Moving away from people: need for detachment, wish to be alone, numbness, observers, need for self-sufficiency, feel superior

Erich Fromm (1900–1980), another theorist who influenced Humanistic Psychology, was born in Germany and became a Democratic Socialist. His theory was based on social values more than the other way around. He proposed that if there is "tension in tenderness" the child will absorb the anxiety of the mother or personal environment around him. In this way, Fromm agreed with Margaret Mahler. Fromm's social/dynamic "theory" is sometimes known as Humanistic Psychoanalysis/Humanistic Communitarianism. It is an attempt to widen the narrowness about human behavior that had come through the popularity of Behaviorism; Fromm's view was much more focused on self-awareness, for instance, than the previous behaviorist theories of Watson or Skinner. Fromm coined the term "Dynamisms", which are kinds of living cells which compose the organism and qualify the relatively enduring pattern of energy transformation. [We can see the influence of chemistry and physics here].

I started my clinical training as a therapist and psycho-diagnostician, giving Neuropsychological Evaluations, Intelligence tests and personality assessments using the Rorschach inkblot test. I also gleaned a lot of information from the Thematic Apperception Test (TAT), developed by Henry Murray (1930s) and based on the theories of Gardner Murphy (1895–1979). Murphy's "three levels of complexity" included the concept that the evaluator should look at the Object or Other in a larger context, keeping aware that it has internal structure for the subject given their history (UFT), and that the boundary between the world and Self is permeable and flexible. Therapeutically, a projective test measure of the individual's "field view" could define the direction of best therapeutic action ("flow") to take.

Murray believed the ambiguous nature of the TAT cards could elicit "information about past experiences and current motivations." Each of the cards presented shows a black and white scene of ambiguous theme, from love to abandonment to fear. The story elicited by each card is what provides the projective information to the examiner. Murray felt this content could be best assessed through the projective technique of responding to pictures of emotionally laden scenes, removing many of the defenses as Freud defined them. Social factors and emotionality that was uncovered could then guide the subject to psychological change through Self-discovery.

Gordon Allport (1897–1967) was one of the first psychologists to specifically focus on the development of the personality. He felt that this process was a "dynamic organization within the individual of those psycho-physical systems that determine his unique adjustments to his environment" (Allport, 1955). This dynamic organization was constantly evolving, reflected deeper motivations of the "psycho-physical systems", was unique, and spontaneously allowed for creative behavior that adjusted to "functional and evolutionary needs."

> Motivation entails one and only one inherent property of the organism: a disposition to act, by instinct or by learning, in such a way that the organism will as efficiently as possible reduce the discomfort of tension. Motivation is regarded as a state of tenseness that leads us to seek equilibrium, rest, adjustment, satisfaction, or homeostasis. From this point of view personality is nothing more than our habitual modes of reducing tension (ibid, 1955, p. 48).

One's behavior varies according to Self or task involvement. Present-day therapy is chiefly devoted to leading the patient to examine, correct, or expand this self-image, i.e., the way the patient regards his present abilities, status, and roles, and what he would like to become, his aspirations for himself [Horney's idealized self-image]. We are still viewing the client from a psychodynamic perspective here. These goals are not used by behaviorists.

Allport attempted to integrate philosophical bases of behavior with the psychoanalytic belief in ego development and need for attachment. "The early affiliative need (dependence, succorance, and attachment) are the ground of becoming even in their pre-socialized stages. They demand a basic rapport with the world before a growth proper can start" (ibid, 1955, p. 32). This position reminds me of how Kohlberg felt moral development is a task specific to altruism over initial affective social behavior; this is where true transformations of motivation are seen.

Allport also felt that development of temperament was constitutional or a habit of mind; it is a phenomenon of "an individual's emotional nature, susceptibility, strength and speed of response prevailing mood." This existentialist point of view allowed for the acceptance of one's own personal experience of phenomena and the ability to reflect on one's own Self and experience. Having become aware of one's own being, one can become more goal-directed.

At this point, the reader may have come to recognize that this very brief survey of several of personality theorists from the "Second Force" of psychotherapy provides only the briefest outline (if that) of their theories. The reason for even taking this detour in our overall discussion of psychological aspects of human experience is to make the CONNECTION between the founding fathers of psychodynamic theory and the initial influences on my own training and eventual development of my UFT. One of my graduate school professors knew Allport well; thus, I was strongly influenced by his theory. During the time I was being trained, the humanists and proponents of a "Third Force" in psychology were coming to the forefront.

This "new wave" of theorists and their ideas were interested in Self-actualization, an integration of Eastern and Western philosophy, and the use of the relationship itself as supportive for the most powerful of all transitions.

Founders of "Third Force" Psychology

Most people think of Abraham Maslow when discussing "Self-actualization". However, it was Kurt Goldstein's (1876–1965) theory of the organismic development of the personality which first helped me blend the ideas of Hegel mentioned in Chapter Three with the ideas of the organism in each environment as described in Chapter Twenty. Then, from that point of view, I saw the developing individual and personality as a whole (Gestalt), as had Goldstein and Fritz Perls after him (1969). Basically, Gestalt theory is about the "personal process of alienation and identity." It assumes that we all identify only partly with what we are and the potential within us. "We look to find from others what we cannot mobilize in ourselves and therefore fight being drawn down into alienation'" (Perls, 1969, as quoted by Hardy, 1990, p. 203). Also a student of Goldstein, Perls conceives personality as comprising three layers:

> The surface is constituted of the roles we enact in manipulating the environment, the games we play; when we do away with such 'phony personality' we are confronted with an area of deadness, nothingness, emptiness (the 'implosive layer'); and only by working through and giving in to that deadness can one come to the real life—the 'explosive' layer of true feelings and strivings (Otto, 1970, p. 132).

Fritz Perls said, "Don't be an observer, merge with your actions: maintaining the duality is the source of the conflict, the end of the conflict will be through the synthesis [Hegel]" (op cit., 1990).

Sidney Jourard (1971) proposed a theory of Self-disclosure based on the idea that each of us needs at least one significant other in our lives to disclose our feelings and opinions to. His theory is based on a general phenomenological study concerning man's relationship to the world. Those of us who have a hard time disclosing, perhaps as an outgrowth of the way we were socialized, often find neurotic and/or unusual ways of expressing ourselves.[113] Each of us has this need

---

[113] How is one's vastness sensed? Jourard would define "knowing" as that which is fixed in the mind, which is understood as "truth," whereas "awareness" comes more from consciousness, having knowledge which is watchful sensitive, and often without specific intention. "Your power to sense potential and imagine possibility—is one secret of your growing. Those individuals of the greatest maturity are also those who

to disclose, and many of our behaviors can be explained in terms of this need, regardless of how awkward it feels.

Some people, perhaps the reader, view life as an endurance test. A check in the Thesaurus verifies that the words "cautious" and "nurturing" are truly antonyms. Nurturing implies the type of attentiveness, perhaps the ability to encourage and be thoughtful, considerate and/or earnest. Caution is exhibited when the need to avoid CONNECTING and/or to protect one's own boundaries prevails (Mahler's theories, for instance). When I finally started teaching Developmental Psychology, I called these ideas my Unified Field Theory of Development because I had tried to integrate so many ideas, from Freud, Erikson, Jung, Piaget, Mahler, Kohlberg, Rogers, and Maslow. The Rogerian and humanistic psychologists (known as the Third Force in Psychology) had been a great influence upon me because many of them were still actively teaching, some even at my university (or came as a visiting professor for a lecture or two).

It was a time of great growth in the field of psychology; I was blessed to be part of it, just as my mother had been part of the growth of psychoanalysis in the NY scene in the 1930s.

Given my unique, and sometimes complex, point of view toward psychotherapy, I created a chart for my students early on in my teaching career. It was a Developmental Psychology class. I wanted the students to understand the strengths of both Freud and Erikson, but also be able to contrast and compare them through each of the developmental stage. I instructed them to note where they thought their own development, theoretically, would lie on this treatment-oriented chart. I also began to get feedback that they found the chart very helpful in dealing with their own children or students, as many of them were teachers or worked with addicts. As I've mentioned in other chapters, they often asked me, "Why don't we learn this stuff in high school, before we're adults, with children, ourselves!"

Victor Frankl taught one of the particularly meaningful classes I had. He came to speak to my class while in his 70s. Survivor of the Holocaust, his writings (*Man's Search for Meaning, The Unconscious God, The Doctor and the Soul*) and his physical presence gave me an inspirational start to my growth as a teacher and as an individual. I accepted his mantra (of sorts) as my own: "I accepted a Higher Will to which I have surrendered pain and sorrow as meaningful and ultimate, not needing explanation. From here on, I have undergone a tremendous recovery" (*The Unconscious God*, 1948).

Frankl called his form of therapy "logotherapy," in that it gave existing forms of therapy an even more existential analysis. He felt therapy should deal with meaning in life and that this meaning can be accomplished through finding creative values (meaningful tasks), experiential values (knowing the Good, True, Beautiful or Uniqueness) or attitudinal values (right kind of suffering) for oneself. The outcome, therefore, would be a sense of responsibility and use of this responsibility for finding meaning in one's life, actualizing one's freedom and one's spirituality.

---

have been inspired to the greatest passion, and usually for one specific something" (Jourard, 1975).

To explain man's being free, the existential quality of the human reality would do; however, to explain his being responsible, the transcendent quality of conscience must be considered...This unconscious religiousness, revealed by our phenomenological analysis [translating the wisdom of the heart into scientific terms], is to be understood as a latent relation to transcendence inherent in man [emphasis added] (ibid, 1948, p. 61).

Another of Frankl's particular emphases was his focus on the meaning of death. Frankl show that by accepting the intrinsic meaning of death one's responsibility toward life deepens. The uniqueness and spirituality of each moment in life gives a meaning that helps us accept our mortality. "Man works the matter with which fate has supplied him; now creating, now experiencing or suffering, he attempts to 'hammer out' values in his life—as many as he can of creative or experiential or attitudinal values" (Frankl, *The Doctor and the Soul*, 1986, p. 65). I have found Frankl's ideas particularly helpful with patients whose basic problems stem from "anticipatory anxiety", the result of their own intentional mis-directions or obsessions (which create undoing and isolation).

Research has shown that even at a young age children develop a natural, healthy curiosity about death, knowing that they will not live forever.

"When a death in the family does occur the behavior of the parent and other adults will be a model to the child. He will imitate the grieving behavior of the adults around him. Mourning is a necessary and therapeutic method for overcoming the effects of loss. The child should be integrated into the mourning process and taught how to express his feelings of loss, anger, and fear" (Searby, 1986, p. 7).

Observation of how the child goes through Kubler-Ross' five stages of grief (denial, anger, bargaining, depression, grief) can accommodate healthy and unhealthy signs.

Finally, the child's loss may not have been caused by death, but rather by a divorce, where a child may be seen as a "complication", whose feelings are completely ignored. They may not be treated with the same understanding that they would have received if there had been a death in the family. "Research has consistently found that boys experience more maladjustment from divorce than girls. They show more aggression, dependency, disobedience, and developmental regressions. Because children are almost always in the custody of the primary mother, there is typically more problems with the mother/son relationship than with the father/son relationship" (ibid, 1986, p. 11).

Selfhood Reached

We grow as we learn to assimilate and accommodate which information is necessary for "survival" (Piaget). Darwin felt that a few superior individuals in every generation would affect the entire culture. As we discussed in the last chapter, Piaget's great theory of how children learn is based on ideas of assimilation, accommodation, and equilibration, which are all necessary for using a dialectic to move through his six stages.

Bruner (1966) wrote a great summary of Piaget's theories, and he added that learning, as cultural and the impact of culture, is an integral part of his theory. He believed that there are culturally transmitted "amplifiers" of motoric, sensory, and reflective capacities. He also explained his view of evolution, described as a gradual process of "de-specialization". Bruner maintained that Behaviorism cannot account for the complex behavior of the individual engaged in concept attainment, problem-solving, or language production, or more importantly for the degree of intention shown by the individual as early as infancy.

As Goethe said, "a person is his deeds." Goldstein's (1973) ideas unified the concepts of how humans adapted to their environment (Darwin); part of the process of "actualization" was to determine "the figure from the ground." Goldstein believed normalized behavior might be seen in behavior had been conditioned to avoid catastrophic stimuli. If the stimuli could not be avoided, Goldstein observed subjects: a) voluntarily withdrawing; or b) busying themselves with substitute reactions (Goldstein, 1973). These findings were discussed in terms of attachment behavior (avoidant or anxious).[114]

The "normal" tendency of personality development would be toward Self-actualization from within (having overcome anxiety). Although this is a natural tendency, according to Goldstein, performing at one's "greatest efficiency" is a learned behavior, dependent upon environment cues and appropriate socialization. The actualization process is considered the "preferred" method of performing culturally determined actions, demonstrating an execution which is exact and an execution which is comfortable and easy.

How one knows, especially women, has been researched by Belenky, et. al, in a study on women's ways of knowing (*Women's Ways of Knowing*, 1997). Someone who expresses "received knowledge" assumes that for every question there is only one right answer and is impatient with "ambiguity, intolerant of complexity." Such people rarely compare their thoughts with alternatives and are specifically outer-directed. Such a person may be a good listener, but she rarely changes her point of view from the information received. A "subjective" listener is more inner-directed, using intuition and often deciding "if it feels right, it must be right."

"There's a part of me that I didn't even know I had until recently—instinct, intuition, whatever. It helps me and protects me. It's perceptive and astute. I just listen to the inside of me, and I know what to do" (ibid, 1997, p. 7). The third type

---

[114] In avoidance conditioning experiments the fear theoretically does three things:
1. It energizes behavior.
2. It cues or directs behavior.
3. It reinforces fear reduction.

Because of the last factor, avoidance responses are extremely resistant to extinction. In other words, if the thing or issue being avoided is removed, the individual cannot know whether he still needs to avoid it. Likewise, the reduction of frustration is reinforcing. On the other hand, frustration can have an energizing effect, better known as <u>anticipatory anxiety</u> "Coping" or managing stress is found to be most successful when there is a sense of environmental control (AATBS, 1978)

of knowing is "procedural knowing", which includes separate knowing (separation and detachment from incoming information, can sometimes be adversarial) and CONNECTED knowing [emphasis added], which requires trying to imagine oneself into the other person's situation and responding collaboratively.

Belenky et. al. refers to the "imaginative attachment" that comes from being able to see the other person's point of view and uses the other person's own terms and experiences to understand in an uncritical way. Hopefully, a good therapist uses this type of listening all the time, "detached, critical yet accepting." Good therapy also has a bit of the three R's: receiving, remembering, and returning truths that might be too dogmatic. I enjoyed this book and agreed with its basic thesis; however, I do not think it has to be limited to women.

It is important to me as a therapist to acquire information in specific areas, especially when working with women (about 60% of my practice—although these questions also adaptively apply to men). I need to know what messages about role identification they received in childhood and how they feel about their sex role orientation. The answers usually come from discussions about their family life. I am also interested in how a client experienced health, mental and physical, as a child. What made them feel happy and whole? What were the family roles and rules and how did each family member relate to each other? How have those experiences continued into adulthood? How do they identify that part of them that is centered and knows their "true voice?" In my case, I had experiences of spirituality and CONNECTENESS very early and I could draw at will upon my experiences of earnestness and a tendency toward healthy choices.

Maslow's Contributions and Humanistic Approaches

Abraham Maslow (1908–1970) is best known for his work on a hierarchy of needs and the concept of Self-actualization, extending Goldstein's organismic ideas of the Self. In the process of actualization within social influences, Maslow considered an individual's state of need (Adler). Maslow believed that "the human being is motivated by a number of basic needs which are species-wide, apparently unchanging, and genetic or instinctual in origin" (Maslow, 1968, p. v). He proposed that if any of these needs are not met at a basic level they lead to dysfunction within the individual's behavior or personality. In my mind, his theory was a culmination of Freud, Adler, Erikson, Mahler, Horney, and Goldstein (plus others) or, as others have described it, one of "Meta-Motivational" concerns. Because Maslow believed needs to be instinctual, it followed that the ideals were also innate. One works through a need "hierarchy" to obtain an overall ideal state of development of Self or Self-Actualization.

Maslow defined how having each level of needs fulfilled provided an additional experience of survival. As each level was fulfilled, one could eventually move up into a healthy experience of meaning in life and the joy of love and bonding.

If a child is stuck because of failed early need gratification, the "acquaintance function" is disturbed and he or she has trouble interacting with an emotional investment. On the other hand, it is gratification of these very instinctual needs that lead to Self-actualization, the act of reaching spontaneity and autonomy rather than being "stuck" in the need for prediction and external control. Loss of the basic "need satisfactions" as one attempts to rise through Maslow's hierarchy will create illnesses and deficiency diseases.

"A child prefers consistency, fairness, and a certain amount of routine. When these are absent, he becomes anxious and insecure" (Goble, 1970, p. 39). As with previous attachment theories, Maslow's theory stated that the child has a much harder time reaching the higher levels on this need hierarchy. The basic needs are physiological, safety and security, love and belongingness, self-esteem, growth needs (among which is included individuality and meaningfulness), and finally the need for Self-actualization.

Interactions with others (who were moving up on their own hierarchy!), create a trusting, open and loving CONNECTION. Whether a person's core is developed and reinforced by love or by pain will be demonstrated in how they look for dependency in others or push them away as symbols of rejection and pain (UFT). Because we all want someone to love us and pay attention to us, it is also a fearful thing to get just what we want and then risk losing it again.

Maslow calls these variations the "growth choice" versus the "fear choice", in that individuals are afraid of experiencing feelings and values for which their environment during development did not prepare them. Thus, the same energy that goes into guilt, worry, and doubt can be used toward success. To form a healthy habit, one must keep goal-oriented rather than failure-oriented (Maltz, 1960). The failure effect especially happens when we abandon the work we have chosen, due to depression or a lack of any further "feeling" for it. Likewise, we are most likely to manifest dependency symptoms when we are tired, hurt, vulnerable, ill or under stress.

Maltz (1960) believed that it is human nature to be goal-striving. In fact, it is important for humans to stress goal orientation because, if errors are given more attention than the pursuit of goals, "the error of failure itself becomes the 'goal' which is consciously held in the imagination and memory. We should not consciously focus upon the error, or consciously feel guilty about the error and keep berating ourselves because of it…Emotional habits of resentment and self-pity also go with an ineffective, inferior self-image" (ibid, 1960, p. 61, 93).[115]

Maslow felt that humanistic aspects of behavior were innate, but not predetermined. "Man has his own unique type of innateness" (Maslow, 1968). Although he was writing at a time of strong democratic ideals, an analysis of his theory underscores how "aristocratic" the formulation of his hierarchy is. "Maslow argues that divisions and arguments within the personality parallel those between his [own] sense of person and groups. These disagreements can grant him a more elite status, which is what aristocracy stands for after all" (Shaw & Colimore,

---

[115] Maltz believed that "emotional scars" to our ego also have another adverse effect. "They led to the development of a scarred, marred self-image; the picture of a person not liked not accepted by other human beings; the picture of a person who cannot get along well in the world of people in which he lives…The self-image is the key to human personality and human behavior. Change the self-image and you change the personality and the behavior…expand the self-image and you expand the 'area of the possible'" (ibid, 1960, p. 139).

1988, p. 55, 64). His theory indicates that man is reaching for an ultimate "harmony" where his experience of Self-actualization can provide him more hope and an ability to cope with the dialectical nature of his life.

Because a healthy person lives by inner laws rather than outer pressures, he or she has a free choice of behavior which they pick from a wide range of possibilities, providing them with spontaneity, release, naturalness, self-acceptance, impulse-awareness, and gratification. These areas are the lessons of therapy, and the most common methodology used includes (generally) an eclectic view toward personal growth, with frequent behaviorist techniques thrown in, based on immediate observables.

As mentioned above, there is a difference between being inner-directed and outer-directed, sometimes correlated with personality type and possible exposure to early traumatic experiences. I used the Personality Orientation Inventory (POI), which is a measure of these differences, as a basis of my master's thesis on creativity and Self-actualization traits.

The POI measures whether a person, and his or her interactional behavior, is inner-directed or outer-directed, and whether his or her time orientation is present-, past- or future-oriented. The relationships and interactions among all these characteristics are evidenced in a sample of any reasonable size. In addition, Rorschach's inkblots can also be correlated with Maslow's characteristics of Self-actualization, in that the scoring results are conspicuous for signs of inner creativity in thought and perception. These signs include components of intelligence; one's CONNECTIVITY to the emotional process; ability to create new, individual products; artistic inspiration; and religious experience.

In more recent years, the concept of Emotional Intelligence (EI) was developed by Goleman (1995), presented in a book by that name. Emotional intelligence is the ability to approach emotions (and emotional-laden situations) with more sophisticated processing, including the influences of both thinking and behavioral responses to emotional stimuli. The higher one's use of their personality traits in a flexible and eclectic manner, the more they are using empathy and a collection of knowledge from observation to formulate a response based on this "emotional" knowledge. Emotional self-awareness is a trait that is cultivated over time and life experiences. Thus, a measure of EI is "one's ability to recognize, process, and utilize emotion-laden information" (Mayer, Salovey, & Caruso, 2008). Another name used for this process in the past has also been "social intelligence" (Thorndike, 1920).

Goleman and others had always thought that reasoning and the use of emotions could co-exist (Gardner, 1983; Guilford, 1959; Sternberg, 1985), but it was the more specific refinement of the concept of EI to mean a type of Kohlberg Stage Six reasoning, that related to "universal meanings". The more one becomes goal-oriented in Erikson's Industry versus Inferiority stage onward, incorporating Kohlberg's stages Four through Six, the more likely they are to use relativistic thinking and empathetic responses. "These higher EI individuals are better able to recognize and reason about their emotions, as well as about the emotional consequences of their decisions, and the emotions of others" (Mayer, Salovey, & Caruso, 2008, p. 512). CONNECTING these concepts to my UFT indicates that it takes functional intelligence and problem-solving along with EI to create an emotionally healthy individual. Lifelong periods of growth, reactions to trauma, and adjustments in Self-perception all contribute and CONNECT to one's UFT, to functional, social, and emotional intelligence.

Carl Rogers (1902–1987) extended Maslow's ideas, combining them with the phenomenological basis of his own theory, and particularly focusing on the "humanness" aspect of Maslow's many ideas. Rogers' general approach was based on three core issues: the use of unconditional positive regard; reflective listening (genuineness); and empathy. Clients were provided the opportunity to heal from trauma, attachment disorders and limited development of a healthy Self. A therapist is looking for expression of the fullest range of "humanness" available, and beyond serving as an objective observer ("3rd person impersonal"), will also provide as much positive, compassion feedback as required for support and effective change to take place.

This type of "Nondirective Counseling" was based on the idea that there is no single problem or complex that can be the seat of a neurosis; rather the effect from how a client experiences reality to be true, to them, will determine their personality development. Rogers was looking for congruence between the different sources of phenomenological clues to clients' issues. Also based on Goldstein's Field Theory, Rogers was using his experiences and conceptual knowledge of the structure of the Self to formulate his own theory. The individual was viewed with respect, and his or her own center and private world of experience was acknowledged. He understood the basic tendency of individuals to actualize and experience life, where behavior is goal-directed and reflective of an internal frame of reference.

The Necessity of Boundaries

Now there is a Self, internalized (UFT) from the parental patterns, co-mingled with genetic predisposed temperament and secured by adequate parenting or suffering from PTSD from trauma loss or a prevalent anxious attachment. Next, how does that Self appear to others in social interaction? We all have heard or even had close contact with the drama of a Narcissist (Note that sometimes I use the word narcissism or narcissist with a small "n" and sometimes with a large "N". The small "n" is meant to be descriptive, the use of the large "N" refers to an actual diagnostic category). Narcissism is a special case of delayed personality development. The reaction or tendency to always feel what the Other needs us to be will ultimately lead to detachment or lack of interest in interactions out of fear. This is called "inverted narcissism", because the individual has been trying, in his own way, to still be special by being the only one the Narcissist can trust or really relate to (think Trump's initial inner circle, or Sherlock Holmes' relationship with Dr. Watson).

But eventually the Narcissist will become disillusioned with each one of his confidants. A Narcissist may have made you feel "intimidation, resignation, and disillusioned self-doubt", resulting in an inability to have a genuine/authentic sense of Self. It is his nature based upon his own, deeper level of insecurity. The Narcissist just wants to be right (Axis II); Narcissists are "unreasonable people". As a therapist, it is easy to spot these people upon intake; in training we used to say we'd get the "heebie geebies" because they'd act like a child but want to dominate like an adult, showing a marked incongruence between the public and private way they are trying to be the "center of the universe". [Having a therapist for a mother was tough on my kids in many ways, but early on they learned to differentiate the jerks from the people who wanted to be "center of the universe" based on how I labeled other drivers as we drove around in the car!]

One way to protect ourselves from others who would harm us or not respect the reasons for our "attachment" to them, is to establish appropriate boundaries from the beginning. I quoted earlier from Anne Katherine's book, *Boundaries: Where You End and I Begin,* who wrote about manipulators. She also wrote that "a boundary is a limit that promotes integrity" (ibid, 1991). In the physical world, natural barriers separate organisms, delineating them as unique.

However, emotional, spiritual, sexual, and relational issues between the CONNECTIONS humans form can be "…rigid, flexible, permeable, or impermeable. We respond to the world uniquely based on our individual perceptions, our special histories, our values, goals, and concerns." She calls the need for boundaries during CONNECTIVITY relational boundaries: "the roles we play define the limits of appropriate interaction with others, boundaries bring order to our lives (self-concept separate and unique from others), boundaries that are too permeable lead to enmeshment" (Katherine, 1991, pp. 14–15).

As the adult personality is developing, authenticity can also be reached if narcissism is kept in check. Colarusso and Nemiroff (1980) state that authenticity is noted in people (interdependent and capable of staying in the present) who are also capable of making and accepting a realistic appraisal of life, including suffering, limitation, and personal death. The development of narcissism, on the other hand, shows intrapsychic conflict or psychic numbing, which inclines us toward dangerous behavior and sometimes addictions. Narcissism involves "opposing tendencies [trying] to unrealistically inflate or deflate the self… [the goal is to] replace [these tendencies] with acceptance of the self as special but not unique, a part of the mosaic of humanity…acceptance of the Self as imperfect."

Theorists claim there are two types of narcissism—grandiosity and vulnerability. Although the behavioral presentation of narcissism may seem straightforward, the clinical interpretation is divided into these two types. "Grandiose narcissism is defined by self-entitlement, a sense of superiority, and a need for admiration. Vulnerable narcissism is characterized by a sense of entitlement but also an anxious and avoidant nature" (Ellwood, 2022).

Some of the case studies presented within these chapters can be differentiated by thinking about these attributes; for instance, vulnerability can be measured as a trait on personality tests. The higher the level of grandiosity the more likely that there is some underlying vulnerability associated with the noted behavioral cues. "It seems that grandiose and vulnerable narcissism are relatively independent when grandiosity is low, but co-exist when grandiosity is high" (ibid, 2022).

I return to the "Magic Lady" story told earlier in this chapter. After the eighth grade, I continued to demonstrate my skills at perceiving others' needs, issues and anxieties. And I also noticed boys for myself! This gift of perception was generally unnerving to any potential suitor, particularly as high school boys aren't as willing to self-disclose as are girls of that age (and perhaps adult males either!), but I could not be me. My mother, the parent and therapist, always told me that it is a compliment to let someone know you like them; what they want to do with it is their business. Of course, this theory of life often set me up for rejection as well, but those experiences were part of becoming the survivor that I am today.

We all mourn something from time to time, and therapy often requires working through and restructuring of the Self's perspectives. Ego Psychologists call this process the wish for "fusion", a longing for the actual or fantasized ideal state of Self. Mahler would have called it fusion with a representative all-good symbiotic "mother" or Other. Once the symbiotic union is intact there is gradual differentiation with locomotion (initiated by crawling), a sense of Self (language and relational skills), and a secure concept of the Other (object permanence according to Piaget). Through being empathically soothed and attended to in a consistent way, the child develops an internalized image of the parent and ultimately can consistently soothe and attend to himself.

Thus, a securely attached child will more readily explore, knowing his "base" will be there when he returns (rapprochement). The explorations or separations reflect the beginnings of the child's development of a personality which is separate from his parents. The explorations are ways in which the child learns about things, learns about himself in relation to things, develops his/her own unique thoughts and feelings. The quality of the attachment at this stage of development is a good predictor for future behavior and adult attachment style with their own children.

All of us are happiest, from infancy to death, when life is organized as a series of excursions, long or short, from the secure base provided by our attachment figure (Myers, D., 1990). In an unhealthy relationship, this can look like Codependency (Beattie, 1986). But if there is a mutual fit, there may be a denial of the imperfection of the Self by selective identification with the Other and the sought for interdependence. Men tend to define their maturity in terms of autonomy and achievement. Women should not see lack of completion in these areas as a weakness; rather, concerns about responsibility and intimacy often come much earlier than the later development of these concerns for men. Women learn to understand and use the knowledge they gain about themselves, which informs their growth, intellectually and emotionally.

Codependency is a term used loosely in many circles, especially in addiction studies, as we will see in Chapter Sixteen. The term can refer to: 1) the pattern of being other-directed; 2) taking care of others to "earn" rights and affirmation; 3) an ongoing lack of resolution about Self (who will care for me if I show my deeper, vulnerable, Self?); and finally, 4) a projection onto a significant other outside the Self to provide comfort and aid for one's escape behavior. Escape into Codependency may appear to protect one's inner child, but it is also only valid if one or both individuals do eventually attempt differentiation behaviors.

In assessing themselves for Codependent behaviors, an individual may have asked: 1) How did I experience life as a child? 2) Was I ever given an opportunity to express my real needs? and 3) Do new painful experiences reorganize and present older deeper feelings? These questions are basically saying: "If I trust you, it is like giving a piece of myself to you. And I don't know what you will do with it. Will I overwhelm you? Should I trust my feelings? Do I have to take care of you to be loved? Can I get you to intuit my needs?" These are codependent questions not found in healthy relationships with others.

The goal here is to release negativity and to build positives into a relationship (beyond just the physical). We are searching for skills for personal growth ala Maslow, without the need for superiority that often comes with stagnant gender roles. Are there gender differences in relation to inner or outer experiences of space? How is the couple attached? Does their CONNECTION have a special variant? I cannot overstate the role of respect, especially when one or the other in the couple still has PTSD triggers. To get rid of harmful or addictive attachments, it is helpful to start with one's own self-image. Awareness includes the personal, social, and historical. Change may be a means to an end, but if one attempts to change one's process to achieve a different end-product, it is better to start with a solution-oriented strategy.

I am often asked, "Why are more narcissists men?" Gender-related qualities such as aggression and competitiveness can start very early in childhood, after limited attachment to others, or an experience of dominance by a parental figure. With women, signs of narcissism may be found more in the domains of "personal appearance or vanity, status of their children or household and value as caregivers" (ibid, 2008). In her book, *Disarming the Narcissist*, Behary describes how female narcissistic behaviors can be more covert; they become "martyrs, whiners and gratuitous victims, aggressive quest for attention and admiration." Regardless of gender, narcissists usually show an "inability to adequately fit in, conform, or adjust to conditions in the environment or basic expectations within relationships...self-absorption can leave them without a true and intimate CONNECTION to others" (ibid, 2008).

The diagnostic categories of the DSM-5 are often viewed as influenced by prior parenting style, generally divided into three types. Authoritarian parenting requires respect for work, order and authority, structure is of utmost importance. What the parent sets up as standard family procedure he expects to have followed. Any threat to structure is a potential loss of control. In contrast, the authoritative parent, sometimes known as a nurturing parent, sets up realistic guidelines for the child. Control is necessary, but respect for the intellect of the child and his/her decisions is also included in parental influences; the parent has communicated with the child and explained his reasoning, which models good problem-solving. There is a use of rational, issue-oriented methods, give and take, sometimes referred to as "logical consequences". Giving time and attention to the child is the main characteristic of the authoritative parenting style. Finally, in permissive parenting, the parent avoids outright boundary-setting and consults with the child on decisions, even at an early age, which can result in manipulative patterns in parent, child, or both. These children often do not accept rules at school or laws in the community. Busy parents often become permissive parents, not having the time or energy to be firm with limit-setting. They may use gifts and privileges as substitutes for healthier forms of attachment behavior. The child may grow to be anxious, self-centered, non-conforming and unable to form meaningful friendships.

Theoretically, it is held that the children of both authoritarian and permissive parents are alike in many ways because both kinds of parents tend to take control of shielding the children from stress, responsibility and having to be assertive or self-disciplined, all of which may lead to low self-esteem. Likewise, rebellious children, and then teenagers, usually come from one of these two types of parenting. I refer to the necessity of parenting in the authoritative style as the inoculation theory, where there are hard situations and hard decisions to be made but children must learn that life is not fair. By experiencing problems, conflicts, and the unsolvable problems in everyday life, they are inoculated to deal with life as it really is. These strengths will carry through to adult choices and relationships. To reflect the child's point of view, Behary came up with her own labels, which include:

- Spoiled child (expect specific privileges, can't tolerate discomfort).
- Dependent child (wants attachment to be as pain free as possible, achieves no personal competence and learns instead that he is helpless and dependent, any frustration feels like a failure).
- Lonely, deprived child (love was conditional), feels if he is not perfect then he must be flawed, inadequate, and unlovable, has a fear of shame/embarrassment, may have been surrogated, not taught empathy because not shown any empathy, there is a sense of defectiveness.
- Mixed bags: spoiled-dependent (avoids taking initiative and making decisions/exposes his limitations), deprived-dependent (needs constant reassurance, hypersensitive, addicted to self-soothing in any form, uses defensive "hiding" as coping mode, may perceive he's being attacked or has an inability to escape from humiliation or failed attachment (ibid, 2008, pp. 14–17) [there is also an excellent therapeutic example in her book on page 48 and 70].

Narcissists in Recovery

Narcissists who attempt recovery, a rare occurrence, will have to take lessons in "tolerating frustration, setting limits, and developing reflective self-regulation" (ibid, 2008). Behary uses Siegel's stages of schema recognition to outline recovery in gaining appropriate boundaries for oneself in recovery:

1. Observation: notice if you feel blamed or triggered in any other way, "identify threatening conditions" and steer yourself back to a core sense of safety.
2. Assessment: gathering of UFT information.
3. Identification: name the schemas "embedded in memory", do you feel provoked to give ineffective responses?
4. Differentiation: are the memories or experiences driven by memory or temperament traits?
5. Ability to self-soothe.

As narcissism is originally a response to fear of rejection, I always encourage my clients to look at their experiences of Fight/Flight/Freeze as an opportunity to notice how they dealt with the "fight" in them when they were first triggered. Why didn't they just express their anger in the first place? Who trained them not to? If you move on from "fight" to "freeze", usually by isolation or denial, the theory is that you probably skipped over some important cues on the way. These responses were stuffed away, even though they were evident at the beginning of the trigger. As noted by Siegel, Behary, and many others, the signs of a Fight/Flight/Freeze reaction can be any or most of the following:

- Increased heart rate
- Elevated blood pressure
- Increased skin temperature
- Faster breathing rate
- A damp brow or palms
- A queasy or achy feeling in your stomach
- Tightness or a lump in your throat
- Dry mouth
- Quivering lips
- Tingling in your hands, feet, or legs
- A sudden stiffness in your neck, back or joints
- Dizziness
- Welling of tears
- Sleepiness
- Pain or numbness in parts of your body, and perhaps even your thoughts going blank
- A heightening or dulling of your senses: sound, smell, visual recognition, taste, or touch (Behary, 2008, p. 82)

Self-Psychology

A useful explanation of the concept of executive functions, and how a client can regain an experience of composure, security, and Self-containment, is the Self-psychology explanations of personality developed by Kohut and Kernberg (1977). I integrate Kohut's Self-theory, developed post WWII, with client-centered counseling (Rogers), which seems particularly suited as an intervention strategy with narcissistic clients. I later learned the methods of Dialectical Behavior Therapy (DBT), which was developed by Marsha Linehan in the late 1960s and is particularly useful with borderline patients as we will discuss in Chapter Twenty-One.

Kohut's beliefs diverted from the standard psychodynamic/Freudian theories of the time; he looked at one's "sense of Self" from a different point of view. He viewed one's Self-esteem and how this develops in terms of relationships with others (ibid, 1971).[116] His work focuses on the "development of the ego in relation to significant others in early childhood" (Hardy, 1990) and the lessons of attachment (Bowlby).

Because one's sense of worth seems to me to be the core issue that derives from a healthy attachment history, this theory of Self became a solid starting place for many of my treatment plans with clients as a Child Psychologist and later as a therapist who focused on issues of aging. Kohut's ideas of "mirroring" and use of empathy, much the same as Rogers, was one that could be successfully used with clients of any age. Some of the salient points of his theory about narcissism blend well with those of Behary and include:

1. An exaggerated and grandiose sense of self-importance or uniqueness.
2. Fantasies involving unrealistic goals.
3. A craving for constant attention and admiration.
4. Cool indifference or intense feelings of emptiness, humiliation, inferiority, rage or shame in response to criticism or disappointment.
5. Disturbed interpersonal relationships characterized by at least two of the following.
6. A sense of entitlement without a corresponding sense of obligation or reciprocity.
7. Interpersonal exploitation serving to indulge personal desires or for self-aggrandizement.
8. An absence of sustained positive regard for others, resulting in relationships that fluctuate between interpersonal idealization and devaluation.
9. A failure to recognize or empathize with the emotional experience of others.

(Kohut quoted in Behary, 2008)

Relating to a Narcissist

Behary finds that those in a relationship with a narcissistic person fear the loss of a sense of Self (as they should!) when entering this possible emotional merger:

---

[116] Kohut observed that narcissistic clients frequently report vague feelings of emptiness and depression. Clients may also experience derealization and emotional dullness and may require routines to compensate for a lack of initiative. The grandiose self is expressed in unrealistic aspirations, attention-seeking behavior, and extreme sensitivity to slights. The idealized parental image is manifested in the excessive idealization of others. "The counselor may be idealized or denigrated during the course of therapy; denigration is the client's defense against the experience of envy…Unacceptable aspects of the self, especially the rage that the child experiences in response to frustration, are projected onto external targets, which are then devalued…When external adulation becomes too predictable or is depleted, narcissists feel restless and bored, and seek new sources of admiration. As a result, narcissistic relationships tend to consist of brief, serial, and shallow attachments." There may be a tendency to exploit others for need gratification and self-enhancement (Behary, 2008).

If you're in a romantic relationship with a narcissist, he may feel the threatening emergence—of that lonely little child the minute you ask him for a tour of his inner emotional domain (Mahler's theory of merger), or even when you invite him to wander through yours. It's likely that he fears making contact with [his own] child, viewing him as a defective, lonely, and shameful little pest, so he'll push him ever deeper out of his awareness any way that he can. In so doing, he pushes you away as well. This absence of emotional intimacy can leave you experiencing loneliness, even when your narcissist is right beside you (ibid, 2008, p. 22).

One dramatic signal that a narcissistic response is conditioning a relationship is the "splitting" that occurs, seeing things in only black or white terms (in contrast to black and white, plus hopefully gray). This narcissist coping mechanism has a slow onset, possibly reaching pre-psychotic symptoms in late adolescence or early adulthood, with an ultimate diagnosis, in some cases, of Schizoid personality disorder or even schizophrenia. Early in the relationship/attachment (or lack of) to a parent, the emergent idealized image necessary for feelings of safety and survival in the child results in a "representation of parental perfection and omnipotence," with which the child later seeks to identify (even though it may be a creation of fantasy and yearning for attachment).

Therefore, all is either good or bad, black or white, with the splitting between acceptance and lack thereof being obvious. Until the child can see a little good in the bad or a little bad in the good (resolution of the dialectical), the child cannot move forward on Erikson's stage of development for initiation of successful experiences in life. Without the ability to seek and see change as positive, the grandiose Self becomes defensive as the child attempts to control anything that might cause changes that would be seen as threatening or even as "loss". Sometimes this need for perfection and control will be projected onto an external transitional object or behavior that can become addictive as part of this defensive process, as we will see in Chapter Sixteen on addictions.

When a Narcissist does feel anxious, depressed or emotionally unstable, his solution is to find the special Other who can anchor him with attention and Self-esteem. Narcissists need reaffirmation that they are "special" and that their Self-esteem is as valuable as they themselves would like to delude themselves that it is. Therefore, they have the "inverted Narcissist" provide them stability by erasing the bad feelings, reassuring them, or worst, becoming the bad "trash can" for the Narcissist's secret bad thoughts about themselves, which can be brought about by "either a minor slight or an overt rejection."

The example of this interactional process that I use with clients is the relationship between Sherlock Holmes/Watson and Dr. House/Wilson (TV show). In both parallel relationships, Watson/Wilson gains his own (internalized and narcissistic with a little "n") sense of importance by being the only person Holmes/House can be their real Self with, being the only person who can deal with either of these two Narcissists. In both stories, however, Watson/Wilson will eventually find that he can no longer stand the abuse and loss of his own boundaries to be the "trash can" of negative feelings and actions by his "hero". I see this dynamic often in the relationships in my office, where one person has dutifully lost a sense of Self over the years but has gained some sense of importance and Self-meaning by being the only one a spouse or child can stand to trust. It does not usually turn out well, with the inverted narcissist becoming depressed, avoidant, isolated or even psychosomatically sick.

As the triangulated therapist in these situations, I am often the subject of what is called "Narcissistic rage". I observe this type of response (to need frustration) as basically a "tantrum", and instruct the Inverted Narcissist to read Behary's book and to learn to reparent the partner/adult child if they choose to maintain the relationship, for they are truly dealing with a five-year old. Remember: Narcissists are those who act like children but want to be treated like an adult.

The Narcissist, of course, will go for every perceived imperfection in the counselor, and we have a name for this also, "transference", a process which is sometimes reinforced as part of the therapeutic alliance, but which can also reflect too much unhealthy merging or over-bonding with the counselor, or even poor boundaries on the counselor's part.

Reparenting Tools

Another of the characteristics of treatment with Narcissists is the "re-parenting of immature, delayed or ill-equipped" personality characteristics. My favorite methodology is to provide examples through the stories of past or similar clients who have already worked through an issue. On occasion, I have used myself as a model, increasing the possibility of transference. Analogies work very well to aid processing of past behaviors and to encourage the rethinking of outcomes.

One could ask, is the therapist just like a biological parent? Not really, but consideration of the psychological emergencies of childhood, and the resultant UFT variables that have traumatized the client, can facilitate mastery, which is of primary importance in the therapeutic process. The therapist is assessing how parents unwittingly trained antisocial behaviors, and how coercive parental interactions affected self-esteem, peer relations, academic performance, and the impact of stressors on opportunities for attachment.

During the thirty years I worked specifically with children who had been abused, consideration of these factors enabled me to make the best treatment plan for them. One must match the child to the treatment best suited to address his symptoms. Specific questions to be used to understand the child's UFT are:

1. Who is this child?
2. What are his relationships with the important people in his life?
3. What is the sum of his experiences so far?
4. What stage of development had he reached before his illness, experience with death, loss, abuse, etc.?
5. How, and to what extent, can he be helped to master this experience? (Lindquist, circa 1980)

What an excellent summary! I have observed over the years that, whether the client was a child or adult, finding a new "parent" in terms of attachment behaviors and projection of trust needs would demonstrate a repeat of past patterns. These areas might include expecting to be scapegoated, wanting a codependent relationship, or shyness and withdrawal. The new "parent", whether in individual treatment, group treatment, or even a group home, should provide a permissive environment in which the child can regress and work through intrapsychic conflicts, reverse learned behaviors, and work to gain better "insight".

Trust Regained

In conclusion, we now see that children benefit not just from how they are treated but also from how parents treat themselves and others. "Show them how to apologize to one another and forgive each other, use stress management practices, organizational skills and ways of managing stressful thinking, don't be too obsessive about keeping children safe" (Epstein, 2016). Be a facilitator, not a controller.[117]

An excellent summary of what we have been considering here is the famous poem by Robert Fulgum (1986), "All I Really Need to Know I Learned in Kindergarten." It sums up the totality of a childhood well lived.

Most of what I really need to know about how to live, and what to do and how to be, I learned in kindergarten. Wisdom was not at the top of the graduate school mountain, but there in the sandbox at nursery school.

These are the things I learned: Share everything. Play fair. Don't hit people. Put things back where you found them. Clean up your own mess. Don't take things that aren't yours. Say you're sorry when you hurt somebody. Wash your hands before you eat. Warm cookies and cold milk are good for you. Live a balanced life. Learn some and think some and draw and paint and sing and dance and play and work some every day.

When you go out into the world, watch for traffic, hold hands, and stick together. Be aware of, wonder. Remember the little seed in the plastic cup. The roots go down and the plant goes up and nobody really knows how or why.

Goldfish and hamsters and white mice and even the little seed in the plastic cup…they all die. So do we.

And then remember the book about Dick and Jane and the first word you learned, the biggest word of all…LOOK! Everything you need to know is in there somewhere. The Golden Rule and love and basic sanitation. Ecology and politics and sane living.

Think of what a better world it would be if we all…the whole world…had cookies and milk about 3 o-clock every afternoon and then lay down with our blankets for a nap. Or if we had a basic policy in our nation and nations to always

---

[117] Epstein also focuses specifically on attachment patterns. With distant parents who provide too little emotional contact, "children will receive insufficient mirroring, guidance, closeness, or feedback to develop a sense of their emotional selves. A child of enmeshed parents, on the other hand, gets filled, not with her own feelings, thoughts and values, but with theirs…Do not expect the child to take care of the parent, ask the child to make adult decisions, or create an enmeshing environment with the child (which comes from a parent's desperate feeling of emptiness, i.e., the need to feel validated)" (ibid, 2016, p. 72).

put things back where we found them and cleaned up our own messes. And it is still true, no matter how old you are, when you go out into the world, it is best to hold hands and stick together.

(Fulgum, 1986)

If we return to consideration of Maslow's need hierarchy, we can see that after achieving the "basic needs" of trust and safety, the developing individual next strives to fulfill the "psychological need" of belongingness. This "need" extended to therapists in training as well, as many of us found ourselves following our elder practitioners to become, hopefully, as self-assured as they were and as grounded in a particular theory. Because there were so many theories abounding at that time, it seemed pragmatic to do so, but some more adventurous new therapists grounded themselves in an eclectic style, learning about all the methods and then becoming adaptable to use whatever theory best actually suited the problems as presented by the client. I generally present myself in such a fluid manner, seeing myself as more of a problem-solver than as a sage. I am willing to listen to one's distress.

We have come to realize the unconscious processing does influence behavior, but perhaps in only a limited way (Bigthink.com, 8/18/2011). Even in higher-order cognitive tasks, addressed by the neocortex, brain scanning can show when we are engaged in unconscious information processing. The processing creates meaning that can be used in an emotional context or to make sense of images that were formerly unconscious, but perhaps triggered by conscious experiences, that the symbolic nature becomes available at a higher-level stage of processing. The visual pathway is known as a great source of such triggers. Our conscious awareness is preloaded with all kinds of meaning-laden signals and symbols, even ones which we noted were triggered by our unconscious.

As society changed toward more Self-realization, developing and sustaining CONNECTIONS have become the key (especially within a marriage). Virginia Satir, with whom both my mother and I studied and became personally friendly, was the optimistic, charismatic, and caring version of the Wizard of Oz. She never tried to replace a clergy or other confident (nor did I); rather she was just a naturally gifted listener. I watched her draw a reluctant participant out of the audience and within 10 minutes she (and the rest of us) would know the significant history, presenting issues and enough to ask just that right question to get the individual to emote. She saw the untapped potential in every person, but her technique went beyond just nurturing communication.

As we will see further in Chapter Nineteen, on the therapeutic process, the position of Satir and others results in a composite view that the developmental level and progress of the patient is more important than their diagnosis. Family dynamics, and even hyperactive symptoms, cannot overtake the sense that the presentation of a problem is multiply determined. We look for continuity between the temperament seen in the first two years of life and later behaviors (but not necessarily in a linear fashion, example: high-risk children do survive!). The most essential ingredients of the therapeutic process as a factor in personal change are realistic perceptions to start with, genuine feelings of respect between patient and therapist, compassion, empathy, and a deeply felt friendliness and attachment. This dyad is meant to savor the work accomplished together.

"If I can convey to the person that I am trustworthy, then we can move on and go to the scary places" (Simon, 2012, p. 36). In working with a client, this needs to summarize Erikson's stages up to that "scary" point becomes even more important as one developmentally reaches Mahler's secondary phases (differentiation, narcissism, and rapprochement) better known as adolescence.

Chapter Fifteen
Developmental Issues of Adolescence Through Old Age
(We Grow Up and Grow Old)

Children need a solid emotional basis for their higher development (control, decisiveness, and discipline). A child lacking in fulfillment of the safety need (weak boundaries or over-indulged) will show security and safety issues as an adult. Maslow presented these needs as a prerequisite in his need hierarchy, enabling the person to become Self-actualized, a concept directly related to my theory about CONNECTIONS. Many troubled adolescents carry an overwhelming ideal of themselves, which is much too perfectionistic and measured by failures avoided rather than by successes achieved. Comparing oneself to this perfectionistic ideal can only lead to a sense of inadequacy and insecurity, the very thing the compensating parents were trying to avoid. I agree with Behary, who states that by the time adolescence is reached, the concepts of "reciprocity, responsibility and empathy with others" should be well founded but are not always prevalent. I have often noted in my patients that these skills were often unavailable, leaving the individual ill-equipped. For instance, failure to progress in school is extremely stressful for primary school children. The four leading causes of school failure are learning disabilities, emotional disturbance, ADD, and chronic illness.

A future "attachment failure" in the adult started long ago in the child's experiences. A "false self" (Winnicott, 1971) has developed, which is just another word for "disguise". If we start acting under false pretenses very early on in our lives, it will become very difficult to undo the habit and process. A therapist may collect information about your UFT to investigate past influences and to "sum you up" into a therapeutic label. But, in truth, your label may present differently for different people because you only present what you choose to have anyone focus on: "my partner, my job, my fears, my label, my life."

My perception, based as well on my own experiences, is that we want and need "attention", but we do not want to bring attention to ourselves. This trickiness about attention-seeking may be associated with early moments of shaming. We can internalize that our Self has chosen the "mask" freely, but we do not have to identify with it completely. To quote Adler, "man knows more than he understands."

Adolescence Takes the Family by Storm

When I was teaching, one of my favorite lectures was about how adolescence explodes the family's myths. I could see in the students' faces recognition of their own history, the complications and angst of adolescence as they had experienced it. It is a time when teenagers try to break free of the rules established by their family and challenge their parents' control. Often this challenge will threaten to expose long-held secrets about sexuality, alcohol or drug abuse, or even domestic violence. The parents will need to brace themselves for a betrayal, but one which will enable the child to grow away in a healthier way and may even provide a troubled family with some healing. Up to this point the family may have manifested unspoken, yet silently reinforced, fantasies and contracts toward each other to maintain a type of symbiosis. But as the eldest child/children reach adolescence all agreements now are off!

Anger is a natural part of growing up; employed by teenagers like a weapon to blast themselves loose from the family. The best sign that the adolescent is about to make the break from his/her family is when the anger begins to abate, no longer being needed to create independence. Because of the fear of losing the little bit of control they may have gained, the adolescent will often assert competitive dominance while also trying to maintain emotional isolation as a form of distance, an appropriate boundary at that age. We saw earlier a description of the different types of parenting (authoritarian, authoritative, permissive). Now as the child reaches adolescence, the effect of whatever type of parenting was used will show up. For instance, the parents may displace hostilities of their own, signaling an underlying jealousy or the beginning of a midlife crisis due to the parental loss of their own childhood fantasies of success or hope for power.

Preoccupation with their own needs may make the parents unable to make adequate room for their children's needs or they will see the child's needs as threatening, i.e., having to give more support to the teen during adolescent transitions. On the other hand, the parent may feel guilt over a failed attachment or loss of opportunity to provide for the child; this may mean a tendency to pacify or overindulge by giving the adolescent power in the home.

Psychosexual development of adolescents also brings up the possibility of the parent living vicariously through the child's "acting up" and sexual experimentation. This direct sign of maturity in their child often sets off feelings of confusion for the approaching "empty nest", when a couple must return to their own intimacy issues.[118] The best approach is for parents to set realistic limits, assert the family's value system as necessary, and wait for the storm to blow over.

Is acting out during adolescence normal? Yes, to a point if it is transient, benign, and leads toward maturity. Behaviors which are progressively more lethal or consistently negative should cause parental concern. Again, dysfunctional families impede healthy adolescent resolution of identity issues by trying to live vicariously, needing the child to stay dependent, or using the child as a scapegoat.

---

[118] Just at the time that children blossom sexually, feeling all the excitement of new sexual attractions, parents begin to lose confidence in their own sexual desirability. Observing the maturity of their children, parents begin to realize that they are growing older. They protest aging and often become enmeshed in extramarital affairs, trying to relive the excitement of their own youth. Parents with adolescent children are especially vulnerable. As adolescents break away from the family and seek refuge among their friends, parents are alone together for the first time in years. Marriages are pressured and tested. For couples with secure but unexciting relationships, sex vibrations in the family may produce waves of disenchantment. This is one way adolescents expose family secrets: marriages dying from boredom are shown up in the light of intense adolescent sexuality.

A more positive response may be giving protection by taking unpopular stands when necessary.

What dynamics within the family contribute to an impasse in an adolescent's development? When a teenager is used by his family for vicarious excitement, or as a scapegoat for family troubles, he may experience an unrecognized burden. But where do you draw the line? I think the parent should determine how the adolescent genuinely feels and try to respond accordingly. For instance, adolescent sex is a private experience that a teenager shouldn't share with parents. At this time, they are supposed to be creating intimate relationships with other teenagers, not with their parents. Adolescent sexuality is already a source of uneasiness for all family members involved. If the adults in their life are also acting out sexually, the adolescent's needs for secondary differentiation get upstaged.

Early dependent tendencies, which are part of developing a secure base [according to Bowlby], seem to be seen against an underlying issue of control. In a situation where one person is dependent, the other person cannot be "independent;" symbiosis is ongoing because he is just as "dependent" upon the other's dependency for his ego-strength as the first person is on him to care for them. That is why it is seen as Codependency. The adolescent is trying to break away from this dichotomy, sometimes in ways that are too extreme for the situation presented.

Because dependency is based on a need for love, affection, attention, survival (or negatively with being debased, made to feel guilty or unworthy), the dichotomy of an adolescent's struggle to create his own independent identity is exactly the kind of thing Erikson was trying to describe in his theory of this period of development: Identity versus Role Confusion. The goal, often arising in therapy with a family of a teenager, is for the entire family to develop in the direction of mature interdependence and away from the pathological dependencies mentioned above.

Setting limits requires a balance between permissiveness and restriction. Teenagers will try to stretch the limits of what is permissible; it is up to the parents to deal with their own crises and values. Up to now we have tried to teach our children about right and wrong and have given them a set of values (loyalty, fairness, and honesty). Now we must prove, as parents, that we are living by all these standards as well.

Here is an example of how I used to instruct my students to talk to their parent-clients: "Tell your children: 'Until you're six you do exactly what we tell you—no questions. From six to twelve, we'll try to explain why you do exactly what we tell you. From twelve to seventeen, we'll talk it over and try to reach a mutual agreement, but Mom and I have the final word. After eighteen, I hope we'll still talk it over, but you make your own decisions.' It seems to work pretty well." These are examples of how we move through the three types of parenting, authoritarian, authoritative, and permissive. Each type has a stage and context with which it will work best. Parents offer this protection by taking unpopular stands when necessary.

Often there is a period when our children are partially independent but still more than a little dependent. They aren't children anymore, but they aren't yet adults. This state is enormously frustrating. You get used to a child being gone, and suddenly he comes back asking for protection (or to do the laundry at your house), behaving like a ten-year-old. It seems that the whole family must constantly readjust to accommodate this teenager. Adolescents want all the privileges of adulthood and none of the responsibilities; often we've given them responsibilities first to make them earn the privileges, which they in turn resent (secondary narcissism).

"We have trouble reading signals from these aliens who only yesterday were children whom we understood perfectly. 'I know my kid's trying to tell me something, but I'm damned if I know what it is!'" The situation is even more difficult for single parents, who tend to be overly protective of their children and who identify with them more closely. The child, too, finds it more difficult to grow up and feels guiltier because the parent will be alone after they leave. The attachment may change from a loving one into a negatively charged one. Ultimately, however, parents can move into the final stage (secondary rapprochement); it is important to keep boundaries flexible and drop some of the parental role playing behind where they have been hiding their true selves.

Failed Developmental Sequences and Grief

In Chapter Sixteen, we will be further discussing how the amalgamation of a developmental sequence and UFT of factors resulting in an outcome called an adult, individualized or not, can sometimes go awry and create an Outlier, either emotionally or through physical and psychological addictions. But what if the anomaly shows up even earlier through special needs or trauma so that early on there are clear signs of trauma?

Dealing with the outcomes of these traumas, emergencies or chronic illnesses requires a focus not just on the primary "patient" but also on the other family members, guilty parents perhaps, and especially siblings who may feel set aside or burdened by their lack of problems. Later they may act out for the attention they never got as displaced children and become "professional patients", going from one mental health professional to another. This neediness may also reflect unresolved grief, the outcome of which can manifest as either destructive or life evolving.

Grief can be an enforced interlude for reassessment. Life will never be the same, so one must take time to plan how to cope with a world that has been turned upside down...Bereaved people find that they ache all over again every time they discover another habit to unlearn, like setting out an extra plate or buying groceries for two. And blaming oneself is a common symptom. But the pain of grief makes planning harder, not easier, and is too extreme and long-lasting to be useful as a strategy session...Grief is the other side of love (Pinker, 1997, p. 420–421).

Sometimes it seems that every patient I deal with presents with some variation of grief: loss of job or relationship, loss of identity due to serious illness, loss of boundaries due to toxic relationship or early attachment disorder. Early in the treatment I try to address losses as well as the symptoms of PTSD that I notice have arisen following what they clearly experienced as a "trauma" in their life. In his book *Good Grief* (1962), Granger E. Westbury presents a model which works well for me and my interventions. He attempts to strike a balance between the negative side of grief and possible positive outcomes.

For instance, a loss can be balanced with the recognition that one has unique gifts, the shock or denial of the loss with an attempt at affirmation of what can be turned around and meeting the experience of negative emotions or depression with hope (ibid, 1962). Westbury acknowledges that many physical symptoms of grief are inevitable such as anxiety, guilt, resentment, or resistance to asking for help. Many of these patients, especially with anxiety, reflect a fear of the unknown or the projection of an unwanted condition, i.e., feeling a lack of control. All these areas of concern can be addressed directly within a supportive environment, where one learns how to release the pent-up tension in a healthy way.

Sometimes, however, one's environment is not supportive enough, at an initial assessment, to do this grief work. Many of my clients come for support because they literally have no one else to trust, no partner, children, parent, or friend with whom they would entrust their secrets or their needs for attachment. On the other hand, relationships provide my clients the best chance to find someone with whom they have a lot in common—shared interests, similar values, kindred goals, comparable backgrounds, roughly equal intelligence, and a somewhat parallel way of looking at things goes a long way toward providing the "basic needs" on Maslow's hierarchy.

Another ultimate manifestation of a failed developmental sequence can be the actual removal of the child from the home due to abuse (physical, sexual, emotional, neglect, abandonment). Subsequently many of these children have multiple factors influencing their UFT data in that they may have been special needs in some way to start with. This additional trauma will have contributed to long-term symptoms (more stress in the family, et cetera). And their "long-term" is very long term indeed, as they are also more likely to stay Outliers for life, in the mental health system, with addictive patterns or even with sociopathy that may even land them in the criminal justice system.

Although this type of PTSD may be different in cause and manifestation, the symptoms of the stress disorder (SD) part of the PTSD are as similar to and valid as that of any returning combat veteran. It is important to understand how the executive functions of the cortex will be disrupted from achieving healthy educational, emotional, and relational outcomes.[119] It all starts with the perception of threat.

---

[119] Trauma activates the lower subcortical portions (the brain stem and limbic areas). "Once the assessment of a threat is received by these subcortical areas, including a part known as the amygdala, messages are transmitted to the body, creating a sense of distress, and readying you for action. Part of the response involves a discharge of excitatory hormones, such as adrenaline. This all occurs very rapidly. This hardwired system engages in a fight, flight, or freeze response that is invaluable for survival for most animals (including humans) when confronting a truly dangerous or life-threatening moment… [there is] what he calls a 'low road' of function in which a state

Trust builds from consistency and CONNECTION. Thus, each member of the relationship experiences autonomy without symbiosis. However, relationships lose CONNECTION, and symbiosis, as described by Mahler as a healthy infant need for safety and security, is not a healthy adult intimate relationship. One should be chosen, not just needed. Many of the marriages I see (in my clinical setting at least) do not reflect the hope that was there at the beginning, after the wedding.

If a person is experiencing symptoms of grief/loss/PTSD, then their issues about power, individuality, control, separateness, and intimacy will all be magnified. I have found that, to show empathy for the symbolic meaning the wounded survivor is trying to communicate, it is sometimes very helpful to use metaphors in our discussion; indeed the "wounded body narrative" is one most readily accepted by my PTSD patients, whether the actual injury was physical or not. Bonding, long-term attachment, and completion of the process of individuation before re-attaching through intimacy needs often have been severely disrupted. People must ultimately heal themselves, using available tools, as they are the only ones who know how truly deep the trauma goes. Sometimes even "tolerance" can be used as a weapon, albeit at a cost to the individual over-using it. Even when an affair is discovered, the partner may commence upon "soothing, ministering, arranging, placating" (Seymour, 1988); as I often tell my clients, "Sometimes person can be too tolerant!"

Transition

In America, the adolescent style leans toward openness and a search for "other" roles than just those modeled by the parents. When encountering an adolescent, it can be helpful to structure your thinking around the "4 Fs" which identify issues that are active in adolescents: family (relates to emancipation from parents), friends (relates to ego identity within relationships), fertility (relates to newfound sexual identity), and future (relates to life goals and lasting relationships). Human CONNECTION is paramount but so are age-appropriate skills for managing tasks and social interactions, obtaining a sense of personal competence (Behary, 2008).

The narcissism later seen in adulthood has symptoms that are also identifiable in adolescence, mostly as depression and attachment failures. Sometimes, however, feelings of alienation have led to the adolescent's separation from the primary family into a culture in which drugs, alcohol, and violence have come to substitute for love, feelings, and shared understandings. Major contributing factors to serious teen problems will also be trouble at school, drug, and alcohol abuse, sexual acting out, pregnancy, running away from home, and suicide attempts. As

---

of threat can sometimes shut off the higher functions of the prefrontal cortex. This prefrontal area serves as the chief executive officer of your brain, helping to soothe your mind, regulate your body, engage in thoughtful reasoning, and reflect clearly and insightfully on what is going on. Immersion in the low road means a loss of these executive functions (Siegel, 2007).

part of adolescent culture, a suicide attempt is the most disturbing and least comprehensible of all to adults. Suicide scares people: it threatens them because as a self-destructive act, it makes others question the very meaning of life itself. These problems are all externalized symptoms of the internalized rage and then the depression that comes from adolescent feelings of helplessness and hopelessness.

Addiction and narcissism are an attempt to Self-soothe or Self-medicate. In many instances, a depressed teenager will seem much like any normal moody, rebellious adolescent. How can a parent tell what is a temporary stage and what is a crisis? It may be easier to deny and ignore these symptoms, but a suicide threat, for instance, should not be ignored. It is a myth that one who threatens will not attempt suicide. "In studies of suicide, the term 'cry for help' has been coined to describe many suicidal acts. The suicidal adolescent uses an attempt at self-destruction as a plea to be noticed and helped. Usually, this desperate cry for help comes only after quieter calls and less dramatic messages have brought no results" (Sullivan, 1986). The state of severe depression, worthlessness and lack of self-esteem lie at the heart of many suicidal thoughts.

Parents are of vital importance to a depressed teenager. Rather than feeling guilty, or even taking on the blame for the teenager's problems, sometimes teens' own nature (developing UFT) also plays a vital part in determining how they will react to family and environment pressure. As a parent, you can be your child's best initial source of help if you understand the dynamics, the causes, the symptoms, and most constructive ways of coping with teenage depression. Listen carefully; use active nonjudgmental listening to unpack the child's loss of identity and possible feelings of shame. Let your child know that "we are in this together and we support you. We do not expect you to be perfect; if we have been putting too many expectations on you, we will re-evaluate our own behavior."

Help them see that risk-taking may be unconscious and their self-destructive attempts driven by wanting to die. This maybe the beginning of drug abuse as a form of risk-taking mixed with self-soothing that eventually results in major drug addiction if help is not forthcoming. Getting help from other family members, or professionals, may be a good idea. Also, it is important that any circumstances presenting a grief reaction, to the adult family members as well, will be seen as a significant loss. "A child is constantly in the process of developing—cognitively, emotionally, physically, socially, and sexually (UFT). The skills and concepts he has acquired, those he is in the process of learning, and those not yet developed must be taken into consideration when evaluating the effects of parental or other significant relational loss."

Loss can be due to death, divorce, separation, or loss of an important friend or romantic interest. Loss can also be subtler—the loss of childhood, of a familiar way of being, loss of goals through achievement or of boundaries and guidelines. Even the loss of childhood and a family-centered life can disrupt a teenager sense of Self. In forming strong new ties with their friends at school and away from home, they can start questioning family values and traditions. This separation helps them grow emotionally and grow away from parental influences. Their bodies are changing too, and these internal changes along with changes in their social CONNECTIONS can cause disequilibrium or even a state of mourning.

The emotions that arise in the troubled adolescent are highly volatile. Adolescents are craving a CONNECTION to something which can identify (for example, some teens may join a gang, preferring any value system to none). "If there is no adult value system, then a child or adolescent will embrace the value system of peers" (Winnicott, 1971, p. 245). This act parallels Maslow's need for belongingness. But these emotions can also be used more appropriately to reflect reality without carrying a qualitative value. Therefore, the old maxim is true and useful, one may dislike what a person does, but certainly that does not necessarily imply that they dislike the person. As Maltz states, "one of the biggest mistakes we can make is to confuse our behavior with our 'Self' ...to conclude that because we did a certain act it characterizes us as a certain sort of person" (ibid, 1960, p. 150). I believe the way to short-circuit the failure syndrome is to make a conscious decision to change the method of responding to the results of one's actions, and the best way to change, to change the response, is to change the emotional investment which should be in the accomplishment of a goal.

> Gregory Bateson believed that it is not really the "before or the after", it is the change that matters. "That there are various psychoanalytic and religious correlates to these procedures is perhaps obvious. In a spiritual interpretation, all personalities are trying to reach their true nature, trying to transcend the weight of their past. And old reality decays for me. I stink and feel rotten, but this change in matter is ultimately good, for it is change in what matters. Old realities die, new things become my reality. The rigidity of my personality is dissolved, a new pattern is slowly allowed to coalesce. The ferocious desire for pattern itself is tamed, and I begin to look at my former pattern as just one possibility among many. I become less rigid, more tolerant. I see that all that really exists is fusibility and creativity (mercury)" (Bateson, 1972, p. 79–80).

Even if the goal is not reached, there is effort and movement in the direction of growth, both of which are reinforcing, perhaps as much as success itself. And when success is forthcoming the goal takes on even more emotional investment.

Hormonal Influences

Returning to our study of the lifecycle, how do adolescents make it out of their storm of hormones and oppositional defiance? For males, their testosterone gives them a constant readiness for sexual responses (mental and/or behavioral) which cycle throughout the day, month, and possibly even the seasons. Males' sexuality affects their moods and sexual desire as much as females', hormones just manifest in a different manner.

> Men's testosterone cycles fluctuate from higher in the morning to lower each evening...Testosterone also declines as men age, and as their levels drop, they experience increases in moodiness and irritability. The amount of testosterone, and men's response to it, appears written in their genetic code—in particular, their androgen receptor gene sequence. The stress hormone cortisol also appears to play a role, squelching testosterone levels when men get stressed (Sapolsky, 1994).

A study by Glass and Wright (1992) reported that although "only" 25% of respondents have had an extramarital affair, for men the number having sex outside of marriage is 44%. But she underscores that often that is all the affair is— sex. These men are looking for an outlet when they have become unable to perform with their wives or are uninterested in their wives' bodies, i.e., not the relationship. Another explanation might be psychological, with the underlying message, "I am avoiding our DISCONNECT. I won't make you grow up if you don't make me feel weak."

The husband may only be temporarily placating the facts of his behavior so that the wife does not indulge in her feelings. I often start counseling in these situations by explaining such findings by looking for sources of anger and supporting men who are having issues with impotence or even just disorders of desire. It near impossible to feel "sexy" when you're mad at your partner. Well, it's possible but we call that rape.

In females, oxytocin seems to be the hormone which provides signals for relationship-building, and when relationships are in distress, oxytocin may even contribute to females paying closer attention to subtle social cues. Oxytocin is like a "molecule of CONNECTION", signaling the need for social contact. These hormonal and behavioral findings have led me many times to statements about the hormonal differences between men and women as a key to healthy heterosexual relationships.

Gender Differences

Bandura (1997) found that children imitate those who appear powerful and competent and who share a warm, loving relationship with them. This identification process has often been viewed as the beginning of moral development (Kohlberg, 1964). It is also important to differentiate between gender identity (knowing one's own sex and that of dolls), gender stability (you always stay the same sex), and gender consistency (sex does not change regardless of actions and clothes). Same sex preferences and transgender identities are usually noted in children's behavior by the age of 4 or 5, but there is a great variation in the research on this subject. Societal attitudes have been changing, as well as society's influence over sex role preferences.

However, much we would like to support equal rights for women and politically correct stances on equalization issues, Title 9 and otherwise, it just is true that there is a gender difference in how men and women go through the developmental sequence. For instance, one belief is that women are more creative. This creativity is delineated by their nurturing behaviors in family CONNECTIONS and in parenting, their work at home tasks (decorating, cooking, stretching budgets, scheduling, organizing), attention to personal appearance, service to others, friendships and personal relationships, and practice of spirituality.

Women are cooperative, while men are more competitive. That is not to say that any man who is high in these areas isn't "masculine"; these are just statements of frequency and gender specific roles, perhaps having developed over the years within family dynamics. On the other hand, allowed more freedom and acceptance in the workforce over the last 50 years, women have taken these creative skills into the corporate world as well.

I have a friend who wrote a book about women athletes, *Sisterhood in Sports: How Female Athletes Collaborate and Compete* (Steidinger, 2016), which confirms this idea about the collaborative instincts of women. Many books, including *Running as a Woman* (Matthews, 1994), which is about women in politics, have focused on the positive differences between men and women. Therefore, if we were interested in reviewing Erikson's 1950s theory again but we focused specifically on the challenges that face females as they develop, the study might take on a new design within the same framework.

A psychodynamic viewpoint (Freud or Erikson) of women, and their use of defenses, is more evident in the lower stages of Erikson's theory, as expanded by Levin-Landheer (1982).

EIGHT STAGES OF WOMEN

1. Trust vs. Mistrust: During development there is an awareness of environment outside of the basic instinctually driven impulses and behaviors.
2. Autonomy vs. Shame & Doubt: Limits are set, which hopefully lead to a sense of being valued and loved. Boundaries are being established which help the ego develop out of id, along with the necessary awareness of Self/Other. On the other hand, if the female child is instilled with a fear of loss of control, or worse, punished for expressing rage or more externalizing "masculine" behaviors, autonomy (and the implications of its underlying power) might be taken away. We become concerned about when to take initiative or when to be inactive. Gaining a new sense of independence is the goal.
3. Initiative vs. Guilt: Development of the Superego is reinforced. "Male initiative or their version of creativity, may seem more relevant to parents than the female version presented in transformative processes, intuition, and the ability to readily synthesize."
4. Industry vs. Inferiority: The school-age girl has now had to learn to navigate the world where "compensatory behavior" will help with survival in the environment. If repression is achieved, then fulfillment of a concept of Self results in the experience of Freud's stage of Latency.
5. Identity vs. Role diffusion: Secondary narcissism, found in every middle-aged child, results in a need for structure and direction. In girls, sexual identity may develop sooner than in boys, partly because of an easier time having resolved the Oedipal issues (no shift in attachment from Mother/Other required). Early issues of "falling in love" [see the concept of limerence below], represent a "projection of identity onto another, love for same reinforcing to Selfness, and love identified with mother or father (need for externalized control/attachment meaning)." By high school, young adolescent women may be able to understand romantic love, and other Phallic Freudian stage issues, whereas male adolescents are still navigating their puberty issues and focused on peer experiences. Love

comes initially from fantasies and expectations, a search for a sense of relatedness in the context of another.

6. Intimacy vs. Isolation: The self-absorption of young adults may equalize female and male individuals for some time. Many of both sexes are caught up in overcompensation, building careers, and learning self-regulation. This is the period when individuals are beginning to figure who they want to be but may still be stuck in adolescent behaviors as well, such as acting out with sex or substance abuse.

As noted in Steidinger's book (2016) mentioned above, socialization, conscience, complementarity, and a realistic view of love may rise above any experimental period that initiates this stage of development. The individual is finally learning about adult trust, in Self and others, i.e., "trust your feelings to guide you," which will enable surrendering of the need for parenting/mentoring and creating companionship with other age-appropriate adults instead. Both Thoreau and Joseph Campbell tested the need for isolation to focus on Self and work, while still taking note of feelings of loss of intimacy and how these experiences changed their view of Self. Campbell's book, *The Hero with a Thousand Faces* (1949), presents a cross-cultural survey of new adult tasks, mythology, and cultural ritual that represents this journey during early adulthood.

7. Generativity vs. Stagnation: Again, as in infancy, men and women seem to move more toward each other psychologically. Both can be creative or depressed. Addictive or self-destructive behaviors are not gender specific; healthy survivors of a lifetime relive their lives through children, their own or those of others. Erikson would describe this period as a "process of seizing potentiality and overcoming a tendency toward personal passivity." Having finally developed new skills and a firmly established set of values, the young adult is ready to learn from mistakes, including those of being a young parent. Staying flexible is the solution, coming into one's own with the intention of caring for others and producing meaningful work. (Psychotherapy is "generative" by the very nature of its intent and attempts to produce new life and positive energy in our clients.) "We are concerned here with defining reality, dealing with authority, arguing and judging, and skills appropriate to our gender" (Levin-Landheer, 1982, p. 133).
8. Ego integrity vs. Despair: Real CONNECTEDNESS has finally resulted in understanding and a sense of completion. Whether a person, male or female, experiences liberation, equality, and identity satisfaction will be decided by how well they have learned to handle experiences of suffering (which we all must accept in life) and have found a reckoning with issues of death. The experience of love between partners can be "truly sacred" and an expression of total commitment.

We would hope both genders are looking for a global set of individuated and life-affirming traits. These traits include courage and consciousness in the face of conflict, dependability, and eagerness to please (regardless of gender), and cooperative behaviors with both genders. If an individual has achieved Maslow's basic needs of safety and security, then sexual orientation or "lability of Object choice" will not create a conflict. Adult bonding is still based on a search for protection.

Helen Thompson Woolley (1903) wrote in "The Mental Traits of Sex" that "the psychological differences of sex seem largely due…to differences in the social influences brought to bear on the developing individual" (quoted in Milar, 2010). As she showed in her applied research (eventually becoming the director of the Child Welfare Institute, Teachers College, Columbia University), this statement hits directly at the core of the whole basis of the UFT, that it isn't just gender, attachment, developmental safety, or parenting style within any context that affects the outcome of personality—it is all of these.

Issues in the Marital Relationship

If these attributes create success in early adulthood, then finding joy and intimacy in the partnership of marriage is more likely; if the CONNECTION is primarily based on sexual attraction, then the limerent effect will predominate, usually to a negative end; a strong sense of attachment can become obsessive (Tennov, 1979). On the other hand, marriages seem to have the best chance if the partners have a lot in common—shared interests, similar values, kindred goals, comparable backgrounds, roughly equal intelligence, and a somewhat parallel way of looking at things. Too much difference builds in too much distance, the opposite of enmeshment which is the experience of family dynamics lacking boundaries at all. For instance, men expect to be blamed for everything that goes wrong in the relationship (feeling like a failure), so "why try explaining themselves or talking about how they feel?" (Stosny, 2009).

Even with adequate and supportive dynamics, how do we deal with issues in marriage? When both partners will feel valued and CONNECTED, communication rules can be agreed upon early in the relationships, such as asking: "Are you done?" "Can I tell you/answer you…?" What we are looking for is co-creation of a dialectic that can be eventually resolved, avoiding boredom. "Couples in dull marriages avoid meaningful discussions, meeting new people, participating in challenging activities and even thinking about their problems. Since boredom isn't a malignant problem, like alcoholism or wife battering, there's a delusion that it can be safely ignored. But boredom is the greatest threat to a fulfilled life" (Groder, 1991).

Using the transactional theory presented in a previous chapter, each member of the partnership needs to identify if they are being Parental, Childlike, or acting from their Adult. "The Child has the feelings, but the Adult is encouraged to respond. Even with the weakest process, the quality of the Child can be supported, because the unadulterated Child also evokes empathy [and joy]" (Habib, 2011, p. 75). Ultimately, there is the question each member of the marital dyad is thinking: "Will you take care of me?" Imagining better outcomes is imperative, but one must not confuse fantasy with hope for the future. Mindfulness of one's role, actions, and renewable promises is a core function of a successful marriage.

Since each partner may be the one who is terrified to bring up his/her feelings, the marriage based on boredom can go on for a long time with symptoms of depression and its consequent loss of energy and creativity. Groder goes on to detail how to revive a marriage; it starts when a partner stops pretending that everything is okay and initiates a conversation about it ("I want to be married to you, but I don't have to be married to you!"). The revival may not feel safe, but the nature of the dull marriage is not safe either.

The steps to RECONNECTION include a slow and supportive process of communication that may even require outside help from a therapist, where it is more likely that both partners will feel safe to be open, especially given the therapeutic nature of "structure, support and guidance." This need for openness is where the theory of "love language" comes in, including: 1) acts of service; 2) quality time; 3) gifts; 4) physical touch; and 5) words of affirmation (Chapman, 1992). It is also important not to confuse intimacy with Codependency (merger) caused by underlying anxiety.

Most of us are looking for support, understanding, companionship, affection, loyalty, financial balance, security, the opportunity for self-expression, and sexual passion and fidelity, "…. heart to heart, not heart to mind" (Stosny, 2009, p. 160). Symbiosis, however, is not intimacy. One is chosen. During my own wedding, our vows included, "I choose you," as the emphasis, not just "I love you."

In paying attention to one's partner, both will feel valued and CONNECTED. Stosny states that there are four times of the day during which validation should be reinforced: waking up, leaving the house, coming home, and going to sleep. These can be times of CONNECTION or times of dread and feeling "emotionally stranded, isolated, and uncared for." Men may have a primary fear of failure, but both partners must learn to "hold onto self-value and value for each other even when the other's behavior stimulates core hurts" (ibid, 2009, p. 68).

Issues about power, individuality, control, separateness, and intimacy can be determined during an interview process or self-analysis project within the marital CONNECTION. Because men tend to want to respond as a "relational hero", which is the training they received from a father or surrogate father figures among their friends; a woman who truly wants to make a man feel understood should use appropriate metaphors that speak to the male journey. I have found this method very successful when treating male patients.

On the other hand, lack of intimacy to most men means, "'I am not known.' [Perhaps], he makes himself unavailable to his partner, when he's focused primarily on work or alcohol or chemicals or acquiring things or getting ahead, or when he lets stress mount so high that he can't come out of himself to see the other…we know ourselves and our feelings. If a child is taught to ignore his inner self, his inner self won't develop" (ibid, 2009, p. 66). The key narrative here is to see relationship-building as a true test of "courage", from the Latin root "*cor*", meaning heart. This intimacy work presents the concept of how much courage and CONNECTION it really takes to generate a loving, trusting relationship (Wexler, 2003).

We begin to see clearly how attachment patterns, developed from early vulnerability in childhood, predict the resultant nature of the adult relationship. Distant parents provide too little emotional contact. Children receive insufficient mirroring, guidance, closeness, or feedback to develop a sense of their emotional

Selves. "A child of enmeshed parents, on the other hand, gets filled, not with her own feelings, thoughts and values, but with their parents," such as:

- Expecting the child to take care of the parent
- Asking the child to make adult decisions
- Enmeshing with the child (from a parent's desperate feeling of emptiness, need to feel validated) (ibid, 2003, p. 72)

Women with a deep desire to be like their mothers are often "faced with the choice between accepting a beloved image that carries connotations of inferiority and dependency or rejecting it and thereby losing an important sense of closeness…Be aware of the invisible contributions, of the dynamic that cannot be defined in these relationships, just as that often found between parents and children, based on the commonality of goals" (Bateson, MC, 1989, p. 39). It is important that memories of childhood be memories of respect and confidence.

During early marriage, changes in entrenched gender roles are taking place. Men often become less rigid in their sexual, corporate, and familial dominance. "Men probably say, 'I feel,' much less often than women say, 'I think' but they certainly also identify with their feeling exactly as women do with their thought" (Hannah, 1981, p. 111). Robert Bly (1990), a storyteller who uses myth and ritual to help heal wounds inflicted upon some men by negligent or abusive fathers, writes about the "politics of the masculine." He finds men can become "masculine soulmates [even though they] exist in a community that has turned the family man into an alienated father who renders his male offspring emotionally impotent" (ibid, 1990).

Such men suffer from what Bly calls "father hunger", and it is his belief that our "therapeutic society" has created a derisive outlook toward men's emotions, maintaining "men's unwillingness, or inability, to communicate profound emotions (which are different from beliefs)."

If the goal is to maintain a healthy meaning, within CONNECTION and relationship, then the same techniques that are used in any graduate school "Management" class probably can instruct this process, which also includes anger management. David J. Decker developed a training manual called, "Key Ingredients in Having and Maintaining a Healthy Relationship" (2013), which he used for his year-long anger management classes. Unit classes included:

1. Develop self-knowledge, self-awareness, and self-esteem to be ready to be involved in a healthy relationship.
2. Be clear with yourself and with prospective (or current) partners about what you are looking for in a relationship with another person.
3. Develop and maintain a spirit of integrity, trust, commitment, and love.
4. Maintain clear and healthy boundaries to promote tolerance, acceptance, and respect.
5. Develop and use conflict resolution strategies to promote safety and cooperation.
6. Provide emotional support for one another to promote nurturance.

7. Develop and share a vision for yourselves in the context of the relationship.
8. Strive for equality in family decision-making and tasks (Decker, 2013, p. 14).

Progress not Perfection

The therapeutic process is another form of this CONNECTION to Other, the therapist as a parental figure (one expects), a trusting companion and listener without narcissistic needs (one hopes) or expectations of "healing" only in the therapist/listener's direction of interest. Rather, the person needing support and wishing for change will use a therapy session for the purpose of increasing emotional growth, modeling more appropriate social contact, and anger management and life planning skills within the supportive environment before going out in the world to manifest these changes. It is true that therapeutic contact reinforces dependency to some degree (we often just want to stop for a while and let someone else take over!), but it also allows practice in the use of maturing skills in the outside world.

All roles have built-in limits. Respecting these limits creates order in relationships. Crossing these boundaries yields confusion and disorder. I often point out the unfortunate potential for triangulation within the stories I listen to (usually gossip or manipulation), which harms relationships. The developmental goal of my type of therapy is to provide an outlet for the unresolved stress, grief, pain, and anger that has derailed developmental progress.

Sometimes a bit of regression early in the process is even needed to get a person back on their developmental "track". I often must tell a new client, "This may feel difficult at first, or you may even get worse before you get better. But we have established goals and you will see a difference soon." As Everett Shostrom puts it, do not make yourself a 'thing' as a way of allowing manipulation in the relationship, rather be an actualizer, who appreciates himself, trusts himself, and has recognized and changed self-defeating behaviors (Shostrom, *Man the Manipulator*, 1967).

As we have passed through these stages and ended up in a (healthy or unhealthy?) place, we can't help but be chronologically an adult. We may not be mature, we may not be sober, we may not have money, we may not be married. We certainly may still fight the good fight to stay happy or fulfilled moment to moment. The division of the process of reaching adulthood is often developed into seven cycles.

There are counterparts in all religions, in the ancient Egyptians and Persian doctrines, in the Kabbalah and in Taoism. Plato, too, speaks of seven phases. They are part of the Hermetic doctrine, of Buddhism and of the alchemist great works, as well as the *I Ching, Chinese Book of Changes*…All movements are accomplished in six stages and the seventh bring return [recycling or renewal]. This author summarizes the seven phases, by asking us to "pay attention to our normal body clues", such as:

- To *exist*, to live and to be.
- To *act,* to do things.
- To *think,* using logic and concepts.
- To have an *identity* and know who we are.
- To develop *skillfulness* through structures and values.
- To *regenerate*, producing life anew, and
- To *recycle*, developing effectiveness at every age (Levin-Landheer, pp. 136–138).

Likewise, just like the phases of the moon, our psychobiology will take us, and even our relationships, through phases which may reflect the differing influence of values, evaluation of Self, and need for dependence upon another. Gail Sheehy wrote *Passages* (1976) to present the Eriksonian idea of stages in the vernacular. It was named one of the ten most influential books of our times by the Library of Congress and was a major hit because people were trying to understand what had and was happening to them in their daily lives. She subsequently wrote *New Passages* (1995), in which she extended her focus onto the issues of later adulthood, a stage into which she herself was then passing.

Issues in Aging

Issues of aging reflect a generally accepted definition of mental health, seen in the relationship of the individual to himself and the relation of the individual to his environment. Issues generally include increased life-stresses, chronic use of medications and medical problems affecting daily functioning, developmental issues specific to late life and changes in one's level of socialization and family obligations, a lessening of resiliency, and issues in mental health. Of course, one must keep an eye out for Alzheimer's, syndromatically defined as "individuals with progressive cognitive impairment in memory functioning and at least one other cognitive domain coupled with functional impairment and the absence of other pathologic features that can fully explain the syndrome" (APA, 2014).

Of the roughly 5 million people in the United States living with some form of dementia, 60 to 80 percent is caused by Alzheimer's disease. After screening for abnormal protein clusters in the brain, one can differentiate Alzheimer's disease from other types of dementia, such as Lewy-body disease (abnormal deposits of protein alpha-synuclein in the brain). Can we tell how dementia in old age is caused if there are many different types of pathology? Reference to the four "M"s (mobility, medications, mental activity, what matters), are often the first focus during assessment. Treatment thus includes plans when receiving medical care concerning medications, mobility, thinking disorders, depression, and the ability to maintain previous rewarding activities, which are strongly a demonstration of the person's goals, values, and preferences (Novotney, 2018).

Because exercise, cognitive health, and psychological factors so strongly affect the outcomes of aging in working with elders, clinical issues must include "consideration of the client's age, gender, cultural background, degree of health literacy, prior experience with providers and usual means of coping with life problems" (Wolf, Gazmararian, & Baker, 2005). High on the list of influencing factors includes genetic, health, sensory, personality and poverty, discrimination and oppression, affective, and other variables (APA, 2014). [Also see Chapters Ten and Eleven].

Man's environment is a related set of "communities" that represent definite structures, which must be responded to in socially significant ways. Healthy community adaptation (or noticeable changes and difficulties with adaptation) describes the individual's lifestyle within his environment and emphasizes his performance and productivity. In dealing with elders, confidentiality issues will come into play, especially with health care providers. Information can only be shared with adult children or other care givers if permission is granted, which can sometimes lead to difficulty in coordination of care.

"It is important to balance the person's need for autonomy and quality of life with safety." Elders must be taught to pace themselves, and to accept predictable changes such as the necessity of downsizing; overall, therapy can help them deal with the greater uncertainty of the aging process (Mullin & Terrill, 2014). In my own practice, the development of a treatment plan for an elder requires my attention and synthesis of these issues and to counsel them on a new set of tools that will help in their adaptation to the current changes which they are experiencing—how is their balance? How many medications do they take and when do they take them? Are they amenable to the disclosure process of therapy overall?

Continuing research is focused on normal aging, particularly the differences between current elders and those upcoming due to the large cohort of Baby Boomers. This research can include "the biological and health-related aspects of aging and mind-body interactions; the psychology of aging, including changes in sensory processes, cognition, personality and emotions; and the social dynamics of the aging process, including work and retirement, friendships, roles and family relationships" (Novotney, 2018, p. 66).

We have all heard of the "use it or lose it" concept of aging; the recent development of complex problem-solving/cooperative internet learning sites, which reinforce such strengths, are a hopeful process toward lessening incident rates in the future. "Cognitive reserve is something that builds over a lifetime" (Weir, 2017).

Beyond managing general therapeutic issues, if neurocognitive disorders are discovered, then creating training in the tools to self-manage, especially potential depression and anxiety, will become primary within the support their therapy may be giving them. I have seen many cases of positive psychological growth, even in patients over the age of 75! It is true that a shortened "time horizon" creates a sense in urgency in them, but in truth, almost all my clients with PTSD, a chronic or life-threatening illness, or a debilitating depression will experience this same sense of fore-shortened life, and thus strive for more meaning on a day-to-day basis.

> People today are leaving childhood sooner, but they are taking longer to grow up and much longer to die…Recent research also suggests that developing multiple identities is one of the best buffers against mental and physical illness. When a marriage blows up or the company shuts down or the whole nature of a profession is changed by technology, people with more than one identity can

draw upon other sources of self-esteem while they regroup...Such resilience is essential.

We are all hungry for CONNECTION. CONNECTION was a word that came up again and again in my discussions with groups of middle-aged men...An impressive study of the sources of well-being in men at 65 found that the harbinger of emotional health was not a stable childhood or a highflying career. Rather, it was much more important to have developed an ability to handle life's accidents and conflicts without passivity, blaming or bitterness...The traits important to smooth functioning as we get older are being dependable, well-organized and pragmatic. [Those who] mastered the art of 'letting go' of their egos gracefully, so they could focus their attention on a few fine-tuned priorities...they concentrated on what they could do rather than on what they had lost...quality of directness...nothing left to lose... [emphasis added] (Sheehy, 1995b, p. 69).

However, when we look at these "passages", we cannot avoid one unalienable truth, we can't make it alone. Who we are and what we do may have been formed and developed by the past and sequences of positive or negative events that formed that UFT of our current existence. But it is what we choose to do, think and how to make CONNECTIONS going forward into the future that will define us. Bronowski defined creation as "a sense of exploring one's own activity, what science has to teach us is not its techniques but its spirit: the irresistible need to explore" (Bronowski, 2011, p. 72).

Creation being the result of any thought, it qualifies the unique potential in each of us...it is striving which gives meaning. Self-expression gains new dimensions when experienced again through someone else. These people cannot realize their potential without a SECURE BASE of reinforcing past experiences. Worrying about the future creates barriers which only confine existence. "One of the great and all-too-common distortions of spiritual life is to neglect or mistreat the body because of a yearning to develop the soul. Quite the contrary, we should treat our body with great respect, for it is the temple of our soul" (Tart, 2008, p. 35).

As we age, we are still just looking for someone or something to bond to. Often at this stage, we also see an increase in spirituality and reflection upon life as a measurable symptom of this need. "You are a puzzle to yourself as something to understand. Life is all too short to bring that off. You will continue to be a puzzle to yourself. And of great interest...No one else can give you an identity—your own sensing of who and what you are" (Snyder, 1985, p. 41). Why is it when you are grown and better able to appreciate your parents, you somehow lose your youthful frankness and neglect to tell them half the pride and love that is in your heart? When it is too late and you lose one, you can only take consolation in the hope that perhaps "they may then know, even better than you could have told them, what you really feel."

What is a person's true passion? Many who believed they knew and acted accordingly found a major incongruence later in life; many who were afraid to acknowledge their true passion for fear of loss or disappointment later found that their desire lay right before them in later in life and they had failed to learn the effective skills for reaching out and grabbing their passion because they did not believe they would ever need such skills. Or…we may have had supportive relationships with others only to have struggled with lingering inner demons and addictions of our own, as we will see in the next chapter, on addiction and other compulsive behaviors.

Then in Chapter Seventeen, about Jungian psychology, we will investigate how myths are the structure we give to our symbols and our dreams—if we want to change our path, we must give up the safety of our old myths, figure out how they were formed in the first place, and replace them with positive energy, affirming the lessons learned to move forward with new strengths and abilities that are part of the new myth about ourselves.

As I end this reflection over the developmental process and my own life during aging, I think of what I want to pass on to my children, which was in fact a major motivator in writing this book. As a family therapist herself, one skill among many that my mother passed along to me was the importance of taking a good family history/intake. Now I feel these questions make good prompts for journaling/self-reflection as well. Some of the questions, whose answers best define the initial therapeutic process are just as valid for one's own life review and include:

LIFE REVIEW QUESTIONNAIRE

Medical history: Epilepsy/neurological/headaches
Breakdowns: hospital/institutionalized/recovery patterns
General Health: diabetes, gout, obesity, glands, tumors, cancer, twins
Insights: Feel need; loved (Adler)
Attitude toward mate; offspring; opinion of self
What do you think is your weakest point and how do you compensate for it?
What are your assets? Liabilities?
To what do you have to adjust?
Are you afraid of being hurt/laughed at?
How do you feel about your illness? Are you afraid of being hurt?
Do you have any significant task you want to work on?
Do you have anything on your conscience? (Stolen anything, ever been in jail)
What do you think you need?
What did your parents want you to be? What did you want to be?
Of what are you the most afraid? Anyone you are afraid of?
Do you think you are different than others? Same as used to be?
Do others understand you?
Do you hate anyone? Are you bitter toward the world?
Has anyone tried to harm you? Have you harmed anyone?
Do you like caring for your home?
What would you like to accomplish? What have you ever failed at?
What do you think about most? Can you get it off your mind?
What would you like to change? What irritates you most?
Do you feel compelled to do anything oftener than seems logical?
If your life were a book, what pages in the past would you like to tear out?

What do you pray for?
If I gave you three wishes, what would you ask for?
What has life denied you?
What do you feel that you have most missed?
Important to you to have attention? Does isolation bother you?
Does it trouble you not to finish things?

Chapter Sixteen
The Disconnect and Inward Suffering

> The great enemy of truth is very often not the lie—deliberate, contrived and dishonest—but the myth—persistent, persuasive, and unrealistic.
> – John F. Kennedy

How and when do unhealthy CONNECTIONS start? We addressed the importance of attachment patterns in Chapter Thirteen. Although one is prone to avoid the tendency to blame one's parents for the end-product in one's personality development, our unified field theory of development (UFT) certainly points to several clear areas of causation. In psychology, we call these the "precipitating factors".

Addiction is a symptom of a relational disorder; rather than a healthy interpersonal relationship, the relationship is with an "It" (action or thing). Loss of the human relationship as a source of soothing results in more awareness of the underlying triggers to anxiety. In recovery, it is important to check one's actual reactions against possible implanted fears, even at an epigenetic level, from one's family of origin as well as family of choice. Failed relationships and resulting attachment disorders are the most probable sources of grief. Based on 45 years of experience with addicts, working in a county jail and in- and outpatient mental health facilities, it is my belief that underlying any addiction is a severe anxiety disorder.

> The essential feature of Generalized Anxiety Disorder is excessive anxiety and worry (apprehensive expectation), occurring more days than not for a period of at least six months, about several events or activities. The individual finds it difficult to control the worry. The anxiety and worry are accompanied by at least three additional symptoms from a list that includes restlessness, being easily fatigued, difficulty concentrating, irritability, muscle tension, and disturbed sleep (DSM Manual of Mental Disorders V, 2013, p. 222).

Milkman and Sunderwith (1998) wrote an excellent book, *Craving for Ecstasy: How Our Passions Become Addictions, and What We Can Do About Them*. These authors emphasize the human compulsion and loss of control found in all addicts. It is a viewpoint that has greatly influenced my own work, and even more so since reading their book.

We all want to feel good. In addicts, the repeated compulsive response to a trigger has been explained as "a function of a weakness of character, chemical imbalance, or spiritual defect." The brain is an "enormous switchboard housing trillions of interconnected pathways; it is a giant pharmaceutical factory that manufactures powerful, mind-altering chemicals" (ibid, 1998, pp. xi, xiii). But for some (addicts) this switchboard has gone awry. Children are supposed to be thrill-seekers, but the "non-productive" result of compulsive pleasure-seeking can ultimately show up in one or more of many neurochemical reactions during the formation of an addiction in an adult.

In addition, the "drug of choice" is craved as the id takes over the ego's defense mechanisms, with a new and ineffective commonality of anxiety and "need for more". According to Milkman and Sunderwith, the process of well-being is divided into three categories: relaxation, excitement, and fantasy.

1) Relaxation: reduces discomfort from external events or internal conflict, search for tranquility, maintains control over their own hostility. Shuts down internal or external world (Addicts seek sedative-causing drugs, including alcohol and THC).
2) Arousal: compensates for deep-seated feelings of inferiority, demonstrates physical prowess or intellectual ability. Have an overinflated sense of self-worth. Feel active and potent when the environment is viewed as overwhelmingly dehumanizing (Addicts seek stimulants). Fear of helplessness (Seligman), i.e. 'I am not helpless and vulnerable; I am powerful and feared (invincible).'
3) Fantasy: pursue mystical experiences and have adolescent preoccupation with the quest for cosmic unity or spiritual oneness. Special reverence for subtle nuances in interpersonal communication and are prone to find special meaning in accidental occurrences. This process is a very strong method for reducing stress (Addicts seek psychedelics or other mind-altering drugs) (ibid, 1998, pp. xv, 19).

Responses to Anxiety

At some point, normal levels of becoming excited (being energized), relaxed or using one's creativity becomes a compulsive behavior. Anxiety is often viewed as being set off by that which is contrary to established patterns. Another way to define addiction is "self-induced changes in neurotransmission that result in behavior problems" (ibid, 1998). This process can become life-threatening when the neuronal impulses become insufficient to support vital functions such as breathing, heart rate, and blood pressure.

Not only are the new set of behaviors compulsive, but they will eventually make the addict's life "unmanageable". It is also important to consider what type of personality may be a factor in the development of an addiction. Personality disorders reflect malfunctioning expressed through inflexible and limited patterns of behavior which may or may not be compatible with society's definition of success (AATBS, 1978a).

Some of the other personality disorders, as defined by characteristics, in the DSM 5 include:

- Paranoid personality disorder: a pattern of distrust and suspiciousness.
- Schizoid personality disorder: a pattern of detachment from social relationships and a restricted range of emotional expression.
- Antisocial personality disorder: a pattern of disregard for, and violation of, the rights of others.

- Borderline personality disorder: a pattern of instability in interpersonal relationships, self-image, and affects, with marked impulsivity.
- Narcissistic personality disorder: a pattern of grandiosity, need for admiration, and lack of empathy.
- Avoidant personality disorder: a pattern of social inhibition, feelings of inadequacy, and hypersensitivity to negative evaluation.
- Dependent personality disorder: a pattern of submissive and clinging behavior related to an excessive need to be taken care of.
- Obsessive-compulsive personality disorder: a pattern of preoccupation with orderliness, perfectionism, and control (APA, 2013, p. 22).

In the long run, these behaviors are self-defeating and immature. Those individuals most susceptible to compulsive patterns are those with low self-esteem, dependence on external cues to prior anxious attachment patterns (Bowlby), and fear of failure which may be projected onto outside issues. There is some evidence that genetic factors (alcoholism and/or OCD in near relatives) may also play a part in both childhood and adult compulsive tendencies. Milkman and Sunderworth present Wikler's two step model as an excellent way to understand how behaviors become compulsions.

1. Acquisition phase: continuation due to pleasurable sensations (rush) or sense of well-being. Cue-dependent to stimulate craving for the need-satisfying activity. The human body eventually adapts to this stimulus-response effect.
2. Maintenance stage: no longer motivated by any sense of pleasure but now serves to relieve the sense of despair and physical discomfort that is felt when the mood-altering action or substance is not present. Loses power of choice (Wikler, quoted in ibid, 1998, p. 3).

The development of an "irresistible craving" for food/drink/activities seems dependent upon the need to lessen the impact of physically or psychologically arousing stimuli. Milkman and Sunderwith report that behaviorally the addict is trying to recreate the successful self-soothing patterns from childhood. In substitution for the care or nurturing needed which is not available, an attachment to an "It" is formed.[120]

---

[120] Relaxation <u>decreases</u> neurotransmission, which may follow a fight or a need to repress hostility (think of how carbs affect us). Risk taking is a form of seeking out stimulation to <u>increase</u> neurotransmission.
"If enough receptors on the postsynaptic membrane become occupied by neurotransmitters, there is a change in the electrical balance of this membrane that results in a transfer of the impulse from the presynaptic neuron to the postsynaptic neuron. The impulse then travels to the soma of the other synaptic junctions. The soma of the postsynaptic neuron must now make its own 'decision' of whether to fire based upon the multitude of synaptic inputs.
"Why is the initial excitation of the nervous system followed by 'depression?' There are two types of synaptic CONNECTIONS: "inhibitory synapses are depressed first, excitation momentarily predominates, then excitatory pathway is also depressed.

A Substitute for Attachment

The need to feel attached, albeit addictively, also shows up in "love addiction". The authors write:

> Love can be experienced as a synchronized blend of arousal, satiation, and fantasy, giving rise to life's most fulfilling experience. This adaptive, life-enhancing behavior, however, can become as much a self-destructive outgrowth as any other behavior turned addiction. Based on elaborate fantasies of lovemaking and courtship, there are feelings of elation, reciprocity, limerence, umbra of uncertainty or doubt about the future of the relationship (ibid, 1998, p. 43).

Likewise, as much as we can get addicted to another person or the very idea of "love", many of us have also experienced this transfer of the need to feel nurtured to the intake of food. Eating can become a method of mood control, whereas the addict (usually females, but certainly not always) are likely to "increase intake when under stress and are more likely to eat excessively when tempted by appealing food presentations. Those with attachment disorders seemed to increase their demands for food as needs for gratification and security in other areas remained unfulfilled" (ibid, 1998, p. 82). All the above is obviously true to addictions to alcohol, drugs, etc. Food may become a way of "mothering" the Self and/or rebelling in an oppositional expression of feeling trapped, angry, or insignificant. An ongoing internal conflict arises from low Self-esteem and passive-aggressive tendencies in the expression of anger, which creates a vicious cycle in those who already feel like they do not "belong". According to Jungian psychology (next chapter), opposition to one's deeper archetypal influences, including from one's family, does not change the inherent pattern, it just makes one feel bad about oneself for having the traits and interests in the first place—a form of inauthenticity (and acting out). The individuating person learns that choices do matter, "it is not what happened to you that shaped who you are, but what happened in you that made the difference…To hold the dilemma in consciousness, wait for new insight or changed circumstance, and meditate or pray for clarity" (Bolen, 1984, p. 291).

The struggle for domination is evident in the see-sawing between one side and the other of the committee of opinions at the conference table in one's head that we have previously talked about. Conflicting life demands can also contribute—work, home, love, commitments. The best solution is one where the individual can revise and reframe issues to make them a coherent representation, sensitive to any context.[121]

Whether the addiction takes place is dependent upon genetic makeup and whether the formation of enzymes ultimately take place in the body" (Milkman & Sunderwith, 1998, p. 11, 69).

[121] Ambivalence can be good. "The undiscovered self is an unexpected resource. Self-knowledge is empowering. Build an image of a quest, a journey through a timeless landscape toward an end that is specific, even though it is not fully known. Come up with a new and fluid view of the future…don't hold on to a flawed commitment for

We all get worried sometimes; experiences of compulsion or rituals may not always be seen as negative. Some compulsive behaviors can also add to our sense of Self. Meaningfulness can come through fantasy work which is separate yet Self-defining by its Bisociational quality (Salk's concept of I/not I = I/I). Some compulsions result in loss of control and the continuation of addiction/harmful consequences, but some are signals of commitment and challenge in ways that make life more exciting and meaningful. A real tendency to ruminate is probably genetic in some ways as a survival mechanism; we may even be wired for "good worry" in the anterior insula.

Suffering is experienced as the opposite of CONNECTION. It is the unfiltered release that is available to us when we "flow with the moment" of felt anxiety instead of thinking we must do anything about it and/or suffer. Pain that starts in the mind will eventually move to the body anyway. "Alienation, worry, anxiety, humiliation, sorrow, anguish, depression, fear, and panic become as stressful as bodily pain" (Siua, 1988, p. 9). At least in Western societies, we are more interested in "doing" than "being". Many individuals, however, know how quiet and meditation can lead to self-acceptance, especially for those who have experienced a period of planned recovery.

Documents found in the Pali language of India show that the Buddhists not only described the sources of suffering, but suggested ways of palliative care for the pain that was felt. On the contrary, the feeling that we must "obey" through some type of moral contract with ourselves, and others, creates a sense that we are supposed to suffer, that somehow it shows worthiness, when in fact suffering marks a loss of Self.

Buddhists and other enlightened figures in recovery will tell you anxiety is a "human" thing, that we are all suffering. It comes with the territory of being alive in a world where we have no control over others and little control over ourselves and our reactions as well. I believe that "pain" can be observed and measured on two 10-point scales, one number 1–10 for experienced pain, and one number 1–10, for experienced suffering. Anxiety causes great amounts of this second type of suffering, and sometimes the experience of depression or anxiety just magnifies the other experience of bodily pain as we experience a loss of control and a high state of infliction. Thus, a person whose pain=6, plus suffering=8 would be a miserable person.

Fear of Abandonment

We need CONNECTION to grow. Underlying most anxiety is the fear of abandonment or loss of an attachment. Because we have this drive toward attachment, we will seek that CONNECTION; with the sense of loss of that psychosocial gratification we will turn toward body gratification, which normally starts first with oral needs/seeking out food, then perhaps alcohol and drugs, and sometimes even controlling behavior toward others because we cannot control our own internal needs for CONNECTION. Our failure to successfully navigate our

---

continuity…discontinuity may be a move from stagnation to a new challenge and growth" (Bateson, MC, 1989, p. 5–8).

outer world results in us trying to find some control through retreat into an inner world, a world where pain also resides.

Our Self begins to deteriorate because we have little outside relational feedback to help explain our need for CONNECTION; we feel desperate and needy, and this fundamental state of anxiety creates frustration and even aggression toward that which we cannot control. Understanding the powerful effects of mood, expectation, and other psychological factors on pain is important for helping friends, patients, or loved ones deal with someone's pain, and these variables are part of any pain management curriculum. In many chronic pain programs, there is "family night" during the typical 12 session training. On the other hand, pleasure-seeking may even show up in our use of computers and cell phones to structure our waking day. We want to control life because we are afraid of its spontaneity (Fromm, 1968); we see our computers as an externalized Self that has perfect rationality and can be always controlled.

But who is really the robot, the artificial intelligence we choose to turn our lives over to, with all its algorithms and choice-paths, or ourselves who eventually will lose our freedom of will because we just can't think on our own anymore? We will still have our instincts, which sometimes get us in trouble, but we will have turned reason completely over to our computers? Also, in our current society, hoarding behavior may have increased because our things represent that which is still ours, we have no faith in the attitudes and feelings which we are afraid to show. The idea of whether man is still the "decider", when he could just ask Google, begins to cause a loss of his full intellect and the ability to make any emotional commitment to life.

Instead of making the necessary decisions, he may instead turn to that which is pleasurable or helps him avoid his life altogether. As Hoffman puts it (in his biography of Maslow), "Getting along well within one's inner world may be as important as social competence or reality competence" (Hoffman, 1988, p. 30). This phenomenological inner experience reflects one's deeper instincts which should be listened to. Some addicts do not listen, some neurotics listen too much (obsessives). The influence of instincts is reflected in almost every decision we make.

Treatment for anxiety is often complex and focused initially and directly on symptoms. When the primary symptom is addiction, the treatment may inadvertently get side-tracked from the real issue, the underlying anxiety, its causes and/or symptoms. Often therapies for anxiety, including 12-step meetings, help focus the anxiety into a successful decision or plan if it is the future that is creating the fear. Addicts have often been most comfortable with letting others give them the right advice, but without any depth to ameliorate the exile they feel from their initial family after being abandoned. Their anxiety has caused a shift from the initial heroic fantasies of childhood to fantasies of revenge and being a victim.

"What ifs" will not help, however. Rather, it is a function of successfully letting go—to plan and stick to the plan—one day, one week, one month, or one year from now. One begins to realize that clues to the dynamics of the addict's personality (the psychological defense of projection for instance) are always on display to others; it is up to the addict to rein in his/her expectations and live in the moment. Due to PTSD, the addict may have been living in the moment anyway, but in a negative and fearful way due to an unsuccessful attempt to suppress negative memories.

Contributing Factors of PTSD

In an addiction, there is often the mitigating factor of trauma, a condition whose resultant neurochemistry we discussed at length in Chapter Ten. To recapitulate in a shorter version, the essential feature of Post-Traumatic Stress Disorder (PTSD) is the development of characteristic symptoms following exposure to an extreme traumatic stressor. These include catastrophic body sensations and difficulty assessing safety issues. "The person's response to the event must involve intense fear, helplessness, or horror. The characteristic symptoms resulting from exposure to extreme trauma include persistent re-experiencing of the traumatic event, persistent avoidance of stimuli associated with the trauma, numbing of general responsiveness, and persistent symptoms of increased arousal" (APA, 2013, p. 271).

David Clark goes on to define three processes that also play a particularly prominent role in the disorder: "(a) excessively negative interpretations of the trauma; (b) a characteristic disturbance in the nature of autobiographical memory linked to the trauma; and (c) cognitive and behavior strategies that are intended to reduce the sense of current threat but have the consequence of maintaining the disorder by preventing memory elaboration and reappraisal of negative beliefs" (Clark, 2010, p. 712).

Much of the psychological numbing we see in addiction is the result of early trauma impacting the developmental process. Repeated dysregulation can cause "developmental trauma disorder" and set a child up for victimization in the future, such as depression, suicidal ideation, social phobias, underachievement, poorer medical outcomes (Sparta and Kinscherff, 2013).

For instance, my own granddaughter was diagnosed with a rare brain tumor, when she was only three, an ependymoma at the base of her skull. She had apparently had it for many months (or even years?) but because her symptoms manifested in nausea and poor coordination, she was misdiagnosed several times before the tumor was found. Because of the ongoing MRIs and other treatment, there is no doubt that she remembers her original hospitalization, surgery, and follow-up treatment. Now, at nine, however, she is a vibrant, active three grader. Did this trauma impede her development?

Physiologically she appears normal; psychologically a fuller assessment will be required later to assess how resilient she has been and what are the outcomes of the excellent support she got from her family, extended family, and medical providers. It is also important to assess the meaning she has placed on herself as a "cancer survivor" and the ongoing consequences that may arise from the trauma. We can only watch her and pray she will use her traumatic experience to develop strengths and adaptive personality characteristics.

> Trauma assessment must extend beyond consideration of the impact of a single or series of events to include description of the developmental trajectory of the child, past adverse events, and their impact upon the child (including any

positive adaptations and activation of resiliency factors), any pre-existing or co-existing risk, and mediating or protective factors at the time of the assessment. Analysis of the availability and quality of psychosocial supports both before and after exposure is crucial in understanding the impact of trauma and the prognosis for recovery (APA, 2013, p. 12).

Often, we see "emotional hoarding" in addicts. They have little sense of who they are without acting on their fears and emotional reactions to help define their boundaries. Their boundaries may have been erased a long time ago, through alienation from their parents and the resulting lack of individuation. Detachment may protect them, but it is a mixed solution, with both positive and negative results. If they begin to feel impotence and depersonalization, these feelings can lead to a sense of rigidity in their personality [I recommend *Drama of the Gifted Child* (1981) by Alice Miller for more on this process].

Eventually an introverted personality may develop, one that creates total surrender to the undertow of what is, however negative. There is an internal ache, or yearning, which creates the addiction we will be talking about in this chapter, especially to oral behaviors, such as drinking alcohol and eating. "I'm in a race with my emptiness," addicts say; it is automatic and uncontrollable.[122]

The effect of the stress disorder (the SD in PTSD) will be magnified by any pre-existing problems dealing with stress, frequently the result of anxious attachment, narcissistic parenting, physical, sexual or emotional abuse, neglect or major family loss/trauma, or all of the above. [Believe it or not, in the last 45 years I have had many clients in the "all of the above" category].

This list formulated our menu of important contributing factors to the UFT in Chapter Thirteen because it is through accumulation of nature (and epigenetics) and nurture that a child sequences developmentally from infancy to adulthood. This conditioning leads to tendencies for denial, focus on the pleasure of endorphin release, and the cravings when that release is not forthcoming. During these "hyper-stimulating times" it is even more common for individuals to search for something to calm or control their internal drives, especially when they have been taught not to express feelings. They are trying to "manage their feelings rather than experience them" (Simon & Dockett, 2017, p. 33–46).

Feeling the feelings instead of quieting them with drug of choice is the main target of the 12-steps. It is the internal impact of feelings that can result in a DISCONNECTION from the Self, our bodies, and our gut feelings (ibid, 2017). Problems with DISCONNECTION can result in lowered vitality and clarity; eventually lowered self-worth will also correlate with these isolative behaviors.

---

[122] Throughout much of Hellenic, Renaissance, and New Age philosophy the phrase "recreate yourself!" resounded, urging people to continue a search for skills to take on this process. But what real skills for this process are we given? Why are so many people responsible toward others, not themselves, and thus have trouble clearly mirroring their own needs into the external arena of meaningful CONNECTIONS? Can we teach other-directedness, and if so, why do so many people expect others to be responsible for them? More questions and so the searching continues…

And it is not just the addict who suffers, their children do as well. An increase in reported abuse has come from the prenatal or neonatal care of infants in hospitals which treat babies born to addicts, and through regional centers responsible for developmental evaluations of children after their initial periods of bonding and/or attachment may have passed. Deficits in cognitive, social, and behavioral development due to fetal drug exposure continue to be noted. [I worked in one of these care facilities in the 1990s]. These deficits may result in the diagnosis of a learning disability (hyperactivity, short attention span, and emotional lability). This exposure can also manifest in poor organization skills, reading problems and difficulties in acquiring satisfactory mathematical skills due to pronounced alteration in visual processing, quality of alertness, tremulousness, and startle reflex.

Treating Anxiety

Sometimes, the parents of future addicts are angry, aggressive, and difficult themselves. They have strong denial mechanisms and chaotic lifestyles. As noted, underneath all addiction is anxiety, an effect of the negative parenting and resulting attachment failures. Identifying these high-risk parents, pre-pregnancy, prenatally, or even during their own adolescent years due to pre-existing psychosocial factors, is the long-range goal of addiction programs. As the drug-exposed infants mature, areas of self-identity and social adjustment may be dysfunctional; there may be uncontrollable temper, impulsiveness, poor self-confidence, aggressiveness, and difficulties in making and keeping friends.

A major shift away from the escapism created by the powerful euphoric effects of their own addictive choices will depend largely on the level of CNS release of dopamine. The initial release is followed by depletion of that compound, which leads to the 'crash' or abstinence syndrome characteristic of the drug. This withdrawal was also an early psychosocial experience for these individuals, where no strong feelings of pleasure, anger, or distress in response to parental abuse or neglect were allowed during separation. Exposed infants had very few Self-protective mechanisms for avoiding overstimulation and required considerable assistance from caretakers to maintain control of their hyperexcitable nervous system.

Sometimes the need to "numb" the experience of heightened anxiety from immediate stress, through addictive behavior, starts as early as eight or nine (through drinking, sexual acting out). We see these early moments in an addict's life as just periods of high activity, which is really anxiety that can then lead to an obsession (addiction) to do anything to escape the underlying feelings. The intake examiner or counselor will ask about the current presenting problem that makes the client feel "in crisis". However, any psychotherapist providing support and/or behavioral intervention will also need to know about these prior traumas.

The influence of traumas on long-term anxiety may have led to addictions and self-abuse, and possibly even neurological changes in the patient. Lisa Najavits (2002) writes that women as much as men use drugs to numb out, and at least one-third of all patients Self-medicate to ease the emotional pain of trauma. Her self-help group model, *Seeking Safety,* is not only based on safety; this target group is more likely to have experienced repeat trauma throughout their lives, such as rape and domestic violence. *Seeking Safety* groups exist to help patients develop "safe coping skills" such as compassion, honesty, asking for help, taking care of oneself, and setting boundaries. In AA and other 12-step groups, they call the formulation of these types of group boundaries a "fellowship".

Creating Boundaries in the Crisis

Where is the boundary between what depends upon us and what we depend upon? How do we represent the difference? Many individuals lack the ability to express themselves well (if the skill is not gained during Mahler's rapprochement stage), thus they symbolically lose life's most precious ability, to communicate messages and insights. In addition, an addict may not feel appreciated by others. The AA 12-Steps model would call this type of modeled "appreciation" acceptance.

Avoidance of anxiety is an example of a successful defense system and boundaries. In addicts, defensiveness becomes "over-reactive". This hyper-excitability is almost like the development of an autoimmune response (Singer, 2006), where the reaction (attachment to the drug) persists "after the noxious stimulation had been withdrawn" (Fordham quoted in ibid, 2006, p. 11). AA is successful because it switches the triggered system away from runaway behaviors to the boundary of Self-correction. Early in recovery, however, defenses are seen in strong internalized processes and will be less responsive to initial rational intervention. This defensive response is particularly common when anxiety seems to have no known source, but danger is somehow still signaled, as in "signal anxiety", a term used in Ego Psychology.

A Mysterious Force — Compulsions can Take Many Forms

Why do we keep doing what we know harms us? On pages 58–88, the Big Book of AA (2001) begins to answer that question, but addiction is still a troubling disease, one which impacts all facets of being: physical, emotional, and spiritual. It is baffling and elusive to fight and impossible to cure. Gary Zukav reviewed Freud's theory of personality to explain how the "It" involved in addiction comes from unconscious motivations.[123]

My mother, Virginia Haradon, used to say, "The best rehabilitation is arrest." As an admirer of William James, she went on to push the idea that, "The will is in conflict when we can't stop doing what we don't want to do," a thought which can

---

[123] Freud defined three psychic functions that work together to make up one's personality—the id, the ego, and the superego. The id comprises the instinctual side of a person and operates primarily at an unconscious level. The superego is made up of parental idealizations as well as one's own idealization of the parents. It becomes one's conscience, dictating one's behavior via morality. The ego develops as the child begins to acquire a sense of self—that is, of being separate from another. The ego operates at a conscious and a preconscious level, serving to regulate the impulses of the id with the accountability of the superego. "Ego is not the same as the whole personality…it is more what the person thinks of himself" [emphasis added] (Zukav, 1989).

also be found in the Big Book of AA on page 552. A large part of the struggle against addiction begins with the fact that it is based on an attraction to an "It" which can change and have substitutions; this year's drug addiction might be replaced by a preference for only drinking and smoking, or compulsive spending, or whatever. There is a directional change, a clearing out of "mental debris". One feels more righteous about better behavior, but it is all compulsive. The dependencies that develop as a form of what Freud calls "reaction formation" in childhood no longer protect us from previous taunts or rejections. Guilt creates inferiority which, in turn, feeds feelings of guilt; it is a vicious cycle. The aching apprehension we call anxiety becomes the mysterious need for an "It".

As noted above, in *The Seat of the Soul (1989)*, Gary Zukav describes addiction to an "It" as follows:

> Dressed in attractive clothing, the 'It' presents as desirable or beneficial; look clearly at the places where you lose power in your life, where you are controlled by external circumstances. There is attraction plus fear, plus a jolt of energy that is out of proportion to the situation... Attractions are a pleasing part of life. They can be satisfied and left behind, but addictions cannot...A sexual addiction, for example can be made dormant within a relationship by a fear of losing the security of the relationship, but it cannot be healed without a recognition that it is there, and an understanding of the dynamic that lies beneath it. Unless this takes place, it will break through the relationship, or the façade of monogamy, at those moments when the personality feels most insecure, or most threatened.

> At these times, the personality will feel a sexual attraction to others...That is why each human being who is sexually out of control actually has issues of power in which he or she is out of control with his or her own power. At heart, they are identical. A person cannot be in his or her own power center and be sexually out of control or dominated by a sexual energy current. These cannot exist simultaneously...The experience of addictive sexual attraction is a signal to the experiencer that in that moment he or she is experiencing powerlessness, and is desiring to feed upon a weaker soul...when it locates a person who is weak enough to be susceptible to you, to be seduced by you, it triggers within you the experience of sexual attraction...

> When one soul seeks to prey upon a weaker soul, and a weaker soul responds, both souls are the weaker soul. Who preys upon whom? The logic of the five-sensory personality cannot grasp this, but the higher-order logic of the heart sees it clearly. Is there truly a difference when two consciousnesses are trying to link into a dynamic that ultimately will lead to balance when both have identical missing pieces? What causes the need to dominate, for example, is the same as what causes the need to be submissive. It is merely the choice of which role the soul wishes to play in working out the identical struggle. Hold onto the thought that you create your experiences. Your fear comes from the realization that a part of you is creating a reality that it wants, whether you want it or not, and the feeling that you are powerless to prevent it, but that is not so.

Your addiction is not stronger than the soul or the force of Will...By the magnitude of the costs of your addiction you can measure the importance of healing to your soul, and the strength of your own inner intention to do that (Zukav, 1989, p. 148–154).

Because Hegel said, "insanity is inherent in the soul's nature," it is more helpful to consider Hillman's point of view: "It is not a reality or a stratagem. In insanity the soul strives to restore itself to the perfect inner harmony out of existing contradiction" (Hillman, 1997, p. 63). A great deal of distorted reality depends on how our expectations are or are not met, (and how willful we are to begin with). Sometimes individuals who are depressed can even begin to "ritualize" their negative experiences, particularly in an obsessive/compulsive manner.[124] Our subjective, our spiritual Self/God experience, tries to explain (if not justify) our experiences of guilt. This experience is the outcome of our subjective Self. Our Self, or soul, is created through how we explain our experiences to ourselves, internally (meditation) or externally (relationships).

One's CONNECTION/attachment to an "It", predominant over any other person or life goal, can be rewired through a blissful limerent sense of re-CONNECTING and re-powering to Self and fueling improved self-esteem (Tennov, 1979). A person with good self-image can create good Self-esteem if his or her developmentally appropriate narcissistic needs for mirroring, understanding, sympathy, and respect have been satisfied without being over-indulged at each crucial period of development. Issues with self-image or ego defenses result in difficulty experiencing/owning one's negative feelings of jealousy, envy, anger, and loneliness, creating instead a "need-gratifying orientation" to the social world where values, ideals, and committed relationships are the norm.

12-step programs use the mnemonic HALT (don't get too hunger, angry, lonely, tired) to remind newly recovering addicts to pay attention to their state of mind. This self-awareness helps them in following a learning curve or making appropriate gains in social skills development using an accommodation process in their recovery (Piaget, 1962).

Many sociopaths "know" social rules but lack an affective-motivational style (Weston, et. al., 1990). I am thinking of one client now. A false self may develop and the addict: 1) learns to respond as others expect; 2) needs to "medicate;" and 3) repeat. This ongoing repetition results in guilt and shame. Projection of negative feelings onto objects outside himself is common. These individuals will learn to use escapism quite early. These patterns become entrenched over years of repeated

---

[124] "Although there are 12-step meetings that vary in focus, they are all generally based on the same principles. People can be addicted to anything if it helps soothe their anxiety; the "it" functions as a pacifier, a substitute for the thumb. People can be addicted to anything from religion to sex to activities and even to other people. Theories presented to explain these addictions cover biological, cultural and social models, but generally the profiles are similar" (Kammersgard, 1989).

use as a system of defense, making it difficult to "untrain" the internalized system of Self-protection and chosen identity traits, even if they have been used to hide one's true needs.

Low self-esteem, perfectionism, denial of rejected feelings, oversensitivity, restlessness, and a readiness to feel guilt and shame may ultimately prevail over the basic human instinct for love, which requires adaptation to others. We have been trained from childhood that "living" is the constructive, productive part of life; we lose sight (oftentimes in an attitude of defeat) of that which brings us joy in the moment.

Although one often thinks of shame as paired with guilt, the two concepts are quite separate. Whereas guilt is experienced after an error, a mistake, or even a premeditated act, shame is developmentally a younger feeling, a yearning not to be exposed. Because of this fear of exposure, we sometimes see the same defenses: control, depression, panic, and confusion. The individual experiences a need to run, to escape or shut down these feelings, therefore the tendency toward the use of mind-altering and addictive behaviors. The vulnerable and threatening ideas are also couched in the deeper feelings that one will be abandoned and rejected for their core, but uncontrollable, Selves.

This fear is also at the center of how the 12-step model works; we are all here at a meeting because we are all feeling the same type of shame, just with a different story about our "shortcomings" attached. We experience a different type of spontaneity than that which usually accompanies shame and fear of loss or abandonment. And because shame and spirituality cannot exist at the same time, the search for Higher Power is also at the center of the healing process (Stephanie E., 1986). We learn the consistency and accountability that occurs by just showing up at the meeting.

Frankl (1946) asserted, "When a person loses touch with how he actually feels about events and substitutes what other people tell him to feel, when his capacity to feel is eroded, when he loses his sense of being needed by some loved one, he quickly dies. For he has disintegrated as a person" (Frankl as quoted in Synder, 1967, p. 28).

Most of the great religions urge us to pay attention to what our impulses tell us about ourselves.[125] However, an old Korean saying illustrates the variance of that point: "A person's true character is written on their back; everyone else can see it but them." In the Self-help, AA, and other types of healing groups, the belief in character defects that one cannot easily see is a deeply imbedded concept.

---

[125] An integrated individual is one who carries his own dark shadow of undesirable qualities and frees those around him from his projections. "When he carries his own bright shadow, he takes up his courage, his strength, and his dignity, and his own imaginative thought, and refuses to be bowed down by burdens which others are unknowingly projecting on to him…To accept one's own personal shadow means to accept responsibility for its behavior…It demands not only self-knowledge but the utmost vigilance to see it does not break out unawares…What one does, one is. It is not only the concern of an inner invisible process which we call being, but also the quality of our being which will depend on the value of our actions" (de Castillejo, 1997, p. 31).

However, the search for Self must transcend this basic concept—it is not another's reactions to us, but the urges from the inside that will best guide us in the end.

While self-regulation may look like self-control and will power, what is important is strategies for physical as well as emotional health. Often the addict has turned to the drug of choice to cope with symptoms of past or current trauma and to manage underlying and overwhelming feelings. This unbalanced state sets the stage for addiction. But the "solution" can also come from identifying the problem which is trying to be resolved. Liberation from the punitive "inner critic" can help in the resolution of conflicts, whether with Self or others.

We are hoping soon to use the advances in neuroscience to understand how an "alarm state" can add so much more stress to the neurological system that, eventually, even the DNA is altered. This situation is possibly the result of methyl groups (see Chapter Eleven) attaching to the DNA, which turns off certain gene responses.

Developmental Issues

When one does finally feel safe to attach outside of oneself, it is probably because he/she has started with an "It". How does this early this transfer of "need gratification" begin? My belief is that compulsions could start as early as the undifferentiated ego states before the age of six months old. Addiction is constructed from, and is equal to, weak ego; little accommodation strength has been developed from external feedback and social skills development. Very little sense of a Self may exist. Personal boundaries must also have "permeability" or enough flexibility for sufficient social functioning. Self-destructiveness can begin to emerge due to a lack of acceptance (or availability) of this attachment and a lack of any experience of real love.

Uncovering a history of obsessive thoughts/compulsive behaviors will clearly foreshadow later addictive behaviors. This is where a therapist may ask the deeper question: "What is the client really grieving?" [How far back do they remember feeling abandoned, needing an "It" to CONNECT to?]. Others (friends and family) may notice the alternate symptoms of a building narcissism that often comes with addiction and self-alienation: anger/rage, shame/guilt, boredom/emptiness, loneliness/depression, or vague sense of wanting 'excitement' (Wurmser, 1978).

I had one client whom I had been seeing for over two years before he clearly disclosed to me that he was a sex addict, although it had been revealed previously to me by his wife. When we began to work on the underlying anxiety that admittedly prompted his need to "act out" sexually, he disclosed that all the factors on the above list (particularly anger, shame, and the need for excitement) fueled his narcissism and made him feel "wanted", which he mislabeled as "loved and important". Once he identified this need for excitement, which he referred to as "recess" from his "normal" life, then he was able to understand why he had the need to act out for attention, and at other times to distract himself from anxiety, shame and/or anger. We could think of this cycle of shame/addictive behavior as a "pacifier"/substitute for his thumb (Milkman & Suderwith, 1998).

Seligmann's (1975) theory of Learned Helplessness maintains that where there is no competence to deal with repeated stressors, often there is also a complete absence of control of underlying impulses on the part of the individual. As a result, the stressed individual "learns not to bother paying attention" at all. This attempt to deny or ignore that which is around us varies based on our temperament style (Chess and Thomas, 1965).

Laura Shepherd and Jennifer Wild (2014) present several theories of arousal that can help us understand how helplessness starts in the first place. Each human has a "median level of arousal" that may be considered normal for them. I have had patients explain their drug use as just trying to get to this "place", often referred to as "the click". Having been depressed for most of their post-pubescent lives or longer, their first serious drug use experiences reset their "thermostat" of arousal to a medial level of arousal that had never been experienced before. "This is what normal feels like? No wonder I got hooked so easily; I had no idea it's what other people had been feeling for their whole lives!"

Some people continue to suffer because of their belief that getting help (12-step), or seeing a therapist, will bring on more feelings of shame and uselessness than they already feel. "Alcohol is expected to result in increased relaxation, power, sociability, behavioral impairment, and sexual enhancement; in general, people believe that alcohol changes them in many ways. If people expect this to occur, does it occur because it is expected? Or does alcohol really increase relaxation, sense of power?" (Kammersgard, 1989).

This circular experience about changes in arousal can quickly result in dependency, or even what an outside observer would consider addictive behaviors. A totally independent life is a myth because we all look for a dependency on something, that which can also take the form of giving mutually rewarding experience. That is why one's "dependence" upon a Higher Power is a popular solution both in and out of AA rooms, where "addiction is seen as constriction and recovery is seen as expansion" (ibid, 1989).

With overeating and obesity, distinct impulse management techniques for "inhibition training (go/no go)" requires a clear motivational process to address the appetitive and aversive motivational processes (Field, et. al, 2016). Usually, addictive behaviors are based on some kind of aversive or avoidant processes; the craving experienced is commonly related directly to levels of dopamine transmission in the brain. Over time the dopamine response becomes "over-sensitized". What the addict is looking for is improved wellness feelings, but what he gets is poorer self-care. This finding is true for all addictions; however, the reality is that people cannot abstain from eating as they would any other addiction or vice, even sex addiction. The ambivalent pattern between approach (I'm hungry, I earned this!) and avoidance (I'm so fat, it's not a healthy choice) creates an ambivalence where the sensitization of the dopamine, which might have guided an appropriate choice, is not as actively in play anymore.[126]

---

[126] Is there one center of "craving" for all addictions? "All addictions are characterized by an excess of norepinephrine, which is concentrated in a small area of the brain called the locus ceruleus. A person may subdue biochemical excitation in this area of

Once addicts are getting help, their anxiety can be slowly abated and they may become more interested in controlling their bad habits, substituting instead many better ones. This process may start with the simple tool of compassionate self-talk, a relating to and acceptance of that which is, and recognizing that one's inner fears cannot truly be allayed through the addiction. This is the cognitively based process of CBT therapy. The path to recovery may not be smooth or easy, but a clear look at the personal factors which are the cause of the anxiety will inevitably ease the trauma and the shame.

Can the notion of recovery allow us to "recover our future?" This notion seems to be the one most binding social construct of our times. In other words, to create our own path means to compose our Self and our beliefs in outside CONNECTIONS.

Levels of Arousal, Seeking Intimacy

As much as addiction can be viewed as the result of chronic attempts to change or maintain a certain level of arousal, ultimately it is the changes in behavior that are the most noticeable (all are a part of the stress regulation process) if one wants to return to a median level of socially acceptable and responsible behaviors. Disrupting behavior must be the first to be challenged by the nonaddicted and non-aroused parts of our brain. Instead of using an external substance to deal with anxiety, the addict must become a "warrior" and learn to challenge his or her addiction to a daily fight, responding to the inadequacies within, because addicts will always have their inadequacies. "Release the attraction, take on the appropriate form of learning [pause and reflect], whatever it is that will help you with your sensibility. There are times when there is wisdom waiting as the rest of you prepare for the journey. There is no shame in this decision" [emphasis added] (Zukav, 1989, p. 159).

Some forms of comforting ourselves are a translation of normal cravings for intimacy into another satiating form of need-satisfying and over-dependency, where the object of addiction becomes a projective recipient of needs, dreams, fears, inadequacy, and rescuing behaviors. Known as Codependency, it is defined as a "symptom" in individuals who organize their lives—decision-making, perceptions, beliefs, values—around something or someone else. Often there is a pattern of dominance/submission in the dyad and a loss of independent autonomous self in the Codependent person within the relationship. Just as a child learned through accommodation as an infant (Piaget, 1962), in an intimate

---

the brain by using cigarettes, alcohol, or opiates. During withdrawal, however, the locus ceruleus over-fires, producing too much norepinephrine, which results in the common experience of craving. The fact that stress elevates the level of norepinephrine in the brain may account for the increased craving and frequency of addiction relapse during periods of duress or conflict. The model may also help to explain the high frequency of dual addictions, as in the upper-downer cycle of cocaine-heroin dependence, and the various combinations or switches between risk-taking, alcohol, cigarette, and opiate abuse" (Milkman and Sunderworth, 1998, p. 110).

relationship where Codependency is apparent, the major accommodation is loss of Self, turning the craving for CONNECTION into a need coming from a false Self, often based on role reversal and a feeling of responsibility for the Other.

> The all-or-none view, and the loss of self required in the codependent position underscore one of the most significant themes in the treatment of the [codependent]. This gives the illusion of control. 'I was always on guard, always ready for the next crisis or disaster, the next drunken binge. Now the only time I feel off duty is when I'm alone' [emphasis added] (Kammersgard, 1989).

Hopefully these wounded individuals may eventually turn to others and attempt attachment as a satellite bond of sorts to the relationship they already have with their primary "It". As a partner, they may show behavioral problems while trying to maintain intimate behaviors; the thought disorders often common among addicts create shame and isolation. Even within a committed relationship they may continue to be preoccupied with their family of origin issues even after leaving home, which can cause them to fail at school or jobs. "To focus on themselves is to run the risk that a calamity will occur in their family, and they will not have done all that they could to avoid it. Such children feel abandoned and are constantly frightened about the loss of one or both of these parents" (ibid, 1989).

Psychological providers try to treat this fear and dependency by examining the environment, the inhabitants, the age at onset of the addiction, the resources outside of the family, the innate constitution, and the interactions of all these factors, which creates a systemic evaluation, or Unified Field Theory (UFT) of the developmental issues influencing addictive behavior. Usually there is a discovery that the CONNECTION of the child/individual to the family of origin is based upon some (mis)understanding about what is expected in the family to maintain homeostasis and/or their definition of normality, even though it might be at a heightened level of arousal, as discussed above. There can be no real escape from the "disability" of addiction, but a new adaptation may develop, a new normal.

Likewise, we might want to take a moment to look at the "introverted" narcissist (co-addict), or the person whose Codependency is based on being the one person who can help the addict, therefore giving the co-addict a sense of purpose and meaning. This type of Codependency is very common, and I often see it as a secondary diagnosis in the women I treat.

> There are hundreds of self-help books written on this problem and it might be self-evident that a person willing to throw themselves into dependency onto another non-gratifying individual might have no problem with a system of recovery spelled out in a non-threatening, but also non-intrusive and non-demanding way. I recommend the living, breathing, we are here for you unconditionally format of a 12 Step Program, but hey—that's me (Beattie, 1986).

Addiction as a Form of Defense

Can addiction be viewed as having originated as a psychological defense? It seems to me that the activity of addictive behavior is as protective and distracting as any other of the Freudian defenses (such as denial or projection). In addition, by taking away the experience of anxiety, by changing the defense structure, an addiction can produce a perceived higher level of adaptive functioning, at least temporarily.

If you add addiction to the list of other defenses such as denial, disassociation, projection, and externalization, you have a picture of avoidance and protection, which these defenses serve. As the practice of avoidance of anxiety can start at any age, sometimes very early, lack of recovery from the need for dependency can intensify the experience of anxiety in the subsequent Freudian stages. If mirroring, and attachment, has not been achieved in each developmental stage, then there will be a further weakening of the ego's ability to grow in a healthy way.

It is important to differentiate between love and projection (which causes an illusion). Children project their needs upon the mother, and the need for wisdom and power upon the father, whereas the mother and father will project their inner image of the future and immortality onto their children. It would be hard to grow within a world without projection, yet if one wants to experience a purer love, then the removal of projections (if possible) is imperative. Part of the unified vision of CONNECTIONS is that one can assimilate the paradox of the opposites as they are experienced—experience life without preconceived notions. We often pressure ourselves with logical thinking that turns into compulsive action. We are healthier when we listen to all the voices within and take note of all the reactions of our bodies. This is CONNECTION and integration.

The many aspects of the UFT will add complexity as each stage advances, as does the nature and condition of the parental influence. Kammersgard agrees we should look for all these symptoms during and/or by the period of development Freud called "latency" (approximately six to twelve years old/puberty) when "consolidation takes place, and peer group (hopefully healthy) could be an 'It'."

I once had a preteen boy who was brought in for therapy by his father because he had gotten in trouble for sneaking into a movie theater. The parents were divorced, and the mother not only admitted to a drug problem, but often had cocaine in the house where her two children could have accessed it. She didn't seem to think the issue of "sneaking" was such a big deal. I finally got the boy to admit he hadn't even wanted to see the movie; it was the "rush" of sneaking into the movie he was enjoying. I immediately set up a meeting with both parents and pointed out the importance of getting the boy into sports, collecting something, or more social opportunities because if he didn't discover a passion for something legal, he would be distracting himself very soon over his anxiety about his home situation with drugs, or behavior even more lethal. The father agreed, the mother didn't (sic). The liveliness of one's CONNECTIONS is rooted in the trust and wonder seen in even the youngest infant. What inspires gives one passion, which is what one lives for. On the other hand, suffering and injury are an obstacle to maturation.

William Styron wrote a book entitled *Darkness Visible* (1950); it joins the handful of books written in my field that truly moved me and helped me help others. He writes about his own long period of suffering and how depression is "the great self-loathing, the sense that it is the way it was, and would be, forever." It is our society's most common form of stress-related disorder and self-alienation. As the author was himself the victim of suicidal ideation and debilitating depression, he is best able to describe how the Self, which he defines as the mediating intellect, was helpless to protect him. "The ferocious 'inwardness' of the pain produced an immense distraction that prevented my articulating words" (ibid, 1950, p. 20).

Styron refers to the myth of Sisyphus, who was fated to roll a boulder up a hill over and over without final success; he states that in the absence of hope we must still struggle to survive, and we do—by the skin of our teeth. It is likely that the sense of abandonment in the chronically depressed stems back to childhood losses, learned helplessness, and fear of intimacy, all enhanced by the current expectation of loss and abandonment.

> Loss in all its manifestations is the touchstone of depression and the cause of its origin…The loss of self-esteem is a celebrated symptom, and my own sense of self had all but disappeared, along with any self-reliance. This loss can quickly degenerate into dependence, and from dependence into infantile dread…One dreads the loss of all things, all people lost and dear. There is an acute fear of abandonment (ibid, 1950, p. 56).

As noted, Freud established a hierarchy of defenses; Blanck and Blanck (1974) and several other theorists (Adler, 1907; Jung, 1934; Erikson, 1950) built on this hierarchy. I have long believed that depression is also a defense as much as a pure "emotion" as it has so much cognitive undertone activating it. So much of depression is driven by anger, or what we believe about a situation, what has happened or been "done to us" by another, or our sense of disappointment, also a cognitive process. On the other hand, true loss is really grief, isn't it? Any of us who have experienced real despair do not need me to explain the difference between that ordeal and an ordinary sense of "depression" about something. During despair/grief we tend to shut down automatically; the depression that comes from anger turned inward is the feeling that could send us to a bottle, a cookie, or the casino. You don't eat while in despair, trust me!

Commonly, alcoholics, compulsive eaters, and those with other substance abuse disorders attempt to hide from the pain and feelings of fragility through their substance of choice. For Styron, and thousands of others who have been successfully treated for depression, survival seems rooted in a deeper sense of Self, a cognitive base for decision-making, as opposed to the emotional base of most impulsive decision-makers who then regret their decisions and become depressed. An understanding of personal needs for fulfillment is what Adler calls "lifestyle" (See Chapters Three and Thirteen).

Further Treatment Issues

Sometimes addictions, which may begin to quell anxiety, also need to be seen from the position of a causative/specific injury and subsequent PTSD point of view. For the purposes of our discussion, the term Outlier refers to those individuals who either do not fit in socially by social or life experience, or may indeed fit an external criterion, but they themselves feel they don't fit in.[127] Life becomes unmanageable and, because they are unable to "fit in", the urge to escape pulls them further and further away from healthier CONNECTIONS and into a powerless need for isolation and the use of substances to control stress and anxiety.

As noted in Chapter Twelve, the quantum events of anxiety do not just exist one particle at a time; experienced as waves, they persist! [If the "drug of choice" is food there can even be a result of "acquired dopamine deficiency", repeated exposure to drugs of abuse or fatty foods which leads to down regulation of dopamine receptors, where the food is sought out despite obvious negative consequences (Davidson, et. al, 2013)].

For a few paragraphs, I would like to address molest specifically, not only as a trauma that can cause childhood PTSD, but as a specific cause of identity crisis and the need for ego defense by searching for an "It". After the child has attempted to tell an adult, a lack of validation by the receiver of this "secret", which often happens, is seen by the victim as condoning the acts.[128] Henceforth anxiety about Self as victim begins and can be repeatedly reinforced.

Part of the long-term effects, impacts, and causative factors of PTSD from a sexual molest is how the child defines the molest in his or her own mind. Memories are painful and a great deal of resistance and repression aids denying or not identifying past sexual experiences. The child may confuse the prompts of the sexual molest with the outcomes of their feelings about the molest; ultimately a confused paradigm about themselves, their sexual feelings and their secrets becomes permanently damaging. "What does daddy do with that (penis)?" "What does he do to mommy, I am like mommy, will he do that to me?" or "He does it to mommy and they are close. If he does it to me, will we be closer? If not, he must not love me." A feeling of rejection is then experienced. This type of thinking is often the justification that step/or birth daddies use to convince little girls why he needs to do what he's doing to her during the molestation.

---

[127] In Outlier analysis, although outside the normal curve by one standard deviation or more, an Outlier can have a highly significant impact on the total outcome of the statistical average of the overall measurement. In a likewise manner, a social Outlier can easily affect the outcome of any social or family situation by his or her behaviors or lack of attachments.

[128] "The earlier the trauma in a women's developmental stages, the more resistance to facing those past painful experiences. The mother may choose to use denial as her defense mechanism because of her fear of confronting the male, frequently her marital partner. Confrontation may lead to separation or divorce from her lover; or often worse for the child, facing herself and child if she does not leave the offender" (Lerma, 1988, dissertation).

Although there will be an entire chapter devoted to deeper treatment issues (Chapter Nineteen), specific therapeutic techniques have been found to be helpful to those individuals dealing with addictions who reach out for help. Changes in consciousness are seen as the area of best practice, because addiction is known to be the outcome or side-effect of underlying anxiety. Author Harold Bloomfield (1976) writes that it is the inner energy gone awry that leads to stress (anxiety) and it is in treating anxiety, then PTSD, then the actual substance being abused which becomes the order of emphasis to find ways to handle this stress that can help overcome the negative behaviors we have used to deal with it.

We really are "slaves" to our habits. When a habit is first established, we never anticipate what the long-term result will be. Later, we never ask ourselves what the original purpose of establishing this habit was. We only know that compulsive behavior relieves anxiety. For instance, we know many people use food to change how they feel. They have developed an "automatic habitual behavior". But as they learn to inventory how they use food as a coping tool, they can learn other, healthier, tools to assuage the original anxiety. This is the simplest definition of addiction: "use of a mind-altering substance or behavior, in spite of its negative consequences."

The only exception to this relief of anxiety might be found in cases where anxiety has become part of the individual's identity, and pathology is framed within his or her personality diagnosis. In this case, such as with obsessive-compulsive disorder, for instance, meditation may help with symptoms, but it may have slightly fewer positive results. I am familiar with the Personal Orientation Inventory (POI), a measure of self-actualization (used in my own thesis, see Haradon, 1975), which shows that frequent meditators' sense of inner directedness increases. Likewise, it can show their ability to express feelings through spontaneous actions, to accept certain levels of anxiety or anger management as "normal".

Hypnosis

Another methodology sometimes sought by those suffering from addictions is hypnosis (also briefly mentioned in Chapter Nine). Not as common in this country today as in other parts of the world, variants to hypnosis also exist, such as mindful meditation to begin a session, EMDR, and other breathing techniques. Why is it possible, beyond a form of suggestibility and relaxation, that hypnotic treatment forms can help with addictive behaviors? Initially, there were two schools of hypnotic belief existed—the Nancy school, founded in Nancy, France, by Bernheim and Liebeault, explained the behavior of subjects in a trance, not in physiological terms, as the Paris school did (followers of Mesmer led by Charcot), but in terms of a conscious and an unconscious level of the reaction.

Freud would also incorporate hypnosis into his treatment, comparing hypnosis to the quiescence of being in love. He found the same compliance, and absence of criticalness during and after the trance experience.

If one looks at the methods of induction used in hypnosis, we can see the similarity between the process and certain forms of meditation. Clients can draw their attention away from distress or pain and instead put it on a "chosen" increase in dissociation, changes in physical sensations, and even heightened integration of Self (Marcus, 2015). Disorientation can become mindful; new attentional skills and the establishment of a link to new experiences can arise.

> The client collaborates with the therapist about which relaxation imagery to use, thereby increasing client involvement and the likelihood that the client will follow through on new suggestions. The basic skills of hypnosis—including relaxation, imagery, and suggestion—are taught. These skills can then be practiced preparing for anxiety-producing situations and ultimately, in vivo exposure (including depression and/or rumination (ibid, 2015, p. 6).

Ultimately, hypnosis is just an alternative method for offering suggestions to create "changes in perception, behavior, and coping." Indeed, I often think of teaching my patients mindfulness meditation as a form of "self-hypnosis". Typically, the subject's need for compliance is balanced with his or her need to assert autonomy, and this combination of needs will ultimately result in a passive resistance during the induction. Suggestion is usually implemented by definiteness and emphasis of statements but may be given in a more indirect manner to induce the lighter stages of hypnosis.

Use of hypnosis in psychotherapy usually falls under two major areas, either to enhance the patient's control over himself, or to uncover the material the patient has repressed. In enhancing his control over himself, involving the patient as an active participant in the hypnotic process, in detailing the methods of induction and perhaps even teaching the patient self-hypnosis, the subject will become more convinced that, with his cooperation, he has some control over desired changes in his life and in the hoped-for resultant factors in his therapy.

> The use of active psychotherapy with hypnotherapy and self-hypnosis has been found to lead to an understanding of the precipitating factors of the neurosis or anxiety reaction, and to a resultant synthesis of the various factors which will offer security and change in the patient, i.e., a secure center. If nothing else, the idea of placing the patient under some degree of personal responsibility for his change and health is nicely facilitated through trance induction. It draws the therapeutic relationship away from the dependence upon the doctor as an authoritative figure into one of collaboration and cooperation (Haradon, 1975).

The goal of hypnosis, ultimately, is to replace a negative compulsion with a more adaptive or perhaps even consciously controlled compulsion, because the bottom line is that an addict is dealing with having a compulsive personality, which cannot be "cured", only remediated. Often a compulsion may even seem "psychically" driven, or at least the leading obsessive thoughts tell the patient so. "Healing" is viewed through a new sense of self-awareness and willingness to acknowledge how external pressures cause over-reactivity. It is most constructive to focus on causes or behaviors about anxiety, on the interpersonal aspects which feed into individual's vulnerabilities.

Impulsivity, especially that rapid, unplanned reaction to stimuli without awareness of negative consequences, is usually emotionally triggered. Difficulty with self-control, as well as impulsivity, is seen as a part of the trait view of personality and can be an underlying influence on the addiction process. Sometimes one experiences the internal cues as a sense of urgency (compared to the external behaviors that everyone else can see).

Emotion regulation abilities and "strategies" contribute to psychological well-being; how the strategies become effective, however, varies according to whether the stimuli are inner-directed or outer-directed (Naragon-Gainey, McMahon & Park, 2018). Outer-directed responses require attention to factors such as engagement, which is found to be more successful than avoidance. Emotional expression and external support, which leads to relief from anxiety overall, will result from the creation of more secure feelings and finding a "still place" that gives security and puts us nearer our Soul (Sullivan, 1953).

Dual Diagnosis and DBT

Practical considerations for the behavioral components of addiction (bereavement and anxiety due to loss of control and attachment) are particularly complex in a dual diagnosis situation. "Dual Diagnosis" is the psychological term for an individual whose presenting symptoms have a classification under the Diagnostic and Statistical Manual (DSM-5), but are exacerbated by underlying addictions, especially drug or alcohol abuse (the abuse formulates the secondary diagnosis). These diagnostic situations usually respond best to Dialectical Behavioral Treatment (DBT).

In DBT, there is a treatment "target hierarchy" (Linehan and Dimeff, 2001) that has been determined through an organized interview and set of criteria which look for self-injurious and suicidal behaviors commonly found in individuals with dual diagnosis. Obviously, these dangerous behaviors take priority in building the treatment paradigm. The "dialectical" nature of the behavioral treatment is based on strategies which acknowledge the reality of the addict's conflict and skills-deficit in self-care, while at the same time providing a challenge to the self-destructive and circular nature of the negative thinking process. Some of the techniques employed include improving skill use, effective strategies for asking for what one needs, saying no, and coping with interpersonal conflict. The skills taught are intended to maximize the chances that a person's goals in a specific situation will be met, while at the same time not damaging either an important relationship or the person's self-respect (ibid, 2001).

A second set of skills includes distress tolerance, such as learning to bear pain, which is a very difficult skill for addicts, who usually began their addiction to an "It" as an escape from pain in the first place. Depression severity can be concurrently measured in pain-management situations (behavioral or physical) by measuring: 1) anger regulation skills, 2) pain-related guilt, and 3) the level of dysregulation in behavioral skills utilization. Coexistent anxiety disorders are often discovered. Learning to accept in a non-evaluative and nonjudgmental fashion, both of oneself and of the current situation, includes acceptance of reality as is. Linehan, the founder of most of the organized aspects of DBT, refers to these acceptance skills as "radical acceptance", because the act of turning the mind toward acceptance, even when one feels willful and angry, can indeed feel like a radical and miraculous act of "willingness".

Assagioli includes acceptance as one of his five stages of growth with "subpersonalities" (recognition, acceptance, coordination, integration, and synthesis) and suggests an "evening review" of one's life for that day (Hardy, 1990). This review process is strikingly like the 12-step model of the acceptance process, as well as doing the 10th Step daily, to review one's behavior and/or need for immediate amends. Tolerance is the key, and acceptance is "the key to all our affairs" (*Big Book of AA,* p. 86).

One final set of skills—emotional regulation—is an important process, especially for individuals with borderline personality disorder and suicidal individuals who are frequently emotionally intense, easily aroused, labile or unstable. Suicidal ideation is caused by a negative interpersonal state, where belongingness has been thwarted and the individual's sense of being a burden to others has been enhanced. Given the high statistical interactive effect found between these two factors (in research by Joiner, 2005), treatment should raise positive interdependence during a period when social competence and belongingness skills can be addressed therapeutically.

These skills are particularly important for creating the surrender to "powerlessness", which Step One in the 12 Steps requires. A lack of these skills would make accepting the intensity of one's powerlessness more threatening. During this act of surrender, individuality is temporarily stripped away and the person becomes "willing" to turn desire away from the addiction and toward a spiritual experience. "Not the saint, but the sinner that repenteth, is he to whom the full length and breadth, and height and depth, of life's meaning is revealed" (James, Wm., *Will to Believe,* 1897, p. 169).

AA and the 12-Steps

We have been leading up to one obvious paradigm for addiction treatment and solution, which is 12-step programs. First founded by two men, one who got sober and stayed sober by helping another, the program has grown from 100 members in 1935 to 100,000 members in 1950 to over 2 million members worldwide in 2005. It has been extended to almost all possible areas: GamblersA, NarcoticsA, OvereatersA, and so forth. Even without a specific meeting, the "steps" can be worked on with any problem: admit powerlessness, surrender, do an inventory, acknowledge character defects, and ask for them to be removed, make amends, and reach out to others.

This is where love comes in, love for others and self-love. "Surrender is yielding inwards to one's own feelings, vulnerabilities, intuition, and aliveness— the hidden garden of you to the unknown you. Surrender is falling love with yourself" (Mandel, 1985, p.10). In fact, these twelve steps don't have to be organized specifically according to the outline of the AA Big Book but have been used by many subsequent theories, including psychological ones. For instance, in the spring 1990 edition of *Meditation,* "An Esoteric Interpretation of the 12 Steps," presented a relabeling of the steps as:

1. Consciousness
2. Recognition
3. Surrender

4. Acceptance
5. Disclosure
6. Will to change
7. Forgiveness
8. Law of Karma
9. Correcting Karma
10. Commitment
11. Prayer and meditation
12. Service

The point is that the work of the 12-Steps gently and courageously can lead all of us, addict and "sober" student of life alike, out of a state of Self-centered destructiveness and into a state of freedom and responsibility. The addict may find himself/herself not only sober, but soberly walking a spiritual path that leads, eventually, to an initiation into a new life, a new awareness. This "initiation" is a spiritual awakening and marks a lifelong commitment if he or she is willing to make it. The Ancient Wisdoms describe "Initiation" as a symbolic indication of inner attainment, as expansion of consciousness wherein the aspirant/disciple enters a new and wider dimensional world.

> We are led to a mystery that is embedded in all initiations and in every rite of passage: the end of a previous form of existence is felt as a real death...He discovers by his own experience that he is lovable. Further, he loves himself as an object... "I am stuff. I am made up of things and qualities, and in loving these things I love myself. '[I] can be a piece of a larger scheme of transformation...I see this as a movement away from human subjectivity and into nature.' Narcissism heals itself away from loneliness into creation: in our narcissism we wound nature and make things that cannot be loved, but when our narcissism is transformed, that result is the love of self that engenders a sense of union with all of nature and things" (Moore, 1992, pp. 63–74).

Sometimes, with sobriety, our new life may present a possibility of loss; our old selves may have been destructive, but they were our old lives—fear of loss can block the potential of hope and growth in our new lives. We learn to deal with loss, with trust, with disappointment and with hope. The reaction to this loss varies from person to person; some rage with an exaggerated sense of total loss of Self, others just feel displaced and isolated, without a newer set of behaviors to deal with shifts in hope and trust.

Some, who are recovering, shut down completely, surrendering totally to the anxieties of the world and the need to reduce their demands upon the world. For many people who have never experienced elements of an esoteric life or even concrete spirituality, the 12-Steps are the first step into this world. Obviously, we do not want people to become hardened, to lose compassion or empathy. But by this act of surrender, the 12-Steps become the First Initiation.

The goal of healthy Self-discovery is to turn concealment into revelation, silence to expression, and isolation to intimacy (Erikson). One states, "I care about maximizing my experience of life, and I am able to develop inner resources to create separate 'needs' and 'fantasies' from 'wishes' or even 'dreams'" (Milkman and Sunderworth, 1998, p. 188). Having become open to this experience, the next step in an individual's journey of Self-discovery will be through healthy Self-care and centeredness. Experiences of wounding turn into healing, and we find we can be open to life coming to us; we all get a call to adventure. These are the options of Self-actualization. However, let us first collect our Selves, and perhaps even our Shadow sides; presented in the next chapter, it is through C.G. Jung's work and the study of symbols, myths, and archetypes that he has helped us interpret the Collective Unconscious.

Chapter Seventeen
Carl Jung Archetypes and the Unfolding Spirit of the Self

> Only one thing is effective against the unconscious, and that is hard outer necessity...the 'simple life' cannot be faked...Only what is really oneself has the power to heal.
> – E. Abdill, 2003, p. 117

Introduction

As we have seen in Chapter Sixteen, in some ways we are all Outliers. Each of us probably has an "addiction" to some thing or some compulsive tendency. We relate better to our peers, perhaps, because of these mutual types of experiences. Each of us has developed into an individual person with some system of values, beliefs, and character from which we react, decide, or hide, and to which our immune system reacts during daily stresses. How we adjust (some people better than others) is based either on accommodation or assimilation. If we cannot help ourselves and/or if we have recognized that over-dependence on an "It"/substance has not rescued us, then we may turn to some theory or significant healer outside ourselves to "fix" us.

There is a well-held theory that one can understand nothing psychological unless one has experienced it oneself. This concern for truth brings into focus the concepts of prior contextual training (UFT) and epigenetics, both ideas that address influences (conscious and unconscious) which impact and CONNECT judgment and experience every day. Time and space considerations may have immediate effects, but our level of observation also determines our ability to "fit in". Extroverts may have an easier time with social functioning, but introverts may have higher adaptive skills. How the unconscious responds to the need to adapt is usually much more "egocentric".

Carl Jung created his theory using input from instincts, including Eastern thinking, wisdom and language studies, myths, and ancient knowledge along with modern scientific findings (Hardy, 1990). He was drawn to both the Kabbalah of Judaism and the Gnostic writings of early Christianity. He came to believe that identity can be found through mysticism as much as through psychiatry. I love Jung's inclusion of the perspective of time and space into his psychological theory of the Soul; the Soul seems no longer to be an "It", but an Intelligent Being which can be accessed.

This early nod to dualism, physics, and the inclusion of metaphysics into a general theory of psychology (or Unified Theory!) explains his attempt to integrate the many influences in his life from spiritualism to Schopenhauer to science. Given the core theme of this book, how we achieve the integration of all developmental aspects of experience through CONNECTION, this theme also explains my overall emphasis on Jung in this chapter.

In Chapter Thirteen, we discussed several theories of psychological development that attempt to explain the sequence of healthy human evolution. We began to describe similarities and differences between two theorists in particular—Freud and Jung. The history of friendship, collegial partnership, and eventual theoretical falling away from each other of these two giants in the history of psychology is commonly known and found in many other sources. The following initial history is a summary of their relationship and Jung eventually breaking away to develop his own theory, which was more spiritually based. Much of it is based on my own exposure to Jungian theory while in graduate school.

Jung first met Freud on May 24, 1907. Freud was much impressed by Jung's analytic methods and his fresh approach to psychoanalysis. Jung became known, also, for his amazing ability to get people to comfortably be themselves. Many who knew him came to see him as a Renaissance man due to his varied interests, which is probably what drew me so strongly to his theory. This "combination of charisma, simplicity and directness" created an excellent balance to Freud's academic style. Freud invited Jung to go with him on a lecture tour in America in 1909 (Hayman, 1999).

Both Freud and Jung found that the dream was the richest area from which repressed wishes were uncovered. They also both believed that when the individual shows regressive thoughts and behaviors, it is to a stage before any trauma during his development; his safety, his dependency and his security disrupted. This period of dependency is not usually found to be in direct relationship to his parents, but to images or symbols which represent the father or mother, because the fantasy usually deals with a distorted image created (archetypes) by the individual and not an actual memory.

There was, however, an undercurrent of disagreement between Freud and Jung almost from the beginning. I think Jung recognized it even more than Freud but tried to maintain the friendship, nevertheless. Although they continued their relationship, professional and personal, for another two years, in 1911 Jung found that he had to make clear to Freud his disagreement with Freud's sexual interpretation of libido. Freud believed that the relationship between members of a family were caused by Eros, but they were maintained by the libidinous energy of the id, necessarily leading to incestuous feelings. By 1912, Jung disagreed openly and clearly saw that his own view of the libido would be divided into three periods:

> a pre-sexual phase which ends at about the age of three; a stage at which boys normally develop the Oedipus complex (a term he disliked) and girls develop the Elektra complex (a term he invented); in the third phase, the adolescent should direct his libido away from the family. If it leaks incestuously backward, regression and neurosis ensue…Jung redefined libido in terms of energy conservation. When too much libido is invested in one activity, too little goes to another, and the task of psychoanalysis is to adjust the balance (Hayman, 1999, p. 157).

As the differences between the men and their theories grew, Jung received his last letter from Freud on January 3, 1913. By then, Jung had already begun to ask himself deeper and more personal questions about what his study of psychological types had begun to show him. Much of the source of his questioning came from his use of the Word Association Test.

After using over 25,000 stimulus words on 150 normal subjects, he discovered that "the quantity of associations depended on the sound of the stimulus word (as opposed to its meaning) and was inversely proportional to the subject's attentiveness, which could be reduced by illness or exhaustion" (ibid, 1999, p. 77). Jung began to not only use a stopwatch to accurately track the period before response, but he also noted the silences, slips of the tongue, voice tone, and volume, along with any involuntary or unpredicted bodily movements. Eventually his use of word association shifted to the process of "free" association, which he called transposition, and which allowed him to talk with the client about whatever topic that came to mind.

These experiences led Jung to ask himself the question, "What is your myth by which you live?" (Arraj, 1985, p. 105). Throughout his career, and especially in his private life, Jung focused on the "heroic deed", both in himself and others; eventually, almost everything he analyzed was couched in terms of these ideas of myth. While the extrovert can lose himself with the myth, the introvert could lose his soul through the hero's journey, creating an experience of Self-transformation.

Jung called this being "controverted", where the perils of the Soul could threaten the individual from within, but the Soul was ultimately protected through stability and indestructibility. The individuation process was a fight for transformation, not in a corporeal sense but as a totality of the personality, which must take responsibility for a projection of one's internalized prior experiences (UFT) onto present processes.

Thus, individuation is the process whereby a person discovers and evolves his Self, as opposed to his ego. The ego, of course, is a "persona", a mask created and demanded by everyday social interaction, and as such it constitutes the center of our conscious life, our understanding of ourselves through the affirmation from others. "The Self, on the other hand, is our true center, our awareness of ourselves (ala mirroring from the mother/parent) without outside interference, and it is developed by bringing the conscious and unconscious parts of our mind into harmony" (Berman, 1981, p. 69). This harmony is becoming yourself as you were meant to be from the beginning. The more central the core of Self/Soul, the more whole the personality, with a sense of security coming through being able to retain identity/integrity. This goal is the ultimate purpose of a long life lived fully.

Jung believed that myth gives us knowledge of the living psyche, in the Collective Unconscious and in an analysis of individuation, concepts which will be discussed in detail below. Unconsciousness was broken up into a Personal Unconscious, a Cultural Unconscious, and finally the Collective Unconscious, a term for which he is perhaps best known. Within the Collective Unconscious, we see motifs of the archetypes: mother/father, fear/joy, and so forth, as well as fire, theft, deluge, land of the dead, virgin birth, and the resurrected hero, which have all built a fund of mythological beliefs and experiences (Campbell, 1988).[129]

The basis of Jung's studies, unlike Freud, was that every individual alters and expresses their "archetypes", or symbolism, in their own unique way. He defined an archetype as "composed of an instinctual factor and a spiritual image," signifying a particular spiritual reality for that individual as he manifests a constellation of symbols in his consciousness (Ostrowski-Sachs, 1971). It is like having had a "prime imprinter" or possibly even an inherited [epigenetic] experience of functioning. To Jung, it is the most basic form of the schemas to which one adapts in life.

In *The Interpretation of Nature and Psyche* (1955), Jung states that archetypes are "active, living dispositions, ideas in the Platonic sense, that perform and continually influence our thoughts and feelings and actions…to the extent that the archetypes intervene in the shaping of conscious contents by regulating, modifying, and motivating them, they act like the instincts." Over the years he would hold his own lectures and full conferences to formulate a broader view of psychology. He began to focus specifically on affect (emotional experiences) and periods of emotional imbalance, rather than the sexual repression that had been so important to Freudian theory; as we will later see in detail, Jung considered the central archetype to be the Self.

Jung came to call these early years the most important period of his own "individuation". Individuation comes from an integration of consciousness in the individual, where the relationship of the conscious to the unconscious becomes clearer (Arraj, 1985, p. 109). In other words, one becomes what they were "meant to be". The Jewish Kabbalah refers to the *En-Sof*, God reposing in himself; the unconscious, like gravity or other field forces (numinosity), can only be apprehended indirectly [and with uncertainty]. Jung thus believed individuation is made up of three states: God, the Self, and the ability to relate beyond the illusion of daily life [I can see the influence of Eastern religions here]. The word *in-dividius* means un-divided. Jung CONNECTED myth, mysticism, and religion (Drob, 2010).

Eventually, Jung became interested in alchemy (separation and unification/*Solve et Coagula*), or *kimia* (Persian word for elixir). Alchemy came with a long history. The practice of alchemy had traveled from the Greco-Roman world, to the Islamic, to medieval Europe. Chinese alchemy was connected to *Taoism* and Indian alchemy and with the Dharmic faiths of *pao zhi* and *Ayurveda*.

The study of alchemy had also been a long-time influence on the Kabbalists and even CONNECTED Jung to the study of the Gnostics (third century *Zosimos*), whose spiritual "unity" was the *pleroma,* a totality of the divine powers and

---

[129]Turning spiritual experiences into creative mythology is one of the most important mythological traditions of the modern world. "It can be said it had its origin with the Greeks, to have come of age in the Renaissance, and to be flourishing today in continuous, healthy growth, in the works of those artists, poets, and philosophers of the West for whom the wonder of the world itself—as it is now being analyzed by science—is the ultimate revelation" (Berman, 1981).

emanations. In short, alchemy is believed to provide the possibility of unity of the Soul with the body. The idea of gnosis and Jung's study of the Gnostics proved the intuitive knowledge of God was possible. "With respect to the Gnostics, the process of self-perfection is essentially one of self-discovery" (ibid, 2010, p. 103).

This triangulated study (Kabbalah, Gnosticism, and Alchemy) was to provide Jung with a core set of beliefs. They carried him into studies during the second half of his life, where he searched for his own "philosopher's stone" (By the way, this is also the process of "Bisociation" that Koestler referred to in his book *The Act of Creation*, 1964). To Jung, the philosopher's stone equaled enlightenment and individuation itself. It was an alchemical process because parts of the unconscious became a unified Self (the Persian word, *Chymical*). However, where the Gnostics looked for escape from the world [see the Gospel of Philip], ultimately Jung looked for redemption in the world. "If he is to achieve enlightenment, he must be submitted to the painful process known in alchemy as *divisio, separatio* and *solutio.* 'Every step forward along the path of individuation is achieved only at the cost of suffering'" (Hayman, 1999, p. 372).

Jung's primary studies in this area predated Heisenberg's major contribution to physics, the "Uncertainty" principle. Jung based his early beliefs on structured and empirical facts and felt that evidence would vary dependent upon the nature of the observation, nature of the measurement, and where on a spatial to non-spatial continuum the measured observation was to be placed.

The more we turn from special phenomena to the non-spatiality of the psyche, the more impossible it becomes to determine anything but exact physical measurement…(An) experiment consists in asking a definite question which excludes as far as possible anything disturbing and irrelevant. It makes conditions, imposes them on Nature, and in this way forces her to give an answer to a question devised by man (Jung, as quoted in Arraj, 1985, p. 111).

Jung believed that emotionally charged ideas, originating from the ego, tend to cluster together (emphasis on the influence of social values and individual experience) and tend to seek out the source of man's identity for sanctuary or comfort (we think of this as the Self or ego-consciousness). This knowledge is given to the psyche through the subject's relationship to the Collective Unconscious, which Jung stated stored the history of humanity. "It is only individual ego-consciousness that has forever a new beginning and an early end. But the unconscious psyche is not only immensely old, it is also able to grow increasingly into an equally remote future" (Jung, 1939, p. 24).

Basic Psychological Concepts

As mentioned, the basic psychological concepts which distinguish Jung's thinking from Freud's original concepts are these beliefs in a Collective Unconscious and the belief in archetypes, complexes, and symbols. While archetypes are a "thought form" created out of images that "correspond in normal waking life to some aspect of the conscious situation" (AATBS, 1977), complexes are more organized groups of feelings, memories, or perceptions (creating the UFT). Other important concepts in Jungian psychology are that of the personal unconscious, from one's UFT, and the four functions (thinking, feeling, intuition, and sensation) which expand his two basic personality types (extrovert and introvert).[130] Core issues also include the concepts of the Soul-image and the persona, which mediate man's relationship to himself and to society. "All of the contents of the conscious mind are compensated for by the contents of the unconscious mind" (ibid, 1977).

The introvert is more strongly affected by archetypes (external symbols) than the extrovert, and the extrovert is slower to recognize similarities between "things" or abstract concepts in general; introverts are much more likely to use reason and intuition to develop ideas and judgments into conceptual responses rather than basing their responses on experience or sensory input alone.

Sensation comes from perceiving things as they are and not otherwise. Intuition also "perceives", but less through the conscious apparatus of the senses than through its capacity for unconscious "inner perceptions" of the inherent potentialities of things. Jung defined two concepts to explain how the ego relates to either the subjective or the objective world, according to the different functional types, superior functions, and auxiliary functions. Therefore, ultimately there are two 2x8 possible combinations of type and function, combining into 16 possible type combinations. The 16 Personality Factor Test (16PF) was created by Raymond Cattell in 1946 to test for these concepts; the Myers-Briggs Type Indicator (MBTI) was created in 1962.

Jung's concept of the persona describes an organized sense of Self which is exclusively concerned with the relationship being formed with the object or the outside world. Persona is "the mask worn by the collective psyche to mislead other people and oneself into believing that one is not simply acting a role through which the collective psyche speaks" (Hayman, 1999, p. 207). Conscious development is through ideals, goals, and recognition of our social roles. At this point, it is important to understand how Jung used the ancient Greek concepts of the soul-image (*Anima* and *Animus*).[131]

---

[130] For instance, the attitude of the unconscious as an effective complement to the conscious extroverted attitude has an introverted character. It concentrates the libido on the subjective factor, that is, on all those needs and demands that are stifled or repressed by the conscious attitude.

The extrovert is someone whose energy and attention are directed outward to the people and things in the world around him; adaptation is decisive…His own inner world is less real to him and a secondary influence on his conduct. In contrast, the introvert's energy and attention are directed inwardly. His own inner world is that which he adapts to…(The) outer world is less real for him and therefore of less influence than the inner world (Arraj & Arraj, 1985, p. 19).

[131] "These two basic archetypes were added to the persona, or presentation of personality, as were the Shadow, the Self, the *Senex* (Old Man), *Puer* (young man),

The archetypes might be described as "self-portraits of the instincts." They are meant to denote an inherited type of psychic functioning which may often go around consciousness to lead to behavior. This work-around is psychologically necessary, although not consciously recognized (Jung, 1939). Jung discussed two core archetypes most frequently; they were the *Puer* (vitality youth/conceit) and *Senex* (wise old man/complacency). Because he was aware of the danger that implicitly lies in opposites, which instruct us but can also split us, he was also aware that *Puer* and *Senex* cannot CONNECT; our task is to heal the split to repair the soul-rending *puer-senex* opposition. These were the main archetypal images that Jung felt corresponded to mythological motifs and brought familiarity into our everyday lives. They compensate for the outer personality and provide a link between the personal and the impersonal, between the conscious and the unconscious.

When Jung broke with Freud, he had already begun to find substitute father figures in William James and Theodore Flournoy. James' work on mysticism and his seminal book, *The Varieties of Religious Experience* (1902) influenced Jung's growing inclusion of subjective experiences and their analysis in his theory. James' use of the terms *I* and *Me* (and later Martin Buber's book, *I and Thou*, 1923) may have directly influenced Jung's newly developing differentiation between the terms Ego and Self, even though he continued to refer to many of the original psychodynamic terms. Theodore Flournoy (1911) was developing his own psychology of religion, and believed that awareness of one's subliminal cues beyond the metaphysical was important for human experience, psychological and biological. "Analyzing dissimilarities between himself and Freud, [Jung] had concluded that he was introverted while Freud was an extrovert. Freud, the extrovert, had produced a theory 'which is essentially reductive, pluralistic, causal and sensualistic.' It is 'strictly limited to empirical facts, and traces back complexes to their antecedents and to simpler elements'" (ibid, 1999, p. 168).

The concept of the *libido,* which Freud had originally meant to be analogous to "energy" (as used in physics), had begun to provide a dynamic, not static, picture of energy for the way in which individuals view their behaviors. Jung stated: "I am a point that requires space and time to expand into consciousness [the idea of relativity in quantum energy which he called the *pleroma*]." Jung adapted the principle of entropy from physics to describe personality dynamics, as energy is distributed and always seeking balance or equilibrium. "If I am all things, I cannot distinguish myself from the rest or recognize what is different from me. Man is the dividing line of the acts of consciousness; he illuminates the night of the unconscious around him."

"There is no balance, no system of self-regulation, without opposition. To be whole is to be full of contradictions" (Jung as quoted in Ostrowski-Sachs, 1971). Jung believed that man, ultimately, was indescribable because his Self could not be completely grasped. As I have indicated, individuation is a term used in Jungian psychology to represent the achievement of total Self-realization, "the process of

---

the Mother, the Father, the Hero, the Trickster, etc., all seen as projected mythological expressions" (Drob, 2010, p. 119).

fulfilling potential by integrating opposites in a harmonious whole...if madness divides the self, sanity is unity" (Hayman, 1999, p. 217).

When we discuss archetypes, it is important to see how a description of an archetype provides an opportunity to create "the natural balance of masculine/feminine polarities" (Bolen, 1984). This recognition of our opposite Self, or "Shadow", can help guide us on our path of self-awareness. We try on different identities, a recognition of our many selves which sit at the conference board table of life and help guide our inner thoughts into our outer voice. This view of the personality "personifications" which develop through the *anima* (in the man) or *animus* (in the woman) sets us up to understand how individuation proceeds.

The *anima* is a female image/archetype that arises within a man's soul and is viewed as his spiritual counterpart or completion; "being essentially feminine, the *anima*, like the woman, is predominantly conditioned by eros, that is, by the principles of union, of relationship, while the man is in general more bound to reason, to logos, the discriminating and regulative principle" (Jung, E., 1957, p. 59).

The *animus* would be the similar image for a woman's internalized view of men. The animus or male archetype in a woman directs the need for power toward something of "great significance", using intellectual tendencies and spiritual guidance that is not coming from a "feeling" function, but rather from "suppressed feminine interests."[132] For either *anima* or *animus,* the loved one, (who is the spiritual intermediary), is also at the same time perceived as a "human being to whom one has a positive, human relationship."

Our search for the archetype, however, may cause us to deceive ourselves about CONNECTION and will blur our powers of discrimination. The error is based on the original "limerence", where in early love we enjoy the pursuit of a sense of ecstasy caused by the Other invested with *anima* or *animus* qualities.[133]

---

[132] "Since each archetype speaks for a particular instinct, value, or aspect of a woman's psyche (the totality of her personality), the amount of say that any one voice has depends on how strong that particular archetype is, how involved it may be in that particular agenda item, and how much of the floor the ego (as chairperson) allows the archetype to have" (Bolen, 1984, p. 267).

[133] "If the possibility of spiritual functioning is not taken up by the conscious mind, the psychic energy intended for it falls into the unconscious, and there activate the archetype of the *anima* or the *animus*. Whereas feminine thinking is driven by 'thinking, imagining, wishing and fearing,' a man's experience of his *anima* is where 'she' is destined for him that he cannot live without, she is his other half. He gains a sense of CONNECTION by giving help and protecting; unfortunately, there are signs that many men take pleasure in women's 'unconsciousness.' They are bent on opposing her development of greater consciousness in very possible way because it seems to them uncomfortable and unnecessary. Because the anima, as the feminine aspect of man, possesses this receptivity and absence of prejudice toward the irrational, she is designated the mediator between [his] conscious and unconscious" (Jung, E, 1957, pp. 25, 56).

If we think of the internal voices of our "many selves" forming a council of intentions, then the *anima/animus* may show up as judgmental and even counterintuitive to the more basic personality tendencies. Adolescence, for instance, is an unbearable age because puberty brings differentiation from parents and the eruption of sexuality; internal/external impulses oppose each other.

Consciousness and Imagination

Much of the process of imagination is stimulated with reminiscences and instincts or impulses generated from what Jung believed was the Collective Unconscious. This concept was like the "eternal" ideas of the Greeks. Jung had been influenced by the Greek historian Herodotus, and a book on Babylonian excavations, as well as four volumes by the classical philologist Friedrich Creuzer, *Symbolism and Mythology of the Ancient Peoples Especially the Greeks* (Hayman, 1999). He claimed his favorite reading was "Egypto-Hellenistic with a Gnostic coloration."

> He always tended to mythologize his experience. [In addition] Jung was reading voraciously as he worked on *Psychological Types*, which was to be published in 1921. The enormous range of reference shows how carefully he had studied Gnosticism, Tertullian, Origen, Lao Tse, Meister Eckhart, *The Shephard* by Hermas, which dates from AD 140, a Latin translation by Ficino of *De Insomniis* (*Concerning Dreams*) by Synesius, the Cristian bishop of Ptolemais and pupil of Hypatia, Rousseau, Schiller's *On the Aesthetic Education of Man*, Carl Spitteler's *Prometheus and Epimethus*, Worringer's *Abstraction and Empathy* and Otto Gross's books (ibid, 1999, pp. 118, 178, 218).

Jung determined that perceiving was an act of sensation, whereas conceiving was an act of imagination. Thus, a creative imagination gave birth to much of the lineage and artistic representations so deeply cherished in Judeo-Christian heritage; an example of this giving of lineage was Isaac passing on his blessings to Jacob. In that Jung's father was a Swiss clergy man, from whose strong opinions and practices Jung tried initially to distance himself, this eventual coming to a reconciliation between imagination and religion was a powerful influence in his life.

Jung traveled to India and Africa, practiced the Chinese *I Ching*, and studied the American Navajo culture. His experiences helped his cause of putting forth the idea of tribal influences in mythological/archetypal material; at about this same time Bronislaw Malinowski was also presenting his research of the Trobriand Islands off New Guinea (1920s). Likewise, Levy-Bruhl's (1910) idea of "participation mystique" was changing views of primitive mentality. Both men contributed studies that would change anthropology forever. Jung's own main point at this time, I believe, was that while science and technology had ever increased our productive directed thinking, the thinking of antiquity (as Malinowki showed) was of the "fantastic" type, and that this is the kind of thinking we turn to during dreams or regression (what he believed was a method of "direct access" to the unconscious).[134]

> The instincts and archetypes together form the "collective unconsciousness... and the archetype recurs constantly throughout history and appears wherever creative fantasy is expressed freely." Each archetypal image contains "a little piece of human psychology and human fate—residue of the pleasures and sorrow that are recurrent throughout our ancestral history...The collective unconscious comprises in itself the psychic life of our ancestors right back to the earliest beginnings. It is the matrix of all conscious psychic occurrences...The archetype is a kind of readiness to produce over and over again the same or similar mythical ideas" (Jung, 1929, as quoted by ibid, 1999, p. 227, 348).

Jung maintained "the primitives were better than we are at releasing the powers that lie dormant in every human being" (Jung as quoted by Hayman, 1999, p. 292). He made the CONNECTION between the civilized and the primitive by seeing the polarity and the inter-CONNECTIONS that could come close to a unified explanation for everything.

Koestler cautions us to not equate "underground" processes with "repressed" as per Freud. Dreaming, for instance, is the psychic metabolism, the stuff of which our sequences of understanding are constructed. "In essence, the brain areas responsible for executive control, logical decision-making and focused attention shut down during dreaming, while sensory and emotional areas come alive" (DeAngelis, 2003, p. 46). And dreaming does not just refer to what we do in our sleep, but rather more broadly to that which we do in our waking life with our symbolic Self. "As the dreaming mind works to process feelings, concepts and to potentially solve problems, the conscious mind can give it an extra boost...The key is to translate dreams' messages into creative urges and products" (ibid, 2003, p. 48).

Jung believed that dreams predict the greatest transformations or fantasies—images that are facts to the one who experiences them. He stated that we should observe the stream of images, looking for archetypal symbols and patterns within them, especially in the introvert personality type, whose fantasies are especially factual, certain, and part of his dignity. (The goal is to differentiate delusions, hallucinations, fantasies, and dreams one from the other!) One could say that while

---

[134] "It is the subliminal Self which knows how to divine, to choose. Pictorial thinking is older ontological ideation than verbal thinking (which can be more virtual in meaning). 'Thinking in pictures dominates the manifestations of the unconscious—the dream, the hypnogogic half dream, the psychotic's hallucinations, the artist's vision.' (The visionary prophet seems to have been a visualizer, and not a verbalizer; the highest compliment we pay to those who trade in verbal currency is to call them 'visionary thinkers'). But on the other hand, pictorial thinking is a more primitive form of mentation than conceptual thinking, which it precedes in the mental evolution of the individual and of the species" (Koestler, 1964, p. 168).

man is sleeping, he is most truly alive. The symbols and insights that are created during a dream are the closest truth about a man's personality that we may get (Fromm, 1968). Fromm (1941) added that dreams were the method by which man transcends his awake societal boundaries. In dreams, man "becomes fully human".

The Sensate personality type focused on the experiential tended to interrupt awareness of the individual pattern of reality. Jung believed that these clues help us widen our mental horizon out of the present into timelessness. Because he also included a spiritual viewpoint in his developing theory, Jung approached ego development through this lens as well. "I am not whole in my ego, just a part, center is the whole; an acorn cannot become a horse, you will become what you are meant to be. He ought to get there, but most get stuck; the way there is to spend time on oneself" (Friends of Jung, lecture, 1990). These positions became strong within the psychological community at the time of Jung; we see influences of his ideas and work throughout 20th century culture.

Jung believed that the unconscious personates the "fluid boundaries of the self" as represented in the unconscious mind. It confers on it the gift of empath (*einfuehlung*), of entering a kind of "mental symbiosis with other selves." In some cultures, this is the gift of the Shaman, whose role is "to induce the patient to an act of faith, to submission, worship, transference, catharsis" (Koestler, 1964, pp. 181, 188). Likewise, to make this meaningful CONNECTION is the bliss experienced by client and therapist alike during a powerful and rewarding therapeutic session.

Jung took some of his ideas of energy from the growing field of physics (de Broglie had introduced particle-wave duality for matter in 1927); he also incorporated his own studies of alchemy and spirituality (and even spiritualism). Others might currently call this type of theoretical formulation about ongoing cultural influences as the idea of epigenetics, but at the time, Jung maintained that God is simply representative of the sum of energy like the Kabbalah *scintillae* or "sparks" (Freud's *libido* or early stages of conscious development). Jung's idea of the energy from the Self's discovery and CONNECTION with the energy of the unconscious was almost one of making God-consciousness incarnate. This experienced need for continual CONNECTION and spiritual searching may be one of the reasons why he took up and continued the study of alchemy for the rest of his life. "The opposites were so much united in him, and he was by this time so whole, that more one-sided people were inevitably drawn to him to get at least a glimpse back into their own lost wholeness" (Hayman, 1999, p. 298).

This energy, then, is projected [as a wave] from the unconscious outward, the first level of which is the father transference (although Jung did not personally like this term). It is not God's form which is important, it is His power (*libido*). Longing for God is a desire to reach and understand potential, the vital force within. This channeling out of libidinal energy, therefore, facilitates individuation, and while there can be a lack of energetic balance, which is experienced as depression or negativity, there will also be a balancing experience through awareness of the archetypes. We are searching for what touches and inspires us, and from which our imagination creates and recreates something personally relevant. The individual finds himself surrounded by symbols which soon become organized into a system.

Jung's use of symbols was intrinsic to his method, regardless of how all three major theorists of the time (Freud, Adler, Jung) tended to use material uncovered by patients looking backward into their histories for signs and symptoms, often direct links to painful and repressed material. Jung used these recovered histories to develop an intricate pattern of symbols and myths about the person, "while depersonalizing and demystifying personal or sexual material" that Freud might have focused on. Not that Jung did not influence Freud somewhat, at least in the initial years.

The Function of the *Libido*

The primary personification of the *libido* in mythology is in the hero, conqueror, or demon. Heroes are almost always wanderers, which is symbolic of the [libidinous] longing, the desire to return to the deepest sources of our own being, the mother image. "Any man will be afraid of the woman who enslaves him so that he can no longer free himself and will follow his own path to self-sacrifice and rejuvenation" (Haradon, 1972a). Jung felt that the will, which may become completely introverted in relationships, therefore loses productivity, and becomes completely subjective. We are each of us looking for our Other who will, however, not limit our pursuits but only contribute toward our rejuvenation.

Man's tendency toward fantasy thinking can be creative, but complete introversion leads man away from knowing God, or our own *libido* as we are searching for it in the context of reality. Directed thinking, on the other hand, is productive and leads to the advancement of the species, but we should not completely lose touch with our creative and symbolic past (Campbell, 1988).

An equilibrium of these two aspects of human nature can lead us to an exciting and satisfying search for our own identity in the common and CONNECTED cosmos of which we are all a part. Jung felt that an "uniform field of symbolic presentation" required awareness of man's nature and tendency to use both logical thinking (Freudian perspective), where the analysis is outer-directed, and analogical thinking (Jung's preference).

As Adler had addressed the formation of needs, Jung discovered the source of many "secrets" by deconstructing the patient's archetypes. Often, he believed that what is secret is what is the most sacred. On the continuum of experience, secrets of the Ego (at one end) were part of the dichotomy of secrets of the Self (at the other end), which he called the Great Mystery. Secrets did not have to be seen as repressed or pathological but could be viewed as helping the individuating person learn to discern, perhaps considering as well that some secrets would still need to be hidden. Jungian therapists believe that revealing the secret is a form of dualistic experience (open-reveal/closed-hidden).

Sometimes as knowledge of the archetypes and the psyche's secrets become revealed, the result is transcendence (the archetype having served its function as intermediary). Again, wholeness is only a hypothetical end of a continuum of experience, perhaps approachable after moving in that direction through a heightened state of awareness and acceptance of one's spirituality, sometimes known as Higher Power. Much of the impetus for this growth is the result of intuitive and synchronistic experiences of the "mystery of life, a psychological reality beyond words" (Friends of Jung lecture, 4/6/17). Therefore, although not always on a conscious level, unveiling of one's secrets can be a catalyst for change, even if it cannot be verbalized.

In summary, to delve deeper into Jungian concepts here, or further on one's own, it will be important to understand certain key concepts:

1. Collective unconscious—universal or unconscious mind shared by all members.
2. Personality types—a) extrovert b) introvert
3. Archetypes—complexes, symbols
4. Personal unconscious—at one time in consciousness
5. Ego—reference point of consciousness
6. Self—total personality
7. Shadow—negative side of impulses (birthplace of projections?)
8. *Anima* and *animus*—female aspect in male and male in female.
9. The ego—assimilated by the Self
10. Persona—identification with societal personality, outer attitude.
11. Four functions: a) thinking b) feeling c) sensation d) intuition
12. *Libido*—psychic energy
13. Individuation process

(Haradon, 1986)

Within the study of such concepts, however, I believe it is now most useful to have a context for understanding Jung, the man. Who was Jung?

Jung, the Individual

Like many others who are driven by their innovative spirit and a renaissance view of the world, Jung used his study of the classics—culture, values, art, and humanism—to guide him in his search for the psyche. C.G. Jung was like his grandfather before him, Carl Gustav I (1823), who went to Basel and developed a curriculum in "*Therapie,* a combination of the latest medical technique and philosophy that was used to treat mental conditions," and his father, Paul, whose dissertation was "on the tenth-century scholar Jephet Ben Eli's Hebrew commentary on Solomon's Song of Songs" (Bair, 2003). As a renaissance personality, Jung's interests went everywhere, and he grew within and beyond that great shadow under which he was first nurtured.

It was his maternal grandmother Gustele, however, who was to first influence his ideas for the "collective unconscious" and his own personality theory. Her spiritualism, belief in multiple personalities, and in an "omnipresent, unchanging and everywhere identical quality or substrate of the psyche per se" had the strongest effect on him (ibid, 2003, p. 15–16). Thus, Jung's personal development was balanced between mother/father aspects: spiritualism and religious theory. "He was already building the foundations for his theory that the psyche's most important relationship is with itself, that the path to spiritual maturity is through integration of the self" (Hayman, 1999, p. 33).

If one were to think about the transition to the "I am...my Self" moment in therapy, where the individual no longer is outer-directedly measuring and evaluating (Self), one might assume, from a Jungian point of view, that there is also a spiritual factor at work, experientially "possessing authority and value" (taking charge) (Bair, 2003, p. 33). Some think God controls this awareness, some call it Dharma. The process may even lead to the need for tests of courage, as in the hero's journey presented by Joseph Campbell (1949). The heroic way (often willfulness) usually starts with a cause, but the hero can lose his way trying to be of "service".[135]

A hero's journey is a life lived in self-discovery. The hero's journey is not to deny reason; "to the contrary, by overcoming the dark passions, the hero symbolizes our ability to control the irrational savage within us...The ultimate aim of the quest must be neither release nor ecstasy for oneself, but the wisdom and the power to serve others" (Campbell, 1990, p. xiv). Campbell says that atonement is about sacrifice and from this sacrifice comes one's bliss.

The hero's quest is a way of action, as mentioned in the 12-Steps described in Chapter Sixteen, and about involvement in the world instead of withdrawal, even within an element of danger; the hero gives his "devotional way" to himself and to others, usually through ritual or ceremony of some kind (ergo AA meetings) (Hardy, 1990). For me, this journey was my international travels, starting with South America at 11 years old, Europe at 26, 31 and 43 years old, Russia at 49 years old, and two trips to India at 50 and 68 years old.

The demonstration of high-risk behavior CONNECTS with the recklessness of youth and "curse of 27 years old" theory. Many famous and/or gifted young adults die recklessly or commit suicide around that age out of a sense of *ennui*, need for more excitement, or both: Jim Morrison of the Doors, Brian Jones of the Rolling Stones, Jimmy Hendrix, Janis Joplin, Kurt Cobain, Heath Ledger (28), and Amy Winehouse. Is this finding also a result of some unusual form of synchronicity? Synchronicity was Jung's term for repeated experiences that indicate events do not always obey the rules of time-space causality, sometimes even seeming like "prophetic foresight." Unfortunately, many young people have died under similar circumstances who are not nearly as famous...

Jung spent time with Eugen Bleuler (1908) and learned about *Affektiver Rapport*—Bleuler's method of working with patients through a process of making a schedule, establishing contact, and developing rapport, all of which would result in a meaningful human relationship (CONNECTION). This CONNECTION could give experiences to the patient which counteract experiencing shame due to a lack

---

[135] Having achieved the awareness of one's willfulness, one can begin to ascend to the true crisis of the hero. The hero myth, as proposed by every culture in every generation, is basically as follows: "According to this universal myth, the beginning of growing up (of being no longer a child) is to go on a journey of your own, leaving—when necessary—the support of friends and familiar community. Find yourself in a situation [new CONNECTIONS] where you have to depend on what you can do, nobody's going to rescue you. You have to stand up and bring off the enterprise...The hero is only a shadow on the screen and as he daydreams his fantasies are awareness which he creates for his own benefit" (Allport, 1955, pp. 72, 179).

of skills (skills-deficit or having been ill-equipped as I often call it in my office). Jung's studies and theoretical formulation came from balancing his social needs with his need for asceticism, a religious CONNECTION which gave these very concepts meaning, "[he had] the soul of ascetic refinement" (Bair, 2003, p. 57).

During these early days, Jung brooded, increasingly about life itself; that is, "the idea of the life he had not yet lived." Jung came to believe we all go through this experience. He considered the question: "What role does yearning play?" As someone who had often felt like an Outlier himself, he was aware that everyone has their own level of philosophical consciousness; perhaps because of his own upbringing, Jung was curious about whether there was more evidence of Father's influence versus Mother's? He began to have a keener interest in myths and archetypal images that might give evidence about this point (ibid, 2003).[136] He set himself the task of developing a theoretical basis that would show where the bridge lay between "inner life" and actual realized and external "self-reliance".

Most of us continue to view the "norm" as a goal; a successful life as an important outcome for which to model to our children. But given the possibility that we have been blessed with a creative child, later perhaps to become an Outlier, what is the youngest age a child could first be shamed by their unusualness and therefore begin the process of self-loathing/rejection? In Chapter Thirteen we saw that Erikson's theory would say 18 months, given the second of his seven stages at that point is Autonomy versus Shame.

Sometimes untangling possible factors can be a matter of discriminating between anxiety from shaming and whether the reaction is a State or a Trait experience. Spielberger (1983) proposed that discrimination between experiences of anxiety shows that there is more than one type of anxiety. State anxiety is a result of the autonomic nervous system and, as we have seen in Chapter Ten, probably uncontrollable by the subject.

Trait anxiety is different, more longitudinal, and a daily type of anxiety that most people would describe as a pervasive experience of stress or worry over longer periods of time. In summary, a child may be taught that he possesses unlikable traits (feels unworthy, undeserving), but didn't those attributes really start out as momentary states of reactivity/impulses? Jung began to include this thinking when he was constructing his theory of Psychological Types (Campbell, 1971).

Jung came to believe that, although one's character and temperament exist at birth, society has much more to do with the outcome of individuation than Freud originally proposed. "The Freudian unconscious is a personal unconscious, it is

---

[136] As a side note, for now this raises the question whether it can ever be a healthy choice to be an outsider/Outlier? The "normative" group of individuals in socialized and structured society view those "outside" normative behavior as too "creative," unhappy, unproductive, or even mentally ill to be accepted. But "exceptional" does not lie far from "unacceptable" in terms of this viewpoint, and many individuals I have interviewed have just seen it as a waste of time to try to "play the game" of fitting in when they have so many better or productive (in their own point of view) things to get on with.

biographical. The Jungian archetypes of the unconscious are biological. The biographical is secondary to that" (Campbell, 1990, p. 51). Jung also believed that an individual could, by way of his archetypes and their influence, have a sense of more than one Self at work at different times. By studying ancient writings, myths, fables, novels, and novelettes (anything of value with a story of meaning to tell), he discovered and labeled certain archetypes that describe the way in which we come to believe a person should behave.

He described the Persona as being developed from the "complicated dictates of society and what one believes that one should be," which could be discovered and controlled only after a period of treatment and the unveiling of the personal unconscious. He defined his concept of Shadow as an unconscious part of one's personality containing those elements the Ego considers negative or unacceptable and would like to annihilate, and that from which the Ego defenses are created to protect consciousness (Knapp, 1995).

When the Shadow is not faced, we are left with a two-dimensional reality. Jung also believed that the act of DISCONNECTION, or even dissociation, was the result of unresolved regressed parts of personality, thoughts, dreams, and particularly compulsions, which are inhibited but create an unconscious that has an independence all its own (Hayman, 1999). In his work, *Coincidentia Oppositorum*, Jung compared the Shadow to the Kabbalistic concept of "the other side (*Sitra Achra*), negative, discarded and evil aspects of Self." Our job is to work toward control of baser instincts, as seen in the Biblical Book of Job. In his work, *Answer to Job* (1952), Jung describes the purpose of creation, how darkness was part of the divinely created world, and that the depths of the human soul, as well as the need to be aware of inner opposites, facilitated individuation.

Individuation

For Jung, every story has a beginning (coming from the unconscious), a middle where the individuation takes place (driven by incidents with progressive complications that increase more confronting of Self and result in the building to a climax, crisis, and resolution), and an end (information is conscious now/completes the process) (Friends of Jung, lecture, 2/13/2009). The individuation process is the result of achieving command of all four functions (thinking, feeling, intuition, sensation).

> In addition to the two basic attitudes, there are four functions which are the ways in which the psyche makes contact with either the inner or outer world. He paired sensation and intuition together as two opposite ways of perceiving. Sensation is the perception of the immediate and tangible reality around us by way of seeing, hearing, touching, etc. Intuition is also a perception, but of what is in the background, i.e., hidden possibilities and implications. Thinking and feeling go together as a pair of opposite ways of making judgments. Thinking is the way of judging about the nature of things by means of our ideas and their organization. Feeling is an equivocal word and means instincts, emotions and hunches as well, meaning a sense of rapport or lack of it by which we decide whether we like or dislike something (Arraj & Arraj, 1985, p. 21).

There are several stages involved in the individuation process. The first stage is the experience of the Shadow, symbolizing our "other side", which is an inseparable part of our psychic totality. The nature of the Shadow is most often inferred from the contents of the personal unconscious. Recognition of the Shadow is a moral problem in that it requires becoming conscious of the dark aspects of the personality as real and as affectively influencing the personality. Affects/feelings occur usually where adaptation is weakest. The second stage of the individuation process is usually an encounter with the soul-image, either the *anima* in a man or the *animus* in women.

This archetypal figure stands in our mind as the complementary part of the psyche, reflecting both our personal relation to it and the universal human experience. Through reflection upon the soul-image, its relationship to the persona becomes apparent. If the persona is intellectual, the soul-image is most likely to be sentimental and sensitive in nature. The persona designates man's habitual outward attitude, while the *animus* or *anima* reflects the habitual inner attitude (Haradon, 1972b).

The transformational process is like the "letters of transit" in Casablanca. It is our yearning and Dharma to search for it, but it may or may not be our destiny to find it (Friends of Jung, personal notes, 2/13/09). This transformation is such a difficult process because as the unconscious leads to conscious awareness of the Shadow, it is viewed as defeated by ego defenses.

Jung and Joseph Campbell's Hero's Journey

Of all the individuals who were influenced by Jung, probably none has had a greater influence than Joseph Campbell. Although Campbell edited a famous tome about Jung, *The Portable Jung* (1971), he felt himself to be his own "theorist, not just a Jungian". His book, *The Hero with a Thousand Faces* (1949), explains the "monomyth" of how we all go into our adult lives seeking to resolve individuation through some type of "mythological journey". During the Depression, alone in a rented cabin in Woodstock, New York, he undertook a five-year study of most of the great literature of history (1929–1934), which led him to conclude that almost all prior Pagan and Greek myths had this aspect of the mythological journey of the hero at their center. This belief in the "power of myth" included, as well, the true stories of Buddha, Christ, and Mohammed.

Campbell's work underscores the need to bring spiritual energies forward, whether within a relationship or in one's own inner imagination. However, our current societal influences, including those from external stresses, tend to "cut away" one's inner world from our basic attitudes, attachments, and life patterns. One's deepest creative sources may not have enough time away from stress to be revealed until retirement or if the individual chooses to take a personal retreat, as Campbell did. I, myself, take one week (and sometimes two) a year, to regroup, meditate, and re-CONNECT with my deepest inner Self. These retreats allow us to find the path of our journey and submit to the energy from one's shadow which we are usually side-stepping or are too busy, or avoidant, to investigate. The symbols, archetypes, and fears that manifest upon reflection, are usually oppositional to everyday consciousness. Detachment facilitates underlying realizations.[137]

Campbell reiterates that the first work of the hero is to retreat until contact with inner is found. "The hero is the man of self-achieved submission" (ibid, 1949, p. 18). From the clearing of Shadow-caused confusion will come a deeper awareness of the meaning of one's archetypes. After he/she leaves home to achieve some great deed, the individuating person returns having experienced more lessons about themselves than just surviving the danger, or even near-death experiences in the greater world (think Achilles and his heel!). They will have gained an improved "personal power"—awareness of a guiding inner voice, and CONNECTION to the Collective Unconscious. This is their transformation experience; "the time for passing of a threshold."

One factor in this path to transformation is an understanding of one's dreams, for the dream is the "personalized myth". Dreams can represent a whole range of daily activities: creative working, decision-making, emotions and even reactions to stress (DeAngelis, 2013). For Campbell, nothing is more important than understanding one's myth, and dreams assist in this process. Understanding inner knowledge can help one reevaluate the "chain of causation" and find redemption and liberation from past parental influences. When underlying forces are not understood, then desires and conflicts may go on being suppressed. In referring to the "call to adventure", Campbell tells us we must face our destiny (Dharma) and find a truer CONNECTION to the deeply felt Soul.

This journey varies according to one's typology, i.e., introversion or extroversion, and everyone's creative genius is expressed differently. Sometimes there is a need for a protective figure (therapist, priest, special friend) to bounce off new insights and reveal archetypes. When one finds their archetype for guardianship and protection, they can unite uncertainties. CONNECTING one's spiritual sense to this new certainty creates a greater sensitivity and light to the "darkness of the Shadow" and its personal meaning.

Where [therapeutic] support is experienced, personal power can begin—in a redemptive action, old messages of abandonment can fall away and be replaced with hope and belief in Self. One of my sisters-in-law once gave me a homemade goblet for putting special what-nots in. Around the rim she had etched, "Turning a crisis into a circus." It sits still today on my bookshelf and has great meaning, today as much as the day I received it. Using symbolic figures and ritualized moments of Self-care, a new experience of purification can come out of the chaos and messiness of everyday life. Our personal past and its dualistic nature can be reconciled into the One which heals. The goal, then, is to discover and assimilate

---

[137] "The inflated ego of the tyrant [narcissism] is a curse to himself and his world—no matter how his affairs may seem to prosper. Self-terrorized, fear-haunted, alert at every hand to meet and battle back the anticipated aggressions of his environment, which are primarily the reflections of the uncontrollable impulses to acquisition within himself, the giant of self-achieved independence is the world's messenger of disaster, even though, in his mind, he may entertain himself with humane intention" (Campbell, 1949, p. 16).

our "opposites" (by bearing the unbearable) and organize our inadequacies to make life more manageable.

Sometimes that which is missing and/or desired is projected onto a Higher Power which is arbitrarily seen as merciful, graceful, and just, thus making available the very attributes missing from early experiences and sought in the Other. By this projection onto Other [Codependency], the ego can abandon its attachments to itself and its laundry list of anxieties. The "middle way" and eightfold path provides balance, self-awareness, and safety.[138] One CONNECTS with Soul through the "satisfying secret of release" (Bhagavad Gita quoted by Campbell, 1949, p. 166).

Spirituality and Symmetry

Campbell proposes that since "time and eternity are two aspects of the same experience, then the essence of life is time." In our review of physics in Chapter Twelve, we verified this spiritual principle through the study of physical properties of space and time. As Buddhists have proposed for over 2000 years, life really is uncertain (Heisenberg) and all existence brings some suffering (chaos theory). The "One God" can be reached by any of man's paths to spirituality; the world is CONNECTED by its atoms and energies. We are each other's mirror, just as God is our mirror until we become our own mirror. "The divine being is a revelation of the omnipotent Self, which dwells within us all. The contemplation of the life thus should be undertaken as a meditation on one's own immanent divinity" (ibid, 1949, p. 319).

Myth, psychology, and metaphysics were first combined into a close relationship in the Orient, including India. "The transcendent function is endowed with the capacity to unite all of the opposing trends of the several systems and to work toward the ideal goal of perfect wholeness (selfhood)" (AATBS, 1977, p.12). As often as there is a balancing of these realities, there is also a need to accept the asymmetry found. Asymmetry is the between of our awareness: movement, the unfinished, the unexplained temporality of life, and transcendent experiences.

Through a search for authenticity the Self becomes assimilated and the Other fades into a supportive position. There is awareness of now, God at a standstill for "God controls time." We must experience disillusionment and bear the unbearable. The hero returns from his search to understand his destiny or Dharma. Going forward, our job is to understand that life is impermanent and immutable, as well as sometimes asymmetrical. "That's what you have to strive for every minute of your life: to get rid of the life that you have planned in order to have a life that's waiting there to be yours…Our spirituality is of the individual quest, individual realization—authenticity in your life out of your own center" (Campbell, 1990, pp. 88, 90). On the other hand, addictive behaviors most certainly block this CONNECTION.

---

[138] The Buddhist Eightfold Path includes Right Belief, Right Intentions, Right Speech, Right Actions, Right Livelihood, Right Endeavoring, Right Mindfulness, and Right Concentration.

How does the "call to adventure" become "illumination?" Campbell explains that the journey must pass through atonement and sacred CONNECTIONS, and one keeps for oneself the gifts which can heal suffering. From here the return (resurrection) unites experience into meaningful expression (of feelings, beliefs, and Soul). Thus, any ordeal leads to a reward, an expansion of consciousness, and freedom. New archetypes are created. Integrity and fortitude are enhanced, from which come evolution of the original mythic (+/-) influences into just being one's "history".

From our ability to embrace silence and an inner Truth comes a sense of mystic or ascetic experience. This is the ultimate outcome of Self-Actualization. One's true character has conquered isolation (outlier experiences) and turned it into something rewarding. Impediments from the unknown have been redeemed and freedom gained. External abandonment and the obscurity from fear and loss have brought one to a knowledge of Self and the ability to even face Death, in others and oneself. Archetypal stages have culminated in acceptance: of aging, of loss, and of the final separation from Self and one's true essence altogether.

Only by belief in fantasy/destiny can the hero cross many thresholds toward resolution of his spiritual trials; readying himself through purification for surrender of the Self to gain transcendence. It is at this very moment of surrender that the hero learns how to assimilate his many selves, to embrace his opposite or "dark side", to gain atonement after he has abandoned attachment to his Ego (Campbell, 1988). Campbell felt that the hero's journey or quest may be "hard-wired" in us all, and he provided many simplified explanations for the complex concepts that are typical in Jungian theory.

For instance, Campbell describes unconscious psychic contents as autonomous carriers of memories lost to consciousness. Unconscious material has teleological significance and acts as "an intuiting agent of a receptivity" (Campbell, 1971). In my practice I have found that a Highly Sensitive Person (HSP) can have much more unconscious sensitivity than average. But the good news is that this sensitivity is also often a source of creativity, i.e., originality and functionality. On the other hand, consciousness is a turning away from instinct and may lead away from the sensitivity and creativity found in the shadowy unconscious where the ability to adapt originates.

Before Campbell's in-depth explanations, Jung tried to restate Kant's concepts (1786) in everyday language, particularly the ideas of attraction and repulsion (Hayman, 1999). We see these ideas especially in Jung's book *Psychological Types* (1921). Kant famously said, "I had to nullify knowledge in order to make space for faith." He called transcendental ideas "things-in-themselves" or "concepts of pure reason". Jung readily accepted Kant's other term for these concepts, *noumena* (as opposed to *phenomena*, which exist tangibly and visibly in time and space), and took the concept further, stating that "instinct is a Kantian interruption of the continuity of consciousness, an abrupt psychic occurrence" (Jung quoted in Campbell, 1971, p. 48).

Finally, Jung went so far as to CONNECT psychology and physics, showing how the unconscious exists in Einstein's time-space continuum. He often thought about unconsciousness in terms of "space", and the human psyche as a form of structured consciousness. In another CONNECTION between psychology and physics, psychology's "law of participation", where a thing can be itself and something else at the same time, is close to the idea of simultaneity in physics, where a thing can be two places at the same time.

Intimacy

"Not feeling like 'myself' is probably just the experience of the unconscious"
–Johnson, 2009

As proposed by Haeckel (1866), ontogeny recapitulates phylogeny—the development of a species over time can be compared with the development of any individual ovum after insemination. Not really a scientific "law", Haeckel's theory was expanded into a "phylogeny of the soul", meaning that "if the development of human thought could be shown to parallel biological evolution as well, the new science of psychology would illuminate the history of psychology" (Hayman, 1999, p. 30).

Having influenced Darwin and others of his time, Haeckel's ideas were embraced for over 100 years (although disputed by others) and eventually were applied to child-rearing, particularly by Dr. Benjamin Spock in the 1960s. "Each of us is a microcosm in which the universal process actualizes itself… Each of us must, in an individual lifetime, recapitulate the evolution of the human race, and each of us must be an individual container in which the evolution of consciousness is carried forward" (Johnson, 2009, p. 7). This point of view reinforces the more current view of humanity's inter-CONNECTEDNESS to the whole cosmos and the importance of CONNECTION with others to serve as a background to the process of our work of bringing "ourselves together".

Although many people relate to the outer cultural imperatives of their childhood, to grow/individuate they must find the path of the inner journey. Inner work requires a lot of careful observation of one's own behavior and is an opportunity for self-awareness and self-reflection. "One of the best ways to discover what you really believe in, what value you are really serving, is to watch your own behavior" (ibid, 2009, p. 75). Because Jungian analysts use archetypes extensively for this process, it is often called "archetypal amplification", and can demonstrate fragments of information that ultimately give us an ability to formulate a unity [or what I am trying to build into my own version of a psychological and developmental Unified Field Theory (UFT). Johnson states that clarity can come from asking questions such as: "What is this archetype doing today in my personal life? What does this have to do with me, as an individual?" (ibid, 2009, p. 64). Is there a committee meeting taking place in my head every time I must plan? Look to the dark, Shadowy side for some of the best parts of yourself!

Archetypes and Dreaming

The inborn mode of acting has long been known as instinct, and for the inborn mode of psychic apprehension I have proposed the term archetype.

– C.G. Jung

The idea of archetypes was not born from Jung; archetypes probably originated as far back as Plato's ideal forms. Inborn symbols and a growing awareness of the unconscious, beyond just that experienced by mystics, encouraged the average dreamer to pay more attention to his/her dreams (think of Joseph and Moses and other characters in the Bible, besides the numerous historical and fictional characters over the last 4000 years). Dreams take archetypal symbols and create a view of the individual's personality dynamics which can guide one toward an inner "energy system".

> The dream is, so to speak, a pure product of the unconscious. The alterations which the dream undergoes in the process of reaching consciousness, although undeniable, can be considered irrelevant, since they too derive from the unconscious and are not intentional distortions. Possible modifications of the original dream-image derive from a more superficial layer of the unconscious…They are further fantasy-products following the general trend of the dream. The same applies to the subsequent images and ideas which frequently occur while dozing or rise up spontaneously on waking (Campbell, 1971, p. 283).

Jung felt that the dream, as a direct link to the unconscious, was an important source for this information. Also, the client histories were a way into what he called "the ancestor component". Beyond how Freud thought of consciousness as "a highly organized internal perceptual process," Jung saw the unconscious "not as an adjective but as a noun" (Schwartz, 1999, p. 137). Jung was the first of many to claim psychoanalysis for purposes other than those Freud had in mind. He wanted to position psychoanalysis as an extension of philosophy.

In studying Tibetan Buddhism, I have come to recognize their belief in something they call the Night Soul. The night soul is one's experience of vulnerability that especially happens during dusk or dawn periods, when one can be more easily and emotionally vulnerable because the sun, light, and experience of time/space continuum is shifting. Just being vulnerable can be valuable.

Jung believed that each archetype has its own "energy". Our developmental job is to translate the dream or other symbolic messages passed along to us and, with this archetypal guidance, discover behavioral and cognitive functioning that works for us. Certainly, the influence will have been matched with, and filtered through, our own personality style. For example, in the Introverted type, psychic adaptation is grounded almost entirely on intuition.

"Thinking, feeling, and sensation are then largely repressed, sensation being the one most affected…When it is the dominant function, every ordinary situation in life seems like a locked room which intuition has to open" (op cit., 1971). As I, as well as many of my friends, are Introverted/Intuitives (INTJ-Myers-Briggs Type Indicator/MBTI), I have long been aware of the archaic sensations that can either lead to empathic experiences and even mystical experiences, or at times highly sensitive compulsions.

In the Introverted type, fear of intimate connections with others can develop into a peculiar kind of cowardliness; the individual shrinks from making himself or his opinions felt, fearing that this will only increase the Other's power over him. This behavior is the singularly most common cause of patients seeking out my help for therapy. These individuals are initially very intense, and all their process and experience of emotional pain is internal, where they see the Other as a kind of opponent who can harm them, even if this is because of a projection of their oversensitivity.[139] Because the Introverted Type presents with some devaluation of the Object (It), introverts' egos can be more fragile and are often well-defended. Friends and loved ones observe compensatory reactions in the introvert and a difficulty with intimacy at times.

In the Extroverted type, the psychic relationship is "always governed by objective factors and external determinants" (Campbell, 1971, p. 229). If one adds, to either of these two types, the function of Thinking, then we see a complex where the individual just wants to be left alone "in peace to pursue his ideas." Jung believed that "degeneration of the personality sets in" if a patient is left to himself; however, with this person's intelligence, he can also reject criticism, and external causes of isolation do not necessarily bother him if he has a sense of protection by ego defenses to pursue his ideas and plans. "He lets himself be brutalized and exploited in the most ignominious way if only he can be left in peace to pursue his ideas…Only with the greatest difficulty will he bring himself to admit that what is clear to him may not be equally clear to everyone…" (ibid, 1971, p. 243).

In considering individuation, Freud proposed that a regulating "counteraction" will always develop in the unconscious as well. Jung, on the other hand, liked to think of the dream as the expression of the process of individuation and growth, its symbols "embedded" in a *mandala*, a circular drawing of one's own making. It is the visual symbol to which one is drawn, due to its ability to nonverbally express an inner sense of Self or "Journey toward Individuation". Just as the *mandala* usually contains one's symbols of peace or discord, one's symbols of individuation are represented in discovery, growth, and recovery, as we will see in the next chapter.

---

[139] Our depressions, jealousies, narcissism, and failures are not at odds with the spiritual life. Indeed, they are essential to it…they provide their own seeds of spiritual sensibility. The ultimate marriage of spirit and soul, *animus* and *anima*, is the wedding of heaven and earth, our highest ideals and ambitions united with our lowliest symptoms and complaints (Moore, 1992, p. 263).

Chapter Eighteen
After Individuation
Discovery, Growth and Recovery

> Often men are more afraid of the [heroes'] trail, of failing the ordeal, than of death itself. Impotence, Powerlessness in any of its forms, is worse than annihilation…work, war, worry. Beneath displays of power is the complex, beneath the complex lies fear. Sharing has its place, but personal change is primary.
> – James Hollis, 1994

As a Hegelian, Jung proposed that "every form of life contains its own inner antithesis" (Jung, Collected Works, Vol. 12).[140] I often think of therapy as a dialectical process between the therapist and patient. Conflict helps to articulate "polarity and paradox", which are the core personality concepts needing dialectical balance and synthesis; the real working through of the conflict takes place to achieve a form of core resolution of divergent parts and thus unification. Reciprocity is modeled by the therapist during the treatment and can subsequently be used in everyday life by the patient, as in the Self-made manifest. Man reflects his own collective unconscious in a type of reciprocity and clarity by resolving paradoxes.

In Jungian terms, this process is the cornerstone of his entire psychology and is found largely in the reconciliation between the *anima/animus* process, where indeed the unification of the Self mirrors the Kabbalistic concept of ethics, because everything is transformable. Things fall apart, true, but then they can be reintegrated. In Chapter Fifteen, I wrote of how adolescence causes the youth to "blast themselves" out of the family. Separation is a natural progression at this stage; it is also a symbolic death of childhood dependency that still temporarily traps the adolescent and the parent alike, sometimes causing a rift that may never be healed within the family.

Once separated, the adolescent/child is now free to learn the practical lessons of the world—responsibilities of adulthood and some of the mysteries of personal and private functioning, not unlike the "Magic Lady" story about my own childhood told elsewhere. In a kind of rebirth process that Margaret Mahler (1973) called secondary individuation, the adolescent learns that intimacy and trust for himself leads to trust in others. A true sense of Self and identity can be formed. This process is the evolution of Life itself.

---

[140] "For Jung, the dialectic or coincidence of opposites is a mythological progression, one in which a collaborative, archetypal, mythological mind (the collective unconscious) becomes estranged from itself in a conscious, personal, and rational ego…ultimately returns to itself through a series of symbolic unifications that merge unconscious and conscious into a united 'Self'" (Drob, 2010, p. 236).

Both Campbell and Hollis talked about how an "ordeal" would provide a young person an opportunity for growth and the necessary closure of prior dependence upon the one's family in preparing for adulthood. "The essential part of being an adult means not only that one can no longer turn backward to the protection of others, but that one must learn to draw upon inner resources" (Hollis, 1994, p. 19). After the resolution of this primary ordeal, the heroic return occurs (Campbell, 1949). The [boy] is truly an adult, there is a period of tertiary rapprochement (Mahler), indicating that the bonds have not been totally broken.

However, the *ennui* and disastrous outcomes for many men who turn to alcohol, or to lives of other addictive behavior, is reflective of their Shadows having threatened the better intentions of their egos. I have seen many patients act out this process of splitting off part of their Shadow/soul. Never having gone through the process of separation outlined above, they are not psychologically integrated, and what is not integrated will be projected onto others or show up in other dangerous behaviors. In contrast, it is in the moments of self-sufficiency that one best finds their true Self and regains their full Power and Strength.

In a splitting between the acquired personality and the natural Self a need for falseness is created. In the seriously mentally ill, splitting as a factor of personality flaws (or character defects) shows unresolved internalized fears and boundary issues during the therapeutic process. What happens to the individual whose internal and external processes may be going through an arbitrary "splitting" during this attempted adaptation toward balance? Indeed, as Freud stated, this splitting may be seen as a period of "regression" in individuation until there is an adaptation in moral development and an understanding of the Self's needs to gain balance.

The Shadow may be revealed, the patient (through skills training) becomes equipped to deal with daily stresses, and the splitting of black or white thinking is allowed to be gray if necessary. Splitting is never the solution and can be a serious long-term symptom, for all parts of the persona must be developed and maintained. This process is aided by journaling, both life experiences and dreams, to provide daily structure and to develop a roadmap toward uncovering that from which one might be forced to split off.

A good example of a creative person facing their shadow is found in the life of the writer Herman Hesse (1919, 194e, 1971). Jung met Herman Hesse in March 1916, when Hesse was thirty-eight years old. Hesse had been interested in psychoanalysis for several years and had already read both Freud and Adler. Hesse's childhood, like so many gifted children, was often difficult. His parenting was full of rules and regulations which trapped Hesse's sensitive nature and intensity of feeling. Later reviewers (Stefan Zweig and others) felt strongly that it was Jung's influence that finally deepened the metamorphosis in Hesse's "poetic nature".

Hesse no longer had to avoid his negative emotions. *Demian* (1919), and its focus on the newer concept of "inner space" where transcendental vision can be experienced, was Hesse's first real Jungian novel (Hayman, 1999, p. 242). In this novel, Hesse quotes the Greek historian Herodotus, a great favorite of Jung, and shows the influence of other favorites such as St. Augustine, Nietzsche, and

William Blake. "Whoever wants to be born must destroy a world [Shadow]," Hesse states. This comment alone shows the Jungian heroic journey that was later also noted in the analytical Jungian writings of Joseph Campbell and James Hollis.

Even Hegel had been influenced by a pre-Jungian view of "thesis versus antithesis", that analysis cannot be black and/or white but must be evaluated in a more "relative" and global view of total effects, values, and outcomes. In fact, Jung discussed the transcendent function of opposites as the aim of active imagination, where the subject is required to "concentrate his attention on an impressive but unintelligible dream-image or visual image" (AATBS, 1977, p. 13). Here the middle position (synthesis) supports the realization of the whole, despite the Self's paradoxical nature. Here we can also see the influence of Einstein and physicists of the time, who Campbell enjoyed reading (as do I).

The Male Psyche: Work, War, Worry

Does the manifestation of individuation and Self-building vary dependent on gender? Do men react to archetypal stimuli differently than women? James Hollis wrote a wonderful book regarding specific issues in men, *Under Saturn's Shadow: The Wounding and Healing of Men* (1994). In the Greek myth, Cronus hated his children for he feared their potential. Legend tells us Cronus was "the first to devise shameful actions" toward male children for outgrowing parental control. Hollis goes on to delineate the outcome of this shaming by a parent to be deep-seated feelings of self-rejection and fearfulness, which the author feels is universal within the male gender. He summarizes his findings into the following list:

The Eight Secrets Men Carry Within

1. Men's lives are as much governed by restrictive role expectations as are the lives of women.
2. Men's lives are essentially governed by fear.
3. The power of the feminine is immense in the psychic economy of men.
4. Men collude in a conspiracy of silence whose aim is to suppress their emotional truth.
5. Because men must leave Mother, and transcend the mother complex, wounding is necessary.
6. Men's lives are violent because their souls have been violated.
7. Every man carries a deep longing for his father and for his tribal Fathers.
8. If men are to heal, they must activate within what they did not receive from without (Hollis, 1994, p. 11).

As much as our society, or our socio-cultural traditions, might support these positions, academically one question still exists—how can we teach our children the skills and strengths to break free from this pattern?

"The male child desperately hopes for information, for modeling, for leadership, for instruction, for help in coping with that which will shortly confront and perhaps overwhelm him…the youth desperately hope that 'they' will take him aside and teach him what he needs to know." Hollis describes how "they" never took him aside and told him what it meant to be a man or how to conduct himself as an adult (ibid, 1994). Our society, and societies across the globe, have rites which provide us with archetypal encounters to give us a sense of, and movement toward, the richness and depth of the cultural values which we are meant to absorb.

The real development of an individuated personality requires the dialectical "separations and evolutions" Jung spoke about in *The Symbolic Life* (1939). Likewise, this concept of evolution is shown through Campbell's concept of the hero's journey. Long before Hegel, the Greeks related concepts in dialectical paradigms and, just as Jung was influenced by Hegel and the Kabbalists, the Kabbalists themes were influenced by Plato and Neo-Platonism, Christian mysticism, both Hindu and Buddhist thought, and the German idealists such as Schelling and Hegel (Drob, 2010).

The Path of Manhood

For many of my male patients, the primary symptoms of dis-ease are the issues of control. I look for symptoms of how the patient tries to control his environment, ways in which he demonstrates feeling "sentenced to life", defending against life, against risk and commitment, and how addiction is a very active method of projecting his anxiety and angst onto the "It"/Drugs/Sex/Food which he can so readily obtain and control. Jung describes the way this process might even feel heroic to the addicted person, because he is controlling the process of losing control.[141]

Hollis feels the easiest place to look for symptoms of this pattern is through the man's *anima*, or projected female *yin* side, which he has internalized from the maternal bond. [Yet inside he still is seeking to serve Her, win Her favor, be Her good child].

> One of man's greatest developmental tasks is to achieve a healthy separation from the bond with his personal mother. He must also develop an awareness of the importance of the image of the archetypal Mother…Unlike the daughter, the son lacks a primary identification with his mother, especially as he begins to psychologically emerge from her. In adult life, remnants of the original attachment/separation problem are conveyed by a man's internal anima image (Loren Pederson *Dark Hearts: The Unconscious Forces That Shape Men's Lives*, quoted in Hollis, 1994, pp, 47, 74).

I have long proposed what I call my "two speeds theory". It states (not so tongue-in-cheek) that men generally have two speeds: "I don't care" and angry. Both are attempts at control, as in following example: You ask a man want he

---

[141] "Dissolving an image means that you become that image [the positive hero]. Doing away with the concept of God means that you become that God. This is so because if you dissolve an image, it is always consciously, and then the *libido* invested in the image goes into the unconscious. The killing of the hero, then, means that one is made into a hero, and something hero-like must happen" [emphasis added] (Jung as quoted by Hayman, 1999, p. 176).

wants for dinner: response, "I don't care" (Repeat question), "I don't care, really anything is fine" (Repeat question, give several choices), "Look, I told you I don't care, you pick" (not wanting to decide or upset the other person, usually a spouse.) (Repeat question, now with a sense of urgency as the other is getting hungry and this isn't the first time they've played this game!), he responds, "G*d damn it! I told you to pick. Go get anything, go by yourself, see if I care…whatever!" Sound familiar?

In this example, the man's *anima* is speaking to the Other, his need for nurturing and fear is couched in not wanting to make the decision, but he shows it through his long gender-developed skills of assertiveness, competency, and empowerment. There isn't much unconditional acceptance and nourishment for the Other, nor does he know how to obtain it for himself in this situation, where he feels the other should know what he wants! Over time, even sexuality can be an infantile need for bodily contact and nurturance, although most men may not be quick to admit this fact. But the greatest loss is when men "fear" their own *anima* and therefore abandon their need for relatedness, expression of feelings and CONNECTEDNESS.

One of the saddest sources of anxiety, addiction, or even mental illness I see in patients is the burden of an underdeveloped [unconscious] adult male trying to compensate for the unlived lives of his parents. The telling of this story goes all the way back to the beginning of written history, when Sophocles (409 BCE) had the Chorus in his plays tell us how heroic it was not to be Self(ish), even though most of his characters, and the majority of characters in every great novel (and play) since then for that matter, seem destined to face their own regressive and powerless nature within which lies loneliness, fear, anxiety and self-pity.

As we saw in Chapter Sixteen on addictions and mental health issues, these negative attributes are the source of most character defects because of our inability to be self-compassionate, Self-nurturing, and Self-determined. We must learn to accept our negative emotions, to refine them and, through taking a sense of responsibility, to find authenticity. Intense separation anxiety early in life will show up in the ways in which the body reclaims the same fight/flight/freeze sensations due to loss of attachment (with fear of abandonment); the need to mask these feelings may be deferred to addictive behavior.

But if the individuation process has never been completed, and the man's *anima* accepted and internalized, this process of Self-identification cannot have been achieved. Hollis points out that in the adult male, the ambivalent pull toward the dark side (exploitation/domination of others), may make the macho, loneliness, or Codependency/addiction behaviors into *anima*-oriented ones which are projected onto female relationships, or "It" addictions (fear of unconscious material).[142] Attempts to change such a situation by a woman/partner may lead to abuse.

---

[142] "As his personality is a protection from his pain, he cannot bear to turn within and suffer that pain, thereby lifting it off the Other. Sadly, that historic pain becomes the constant buffer between himself and others. No matter what his external accomplishments, he is a terribly frightened man. He is so frightened that he cannot

The typical reaction would be better the devil you have known than the ambiguity and tension of the unknown! Therefore, does an individuating male have to break away from his maternal CONNECTION as a matter of course? For the Hero archetype to flourish, not only must the ordeal of separation and return be accomplished (out of separation comes duality and purpose after all), but the "demons of despair and depression" must be overthrown through meeting the world without the council of the external mother, rather with an internalized *anima* that is successfully attaching, intimate and nurturing.

We find ourselves circling back again to the two-speed theory: "I don't care" or angry. How does the schema of anxiety versus ability for emotional CONNECTION begin to transfer from the nurturing (or not) biological mother to the internalized, and experienced, and utilitarian *anima*? We know from the neurological process of fight/flight/freeze that the constriction of feelings [*angh*: Indo-Germanic root for "to constrict"—anxiety, angina, anger] results in these feelings still manifesting themselves, only as expressed unconsciously and undifferentiated. Some examples are:

1. Depression—anger turned inward and learned helplessness (internalized in the body)
2. Repression—general irritability, displaced anger
3. Self-destructive—violence toward others, intensity of injury to a man's Mother complex
4. Pleasing and placating—tries to keep Her happy, often sacrificing his own well-being in the process, or indulges the double urge to get his own way and still avoid confrontation through passive-aggressive behaviors that seek control and revenge (I became a ___ for her but it screwed it all up for me!); Self-estrangement (ibid, 1994; p. 59).

In psychotherapy, many patients (male and female) present with a primary trauma that has not been resolved and it is their very strength and ability to avoid through denial (flight), avoidance (freeze), or addiction that covers up old wounds. Alice Miller writes about this process in *The Drama of the Gifted Child* (1981), but the theory of repression and the harm it causes to the soul is not a new idea. Many treatment strategies focus on the exposure of underlying or repressed issues, and having uncovered them, move on to development of tools to accept previously intolerable thoughts or behaviors on which the patient's energy had been focused. According to Jung, a wound can cause us to have our soul crushed, or cause us to grow up, because as we face our demons we are able to accept our true Selves (the 12-step process has us look at character defects while doing an inventory in Step Four).[143] When this process has not been completed, or even begun, the individual is ill-equipped to solve his or anyone else's problems. According to Mahler (1973) these individuals make poor spouses, employees, and especially poor parents.

---

bear to look at his pain and can only see the Other as the source or continuance of it (Hollis, 1994, p. 43).

[143]"An archetypal pattern requires that something be given up for something to be gained. Childhood dependency must be relinquished for adult self-possession and creativity…all are summoned to grow up; not all are up to the task" (ibid, 1994, p. 70).

They have difficulty dealing with the issues of rapprochement (verbalizing their feelings and needs) because of intimacy issues and fear of failure.

When Hollis speaks of this period, he specifically points out the ways in which men, who have been shamed or isolated in childhood, can become ill-equipped, just as those who are drawn toward images that stimulate the *libido* may become overly sexualized. The problem is that even though men feel like children within, they must begin to play "adult" games; navigating mysterious rules that don't seem to apply to them is often difficult and intrinsically punishing. If they must learn how to live "out there" with integrity, they may find themselves either taking shortcuts, like criminal behavior, or isolating altogether.

Determining one's path is what Rilke called the "sacred nature of the journey". Having successfully determined the path, even if not completed (for is it ever complete?), one finds that having a healthy relationship becomes more tenable. "Men and women may be more comfortable with each other when they have become more comfortable with themselves" (ibid, 1994, p. 93). On the other hand, as Campbell aptly stated, "One can spend one's whole life climbing the ladder, only to realize that it had been placed against the wrong wall" (Campbell, 1991).

Women and Their *Animus*

Knowing theoretically these specifics about male development and unconscious structure, in contrast, what can we now speak of more definitively about women? In reviewing Hollis, we find his view about men can also summarize men's view toward women. "Man's relationship to his beloved can never be better than his relationship to his own *anima,* because what is unconscious in him will be contaminating his relationship with the Other, just as the Other is projecting onto him in turn" (op cit., 1994, p. 49).

Because of this blockage, *anima*-possessed men may have unwillingness or refusal to do what is necessary right now, at this moment, often an important virtue desired by moment-grounded women. But, by rejecting CONNECTION with a man's *anima*, or rather a woman's *animus* CONNECTING with a man's *anima,* we may be rejecting psychological needs that will later become "imprisoned in the body". The way for women to deal with male *anima* is to "not be overwhelmed by it".

As a separate gender, women have their own way of attaching. Laurie Schapira has written about this difference in *The Cassandra Complex: Living with Disbelief* (1988). Cassandra, the daughter of King Priam and Queen Hecuba, was banished by Apollo after she resisted his advances. Having previously received the gift of prophecy, her punishment was that no one would believe her prophecies anymore; in several versions the situation causes her to experience insanity. It was her fate to know what disasters were coming and be unable to avert them. As a therapist I often feel the pain of wanting a client to really hear me tell them, or even warn them, about the outcome of some of their decisions, but to no avail.

I am a Cassandra, powerless to avert the disaster inevitably on the horizon but bound by ethics and professional choice to stay and help them out of yet another "mess". This type of story and process is at the core of many tragedies about female heroines, whereby some great potential goes unfulfilled, even turning destructive, making them into the "tragic figure". For Cassandra, was her "tragedy" a need for control? Being a sexual tease? Not dealing with the basic drive behind her behaviors and in response to Apollo, who wanted her for his god bride, to be his "divine inspiration?"

The development of a healthy feminine side in women starts early. The child's experience of the strong archetypal force and the primal relationship (think Margaret Maher) creates dependency during the pre-differentiation stage, when the formation of archetypes begins. A healthy Self is the synthesis of the opposites revealed during developmental shifts out of dependency. The individuation process was seen as a paradox symbolized historically by alchemists as the snake eating its own head, the *Ouroboros*. That which was incomplete would always try to complete itself, if not consciously then through dreams, archetypes, or unconscious material (super-personal or sub-personal level). Most times it is one's own attitude, not the relationship on which one needs to work.

In *The Cassandra Complex,* Schapira discusses in detail the effects of being abandoned, particularly by the "needy" mother, who is focused on her own problems. This loss of intimacy is then later, in turn, projected onto the primary love relationship between the woman and her significant Other, man or woman.[144]

As discussed earlier, Miller (1981) believes early abandonment results in overwhelming anxiety, due to the failure to separate (at the developmentally appropriate time) from the early symbiosis with the needy mother, not having formed a secure attachment in the first place. No wonder there may be a future searching for love from one whom is very much the *animus* of the Mother projected onto a masculine figure. No matter which way she turned, in her myth Cassandra was neglected, attacked, or asked to give up her own identity to mirror another, as in childhood. This concept is a frequent one with females I see and is of primary importance.

Jung described the Intuitive type as often being like a Pythian/Cassandra oracle of antiquity. He concurred that transference in the therapeutic situation mirrored the patient's experiences like Cassandra's process as an oracle. It did not guarantee, however, a positive symbiotic bond, which he felt was necessary for a healthy sense of Self.

---

[144] "A myth may be read as referring to many different levels of experience at once. The story of this mother and daughter is lived out between actual mothers and daughters, but it is also at work in interactions between ourselves and other maternal figures—men and women, or sometimes even those institutions, such as schools or churches, that serve as mothers for us. And internally, the story describes tensions between dimensions of our own soul.
Mother anima affirms her attachment of her own wishes for her child, while at the same time remaining loyal to her as she goes through a transformative experience. "Women may be drawn to wounded and sensitive men, boys not ripened by life; men may be drawn to fragile women who seem to need protection and guidance of a maternal kind. These problems of a "mother complex" require a deeper sense of what mother is, and the knowledge that often we can best give maternal care to another, not by being mother ourselves, but by finding ways to stir the maternal impulse in the other" (Moore, 1992, p. 40, 45).

In the internal sense, it is the loss of the "participating consciousness" that allows the identification or merger with a psychic or healing Self to take place. In many processes, becoming aware of what is "not-me" is the beginning to the path of Self-knowledge. Because the locus of control is external in these parenting situations, with the child carefully watching for cues, the children become highly sensitive and perhaps hypervigilant into adulthood.

In place of a lack of nurturing, on the other hand, the child may respond to the strength she sees in the mother's Apollonian *animus,* and she may come to idealize the masculine, causing further Codependence in adult heterosexual relationships as an adult. Thus, the ego is created in the service of the *animus.* "The woman's ego is reduced to playing anima to her own animus" [!] (ibid, 1981, p. 64). What has happened to the intuitive insight in these women? It fails to be grounded, due to a lack of personal experience and a failure to guard the ego from the Shadow. The result may be deep-seated feelings of unworthiness in a woman of this intuitive type, who has had hysteric or rejective parenting.

Although Schapira focuses most of her studies on Cassandra's story, she completes her book with a summary of other Greek goddesses and how their personalities can also illustrate the Jungian concepts we have been discussing.[145] Looking first at Athena, we see a Goddess who denies any experience of inner needs or even of depression. Rather, her power is outer directed. Because of this focus, as an archetype, these women often do little to take care of their inner Self or of the development of their "feminine sides". In the Intuitive type, this lack of Self-care leaves the woman unfulfilled and overly idealistic. In some individuals,

---

[145] Jean Bolen also has written a whole book on these *Goddesses in Everywoman* (1984), in which she outlines these common themes: virgin; vulnerable; alchemical (or transformative); modes of consciousness; favored roles and motivating factors; attitudes toward others; need for attachment; and the importance of relationships. For instance, although the "virgin" role can be seen as vulnerable it can also be seen as independent and a "sufficient enough" quality in women. It is an archetype of autonomy, goal-directedness, and logical thinking. Bolen sees Artemis, Athena, and Hestia as the "achievement-oriented" goddesses. "Hestia avoided power altogether…[she] represents a spiritual component that a woman does well to honor." Other vulnerable goddess archetypes are Hera, Demeter, and Persephone, where traditional roles, relationship-building, and being well-meaning create significance and "reactions to loss and growth through suffering." Bolen translates her view of the role of each goddess into one which she sees as innovative and useful:

- Athena—help me to think clearly in this situation
- Persephone—help me to stay open and receptive
- Hera—help me to make a commitment and be faithful
- Demeter—teach me to be patient and generous, help me to be a good mother
- Artemis—keep me focused on that goal in the distance
- Aphrodite—help me to love and enjoy my body
- Hestia—honor me with your presence, bring me peace and serenity (ibid, 1984, pp. 26, 33)

there may even be grandiose fantasies toward men that interfere with healthy relationship-building.

Persephone's archetype represents the parts of a woman which are more patient and observing, being able to show empathy toward herself and others with the important characteristics of listening and mirroring. Largely mental and based on rational understanding, this archetype evolves from a relationship with "a good mother, based on an empathic connection and [being] more emotional" (ibid, 1981, p. 87).

Hecate (Hestia), the protective Goddess of the household, sometimes seen as having magical powers, represents how a woman can feel misunderstood and experience the need to protect herself or her position. Boundary skirmishes are evident; the woman can become enraged because of narcissism on her part. This experience is an expression of her Shadow. In working with this archetype, it is important to build a newer, healthier ego, which can help her deal with the residuals of her prior defenses. "The difficult separation-rapprochement phase of development [Mahler] is worked through and the depressive position negotiated. The separation becomes a rebirth in which something is lost, and something is gained" (ibid, 1981, p. 97).

Finally, Artemis, twin of Apollo, is the huntress, the wild-side archetype, representing virginity, young girls, and then childbirth; she is another side of the Protector myth. Artemis has the power of positive thinking, integrity, independence, and strong ego boundaries. Women who relate to this archetype protect themselves and refuse to be victim, even of their own unconscious material. They are rarely narcissistic, rather preferring hard work and discipline. Their Shadow may not be easily accessible to them.[146]

Not a Goddess, but an archetypal symbol or typology that represented Wholeness itself, Quaternity was the Jungian term for the structure, sometimes a cross or even a circle, that was symmetry itself. It included the four aspects of "Creator-God" discussed above, "space, time, causality and meaning" (Ostrowski-Sachs, 1971). Quaternity pointed to the center of morality and the workings of the human soul. In his *On the Genealogy of Morals* (1887), Nietzsche had declared that "moral maturity" was a very important concept; such wholeness could only come out of seeking one's true desire.

Ultimately, the search for wholeness is subliminal; Unity resides in the unconscious in a way that may or may not be reachable by the conscious mind.

---

[146] When we are narcissistic, we are not on solid ground (earth) or thinking clearly (air) or caught up in passion (fire). Rather, the very positive outcome of knowing oneself is possible, as well as loving oneself (a deeper version of itself, a true stillness, a wonder about oneself, a meditation on one's nature). But if one is obsessive, there is no room for anyone else. "The hardness/dangers of narcissism is its inflexibility and rigidity, suppleness is an extremely important quality of soul…Echo anima, the soul in desperate need of attachment to the boyish beauty. Talking to nature shows that his grief is giving him a new CONNECTION to the soul. When soul is present, nature is alive." He discovers by his own experience that he is lovable. "Further, he loves himself as an object…'I am stuff. I am made up of things and qualities, and in loving these things I love myself'" (Moore, 1992, pp. 61, 73, 74).

Externalization comes when we project onto an "It"/addictive, self-soothing factor, upon which we become too dependent. Our desire may also be delayed until some future time. The path to discovery of our true desires comes from kindness rather than Self-criticism or being judgmental. This is the way of Creation of the Self. Delineate and embrace your values for moral maturity; this process will guide you on your path of differentiation of Self, something that requires work over and over and over.

To begin healing, an individual becomes more acutely aware of issues arising from unresolved *anima/animus* influences. Sometimes falling apart ("Breaking of the Vessel" in the Kabbalah) will demonstrate the very uniqueness that is one's Self, especially for an Outlier. Archetypes can serve as symbolic "containers" of the fragmentation that might take place during treatment or even during life in general. Weaknesses and uncertainties are viewed, not only as diagnostic, but also as signposts along the way to making what is negative more positive and to becoming aware of how the Self is not the only goal of development.

The Self is an organizing center of the more complex system of unconscious/Shadow, ego, Self, and higher supra-personal information. If gathered, the balance gained will enable the subject to feel unified, for the weak and uncertain parts of the personality to be able to follow healthier instincts and to give negative impulses a positive source of individuation material. This process is the very transformation we have been seeking through a deeper awareness of our UFT of development; it has impacted our beliefs and behavior through contextual ideas, beliefs, and emotions. This introspection can lead to "meta-awareness" and a deeper mindfulness.

Active Imagination

Jung taught his patients the skill of "active imagination", that is, to make conscious what is disturbing us or has too much emotional weight. The process of active imagination is revealed through dreams, myths, or mystical experiences. Jung discovered that even the *Taoist* alchemists had practiced something like "active imagination". Whatever the process, the goal was to make the negative positive. "The process of individuation is furthered precisely by not taking part in the battle but rather walking out of it; 'the way to deal with serious problems in life is to outgrow them'" (Jung as quoted by Von Franz, 2002, p. 21).

Jung felt that the dream was always ongoing in the unconscious; it usually needed sleep and the complete cessation of attention to outer things for the unconscious to register in consciousness. Bringing the unconscious to consciousness is the helpful purpose of meditation and other forms of reinforcement of Inner Work. It can be the first step of active imagination practice, to rest and to just let things happen. One will cease to see dreams, even nightmares, as frightening or as a punishment. Rather they are an opportunity for adventure and information. Active imagination allows us to heal ourselves from within. Freud likewise felt the dream could "compensate", allowing transcendence.

Dreams and their mythical symbols can help reconcile opposites into unified functions (outer/inner; macro/micro; theological/psychological) (Drob, 2010).[147]

Jung conceived the idea of active imagination during the years 1913–1916, following his break with Freud (1912) and after which he began experiencing one of the most significant traumatic periods of his life. He learned that Self-confrontation was constructive, and much of his increased understanding of his inner turmoil came through the active imagination process. He believed that throughout the process of analysis, whether with a guide or Self-driven, operating in the opposite attitude of one's Psychological Type requires the expenditure of energy, while operating from the person's natural attitude replenishes that same energy. Of course, one's occasional necessity of "inferior" functioning provides balance and helps with the development of Self.

Heraclitus said, "Everything in time turns into its opposite…Good and evil are one;" and "God is day and night, summer and winter, war and peace, surfeit and hunger." Jung called this the rule of *enantiodramia* (a running toward the opposite). "Where danger is, arises salvation also…God is also our own yearning, which we honor." This dualism shows that the "forces of nature have two sides, creative and destructive."

As we know, Jung studied the Greeks; his own belief in the "One", whom he called the "inconceivable God", came from his study of ancient cultures and religions. This study proved to him that the One is manifest in many forms, many of these appearing as "pairs-of-opposites". Jung transitioned his view of God in three stages:

> In the first stage (roughly 1900–1921), Jung understood religious experience to be a projection of the individual's emotions; in the second stage (1921–1945), such experience was understood as corresponding to the archetypes, and thus a projection of the deepest layers of the collective psyche; and in the third stage (beginning around 1945), Jung appears to have suspended judgment regarding the objective nature of that which the archetypal patterns of the psyche represent (Drob, 2010, p. 214).

I propose that our relationship with the therapist is likewise a "relationship with opposite/Other", where conflict arises needing resolution and synthesis to a higher gestalt of understanding for both participating members of the partnership. Synthesis certainly is both an attachment and a CONNECTION. Jung believed that in treatment the relationship with doctor/therapist becomes a quasi-ideal solution of the conflict where opposites unite. Although religion or "spirituality" may not even be mentioned, there is a wish for a spiritual CONNECTION of sorts

---

[147] "Reality is paradoxical, in the way that things and their opposites are closely related, in that attachment and resistance have the same root. We know this on an intuitive level already, in how we speak of love-hate relationships, in how we recognize that which frightens us is likely to liberate us, and in how we become suspicious if someone accused of wrongdoing protests his or her innocence too hotly…A thing can be and not be at the same time, and as Jung, Freud and apparently the alchemists all understood, it usually is" (Hannah, 1981, p. 71).

in every meaningful relationship; the therapeutic one is high on the list of importance.

Self-realization inevitably brings into consciousness the contents of the personal unconscious, thus enlarging the scope of one's personality.[148] Piaget (1962), for instance, pointed out that one's moral development could not exceed his cognitive development, meaning that until one's level of consciousness could expand into a certain level, but one's knowledge of oneself could not, in turn, expand beyond the cognitive level of functioning into social functioning which would demonstrate behavior and awareness of others' expectations. Much of this morality and social justice was taught initially through the Scriptures, particularly the Proverbs (think "Pride goeth before a fall", for instance).

Probably the most important goal of treatment is to put into practice some evidence of one's insights even with patients who believe themselves to be "ill-equipped" to navigate social cues and face the moral dilemmas presented in everyday life. The therapist can help them to understand the contextual training available from seeing both sides (*Tao* again) and learning to think in gray instead of black or white. Epigenetic influences, from historical events (UFT) or familial traits, can be overcome through practice and goalsetting. Although Piaget made a distinction between assimilation and adaptation in the process of learning sequences, I would differentiate adjustment from either assimilation or adaptation.

Adjustment is not adaptation; adaptation draws in the level of consciousness where morality resides and requires far more than merely going along smoothly with the conditions of the moment. It requires observance of laws more universal than the immediate conditions of time and place. In all psychological types, there is a markedly egocentric tendency in the unconscious because the Shadow is invested in protective maneuvers. We have discussed the importance of balance; for instance, the opposite of an extroverted behavioral adjustment would be awareness of unconscious introverted needs.

Jung was particularly taken with the idea of a cultural persona. This idea of the "persona" or mask that hides our individuality long enough to protect us, allowing us to appear as we believe, or have been taught, we "should be" in response to social cues, a compromise of sorts. Many of my clients who report feeling ill-equipped actually come into therapy with the role or persona of family hero. This persona may have started early in response to birth order issues.

---

[148] "Likewise, the unconscious contents that are released and brought into consciousness by analysis are usually unpleasant—which is precisely why these wishes, memories, tendencies, plans, etc. were repressed…It is not a question of inherited ideas, but of inherited thought-patterns…at its deeper levels the unconscious possesses collective contents in a relatively active state. That is why I speak of a collective unconscious.

"By raising the personal unconscious to consciousness, the analysis makes the subject aware of things which he is generally aware of in others, but never in himself. This discovery makes him therefore less individually unique and more collective. Moral sense comes from the freedom to understand the choices" (Jung quoted in Hayman, 1999, pp. 81, 94)

Addiction within families also requires children, especially the oldest, to grow up quickly and take over the hero role. Many of my patients with Post-Traumatic Stress Disorder (PTSD) also take on a persona of hero/survivor when internally they really have none of that strength available to them.

The Shadow as Guide: Making the Invisible Visible

Now that we have come to view the Jungian typology as capable of coming into balance, let us also look at how Jung believed the Shadow can be reintegrated into conscious awareness during the individuation process. The following quote, directly from Jung's *Collected Works*, is included at length here because of the importance of every point detailed.

> Recapitulating, I should like to emphasize that the integration of the shadow, or the realization of the personal unconscious, marks the first stage in the analytic process, and that without it a recognition of anima and animus is impossible. The shadow can be realized only through a relation to a partner, and anima and animus only through a relation to a partner of the opposite sex, because only in such a relation do their projections become operative.
>
> The recognition of the anima gives rise, in a man, to a triad, one-third of which is transcendent: the masculine subject, the opposing feminine subject, and the transcendent anima. With a woman the situation is reversed. The missing fourth element that would make the triad a quaternity is, in a man, the archetype of the Wise Old Man, which I have not discussed here, and in a woman the Chthonic Mother. These four constitute a half immanent and half transcendent quaternity, an archetype which I have called the marriage quaternion (Collected Works, Vol 16).

Because understanding the concept of the Shadow is such a prominent aspect of Jung's theory, many other psychological writings and theories of personality development further define his initial ideas. For instance, Reeves (1981) defined what certain aspects of the Shadow represented to her. I found this passage descriptive of how active our Shadow sides are in our daily lives, whether we recognize it or not.

> The Shadow, Jung tells us, is a personification of the repressed contents of the personal unconscious. The Shadow functions as a kind of psychical magnet, attracting to itself all manner of repressed or forgotten experiences which constellate into a complex of feelings and have a tendency to emerge autonomously, coloring consciousness and even taking it over…Working together, Shadow and ego produce vitality and great energy, which is why creative and athletic people (and young children) exhibit a kind of animal spiritedness…fear can seriously distort the ego's attempts to wisely use experience or rationale…"Find a friend and share your fear." (her grandma said) …Some call their search therapy, others communion; children call it love…Eventually we are confronted with the paradox that any journey toward

spiritual and psychic wholeness requires the acknowledgment of how [CONNECTED] each of us is to all of mankind (Reeves, 1981, p. 3).

For Jung, another important variation on treatment was the use of creative endeavors to express the unconscious, making visible the invisible. He felt that drawing, painting, molding, sculpting, or making a mandala all presented deepened opportunities for individuation and could make "vague" content clearer. He believed that the creative process itself got the individual in touch with a CONNECTIVITY of spirit and creativity in the Other as well, allowing higher levels of intimacy and openness from the personal unconscious, often using active imagination.

"Bisociation: The transcendent function manifests itself as a quality of conjoined opposites" (Salk, 1983, p. 297–298). We find ourselves back at Hegel and our *Taoist* theory of reconciling opposites again, of finding balance within, but not necessarily in a binary manner. According to Jung, individuation requires blending, shaping, graying, the awareness of and uncovering of things long repressed. Most importantly, being oneself takes courage.

In October 2011, I attended a monthly meeting of my local group, Friends of Jung (FOJ). We regularly hear a speaker of some national reputation in Jungian studies, and then the lecture is followed by a lively question and answer period. That month the speaker, Jungian Analyst Dr. Ronald Malashock, spoke on the specific attributes of active imagination that can be useful to the individual in search of Self. As I have mentioned, active imagination is somewhat like dreaming, and it gives us an important skill in grasping the dream's meaning, for "a dream that is not understood remains a mere occurrence. Once understood it becomes a living experience" (Jung quoted by Malashock, FOJ, 2011).

Dreams provide specific symbols as guides to unconscious material and as guideposts to the world where the opposites that need reconciling, as we have been discussing, can come together. "The symbol is the middle way along which the opposites flow together in a new movement, like a watercourse bringing fertility after a long drought" (ibid quoted by Malashock, FOJ, 2011). Jung believed in a spiritual content to our unconscious and our dreams, or even our mystical potential which, again, he referred to as the Collective Unconscious. We are driven into behavioral responses by the needs and trait-based predispositions of our "types", much in the same way as neurologists and behaviorists might say we are affected by our epigenetic influences. "To transform itself in us the future enters into us long before it happens" (Rilke, as quoted by Malashock, FOJ, 2011).

Malashock asked us to consider that our persona may be giving us some privacy, and in fact that our personality is dependent on privacy, but it can also give us the opportunity to try on different types, so why not go for it? Our Shadow doesn't have to be feared as the "dark side" but rather can be seen as just the underdeveloped part, and he challenged us to use our active imagination to work on developing it. "What you can't see on the inside, you can see on the outside and vice versa."

Active imagination concentrates on symbols in a dream and lets whatever happens passively come to you through writing it down, known as objectification. You will find that things tend to show up in their opposites (Jung called this compensation, Freud called it reaction formation). In the long run, working on active imagination skills through journaling your dreams will help allay repression; for the Jungian, this is the same as working on the complexes, the center of which is the archetype. Malashock closed his talk with the belief that whatever we discover will be coming from the "one Psyche which encompasses all, and [of course] the Self/Soul is already perfect" (Malashock, FOJ, 2011).

Dream themes often concern death containing the seeds of life, death as marriage, as an ecstatic experience at the end of life, death as rebirth and resurrection through darkness, death as the stronger, welcomed or feared, who comes to collect the one who must die. "Active imagination is a certain way of meditating imaginatively, by which one may deliberately enter into contact with the unconscious and make a conscious connection with psychic phenomena" (Jung, 1964, p. 206–207).

Jung believed that all these powerful symbols came from a "somewhere", an inner space which CONNECTED to a greater "there" collectively. He also believed this process created a historically relevant depository of unconscious material, mostly presented through symbols. Our responses, emotionally and behaviorally, of course, are supported by our initial affective state at the time that the symbols are revealed to us. As noted by the idea of a developmental UFT being presented throughout this book, culture, history, and mythological orientation influences one's process of individuation, and archetypal themes, the framework of explanation during Jungian analysis.

Religious Symbolism

We now turn to a more intensively studied side of Jung. His spiritual influence and his struggles between religious belief as organized practice versus a response to mystical experiences are well known. Of course, in some ways, this dichotomy is not so much a dichotomy as a continuum. Much of early organized religious symbolism was basically a "collective mythology". St. Augustine famously alluded to the "happy fall of man, *felix culpa*," an understanding which Jung saw as primary to one's individuation process. Thomas Aquinas, on the other hand, believed that God allows evils to happen to bring a greater good therefrom; "the acceptance of the shadow is a sacrifice."

This perspective is closer to that of current addictive treatment and 12-step work, where one becomes aware of one's character defects through a 4th step inventory. Through acceptance of God's will for them (3rd step prayer), the addict gains victory over the suffering caused by the addiction and the past. The formation of AA was influenced by Jung's belief that any of these types of rituals could gather the lower, instinctual forces of the psyche into symbols, and in this way integrate them into a hierarchy of the spirit (Jung, 1928). This emphasis on "metaphysical and meta-psychical affirmations" would go on to have a great influence on the Oxford Group in England and the formation of AA in the United States.

In Chapter Eight, we discussed how the formulation of religious structures were often reinforced through liturgical stories (Psalms), poetry, and personal imagery during sermons. Christianity was noted for its use of collective mythologies, many of which drew on much older Egyptian stories, as old as Moses (see the Egyptian story of *Orisis/Set*), and the Greek tragedies of Sophocles. Jung believed these mystical cues led "worshippers" to consider the personal unconscious, including its complexes, and a collective unconscious, with its archetypes' feeling-toned complexes. Jung worked directly and closely with patients to help them achieve "self-understanding and self-exploration." Similarly, church leaders, whether priests, pastors, or lamas, have used the guidance of symbols to construct anchor points in their liturgy.

As noted above, one CONNECTING principle between Jung's ideas and those of religion was the reward gained from the "inner search". Whether through prayer, meditation, congregational practice, belief in archetypes, or even alchemical studies, rewards could be great. For Jung, it was a search for "Soul". For James Hillman (1999), an archetype is "a psychic premise with many heads: one we see in our dream imagery, another in emotion and in symptoms, another styles our behavior and preference, while still another appears in our mode of thought…The same archetype dominates our individual choices, our messes, and our ideas" (ibid, 1999, p. 131).

Wolfgang Pauli, the Nobel Prize winning physicist, wrote an article about man's wholistic nature, entitled "Synchronicity: An Acausal Connecting Principle", which was published in his 1955 book, *The Interpretation of Nature and the Psyche*. Pauli, Jung cited, called the "ring" or Unity beyond particle and wave as "*i*" or the "imaginary element" that unites us all, in love, and during individuation in the psycho-spirituality of everyday life. Part of Jung's concepts of the archetype and synchronicity could be viewed as expressions of *unus mundus,* a kind of unity of character; the archetype was a specific expression of *unus mundus* and synchronicity, or "meaningful coincidence" being made possible by the fact that both the observer and the CONNECTED event ultimately stem from the same source, the *unus mundus*.

"Synchronicity means the simultaneous occurrence of a psychic state with one or more external events, which appear as meaningful parallels to the momentary subjective state" (Ostrowski-Sachs, 1971). For Jung, "divine intention" was not just his way of looking at spirituality but rather an avenue for reaching the collective unconscious itself (Hayman, 1999).

Discovery and Recovery

I am not my wound or my defense against my wound. I am my journey.
– C.G. Jung

During his own process of aging, Jung's writings became more and more spiritual, intuitive, creative, and even full of his own fears. It was natural that it should be so. Jung found great enjoyment in the process of CONNECTING. He allowed a documentary to be made about his life during which he was interviewed. He sponsored and involved himself in many seminars and international symposiums. And yes, there was more than a bit of "guru" in him. As we pursue inner work, specifically from the "Jungian" point of view, we see all types of symbolism, including Buddhist foundations of following a leader with spiritual practice. These symbols help teach us Self-care and to invest in the individuation process.

We are on a path; regardless of what we think our destination may be, all paths will and must lead us to our essence. However, the problem may still exist in our tendency to fight this revelation along the way. Jung wrote a paper entitled, *Adaptation, Individuation, Collectivity,* which reflected some of his thoughts on this subject. We are created, we evolve and CONNECT, we hide and escape or manifest an awareness of the greater (collective) unconscious, a special type of knowledge Jung called Gnosis.

Sounds good in theory, sounds good on paper. How do we follow the path, day to day? One day at a time? We started an overview of recovery in Chapter Sixteen; now we will proceed to a fuller discovery of the Self. Jung believed that:

"a certain amount of suffering and unhappiness is our lot and no one can escape all the dark phases of life;" we grow through conflict…Real security is in returning to the understanding that—yes—there is suffering and danger and—yes—there is tremendous beauty and tremendous possibility for compassion…To live a life of fear is to lose the freedom that is our birthright…Our practice is to deal with our fears and our sorrow with tenderness, so that we don't project them out into the world. To the extent that we're willing to face our own pain, and only to that extent, can we be a source of peace for the world around us [CONNECTION and Inner Work] (Ostrowski-Sachs, 1971).

One useful technique for facing our fears is to watch for how "re-" in front of a word changes it, for example what one re-sists, persists; other words that come to mind are re-sonance, re-cognition, re-membering, re-spiration. Greatness comes from approaching fear, which is not death, but rather not living one's life. Jung believed in asking his *anima,* "What's the matter with you now? What do you see? I'd like to know!" He felt there were answers inside each of us if we really wanted those answers and were not afraid of them. Before we can make global CONNECTIONS and changes, we must locate ourselves in our own personal CONNECTIONS.

Jung stayed CONNECTED to the end, ever searching, and always invested in the mythology of any experience around him. He felt the human adventure represented in the myth shows us the purpose of CONNECTIONS between life and the soul. "The reflective moment is the soul-making moment, deepening of events into 'experience,' derives from relation with death and is reflective through dream-image, and fantasy" (Hillman, 1997, p. x).

It was as if Jung was searching for that state of meditational bliss that might help him cross into permanent unconsciousness. Although he had been successful in combining Christianity and mythology into a new "depth" psychology, he may best be remembered for his contributions to a vernacular conceptualization of consciousness with such terms as synchronicity, archetype, and Collective Unconscious.

Be patient toward all that is unsolved in your heart and try to love the questions themselves…Do not now seek the answers, which cannot be given you because you would not be able to live them. And the point is, to live everything. Live the Questions now. Perhaps then you will gradually, without noticing it, live along some distant day into the answer.

– Rilke, *Letters to a Young Poet.*

Chapter Nineteen
Discovery of Self
The Art and Science of Growth

When you're reaching out for something you want, be careful you don't destroy the things you already have.

– John Abbott, patriarch
The Young and the Restless

We have previously explained the sources of biological or biochemical breakdowns that affect cellular or neurological systems when we experience pain, loss, worry or illness. These breakdowns are also, therefore, the cause of a breakdown of CONNECTIONS. These DISCONNECTS result in a sense of alienation, aloneness, and isolation, as if we are the only one ever to have had our experience and (perhaps) the sense of guilt, failure, and loss of identity we are experiencing. We blame others. We blame God. But ultimately, and most usually, we are blaming ourselves for the outcomes of our prior lives, behaviors, choices, lost opportunities, or failure to "grow up". This composite of history, experiences, behaviors, and emotions may be formulated into a unified field theory of personality development (UFT) but is often experienced and labeled as Depression.

As noted in an earlier chapter, much of the growth in psychotherapeutic techniques during the 1960s was based on a process called Transactional Analysis (TA) (Stewart, 1987). In this process, the old Freudian terms of Id, Ego, and Superego were modernized into the terms Child, Adult and Parent for a refreshing and regrouped view of Self that allowed millions of new followers of self-psychology to look at Self-care and Self-discovery. Paralleling the growth in the self-help industry, Thomas Harris wrote *I'm OK, You're OK* (1967); Berne's book, *Games People Play* (1964), outlined behaviors in terms of "games".

The author explained these games as Jungian-type Personas people use to hide their fears and depression. Even if the experience of loss had originally precipitated much of the depression, over time the remaining anger with the abandoning individual was turned inward by the depressed person.

Symptoms of depression include a dysphoric mood or a loss of pleasure or interest in usual activities (anhedonia). Most importantly, mood disturbance is prominent and persistent, which distinguishes it from short environmental periods of reactive depression or grief in response to distressing events. The individual may be plagued by feelings and thoughts of worthlessness and excessive guilt and may express an intense sense of responsibility for his or her thoughts and feelings and for events in his or her environment.

The sense of vulnerability that comes with loss also creates a tendency to feel as overwhelmed and helpless as she or he did in childhood. Therapy usually focuses on the patient's vulnerability to loss and related behavior, such as their tendency to avoid ongoing close relationships. Cognitive therapy emphasizes the role of how one thinks about oneself and the environment as the genesis of depression. Berne takes the position that people can change (openness), whereas the loss of freedom to change (closedness) is Freud's definition of "neurotic process".

Berne's book not only made a big impact on psychotherapists, but self-help support groups also sprang up all over the U.S. and around the world. "Game" terminology and theory joined the vernacular of the day. Individuals were able to understand, in everyday language, how they got to be the way they were (UFT) and in which of the three main positions of triangulation (Victim, Blamer or Rescuer) they usually found themselves.

> Personal inadequacy, worthlessness, inferiority, failure, and guilt…intense rage and indignation…In claiming depression, you cry for love, and no one answers, you get angry in response to the frustration. Self-criticism is primary and the mood follows…a lower script, in which you used the game of Kick Me to perpetuate a basic lifestyle of suffering or self-destruction…this script said, 'closeness and intimacy are dangerous.' The constant barrage of self-criticism and self-ridicule led to intense depressive illnesses, which resulted in withdrawal from people important to you and enabled you to maintain your basic life plan of avoiding intimacy. In order to stop the self-punishing game, you would have to change your life script to something like 'it's OK to be close' (Arieti, 1962, p. 397).

Whether we are actively in addiction treatment or are on the path of Self-discovery for its own outcome of growth, we learn that old guilts can continue to make us suffer. Buddhists maintain that we are all suffering (see Chapter Nine), but they also believe there is a cure for the source of the suffering. Many of us have been raised to find "feelings" experienced in the Child/Id state as unacceptable or problematic (having internalized these blaming "Parent" messages, according to TA, along with the history built into our UFT). The Child then reacts with feelings of guilt. In TA terms, when you look at guilt, you see that it is a form of the Kick Me game, with the internalized Parent blaming the Child (Self) for wrongdoings.

Because it is against themselves that the Child state holds these feelings, they are causing and are the source of the guilt. Occasionally the anger rises to such intensity that it bursts out toward others and becomes almost a rage attack. "These people then feel guilty about having expressed unjustified and irrational hostility and become more depressed. It can be a vicious circle of guilt: blowing up with anger, then feeling guilty over the anger, and so becoming more depressed" (ibid, 1962, p. 4).

On the other hand, the Ego/Adult state in recovery is seeking self-worth and Self-esteem, which are expressions of a healthy and nurtured Child state.

There are many ways to achieve personal satisfaction and fulfillment. Ultimately, the goal of Self-care work is the avoidance of reinforcing the "helpless Child", the part with issues of dependency and inferiority. This personality type usually starts very early in childhood, with reinforced experiences of learned helplessness. We avoid that which makes us stressed, uncomfortable, or anxious. Most anxiety disorders, by definition, involve some level of avoidance because of prior trauma.

Since the absence of attention (TA calls this "stroking") is intolerable, children settle for negative forms of recognition instead. They get attention for misbehavior, sickness, and suffering. Behind every negative emotion there is a longing, and within that longing there is a positive need. Negative attention is better than no recognition at all. In fact, children will choose immediate gratification, even with a negative consequence, over being ignored, every time. This DISCONNECT between logic and emotion is usually obvious.

Sometimes the dependent tendencies turn into full-blown "Codependency", a term I usually dislike using because it has become overused in the vernacular of our times. I would define Codependency as a pattern of using compulsive attention-seeking or dependence on the approval from another with whom there is an addictive type of CONNECTION. The addict searches for Self-worth and identity through dependence upon the Other and the Other's boundaries, instead of using her own UFT. This desperation is a cue that the Codependent individual may have other types of diagnostic symptoms. A higher percentage of individuals with Codependent features seem to be women, which might imply that "such women were often socialized to be dependent, have no self-esteem, and live vicariously through others" (Anderson S., 1994, p. 679).

Self-denial and negative Self-image are also common co-morbid symptoms. Therapeutically, Anderson supports the idea, focusing on empowerment through acceptance, that femininity does not have to equal sensitivity. Quoting Krestan and Bepko (1990), Anderson focuses her research on the idea that "over-responsibility needs to be understood as a positive impulse gone awry. Relational responsibility needs to co-exist with responsibility to Self" (ibid, 1994, p.682). [I feel like repeating the typing of this sentence, making it a mantra. That is how valuable it is in my work].

As I have already mentioned in Chapter Sixteen, many addictions start with a type of anxiety generated from mourning the loss of something and/or a trauma. Even though as more mature adults we can accept sadness as natural and appropriate, early loss and resentment do not get easily assimilated. Sometimes your path gets rerouted without your consent, but the initial path is still there. Even after seeking therapy, part of you may want to leave the experience; maybe the reason you are reacting so strongly is because the intuitive part of you realizes something valuable is happening in that room!

Even though we experience dependency and helplessness, it is imperative that we recognize the penalties for avoidance. It is a choice after all, to avoid, even if it is a choice we make by default. Healthy decision-making skills are formed through the resolution of more primitive tendencies in our libido toward aggression and the anxiety of abandonment. But these feelings are at least the ability to feel something.

I constantly work with my clients to "stay in the present" as one method to fight depression. In Chapter Nine I discussed how useful the practice of Buddhism (or even just using mindfulness) can be to be present with oneself. Being responsive to one's Child state—even if it brings feelings of depression, anger, or fear—will give one the opportunity to clear out old repressions or sources of one's Persona.

One of my many mantras with clients is: "No one ever died crying to death!" I have enough respect for my clients to let them express themselves, to be a good listener and to know they will not fall apart, giving them the benefit of the doubt that they are much stronger than others treat them (Outlier or not), certainly much more precious than they usually treat themselves. What I am looking for is a genuine experience. And the aloneness that may result from the self-imposed DISCONNECT becomes even more pronounced if illness or end-of-life issues surface. An accumulation of our aloneness, pain, or lack of self-care demonstrates the creative ways many of us have designed our lives to experience suffering.

In the 1990s, the Robert Wood Johnson Foundation (RWJF) created a $12 million initiative to respond to overwhelming evidence that too many Americans die alone, in pain, and receiving aggressive medical treatment not justified by its likely benefit. In many ways, just as we look at the palliative portion of hospice care as humane and compassionate, what if we began to treat ourselves with "palliative care" early in our lives?

Living in the now, accepting that we are all suffering but that we all can also find immediate solutions to our immediate needs, one day at a time, might work as a better solution than many of the other current high-cost ways we spend money to treat our anxiety and addictions (drugs, alcohol, gambling, compulsive spending, unnecessary medical treatment, and so forth). Again, I am thinking of "palliative" in terms of day-to-day self-care. I would be overjoyed to see the outcome of some of these goals on the current population of patients with whom I work.

When I first start working with a client, often it is necessary to allow for long periods of silence, during which the client will settle into his or her natural relational response pattern. I try to be aware of any cultural factors that might assist the client, as well as intergenerational factors, the importance of dreams, or personal beliefs about doctors and treatment. Family and friend relationships will often be the source of the problem; mapping these patterns is important but may take time to unravel because it is important to stay away from interrogation methods, which may or may not be satisfying in the long run.

Ultimately, I will have collected a type of content analysis of the client's stories and concerns that then allow for the further "real" investigation into the client's values and beliefs [UFT], how they may not be in harmony with their world. Finally, together we make goals that reflect how they can feel more CONNECTED. I reflect their ideas about goals and how to gain balance, not mine. The clearing of emotional blocks and the expression of anger will not usually come in the first few sessions, but they will eventually appear.

We all walk around with some internal dialogue going on, and some ideas are more disturbing than others. If we think, irrationally, that: "I must be loved or approved by practically every significant person in my life; I must not make errors or do poorly; people and events should always be the way I want them to be," then we will be creating a state of disturbance by our own will (and perhaps narcissistic thinking). If rather we think: "It's definitely nice to have people's love and approval; doing things well is satisfying; people are going to act the way they want, and they have a right to do so" then we will function more effectively.

> Successful treatment should not only relieve symptoms but also foster the positive presence of psychological capacities and resources. Depending on the person and the circumstances, these might include the capacity to have more fulfilling relationships, make more effective use of one's talents and abilities, maintain a realistically based sense of self-esteem, tolerate a wide range of affect, have more satisfying sexual experiences, understand self and others in more nuanced and sophisticated ways, and face life's challenges with greater freedom and flexibility (Shedler, 2010, p.100).

Attachment Patterns in Women Versus Men

Before we look at how the causes for DISCONNECT/depression may affect relationships, it may be useful to first point out the difference in gender attachment styles overall. The CONNECTIONS we need grow from our primary attachment patterns and the meaning we took from them for developmental strength: security, safety, nourishment, and so forth. These attachments create very powerful feelings, with meanings very personal to us based on the UFT we have built throughout the cultural "heritage" of our upbringing (Chodorow, 1999). Chodorow's research (*The Power of Feelings*) showed that because girls separate from their mothers much more slowly and less completely than do boys, they do not form as strong ego boundaries between "Self" and "Other".

"As adults, women live out their psychic lives in the reproductive realm and readily empathize with others." There is a clear differentiation during preschool ages where we see the basic masculine "sense of 'self' as 'separate' and 'the basic feminine sense of Self' as 'CONNECTED to the world'" [emphasis added] (ibid, 1999).

Women, therefore, grow up with a more complex set of variables regarding attachment, caretaking, and care-receiving, and are socialized often in contradiction to that which they observe around them. The "do as I say, not as I do" script can weaken their Self-esteem and their development of Self in the first place; women experience a "double bind" when their sense of Self is organized around relationships. Too often they are socialized to acquire Self-worth through relationships, but also women are led to believe that such Self-definitions are unhealthy and/or immature (see Chapter Eighteen for in-depth discussion of male development).

Initial investigations of presenting problems may only be confounded by possible pre-existing histories of underlying sexual abuse and eating disorders, two of the more challenging therapeutic concerns [although men can also present with these histories as well]. A history of emotional abuse is as painful as physical assault, with a pain that can last a lifetime even though there may be no physical scars. "When your self-concept has been shredded, when you have been deeply injured and made to feel that the injury was all your fault, when you look for approval to those who cannot or will not provide it—you play the role assigned to you by your abusers" (Vachss, 1994, pp. 4–6).

This search for approval is why these women frequently request a female therapist to deal not only with the litany of problems, but also with the attachment disorders that originated their depressions and identity issues in the first place. Even if they have been successful in the professional world, they may have had to hide deeper insecurities. And it is very hard to solve problems with the same kind of thinking we used to create them.

I have heard it said, "A mother is only as happy as her least happy child." Thus, it may be very hard for some mothers to maintain a balance in their life. Just yesterday, I made a home visit to give support to a woman with six children under sixteen years old, all wanted and loved, but with whom she found herself overwhelmed and under-supported by her husband. Her problem wasn't the parenting, per se, it was the rest of the domestic responsibilities and maintaining some type of structure and schedule, including doctor appointments, homework, and her own attempt to return to college classes. "[such women are] …entrapped by the 'superwoman phenomenon;' they feel they must perform each role perfectly, leaving them emotionally drained and depressed" (Gilroy, et. al., 1998, pp. 402–407).

On the other hand, there is a difference between perfectionism and the desire to excel, found to be hard-wired through genetics in certain individuals. One must differentiate between the 1) "socially prescribed" perfectionism, where one's value can only be experienced through another's perception of them, and 2) their drive to excel as their form of coping with stress, or even a healthy form of ambition. Although Self-driven perfectionism may be a factor in avoidance behaviors or deeper psychological disorders, it is not necessarily a disorder.

My mother, who I have mentioned was also a therapist, collected many sayings to use as handouts, most of which I inherited. Often, she worked with women whose men had cheated on them, but rather than focus on the failure of trust, she chose to reinforce the woman's own Self-esteem, purpose, and realignment for Self-care and a better future of health and productivity, regardless of her partner's failure. She gave them this handout:

If there is a way of bringing man to repentance, it is the way of the woman who refuses to let herself be corrupted and made disobedient by his disobedience, but who despite his disobedience maintains her place in the order all the more firmly, …

V. Haradon handout

Then she would proceed to ask them, regardless of their trauma and the current situation in which they found themselves, "What do you want to be able to do that you're not doing?" It is clear, to me, that in a world that is economically and politically male dominant (still!), continual assignment and realignment of strengths can help make a woman become more successful. Women's part in shaping civilization has been underrated for too long, and there are many specific ways in which women demonstrate their needs. For instance, women need mothers who will be role models (ego ideals) and show them that there can be alternate career paths and even guide them toward counseling if necessary.

Part of this process of reinforcement by a positive model is to have the changing and growing woman acknowledge her history: my mother frequently did this as a reveal of her life story in front of me—a professional and highly involved community volunteer. After serving my internship and post-doctoral time at Mercy Hospital and Outpatient Mental Health Department in San Diego, CA, I likewise went on to use my history to help develop a job seeking skills program and mental health support network at the woman's jail in that county. Later I started my own clinic, Psychology and Professional Center.

In addition to a healthy personal and career path, one needs to continue self-care. The continued use of a mentor/ego ideal will provide the feedback necessary for keeping on track, excelling, and developing CONNECTION skills and personal strengths; it is also important to be able to accept limitations. As one recognizes ways to become resilient regardless of the obstacle, then difficulties give us opportunities to RECONNECT with our philosophy and value system [UFT], ultimately achieving and keeping the balance that we all need.

If we pursue therapy, we can see it as a teaching tool that also results in building strength. The therapist can become our "historian, reality test, anchor, cheerleader." As providers, therapists can get mutual feedback by such simple questioning as the *Session Rating Scale*, a 4-question form which asks: "How heard and respected have you felt in the session, how much has the session addressed your goals, how good a fit was the therapist, and how the session seemed overall?"

Defining Wellness

In many cultures, there has been a growing split between cerebral-intellectual function and affective-emotional experience (Fromm, 1968). Fromm describes a split between "thought from feeling, mind from the heart, truth from passion." Rationality is fine and can prove to be quite productive in our current techno-industrial world, but the heart will continue to want things that the intellect may know nothing about, such as a need for balance and growth. Signs and symptoms of this unmet need show up as anxiety and an abiding sense of loss that cannot be pinned down to any one cause (nor abetted by one's social media account!). Even "love" can become Codependent and lose a rationality that might give it balance. Love without independence is not freedom to choose and grow.

Prominent among these issues of resilience was generativity and giving to future generations, as well as being able to accept one's age, to find meaning and purpose, and to not yearn for the activities of youth (Jung, 1934, Erikson, 1950). To resolve one's fear of death (Jacques, 1965) and to loosen up and seize one more chance of rebirth (Vaillant, 1977) helps one to form a realistic picture of oneself and the world (Levinson, 1978). I often ask my patients, "What would a reasonable person do?" reminding them of all the work we have done to put anxiety and loss of control in its proper perspective.

Having looked at symbols and meaning for identity formation, mostly in male subjects, male writers (Jung, Jacques, Erikson, Vaillant, and Levinson) also looked at midlife issues in women. Along with the picture of men's development toward productivity, versus women's possible Codependency, came a parallel awareness of health concerns, physical and mental. Even when adult midlife issues bring these concerns regarding control and fear of death, there are structured methodologies for treatment support. Women (and men) can impact, shape, and even lead their families, their communities, and their immediate world when their consciousness is one which has developed an attitude of health, Self-acceptance, social competence, and resilience under stress.

Finally, in her 1998 article in *Social Work,* McQuaide presented the results of her research about women at midlife. Bringing her outlook as a female researcher, she found that 72.5% of the women studied described themselves as happy or very happy. "Wellness was defined as not being sick and as an absence of anxiety, depression, or other mental disorders...new conceptions of psychological well-being emphasize positive characteristics of growth and development, such as caring and trusting ties with others, a purpose in life, self-acceptance, and personal growth" (McQuaide, 1998, pp 21–31).

The therapeutic alliance can also be evaluated based on whether the client tends to be more trait-based or state-based (Zilcha-Mano, 2017). McQuaide confirmed that not only will the development of a "therapeutic" alliance bring benefit from working directly with a client, but the client can have their own "collective alliance", working with their many Selves and Personas to create safety and peace. The role of the therapist can be auxiliary parent, educator (prompting growth and increasing mastery), or therapeutic agent through transference of deeper neurotic tendencies. These outcomes may also be based on the original attachment patterns, i.e., whether they had "secure attachments" according to Bowlby's theory (1988). More secure histories enable more "here and now" states of the interpersonal relationship with the therapist to be formed.

McQuaide also quotes Apter (1997) as another of the few scholars to examine the actual experiences of women during midlife. Apter found the greatest challenge for a woman was dealing with messages from teen years about their upcoming roles in an adult world. She concluded that women must "at least listen to her own voice." Having found her voice, a woman is then able to be more active in designing an environment within which she can find fulfillment.

McQuaide notes one Self-in-relation theorist (Miller, 1976) emphasized the following as important to a woman's identity: "having CONNECTIONS with others...[creating] a friendship network...having the temperamental traits associated with resilience and vulnerability" [emphasis added] (Miller as quoted in McQuaide, 1998). These additional outcomes were also emphasized:

- To have the ability to grieve and let go of the past.
- To have the ability to construct a new midlife self.
- To believe in a protective, spiritual force outside of herself.
- To have the ability to find purpose and meaning in her life, to have a vision for the future.
- To believe that she has a right to a life and is not obligated to a life of self-sacrifice.

- To be accepting of herself, self-forgiving, and have a benign (not harsh) superego.
- To be accepting of her own body.

Much was discussed about male psyche in the previous chapter on Jungian psychology. I believe the above list of outcomes are also good goals for men as well. McQuaide's methodology came from scores collected in 17 areas: having friends, dealing with fear and anxiety, dealing with depression, dealing with anger, dealing with guilt, family relationships, job and career, spirituality, intimacy, money management, creativity, leisure time, finding satisfaction, finding contentment, self-acceptance, acceptance of their bodies, and coping with this stage of life. (Any one of these areas sounds like a good subject for a journal entry to me!) The bottom line is whether your work and daily activities are validating to your deeper values.

Do you work for money only, or also for the value you find in it? Time management is achieved by organizing your day and setting priorities, delegating tasks to others, when possible, then tackling the tough jobs first and controlling spending too much time in meetings or on the phone. You cannot teach values; you must live as an example. Do you achieve Self-mastery through Self-management and/or course corrections, using time effectively and according to some underlying plan? Are you aware of what future you are creating?

By summarizing all the above studies, we conclude that they were designed to gather information on the following constructs, which will give us a beginning format for arranging our lives toward healthy and fulfilling midlife results:

- Self-esteem
- Lack of Self-denigration
- Self-effectiveness
- Optimism
- The ability to grieve
- The belief that one has the right to live
- Having a vision or goal
- A sense of meaning in one's life

A person's act of constructing an identity along the way that will create strength and the boundaries to uphold a "positive narrative" by midlife is very important. And it is also important to not be overly hard on oneself or to a have an overly harsh superego (internal parent). The result of all this growth is high Self-esteem, shown through practice of spirituality, keeping up of personal appearance and health, and not allowing oneself to be marginalized. It will show up in one's personal, financial, sexual, and relational life! Healthy individuals will "develop goals for the future, grieve the past, and compose a positive life narrative" (Frankl, 1946, pp. 21–31). Thus, the real meaning of the word re-form is to form again, with the possibility of transcending that which existed before.

I often ask my clients who show relationship difficulties if they feel irreplaceable to their mate. Most often they feel surprised at the question, as if that sense of CONNECTION had never been considered by them. But it is a prevailing truth that making yourself valuable to someone with whom you have formed a relationship is just as important as thinking of them as important to you. As you value them, they will value you even more.

Brene Brown has long been a favorite writer of mine (listen to her wonderful TED talks!). My review of *Daring Greatly* (2012) found many supportive concepts to my UFT. Her view of the importance of CONNECTION lies in her ideas of "engagement", which is the ability to show vulnerability. "Fear and DISCONNECTION" are not signs of vulnerability, but rather of using defensiveness to "armor" oneself against abandonment and cynicism from others. Brown maintains successful accomplishment of "daring greatly" is the ability to remain "whole-hearted".

Much of one's creating armor may come from one's sense of being unworthy. A concept we have consistently discussed throughout these chapters is that one's early parenting and UFT, from their early history forward, will either create secure attachment and Self-esteem or fear of abandonment, self-loathing, shame, and creation of armor techniques. For Brown, the ability to CONNECT comes from developing compassion, first for Self and then for others.

Resilience is another concept that Brown brings into her study of vulnerability. It takes bravery and a true sense of Self to practice authenticity in response to shame. Brown uses the mantra, "If you own this story you get to write the ending"—which is a variant of Jung's statement, "I am not what has happened to me. I am what I chose to become" (Jung quoted by Brown, 2012, p. 80). Brown finds resilience resources are particularly important in dealing with catastrophizing, which is common in people with low Self-esteem.

People who consistently take a victim role will find themselves "rehearsing" the tragedy, which in turn, Brown writes, will create "perpetual disappointment." Finding gratitude as a resilient response to catastrophizing can be difficult if one is afraid of the fear of loss that can come after finding joy. We all search for the balance between the dark (discomfort, DISCONNECTION) and the light (flexibility, resilience, and tolerance for vulnerability); often this balance is reached through the practicality of studying, knowing, and exercising our values.

I have talked elsewhere about my abhorrence of our "instant potatoes" society. It seems that ever since WWII created the necessity for things, especially cooking, to be quicker and easier (ergo instant potatoes and sliced bread!), as a society we have lost our ability to pace ourselves, enjoy the moment and the activities necessitated by our daily lives. We are always in a hurry. We have lost faith in ourselves, what Brown calls being mapmakers (decide, plan, or come up with a solution, and then follow it to its conclusion without getting side-tracked) (Brown, 2012, p. 216).

Some days I feel like we all have ADD (attention deficit disorder) because our whole society can't get on track! I really like her idea of mapmaking because it fits well with my idea of a UFT, where we can review our map to develop a normal sense of Self and where we want to go next, for ourselves and for our relationships. This ability to "take a moment" helps us recognize and enhance our strengths and our limitations. "When you shut down vulnerability you shut down opportunity" (ibid, 2012, p. 208). Brown wants us to move from controlling to engaging; with vulnerability comes the shift from risk to trust.

Based on Madeo's theory of asymmetry and certitude (see Chapter Two), I ask my patients whether they really need certitude to feel safe or if they can see the positives of a world with no absolutes or judgment. Did our "first families" leave us equipped or ill-equipped to deal with asymmetry, that life is always changing and unpredictable (Heisenberg) just like the weather. Because nature/genetics may have left us more anxious or hypersensitive and/or nurture/parenting left us with difficulty handling shame messages and traumatic incidents, we need to learn, and then teach our children, accommodation skills which come with a sense of belongingness and worthiness.

Brene Brown tells a story about having to call a friend one day in great distress. Her friend was willing to be there for her because Brown had been there for her friend more than once. As the story goes, this friend's mother-in-law could be quite the drunk, but the grandchildren tended not to be aware of this. So, during a particular mother-in-law visit, Brene's friend got her to come over to help with the passed-out mother-in-law before the children got home from school and saw grandma in this condition. When Brene asked her friend about the call, her friend simply responded, "I thought to myself, Brene is my only friend whom I could call to move a dead body and not tell." And so, it was true.

As Brown reported, they had this kind of relationship. Similarly, the relationship, fictional or not, between Grey and Christina on *Grey's Anatomy* is now known universally as having a "person". People refer to each other as "my person". That one and only true friend is a rare commodity and one to be cherished. This process is what defines the real foundation of our society. People who are friends don't just like the same things, they will be each other's "person", even if it means helping move a dead body [sic]. Recently, one of my clients was discussing some relational issue and she spontaneously said, "You know, she would move a dead body for me." The client had been listening to my feedback!

Part of a healthy relationship between partners is the give and take of a balanced power structure. If the man can identify with his feelings and communicate as the woman identifies with her work (somewhat a shift from past traditional values), then that communication and CONNECTION will provide meaning and not alienation. Again, from my mother's handouts we find:

> Some men just shut down when a woman is over-identified with her work, cut off from her personal power and ability to respond, give and take... V. Haradon handout.

The type of individuals in this quote begin to question themselves and their relationship, perhaps even looking to others (or an "It" they are addicted to) to solve their problems (More about this in Chapter Sixteen on addictions). In marital relationships, once there is a clear awareness that something is wrong, both the personal and interpersonal clues need to be interpreted and adjusted for a healthy shift back to a CONNECTION that is personally fulfilling and away from negative personalization. A clue that something is wrong may show up in isolative behaviors or in the use of denial.

Using Affirmations for Growth

Self-esteem building focuses on general self-care, health and wellness building, global consciousness, a well-rounded education through the availability of information on the internet and (it occurs to me), a sense of renaissance-growth and maturity not unlike the Platonic world of the Greeks or that of da Vinci during the Renaissance. One focuses on Self not because one is narcissistic but as a valuable conduit for viability in the fast pace of today's world. Affirmations for Self-esteem could be:

Affirmations

I realize solitude is an opportunity for me to develop my self-esteem.
The more successfully I handle solitude, the more successfully I'll handle my relationships.
The better I know myself, the better I can communicate.
The more I enjoy being alone, the more I can enjoy being with people.
Since there is no one exactly like me, I am interesting to myself.
When I am alone, the potential for my real feelings is aroused; and this is valuable to me.
I am now willing to let my suppressed feelings come up to the surface and to discover new insights about myself.
I find even depression gives me the opportunity to discover something about myself.
I can achieve self-awareness through solitude.
My creativity is enhanced when I am alone.
I can now be alone as much or as little as I want to.
I can stop being alone anytime I want to. (*New Woman* September October 1976)

Eleanor Roosevelt wrote a famous and beautiful prose/poem which expresses her experience of human nature.

Men and women send metamessages to each other: men and women use language differently; women take the attitude that the purpose of a conversation is to explore cooperative solutions to common problems, while men regard speech as an extension of fighting by other means. So strong is the urge to dominance in American men that they will drive right past a policeman rather than stop and ask for directions, because to ask for help is to put oneself in a position of inferiority.

By contrast, according to Deborah Tannen, American women are so accustomed to asking for help that they have been known to ask strangers for directions even when they know perfectly well where they are going. "Nagging", being told to do anything whereas women are convinced men would do what she asks, if he only understood what she really wants him to do, but a man who wants to avoid feeling that he is following orders may instinctively wait before doing what she asked, to imagine that he is doing it of his own free will. Nagging is the result because each time she repeats the request he again puts off fulfilling it...Men resist the intimacy of discussing their feelings, because it implies a need for help, advice, or consolation [emphasis added] (*Newsweek,* 10/1/1990).

These thoughts express in a timeless way the nature of my theme: the Self perceives, CONNECTS, yearns to know, to tend to another and to grow from the experience. Of course, all this hope and peace of mind has the extra benefit of being packaged up within the context of the natural world, where we don't control a damn thing and isn't that a blessing!

For over ten years, I subscribed to *Heron Dance (*Middlebury, VT), which either arrived in the mail or through the internet to provide me with beautiful art color washes of nature scenes, poetry and journal entries from the thoughtful editors Ron MacIver and Ann O'Schaughnessy, and their many contributors. Without fail every month or so, I was inspired to do my own writing (could I paint so beautifully!) and to bring myself back to a point of mindful awareness of just what is important in my everyday work and relationships. Unfortunately, I am no longer getting mail from the site outreach@herondance.org, but readers can search for back issues there. Here is one of my favorites from *A Pause from Beauty #69:*

From Kathy's email.

Come, lay your head down in my lap as I stroke the world-weariness from your mind. Feel the gentle energies pass between us. Listen to the soft breaths that keep us. The fruitful ground is just outside. The soil is sweet with fall's offering. The Grandmother Oak still stands in my back yard. When I feel this way, I go out to stand with her. I say, 'Old one, you're still here...' and it feels like a kind of security. Assurance that some pretty serious history has passed and this old one has weathered it all. I feel small then, and the great clamoring inside me that are trying to work through something huge become quieter.

Finding Balance

Pain and loss will still come, but out of such experiences comes growth as well. It is the balance of life, and this is how the *Tao* works; to keep moving forward one needs the traction of adversity and the knowledge that sometimes comes from shame. As I have been talking about the effects of one's genetic, cultural, and attachment influences (unified theory/UFT), my goal has been to portray the trajectory of one's growth. As one learns to identify with one's Self, amazing truths are revealed: to understand one's *anima/animus* and see glimpses of one's Shadow as defined by Jung (Chapter Eighteen), and to accept that the original path of one's potential may have not progressed entirely to a place of full bloom. Instead, it may have taken another path, one of different Dharma and meaning but also of great treasures.

Working with one's Shadow ultimately creates a fuller "unity of experience". This acceptance of Self as it is, and as productively giving to Self and others, is my definition of mental health in its purist form, well beyond either society's identification with fame and fortune or the rejection of Outliers based on fearfulness. This process is the renaissance of one's inner world.

In a 1981 article, *The Wilderness of the Soul (Part II)*, Peter Monkres talks about this moving from one's personal history to maximizing one's potential.

> [It is] the spiritual supermarket, only a people who have lost their way could possibly create and consume such an anarchistic array of alternatives, of religious and psychological products. Each alternative, each franchise, each school of thought, we hope, will become a password that can be utilized to roll away the stone which bars our access to our own souls...when we react with discomfort, anxiety, irritation, anger, shame, nervousness or even despair (Monkres, P., 1981, p. 168).

Monkres agrees with the Buddhist philosophy that recommends we "…. bend as a tree in the wind and absorb important information from the shadow," a quote which reminds me of Jung and the *Tao*; gaining perspective through the pursuit of awareness, but also through healthy detachment in a manner that comes from a recognition of the impermanence of life.

> Tao abides in non-action,
> Yet nothing is left undone…
> Without form there is no desire.
> Without desire there is tranquility.
>
> Lao Tzu

Detachment/DISCONNECTION allows us to achieve a different type of focus and strength that comes from breaking apart the hard and unyielding. I cannot underscore this concept of reframing strongly enough; it is at the core of my theory and my purpose in writing down my ideas and my approach to helping patients. There is always a new approach, another point of view, or to quote Einstein, "It's all relative." Or as my mother would say, "Every problem has a solution if you just stick with it." Thus, our Soul will become stronger, and we will experience hope.

Dealing with Despair

The next chapter teaches enhanced concepts with which we can each evolve and get the most out of psychotherapy. It is a powerful moment to realize that the "cultivation of hope and the abolition of despair" are the best we can expect if we, in turn, give our trust and self-respect to the process, whether in psychotherapy or not. Assagioli (1980) believed it took work on all levels, diagnostic, personality, physical, and transpersonal to come to synthesis and growth. Therapy can teach the client to cope with the memory of old wounds and provide tools to deal with later disappointments, loneliness, and loss.

Beavers and Kaslow (1981) propose a paradigm where there are two usual outcomes when humans are frightened; they will reach out for help in one of these two ways—either by attempting 1) to establish a relationship with others, or 2) to control themselves or the environment. I have seen this type of approach over and over during my fifty years of being a therapist. Often my patients have even entered "risky" relationships, where a lack of trust was obvious, and the relationship was doomed to fail; my conjecture was that the individual was setting it up this way from the beginning to validate his or her own mistrust issues.

In these cases, the need to control others and feel "safe" takes precedence over the real level of intimacy that might be provided. Because we transform relationships as we transform ourselves, being in healthy relationships requires drawing from all our internal selves. Just as children learn from mistakes, we must hold a healthy respect for how we learn from our relationships, good or bad. As Satir says, "Falling on one's face led to the joy of getting up, control is trustable, people are not" (Satir, 1976).

It is also highly likely that in their families of origin these individuals were "trained" to relate to others like this— "loving means controlling." "Each family member tries to avoid loneliness and despair by controlling and being controlled, each intimidating in his own way. These are reciprocal elements essential to homeostatic balance" (Monkres, 1981). I have a client whose mother was so narcissistic and controlling that the relationship was finally labeled as Munchausen by proxy. A very dangerous dynamic, the mother needed the daughter (her only child) to be sick to prove her dependency upon the mother and that that she (the daughter) would never abandon the mother-daughter dyad/enmeshment.

It took many years of therapy, but the daughter finally moved out. After she did, the mother killed herself, as she had threatened she would. My client was obviously devastated and started a slow regressive slide into Self-harming and even her own suicidal ideation. It took several years for her to regain her own boundaries and sense of a Self with some personal power. I can happily report that, just recently, she was married and maintains a very healthy relationship.

> The riskiest control effort is to isolate oneself to prevent supposedly dangerous expressions of feeling or thought. The intent is that through such heroic means, one may remain unknown and safe. The family messages re: when you suffer a loss, do not complain, do not remember, do not mourn; when lonely, do not speak out, do not search for others; when in pain, be silent, and appear strong and invincible. The problem, of course, is that by becoming an emotional recluse, one obtains nothing from others. Such a person may develop anomie, with no meaning evident in living (Durkheim, 1951); at that stage suicide becomes a threatening possibility (ibid, 1981, pp. 119–126).

Although people do not like to talk about suicide much, when one is called into action in response to an actively dangerous situation regarding suicidal issues, there is a protocol. After first assessing whether the person has a plan (and how lethal and imminent it might be), the next step is to assess how many symptoms of regressed, helpless, worthless, or dangerous ideation the person has.

If the precipitating stress has been extreme, at least in their mind, then giving some stress-tolerance behaviors to practice is suggested, even if it is just sleep and a healthy meal. My mother was famous for this; she would stop an intervention with a suicidal individual and say, "I missed lunch to stay here with you, but I'm sorry I'm starving, and my blood sugar is low. Can we go across the way to Denny's and get a bite to eat?" Of course, the person would comply, despite their crisis, and once they were at the restaurant, they would eat something too; eventually they would start to feel a bit better and showed a willingness to go rest and come back the next day for more support.

Evaluation of possible solutions for losses, separation and divorce issues, medical problems, or financial hardships are the most common areas of concern. If resources can be suggested, it is also important to evaluate at what level of comfort the individual may be with interpersonal relationships and how comfortable they might be with reaching out for support in areas that they might not have previously considered. A boundary, always important, vacillates between the act of union and the separation that necessarily follows. If left to itself, most organisms, including humans, will self-regulate. Goldstein (1973) calls this a negotiation between who I am and what I need.

> "Hope" is thing with feathers
> That perches in the soul—
> And sings the song without words
> And never stops—at all—
>
> – Emily Dickinson

I have always seen my job as the source of another kind of hope: helping my patients develop or rediscover parts of themselves (sometimes using archetypal work or uncovering deeper sources of anxiety), the foundation of their values (UFT of Self), and where they think their own personal journey can take them. Here is a list of Frankl's important areas for consideration in a therapeutic experience:

1. To be heard with respectful attention and pertinent queries by the counselor.
2. To have successes and define reachable goals that are small achievable, and clearly defined.
3. To self-observe, if one is helpless and a victim of circumstances, then one cannot feel hopeful, counselor uses systems orientation and can be an observing ego, pointing out how causes are effects.
4. To develop better interpersonal skills, increasing self-esteem; a high satisfaction quotient and hope go hand and hand.
5. To reduce mistrust and address painful unresolved ambivalence; many clients have a childlike uncritical trust in others, "I can teach YOU to help others avoid hurting you." Kohlberg rephrased the 'golden rule', "If one can manage not to do unto others what you would not have them do unto you, one can create a safe interpersonal environment."
6. To distinguish now from then.
7. To have a transcendent belief system (Frankl, 1970, as quoted by Monkres, 1981).

Given these seven values of the therapeutic experience, there will always be a balance between the need to CONNECT and the occasional need for distance. But if we return to Hegel, we remember that it is in this dialectical tension, which ultimately will require resolution and synthesis, that we find a wealth of information about ourselves: archetypes, dark side/shadow unconscious images, creativity, repressed fears and shames, needs and dreams…all of it.

Love is an Archetype

Over the centuries many have come to see Platonic love as "divine delirium", a communion of the souls and the "misfortune of selfness". Because Eros is the desire for unity, and a yearning for one's opposite polarity, our lives are often formulated upon how to find that "Other" that fits, to create a completion of the dualism. Once this dualism is contained, homeostasis and transcendence become possible. "Eros within the self as a defense against death is narcissism. Eros as a means to an end, ego integration, is unity or non-polarity" (de Rougemont, 1983). Unfortunately, for some, the Other which dualistically completes Unity is only an object or drug of choice, one which can be controlled and trusted within one's own sphere of influence.

Sex may even be a method of numbing current or old wounds, a desperate search for acceptance, regardless of the loss of pride or experience of shame. Relationships are meant to be dialectical, "soulful encounters that temper and enlarge. One of the bridges between the sexes, to be sure, is sex. But men, too often feeling deficient in discourse, place too much emphasis on intercourse" (Hollis, 1994, p. 104). The purpose of a committed relationship, of which marriage is but one example, is not only to take care of each other, but also to grow through and with each other.

Erikson (1950) states there are three processes, the somatic process, the ego process, and the societal process. The integration, transcendence, and understanding of the relativity of these aspects of human experience is the purpose of actualization. "You can lead an expert to the source of his fear and disgust, but you cannot always make him drink of his observation" (Erikson, 1950). As I have noted so often in my practice, narcissism can be the defense of Self against its own ego identification and growth. Likewise, I believe "love" as sexuality, rather than Eros, is the defense of Self against its own ego. "Without defenses the ego disintegrates. With extreme levels of defense, the ego boundaries become rigid and resist change. Appropriate levels of defense, which could be referred to as levels of coping, facilitate growth of the ego" (Haradon, 1975).

What I really mean by coping is that sometimes disintegration, by means of a unification of polarities, also presents the individual with the situation of transcending his fear of self-awareness and/or even death. In the next chapter, we will face our deeper selves squarely and learn that only through true Self-care can we experience a balance, and perhaps transcendence, in our lives.

Chapter Twenty
Self-Care as an Entry to Awareness

He who has resolved his doubts and whose mind is absorbed in the Self lives happily in the world. Realizing that the Self is beyond action, I do whatever needs to be done at any one time and live happily.
– Ashtavakra Gita (quoted in Robert Powell, *Return to Meaningfulness*, 1981)

Difficult CONNECTIONS, at times, might lead one to a sense of anxiety or meaninglessness. Some of this anxiety comes from situational pressure, some from social abandonments or failures, and some from our own internal flawed biochemistry in reaction to fight/flight/freeze or (normal) stressful situations. The core UFT of our Self also shows us the unlived life that might "haunt us, summon us, judge us" (Hollis, 1994). No one else knows what is right for us, but something in us certainly knows. Sometimes we have lost the passion through which our nature sees its own fullest expression, perhaps because we were inadequately supported, or even discouraged by parents. "Whatever the fates imposed—permission, passion, programming—we are summoned to break through the old paradigms, to risk all, to be worthy of the journey to which the Gods have summoned us" [What does the Soul ask?] (ibid, 1994).

Self-discovery (consciousness) is known through expression (creative pursuits, journaling, sharing), not just thinking/dreaming. This process results in the journey to oneness. "Don't be a follower, be an adder" [emphasis added] (Catala, 1998, p. 4). Catala also quotes Nietzsche about how one should take from healthy and inspiring mentors, as far as it goes, and then find their own rituals that will reinforce positive, sacred, and CONNECTING behaviors. We must develop principles we can live by, "an invisible structure which generates [healthy] behavior." This requirement for structure is very much like that which we see in the process of going through some kind of recovery, such as the steps of AA.

Not all treatment is only individual work. Often a client will ask to bring their partner, especially if there is sexual acting out in one or both members of the couple. Infidelities, and their treatment, come from an awareness of the fear that causes them (Solomon and Teagno, 2007). The authors recommend giving homework assignments between sessions to teach the couples to recognize which of treatment paradigms apply to them. In the area of fear of communication, for instance, one good journaling idea for working with couples with problems is as follows: "Times I noticed I withdrew or isolated to 'think' instead of having the feeling and acknowledging it."

Could we make it a goal to "go forward in life together and be partners in the inevitable ups and downs of the future?" Wachtel (2018) identifies the need to focus on what yearnings and CONNECTIONS still exist between the couple rather than focusing on criticism and accusations. "I'm struck by how you're each trying hard today to listen nondefensively" is Wachtel's common rallying call. She maintains "It is a rare person who doesn't respond well to approval."

Even in a couple, Self-discovery can be isolative, loneliness comes from lack of intimacy and Self-judgment, causing low Self-esteem and feeling DISCONNECTED. "Judgment exacerbates DISCONNECTION. Our response to signs of loneliness should be to find a CONNECTION" (Brown, B., 2017, pp. 161, 199). Jung based Self-discovery on a willingness to face the darkness of the Shadow and to integrate archetype insights, as he called them. Sometimes, as I also use my work with the *Tao* and mindfulness to support clients, I think it is the experience of limitlessness, or the unknown, that brings people directly in touch with their fear. Of course, this is Mecca for me as a therapist, for as we investigate our fear, we make the most progress.

We all search for a breakthrough in the discovery process—therapeutic or Self-accomplished—of coming to our own great archetype called the Reckoning. As presented also in a previous chapter, Victor Frankl (1946) became a prominent figure in psychology after presenting his theory of hope and survival as therapeutic solutions. His ideas were formulated from his years in a Nazi concentration camp. It was my honor to see him lecture while a student at United States International University (USIU). The school had installed a special chair in Logotherapy for him. Before his death in 1997 at the age of 97, he came to USIU in the 70s to lecture—sharing his insights from his experiences—including his hope for mankind and its ability to help individuals who suffer while trying to find meaning.

Frankl's founding of Logotherapy, otherwise known as the Third Viennese school (which separated it from Freudian or Adlerian schools of psychology), was focused on this factor of finding meaning in one's life where meaninglessness, hopelessness, victimhood, or feelings of being an Outlier may exist. The theory proposes, contrary to the Freudian tenets of Frankl's time that, rather than a "will-to-pleasure" or "will-to-power" as the source of man's instinct for survival, it was his "will-to-meaning" which created his inner power for self-care and determination to survive. The 12-steps of AA are based on this sense of finding serenity through a Higher Power, even in the face of powerlessness and emptiness.

An addict may have filled his emptiness with his substance of choice, but then, through the recovery process, he learns to replace it and fill it with spirituality. Spirituality is celebrating that we are all inextricably CONNECTED to each other by a power greater than all of us, and that our CONNECTION to that power and to one another is grounded in love and compassion (Fromm, 1968). Frankl approaches man's anxiety by watching how his awareness of his limitedness can put him in touch with his existential anxiety.

One definition of Logotherapy is doing something worthwhile, to experience meaning through such events as a sunset or a relationship; perhaps one could take a constructive attitude toward even the worst situation. Another author who came to USIU while I was studying for my doctoral degree was Rollo May. In his two classic works, *Man's Search for Himself* (1953) and *Love and Will* (1969) [my personal favorite], he agreed with Frankl that the psychological origin of emptiness stemmed from feelings of powerlessness.

Sometimes just relying on basics is important. Contrary to the way standardized mental health treatment tends to pathologize and give diagnoses, Buddhist principles encourage one to look at oneself and others from a positive point view, where individuals are basically whole, complete, and inter-CONNECTED. How can therapists help their clients find hope despite their suffering?[149]

Both the response of avoidance and the response of despair tend to lead to negative consequences. The third alternative, referred to as courage, is more positive. Courage does not remove the anxiety of meaninglessness, but it facilitates the exercising of choice and the taking of responsibility. This courage is 'in spite of' the apparent meaningless of one's existence (Tillich, 1952, p. 66, as quoted in, Ruffin, et. al.).

The Practice of Meaning

People often practice their spiritual belief in the company of others, whether Christian, Jewish or Buddhist (Sangha), in a search for the certitude in something outside of oneself. Robert Powell, in *Return to Meaningfulness* (1981), proposes that creativity is a state of grace, in-spiration requires drawing in something from the outside. When we see this creativity mirrored in the spiritual practice in others around us, we can better face our own meaninglessness.

As an example, many patients find that a diagnosis of cancer threatens to change their lives forever, but within the fear from this diagnosis, positive self-discoveries and insights can lead to powerful faith and a hope to a better future life, however long it might be. These unexpected positive responses to bad news can result in moments of happiness, spiritual awakening, and discovery of artistic and musical skills (right brain) that the patients may not have been aware of before

---

[149] Three alternative responses to feelings of meaninglessness, (moving instead toward Equanimity, one of the Three Jewels of Buddhism—See Chapter Nine), include:
- First, we can avoid that which gives us a sense of anxiety or is overwhelming. Many individuals will block any feelings that trigger being uncomfortable and will seek to escape (those feelings of fight/flight/freeze with which we are all so familiar). This knee-jerk reaction, even panic, will result in a loss of one's authenticity and equanimity in our responses, and can lead to alienation from one's Self. Bugental (1965) defined authenticity as a state in which an individual's needs are in harmony with the realities of the world. "Like an artist standing before an empty canvas, choose to despair at the nothingness or choose to become creative" (ibid, 1965). He perceived therapy as a philosophic venture, it is a facing of infinite. Likewise, Tillich (1952), who we will discuss further in this chapter, believed the Self was lost when one avoided the anxiety of meaninglessness, although meaning might be gained if the individual could hang in there with the pain.
- Secondly, we can face that our despair (Tillich, 1952) or absurdity (Bugental, 1965) are natural parts of life and that trying to avoid these experiences, or to stay in denial of them, could be a kind of self-destructive lifestyle in that they were "forms of self-alienation."
- Finally, we could find the courage to look at one's life history and the consequences of not facing Self authentically to manifest ongoing change.

their diagnoses. This process sometimes feels like a kind of epiphany about how to be able to live simply and authentically.

Instead of the same old self-defeating patterns, we can become more open to successful patterns of responding with awareness, gratitude, integrity and choosing our new life goals with passion. Often, we find honesty, creativity, commitment, and patience in the state of "knowing" that leads us to this "inner sense of integrity" and away from guilt and humiliation (Catala, 1998, p. 850). During growth, whether with the help of therapy or not, a prior manipulative aspect of an individual's personality may be acted out in a more creative manner and can lead to psychological growth and health.

Part of our success, with navigating the stresses or "meaninglessness" of daily life in our current society, can come from self-analysis and the resultant awareness of our needs and whether they are being met. This experience should precede looking for love and approval through a CONNECTION with someone else. The basic needs for healthy development toward this type of trust in an Other, also restudied by Maslow (1968), are: to be cared for, to be protected, to be respected, to be loved and admired, to gain mastery over our environment, to find self-expression, and to have appropriate boundaries that will keep us safe. If these needs are met, then we grow.

The mind has a need to understand, which results in the child's fabricating his or her own understanding if appropriate boundaries are not available. A child has little internal resources for dealing with stress, so the more stress that comes, the less a focus on growth will take place. As they develop, even in an age-appropriate way, then they will be unable to maintain or resolve the state of Self-alienation that is produced. The person may feel "stupid" or out of control.

In psychology and social work assessment, the common term "ADLs" refers to Activities of Daily Living and is considered a primary source of information about how well self-care is being accomplished. These activities (toileting, feeding, dressing, grooming, bathing and physical ambulation, shopping and food preparation, use of telephone, laundry, finances, responsibility for medications) may not be inclusive but they do give a pretty good idea of someone's daily existence and, trust me, more than one of my typical clients has problems in these areas. Knowing their level of functioning is very helpful in reorienting them toward regaining a sense of purpose and "meaning" as daily life improves.

My mother did her thesis on Adler's theory, as first described in Chapter Three. Her obvious influence led me to develop my own set of treatment techniques: 1) to reexamine the initial conclusions that may be protecting the person from buried traumas, 2) to tie this past to the present, 3) then to make peace with the past, taking away blame as a defense (passivity), to protect against fear of failure going forward.

In addition to Maslow's influences on American psychology, ancient ideologies from other parts of the world were also being brought to this country and integrated into our techniques. Confucius (551 BC), and Socrates (399 BC) after him, had already established the groundwork for living a meaningful, authentic, and "self-actualized" life in the Eastern cultures.

In the *American Psychologist,* Tweed and Lehman (2003) contrasted Socratic versus Confucian methods in the search for meaning. The concept of *ren* is the Chinese idea of lifelong striving for any human being to become the most genuine, sincere, and humane person he or she can become. This process is seen as a morality issue, which takes moral courage and a sense of righteousness and intellectual honesty.

> Confucius taught a sense of integrity and a sense of shame and supported recognizing one's wrongdoings and concomitantly amending oneself. The Socratic model may be about truth finding or even knowledge generation, but the Confucian model is about moral striving, which is very different from Western epistemology…[the] idea of a love or passion for learning being an end in itself, given that learning to Confucius was the only pathway toward lifelong moral striving and that moral ends serve no other purposes than themselves "Knowing it (insight, wisdom, understanding) which is not as good as liking to know it; liking to know it is not as good as loving to know it" (Tweed and Lehman quoting Li, 2003, p. 147).

Self-Esteem in the Development of the Self

Many of my patients have as treatment goals to obtain improved Self-esteem by working on improved knowledge of Self. Of course, some people come into therapy with an impatience about looking for a spiritual or metaphysical view of their lives; that reaction may just be in response to the suffering they are experiencing. They are looking for the immediate and the practical. I don't blame them. I must meet them on the level, intellectually and emotionally, where they are and give them some taste in meeting the needs for which they ask. Once they trust that the process of repair and resolution of some of their suffering has begun, then I can backtrack to the other issues mentioned above, understanding their defenses, their anxieties, the influences of their history, the UFT of their cultural values, and ultimately any addictions/compulsions.

Blanck and Blanck (1974) wrote an excellent book on how to help clients with both ego development and managing their various stages of anxiety and defense structure development. I often use this book as a roadmap with clients when building their treatment plan so they can visually see who they are, how they got there, where the "holes" are in their development, and where we are going according to our "team" plan for building their new defense structures for healthy Self-acceptance: powerlessness versus Self-acceptance, and helplessness versus Self-esteem. We work together to construct a reasonable "new normal" of where they would like to end up and look for "developmental trends" that show us we are on the right track. Any movement is viewed as success and reason for celebration!

Safety needs, the basic of all of Maslow's needs in his hierarchy (built upon Adlerian theory), speak to the importance that these needs be satisfied by orderliness and security. The need for stability and dependency requires a sense of protection, freedom from fear, anxiety, and chaos. How many of us do not have our need for structure, order, law, and limits met? In his work, *Who is Man?* (1965), Heschel speaks of man's nature overall as being "a series of ordered events, not only in an order of processes. It is a spiritual order. Moments of insight, moments of decision, moments of prayer—these may be insignificant in the world of space, yet they put life into focus" (Herschel, 1965, p. 43). It is as if our life creates its own "index", an internal, intentional catalogue of the events that give us our humanity (UFT).

Moving up Maslow's hierarchy, belonging and love needs involve "having a place in the world and people who care," while a need for Self-esteem reflects the need "to feel worthy of respect and to escape self…self-confidence, worth, strength, capacity, capability, and adequacy, of being useful and necessary in the world" (Kirkpatrick, 1979). If one has not achieved this level of self-worth, the feelings of inferiority and helplessness affect one's social functioning or community feeling (*Gemeinschaftsgefuhl,* or Adler's social interest). Many theorists believe that the world is becoming less violent and more principled.

This finding is reflective of how each of us, one person at a time, can change the worldview. Self-actualizing individuals can "accurately and efficiently perceive reality and judge people and situations soundly." Initially, many of my patients are not good at adapting to their environments as Outliers because they are not good at assessing the social cues around them. They must be taught better skills of assimilation and accommodation. The dialectical result here is adaptation.

Cognitive Strengths and Phenomenological Information

After the Third Force theorists developed a model for moral development and need satisfaction, Beck (1974) and Seligman (1976) added a broader view on how to use CBT to modify hopelessness or powerlessness. In 1979, George Matheson looked at Beck's (1974) theory that negative expectations were the cause for depressive mood states and Seligman's (1976) theory of learned helplessness, a state of apparent futility, and came to the following conclusion: "Through imagery conditioning, the desired adaptive responses are encouraged or reinforced by associating them with an imagined, pleasurable stimulus" (Matheson, 1979, pp. 61–64).

Unfortunately, even if the "imagined pleasurable stimulus/addictive response works, the resultant helplessness and victimhood can cause severe depressive symptoms and poor ADLs." The field of psychology worked hard to develop a better procedure to modify the negative cognitions and activity level of a chronically depressed patient. Simply "helping people acknowledge the past and then move on was keeping them stuck in the victim role" (Simon, 2012, p. 38).

As Beck and Seligman worked toward what would ultimately become the basis of Cognitive Behavioral Therapy (CBT), many measures of a discomfort/well-being continuum were designed. When I use the Beck Depression Inventory (1961) or Beck Anxiety Inventory (1988), outcomes are primarily assessed by the patient's self-report combined with the therapist's observation. "Anchor points created through re-experiencing a happy event memory from the past helped remediate the experience of helplessness." To the layman, most of learned helplessness may look like depression, so we will return to that perspective diagnostically when we address therapeutic situations; however, it is important to remember that there are other sources of depression besides behavior cues or needs deprivation.

CBT can reduce stress, discomfort, and anxiety in the short-term, and can teach acceptance of the reality of difficult situations in the long-term. It is a collaborative process, known by therapists as the "therapeutic alliance". Avoidance of Self-knowledge and Self-care is the cause of the anxiety, not a solution or an actual way out of the experiential pain or the anxiety that comes from making a difficult decision. Actualizing a positive experiential response, versus hanging onto an imaginary and anticipatory anxiety about what might happen, will allow the client to identify experiences for what they really are.

It is not just famous psychologists that are concerned with this sense of pain and isolation; it is the great subject of writers and poets. I described my love for the poetry journal/publication, *Heron Dance,* in Chapter Nineteen. Many years ago, I read this touching (and to the point) writing:

Under the surface there is a raging furnace in each one, or a cold, frozen hell of despair. A truly brave cheerful man, with living faith and hope, is rare to see…Sacrifice is the core of sacredness. What we sacrifice is what becomes sacred to us…internal power…because I've dealt with what I'm vulnerable to, those issues don't scare me anymore, be honest with myself, I make good choices in my life to be thoughtful, I am aware that I think more, or figure out more or reflect more than many of my friends. I must be building a set of values or a set of guidelines that help me when I come to intersections and choices. "When you're unhappy about the Way, that's when The Way becomes difficult" (MacIver, 2004).

We must all have a sacred place: somewhere where we can go that no one knows where we are, no TV or newspapers, no friends, no bills. In this place, one can be truly creative and out of that creative energy can eventually come something really special.

We are not focused on science or theoretical concerns in this chapter, however phenomenological investigations soon bring us to an awareness of theistic and existential issues. It is important to recapitulate that the human form is also functioning inside a more complex universe. Theistic existentialists such as Pascal (1647), Kierkegaard (1844), and Tillich (1952) studied how unity of action comes first from the dialectical process (thesis, antithesis, synthesis). Of these three philosophers, Tillich (1952) provides an emphasis on individual consciousness and "the mysterious gift of existence" (Tillich,1952, quoted by Yoder, 1982, p. 31). Tillich asks: "How can the realms of our experience, those of the outer and inner world, be brought to a unity within the framework of an evolutionary universe?" [CONNECTION] (ibid, 1982, p. 431).

As I have discussed in several previous chapters, science investigates that which is outside of us, but also that which is inside of us, and we must figure out how to unify mind and matter, past and future, many and one, forming a uni/multi-versal view of our lives that can be understood with the information contained within the UFT of our epigenetic and historical context. A dialectical view emerges "that stresses oscillation and movement between poles," which Tillich viewed as directly moving us toward a synthesis and helpful explanation of human beings, thus an explanation of the basic "rugged individualism" of so many humans.

Life is impermanent; progress is not inevitable. We must work hard in our daily mindfulness practice and our daily shedding of self-loathing to reach what de Chardin calls "choice and discernment". Defining "mindfulness" is difficult, but I would describe it as moments of experience where the "personal" can separate from the Self. Language and intellectualization no longer create safety; rather a sense of being in the Now or *Taoist* One allows emotions to bypass the rational and to create awareness of an unfolding process of compassion toward Self. The goal of Self-awareness, whether through the phenomenological world of Tillich or the humanistic Third Force world of Maslow, is to move toward convergence of suffering and choice, the place where hope and motivation to change lies. My role as therapist is to teach Self-positivity, Self-reflection, and the ability to shift the focus away from Self-criticism. Communication problems with others cannot be the focus of change until the Self is first reinforced. We call this empathy.

A concrete example of empathy would be the process of taking a hurt/situation/problem/fear and then, with eyes closed, gain enough distance from the sensations or attitudes to bring attention to "what is", to organize a new feeling through variations in closeness/distance from the feelings as they arise in consciousness. From here, anticipatory anxiety can turn into an experience of normalized anxiety, keeping the future in the future; the Now gives us contextual solutions which use effective and flexible methods to put ourselves and our reactivity into a new perspective.

Trust as the Foundation

We can use that which we experience, hopeless or helpful, to measure our own current level of functioning, sometimes referred to as phenomenology. My doctoral dissertation on the Rorschach Psychodiagnostic Test (better known as the inkblot test) was a phenomenological one. Many earlier philosophers (see Chapter Two) and psychological researchers, (e.g., May (1958), Rogers (1961), and Frankl (1963)), used this methodology to discern the best way to achieve changes in personality and symptomology. Researcher/therapist Carl Rogers had great success with this method.

An example of this methodology was his use of the Q sort, first developed by Will Stephenson (1935). Through many individual choices, the phenomenological world of an individual was revealed, allowing the researcher to study a single case and still collect quite a bit of information. Rogers had a great desire to test, implement and share what he discovered; he had a great openness to other people's ideas and to life in general (Heppner, 1984).

Of the psychological theorists, Carl Rogers may have also had the most practical influence on everyday functioning of individuals, marriages, education, businesses, and societal values. In my travels to Russia in 2000, I saw first-hand how even Soviets during the pre-break-up of USSR had established counseling centers and used Rogerian techniques in their drug treatment centers, quite successfully I might add (in conjunction with 12-step, daily yoga, and macrobiotic diets after detoxification). Rogers' theory is based on the three therapist behaviors that he believed produced the most effective change in the therapeutic process: genuineness/congruence in the process, acceptance/unconditional positive regard, and accuracy/empathy in therapeutic perception.

> The individual has within him or herself vast resources for self-understanding, for altering his or her self-concept, attitudes, and self-directed behavior…There are three conditions which constitute this growth-promoting climate. The conditions apply, in fact, in any situation in which the development of the person is the goal… [emphasis added] (Rogers, C., year unknown).

It is easy to see how being genuine will lead to a congruent sense of therapeutic CONNECTION between the therapist and the client; but for Rogers it is the second and even more powerful step of showing acceptance, of voicing the unconditional positive regard, that took his methodology beyond the psychodynamic methods of Freud. This sense of caring and sharing may have been in the psychodynamic/Freudian consulting room, but it wasn't in the theory.[150] In fact, based on the pronouncements against transference and countertransference, sharing anything about self to aid in the therapeutic alliance and comfort of the client was strictly forbidden until this new supportive type of therapy came along.

Rogers believed that whatever the client is feeling at a moment of disclosure, the realness needed to be reciprocated by the therapist in some indication of understanding and acceptance. This response was the third Rogerian technique, empathy, being accurate in what is sensed and mirrored back to the client. Having built a basic trust from use of these methods, the therapist can now build on that basic trust, to create a "flow" toward more disclosure, toward complex and complete actualization of the client's inner developmental needs.

> My inner spirit has reached out and touched the inner spirit of the other. Our relationship transcends itself and has become a part of something larger…A basic philosophy rather than simply a technique or a method…It empowers the individual, and when this personal power is sensed, experience shows that it tends to be used for personal and social transformation (ibid, year unknown).

Clients trust the therapist through therapeutic CONNECTION, allowing the clients to trust themselves again, which includes CONNECTING to their emotions and bodily sensations. They need to develop compassion for themselves. Failed attachment and poorly modeled socially adept behaviors had initially caused a loss in the ability to trust.

---

[150] Unfortunately, whatever both Freud and Jung stated as important professional boundaries which should be set with patients, it is known that both these theorists and therapists often had personal relationships with their patients, and even sexual contact with several of them.

With my own clients, once the therapeutic alliance has been formed, the client feels freer to give me feedback; I often have what I call "report card day", when I encourage a give and take discussion about what is working and what is not working in our therapeutic relationship. It is okay for me to "tumble off my pedestal" as an open and transparent therapist.

In this way, I often augment the techniques of Cognitive Behavioral Therapy (CBT), which insurance companies recommend so often (because it's "supposed to be" quicker). But I find that authenticity works better every time! Obviously, I must go with the individual characteristics that the clients present; in turn, they become more of an expert in themselves and develop good decision-making, giving a summary of how they are doing in their personal lives, at work, and in social situations. Otherwise, the anxiety, avoidance, and even PTSD symptoms I see demonstrated may cause short-term and addictive reactions to get a more immediate relief.

People avoid because it reduces distress, discomfort, and anxiety in the short-term even if it maintains both anxiety and the uncomfortable circumstances over the long-term…paralyzed by indecision many people may avoid daily choices that lead to gradual lasting change in factor of choices that offer immediate gratification but are unhealthy (Dobson & Dobson, 2018).

Harold Greenwald, author of *Direct Decision Therapy* (1975), taught another class I took in graduate school (he also taught the hypnosis class). I learned how to prioritize the influences on my decision-making process and how to "let go" of those decisions which it turned out weren't really in my purview to act on. To this day, this process is the "evidence-based" nature of the way I do therapy, and I feel it has a very collaborative effect. Dobson and Dobson call this technique "collaborative empiricism". In many ways, it's not that different from how I've raised my own children (now in their thirties). In therapy, I support the client's sense of control and give them space for a sense of "Self-efficacy", which is about having the right tools.

"Therapy", per se, does not have to take place in a therapist's office, on a couch, or in a group. Many self-help groups through church-sponsored, 12-step sponsored, post-illness, or PTSD-sponsored opportunities can be of assistance as well. The New Thought movement, headed by philosopher Ernest Holmes, reinforced group process and was reflective of the previous teachings of Mary Baker Eddy/Christian Science and Ralph Waldo Emerson. Holmes' writing had an influence on Emmett Fox, who wrote *The Sermon on the Mount* in 1934. Holmes' book, *The Science of Mind* (1922) and the subsequent magazine by the same name, first published in 1935, was to go on to have great influence in tandem with his speaking engagements all over the United States for many decades, starting from 1916. Holmes was able to philosophically combine newly emerging scientific concepts with longstanding religious and philosophical ones, which led to the formal establishment of the Church of Religious Science in 1954.

The experience of studying the writings of Holmes and the tenets of Religious Science while I was in graduate school paralleled what I was also learning about being a therapist; I integrated a deeper spiritual basis to my practice, which my clients have always liked. Most important, I suppose, I learned during this period that growth is gained through trusting, risking, and being vulnerable. Growth comes from freeing the inner Self from judgmental internal processes. Fear is often the source of vulnerability, fear of conflict, of rejection, or of failure. Motivation comes from reconciling the variance between what I "ought to do", the messages from outside influences, with what I want to do. Negative influences take away my motivation to act and I become less trusting. The safer and "in control" I feel the more motivated and willing to trust I will be.

Integrity of purpose and action comes from a congruence of motivations, beliefs, feelings, and the resultant behaviors in any situation. You must trust someone to know him and let him know you, to care and be cared for, to respect and be respected. And trust determines the quality of the response made to another person. "Loving people are living people" (Fromm, 1956). The impersonal nature of the automated world within which we live spurs a renewed need to fulfill our creative nature.

Every Day Slow Self-Torture=Hate

Thomas Wolfe was my high school writing hero (*Look Homeward Angel*, 1929). I envisioned myself in the character Eugene, but I also knew I couldn't "go home again" to that lost childhood where perhaps I didn't get enough nurturing. If I, or millions of others, was ill-equipped, then where was our home to be? And then I learned...I needed to "come home" to myself. In 1983, George Bach talked about this inner "home", of an inner "friend" that ultimately helps us defend against our "inner enemy", the source of our anxiety and self-criticism (*The Inner Enemy*, Bach and Torbet, 1983). Without this friendly inner voice, you can be very lonely indeed.

> You must find your self-respect within, not from friends, family, or acquaintances—for no amount of society's approval of your image will make up for your own judgment of your worth...anxieties are natural: they are what drive you, in whatever direction, for better or for worse. Where do you begin to do battle with the Inner Enemy? The first step is to declare your intent to stand up and fight. The declaration itself is therapeutic, for the Inner Enemy loves it when you pretend it's not there...You feel like an impostor...Have you ever noticed how your free-floating anxieties and self-criticism abate when a real problem comes up and things aren't going very well anyway? (ibid, 1983).

Many of my clients are unable to see much worth about themselves upon first review. They are usually caught up in some type of drama, of which they are not only the "victim" but with which they use the facts (and their negative inner voice) to drive their low self-esteem. When I try to resurrect something of value in their view of themselves there is usually a therapeutic battle, the one predicted by Bach and Torbet.

> The Inner Enemy is a great museum builder. It keeps all the joyless, negative Information on file and can display it at a moment's notice...The joylessness

of the Inner Enemy is boundless. If you are anxious and feel your life is in a mess, chances are your Inner Enemy is acting up in ways you don't recognize. You must look a little closer at the things that go wrong in your life and see if any of them are self-inflicted, not the responsibility of any outside person or situation. Try to capture random thoughts that come to you. You will notice you have two voices in your inner life (ibid, 1983).

As a theoretician writing in the middle of the decades when the "Third Force" of Humanistic Psychology was really taking off, Bach and Torbet built on the work of Rogers, Gestalt therapy, and the way in which Transactional Analysis (Berne and Harris) named the "games" we were playing. Here is one the "names" they gave our inner voices.

The Ally: it reassures you of the benefits and rewards of success and the pleasures of trying. It is also a comforter. It will rescue you from self-recrimination. It is also the voice of reason. [Knows] your inner life, wants the best for you, is sympathetic to your dreams, your feelings, your concerns. It is this voice to whom you confide day-to-day issues and major undertakings; it is your companion when you mull over a problem, try to reach a decision. It is the eternal optimist. It is your biggest fan. It believes in you and what you can do, and its cheers and compliments (ibid, 1983).

However, for some people the very act of having fun can be stressful. They have learned that if things are going well, if they are too successful or having too good a time, they get a feeling of dread, of free-floating anxiety. "The inner Dialogue (Inner Enemy versus Inner Ally) daydreaming allows you to explore your wishes and longings, gives you insight into your hopes and dreams."[151]

A sense of humor, which some of us have more than others, is seen in the archetype of the Fool. Thought of as a medieval symbol and/or subject of the King, as the one and only person who could directly tell the King something he didn't want to hear, the Fool represents life through humor, metaphor, and mysticism. For the Fool, humor means "seeing the dichotomies and the totality at once," which allowed one to play, to communicate, and to express total freedom (Boyce, 2012). "The big moment in the medieval myth is the awakening of the heart to compassion, the transformation of passion into compassion…human values of self-giving in shared suffering" (Campbell, 1990, p. 116).[152]

---

[151] "An effective way to steal the Inner Enemy's thunder is to take away its power to punish. The twerp has its own punishments specially tailored to each person. It makes one person depressed and anxious; it drives another to drink or drugs; it causes another person to worry constantly, unproductively, someone else to give up what she really wants for safety or security or another person always to doubt and undermine others' love. As long as you focus on the negative, you are too anxious, too lacking in self-esteem, too closed to the satisfactions you might seek to make changes in your life. You stagnate" [emphasis added] (ibid, 1983).

[152] Maslow defines "transcendence" as yielding to one's destiny or fate and to fuse with it. "To embrace, lovingly, one's own destiny. This is the rising above one's own

It is often more real as "therapist" to become the "Fool" as a conduit for productive intentionality, although sometimes paradoxically.

How Theorists See Self

I have long made the following point: If we consider these concepts—self-regard, self-esteem, self-destruction, self-determination, self-centeredness, self-awareness…ad infinitum, it is not on the word to the right of the hyphen to which I, as a therapist, first focus. It is the word to the left, Self—with a capital S—that must be discovered, at most times signifying its existence in one's personal reality as controller/determinator, responder/destroyer. The Ego protects and helps us function "in spite of" our instincts, but it doesn't really want to. I (Ego) am telling you what my (Self) wants are. If you want to stay in Self, use "my" sentences. If you want to get out of Self/Inner Child, use "I" sentences.

Going back again to Rogers (1957), we find that, in a perception of the client by the therapist, Self-competence is seen as part of an inventory of assets which a person should have developed. Rogers believed this could only happen in an environment of mutual respect and concern. "Positive benefits accrue when both parties approach a relationship in an aiding, considerate, creative way…seek to develop and retain cooperation" (ibid, 1957, pp. 95–103). Many clients start therapy with uncertainty and confusion that reflects the crisis that they then disclose; Rogers' Client-Centered Therapy can be directly addressed without having to necessarily take a long history of trauma or family dynamics.

Certainly, this historical information will aid the treatment in the long run, but during the initial period of assistance, Rogers believed the client needed immediate regard and support. Often there is a pressing decision that must be faced as well. Just this week a first-time client came in to see me, a man who had found out his wife was having an affair; he had indisputable evidence, but he hadn't confronted her yet. Obviously, a history of how he dealt with crisis and anger management, as well as loss and despair, would have helped me aid him in his decisions about whether to confront and/or then to leave their family home. But I had one hour to support his needs and to alleviate his stress so he could come through the decision-making process with dignity and an appropriate set of plans.

Life demands, choices, and decisions are rooted in adequate, relevant information. Rogers believed that the individual needs to actualize potential and to become a more complete person, perhaps for the long term but certainly for that moment or that week. Thus, his theory that patients have: a) a need for positive regard from the therapist and ultimately from others, and b) a need for Self-regard. When Rogers was interviewed, in a 1975 article, he gave the following advice:

CR: "I drop my own evaluative notion forget the judgments I make about him [the client] try to hear his problem and specially to hear his feelings as he's experiencing and perceiving them…share a rule a thumb…realize that I have

---

personal will, being in charge, taking control, needing control, etc." (Hoffman, 1988, p. 274).

understood it as he feels it and he's glad to find that someone really understands." [I ask myself] "Do I really prize this person of worth?" Genuineness…with sufficient exposure to what I think of as a therapeutic climate, almost any person can be reached…It's good to look at your own feelings, define them as sharply as you can, and express them…If a person is really seeking help, and I'm willing to give myself as a listening, attentive, responsible human being, that can be very meaningful…Treatment depends on individual choice…willingness to submit to a regimen which may be structured but is not controlling in the authoritarian sense…Help a person reach the initial decision…figure out what would reward him enough to prevent him from [addiction]…There is nothing more exciting or rewarding to the intellect, to the feelings, to the sense of creativity than to find you have been able to release some hitherto undiscovered powers or abilities in a person you're dealing with.' [emphasis added] (Rogers, 1975, pp. 97).

In summary, when we as therapists monitor ourselves (evidence-based practices), we believe we should see what Carol Goodheart (2004) calls the "triumvirate of factors". These factors, which contribute to a positive psychotherapy outcome, are the patient's personal factors (e.g., motivation), the therapist's personal factors (e.g., capacity for empathy), and the interventions offered.

CR: "Psychotherapy is a rich process. It is an attempt to reach understanding, ease pain, solve problems, and find meaning, within the context of a trusting relationship…[it] draws on many theories, including behavioral, cognitive behavioral, family systems, feminist, humanistic, psychodynamic, and cultural competency orientations. Psychotherapy is complex: one's predispositions, personalities, preferences, developmental level, and psychological functioning intertwine with their life circumstances and stressors" [UFT] (op cit., 1975).

I have shared so much about how the therapeutic process is "supposed" to work because it is my feeling that woefully too many people in this country have not yet found the right "fit" with a therapist for a healthy support and recovery process. The average individual has not been trained to ask for what he needs as far as this kind of professional help, and if you consider that he or she is in deep crisis or has just had a personal trauma, the odds of asking for what he or she really needs are even lower, even if the therapy is working. The effect of this avoidance may be the result of having learned to overcome such powerful sensations and the potential for fear that they cause. However, sometimes we discover that the individual is also more resilient than initially thought.

The path to experience of resilience is often through "corrective action", alleviating pain because, of course, people mostly just want to live and work. As Joseph Addison stated, "the secret to happiness is something to do, someone to love, and something to look forward to." This point of view is more self-compassionate than that of the usual defensive responses many of us feel when hyper-aroused by the stress around us. That is the secret of "staying present". Acknowledging one's vulnerability can result in better boundaries in the long run;

this is also the secret of the "love response", where there is an anticipation of something not of ethical necessity but rather a personal possibility.

Developing Self-Acceptance

If we have been successful at finding our actualized Self, how does this "knowing Self" help us to relate to others? Certainly, our socially conditioned Self has learned behaviors, but theorists such as Daniel Siegel (2011) believe success may even be hard-wired in our brains. Siegel regularly writes about and presents workshops on strategies to nurture "a child's developing mind". He believes strongly that it is the focus of attention that shapes the CONNECTIONS in the brain, and that these CONNECTIONS link in a way that integrates and shapes our future health. Focusing helps us CONNECT with our "felt Self" [what is the Self telling you, right now, this minute?] and enables us to further ask what we need, reinforcing our insight about ourselves. It is not just whether one has a healthy view of attachment or not. Siegel states it is also important to remember that it is "how you made sense of your attachment history" that will define one's future sources of pain versus Self-acceptance.

In addition to the ideas presented by Siegel, something very meaningful to my practice is a recent movement that has grown out of the work of Martin Seligman (1975), which was discussed earlier. In addition to Seligman's work on learned helplessness, he also researched what has come to be called Positive Psychology. This theory focuses on awareness of Self and one's needs, others in one's sphere of CONNECTIVITY, how to react positively within a group consciousness, and how best to contribute of Self to these others. By making such a contribution, which comes across as enhancing the adult bond, the individual increases his own sense of self-worth as well.

This is often experienced as a feeling of joy, a sense of bliss and, as Barbara Holstein (2006) puts it, taps into a unique reservoir of wellness that resides in each human being. Becoming aware of a sense of integrity and Self-integration allows one to be more introspective and is also a way to re-fuel and replenish. Holstein calls this awareness the ability of a client to tap into their "secret selves". She maintains that it is a healthy attribute which could reflect some Self-esteem regardless of crisis or anxiety. She refers to this process as her clients giving her Wellness Reports.

> I asked clients to tell me about a time in their lives when they had felt most whole, most productive, most integrated…The more I could help a client remember positive states of being, and/or her own talents, strengths, and potential, the more likely she was able to put into action positive changes and behaviors that were good for her. Of course, her positive self-regard was also enhanced (ibid, 2006, pp. 16–21).

> Pray as if everything depends on God, Act as if everything depends on you.
> – St. Augustine

In my own practice, I not only share my own wisdom, hope, and strength, but I set a high bar for acting as if there's an answer or solution available to "bearing the unbearable". Of course, this positivity and Self-discovery is possible because of one's growth in the ability to trust (Self and others) and let others know you. Self-discovery (consciousness) is known through expression, not just thinking/dreaming. This requirement is very much like that which we see in the process of going through the 12-steps of AA.

Fromm said much about the process of trust in the *Art of Loving* (1956) and *The Revolution of Hope* (1968). He wrote about intimacy and how we create long-term loving relationships, relationships which are often based on whether we can first create an attitude of Self-acceptance and positive attitude toward ourselves. It takes courage to disregard that which upsets us and to listen instead to our heart's impulse and act on that. Hope, of course, is defined in the future tense, hoping for a time when, and the future becomes the central category of this kind of hope.

Many of my clients have become passive waiting for the future to bring them their "hopes" without realizing that at some moment in the future when something may happen, that moment will be "now" to them as well. [These concepts tend to be when I also explain quantum time-space to them (sic)]. I agree with Fromm that in this post-technological society we, as a group and as individuals, have exchanged some previous hopelessness for "repression and exploitation".

Our phones tell us what we what to know, and, beyond that, even what to think depending on the algorithms of what we read or watch. Fromm believes it is too Hegelian to accept the either/or of modern-day choices. I choose to work within the framework of therapists like Erikson, Jung, and Rogers, who based their theories on the synthesis of many factors and possible outcomes, all dependent on individual UFTs and current support systems.

Chapter Twenty-One
A Look at Curative Factors
We Find Peace

Because the act of relating to others was also defined as a "transaction" during the 1960s and 1970s, overall awareness of what forces drove the transactional interaction also became an important area of study (see Berne and other Transactional Analysis authors in the last chapter). The idea of outlining one's core values took on a newly defined meaning and "values clarification" became its own area of study. W. Ray Rucker, who was a Dean at U.S. International University when I was a doctoral student there, presented us with the idea that man's experience could be broken down into 8 areas and then his rated values placed on a continuum from low to high synergy. Synergy was a concept Rucker expanded from the writings of Maltz (1960) and Bateson (1972) whereby a systemic Self-image was "the cornerstone of all changes that could take place in a person" (Maltz, 1960). Bateson's "meta-science" did an excellent job of doing just that; it provided an epistemological and systemic view of mankind's evolution (following up on his anthropological studies with his wife, Margaret Mead) as well as an ecological use of mankind's consciousness, where one's values, behaviors and self-awareness could all work together harmoniously.[153]

    Maltz quoted Schindler's six basic needs (from Adler): the need for love, the need for security, the need for creative expression, the need for recognition, the need for new experiences, and the need for self-esteem. These seem quite like Maslow' original needs as well, but they were still less specific than Ray Rucker's continuum, as we will see below. Rucker states, "to these six, I would add another basic need…the need for more life—the need to look forward to tomorrow and to the future with gladness and anticipation" (ibid, 1973, p. 239). He is tying the ideas of needs satisfaction in with his basic theory of success through raised Self-image [to being more highly synergistic]. The relationship between Maltz's ideas about Self-image, and that of obtaining success, will be further seen in our perspective about Rucker's study of values below.

---

[153] The striving for synergy is in general "anti-authoritarian and anti-controlling." Hoffman relays Maslow's integrative focus on a holistic point of view [*Taoism*], "not only as expressed in contemporary ecological and ethological studies, where we have learned not to intrude and control, but for the human being it also means trusting more the child's own impulses toward growth and Self-actualization. This means a greater stress on spontaneity and autonomy rather than on prediction and external control" (Hoffman, 1988, p. 14).

Values Clarification

While Dean of the School of Human Behavior, Rucker did a great deal to influence the students who were taking psychology classes. His class on the theory of values clarification was mandatory, and during that class we were often forced to face our own upbringing and view of ourselves within our small and then larger group consciousness.

> Values emerge from us and are in our organismic life force…It is value deprivation that lies behind our personal and social problems…In it is the force of love, or power, or other inner demands for fulfillment such as physical and mental well-being. We also seek to actualize the compelling needs to be respected as unique human beings, to be right or authentic, to exchange goods and services, to be competent in skills, and to understand the world and others…The universality is the fundamental channels in which people are trying to fulfill themselves through expression of the life force…It is not merely a question of whether the individual is indulging himself in love but, rather, it is the transaction in which love is given and love is returned that is significant and actualizing (Rucker, 1973, pp. 127–139).

As mentioned, the core elements of Rucker's eight basic values are presented as "needs" in the Maslovian sense. The continuum concept shows how each of the needs is either actualizing or leading to dehumanization and DISCONNECT. Behavioral examples of each need are listed. The value corresponds to Maslow's needs and yet are in some areas more diverse, in others more distinct. For instance, the value of affection and personal well-being could be categorized as love and belongingness needs, but self-esteem and growth needs are dispersed among Respect skill and Understanding skill. Here are the steps Rucker recommends:

1. An elemental step in values clarification is to help people to see that there are at least eight different ways of looking at human experience.
2. Another elemental step in clarification is to sharpen awareness of these values as each main type is laden on our behavior and those of others. Identification of the type and consciousness of the transaction helps to strengthen such awareness.
3. One should figure out the base value that he is working from and then he needs to see exactly what he wants to achieve…Our behavior for instance may be based in power but have developed in respect. This is a third technique for values clarification.
4. A fourth technique for values clarification is to discover and estimate how the several value categories which tend to shape behavior in a context affect or condition one another. How are values relative to each other as internal components of a whole?

And so, values clarification as a process helps us to pinpoint what is going on in each category and which other categories are acting in the situation to condition the effect of the outcome. Having this information allows us to optimize expression of appropriate behaviors to match our deeper values to our overt decisions.

The Rucker Values Deprivation—Enhancement Continuum illustrates the positive benefit of living in the "high end" of the spectrum on each of the eight attributes (Note: Trend, condition, projection, and alternative data should be analyzed and appraised in terms of their relevance to the goal, in other words it is all contextual). Thus, Values Clarification can be extended into Value Analysis, including the decision process, making system analysis relevant when someone must choose an alternative, especially valuable to setting up the initial parameters of a decision. Values Clarification can be extended into Value Analysis, including the decision process, making system analysis relevant when someone must choose an alternative, especially valuable to setting up the initial parameters of a decision.

Dehumanization	Humanization
Low Synergy	High synergy

- Affection…Human transactions of emotional warmth, intimacy, and support in love, congeniality, and friendship.
- Respect…Human transactions recognizing admirable uniqueness and individuality in a context of mutual identity.
- Skill…Human transactions that develop talents to the limits of potential ability.
- Understanding…Human transactions that stimulate each person to find his own truth in every issue while gaining understanding of social norms and the significant events of human history.
- Power and influence…Human transactions in which each person will participate in making decisions which concern him and exert in formal influence according to his talents and responsibilities.
- Goods and services…Human transactions providing facilities, materials, and services to promote excellent conditions of living.
- Well-being…Human transactions which foster the physical and mental health of each person.
- Responsibility…Human transactions that share experience enabling the person to develop a sense of authenticity, ethics, and integrity in his behavior within the broad limits of his social context (ibid, 1973, pp. 130–131).

Rucker's measurement reflects our view of values. Our cultural values influence the relativity of our relationships (think Einstein), as well as the potential for problems within our society because of our cultural values. They also suggest the intensity of how the therapeutic relationship is like a "mini society". As Carl Rogers had us remember the importance of unconditional positive regard, I know how important it is that I model for my clients the small, value-laden, acts of kindness and listening that makes our relationship rich and meaningful as a healing process.[154]

It is useful to use a word like dignity as meaning "a high state of actualization" and a word like indignity in the other direction meaning "counter-growth". Here is a very nice short-cut to test what you do: stop to ask yourself the question: "Does this lead to dignity or indignity?" From time to time as human events occur, we slide back and forth along Rucker's values enhancement continuum.

As I have mentioned earlier, with any hyphenated word that begins with Self (determined, destructive, esteem, aware, hatred, and so forth), it is not the words following the hyphen that I react to; first I must evaluate the actual level of development of Self when a phrase is used. I am always aware that people recognize their lives as a task. Some individuals are more aware than others of how much work it takes to direct one's own "becoming" and to have reasonable goals in this area. Indeed, psychotherapy can become one way to fight for your life, to become "more alive" before you die. The humanistic theorists were proposing that we be more fully aware and not succumb to meaningless routines or facades.

Bugental, also a professor at U.S. International University during that period, extended the study of values into his existential method of psychotherapy. He proposed that attitudes and values directly affect awareness. He theorized that values are indexing events within one's daily experiential framework (expression and language). As an interactive human species, we extend ourselves; it requires constant categorization and an "open-endedness" to our system of values.

Therefore, values were not just the reasonable results of analysis, but Bugental believed that they were "concept areas, not just concentration on 'thing' or 'event'" (Bugental, 1965). He was much more likely to consider the role of unconscious or underlying and automatic decisions in the formation of attitudes. In class, Dr. Bugental defined being alive as sensations and emotions, mobility, memory, insight, and empathy…in other words, CONNECTED awareness!

Obviously, no one would deny the benefit of heightened awareness or even self-knowledge. But I have been asked in what circumstance psychotherapy would be warranted due to the potential need for a guide or second "set of ears" to one's

---

[154] Self-awareness results in a rather continuous self-reflective process which not only constantly evaluates where the individual has been…[it includes] becoming aware of the values transactions that are taking place in his own world, then, constitutes the most basic process for self-discovery and examination…What is important about value clarification is that it remain rather objective and detached rather than judgmental, that we try to see the truth of what is going on, that we try to see the <u>what is</u>, and we try to understand it, not to use it for an immediate jump into a judgmental action…and decision is the thing that we are headed toward directly when we talk about a more formalized value analysis process…values analysis is a marriage of the problem solving or reflective process with values clarification. It is an attempt to plunge to the depth of awareness and clarification of value in each step of problems solving or in the thinking process [emphasis added] (Werkmeister, 1967, p. 15).

external Self-disclosing process. Couldn't journaling work as well? For instance, there are basically three types of empathy: cognitive, which helps us to identify and classify another's experience; emotional, when we feel what the other is feeling; and compassionate empathy when we grasp, feel, and are spiritually moved to help in some way. I would predict that a journaling process where we try to include our experience on each of these three levels may not substitute for therapy entirely, although it could provide us with much internal clarity.

OK, so I can't help myself. Let's go back to the therapeutic process for a minute, even if it is only so that if the reader is in it, or considering being in it, maybe some of it will make more sense. The therapist collects apparently subjective information from some values clarification plus empathy; the therapist first builds rapport and then creates a paradigm of positive health and change within that structure of trust. There are as many specific models as there are individual providers, in that each person and therapist create a unique opportunity for sharing and healing, whether the methodology is directive, behavioral, gestalt, psychodynamic or spiritually based. The following is Yalom's famous list of curative factors of additional experiences that sometimes come along, with my own comments in parenthesis:

Curative Factors in Psychotherapy (Yalom)

1. IMPARTING OF INFORMATION (Installation of hope)
2. UNIVERSALITY (Uniqueness of experience but which can also give a source of relief if there are some feelings of basic inadequacy or alienation going on and/or sexual secrets)
3. ALTRUISM (A core concept in AA and other 12th Step programs as well: "The best way to help a man is to let him help you.")
4. THE CORRECTIVE RECAPITULATION OF THE PRIMARY FAMILY GROUP (True as well for Buddhist Sangha experiences)
5. DEVELOPMENT OF SOCIALIZING TECHNIQUES (Provides structure as needed)
6. IMITATIVE BEHAVIOR (Modeling of problem-solving)
7. INTERPERSONAL LEARNING (Monitoring of self-esteem and self-observation, use of 'Motivational Insight')
8. GROUP COHESIVENESS
9. CATHARSIS (Yalom, 1995)

Another influence on Maslow (and Rucker) and thus myself, was Ruth Benedict's concept of synergy (1989) [as noted as one end of Rucker's continuum]. Originally, Benedict did not write a comprehensive piece about synergy, but it was mentioned in one article, written right before she died, and picked up by Maslow in private conversations. Benedict defined high synergy as "where the individual by the same act and at the same time serves his own advantage and that of the group; low synergy represents the group in which the advantage of one individual becomes a victory over another, and the majority who are victorious must shift as they can" (ibid, 1989). This arrangement of the relationship in such a fashion that one person's advantage is the other person's advantage rather than disadvantage is one way of explaining the intense love experience. It is a total merging of desires, of basic needs.[155] Maslow concurs when he states, "high synergy can represent a transcending of the dichotomizing, a fusion of the opposites into a single concept."

Hermann Hesse and his Phenomenological Influence

During this same time during the early 1970s, I read Hermann Hesse's book *Magister Ludi/The Glass Bead Game* (1943) and wrote a paper called "How I Play the Glass Bead Game." Hesse's work was a masterpiece, unifying all aspects of my phenomenological interests into one congruent explanation, as well as a unification of all four of Jung's character types (sensation, intuition, feeling, and thinking). Hesse believed that symbols are what tie us metaphysically to our abstract ideas. Any symbol can affect the figure-ground relation, causing the very center of our "being" to move and fluctuate. Hesse proposed an idea of the relational element between the different aspects of conscious development, similar to Einstein's theory. This relational element is measured and experienced through its symbolic representation. If one is to think symbolically, one also tends to see all things as related and thus relative. Everything is all a part of each other.[156]

The Glass Bead Game was Hesse's last novel, for which he won the Nobel Prize in literature in 1946. The "Game" is a process whereby there is a basic symbol that can be comprehended aesthetically on all levels: music, art, literature. It is a combination of learning, veneration of the beautiful, and meditation. The basic theme is developed through the different variations and then there is a period of meditation, withdrawal into the symbol itself.

Hesse says, "I realized in that flashing moment, if seen with a truly meditative mind, nothing but a direct route into the interior of the cosmic mystery where, in the alternation between inhaling and exhaling, between heaven and earth, between *Yin* and *Yang*, holiness is forever being created" (Hesse, *The Glass Bead Game*, 1943, p. 105).

Thus, the idea of the Game is to arrange and sum up all the knowledge of one's experience [UFT], symmetrically, around a central idea. Although Hesse dealt primarily with abstract questions, I feel that key areas for symbolic representation

---

[155]"Unitive Consciousness" is Maslow's concept that fusion can take place in either of two directions: one, by improving the actuality so that it comes closer to the ideal, the other, by scaling down the ideal, so that ideality may come closer to what exists (universality) (Hoffman, 1988, p. 115).

[156] Not only could we manifest the bipolarity of internal and external CONNECTEDNESS, but we could also use that plurality to concretize "re-being" as historically proposed by Jung (archetypes), Hegel (synthetic Self), Hesse (*Glass Bead Game*), Gestalt theorists (past and future in the now), and meditational religious (Buddhism, Taoism).
As in the Glass Bead Game, a symbol may be used to trigger a sub-self, bringing in into prominence of figure within the background of the many layered Self, especially if the sub-self has been "crystalized" around the symbol. Thus, I recommend creating a symbol for one's sub-self (archetype such as compassion, sensitivity, success, sexuality, creativity, intellectual, fun/Bolen's goddesses), which you can call up at will.

are feelings, anxieties, dreams, and fantasies, as well as specific problems. It may very well be that the most important part of the Game is not the playing of it, itself, but the periods of meditation that go along with it. "The Game as I conceive it encompasses the player after the completion of meditation as the surface of a sphere encompasses its center and leaves him with the feeling that he has extracted from the universe of accident and confusion a totally symmetrical and harmonious cosmos and absorbed it into himself" (ibid, 1943, p. 178).

Communication and CONNECTION with another is another way of trying to reach a unity of spirit. Sometimes we share too much, but usually it is too little due to the fear of becoming vulnerable and thus being hurt. We are afraid of interpersonal contact because we might find out we are real, beautiful human beings, and how it is our journey must continue. If one is always in control, it cuts down on being phenomenologically aware. We must give up fear of change and embrace the creative and productive inside of us. Fear doesn't always have to be negative; Hesse felt fear is also a helpful indicator of where we are on the path to Self-actualization.

Hesse, of course, wrote many other books and short stories. His *Autobiographical Writings* (translated 1971) present many of the symbols he had discovered earlier in his life. Many of them were written after he had undertaken psychoanalysis with Jung and been greatly influenced by Jung's writings. "He [Jung] is interested less in providing a dispassionate account of outer even—'reality'—than in undertaking an agonizing reappraisal of his inner growth—spiritual reality" (Introduction, 1971, p. xiii). To continue, in "Life Story Briefly Told" (1925), Hesse summed up his viewpoint in this way, "I consider reality to be the last thing one need concern oneself about, for it is, tediously enough, always present, while more beautiful and necessary things demand our attention and care" (ibid, 1971, p. 56). Most importantly, to me, Hesse was able to represent the "triadic rhythm of human development," that of the movement of each human individual from childhood innocence, through problems and growth lessons, and even despair at times during the period of adolescence to middle adulthood, to finally the "higher consciousness" of later adulthood and Erikson's period of Ego Integrity.[157] One must not be too focused on the outcome and forget to be successful at playing the Game!

Sometimes we feel as though we have magical powers or wish for them. At least I did. Speaking for most of my clients, and myself, we couldn't have said it better!

> When I look back, it seems to me that my whole life has been influenced by this desire for magic powers; how the objects of these magical wishes changed with the times, how I gradually withdrew my efforts from the outer world and concentrated them upon myself, how I came to aspire to replace the crude

---

[157] "But now I had entered upon that period of life in which it no longer makes sense to continue elaborating and differentiating a personality that is already complete and more than adequately differentiated, in which instead the task becomes that of allowing the estimable I to disappear once more into the universe and, in the face of mutability, to take one's place in the eternal and timeless order" (ibid, 1971, p. 58).

invisibility of the magic cloak with the invisibility of the wise man who, perceiving all remains always unperceived—this would be the real content of my life's story (ibid, 1971, "Childhood of the Magician", 1923, p. 5).

Treatment for the Untreatable

Not everyone is working on themselves or even presenting themselves for therapeutic help. Even once there is initial therapeutic contact, a lack of honesty or failure to be motivated or Self-aware can really interfere or block treatment. In these cases, the techniques of Motivational Interviewing can specifically provide skills and attitudinal assistance, even to the resistant. This process is geared specifically toward making the most of one session, and I think the method could help almost anyone interested in trying the technique. Miller and Rollnick (1991) delineate some of the specific target areas to address as follows:

1. Zero in on a problem: if you wake up tomorrow and the problem is gone, what would your life be like? Simply ask clients what they'd like to focus on first…
2. Unearth hidden resources.
3. Don't cajole.
4. Plan for the future: interpretation of physical symptoms can turn a harmless habituation into an intensely stressful situation (Miller and Rollnick, 1991).

Treatment for the difficult can also go beyond just those who lack motivation. Some patients are blocked by true personality disorders, fears and phobias, and denial of prevailing symptoms by narcissism. In these cases, and what most therapists see frequently in this category are borderline-type personalities, treating the emotional dysregulation and self-harming is the primary target. Individuals with Borderline Personality Disorder (BPD) crave approval, paradoxical to the fact that a small provocation can trigger abusive and even violent behavior toward those trying to help them. A condition that can be diagnosed even in young children, by adolescence these individuals are seen as having uncontrollable impulsivity, mood swings, tenuous relationships, and poor judgment.

Often, theorists studying BPD have proposed a severe trauma experience at a very young age, which creates significant fear of abandonment, poor frustration tolerance and faulty reality testing. Treatment goals include learning skills such as distress tolerance, interpersonal effectiveness, emotion regulation and mindfulness skills. Many people with BPD demonstrate self-harming behaviors to regulate their emotions because it is primarily a condition of emotional dysregulation. "In an effort at self-stabilization, some use physical pain—which has been demonstrated to reduce emotional arousal… (the practice of) mindfulness allows clients to observe their emotions without reacting to them or seeking instant relief through self-harm" (Dingfelder, 2004, p. 46).

Marsha M. Linehan, Ph.D., at the University of Washington, has developed Dialectical Behavioral Therapy (DBT), which provides support and intervention specifically for such thought-disordered people (Linehan, 2013). In DBT, Self-harming equals damaging impulsive behavior. DBT-treated patients more successfully reduced suicide attempts, self-mutilating and self-damaging behaviors than those who received treatment as usual (ibid, 2013). It is important for self-harming patients to specifically identify and address dysfunctional core beliefs.

BPD clients often have a much more difficult time coming back from a conflict or "setback" than some of the other personality disorders defined by the DSM-5. This difficulty comes from the disorder of their thinking and their inability to try new strategies and get beyond their fears of failure.

In cases with PTSD symptoms, use of DBT with or without additional treatment factors (such as yoga or meditation) has shown the need to treat the immobilization that comes with PTSD. We have been socialized to dwell most on the bad parts of our history and our UFT developmental issues additionally reflect difficult epigenetic influences from our ancestors. "When people experience trauma, they may experience not only a sense of emotional dysregulation, but also a feeling of being physically immobilized. Body-oriented techniques such as yoga help them increase awareness of sensations in the body, stay more focused on the present moment and hopefully empower them to take effective action" (Novotney, 2009).

Although acts of meditation may help and certainly should be recommended, these individuals often lack resilience (instead they manifest non-acceptance), as well as any sense of optimism, a very important factor that should be immediately addressed in their treatment. Resilience aids in the development of Self-knowledge as well (Rockman, 2017). Dr. Bruce McEwen, of Harvard University, has been studying the cycle of defeat (which can be aided by building up resilience), by teaching these patients survival techniques.

"Helping the individual with a personality disorder to develop cognitive, behavioral, social, and emotional competencies will assist them to manage day-to-day stressors and events effectively…the habit of trying new approaches when old ones are not working" (Dingfelder, 2004, p. 46). That is why "detachment", a healthy form of functioning in the face of obsession on the negative, can add a resourceful and even spiritual set of guidelines to aid in coping with sources of despair. In this way, "spiritual fitness" can be achieved, and a higher order of spiritual aspirations can be realized. It is by detaching that one can begin to transform. Some of the goals of DBT include:

1. Enhance and maintain the client's motivation to change, reinforce a sense of benevolence toward Self.
2. Enhance the client's capabilities, their ability to focus more in the moment-to-moment rather than the conventional sense of Self.
3. Ensure that the client's new capabilities are generalized to all relevant environments, maintaining first an internal locus of control.
4. Enhance the therapist's motivation to treat clients while also enhancing the therapist's capabilities.
5. Structure the environment so treatment can take place (Siegel and Yapko, 2012).

The clients who do the poorest are those who see no future, and specifically are just getting through the day by addiction (dual diagnosis). They have a type of "validation deficit disorder" where they need increased respect and recognition. They need to learn that they are more than their history. They are often encouraged to take notes during therapy and are given homework assignments like journaling and looking for positives. However, their lack of survival skills and flexibility in the face of stress and conflict makes these patients much more likely to experience episodes of Post-Traumatic Stress Disorder (PTSD), as well as depression.

As we discussed is Chapter Ten, PTSD is not only a physiological, psychological, and behavioral reaction to an unexpected traumatic event in one's life, it can also cause long-term neurochemical changes in the central nervous even after the immediate "trauma" seems to be resolving itself (car accident, death, medical diagnosis, divorce, or other loss). Beyond the immediate symptoms related to the trauma, such as nervousness, isolation, irritability, flashbacks of the event, and fear of reoccurrence, lesser but lingering symptoms such as sleep disruption, risky behavior (smoking, poor nutrition, substance abuse, anger and/or violence), other psychosocial problems can result, causing a biological strain on the individual with PTSD that may even affect their overall health.

PTSD was defined specifically as its own disorder, in the newly retooled DSM-5. As much as PTSD is usually a long-term and somewhat chronic condition, the initial remediation of symptoms comes from alleviation of the "stress disorder (SD)" part of the condition first, demonstrated in the immediacy of experienced anxiety. Self-care and awareness of one's needs can help to re-condition the sense of being overwhelmed and slow the heightened need for being in control—a perfect reason to use Cognitive Behavioral Technique (CBT). In 2007, Lifeline (Spring, Vol. 109) presented the following lists for self-care. I couldn't have made a better list myself, so here they are.

Tips for Taking Time for Yourself

If you have TWO minutes:

- Take deep breaths and think peaceful thoughts.
- Remember the last time you had a good laugh, and it will bring a smile to your face.
- Visualize your Self in a peaceful place.
- Smile at strangers and you will be surprised at the positive response you get back.
- Hum, whistle or sing one of your favorite songs or melodies.
- Eat a piece of fine chocolate. In fact, buy yourself an entire box and look forward to having it as a reward after shopping or work or whatever.
- Cuddle and pet your dog/puppy. Not only will they love it, but you can forget about everything for a bit.
- Take out the hula hoop, we are never too old.

If you have FIVE minutes:

- Reflect on all the things for which you are grateful.
- Email a friend who positively reinforces who you are.
- Listen to a song or relaxation tape that uplifts you.
- Take out the jump rope and let out some stress.
- Sketch or doodle—let your creative side out!
- Express your thoughts and feelings in a journal.
- Ask yourself what you really feel like doing right now, and then do it.

If you have FIFTEEN minutes:

- Soak in a warm tub with aroma therapy bath gel/salts surrounded by candles.
- Go for a walk in the park, by the lake or by the ocean.
- Get a massage.
- Write a poem.
- Take a nap.
- Drive or walk out of your way to find something beautiful in your everyday routine.

If you have an HOUR:

- Volunteer at your favorite charity.
- Go to a bookstore (by yourself so that you can browse to your heart's content) and check out new books, listen to music and maybe have a cup of coffee.
- Have lunch or dinner with a toddler or small child.
- Reread parts of your favorite book.
- 'Do' your hair and makeup on a night you're staying in.
- Go to bed an hour early: put on your favorite pajamas, make some hot tea and crawl into bed.
- Rent your favorite movie and watch it all by yourself (Lifeline, 2007)

Acceptance

As mentioned in an earlier section, one of the useful aspects of using DBT as a therapeutic tool is its focus on "radical acceptance". In 2003, Tara Brach, Ph.D. wrote her book, *Radical Acceptance, Embracing your Life with the Heart of a Buddha.* It is about how radical acceptance works well together with a practice of Buddhist techniques to produce mindfulness, acceptance, and healing. One thing I especially like about her writings is the way in which she integrates so many methods and philosophies. Look at this passage which not only refers to Buddha but also to Carl Rogers.

> We get caught up in feeling like a separate self and an unworthy self...so what we do when we get anxious and insecure is we speed up...'Our fear is great,

but greater yet is the truth of our CONNECTEDNESS' [Buddha]. So, we can remember our belonging at any moment—even facing death—if we can remember the love that holds us. Then we can actually face living and dying and have something that's large enough to hold us...Because if we can begin to bring a sense of peace and care to the life inside us, naturally the circles widen to include other people...Carl Rogers [said]: 'It wasn't until I accepted myself just as I was in this moment, that I was free to change.' So, a pre-condition to true transformation is to accept ourselves in the moment [emphasis added] (Brach, 2003).

The study of noetics is another approach to acceptance and spirituality; it is the study of metaphysical philosophy concerned with mind and intellect, and particularly Divine Intellect. As a science of consciousness, it considers how we experience, internalize, intuit, externalize, and attempt to release our need to control elements of our neurological functioning for enhanced perception, conscious awareness, and acceptance of passing through the death experience by heightened consciousness and spirituality. In this sense, spirituality is defined as higher levels of well-being, lower rates of serious psychological problems, satisfaction with one's relationships, and even greater longevity (Pargament and Sweeney, 2011).

Acceptance is the awareness of our limitations and aspects of consciousness, that which we control and that which we cannot control. Surrendering to "God's will" is the best relationship we can have however one defines one's Higher Power. This surrender leads to true healing of body and consciousness; communion with our own consciousness creates the transformational process wherein a true knowledge of the depth of nature equals the spiritual experience. In the 12-step program, doing an inventory creates transformation through a process of introspection and "pondering—work, failures, and successes".

With the aid of Higher Power/consciousness one creates the conditions for growth. Learning to say "No!" can also give us boundaries and show us a type of affirmation which gives us dignity, teaching us not to go against our own values and principles just to please others.

Anxiety and Vulnerability

Even after graduate school I continued my training. I took workshops, training through work, and continuing education classes whenever I saw one that appealed to my niche of interest. One class, taught by one of my mentors, psychiatrist Allan Rabin M.D., was aptly called "Behavior Viewed from Three Perspectives: Patient, Significant Other, and Treatment Personnel." During this class I learned about signal anxiety, which warns the person that he has an internal conflict which needs resolution: two mutually exclusive forces, usually unconscious (love versus hate), "signal" that a choice must be made, priorities must be determined, and compromises considered. Symptoms of signal anxiety may also have function and utility in stabilizing and preserving the organism, because what is in conflict is the difference between short-term and long-term interests (Blanck and Blanck, 1974).

Although conflict and reconciliation are part of every developmental dynamic, it is during signal anxiety, beyond even the normal use of ego defenses by a person's Persona or Shadow, that the most entrenched defensive patterns may emerge; these manifestations of ego defenses are what makes postponement of reactivity possible [See Blanck and Blanck chart, Chapter Thirteen]. Rabin pointed out that "immature defenses" altered distress which had been engendered either by the individual, the threat of interpersonal intimacy, or the threat of experiencing its loss, while at the same time the individual cannot help but appear socially undesirable and are labeled as misbehaving by the beholder (Outlier behavior).

In common conversational reference (think a Woody Allen movie), a neurotic is someone who gets confused now and then and is overly anxious. But when Karen Horney first referred to *The Neurotic Personality of Our Time* (1937), her definition looked at behavior in a different light. Her concept implied a more global and social assessment, beyond that of a grief reaction to childhood trauma or sexual abuse, which had been Freud's approach. Taking after Adler, she felt neglect of simple childhood emotional needs contributed to the neurotic outcome, and she proposed ten specific needs that fell into three "coping strategies:"

1. Moving toward people: need for affection and approval, need for a partner.
2. Moving against people: need for power, need to exploit others, need for social recognition, need for personal admiration, need for personal achievement.
3. Moving away from people: need for self-sufficiency, need for perfection, need to restrict life practices.

These needs can also be grouped into three broader categories; need for compliance, need for aggression, and need for attachment (Horney, 1945).

I encourage anyone who has a passing knowledge of these categories but is interested in learning more or finds this type of schema to really resonate with them (as it did with my mother and it does with me), to search out Horney's theory and her readings in more detail. My view as a therapist is to notice that patients may present symptoms, yes, and perhaps a laundry list of life traumas, but ultimately there will be an authentic and honest attempt on their part to reveal enough history and vulnerability so that I, as the treating practitioner, can guide them through problem-solving and give them a toolbox of Self-care by using such tools as those suggested by Jung, Horney, and Rogers.

For instance, in treating the perfectionist we find two very different things: the desire to excel and the desire to be perfect. "One set of behaviors is considered more adaptive or 'avoidance coping,' and the other is more 'self-oriented.' Socially prescribed perfectionism—believing that others will value you only if you are perfect—has been associated with depression and other problems" (Benson, 2003, p. 19).

In his book *Care of the Soul* (1992) Thomas Moore concurs that attachment and CONNECTION, or a sense of grief without it, are a determinant of one's ultimate style of coping. The need for attachment can show up through a search for communal love (Sangha), a yearning of the Soul for spiritual experience, for variety and creativity in the passion of activity, and by a search for intimacy through the Other.

Moore comments on why people are lonely when there is no need for a-loneness. He calls this experience "moralistic self-protection" but states everyone requires inclusion, a sense of belonging to the world, not just being in it. "Feelings of relatedness…this is how the soul sends signals [of vulnerability] …[We] love attachment and dependence, to risk the unbearable pain of separation [if the relationship fails], and to find fulfillment in partnership with another" (Moore, 1992, pp. 94, 109). Healthy dependency is seen as finding one's identity through another, which results in the longing to protect the union, whereas envy is desire and Self-denial working together to create a characteristic sense of frustration and obsessiveness.

Moore also points out that, frequently, patients who see themselves as victims have subtle control by using depression; even during bouts of melancholia (as per Freud) some important work is probably going on internally ("brilliance in the darkness"). Regarding creativity, he writes: "The more deeply our work stirs imagination and corresponds to images that lie there at the bedrock of identity and fate, the more it will have soul" (ibid, 1992, p. 185).

Toward Well-Being

Face it, we are all the stars of our own movies and others merely the props. It is the components of the UFT that build the plot, character development, and resolution of our stories. We can plot how each area influenced the eventual outcome and whether our strength, and the ability to experience our memories without fear, is due to nature, nurture, or a combination of both. The very difference between whether we experience nostalgia or negativity from these memories may be directly correlated to those influences.

Sometimes the same sense of well-being can come from the stimulus of music. Some aspects of music engage the left hemisphere more than the right, where nostalgic memories may also lie and thus become stimulated. Music and speech are not as neurologically separate as researchers had supposed. Both Broca's and Wernicke's areas, in the left hemisphere, are CONNECTED to language development and utilization. They are involved in reproducing language hierarchically into sequences according to established rules, aided by "pictures". Research has shown that musical training might accelerate the process of learning to read and possibly even aid in remedying dyslexia.

The point is that the curative effect comes from working with the "pictures in your own head" as we have discussed in Chapter Nineteen and the archetypes we discussed in Chapter Seventeen. "Music, like all art, gives pain and our most wrenching emotions voice, language, and form, so it can be recognized and shared…[it] is the magic of all art: the ability to both capture our pain and deliver us from it at the same time" (Brown, B., 2017).

Like waking dreams, uncovering these nostalgic storylines can feel like grieving losses of the Other, particularly where there are amends or redemption needed, or like the flashbacks experienced by those with PTSD. But on a more positive note, for instance, when we do the type of inventory work required of us in the 4th of 12 steps of the AA model by making amends, we can also be enabling some type of mastery in ourselves with the guidance of our own spirituality and faith in a Higher Power. But faith is not necessarily depending upon some invisible benefactor; it can also be an attitude of non-depending, of understanding, or "trusting oneself to life", which comes from surrender without expecting anything in return (Powell, 1981). My goal is that everyone reading this will respond with an action plan to this quote by William James:

> Once we come into a conscious realization of our oneness with the Infinite Life do we actualize in ourselves the qualities and powers of the Infinite Life, do we make ourselves channels through which the infinite Intelligence and Power can work. In just the degree in which you realize your oneness with the Infinite Spirit, you will exchange dis-ease for ease, in disharmony for harmony, suffering and pain for abounding health and strength. One need remains in hell no longer than one chooses to (James, 1902, p. 115).

Good outcomes can come from bad memories and CONNECTION can come regardless of initial feelings of abandonment. It is the individual's spiritual core that forms the foundation of the human spirit, values, and beliefs. Pargament and Sweeney (2011) list the factors important to understanding the development of the human spirit.

- Self-awareness—reflection and introspection
- Sense of agency—assumption of responsibility for spiritual development
- Self-regulation—the ability to understand and control one's emotions, thoughts, and behaviors
- Self-motivation—the expectancy the one's deepest aspirations can be realized
- Social awareness—realization that relationships play an important role (ibid, 2011, p. 61).

If participation in the mystery of the infinite is supported, you will find the individual to be experiencing the dualism of true happiness and the depth of meaning. The joy reflects the enthusiasm implied by its meaning: *én theos*—a god within. "Happy is he who bears a god within." Koestler's (1964) reference applies clearly to 12-step processes as well, where CONNECTION to one's own personal definition of a Higher Power is enabling in a healthy way to "know thyself;" this knowledge is in juxtaposition to the enabling power of substances or dependency on others. One comes, at times, to "disregard thyself" in response to the pain the meaninglessness life presents. Koestler asks how we can concretize the measure of social communication, and then answers himself that perhaps it is the infinite within us that CONNECTS to the infinite in others, a classically philosophical answer. He believes that the shadows in Plato's caves are symbols of man's loneliness; they lead to man's urge to share, make others participate in them, and thus overcome the isolation of the Self.

We Achieve Balance

What would a healthy and balanced "now" look like? First, because we all deal with losses in our lives, we must construct a method to deal with those feelings of loss, to find the motivation to go on with honesty and directedness. Just because there has been a loss, bereavement, or grief, the objective mind always seems to rebound if the experience is met with a positive and accepting spirit. If one's response to loss is to make it into a "sacrifice", to play the victim, then how could Self-care possibly follow? Mental "health" versus mental "sickness" comes from such a differentiation and a recognition that "realness" is equivalent to love and acceptance. The quicker one gets past fear and avoidance, the less one will experience pain and guilt.

I have a friend who has lost both husband and child to death. This is an experience less uncommon than one would hope for. In her everyday life, she is experiencing more feelings of guilt and depression than actual grief currently. Most of her days are spent trying to avoid acknowledging the loss and experiencing the pain it brings (lots of TV). Then when anniversaries, birthdays, or just nostalgic memories of guilt and remorse in her, she has no emotional backup plan with which to respond. She is emotionally bankrupt.

Think of it like this: if the objective mind rejects a loss, the result in the subjective/emotional mind is to feel abandonment and loss of motivation. On the other hand, we can respond with an effort to go for a reward and not be stuck in fear of loss (like "losing" weight); just start, and of course, become aware of opposing ideas that can get in the way, areas of in which we can get "stuck".

How does the Self teach us well-being? The point I want to strongly make is that the Self-will manifest itself, within any of many contexts, if given the appropriate reinforcement and opportunity beyond the shame and isolation many who experienced an Outlier's childhood may have experienced. On the other hand, in the experience of shame we have often "gone against our own values" and have revealed underlying fear of unworthiness, even if only Self-perceived. Be open to the creative energy which is your Higher Power but is never meant to be binding or a barrier in any way (Science of Mind teachings).

An internal process of naming, revealing, and forgiving is the real source of compassion for us. If we observe anger or fear, the act of observing can turn what is inactive into healthy action, or, as my mother would say, "Just wait, and it will reveal itself." The act of revelation always keeps us on track. Problems are our opportunities to grow if we also use our new strength to serve others as well. Service helps us take our sense of limitation out of fear and, using another set of expectations, we can meet each day with a renewed sense of the intellectual and spiritual side of life.

I have learned over the years that to CONNECT I must understand the larger context of patient experiences and their pain. Having lived with a larger public life myself, traveling throughout the world and studying many cultures and religions, has helped me with this assignment. A fit and balanced Self manifests its needs in all areas, in addition to self-care: mind, body, and spirit. When looking closer at the UFT of my client's lives, I see that their "private lives" have been "shaped by the social, political, cultural, and economic experiences of their daily existence"

(Harvard Medical School CEU Flyer, 2004). Likewise, their suffering, or even sense of meaning, exists as created by these larger contexts. My therapeutic goals for clients include learning to understand one's own UFT.

Self-Actualization

Now that we can identify the birth of the Self, we can proceed with the actualization process that Maslow pinpointed and wrote about in 1968. We are meant to protect its development from negative defensiveness, self-destructive patterns, or neurotic attributes. Maslow proposed that Self-actualization is the highest of the developmental values and meets human need at its most gratifying. It is man's desire for Self-fulfillment, the tendency for him to become actualized in what he is potentially. Integrating concepts such as that which is meaningful, sacred, and congruent results in the experience of becoming an actualized and trusting person.

In a study presented by *Psychology Today* (2008), Karen Wright found that people high on an authenticity profile were more likely to respond to difficulties with effective coping strategies, rather than resorting to drugs, alcohol, or self-destructive habits. They often reported having satisfying relationships. They enjoyed a strong sense of self-worth and purpose, confidence in mastering challenges, and the ability to follow through in pursuing goals. Low scores were found in people likely to be "defensive, suspicious, confused, and easily overwhelmed" (ibid, 2008).

Reclaiming authenticity and CONNECTION are concepts that I pursue with every new client, regardless of presenting history, UFT, or apparent diagnosis. My findings are correlated with many aspects of psychological well-being, including "vitality, self-esteem, and coping skills." Acting in accordance with one's core Self—a trait called Self-determination—is ranked by some experts as one of three basic psychological needs, along with competence and a sense of relatedness. "People feel profoundly like they're not living with who they really are, the authentic self, their deepest possibility in the world" (ibid, 2008, p. 74–77).

The "self-help" craze has certainly continued at a high rate throughout the last several decades. What people seem to be looking for is a sense of their true or core Self as we have been discussing it, especially in the context of current isolation. Self-Awareness, which can come from therapeutic processing, is the knowledge of and trust of one's own motives, emotions, preferences, and abilities. And Self-awareness is necessary for close relationships because intimacy cannot develop without openness and honesty.

Over millennia, philosophers have approached the issue of authenticity with depth and perception. Socrates reminded us: "The unexamined life is not worth living." The Greeks felt it was for a higher good to do so, even though it was expressed differently and unequally in everyone. It is this ultimate expression of Selfhood that can also be seen throughout the writings of antiquity. For instance, in Judaism people do the right thing because they see it as an expression of their authentic Selfhood, whereas in Christianity the eternal Soul is who you really, truly are; sinners are simply out of touch with their core Selves. This idea of nobility reaches beyond eminence in rank or privilege; its meaning implies a quality of mind and character that I believe we are talking about at the highest levels of authenticity and Self-actualization itself.

Philosophers of this century also reflect these ideas. Sartre, the French philosopher of the 1940s and 1950s, stated that "existence precedes essence." To me this statement grabs at the very core of the UFT—we become from that which we were, we are moving toward our true "essence" because we have been contextualized by all that went into the developmental UFT history of our life.

As mentioned in an earlier chapter, during my years attending Science of Mind/Religious Science training, I learned much about myself. I also gained many excellent resources for assisting clients with the questioning/inventory process, and I needed some homework to go with it. This handout was very helpful. I recommend doing this "inner work" for many of my clients as well.

Science of Mind Worksheet

- Up until now _____
- What is it that you want, that you believe is not OK, what will happen?
- What is right about not getting what you want?
- What is wrong with getting everyone/everything I want?

During this training, we were taught that there are stages for processing our experience: demonstration of your trust/need first, then project that trust through the affirmation and prayer, and finally there will be a manifestation in the world. Having looked at these concerns, the process will lead us to a realization of a 5-step process of actualization ending in Release: Recognition, Affirmation, Realization, Thanksgiving, and Release. Practitioners in the Church of Religious Science (Science of Mind) refer to their meditations as "affirmations". I have personally experienced that they work—one can receive blessings, and faith in Self can be restored, for Higher Power and a stronger Self (spiritual fitness) is available if one just asks for that process to start. Here is a Science of Mind Affirmation/Meditation that we were given at the time:

A Science of Mind Meditation

Now is our time for centering ourselves.
Be still. Feel the inner quiet and peace that is your being.
Relax. Feel your breathing.
Be aware of tensions, now let them go.
Feel your body, your mind in a unity of serenity.
Today is yours to share and to know the fullness of realization.
That which is, is yours.
You are all and life is the stream, the source of your doing.
You are the source of your own benefits, the manifestation of pure love and harmony.
As you feel the centeredness, being aware of the peace that is yours,

Enlightenment will be the force that provides your day and your life with all that is good and all that is divine.

That which we believe we can begin to demonstrate, in this projection of our belief, will become a manifestation or outcome for a change in the direction of our life. May you find that sense of Self, authenticity, and peace of mind today.

Chapter Twenty-Two
We Become United

"...the first effect of life is inmost thought, which is the perception of the ends."
– Emanuel Swedenborg, 1763

"We are both spectators and actors in the great drama of existence; Man is his own greatest mystery."
– Niels Bohr

The concept "Collective Communication" was originally a computer term for interfacing systems. But it could also be used to indicate a "global synchronization" of consciousness, the opposite of which would be communication "scattering" and misunderstanding. We use communication and CONNECTION with others to reach a sense of Unity of spirit. Sometimes we share too much, but our sharing is usually too little due to the fear of becoming vulnerable and being hurt. Some of us are afraid of interpersonal contact because we might not find out we are real, beautiful, human beings. Always being in control limits our journey, the one we must always strive to create for ourselves. "Situational awareness" means being phenomenologically aware. If we face our fear of change and embrace our creative and productive side, we will discover that fear does not always have to be negative. Fear is also a helpful indicator of where we are on the path to Self-actualization. Thus, meaning was not in the creation but in the creator.

> To be alive is to face risks. Some of these are physical risks...emotional risks...to be alive fully is to make yourself vulnerable. Suffering, just being alive is a 'struggle' and full of ordinary everyday risks...to be significant, is the biggest struggle of all. Growth is a process of reducing fears and defenses and freeing oneself to love and to trust and to be loved and trusted...The more fearful I am, the more I stay in role or keep things impersonal: the more closed and strategic I am, the more I am inclined to do what I am supposed to do and the more my reactions are determined by my authority attitudes.

> It is when fearful that impersonal, closed, dutiful, and controlling behaviors appear. Conversely, when I am more trusting (less fearful) I am more personal, open, self-determined, and freedom-giving. I open up to the degree that I do not feel fearful at the moment (Gibb, Jack, Proceedings of a Symposium of Training Groups, Renown innovator at NTL, Bethel, Maine).

In this final chapter I attempt to summarize for the reader issues presented in previous chapters, and fully reveal the picture of how our UFT is formed and how through understanding it we recognize our true healthy Self. These issues imply order, where everything is CONNECTED, and in every point, there is the image and information of everything else (Bohm, 1996).

Many believe that man is the only case of life "being aware of itself", and that man's drives are an expression of "a fundamental and specifically human need: the need to be related to man and nature and to confirm himself in this relatedness [CONNECTION]." Fromm's viewpoint makes it evident that he was influenced not only by Freud, but also specifically by Adler and his studies of man's needs (See Chapter Thirteen).

Again, the experience of a polarity, that which has formulated in our brains as a dialectic, can be an important opportunity for resolution and synthesis into a complementary and meaningful "perception" of calm and hopefulness about ourselves and our situations. If we can be freed from our deeper anxieties, we will be truly alive in our sense of Self. We are searching for creative synthesis, something beyond merely personal, which will define ourselves and our values in everything we do. This synthesis is self-reliance (Bateson, MC, 1989).

Jung defines Self as not only containing the deposit and totality of all past life but as a point of departure, the fertile soil from which all future life will spring (Knapp, 1995). Our lives are created out of a healthy, well-adjusted ego, unified, rather than fragmented. It is reality based. As William James writes, "by the merging of the narrower private self into the wider or greater self the spirit of the universe (which is your own 'subconscious' self)," is the moment barriers caused by mistrust and anxiety are removed (James, Wm., *Varieties of Religious Experience*, 1902, p. 126). James wrote this in 1902, today we might call this "letting go".

Living systems require diversity for life and well-being rather than just conformity. Even in a "love relationship", listening to criticism or negative Self-talk is not in the direction of growth; being a good partner comes from expressing Self-compassion and Self-forgiveness. A child may initially experience the necessity of social conformity but will eventually come to realize that putting one's true Self into interactions creates Unity and integrity. "Integrity is that which produces wholeness in your life, integrity is the result of integrating your spiritual self into your everyday behavior" (Mandel, 1985, p. 74).

Transactions require that we "think", then respond; this process provides internal controls that will be necessary as growth continues. For instance, a woman's love and child's gratitude is just a continuation of the dualism we have been discussing. It is also an example of "fusion", where two aspects of natural CONNECTION result in Koestler's concept of Bisociation (the combination of two mentally associated ideas that are not logically related). You might call this "timeless Unity", recognizing the duality of how the world always creates pairs of opposites including the maternal-child bond. The final resolution of this symbiosis may be as difficult for the parent as for the child, especially if the child senses some parental ambivalence or even abandonment. The resolution of this initial symbiosis and then appropriate parenting, to allow and support separation, always depends upon the context of the CONNECTION.

Another example would be the CONNECTION that takes place when two moments (the act of anticipation and the act of creation) are fused and fulfilled (Bronowski, 2011). It is the authentic experience that goes on within an inner space called Self, and we become what we think of ourselves, the great quest! We are always reflecting on that from which we see and learn, searching for a model, developing what Heschel, in his book *Who is Man?* (1965), calls "a human behavior pattern...a drama full of life" (ibid, 1965, p. 9).

Thematically, I am writing about universals and their symbols, which unite us all. Functions which come from the "superconscious", or what Jung calls the "Collective Unconscious", CONNECT us to aesthetic, ethical, religious, intuitive, spiritual, and inspirational states of consciousness. We create changes in both the inner and outer world; what we used to call the "scientific method" can now be supplanted by computer algorithms, but nature and its influences cannot be programmed.

Much of my writings in Chapter Two through Four were based on my perception of consciousness and its contribution to a UFT. From consciousness meaning is born; meaning could be seen as identical with the existential quanta which created it. Any influences, which might create adaptational patterns, are continually reorganized by unforeseeable alterations; the field of my awareness is identical with the field of this fundamental reorganizing [Heisenberg's theory of uncertainty]. In philosophical terms, the moment-to-moment patterning of consciousness determines "the eventual architecture of mind's evolved structure" [UFT] (Atkin, 2007).

Mind and matter are different states of the same thing: the field of consciousness. We become an "organizer" of space, time, matter, and energy in a way that the constant shifting between these interchangeable states creates one source. Ultimately, meditation becomes an act of going "beyond quanta" to the place where space and time cannot be measured. "Consciousness and energy (science) are the same thing somehow...all of life is a meditation, most of it unintentional" (Campbell, 1990, p. 14). Campbell goes on to explain, "as soon as it (transcendent energy) enters the field of time, it breaks into pairs of opposites [point and wave], [then] the one becomes two."

Of course, in childhood we start out with only one, unified unconscious, but then we begin focusing on how that which is lost or missing in life can cause symptoms of PTSD (irritability, depression, and stress), whereas focusing on the future creates anxiety. We are dealing with a circular and cybernetic system. When the system is distorted and the universe no longer joins with each part (in a dualistic yet asymmetrical CONNECTION), then overwhelming "catastrophic anxiety" results. On the other hand, a mindful acceptance of "what is" in the present will allow one to trust, accept, bond, and change outcomes.

In philosophical terms, dialectical reasoning is the mind's ability to reason oppositionally or alternatively. The subjects of the Trivium in Greece favored the art of debate and were focused on the power of grammar and logic to change one's perception and one's point of view. As grammar teaches one to speak, dialectics teaches truth in synthesis, while rhetoric colors words with a fuller meaning.[158]

---

[158] This relates to the Socratic belief that no man will willingly choose falsehood over truth, or evil over good. The assumption here is that ignorance has made the bad choice possible. "The whole of Jeffersonian democratic theory is based on the conviction that full knowledge leads to right action, and that action is impossible without full knowledge...One finds what is right for oneself by listening carefully and Taoistically

Philosophers from Plato to Kant to Hegel to Adler have relied upon this search for truth through dialectics and rhetoric as form of reasoning to generate alternatives.

Abraham Maslow studied the transcendent process and encouraged people to be more "in touch" with themselves, which Erikson had referred to as the experience of immediacy (Schlein, 1994). More specifically, Maslow was somewhat a critic of early psychoanalysis, stating that it tended "to study the worst and the weakest in the human being and to assume that that was all there was" (Hardy, 1990). And yet, transcendent experiences require approaching the unknown as well.

The generative principle drives the world of living creatures and creates a need for beauty and desire, for a Divine Rhythm. The unifying force which CONNECTS the senses with the Divine is exactly what this book is about. We all create actualization through a combination of both mysticism and common experience. From this balance between a yearning for greatness and a fear of what it can bring us, we attain serenity. This lifelong search is the great dialectic between those two opposites and the source of all true spiritual fitness.

As we saw in Chapter Twelve, a balance between potentiality and action (freedom of will) is best sought through a thorough awareness of cosmic forces and influences. This belief reflects the Platonic concept of the "antithesis between Idea and Matter." Action may be limited by a lack of knowledge, but our potential, our cosmic faith, has no limits. Ultimately, we arrive at the humanistic ideal of Self-realization through active involvement, whether it be scholarship, artistic endeavor, or any other way we can develop our full potentialities. There is an impulse to growth and to the actuation of human potential requiring, the sense of an intrinsic ontosophy: the wisdom of the human being as psyche-soma individuality; the individual tends toward healthy harmony-homeostasis of the self-regenerating being (ontopoiesis).

Dogmas, whether religious-based or not, only serve to get in our way as we transverse the cosmic limits of understanding available to us. Our sense of belonging to an Other creates space for us to belong to ourselves. Dogmas of the Reformation may have created the actions of a capitalist society (Adam Smith), but they also exalted the Self as they exalted productivity. Individuals often hold on to their own dogma or ideology as an anchor from which they can move about within their own personal myths, sometimes exploring the fear, anger and suffering that was previously caused.

Marx called "ideology" a methodology by which people can "extol their virtues and ignore or conceal their weaknesses." This experience of overt acceptance of systemic belief can be on a personal level, but it can often be at a community or global level. As I write this in 2023, the effects of the pandemic outside my door still demonstrate how different "ideologies" are causing a

---

to one's inner voices, by listening in order to let oneself be molded, guided, directed. The psychotherapist helps his patient in the same way—by helping the patient hear his drowned-out inner voices, the weak commands of his own nature on the Spinozistic principle that true freedom consists of accepting and loving the inevitable, the nature of reality" (Maslow, 1971, pp. 122, 124).

disruption in our continuity and CONNECTION and in the care for each other that strongly existed a brief 10 years ago.

Philosophy in Review

Before I readdress underlying philosophical ideas, I would like to underscore my predominant view of how the "Outlier" presents in CONNECTIONS. In almost every chapter of this book, the Outlier is seen as a variant, the exception that points to the understanding or truth of the "normal" and healthy individual and system. My personal slant is that the Outlier and unusual individual found in this world should be considered as part of a whole that makes the world unified and dignified. Adler was one of the original psychologists to view the psyche as a social instinct, and he was very involved in helping the poor and less bourgeois than Freud was (more about this Adler and this history in Chapters Four and Thirteen).

Ignorance is no longer a valid excuse when it comes to the mind and the cosmos. It is time to turn crisis into circus and chaos into cosmos. Our culture of hypervigilance has not paid off. Our anxiety does not learn from the genealogy of our experience and our heritage. We are all capable of experiencing empathy, the act of sharing, of "resonating" with another consciousness. "It is my personal opinion that in the science of the future, reality will neither be 'psychic' nor 'physical' but somehow both and somehow neither" (Wolfgang Pauli quoted in Chopra & Kapatos, 2017, p. 213).

As I have discussed in several previous chapters, especially Chapter Nineteen, science investigates that which is outside of us, but also that which is inside of us, and we must figure out how to unify mind and matter, past and future, many and one, forming a uni/multi-versal view of our lives that can be understood within the context of our UFT and our epigenetic and historical data.

As a thinker, Teilhard de Chardin had reached a point where he believed that the entire phenomenal universe, including man, was revealed as part of a process of evolution. He found himself obliged to build a generalized theory or philosophy of evolutionary process which would take account of human history and human personality as well as of biology, and from which one could draw conclusions as to the future evolution of man on Gaia, our Earth, which is a living, evolving organism.

Similarly, and as previously mentioned in Chapter Three, Jonas Salk wanted to reconcile one's relationship to the human mind with that of the cosmos and evolution. His "meta-biology" presents constructs in the realms of mental, cultural, spiritual, and creative. As it existed throughout time, the "metaphysical, implicit, and non-manifest form" of primordial matter took on an "anatomy of order" (Salk, 1983, p. 37). Man's job became having enough courage to be fully alive and to study the meaning of his existence.

For Salk, everything is interdependent, dynamic, and integral for relationships and reactions. Even the asymmetrical within a binary world has its purpose and relationship to maintaining balance (See Madeo, Chapter Two). De-evolving was just the action of remaining unactualized. Actualized creativity is presented in the balanced and constructive nature of any binary system. Evolution is the actualization of the optimum in the relational aspects of the system. Although high tech outcomes in recent years may seem to make us more isolated, ultimately technology presents us with a powerful tool to break out from ourselves.

Fromm (1968) believes that the guiding principle behind our obsession with technology has to do with the maxim "something *ought* to be done because it is technically *possible* to do it." However, he also fears that the choices we are making will be a "negation of the humanist values" we have worked so hard to re-establish for the first time since the beginning of the Industrial Revolution. We are losing our CONNECTIVITY and are feeling more powerless and anxious; we conform to gain validation. But what is lost? Integrity and self-identity are becoming scarcer, the uses of artificial intelligence (AI) more common.

We are victims of our own techno-industrial creation. Our love of "maximum efficiency and output" results in a minimalization of individuality, and our fear due to a "scarcity of resources" causes us to manifest the "smallest possible resources to obtain maximum effect." Fromm called us *Homo consumens*, whose only aim is to "have more and use more…The long-range implications of a cybernated world for mental health are disturbing" (ibid, 1968, pp. 32–33, 94). As part of the world is focusing on regaining optimal health, the rest is planning for "maximum production".

We are the holders of creative possibilities. The difference between "I" and "me" is largely an illusion of memory. Our sense of our totality is part of our whole being, just as the head is part of the body. But at times the head and the body feel at odds with one another. "The conscious universe embraces change, non-change, and the state of potential change" [emphasis added] (Chopra & Kafatos, 2017, p. 217). We are "aware of being aware", and this is "cosmic CONNECTION;" objective and subjective no longer apply.

Ultimately, we are responsible for our view of the world and whether it becomes a place of understanding and solace or a place of drama. The mind may be anywhere or everywhere, but it is how our lives reflect our mind that will guide our choices and how others react to us. We are all linked. This is how the possible becomes actual. "One by-product of this surrender is a new argument for the existence of free will. For if physical events are indeterminate and the future is unpredictable, then perhaps the unknown quantity called 'mind' may yet guide man's destiny among the infinite uncertainties of a capricious universe" [that operates under the Heisenberg theory] (Barrett, 1948, p.28).

Having designed and supported the idea of a UFT of development and Self through illustrating how classical Humanism helped influence the development of Self, we can now add to our review how the symbols of the Renaissance affected later philosophers such as Hegel and Spinoza. Historically, we can trace a line from Plato to other Stoics to the Jew Spinoza (who combined his views with Jewish Rationalism) to Hegel to the development of Psychoanalysis and Behaviorism.

Many of the philosophers focused their readers toward Self-governing and attempted to define a republican view from this position. Some of these positions are based on a historical influence from the past for a solution to their problems.

The destiny of man, a goal of the Renaissance at least for the educated man, seemed to be gentility and clarity. A CONNECTION to, and understanding of, Self then supported more empathy toward others, their need for power, and perhaps even their political point of view.

If we cannot be special, some part of our conscious, our Shadow according to Jung, will revert to Self-sabotage instead. Whether in therapy, 12-step, or the rigorous demands for honesty within a relationship, we face our Self-deception on a regular basis. If we look at our circumstances as a totality, however, we can see a way to integrate the smaller incidents of fear or shame into a greater sense of our strength and willingness to look at the truth about ourselves. The worst experience, I think, is to be shamed about one's shame! "Shame can trigger reactions of rage, withdrawal, humiliation or hurt…we feel unworthy and insecure, with the anticipation of being hurt again" (Amodeo, 2001). Trust becomes difficult, and defenses are brought up.

Marx expanded psychological ideas about this dichotomy—the belief in "naked self-interest", based largely on—Hegel—into a socio-political position, which would support free trade in a constantly expanding global market, ultimately resulting in the interdependence of nations. "A worldwide communal global market would be best" where individuals were Self-dependent (Marx, 1848, p. 91). Most of Marx's ideas went the way of Communism, but there are some lingering influences, such as the idea that there are some "natural laws" (similar to those which govern the natural world), that govern the "growth and flow of wealth". We call this economics.

Ideas against monopolies and for control over the flow of products were entering the general cultural discussion after the French Revolution, including the 18th century ideas of Adam Smith regarding attainment of wealth from the general marketplace. Some of Marx's ideas were in response to what he studied while gaining his doctorate in Philosophy (Boorstin, 1985).

To many, knowledge means more power, more civilization—more comfort. But Heschel (*Who is Man?*, 1965) states: "Our challenge is to remember that each of the traits that disturb us will determine the un-owned areas within, allowing them to be observed and forgiven…more knowledge should also mean more reverence, that the civilization should also mean less violence…Forgiveness holds the vital key to restoring correct vision of who we are" [emphasis added] (ibid, 1965, p. 100). No reality exists externally from, or independently of, the mind because the mind affects reality by the very act of observing it [Heisenberg].

We are now able to map our personal genomes more carefully, but it is the ongoing manner in which the epigenetic changes are being made that will truly express the strengths of resilience or weaknesses of vulnerability with which we are born.[159] This tracking is the value of history, whether it be an accounting of

---

[159] "Genes and environments, especially environments of adversity and inequality, together produce known individual differences in susceptibility, behavior, and disease…Think of the genome and epigenome like this: Your genes are the keys on a piano; each plays a distinctive note. But while a piano has just 88 white and black keys, your genome houses around 25,000 individual genes, making it thousands of times more complex. In the first kind of epigenetic regulation—cell differentiation—these

society, psychological growth, or personal values; we must also consider our UFT as a form of "history" in that we carry with us a personal log of our past and that of our societal influences.

Spirituality and Self-Evaluation

During the mid-20th century, it was re-discovered from Eastern religions that energy should also be equated with spirituality. Our concerns turned from the Bomb and the Cold War to environmental sustainability. System theory not only helped better organize companies, but it led us to a study of metacommunication. Computer systems required "batching" in their backup drives, and so did we, as individuals and as a global society (Our memories are the representative factors resulting from "batching"). According to Heisenberg's theory, we can only think we know where something is or if matter is substantive. How can we live in this world of probabilities? We come to know that empty space and inertia is more than nothing; it is substance, and we see the effects of it just like the wind blowing through a tree. This is partly what Salk meant by the "bisociative" property of "what is". We internalize and thus create stereotypes (archetypes?) which, however, can block bisociative processes and Unity. By the 1960s, the studies of (re)birth of the Self and healthier methods of personal growth enhancement arrived just in time to get us through a global recession and then a global pandemic. We became like multifaceted diamonds, shiny and self-indulgent at times, but basically tough as the carbon we are made from.

Some individuals create and/or carry a dogma regarding their values, familial influences, and spiritual sustenance. In Chapter Eight, I presented a review of several different religions and their core influences. My personal belief system is a combination of the self-awareness gained from Jung and Campbell's study of mythology and magic, Buddhism's presentation of the eightfold path, and the intentionality of a 12-step model.[160]

---

keys can be played in different combinations, sequences, and timings to create a whole variety of different tunes—200 different ones, for each of the different types of cells in the human body. One corresponds to the production of neurons, another to white blood cells, yet another to skin cells, and so on" (Boyce, 2019, pp. 84–86).

[160] "The main drift of mythology, if you want to put it into a sentence or two, is that the separateness that is apparent in the phenomenal world is secondary; beyond, and behind, and within, and supporting that world is an unseen but experienced unity and identity in us all. And the first level of unity that is recognized is that of the family. And the second level of unity, which is deeper, is of the tribe or social unit. But beyond that is a common human identity…you and that other are one, and the sense of separateness is simply a function of the way we experience things in space and time" (Campbell, 1990, pp. 52–53).

We all function within our personally designed views of how history is affected by time and space; that which we find difficult to understand, control or most importantly that which shames us, may be met with through denial. Denial is a very complex term in psychology but generally refers to our inability to face that which pains us the most, as well as that which we disagree with or with conflicts with our values. If I declare something to be "untrue" than I can more easily maintain a perspective within my own

As I noted, I have studied many religions, in college and through personal choice. I have drawn from many of them, especially Jewish foundational principles of conduct and faith in the Kabbalah, The *Sermon on the Mount* by Jesus, and Buddha's teachings. I have come to believe that "the more we learn about emotions the more we learn about ourselves" (Kyabgon, 2013). "Right Speech", according to Buddhism, brings one's attention to one's verbal interactions and away from the "Three Poisons" of greed, anger, and ignorance. If we ask ourselves, "Is it true? Is it kind? Is it harmful?" we will be well on our way to the development of Self that comes from learning that being alone with our thoughts sometimes is the path to our Selves. This core principle defines my therapeutic practices and my personal values.[161]

> Man must not be afraid to release his inner self. To stand up for one's beliefs is man's most important freedom; compromise comes only through the free decision to change one's opinion. If one is afraid of exercising freedom of his will through fear that he will be criticized or that he may hurt someone by being contrary, then he can never truly realize his total potential. Man, as first because of himself, sees everything from only one point of view, which is equivalent to selfishness. Comparing this finding to what moralists would have us think, that to be selfish is a primal sin; rather, it is the primal urge of all men. If one cannot know himself and thereby serve his wants through the available means, then he is neither free nor self-actualizing. Man must be free to express his needs and not have to be afraid of other's judgments (Gerzon, 1997).

Often it seems the meaning of the words "moral" and "ethical" overlap. Broadly speaking, morals are individual principles of right and wrong, ethical refers to a larger system dealing with those principles, some of which may reflect a larger universal view of behavior. "Morals are about personal behavior; ethics are a philosophical view. Who is not for is against" (James, Wm., *Will to Believe,* 1897, p. 109). James believed, rather, in what he coined as the "moral multiverse". A mere escape from suffering cannot be our rule of life. That which we believe can become the source of courage and reward for developing new habits and meeting our most basic needs.

Even though week after week the "crisis" may change, at the core lacking sense of Self and/or Self-determination is what contributes to emotionality. A calmer sense of Self is the antidote to neurosis. Because one can never really know

---

consciousness that it is untrue. This process also works for recent history and its difficult lessons, one reason I have chosen to stay away from political analysis in this book.

[161] "The ultimate Truth, being without attributes, cannot be contemplated by the mind…it lives far from mankind, out in the great loneliness…Just as a man, when in the embrace of a beloved wife, knows nothing within or without, so does this being, when embraced by the Supreme Self, know nothing within or without—*The Upanishads*" (Campbell, 1988, pp. 55, 82). It is Billy Graham's hole for which there is no filling (requires <u>faith</u> alone).

where an experience ends or ceases to be [Heisenberg Principle again], dialectical reasoning may be a necessary process to initiate executive options. "To be human is to intend" (Heschel, 1965, p. 40, 42).

Faith is reinforced by having respect for all religions, cultures and living life on life's terms; it is the ability to, most of all, respect your Self and the unifying force that guides you, whatever your value system. I personally practice Buddhism, fundamental *Taoist* ideas, attend Yoga and *Tai Chi/Qi Gong* classes, go to services at a local synagogue as well as the Methodist church, and even attend a 12-step meeting or two, sometimes all in the same week! All faith is faith, and I can't have too much contact with the Spirit to which I may be guided. I "project" my idea of Divine Power into my own individual method of belief and faith, one which is comfortable for me, and which works.

To experience one thing may be viewed as the end of experiencing the end of the other. Death is and has always been a dominant philosophic theme in my family. We talked about death when it occurred, and we talked about what we wished for with our own death as a way of blending spirituality and philosophy.

Change is inevitable, and resolving dichotomies is the work of a lifetime. We intuitively want to move from that which is imperfect to that which is perfect, healthy, and secure. Sometimes we even sense the fact of our own evolution, not that which brought us here from the struggle of the Iron Age or the elegance of the Renaissance, but rather that which we see revealed through metaphysical certainties expressed during mindfulness and our striving toward individuation. Small daily changes show our ideals and values combine with more global acts of humanitarianism; all are leading toward Unity and an "enlightened society", using symbols to create feeling-images through which we can communicate and CONNECT.

Jung studied alchemy for many years; why was finding the "secret" of this mysticism so important for him? He believed it was the opening of the gate. It is the sure knowledge that nature and the material world are the vessels of eternity, the "'alchemical furnace' in which the spiritual world is revealed." Campbell felt so strongly about Jung's discoveries that he ultimately CONNECTED Jung's findings in *The Portable Jung* (1971). Campbell felt Jung had exhibited a "threefold sense namely, celestial, spiritual, and natural."

Campbell's own spiritual belief was that the human form is holy, as is everything else that lives. I have been inspired by his discussion of "a metaphysical dimension", where "eternity is that dimension of here and now, that all thinking in temporal terms cuts off…the experience of eternity right here and now, in all things, whether thought of as good or as evil, is the function of life" (Campbell, 1990, p. 66). As I have formulated my own spiritual influences, I always seem to come back to the truth of Campbell's statements.

As we saw in Chapter Eight, Tantric training in Buddhism brings together emotion and insight. I had my own personal experience of this during my 2001 10-day training with the Dalai Lama in Ganden Monastery in Southern India. We were taught that our own special insight could give us more control over our emotions, allowing them to then be enhanced to an intense level. Through meditation, we used the simple process of imagery to achieve a strong foundation, a "mindfulness of the details of life" (Chogyam Trungpa Ripoche, 2012).

I have carried this experience forth into my therapeutic activities with patients who are experiencing PTSD or need pain management. It is through the suffering of pain that we recognize our needs and how to take care of ourselves. We don't have to be told that life is dismal sometimes, or that perhaps it is also worth all we go through to possess sensations and desires; we come to recognize, however, that despair and suffering are just an attitude that we can challenge through the experience of gratitude, success, or CONNECTION to find that which is life-affirming in oneself. "The path to fulfillment is paved with the building blocks of not trying to please everyone"; once our mind is consciously available, there is an energy-releasing, life-motivating, and directing agent inside of us called the wholeness of our Self (Catala, 1998, pp, 78, 160).

Scientific Findings

Another point of view about "wholeness" is the one presented by the scientific findings of the last century. We have learned through these diversified studies, for instance, that the glucose in our brain contributes to the processes we call thinking, feeling, and perceiving.

> Chemistry is completely determined; [but] thinking is free. Now you can see why a belief in cause and effect is one of the core beliefs that have broken down in the postquantum era. It just won't do to say that the big bang inevitably led to this very moment, the page you are now reading, the ham sandwich or cup of tea at your elbow, and the spelling of your last name. Strict cause and effect would mean that your next thought or the next word out of your mouth was predetermined 13.7 billion years ago. By turning strict cause and effect into probabilities [Heisenberg], quantum mechanics eased this difficulty. We now live with "soft" causes and effects, you might say. Every event emerges from a set of probabilities, not an ironclad chain reaction (Chopra & Katapos, 2017, p. 61).

Simplification is the act of taking charge of one's life to clean up chaos, focus attention, and practice CONNECTING to the spirit. Suddenly both your outer and inner worlds become the place where you desire to heal from the past by getting rid of some of its possessions and to CONNECT to the future by an increase in quiet and contemplation of opportunities. Time management becomes easier, and disappointments decrease.

Niels Bohr and Werner Heisenberg wrote about one similar factor. Bohr's theory was that of "complementarity" while Heisenberg's was that of "uncertainty". But both were addressing the manner in which cause and effect break down. Likewise, individual experience of culture reflects the initial "mothering function", from thereon the surety of the UFT is being built. One can experience vocational and financial insecurity, threats of war, pandemics, and even moral decline, but there must be a sense of stability, continuity, and CONNECTION for there to be a "civilization".

For some individuals, it is the very essence of spirituality to gain the security and complementarity mentioned above by our awareness of our cosmic selves. Marilyn Schlitz, Ph.D. vice-president for Research and Education at IONS, speaks directly to the issues of matter, energy, space, and time. She proposes they are not the separate entities suggested by common sense but are rather deeply intertwined relationships. Even humans are part of that "vast ocean of energy". One act of complementarity is distant healing, an experience which suggests that causality may not be limited to only its physical properties.

People's intuition derives from a desire to find patterns and CONNECTIONS in—and to figure out how to act within—an otherwise random universe (Greer, 2005). We have come to realize that the universe really is only a representation of what we want it to show us, of how we make the virtual real (see Chapter Two).

Philosophy is written in that great book which ever lies before our eyes—I mean the Universe—but we cannot understand it if we do not first learn the language and grasp the symbols in which it is written. This book is written in the mathematical language, and the symbols are triangles, circles, and other geometrical figures, without whose help it is impossible to comprehend a single word of it; without which one wanders in vain through a dark labyrinth (Bronowski and Mazlish, 1960, p. 126).

"Knowledge that the vastness of the universe might exceed limits previously declared as "Truth" contributed to our internal struggle to understand our importance or nonimportance in the face of astronomical truth. If we accept Heisenberg's theory, which I do, then "nature displays the properties an observer happens to be looking for" [emphasis added]" (Chopra & Kafatos, 2017, 116).

Mind and matter are different states of the same thing: the field of consciousness. We become an "organizer" of space, time, matter, and energy in a way that the constant shifting between these interchangeable states creates that one source. Meditation then becomes an act of going "beyond quanta" to the place where space and time don't exist. "Consciousness and energy (science) are the same thing somehow...all of life is a meditation, most of it unintentional" (Campbell, 1990, p. 14). Campbell goes on to explain, "as soon as it (transcendent energy) enters the field of time, it breaks into pairs of opposites, the one becomes two. Now, when you have two [opposites], there are just three ways in which they can relate to one another: one way is of this one dominant over that; another way is of that one dominant over this; and a third way is of the two in a balanced accord" (ibid, 1990, p. 28).

When Watson and Crick were first studying the structure of DNA, the question most on their minds was "What is life?" The combinations that they found to compose DNA are the closest to the answer as we currently define ourselves. Three billion letters can now be accessed to find out your genome for under $1000, and many genetic diseases can be tracked, even Alzheimer's. The CRISPR project allows us to intrude into our own DNA with the hopes of changing the path of many of these diseases. But it brings up the question: should genomes be altered if mutated—editing genes like typos on a computer? We still have the nature versus nurture argument for many of our Self-imposed diseases and conditions, including addiction and obesity.

Are we really a "blank slate" or not? Research has proven that we pretty much are born genetically (or epigenetically) with our temperament. Therefore, we might be able to change how our neurotransmitters affect our moods and behavior, but I don't think we will ever be able to change our personality disorders. If we begin to see consciousness as a biological process then what are dreams, feelings and even our basic state of awareness? Is everything just a part of science? Too many questions without answers, at least not yet. But my own opinion is that science will never be able to quantify the CONNECTION between two people, each one is unique!

Even so, it is true that DNA, Darwinism, and all forms of differentiation and specialization are affected by a binary system found even in the immune function (self/non-self can equal an autoimmune disorder). In *Lives of Cells* (1957), Thomas' work on biological functioning of the cell reinforces a belief in evolution. "We may begin to view immune reactions, genes for the chemical marking of self, and perhaps all reflexive responses of aggression and defense as secondary developments in evolution, necessary for the regulation and modulation of symbiosis, not designed to break into the process, only to keep it from getting out of hand."

Humans in social situations go through endocrine revisions, for instance, endocrine-producing stress [as do locusts]. Whereas Darwin felt adaptation was driven by a fear of negative consequences while trying to make sense of our world, the "integrative theory" drives us with an open purpose, structure, attitudes, and processes. One creates "entropy and death" while the other creates results that promote our own and the Other's best interests.

In *The Second Brain* (1999), Michael Gershon describes how the nervous system's information presides over the functions of digestive, enzymatic, glandular, muscular, pressure, chemical-physical, and immune hormonal coordination; it produces the greatest quantity of serotonin (95%) present in the human body, by the enteric nervous system. It is not triggered by external stimuli, but is closely CONNECTED to the endocrine system, and is found widespread within the gastrointestinal mucosa. Our nervous system attempts to maintain a balance between the external (food, visual input) and internal (emotions, form beliefs, habits). All living things originate at the electromagnetic level, and the influences here of the quanta can be called a "biofield". "It is the complexity which gives the brain its abilities, including thought and rationality" (Chopra & Kapatos, 2017, p. 191).

As we have seen in previous chapters, DISCONNECTION is probably as harmful to our nervous system as stress, obesity, and poor nutrition. Loneliness and social isolation are a by-product of other phenomena (depression, anxiety, and self-doubt) and are cyclically responsible for poor self-care, but they are not challenged in our society like medical conditions; we refer to them as "mental health" issues. My mother, who lived to be almost 93, used to say she was often alone but never lonely. She had too many things in which she was interested and to keep her busy; she could never "catch up". Loneliness, on the other hand, is the result of something lacking in one's life or due to a skills-deficit, in particular social functioning.

All social risk requires some openness to change and to aloneness and one's individuality. Prepare for periods of aloneness, which may be more painful sometimes than at others. "Allow these alone feelings and states to run their course and don't complicate the whole issue by avoiding or resisting. Resolving your aloneness cannot only aid in your acceptance of your situations but also help you become more in touch with your unique individuality" (Kubistant, 1981, p. 464).

We know stimuli alter physiology; communication always leads to visceral responses in our bodies, which affects our immune system. "Social CONNECTION (or DISCONNECTION) can affect health through biological pathways such as immune function or the regulation of stress hormones. Factors such as anger, hostility, depression, anxiety, and PTSD boost heart disease risk [emphasis added]" (Novotny, March 2018, p. 48–53). Yet few efforts have been made in research to study how social management and vulnerability to social isolation affect the health and well-being of older adults.

One's initial APGAR score at birth may very well be predictive of our whole life to come (in areas such as physical, social, emotional language, and communication domains of development—an interesting algorithm). We are indeed a whole set of complexities [UFT] that cannot be described by any one set of variables. A binary view of outcomes just won't work. But we do know that initial prenatal factors, along with social and physical determinants after birth, are descriptive of benefits to survival and thriving (Boyce, 2019).

A study by Uchino and Way (as quoted by Weir, 2018) shows how "family relationships are linked to favorable levels of the stress hormone cortisol, which plays a role in important functions such a glucose metabolism and immune function," and additional evidence that "the protective role of the neurochemical oxytocin, the hormone released during social bonding, has been shown to reduce blood pressure and lower cortisol levels" (ibid, 2018, p. 50).

Endocrine function, immune function and nervous system activity are a few of the areas I frequently address with my patients, whether these systems were part of the initial concern or not. For example, often a client will come and tell me a story fraught with disaster and a source of fear for them. It may or may not be about their health issues specifically; however, I will say to them, "remind me why you think you come here?"

After a lot of confused looks and unproductive pauses, I go on to prompt them: "You see your cardiologist for your heart, you see your neurologist for your brain, you see your pulmonary specialist for your lungs…so why do you see me?" "Oh, oh," they reply, "for my immune system! To help me cope with stress!" At which point I know my methods are beginning to sink in…

Increases of ATCH (Adrenocorticotropic hormone) will be found at neurotransmitter junctions during stress. Ultimately, Azar (2011) asserts, we can become "a different us", a factor I frequently uncover in my clients who have had social adversity or even abuse earlier in their life. Having been isolated and/or ostracized at an early age could affect the immune system's ability to anticipate "what the body is likely to encounter." She thus affirms that this process is a kind of "developmental plasticity [UFT]."

Getting clients to a point of recognition of these developmental changes, and to a willingness to "remember" a true Self that they might choose to return to is one of the greatest goals of deeper therapy. This action is how we know we are alive, rather than just "drifting toward death" as Jung said. Embracing ourselves may feel scary, like too much change, but it is the most alive thing we can do. It is the completion of our course in learning about ourselves through human suffering that is made necessary through living a full life.

Whether developmental or neurological, plasticity is a real key to maintaining CONNECTIONS. I have historically had clients pick their five-year old self, or perhaps the feistiness of their 12-year-old self, ready to take on the world, as a symbolic representation of their "real Self". We learn the ability to adapt as we experience our whole system "participating" in the act of accepting change as a reflection of complementarity. de Chardin proposed that with full consciousness comes "the specific effect of organized complexity," and he goes on to differentiate between a physicist's definition of energy versus psychology's view of psychic energy.

In neuroscience, we talk about how the brain integrates all new knowledge, information, and sensory input by associating it with what you already know. We saw in Chapter Thirteen that Piaget called this assimilation. It not only leads to our environmental learning but to our moral development as well. Deepak Chopra reminds us that this is an act of "self-organization".

> Whether we're speaking of genes and the brain or solar systems and galaxies, self-organization is present. Existence requires balance, which demands feedback. By monitoring itself, a system can correct imbalances automatically. Every new bit of the universe, however minuscule, must create a feedback loop with what gave rise to it. Otherwise, it wouldn't be CONNECTED to the whole—in human terms, it would be homeless [emphasis added] (Chopra & Cafatos, 2017, p. 72).

This is the meaning behind what I've been calling my united field theory of development, of spiritual fitness, and of the healing acceptance of our existence, as it is. Acceptance has come from understanding the past and letting go of anxiety about the future.

Kant described it well and Buddhism is a great representation of this process of acceptance, using mindfulness, concentration, and insight all to achieve consciousness. Buddhists believe that *Karma* or action comes from the same kind of experiences expressed in such terms as mass, energy, force, and matter used in quantum physics. It is all the same thing.

Psychology Blends with Science

Jung blended his longstanding study of the mystical world with his understanding of the actions of the physical world to expand his view of intuition. Next, the Neo-Freudian theory of Ego Psychology expanded the knowledge of human development and interactions beyond the inner world of instinct. Finally, Einstein's Theory of Relativity attracted us all, captured our interests in science and Science Fiction, and helped create a new holistic perspective about ourselves and the cosmic environment. We now believe that things remain the same regardless of motion (activity) of the source or the motion (activity) of the observer (Kahan, 1983).

In our perceptions of each other, each cannot tell if they or the other is moving [behaving in a causative factor]. All we can be sure of is that each is reacting relative to the other. This is true of relationships; I believe it is also true of nature, and of our pursuit of a relationship with our own Self. Even the electrons whirling around the nuclei inside of us are representative of the theory of relativity. We all have our own internal "clocks" (that knowledge of space-time caused by motion); it is our heartbeat. Literally, everyone lives not only relative to others and the environment but relative to their own private time (ibid, 1983). When we feel bored, depressed, or simply lost in the inertia of our own view of Self, it is really a resistance to change, just like any other of physics' views of inertia. [162]

As we study the evolution of the mind, sometimes we begin to think of minds as being like digital computers (rather than the other way around): neurons are activated through two-way switches, our mind must follow rules, and cannot easily tolerate ambiguity. Intellect shows that versatility in adapting creates a "concept" of similarities between diverse things. Likewise, discontinuity can be tolerated, and quantum leaps (literally) are achieved in evolution during our own lifetimes. Our cerebral cortex evolved because symbolic processes became more complex. By the time the 20-million-year-old Dryopithecus man was found in Kenya by Leakey, his "race" had evolved (Java man at least 700,000 years old, Peking man 400,000 years ago, Neanderthal man 80,000 years ago) to the Cro-Magnon man 60,000 years ago.

He was making cave paintings in France, making tools, burying his dead, communicating, acting cooperatively with others in a social system, and had enough frontal lobe consciousness to show reverence and believe in magic. Thus, we come to realize that our Self-concept is the formulation of this consciousness, the attitude toward oneself, and is the result of a combination of attitudinal factors and competence-oriented goals. "The key here isn't fitness—it's just a feeling of being free, of forgetting for a moment that we are bound by gravity and logic and convention, of letting the magic happen" (Rockmore, 2019, p. 6). As we have been noting throughout this chapter, congruence, consistency, and variability especially relate to one's UFT and changes in personality.

Another way of looking at this concept of CONNECTION is the use of the word "teamwork". In a 2018 article entitled, "Foundations of Teamwork and Collaboration", the authors Driskell, Salas, and Driskell present their model which maintains that successful organizations are based on understanding the importance of team dynamics. As "inputs" are CONNECTED to "outputs" team processes, as well as effectiveness and satisfaction, can be measured through "direct reciprocity", that is, the "accomplishment of a shared goal" [emphasis added] (Mathieu et al., as quoted in Driskill, et al., 2018). I like this idea of sharing, of determining how a CONNECTION can be mutually beneficial, otherwise known as collaboration.

---

[162] Take any one word or factor out of Einstein's equation and substitute that factor with another. Mass is form, energy, or consciousness (See Chopra).

The authors also identified eight core teamwork dimensions: adaptability, shared understanding, performance monitoring, leadership, interpersonal relations, coordination, communication, and decision-making. These eight areas are just as powerful when viewed from a psychosocial viewpoint as from an organization design framework in that they are trait-relevant; success is based on trust and conflict resolution. How our families, our relationships, our marriages, our cultures, and our world view become integrated and CONNECTED is just as powerful, strategic, and dedicated as the goals of any organizational structure. Positive leadership requires a world view in addition to systems and contingency views.

In 2007, Warren Bennis wrote an article entitled "The Challenges of Leadership in the Modern World". In this introduction to a special issue of *American Psychologist*, Bennis presented a cognitive system model of leadership which detailed the need for collaboration among "social-neuro-cognitive scientists" to achieve an integrated theory. What struck me the most about this article was his prediction that if we fail to gain leadership which maintains the values of wisdom, justice and "the common good" we will fall into one of four catastrophes: a nuclear/biological catastrophe, a worldwide pandemic, tribalism, and a failure of leadership in human institutions. Having just experienced the worldwide pandemic starting in 2020, it is clear that at least three of his four predictions have come true already.

The avid narcissism and nationalism that is being put forward in political races throughout the world may "recruit and maintain followers" but these politicians are not worthy of the offices they seek. We do not need leaders who are "masters of performance", who know how to use media and communication to CONNECT; we need leaders who are effective, competent, and trustworthy. Although charisma can have a positive influence, it cannot be the only trait which guides adaptive capacity. Leadership must parallel the complexities of the culture it guides, whether familial, academic, workplace, or on a global stage.

Cognitive ability is not enough, a "leader" must show a sense of morality along with collaborative traits and a flexible personality regardless of the situation presented. Organizations, small to global, are dynamic and require efficiency and effectiveness. Thus, the leader must be able to adapt and change his or her behavior as the situation changes.

Jung's theory of personality was differentiated into the four functions (thinking, feeling, sensation and intuition), as noted in Chapter Nineteen. In 1938, after his visit to India, he said that Indians do not think; he meant that "like 'primitive' man, they perceived their thoughts. 'The primitive's reasoning is mainly an unconscious function, and he perceives its results'" (Hayman, 1999, pp. 225, 427).

It is imperative that in our self-analysis, including that of CONNECTIONS to the physical world, we look for the qualitative, not just the quantitative. This idea was the further concretization of Jung's overall theory, which now had shifted from being based on "psychological" concepts to "spiritual" concepts as well. Heschel concludes (1965), it is self-deception to assume that man can ever be an innocent spectator. "To be human is to be involved, to act and react, to wonder and to respond" (Jung quoted in ibid, 1965, p.68).

Creating Bonds

What, then, is the path to "openness and caring?" The path flows through CONNECTION to and understanding of our personalities through knowledge of others and ourselves. Rather than letting "toxic anxiety" rule us, a solution-oriented viewpoint will be to accept that anxiety will always be there and to find a better way to master it, through what Gerzon (1997) calls the 5 A's: acceptance, awareness, analysis, action, and appreciation. Using these skills presents us with opportunities to learn and grow, relax, gather more information, communicate more openly, act, and use our attitude of gratitude. We become resilient, adaptable, and Self-actualized (ibid, 1997).

Human bonding, like covalent bonding, is a form of binary interaction. It is focused and purposeful. The bonding contributes to (oxidizes) or reduces the original valence or direction of human need (electronegativity). The electron field or Gestalt of individual experience is always the result of predetermined Ego defenses and genetic predisposition, outer shell configuration. But the fact is, every electron is the same as every other. As in $e=mc2$, the energy lost or gained in redox (the chemical reactions where electrons can be changed) is stabilized with or without the other agent's permission.

The shift occurs when life appears. "The universal cell structure of living might be a generality in biology, but when compared to physics, the knowledge of phenomena is 'simple, concrete, and specific,' and yet different in each human infant outside the womb because of its 'unique social environment as in its acquisition of language'" (Schwartz, 1999, p. 143). See this volume's cover for my grandson, Nathan's, first (IVF) "picture".

For instance, if I am like the chemical Hydrogen+, I am alpha and powerfully charged but have no depth or recourse. If I am like the chemical Chlorine-, I am one who strongly bonds and resists outside intrusion at the same time. If I am a Renaissance person, I am more like Carbon+, able to bond freely and to create life. This understanding of modern chemistry and physics is how psychologists differ from the view proposed by Freud, as man being a set of "instincts" alone. "Instead of looking inward at the arrangement of body parts as the origin of the human subject, [the study of man] looked outward at the network of interpersonal relationships as the source of human individuality and selfhood" (ibid, 1999, p. 166).

Bronowski (2011) believes that it was the very search for truth which changed our "bonding" with our immediate universe and moved us out of the Renaissance. Now, according to Maltz (1960), and others, we search for truth out of "cybernetic systems".

There is no longer one Truth. Everything is relative. "Relativity has created a need for standard errors of measurement, for wisdom touched with cynicism, and for the ability to cherish any moments of synergy…The world which the human mind knows and explores does not survive if it is emptied of thought. And thought does not survive without symbolic concepts. The symbol and the metaphor are as necessary [CONNECTION] to science as to poetry" (Bronowski, 2011, p. 36).

The discovery of this type of global truth reminds us that there always was the mythological truth of the collective unconscious, regardless of culture. Making and correcting concepts (schemas) is what pulls us down our paths, whether self-destructive or creative. The CONNECTION, to whatever, will always be there.

A Spiritual Outlook

Jung believed that our experience of "God" is determined by each one's individual need to come to terms with one's Shadow, thus initially creating a tension between opposites but ultimately finding an archetype of "God" which contains both sides of one's nature. Accept that which is experienced as "dark", by releasing dogma and accepting a world of possibilities.[163] One must find a "paradoxical blending of individuality and universality" (Hardy, 1990, p. 56).

It is the recognition of opposites, and their reconciliation, that allows the formulation of a spiritual outlook to CONNECT the beliefs of theology, science, psychology, and myth. Myth is a metaphor, a way into a deeper center. "I do not transcend my possibilities; I only transcend my own concept of what my possibilities might be" (Jourard in Otto, ed., 1970, p. 12). As I resist being in an equilibrium, the tension that creates growth will support my Self-actualization. "The self-actualizing person not only has a more harmonious personality, but he sees the world in a more unified way" (Goble, 1970, p. 26).

This dialectical process of thesis and antithesis is how a personality develops anyway, toggling between the yearning for a continuity with the past and finding the required CONNECTION with one's needs, experiences, and dreams (UFT) to establish appropriate boundaries to move toward (and bond with) the future. We need not live in an "either-or" world, but rather a blended world that encompasses either and or! In *Stranger in a Strange Land* (Heinlein, 1961) "*grok*" means to be identically equal.

"The observer becomes a part of the observed—to merge, blend, intermarry, lose identity in group experience. It means almost everything that we mean by religion, philosophy, and science—and it means as little to us as color means to a blind person" (ibid, 1961, p. 213). Thus, we find the meaning behind Michael's, the main character, words "Thou art God." To blend, to merge, to CONNECT; I was inspired by these words as a young teenager reading *Stranger* in the 1960s

---

[163] We can see Jung's influence on Hermann Hesse, (1926) who wrote, "I know that the value of what we people of today write cannot lie in the possibility of a form emerging valid for our time and for a long time to come, a style and classicism, but rather that we in our distress have no refuge except that of the greatest possible candor. Between these demands for candor, for concession, for surrender of the self and that other demand familiar to us from youth, for beautiful expression, between these two requirements the whole poetry of my generation swings back and forth in bewilderment. For even if we were prepared for the greatest candor to the point of self-surrender—where could we find the means of expressing it?"

and I am still a believer. We are identical to our experience of now as we are identical with our beliefs in the eternal.

Building Boundaries

The technique of creating a Gestalt, used in Dialectical Behavioral Therapy (DBT), is the interplay between therapist and client which continually shows a respect for boundaries. "Building boundaries" lies at the very heart of the methodology of this type of therapy. Some may believe that the mind has no boundaries, that it is an experience of something we are trying to understand and thus control. However, not everyone has the capacity to recognize the internal dialogue of one's own thoughts initially [executive function], and the Dialectical as in "D" (of DBT) represents the back-and-forth attempt to build a balance and a respect while the client is learning to Self-manage prior negative, and usually, Self-destructive behaviors.

Therapists back off when the client's response is one of anger, or emotional withdrawal, or shame, or threatened Self-harm. Similarly, clients would reward the therapist with interpersonal warmth or engagement if the therapist allowed them to change the topic of the session from one they didn't want to discuss to one they did want to discuss. "Acceptance-based interventions [are]...'perfectly normal' messages about behaviors. Clients also must change if they want to build a life worth living...dialectical strategies gave the therapist a means to balance acceptance and change" (Linehan and Limeff, 2001).

This level of mutual acceptance also suggests the concept of resilience, which requires flexibility, a shift away from shaming-blaming-catastrophizing (Graham, 2016). Research shows a direct CONNECTION between resilience and one's ability to control rumination and hypervigilance. How do we recover from trauma? How do we break the bad habits that reinforce the fear and reactivity and loss of faith that is the *Zeitgeist* of our time? What are the basic adaptive skills needed to prepare for recovery or even, unfortunately, another trauma?

Obviously, we need to resolve the stress disorder (SD) in PTSD, but this would mean better mental health in the first place. Even people with compassion toward Self and others can experience PTSD. But these individuals are usually not alone in developing a coping strategy; they have a support system. As we saw in Chapter Twenty, the need to feel CONNECTED to other human beings is hard-wired into our brain's functioning. Small infants and children immediately feel the "pain of DISCONNECTION" and will do almost anything to find CONNECTION, including self-soothing (the initial imprinting of compulsive behaviors later).

Because the largest number of individuals in our country with this diagnosis lies within the veteran population, I share here the VA/TriWest site's description of PTSD:

- Frequently re-experience the traumatic event.
- Experience persistent symptoms of increased arousal not present before the trauma.
- Make efforts to avoid stimuli associated with the trauma.
- Exhibit numbing of their general responsiveness.

PTSD can be understood, if not totally cured. Its course can be predicted. Often, patients use narcissistic defenses to preserve psychic constancy when the ego is overwhelmed by intolerable loss. This signals the demand that caring figures satisfy frustrated needs while providing sustenance. Next, during convalescence, the patient uses immature defenses to alert caring figures that the patient needs support so that he can be enabled to do something for himself above and beyond Self-preservation. In the third phase, recovery, the patient uses neurotic and mature defenses and may even experience the depths of unmodified depression and anxiety, while simultaneously asking caring figures to participate in a mutually gratifying relationship while he becomes aware of the nature of the unconscious purposes of his behavior often based in compassion. Each level of awareness defines the type of psychological problem that has been created by the trauma.

Kristin Neff expands DBT techniques often used with treating PTSD and proposes "self-compassion" practice, where the individual takes on a daily acceptance of reality in the mode of "what is, is; what's done is done." Having reached that "radical" acceptance through verbal or internal repetition of an acceptance mantra/prayer, then a resulting "mindfulness" practice will demonstrate encouragement, nonjudgmental awareness, and acceptance of "life on life's terms" (*Big Book of AA*, 2001).

Regardless of one's personal beliefs about the famous personal coach Tony Robbins, much of his vernacular presentation reflects the current view of mindfulness as a successful response to stress and self-awareness. He states that the past "frames people's belief structures and their value systems," and one must answer the question of "what can I do now to enhance the quality of my life" (Simon, 2017, p. 47–51). Robbins promotes enhanced CONNECTIONS as being what contribute to a richer life, through fear reduction and embracing who you are not just what you want. Because "people aren't their behaviors", Robbins asserts that breakthroughs come from not only Self-acceptance, but also from Self-trust.

Awareness of patterns and then acknowledgement of triggers (without responding to them) is something Robbins and I agree on. In one's search for meaning "meaning equals emotion, and emotion equals life…you can become unconsciously competent." Possibly, this premise is the basis of most therapeutic modalities across the field of psychotherapy. Change comes from awareness, acceptance and embracing a view of strategic change in which one sees himself as honest and trustworthy within the process.

As the 12-step process states, "focus on what you can control, not on what you can't." The structure of socialization is to recognize the talent in our young people and to reinforce it. I can honestly say that most of the people I have seen over the last 50 years for counseling were extraordinary people, but whose talent had either not been recognized or not affirmed for many reasons.

I see the influence of this concept, of a period of hope and a new beginning following a period of degeneration (*fin de siècle*), as the source of excitement, anticipation, and a sense of impending change in our current world circumstances. I see many opportunities to shift opulence and/or decadence, racism, and socioeconomic imbalance into the radical changes that need to be made. I hope in the future we can all commit to building up using the talent of our youth, as each is extraordinary in his or her own way.

Mindfulness Creates Deeper Awareness

How does such a thing as "psychodynamically-oriented meditation" or "mindfulness therapy" bring about a deeper experience of the Self? Meditation becomes more than a refuge from the world; the world is no longer seen as a harsh reality but rather a part of the meditational state—a place to test out new insights, which is the natural development of life (Hesse's *Glass Bead Game*). Of course, viewed as very different from previous "medical models" of neuroses and treatment of symptoms, these therapies focus on clients finding freedom to become their actualized Selves, which is more than just being liberated from historical causes and the psychodynamics effects they experience in their everyday lives.

Yes, mindfulness requires focus and dedication, but the ultimate freedom that is experienced is worth every effort put into practicing the new skill. One could even describe the mindfulness process as Jung's concept of "Collective Unconscious" CONNECTING and making an alliance with one's emerging awareness of peace because of the acceptance of Self-will. This well-being comes when one can see the world's infinite pairs of opposites as a synthesis and complementary, creating a unified world which can be accessed through Self-analysis and/or meditation.

I have discovered when I go into a therapy session with a looser agenda, and an attitude of acceptance rather than looking for information about the past, the client feels free to also go on this journey of discovery and Self-acceptance found in Chapter Twenty. "Unless we are mindful and aware, we will lose precision and accuracy in all the other acts. The whole thing will become an egoistic or neurotic version of activity rather than a genuine sense of spontaneity that develops through the practice of mindfulness and awareness in meditation" (Kyabgon, 2013). This awareness is at the core of all self-reflection; the release from sorrow can only come from within oneself.

Tedeschi and Calhoun (1996) write that supportive relationships create meaningfulness and are of primary importance. These relationships provide a context within which to anchor one's identity and worthiness. In addition, these authors hope for positive changes in education and parenting so that "flexibility, mindfulness and even appropriate risk-taking" can be part of the educational experience. We need to teach problem-solving skills as well, along with impulse control to fight against over-reacting. "Mistakes or setbacks are experience to learn from, not be defeated by." We need to be needed.

My role as a therapist is often based on Yalom's statement: "The honest therapist is one who attempts to provide that which the patient can assimilate, verify and utilize" (Yalom, 1995). Although Yalom's methodology was studied by all psychology graduate students in my day as an introduction to "group dynamics" (still is), I continually find that what I learned is very useful as well in my work with individual clients. The more a person sees himself as an object, the more potential fear of abuse there is at the hands of others (ibid, 1995).

Another model is Gestalt therapy, in which a phenomenological approach emphasizes a person's capacity to impose a pattern and meaning on the discrete events in his life and to organize the phenomena into even more complex wholes. "A Gestalt therapist focuses on 'what, now and how' rather than the psychoanalysis concerned with 'why'" (Perls, 1969).

Finally, the Behavior Therapy model focuses on overt behavior. The theory is that is the therapist can join with the client to isolate the problem behavior (the therapist filling the role of expert); even though the therapist may come across in a very authoritarian, knowledgeable manner, the necessary information, treatment goals, and treatment plan can be developed and shared constructively with the client (ibid, 1969).

Systems Theory

In framing our growth, development, and CONNECTIONS, whether in regard to history, science or psychosocial theories, the purpose and systems symbolize the functional aspects of the ideas. We usually depict systems with a nucleus or origin. In human social systems, this nucleus is the system's control and organizing principle, its reason for being, its purpose. It defines the system's nature. The key issue to remember is that open systems are alive and active; closed ones drive toward static equilibrium.

At the core of every human social system, which includes every social institution, is a transaction between two principal partners (as noted in our discussion of Transactional Analysis). There is often correlation between systems theory and the study of cybernetics in the 1970s. George Land, in his book *Breakpoint and Beyond* (2000), posited that organizational and social systems have two demonstrated phases—the formative and the normative. He also tells us that there is, theoretically, a third phase—the integrative phase.[164]

Ray Rucker (Former Dean of USIU) (see Chapter Thirteen and Twenty-One) maintained that Value Analysis is the most integrative view of human systems theory and includes all the steps of clarification but is also a systematic prelude to a decision (i.e., growth-enhancing). Some of the notes I took during my class with him as a professor in graduate school (1973) brought up the following points:

- With processes of awareness and clarification, we now approach the moment of looking at a value transaction critically, to evaluate it against a criterion.

---

[164] "Formative: concept, idea, philosophy, solution to a problem in someone's mind, manifest that purpose, the formative phase is about 'making it up as you go along.' Decision making criteria are highly qualitative…This phase of a system values people for their creativity, their authenticity. It affirms the unique value of its individual members. People within it feel alive, that they are 'making a difference.'
"Normative: As the system focuses on increasing the predictability and efficiency of its internal operating forms and processes, it becomes more and more concerned only with its own best interests… [it strives to] eliminate diversity and variance…it moves to control them, to make them predictable and interchangeable" (Land, 2000).

- A direction of actualization or humanization, high synergy, or the fulfillment of the person as a human being…Does society develop high synergy in relation to its membership?
- Value analysis depends, then, upon the assumption that we know a direction and have criteria to use…There are many cultural techniques. These techniques are legion and account for cultural diversity and relativity.
- Value relativity is the relationship among value categories based upon a given human event. Difference among people and cultures is difference in cultural techniques for achieving the values, that is, techniques that have been invented by man. "Every civilization finds it necessary to make compromises with its own values." Jungians refer to this as "alchemy of the collective psyche" (Singer, 1972, pp. 23, 26).
- Value deprivation leads to our problems. Value sharing is what we call behavior that portrays acceptance of the obligation of going about in the world helping people to enhance their values.

Systemic CONNECTIONS

We move now beyond the heathy Selves with which we have CONNECTED to CONNECTING with a global systemic consciousness. "The 'life' of the living—personal integrity and authenticity, creativity, insight, meaning, and purpose, the sense of being alive—cannot survive inside closed systems" (Mandel, 1985). It is the piecing together that is important—just as words form sentences, groups of communality and family systems form internal and nontechnical meaning. "There is necessarily something intrinsically good-natured about symbiotic relations."

If we think about the importance of schools, as representative of larger community system, especially during this pandemic period, we will acknowledge that society in general needs these educational supplements to the core values of "family" as social reinforcers. I personally do not particularly value home-schooling, nor even the current phase of online/at home learning, because I fear the element of social interaction and structured testing of boundaries and identity is too severely limited in these situations. The developing child learns by being in a larger society and is reinforced for healthy adaptation. Especially in Freud's latency period, school-age children 7–11 years old, the need for balancing power and achievement is paramount.

In a broader point of view, why does culture have its default to conflict and war? Culture wars are represented in supportive AIDS treatment and for other pandemic responses versus the contrary opinions of the Moral Majority on the Right, inclusiveness versus exclusiveness on the issue of immigration, believers versus deniers regarding the environment and global warming. Time and relativity always put us in a position where comparisons are made to those around us.

Perhaps our competitive nature is part of Darwinian survival? Do we "need" enemies? Can we only appreciate our good through vigilance to our vulnerabilities? Is this yet another dualism? One could say that even "dis-ease" results from inconclusive negotiations for symbiosis, "an overstepping of the line by one side or the other, a biologic misinterpretation of borders" (Sherwood, 1974, p. 89–91).

> The power of guns is not often compatible with truth and very much depends on untruths or lies. So, with guns, there are usually lies and destruction. When governments keep so many state secrets, this is a sign of weakness, despite military strength. If a government is compelled to keep secrets from its own people, this is a sign of weakness.
>
> – Tenzin Gyatso, Fourteenth Dalai Lama

From thinkers in the Hebrew tribes to the philosophers of the Greek city-states and the Roman empire, theologians in the medieval feudal society, thinkers in the Renaissance, the philosophers of the Enlightenment, down to such thinkers of the industrial society as Goethe, Marx, and [in our age, sic] Einstein and Schweitzer, Gates and Jobs, there is no doubt that in this phase of the industrial society the practice of these intrinsic values becomes more and more difficult, precisely because the reified man experiences little of life and instead follows principles which have been programmed for him by the machine.[165]

Society cannot shape us anymore than we allow it to because we are society. Not only were we the society of the past, but Maslow (1971) maintains we are the future, in that "the future also now exists in the person in the form of ideals, hopes, duties, tasks, plans, goals, unrealized potentials, mission, fate, destiny and so forth" (ibid, 1971, p. 53). Maslow's theory concludes that values which an individual develops in respect to his potentials are a result of the ways in which his basic needs (physiological, safety, love) were met, and the person who is behaving badly and feels he has no future is reacting to the deprivation of his basic needs. I like this summary of how one can practice Self-regard:

The Seven Gifts

- The art of mutual respect /generosity: no negative labeling.
- Self-disclosure/courage: securely attached to your inner strength.
- Discernment/Truth: clarity that is based in the present moment, paying attention.
- Collaboration/shared effort: offer the gift of the collaborative "we", ask for what we need, instead of getting annoyed and critical with each other.
- Anticipating clashes/foresight: it is the wisdom of what-if and the memory of how-to that keeps you safe.

---

[165] "It is possible to argue that the tremendous achievements of the modern age, psychological as well as material, were made possible only by abandoning a unified and spiritualized conception of the environment. Even to begin to penetrate the secrets of the universe, it was necessary to cast off anthropomorphic preconceptions, to recognize that the universe cannot be explained as a projection of man's own need or aspirations. An attitude of objectivity toward external reality was both a prerequisite for, and a consequence of, the advance of scientific knowledge. [However], man's unique prerogative and responsibility is the definition of values" (Ralph, 1973, p. 25).

- Apology/responsibility: a genuine apology places emphasis on compassion for the wounded party, not redemption for the transgressor, authentically remorseful feelings are free of self-loathing and a self-centered preoccupation with guilt.
- Reflective listening/balance: extracting hidden sentiments, the gift of balance, handling controversial matters without getting triggered, to feelings about one another that have been closeted in anger, apathy or avoidance.

Our need to "rehumanize" can be seen in one's UFT and its priority to show us how to CONNECT. But we also must speculate about the "root cause" of our discomfort, thereby formulating a "map" or plan for change and rejuvenation/transformation (Brown, B., 2012). We can use mindfulness to create "healthy pictures in our head" as my mother would call it, rather than a shame-based culture. Brown believes that "daring greatly" can lead to societal values of compassion and CONNECTION. Brown also presents Snyder's "trilogy of goals, pathways, and agency" that create a healthy map:

- We can set realistic goals (*I know where I want to go*).
- We can figure out how to achieve those goals, including the ability to stay flexible and develop alternative routes (*I know how to get there, I'm persistent, and I can tolerate disappointment and try again*).
- We believe in ourselves (*I can do this!*)

Now that we are a global society, one must reject the idea of being a victim, stop blaming others for what happens in one's life, and refuse to feel sorry for oneself (or one's "tribe").[166]

How does one accept responsibility more vibrantly for themselves and their own happiness? Martin Seligman moved on from his studies of Learned Helplessness (1975) to a study of happiness and well-being in *Flourish* (2012). He presents a construct that includes five essential parts: positive emotion,

---

[166] Just as the habit of failure or success is developmental in nature, the way to changing these habits is by conscious goal-orientation on all three levels, the social, the emotional and the intuitive. Huxley (1952) states the paradox of what I have been discussing concisely in this way: "The sense of humanity, it is evident, is not something we are born with; it is something we make or grow into. We learn to speak, we accumulate conceptualized knowledge and pseudo-knowledge, we imitate our elders, we build up fixed patterns of thought and feeling and behavior, and in the process, we become human, we turn into persons. But the things which make us human are precisely the things which interfere with self-realization and prevent understanding. We are humanized by imitating others, by learning their speech and by acquiring the accumulated knowledge which language makes available. But we understand only when, by liberating ourselves from the tyranny of words, conditioned reflexes, and social conventions, we establish direct, unmediated contact with experience [UFT]. The greatest paradox of our existence consists in this: that, to understand, we must first encumber ourselves with all the intellectual and emotional baggage which is the impediment to understanding" (ibid, 1952, p. 47).

engagement in life, meaning, positive relationships, and accomplishment. He believes that we have control over much more (40%) of our opportunities for happiness than genetics and life circumstances might predict, starting with expressing gratitude and optimism as well as engaging in acts of kindness toward others and Self. Practicing mindfulness is a good start toward integrating these attitudes.

It may seem that this view is a totally new paradigm shift, but obstacles and problems are opportunities for learning new ways of finding solutions and for strengthening positive intentions (including positive neuroplasticity and immune responses). Seligman believes that this point of view is the whole meaning behind the myth of Sisyphus: to learn from adversity and to find joy from the endurance of suffering. Commit to service; it becomes not only a distraction from one's own problems, but it is also definitely an ongoing need in the world!

If we have been convinced by engineers and physical scientists that windmills will provide enough energy for our global needs, the evidence would have been backed by research and convincing data.[167] But when we view differing cultural views and behaviors, many based on religious beliefs, then the situation is different.

> When any individual, or individual world leader for that matter, claims to have the support of his or her followers to prove a statement of policy, then they are required to demonstrate nothing except some personal credibility which may be weak at best. The achievements of artists, writers, statesmen, and scientists can be explained almost entirely according to environmental contingencies…that 'all these questions about purposes, feelings, knowledge, and so on, can be reinstated in terms of the environment to which a person has been exposed' and that what a person 'intends to do' depends on what he has done in the past and what has then happened'… The question is begged by use of the term 'consequences.' If overpopulation, nuclear war, pollution, and depletion of resources are a problem, 'we may then change practices to induce people to have fewer children, spend less on nuclear weapons, stop polluting the environment, and consume resources at a lower rate, respectively' (Swedenborg, 1749, pp. 7, 150–152).

The fact that this quote originated in the 18th century and could just as likely be about today's environmental issues is even more distressing. How we choose to define dignity going forward from our recent issues (environment, pandemics, political discord, racism) will be determined by how we are influenced and by

---

[167] "The paradox of physics today is that with every improvement in its mathematical apparatus, the gulf between man the observer and the objective world of scientific description becomes more profound…It is not surprising, therefore, that the prime mysteries of nature dwell in those realms farthest removed from sense-imprisoned man, not that science, unable to describe the extremes of reality in the homely metaphors of classical physics, should content itself with noting such mathematical relationships as may be revealed" (Barrett, 1948, *The Universe and Dr. Einstein*, p. 14–15).

what choices and freedom to act that we "think" we have and/or what the consequences will be.

Developmental Integration

"'Ethnocentrism,' which reflects an idea of cognitive tribalism, is sometimes seen in our current views of the same facts. Can something so important be divided dramatically into important reality versus 'fake news?'"

Now here is the surprising fact, this quote is taken from William Sumner, written in 1906! More recent than Swedenborg ideas, but Sumner's ideas were still not integrated into a consciousness of CONNECTION, even 100 years ago. Can the notion of personal and social recovery (racism, environmental issues, immigration policies) allow us to "recover our future?" It seems to be the one most binding social construct of our times.

Finally, America focuses especially on "character development" and moral development as manifested in one's level of sincerity. But consistently we find we are still judgmental. Why are we "intolerant" of others? This question seems to be at the core of our societal difficulties. Cultural differences can also tell us a lot about ourselves. I have two Russian friends (they don't know each other) who are both often overruled by a cultural sense of negativity and mistrust that they got from their first-generation Russian American parents. Evil was seen as a part of the dialectical need to stay vigilant versus learning to live by looking for the healthiest and most consistent patterns to live by. Perfectionism, scapegoating, and blaming were evidently the result of needing to be in control of the "Other"/projection of one's fear of failing, or worse, being judged, particularly by the KGB! These "new" Americans had to learn to drop a concern with image, status, appearance, and their inherited use of denial (of the fact that we must all suffer). Their upbringing is an excellent example of a loss of integrity in the development of the Self due to trying to be something other than what we are.

We see how fear, anger, sadness, and stress tend to narrow consciousness; while love, appreciation, compassion, and joy tend to widen it. In general, what are considered 'positive' emotions are participatory and therefore broaden consciousness; while what are considered 'negative' emotions are defensive. Total commitment to the outer-directed strategies is more simplified and constrictive, whereas the inner-directed strategies are more inclusive and expansive. Not only individuals but also whole societal CONNECTIONS can manifest Self-actualization or in more ordinary terms, "responsible maturation and fulfillment." Our global society will be what we envision it as, and what we are willing to work for.

Kafka demonstrates in his writing that there can be both external and internal processes; in *The Metamorphosis* (1915), Gregor's "bugginess" symbolizes a loss of individualism and sensitivity. It seems to me that man as an objective, rational creature, is free to choose his role, but he will have a role of some kind. Do you manifest what your role defines you as?

"Looking within oneself for many of the answers implies taking responsibility. To be courageous rather than afraid…" (Maslow, 1971, p. 47).

Bibliography

AA. (1939/2001). *Big Book of AA*. Palm Springs, CA: Hazelden, Inc.
AATBS. (1977). *Theories of Personality*. Los Angeles, CA: AATBS Training Seminar.
AATBS. (1978a). *Theories of Marital Counseling*. Los Angeles, CA: AATBS Training Seminar.
AATBS. (1978b). *Learning*. Los Angeles, CA: AATBS Training Seminar.
Abdill, E. (2003) 'Awakening the inner Self', *Quest,* (March/April 2003), pp. 60–64.
Abers, E. and Pearson, (ed) (2004). *Quantum mechanics.* New York, NY: Prentice-Hall Inc.
About.com: Koan study in Zen Buddhism, 10/13/2014.
Abravanel, E. and King, E. (1990). *Dr. Abravanel's anti-craving weight loss diet.* New York, NY: Bantam Books.
Ackroyd, P. (1996). *Blake: a biography*. New York, NY: Alfred A. Knopf.
Adler, A. (1907). *The Neurotic Character*. New York, NY: Bollingen Foundation.
Allport, G. (1955). *Becoming*. New Haven, Conn: Yale University Press.
Ainsworth, M. Blehar, M., Walters, E. & Wall, S. (1978). *Patterns of attachment: Psychological study of the strange situation*. NJ: Lawrence Erlbaum.
Ainsworth, M, and Bowlby, J. (1991). 'An ethological approach to personality development'. *American Psychologist*, (April 1991), 333–341.
Alpert, M. (2007). 'The triangular universe', *Scientific American Mind*. February 2007.
Alzheimer's Disease and Related Disorders Association, Inc. 10 Warnings signs of Alzheimer's disease. (1998). *AAMI Pamphlet*. Chicago, Il.: AAMI.
Amodeo, J. (2001). *The authentic heart: An eightfold path to midlife love*. New York, NY: John Wiley & Sons, Inc.
Anderson, C. (2014). *Personal communication.* San Diego, CA.
Anderson, D. (2004). *The causes of the civil war.* Milwaukee, WI: World Almanac Library.
Anderson, S. (1994). 'A critical analysis of the concept of codependency', *Social Work*, November 1994), 39, 6, 680–685.
Anonymous. An esoteric interpretation of the 12 Steps. *Meditation*, Spring, 1990.
Ansbacher, H., & Ansbacher, R. (eds.) (1956). *The individual psychology of Alfred Adler*. New York, NY: Harper & Row.
APA. (2000). *Diagnostic and statistical manual of mental disorders-IV,* Washington, D.C.: American Psychiatric Association.
APA. (2013). *Diagnostic and statistical manual of mental disorders-5,* Washington, D.C.: American Psychiatric Association.
APA (2014). *Guidelines for psychological practice with older adults*. (January 2014), 34–65.
Apter, T. (1997). *Secret lives: Women in midlife*. New York, NY: W.W. Norton & Company.

Arieti, S. (1962). 'Lessons in empathy: resilience is essential—the psychotherapeutic approach to depression', *American Journal of Psychotherapy*, (July 1962), **16**, 397–406.
Arraj, T. & Arraj, J. (1985). *A tool for understanding human differences.* Chiloquin, Oregon: Tools for Inner Growth.
Assagioli, R. (1980). *Psychosynthesis.* Winnipeg, Manitoba: Turnstone Press.
Atkin, A. (2007). 'How I come about: evolution of my structure about altered trainings of my attention', *AHP perspective*, (August/September 2007).
Ausubel, D. (1963). *The psychology of meaningful verbal learning.* New York, NY: Grune & Stratton.
Azar, B. (2001). 'A new take on psychoneuroimmunology', *Monitor on Psychology*, (March 2001), 34.
Azar, B. (2010). 'Revisiting philosophy with fMRI', *Monitor on Psychology,* (November 2010), 40–44.
Azar, B. (2010). 'A reason to believe', *Monitor on Psychology,* (December 2010), 51–56.
Azar, B. (2011). 'Oxytocin's other side', *Monitor on Psychology,* (March 2011), 40–42.
Azar, B. (2011). 'The psychology of cells', *Monitor on Psychology,* (May 2011), 32–33.
Bach G. and Torbet, L. (1992). *The inner enemy.* New York, NY: William Morrow & Co.
Badya, E. (2003). *Being Zen: Bringing meditation to life.* Boston, MA: Shambhala Publications.
Bair, D. (2003). *Jung, a biography.* New York, NY: Back Bay Books.
Baird, F. and Kaufmann, W. (2008). *From Plato to Derrida.* Upper Saddle River, New Jersey: Pearson Prentice Hall.
Baker, N. (2011). 'Precious energy the ninth Zen precept: Not being angry', *Tricycle,* (Summer, 2011), 79–81.
Bandura, A. (1997). *Self-efficacy: The exercise of control.* New York, NY: Freeman.
Banks, A. and Jordan, J. (2007). 'The human brain: Hardwired for connections', (Spring/Summer, 2007), 2 *Research and action report, Jean Miller Baker Training Institute.* Wellesley, MA: Wellesley Centers for Women.
Barbour, J. (2020). 'Time is the increase of order, not disorder', [summary pp. 1–16]. *The Janus point: a new theory of time.* New York, NY: Random House.
Barker, A.T. (1886). *The Writing of the Mahatma letters to A.P. Dinnett.* Pasadena, CA: Theosophical University Press.
Barrett, L. (1948). *The universe and Dr. Einstein.* New York, NY: William Sloane Associates.
Bateson, G. (1972). *Steps to an ecology of mind.* New York, NY: Ballantine Books, Inc.
Bateson, M.C. (1989). *Composing a Life.* New York, NY: The Atlantic Monthly Press.
Beattie, M. (1986). *Co-dependent No More.* Minnesota: Hazelden.
Beavers, W.R. and Kaslow, F. (1981). 'The anatomy of hope', *Journal of Marital and Family Therapy,* (April 1981), 119–126.
Beck, A. (1967). *Depression.* Philadelphia, PA: University of Pennsylvania Press.

Beck, A. (1975). *Cognitive therapy and the emotional disorders*. Madison, CT: International University Press, Inc.

Behary, W. (2008). *Disarming the narcissist: surviving & thriving with the self-absorbed*. Oakland, Ca: New Harbinger Publications, Inc.

Belenky, M., et. al. (1997). *Women's ways of knowing*. New York, NY: Basic Books.

Bell, J.S. (1992). 'Six possible worlds of quantum mechanics', *Foundation of Physics,* 22, 10, Part I. 1201–1215.

Bell, T. (2011). 'Qigong for meditators', *Tricycle*, (Summer/2011), 70.

Benedict, R. (1989). *Patterns of culture*. New York, NY: Houghton Mifflin.

Bennis, W. (2007). 'The challenges of leadership in the modern world', *American Psychologist*, 62, 1, 2–5.

Benson, E. (2003). 'The many faces of perfectionism', *Monitor on Psychology,* (November 2003), 18–20.

Berman, M. (1981). *The Reenchantment of the world.* Ithaca, NY: Cornell University Press.

Berne, E (1964). *Games people play.* New York, NY: Grove Press, Inc.

Bettelheim, B. (1976) *The uses of enchantment: the meaning and importance of fairy tales.* New York, NY: Knopf.

Bigthink.com (2022). 'Research triggers revision of leading theory of consciousness', *Bigthink.com/neuropsych/revision—leading theory—consciousness.*

Birnbaum, J. (1973). *Cry anger (A TA approach).* Vancouver, Canada: General Publishing Co.

Blair, C. & Raver, C. (2012). 'Child development in the context of adversity', *American Psychologist*, **4**, 309–318.

Blanck, G. and Blanck, R. (1974). *Ego psychology: theory and practice.* New York, NY: Columbia University Press.

Blavatsky, H.P. (1877–1883) *Mahatma letters. Pasadena, CA: Theosophical Society.*

Bloomfield, H. (1976). *Applications of the transcendental meditation program to psychiatry.* New York, NY: Dawn Press.

Bloomfield, H. (1976). *Happiness: The TM program, psychiatry, and enlightenment.* New York, NY: Simon and Schuster, Inc.

Bloomfield, H. (1976). *TM: Discovering inner energy and overcoming stress.* New York, NY: Simon and Schuster, Inc.

Bloor, David. (1976). *Knowledge and social imagery.* London: Routledge.

Bly, R. (1990). *Iron John: A book about men.* Philadelphia, PA: Perseus Books Group.

Bodiford, W. (2006). *'Koan practice', Sitting with koans.* Ed. John Daido Loori. Somerville, MA: Wisdom Publications.

Boehm, Gottfried. (1994) *'Die wiederkehrder bilder', Was ist ein bild?* Munchen, Germany, 11–38.

Bohm, D. (1976). Bridging the analytically continental divide. Philosophical Review 108: 1–46.

Bolen, J. (1984). Goddesses in everywoman. New York, NY: Harper Collins.

Boorstein, S. (2009). 'The suffering we share', *Shambhala Sun*, (September 2009).

Boorstin, D. (1985). *The Discoverers: A history of man's search to know his world and himself.* New York, NY: Random House.
Borgese, E. (1963). *Ascent of woman.* Victoria, BC Canada: Abe Books.
Bowlby, J. (1960). *Grief and mourning in early childhood.* London: British Psychoanalytic Society.
Bowlby, J. (1973). *Separation: Anxiety and anger.* New York, NY: Basic Books.
Boyce, B. (2012). 'Ocean of Dharma', *Shambhala Sun,* (January 2012).
Boyce, W.T. (2019) Orchids and dandelions. *Psychology Today,* (January/February 2019), 80–88.
Brach, T. (2003). *Radical acceptance: embracing your life with the heart of a Buddha.* New York, NY: Bantam Books.
Brandon, N. (1972). *The disowned self.* New York, NY: Bantam Books.
Brenman, M. and Gill, M. (1959). *Hypnosis and related states: studies in regression.* New York, NY: International Universities Press.
Bronowski, J. (1973). *The ascent of man.* London: BBC Books.
Bronowski, J and Mazlish, B. (1960). *The western intellectual tradition.* New York, NY: Dorset House Publishing.
Bronowski, J. (2011). *Science and human values.* London: Faber and Faber.
Brown, B. (2012). *Daring greatly: How the courage to be vulnerable transforms the way we live, love, parent, and lead.* New York, NY: Gotham.
Brown, B. (2017). High lonesome: Braving the quest for true belonging. *Psychotherapy Networker*, (November/December 2017), 30–55.
Brown, N. (1966). *Love's body.* New York, NY: Random House.
Brown, S., Brown, R., and Preston, S. (2012). 'The human caregiving system: a neuroscience model of compassionate motivation and motivation', In Brown, S., Brown, R. and Prenner, L. (eds.) *Moving beyond self-interest: perspectives from evolutionary biology, neurology, and the social sciences,* (75–88). New York, NY: Oxford University Press.
Bruner, J. (1966). *Studies in cognitive growth.* New York, NY: Wiley, Inc.
Bruner, J. (1973). *Beyond the information given.* New York, NY: W.W. Norton.
Buber, M. (1923). *I and Thou/Ich und Du.* New York, NY: Touchstone (Simon and Schuster 1970).
Buck, P. (1945). *Portrait of a marriage.* New York, NY: Open Road Integrated Media.
Bugental, J. (1965). *Search for authenticity.* New York, NY: Holt, Rineholt, and Winston.
Burke, D. Carstensen, L. and Johnson, N. (2011). Boost your memory. *Healthy Living,* (Spring, 20ll), 36–39.
Burnier, R. (Undated). *Delight as a form of yoga.* Handout in yoga class.
Butler, Rev. A. (1866). *The lives of the saints.* Dublin: James Duffy Publishers.
Butler, R.N. (1969). Ageism: another form of bigotry. *The Gerontologist,* 9, 243–246.
Caldwell, R.R. (2002). 'A phantom menace? Cosmological consequences of a dark energy component with super-negative equation of state', *Physics Letters B,* **545** (1–2), 23–29.
Campbell, J. (1949). *The hero with a thousand faces.* Novato, CA: New World Library.
Campbell, J. (1971). *The portable Jung.* New York, NY: The Viking Press.

Campbell, J. (1988). *The power of myth*. New York, NY: The Viking Press.
Campbell, J & Toms, M. (1990). *An open life*. New York, NY: Harper Perennial.
Canli, T. (2008). Code. *Scientific American Mind,* (February/March 2008), 53–57.
Cantor, N. (1991). *Inventing the Middle Ages*. New York, NY: William Morrow.
Capra, Fritjof. (1975). *The Tao of physics*. Boston, MA: Shambhala Publications.
Carpenter, S. (2001). 'How does the brain catch up?' *Monitor on Psychology*, (October 2001), 46.
Carver, C. & Johnson, S. (2018). 'Impulsive reactivity to emotion and vulnerability to psychopathology', *American Psychologist*, **73**, 9, 1067–1078.
Cassella, C. (2022). 'Researchers have a controversial new hypothesis for how civilization first started', *https://www.sciencealert.com,* 5/21/2022.
Catala, R. (1998). *Mysticism of now*. Lakewood, CO: Acropolis Books.
Cattaneo, L & Chapman, A. (2010). 'The process of empowerment', *American Psychologist*, **65**, 7, 646–659.
Cattell, R & Butcher, J. (1946). *The prediction of achievement and creativity*. New York, NY: Bobbs-Merrill Company, Inc.
Chaucer, G. (circa 1400). *The Canterbury Tales*. Middle English.
Chayefsky, P. (1978). *Altered states*. New York, NY: Harper & Row.
Chess, A., Thomas, S. & Birch, H. (1965). *The origin of the personality: your child is a person*. New York, NY: Viking Press.
Chessick, R. (1974a). 'The special theory of psychotherapeutic interaction', *Psychotherapy and Psychosomatics*, **24**, 433–438.
Chessick, R. (1974b). Techniques in the practice of intensive psychotherapy', *American Journal of Psychoanalysis*, **XXVIII**, 1974.
Chessick, R. (1974c). 'Interaction psychotherapy and psychosomatics', *American Journal of Psychoanalysis*, **XXIV**, 1974.
Chessick, R. (1992). *The technique and practice of listening in intensive psychotherapy*, Lanham, MD: Jason Aronson, Inc.
Chessick, R. (1996a). *Dialogue concerning contemporary psychodynamic therapy,* Lanham, MD: Rowman & Littlefield Publishing Group, Inc.
Chessick, R. (1996b). 'Creativity and the sense of self', *American Journal of Psychoanalysis*, **56**, 337–342.
Chodorow, N. (1999). *The power of feelings: personal meaning in psychoanalysis, gender, and culture*. New Haven: CN: Yale University Press.
Chodron, P. (1996). *When things fall apart: heart advice for difficult times*. Boston: Shambhala Publications.
Chodron, P. (2001). *The place that scares you: A guide to fearlessness in difficult times*. Boston: Shambhala Publications.
Chomsky, N. (1971). 'The case against B.F. Skinner', *The New York Review of Books,* 1–16.
Chopik, Wm., Kim, E. & Smith, J. (2018). 'An examination of dyadic changes in optimism and physical health over time', *Health Psychology*, **37**, 1, 42–50.
Chopra, D. & Kafatos, M. (2017). *You are the universe: discovering your cosmic self and why it matters*. New York, NY: Penguin Random House, LLC.
Clark, D. (2010). 'Citation and biography', *American Psychologist*, **65**, 8, 711–714.
Clark, M. (2007). 'Lies and other untruths', *Swans,* 4/23/2007.

Colarusso, C. & Nemiroff, R. (1980). 'Authenticity and narcissism in the adult development of the self', *Annual of Psychoanalysis*, **8**, 111–129.
Colaruuso, C. & Nemiroff, R. (1981). *Adult development*. New York, NY: Plenum Press.
Coleman, J. (1956). *Abnormal psychology and modern life*. Northbrook, Ill: Pearson Scott Foresman.
Connor, J. and Killian, D. (2012). *Connecting across differences*. Encinitas, Ca.: Puddle Dancer Press.
Cooper, David, Rabbi (1997). *God is a verb*. New York, NY: Riverhead Books.
Coote, S. (2000). *Samuel Pepys: A life*. New York, NY: St. Martin's Press.
Corsini, R. (1973). *Current psychotherapies*. London: F.E. Peacock Publishers.
Cozolino, L. (2006). *The neuroscience of human relationships*. New York, NY: W.W. Norton & Co., Inc.
Crick, F. (1984). *The brain*. New York, NY: Scientific American.
Crapuchettes, B. & Crapuchettes, F. (2011). 'Relational meditation', *Psychotherapy Networker*, (September 2011), 42–45.
Cunningham, S. (1992). *Sacred sleep: Dreams and the divine*. Toronto, ON: Crossing Press.
Curtis, J.D. & Detert, R.A. (1981). *How to relax: A holistic approach to stress management*. Palo Alto, CA: Mayfield.
Dalai Lama (His Holiness). (1996). *The good heart: A Buddhist perspective on the teachings of Jesus*. Somerville, MA: Wisdom Publications.
Dalai Lama (His Holiness) Tenzin Gyatzo. (1998). *The art of happiness*. New York, NY: Random House (Riverhead Books).
Dalai Lama (His Holiness) Tenzin Gyatzo. (2001). 'Oprah talks to the Dalai Lama', *O magazine*, (August 2001).
Dalai Lama (His Holiness) Tenzin Gyatzo. (2006). *The Universe in a single atom*. Boston, MA: Little, Brown and Company.
Davidson, R. (2012). *The emotional life of your brain*. New York, NY: Penguin Books, Inc.
Davidson, T.L., Hargrave, S.L., Swithers, S.E., Sample C.H., Fu, X., Kinzig, K.P., & Zheng, W. (2013). 'Inter-relationships among diet, obesity, and hippocampal-dependent cognitive function', *Neuroscience*, **253**, 110.
Da Vinci, L. (1510). *Notebooks*. New York, NY: Braziller.
Davis, K. (1912). 'The origin and growth of urbanization in the ancient world', *Readings in ancient history: Illustrative extracts from the sources*. New York, NY: Vintage Books.
Davis, K. (1998). *Don't know much about the Bible: Everything you need to know about the good book but never learned*. New York, NY: William Morrow and Company, Inc.
Dawkins, R. (1976). *The selfish gene*. New York, NY: Oxford University Press.
Deamer, D. (2014). 'How did it all begin? The self-assembly of organic molecules and the origin of cellular life', *http://www.ucmp.berkeley.edu/education/events/deamer1.html*.
DeAngelis, T. (2003). 'The dream canvas', *Monitor on Psychology*, (November 2003), 44–49.
De Castillejo, I. (1997). *Knowing woman*. Boston, Mass: Shambhala Publications, Inc.

de Chardin, T. (1959). *The phenomenon of man.* New York, NY: Harper Perennial.

de Hamel, C. (2001). *The British library guide to manuscript illumination: history and techniques.* Toronto: University of Toronto.

de Molen, R. (1973). *Meaning of the renaissance and reformation.* New York, NY: Houghton Mifflin Publishing Co.

de Rougemont, D. (1983). *Love in the western world.* Princeton, N.J.: Princeton University Press.

de Saint-Exupery, A. (1943). *The little prince.* Self-Published.

de Salvo, L. (1999). *Writing as a way of healing: How telling our stories transforms our lives.* Boston, MA: Beacon Press.

de Tocqueville, V. (1840). *Democracy in America.* IL: Chicago: University of Chicago Press.

Decker, D. (2013). 'Key ingredients in creating and maintaining a healthy relationship with a partner' *htpp://www.ANGERresouces.com.*

Dell, P. (1981). 'Paradox redux', *Journal of marital and family therapy*, (April 1981), 127–134.

Dell, P. (2014). *A World War I timeline.* North Mankato, Minnesota: Capstone Press.

Dennis, G. (2007). *The encyclopedia of Jewish myth, magic, and mysticism*, St. Paul: Llewellyn Worldwide.

Descartes, R. (1641). *The discourse on method: Meditations of the first philosophy.* Prometheus Books. NY: Amherst.

Desmond, T. (2012). 'The fascinating Buddhist approach to low self-esteem', *Psychotherapy Networker,* (March 19, 2012).

Dichter, C. (2017). 'Personal communication.'

Dingfelder, S. (2004). 'Treatment for the 'untreatable'', *Monitor on Psychology,* (March 2004), 46.

Dobson, D. & Dobson, K. (2018). 'Avoidance in the clinic: Strategies to conceptualize and reduce avoidance thoughts, emotions, and behaviors with cognitive behavioral therapy', *Practice Innovations,* **3**, 1, 32–42.

Donaldson-Pressman, S. & Pressman, R. (1994). *The narcissistic family.* San Francisco, CA: Jossey-Bass, Publishers.

Dreikurs, R. (1959). *Adlerian family counseling.* University of Oregon: University Press.

Driskell, J., Salas, E., & Driskell, T. (2018). 'Foundations of teamwork and collaboration', *American Psychologist,* **73**, 4, 354–348.

Drob, S. (2010). *Kabbalistic visions: C.G. Jung and Jewish mysticism.* New Orleans: Spring Journal Books.

Du Bois, W.E.B. (1903). *The souls of black folks.* Chicago: A.C. McClurg & Co.

Dulles, A. (1987). *The Catholicity of the church.* Oxford: Oxford University Press.

Durant, W. (1968). *The lessons of history.* New York, NY: Simon and Schuster Publishing.

Dyer, W. (1995). *Your sacred self: Making the decision to be free.* New York, NY: Harper Collins Publishers, Inc.

Dyer, W. (2001). *10 secrets for success and inner peace.* Carlsbad, CA: Hay House, Inc.

Ehde, D., Dillworth, T., & Turner, J. (2014). 'Cognitive-behavioral therapy for individuals with chronic pain', *American Psychologist*, (February-March 2014), **69**, 2, 153–166.

Einstein, A. (1954). *Ideas and opinion.* London: Crown Publishers.

Ellis, A. (1973). 'My philosophy of psychotherapy', *Journal of Contemporary Psychotherapy,* (Winter, 1973), **6**, 1, 13–18.

Ellis, A. (2005, 2nd ed) *Rational emotive behavior therapy.* Atascadero, CA: Impact Books.

Ellis, A. & Harper, R. (1961). *A guide to rational living.* Los Angeles, CA: Wilshire Book Company.

Ellison, K. (2006). 'Mastering your mind', *Psychology Today*, (October 2006), 70–77.

Ellwood, B. (2022). 'Narcissism study sheds new light on the relationship between grandiose and vulnerable subtypes', *Social Psychology*, (April 12, 2022).

Emerson, R. (2010). *English traits.* New York, NY: Tauris Paperbacks.

Epstein, R. (2016). 'What makes a good parent?', *Scientific American Mind,* 25, 2,.46–51.

Erikson, E. (1950). *Childhood and society.* New York, NY: W.W. Norton & Co., Inc.

Erdoes, R. (1988). *A.D. 1000: living on the brink of apocalypse.* New York, NY: Barnes & Noble, Inc.

Essex, M. (2011) *Mind training I & II*, Escondido, CA: Drikung Kyopba Choling (DKC) Workshop.

Feiffer, J. (1995). 'Cartoon', *Psychotherapy Networker*, (January/February 1995), 11.

Feinstein, D. and Krippner, S. (1997). *The mythic path.* Hermitage, PA: Energy Psychology Press.

Ferguson, C. (2007). 'A primary human challenge', *AHP Perspective,* (2/3/2007), 42.

Field, M., Werthmann, J., et. al. (2016). 'The role of attentional bias in obesity and addiction', *Health Psychology,* **35**, 8, 767–780.

Fields, H. (2009). 'The psychology of pain', *Scientific American Mind*, **20**, 42–59.

Filipek, L. (2003). 'Thinking on the edge', *Institute of Noetic Sciences,* (December 2003), 24–27.

Fischer, Z.N. (2011). 'Beyond language: finding freedom through thoughts and words', *Tricycle,* **20**, 4, 38–41.

Flor, H. (2014). 'Psychological pain interventions and neurophysiology', *American Psychologist,* (February-March 2014), **69**, 2, 188–196.

Forster, E. (1910). *Howard's end.* London: G. P Putnam's Sons.

Fox, Emmet. (1934). *Sermon on the mount.* New York, NY: Grosset & Dunlap.

Frankl, V. (1946). *Man's search for meaning.* New York, NY: Beacon Press.

Frankl, V. (1948). *The unconscious God.* New York, NY: Simon & Schuster Publishing.

Frankl, V. and Bugental, J. (1984). 'The anxiety of meaninglessness', *Journal of Counseling and Development, (*September 1984), **63**, 40–426.

Frankl, V. (1986). *The doctor and the soul.* New York, NY: Vintage Books.

Freitosa, J., Grossman, R., & Salazar, M. (2018). 'Debunking key assumptions about teams: the role of culture', *American Psychologist*, **73**, 4, 376–389.

Freud, S. (1938). *An outline of psycho-analysis.* New York, NY: Random House, Inc.

Friends of Jung (1985–2019). *Lectures and handouts.* San Diego, CA.

Fromm, E. (1941). *Escape from freedom.* New York, NY: Farrar & Rinehart.

Fromm, E. (1956). *The art of loving.* New York, NY: Harper & Brothers.

Fromm, E. (1968). *The Revolution of hope: Toward a humanized technology.* New York, NY: Harper & Row, Publishers.

Fulgrum, R. (1986). *All I really need to know I learned in kindergarten.* New York, NY: Ballantine Books.

Galileo, G. (1638). *Discourses and mathematical demonstrations relating to two new sciences.*

Gallese and Goldman. (1998). 'Mirror neurons and the simulation theory of mind-reading', *Trends in Cognitive Sciences,* **2**, 493–101.

Garrison, F. (1966). *History of medicine.* Philadelphia: W.B. Saunders Company.

Gebauer, J. and Sedikides, C. (2010). 'Yearning for yesterday', *Scientific American Mind,* (July/August 2010), 30–35.

Geisel, Theodore. (Dr. Seuss). (1990). *Oh, the places you'll go!* New York, NY: Random House, Inc.

Gershon, M. (1999). *The second brain.* New York, NY: Harper Collins.

Gersten, D. (2013). *Integrative psycho-spiritual assessment.* Boston, MA: Pearson.

Gerzon, R. (1997). *Finding serenity in the age of anxiety.* New York, NY: Bantam.

Gibb, Jack. (1960). *Proceedings of a symposium of training groups,* Renown innovator National Training Laboratories, Bethel, Maine.

Gibbon, E. (1776). *The history of the decline and fall of the Roman Empire.* London: Strahan and Cadell.

Gilbert, R. (2006). 'Sacred geometry: ancient knowledge and modern science', *Shift: At the Frontiers of Consciousness,* (June-August. 2006), **11**, 15–19.

Gilligan, C. (1982). *In a different voice.* Boston: Harvard Press.

Gilroy, P., Carroll, L. and Murra, J. (1998). 'Does depression affect clinical practice? A survey of women psychotherapists', *APA Journal*, (August 1998), 402–407.

Glass, S. & Wright, T. (1992). 'Justification for extramarital relationships', *Journal of Sex Research,* **29**, 3, 361–387.

Glasser, W. (1965). *Reality therapy.* New York, NY: HarperCollins Publisher.

Goble, F. (1970). *The third force.* New York, NY: Grossman Publishers.

Goldberg, S. & Sachter, L. 'Zentensive retreat for psychotherapists', *Practice Innovations,* (March 2018), **3**, 1, 18–29.

Goldstein, H. (1973). *Social work practice: A unitary approach.* Columbia, SC: University of South Carolina Press.

Goleman, D. (2005). *Emotional intelligence.* New York, NY: Bantam Books.

Goodenough, S. (1979). *The Renaissance, the living past.* New York, NY: Arco Publishing.

Goodheart, C. (2004). 'Evidence-based practice and the endeavor of psychotherapy', *The Independent Practitioner,* (Winter, 2004).

Gottlieb, A. (2001). *The dream of reason: A history of Western Philosophy from the Greeks to the Renaissance.* New York, NY: *NY Review.*

Gottman, J.M. et. al. (1979). *Marital communication*. New York, NY: Academic Press.

Gottman, J. & J. (2017). 'The science of togetherness', *Psychotherapy Networker*. (September/October 2017), 43–59.

Gould, S.J. (1996). *Full house: The spread of excellence from Plato to Darwin*. New York, NY: Harmony Books.

Graham, B. (2015). 'What is happiness anyway?', *Mindful*, (June 2015), 42–49.

Graham, L. (2009). 'A warm bath for the brain', *Psychotherapy Networker*, (November/December 2009), 23–24.

Graham, L. (2016). 'Is it time to change course?', *Mindful,* (December 2016), 75–80.

Grant, N. (1971). *The Renaissance.* New York, NY: Franklin Watts, Inc.

Greenwald, H. (1975). *Direct decision making*. New York, NY: Edits Publishing.

Greer, M. (2005). 'When intuition misfires', *Monitor on Psychology,* (March 2005), **36**, 3, 58.

Groder, M. (1991). 'The secrets of a good marriage*', Bottom Line*, (August 15, 1991), 1–3.

Gunther, B. (1968). *Sense relaxation: Below your mind.* New York, NY: Collier.

Habib, T. (2011*). Integral marital counseling: The dynamic process of intimacy and regression.* Huntington Beach, CA: Psycho-Legal Associates, Inc.

Haeckel, E. (1868). *The history of creation*. Norderstadt, Germany: Hansebooks, New edition.

Haley, J. (1973). *Uncommon therapy*. New York, NY: W.W. Norton.

Hall, M, Brindle, R, & Buysee, D. (2018). 'Sleep and cardiovascular disease: emerging opportunities for psychology*', American Psychologist,* **73**, 8, 994–1006.

Hall, V. *Brain health: from memory to mood.* Nutritional pamphlet, date unknown.

Hamel-Zabin, A. with Alan X. (2003). 'Disclosure', *Psychology Today*, (July/August 2003), 66–72.

Hamilton, J. (2004). *Events leading to World War I.* Edina, Minn: ABDO & Daughters Publishing Co.

Hannah, B. (1981). *Encounters with the soul: Active imagination*. Nepal: Pilgrim's Press/SIGO Press.

Haradon, S. (1971a). *Philosophy journal, Philosophy 323*, Dr. DeBoe. San Antonio, TX: Trinity University.

Haradon, S. (1971b). *The philosophy of Hegel*. Philosophy 323 Dr. DeBoe San Antonio, TX: Trinity University.

Haradon, S. (1972a). *The crossroads of the cosmos.* Unpublished manuscript, 10/16/1972.

Haradon, S. (1972b). *Jung's theory of the psyche and the self.* Unpublished manuscript, 12/6/1972.

Haradon, S. (1972c). Philosophy journal. Unpublished manuscript. San Antonio, TX: Trinity University.

Haradon, S. (1972d). Philosophy of psychology journal. Unpublished manuscript.

Haradon, S. (1973). *The nature and varieties of eros: Gender and sexuality.* Unpublished manuscript.

Haradon, S. (1974a). *The ideal human.* Unpublished manuscript.

Haradon, S. (1974b). *Hypnosis*. Unpublished manuscript.

Haradon, S. (1974c). *How I play the Glass-Bead Game*. Unpublished manuscript.

Haradon, S. (1975). *A correlational study of creativity and self-actualization: creativity, psychological health, and manipulation*. Thesis. USIU, San Diego, CA.

Haradon, S. (1977). 'The Rorschach Psychodiagnostic Test: A study of interjudge and interinterpretation validity', Dissertation. USIU, San Diego, CA.

Haradon, S. (1995). *The dynamics of maternal-infant interaction in a substance-abusing mother*. Grant proposal for funding to Sharp Grossmont Hospital Neonatal Unit and Maternal Treatment center, Parent Care, La Mesa, CA.

Haradon, V. (1970). *The individual psychology of Alfred Adler and its relevancy to family counseling*. Unpublished manuscript.

Harding, D. (2002). *On having no head*. Carlsbad, CA: Inner Directions.

Hardy, J. (1990). *A psychology with a soul: Psychosynthesis in evolutionary context*. London: Routledge & Kegan Paul.

Harlow, H. F., Dodsworth, R.O. & Harlow M.K. (1965). 'Total social isolation in monkeys', *Proceedings of the National Academy of Sciences of the United States of America,* 54 (1): 90–97.

Harlow, H., McKinney, W.T., & Suomi, S. (1971). 'The sad ones', *Psychology Today,* May 1971, 60–63.

Harrison, J. (1921). *Epilegomena to the study of Greek religion and Themis*. Cambridge: University Press.

Hartman, B. (2000). 'Just to be alive is enough', *Shambhala Sun,* 9, 37.

Hartshorne, J. (2009). 'Ruled by birth order?', *Scientific American Mind,* (September/October 2009), 18–19.

Harvard Medical School. (2004). *Continuing Medical Education information*. Boston, MA.

Havener, C. (2001). 'Fear and anxiety: They're in the system', *AHP Perspective,* (December 2000/January 2001).

Hayman, R. (1999). *A life of Jung*. New York, NY: W. W. Norton & Company, Inc.

Hegel, G (1807) *Phaenomenologie.des geistes.* Wurtburg, Germany: *Joseph Aston Goebhardt.*

Heinlein, R. (1961) *Stranger in a strange land.* New York, NY: G.P. Putnam's Sons.

Heisenberg, W. (1930*).* English translation. *The Physical Principles of Quantum Theory*. Chicago: University of Chicago Press.

Heppner, P., Roger, M, & Lee, L. (1984). 'Carl Rogers: Reflections of his life', *Journal of Counseling and Development,* (September 1984), **63**, 14–20.

Herodotus. (2019). *The Histories* (circa 430 B.C.). WA: Seattle: Amazon/Benediction Classics.

Heschel, A. (1965). *Who is man?* Stanford, CA: Stanford Press.

Hesse, H. (1943). *Magister Ludi/The Glass Bead Game.* New York, NY: Henry Holt & Co.

Hesse, H. (1971). Translated by T. Lindley. *Autobiographical writings*. Toronto: Doubleday Canada Ltd.

Hillman, J. (1997). *Re-visioning psychology*. New York, NY: William Morrow Paperbacks.

Hinde, R. (1997). *Relationships: A dialectical perspective*. Hove, East Sussex: Psychological Press.

Hinds, K. (2002). *Medieval England.* Tarrytown, NY: Marshall Cavendish Corporation.
Hirshfield, J. (2000). 'Kingfishers catching fire: seeing with poetry's eyes', *The American Poetry Review,* (January/February), 9–12.
Hobbes, T. (1651). *Leviathan.* Cambridge, England: University Press.
Hoffman, E. (1988). *The right to be human: A biography of Abraham Maslow.* New York, NY: McGraw Hill.
Hollis, J. (1994). *Under Saturn's shadow: The wounding and healing of men.* Toronto, Canada: Inner City Books.
Hollies, J. (2003). *On the journey we call our life: Living the questions.* Toronto, Canada: Inner City Books.
Holmes, E. (1959). *A new design for living.* New York, NY: Penguin Publishing.
Holstein, B. (2006). 'Origins of a positive psychology for women (The Enchanted Self)', *Independent Practitioner,* (Winter, 2006), 16–21.
Holt, J. (2013). 'He conceived the mathematics of roughness', Review of *The fractalist: Memoir of a scientific maverick* by Benoit B. Mandelbrot. *The New York Review of Books,* (May 23, 2013).
Hori, V. S. (2003). *Zen sand: The book of capping phrases for Zen koan practice.* Honolulu: University of HIwai'i Press.
Horney, K. (1937). *The neurotic personality of our time.* New York, NY: W.W. Norton & Co. Inc.
Horney, K. (1945). *Our Inner Conflicts.* New York, NY: W.W. Norton & Co. Inc.
Horney, K. (1950). *Neurosis and human growth.* New York, NY: W.W. Norton & Co. Inc.
Horney, K. (2013). *Self-analysis.* Paperback edition. New York, NY: Norton & Co. Inc.
Howard, M. (2013). *Understanding dementia.* Workshop sponsored by Concord, CA: INR Seminars.
Hubel, D. (1984). *The brain.* New York, NY: Scientific American.
Hunter, N. (2014). *Life on the western front.* Chicago, Ill: Heinemann Library.
Huxley, A. (1952). *Tomorrow and tomorrow and tomorrow.* New York, NY: Harper and Brothers.
Irwin, M. (2005). *Human psychoneuroimmunology.* Oxford, England: Oxford University Press.
Isaacson, W. (2007). *Einstein.: His life and universe.* New York, NY: Simon & Schuster.
Isaacson, W. (2017). *Leonardo da Vinci.* New York, NY: Simon & Schuster.
Jabr, F. (2010). Neural feedback. *Scientific American Mind,* 21, 61.
Jacques, E. (1965). Death and the mid-life crisis. *International Journal of Psychoanalysis*, 46, 4, 502–514.
Jaffe, A. (1954). *The myth of meaning.* New York, NY: G. P. Putnam's Sons.
James, W. (1897). *Will to believe and other essays in popular philosophy.* New Haven, Conn: New World.
James, W. (1902). *Varieties of religious experience.* London: Longmans, Green and Co.
Jensen, D. (2016). 'Approaches to record-keeping: the super ego, the ego, and the id', *The Therapist,* (May/June 2016), 56–61.

Jetten, J., Haslam, C., Haslam, A., and Branscombe, N. (2009). 'The social cure', *Scientific American Mind*. 20, 26–33.

Johnson, R. (2002). *The making of America: A history of the United States from 1492 to the present.* Washington, DC: National Geographic Society/TV production.

Johnson, R. (2009). *Inner work*. New York, NY: Harper & Row.

Jones, N. (2003). 'If I'm lucky they call me unorthodox', *Shambhala Sun*, (November 2003).

Jones, N. (2004). 'Mind and body at the extremes', *Shambhala Sun*, (September 2004), 56.

Jourard, S. (1971). *The transparent self.* New York, NY: Van Nostrand Reinhold, Inc.

Jourard, S. (1975) 'On being persuaded who you are', *AHP Perspective,* (January 1975), 23–25.

Judd, P. (2003). 'Attachment theory and research: An overview*', San Diego Psychologist*, (October 2003), 13, 9. San Diego: SDPA.

Jung, C. G. (1921). *Psychological Types*. Princeton, NJ: Bollingen Press.

Jung, C. G. (1928). 'Psychoanalysis and the cure of the soul', *Collected Works of C.G. Jung.* Princeton, NJ: Princeton University Press.

Jung, C. G. (1934). 'A study in the process of individuation', *Collected Works of C.G. Jung*, 9, Part I. Princeton, NJ: Princeton University Press.

Jung (1939). The Symbolic Life. In The Tavistock lectures. *The Collected Works of C.G. Jung*, 18. Princeton, NJ: Princeton University Press.

Jung, C. G. (1946). *The psychology of the transference*. London: Routledge & Kegan Paul.

Jung, C. G. (1955). *The Interpretation of nature and the psyche*. New York, NY: Pantheon Books.

Jung, C. G. (1960). *On the nature of the psyche*. Princeton, NJ: Princeton University Press.

Jung. C. and Von Franz, M. L. (1964). *Man, and his symbols*. New York, NY: Doubleday Books.

Jung, E. (1957). *Animus and Anima*. New York, NY: The Analytical Psychology Club of New York. Inc.

Kafka, F. (1915). *Metamorphosis (Die Verwandlung).* Ed. Rene Schickele. Leipzig, Ger: Kurt Wolff.

Kaku, M. and Trainer, J. (1987). *Beyond Einstein: The cosmic quest for the theory of the universe.* New York, New York: Bantam Books.

Kahan, G. (1983). *E=mc2: picture book of relativity.* Blue Ridge Summit, PA: TAB Books, Inc.

Kammersgard, E. (1989). *The defense of addiction.* Paper for National University (Psych 635/ Child and Adolescent Development), 2/3/1989.

Kandel, E. 'Gray matter', *New York Times*, Sunday, September 8, 2013.

Kanfer, S. (1986). 'In all seasons, toys are us', *Time,* December 22, 1986.

Kant, E. (1786). *Metaphysical foundations of natural science.* Originally published in German.

Karel, M., Gatz, M. & Smyer, M. (2012). 'Aging and mental health in the decade ahead: What psychologists need to know', *American Psychologist*, 67, 3, 184–198.

Karen, R. (1990). 'Becoming attached', *The Atlantic Monthly*, (February 1990), 35–70.

Kassel, S. and LeMay, J. (2012). 'Interpersonal biofeedback', *The Therapist*, (January/February 2012), 68–70.

Katherine, A. (1991). *Boundaries: Where you end and I begin*. New York, NY: Fireside.

Keay, J. (1992). *The honourable company—A history of the English East India company.* London: Harper Collins.

Keleman, S. (1985). *Emotional anatomy: The structure of experience*. San Francisco, CA: Center for Energetic Studies Press.

Kendrick, S. (1999). *Holy clues: The gospel according to Sherlock Holmes*. New York, NY: Vintage Books.

Kernberg, O. (1977). *Pathological narcissism in middle age*. Quebec, Canada: American Psychoanalytic Association Paper.

Kernberg, O. (1978). 'The diagnosis of borderline conditions in adolescence. In S. Feinstein & P. Giovacchini (Eds.)', *Adolescent Psychiatry,* **Vol. 6,** Chicago: University of Chicago Press.

Kernberg, O. ed. (1989). 'Narcissistic personality disorder', *The Psychiatric Clinics of North America,* (September 1989), **12,** 3. NY: W. B. Saunders Co.

Kersting, K. (2003). 'What exactly is creativity?', *Monitor on Psychology*, (November 2003), 40–43.

Khong, B. (2010). 'Mindfulness: A way of cultivating deep respect for emotions', Paper presented *118th Annual Convention of the APA*, (August 2010), 1–20. San Diego, CA.

Kiersey, D. and Bates, M. (1984). *Please understand me: Character & temperament types*. Del Mar, CA: Prometheus Nemesis Book Company.

Kierkegaard, S. (1995). *The essential Kierkegaard.* (Eds. Hong & Hong). Princeton, New Jersey: Princeton University Press.

Kim, Y. S. & Noz, M. (2018). *New perspectives on Einstein's E=mc2.* Singapore: World Scientific.

Kirkpatrick, J. S. (1979) 'Silence is beneficial to high levels of thinking: A Maslovian counseling model', *Personnel and Guidance Journal,* (April 1979), 386–390.

Knapp, B. (1995). *Manna and mystery: A Jungian approach to Hebrew myths and legends*. New York, NY: Knapp, Bettina Books.

Koan study in Zen Buddhism, *about.com*, 10/13/2014.

Koestler, W. (1964). *The act of creation*. New York, NY: MacMillan Publishing.

Kohlberg, L. (1964). 'Development of moral character and moral ideology', In (Hoffman, M. and Hoffman, L. eds). *Review of Child Development Research,* (1964), 1, 383–431.

Kohlberg, L. (1981). *Essays on moral development, Vol. I: The philosophy of moral development*. San Francisco, CA: Harper & Row.

Kohut, H. (1971). *The analysis of self*. New York, NY: International Universities Press.

Koob, G. (2013). *Calming an overactive brain*. Workshop sponsored by Haddonfield, NJ: Institute for Brain Potential.

Kornfield, J. (2002). 'A new spirit at Spirit Rock', *Tricycle,* Winter, 2002.

Krauss, L. (2012). 'The Godless particle', *Newsweek*. July 16, 2012.

Kubistant, R. (1981). 'Resolutions of aloneliness', *Personnel and Guidance Journal*, (March 1981), 461–465.

Kuelker, E. (2019). 'Resurrecting therapy: Bit pharma on the couch', *Psychotherapy Networker*, (September/October 2019), 45–49.

Kushner, H. (1981). *When bad things happen to good people*. New York, NY: Avon Books.

Kyabgon, T. Rinpoche. (2003). 'Depression's truth', *Shamabhala Sun*. March 2008, pp. 56–67.

Kyabgon, T. Rinpoche (2013). *The four dharmas of Gampopa*. Woodstock, NY: KTD Publications.

Lao Tzu. (2007). *Tao Te Ching*. Boston: Shambhala.

Land, G. (2000). *Breakpoint and beyond*. Carlsbad, CA: Leadership 2000, Inc.

Lesley, D. and Quintana, S. (1985). 'Recent approaches to the moral and social education of children', *Elementary School Guidance & Counseling*, (April 1985), 256–259.

Layton, M. (2008). 'In treatment', *Psychotherapy Networker*. (July/August 2008).

Lembke, A. (2018). 'How to taper opioid dependent patients off of chronic opioid therapy', *The Therapist: CAMFT*, (July/August 2018), 16–20.

Lerma, T. (1988). *The relationship of sexual molestation before the age of eight on a woman's sexual orientation and sex role identity.* Unpublished Dissertation. San Diego, CA: Professional School of Psychological Studies.

LeShan, L and Margenau, H. (1982). *Einstein's space and Van Gogh's sky: Physical reality and beyond.* New York, New York: Macmillan.

Levine, S. (1997). *A year to live*. New York, NY: Random House.

Levin-Landheeer, P. (1982). 'TA and developmental theory', *Transactional Analysis Journal,* (April 1982), **12**, 2, 129–143.

Levinson, D. (1978). *The seasons of a man's life.* New York, NY: Random House.

Lewis, C.S. (1933). *The pilgrim's regress.* London: J. M. Dent and Sons.

Lewis, C.S. (1955). *Surprised by joy: The shape of my early life.* New York, NY: Harcourt, Inc.

Lewitts, H. (1982). 'Women's development in adulthood and old age: A review and critique', *International Journal of Mental Health,* **11**, 1–2, 115–134.

Lifeline. (2007). 'Tips for taking time for yourself', *OA/Lifeline magazine*, (Spring, 2007), 109.

Lindner, R. (1954). *The fifty-minute hour.* New York, NY: Bantam Books.

Lindquist, P. (1980). *Mastering the Psychological Emergencies of Childhood*: synopsis of professional classwork, personal communication.

Linehan, M. and Limeff, L. (2001). 'Dialetical behavior therapy in a nutshell', *The California Psychologist.* **34**. 10–13.

Linehan, M. (2013). *DBT skills training manual*. New York, NY: Guilford Press.

Llinas, R. ed. (1989). *The biology of the brain: From neurons to networks.* New York, NY: W.H. Freeman and Company.

Locke, John. (1689). *Two treatises of government.* New York, NY: Barnes and Noble (reprint).

Loevinger, J. and Knoll, E. (1983). 'Personality: Stages, traits, and the self', *Annual Review of Psychology*. 1983:**14**, 195–222.

Long, G. (1862). *The meditations of Marcus Aurelius.* New York, NY: Harvard Classics.

Lora, D. (2003). 'A dyadic model of reality: The way of the explorer', *Shift: at the Frontier of Consciousness.* (December 2003), 19–23.

Lorenz, K. (1962). *On aggression.* London: Manthuan Publishing.

Lundeen, E. (2006). 'Heisenberg and psychology', *Independent Practitioner*, Fall, 2006.

MacIver, R. (2004). *Heron Dance,* Issue 42, (February 2004), Williston, VT: Heron Dance Press.

MacIver, R. and O'Shaughnessy, A. (2006) (eds.) *Heron Dance.* Williston, VT: Heron Dance Press.

MacIver, R. (2007). 'Discovering the beauty of the other', (Interview with Hanka, L.), *Heron Dance*: **Issue 51**, 2007.

MacLean, P. (1990). *The triune brain in evolution.* New York, NY: Plenum Press.

McCracken, L. (2014). 'Acceptance and Commitment Therapy and Mindfulness for Chronic Pain', *American Psychologist.* 2014. February-March 2014, 178–187.

McDermott, J. (1977). *The writings of William James.* Chicago: The University of Chicago Press.

McGinn, C. (2013). 'What can your neurons tell you?', Review of *THE good, the true, and the beautiful: a neuronal approach* by Jean-Pierre Changeux. *The New York Review of Books*, July 11, 2013.

McQuaide, S. (1998). 'Women at midlife', *Social Work*, (January 1998), 43, 1, 21–31.

Machiavelli, N. (1513). *The Prince/Il Principe.* Italian publication.

Madeo, R. (2006) *Buddhism and post-modern science: the end of conventional logic.* Unpublished paper, San Diego State University, December.

Madeo, R. (2006). *Michel Foucault and humanity's art: through a pure and simple light.* Unpublished paper, San Diego State University, November 2006.

Madeo, R. (2011). *Beyond the limits of mind, meaning, and myth.* Thesis from San Diego State University, master's in philosophy.

Mahler, M. (1969). *On human symbiosis and the vicissitudes of individuation.* New York, NY: Basic Books.

Mahler, S., Pine, M. M. and Bergman, A. (1973). *The psychological birth of the human infant.* New York, NY: Basic Books.

Maier, S., Watkins, L. and Fleshner, M. (1994). 'Psychoneuroimmunology: The interface between behavior, brain, and immunity', *American Psychologist,* **49**, 12, 1004–1017.

Malashock, R. (2011) *Active imagination.* Lecture at Friends of Jung, 10/7/2011.

Malcolm, J. 'Justice to J.D. Salinger', *The New York Review*, 6/21/2001, 16.

Maltz, M. (1960). *Psycho-cybernetics.* New York, NY: Penguin Books.

Mandel, B. (1985). *Open heart therapy.* Berkeley, CA: Celestial Arts.

Marano, H. (2017). 'From food to mood', *Psychology Today.* (September/October 2017), 31–32.

Marcus, S. (2015). 'How does clinical hypnosis work as a therapeutic adjunct?' *San Diego Psychologist,* (December 2014/January 2015), **29**, 6, 1–6.

Marks-Tarlow, T. (1999). 'The self as a dynamical system: non-linear dynamics', *Psychology and Life Sciences,* **3**, 311–345.

Marx, Karl. (1848). *Communist manifesto.* London.

Maslow, A. (1954). *Motivation and personality.* New York, NY: Harper and Row, Publishers, Inc.

Maslow, A. (1968). *Toward a psychology of being*. Princeton: Van Nostrand.

Maslow, A. (1971). *Farther reaches of human nature*. New York, NY: Viking Press.

Matheson, G. (1979). 'Modifications of depressive symptoms through posthypnotic suggestion', *American Journal of Clinical Hypnosis,* (July 1979), 22, 1, 61–64.

Matthews, G. (1994). *Running as a woman: Gender and power in politics*. New York, NY: The Free Press.

Maturana, F. J. and Varela, F. (1980). *Autopoiesis and cognition: The realization of the living*. Dordrecht, Netherlands: D. Reidel Publishing Company.

May, R. (1953). *Man's search for himself*. New York, NY: W.W. Norton & Company, Inc.

May, R. (1969). *Love and will*. New York, NY: W. W. Norton & Company, Inc.

Mayberg, H. (2005*).* 'Deep brain stimulation for treatment-related depression*', Neuron,* (March 3, 2005), **45**, 5.

Mayer, J. (2014). 'Know thyself', *Psychology Today*, (March/April), 65–71.

Mayer, J., Caruso, D., & Salovey, P. (2008). 'Emotional intelligence: new ability or eclectic traits?' *American Psychologist,* **63**, 6, 503–517.

Meador, B. (2001). *Inanna, lady of the largest heart*. Austin, TX: University of Texas Press.

Melzack, R. and Wall, P. (1965). 'Pain mechanisms: A new theory', *Science.* **150**, 971–979.

Meyers, L. (2007). 'Serenity now', *Monitor on Psychology*, (December 2007), **38**, 11.

Milar, K. (2010). 'Overcoming "sentimental rot."', *Monitor on Psychology,* (February 2010), 26–27.

Milkman, H. and Sunderwith. S. (1998). *Craving for ecstasy: How our passions become addictions, and what we can do about them*. New York, NY: Jossey-Bass.

Millay, J. (2001). 'Thinking about thinking', *AHP Perspective*, (October/November 2001).

Miller, A. (1981). *The drama of the gifted child: the search for the true self*. New York, NY: Basic Books.

Miller, D. (2000). *A biography of America.* Chicago: WGBH Educational Foundation Annenberg/CPB.

Miller, W. R. and Rollnick, S. (1991). *Motivational interviewing: Preparing people to change addictive behavior.* New York, NY: Guilford Press.

Milosz, C. (2007). 'My old love of trees from: Bobo's metamorphosis', *Heron's Dance, (*2007), 51.

Minuchin, S. (1974). *Families and family therapy*. Cambridge, MA: Harvard University Press.

Mitchell, E. (1996). *The way of the explorer*. New York, NY: G. Putnam & Sons.

Molton, I. and Terrill, A. (2014). 'Overview of persistent pain in older adults', *American Psychologist,* (February-March 2014), 197–207.

Monkres, P. (1981). 'The wilderness of the soul: part II' *Pilgrimage,* (Fall/Winter, 1981), **9**, 3, 186.

Montagu, A. (1950)*. On being human*. New York, NY: H. Schuman.

Moore, T. (1994). *Care of the soul*. New York, NY: HarperCollins, Publishers.

Moring, G. (2000). *The complete idiot's guide to understanding Einstein.* Indianapolis, IN: Alpha Books.
Mosley, W. (2007). *The wave.* New York, NY: Grand Central Publishing.
Muscatell, K. (2020). 'Social psychoneuroimmunology: understanding bidirectional links between social experiences and the nervous system', *Brain, Behavior, and Immunology,* **93**, 1–3.
Myers, D. (1990). Personal communication.
Najavits, L. (2002). *Seeking safety.* Oakland, CA: New Harbinger Press.
Naranjo, C, & Ornstein, R. (1971). *On the psychology of meditation.* New York, NY: The Viking Press.
Neff, K. (2011). *Self-compassion: The proven power of being kind to yourself.* New York, NY: William Morrow.
Neumann, E. (1994). *The fear of the feminine.* Princeton, NJ: Princeton University Press.
Neumann, E. (1995). 'The origins and history of consciousness', *The Bollington Series: XLII.* Princeton, NJ: Princeton University Press.
Newton, Sir Isaac. (1953). *Principia, book III; cited in; Newton's philosophy of nature: selections from his writings,* ed. H.S. Thayer. NY: Hafner Library of Classics, 42.
Nicholson, D. (2005). *Remember World War II—kids who tell their stories.* Washington, D.C.: National Geographic Society.
Nietzsche, F. (2017). *Will to power.* New York, NY: Penguin Classics.
Novotney, A. (2009). 'Yoga as a practice tool', *Monitor on Psychology,* (November 2009), 36–41.
Novotney, A. (2012). 'In brief', *Monitor on Psychology,* (January 2012), 17.
Novotney, A. (2018). 'Working with older adults', *Monitor on Psychology,* (December 2018), 60–66.
Oates, W. (1940). *The Stoic and Epicurean philosophers: the complete extant writings of Epicurus, Epictetus, Lucretius, and Marcus Aurelius.* NY, New York: Modern Library.
O'Connor, E. (1971). *Our many selves.* New York, NY: Harper Collins.
O'Neill, J. (2007). *Prodigal genius: the life of Nikola Tesla.* San Diego, CA: Book Tree.
Orloff, J. (2008). The art of remembering and interpreting dreams. *AHP Perspective,* (December/January 2008), 14.
O'Shaughnessay, A. (2007). Removing the veil, exposing your creative spirit. *Pausing for beauty: the Heron Dance 2007, Daybook and Planner,* (2007), 51.
Ostrowski-Sachs, M. (1971). *From conversations with C.G. Jung.* Zurich: Juris Druck & Verlag AG.
Otto, H. (1970). *Ways of growth.* New York, NY: The Viking Press.
Owen, H.P. (1971). *Concepts of deity.* London: Macmillan, 1971.
Pagels, E. (1982). *The Gnostic gospels.* New York, NY: Penguin.
Palmirotta, F. (2013). 'Ontosophy: a holistic approach to therapy', *Psicoterapeuta,* June 9, 2013.
Pargament, K. & Sweeney, P. (2011). 'Building spiritual fitness in the army', *American Psychologist,* **66**, 1, 58–64.
Pascal, B. (1973). *The physical treatises of Pascal.* New York, NY: Octagon Books.

Paul, C.K. (1901). *The thoughts of Blaise Pascal.* London: George Bell and Sons.
Pauli, W. (1955). With Jung. C.G. *Interpretation of nature and the psyche.* London: Rouledge and Kegan Paul.
Pavlov, I.P. (1927). *Conditioned reflexes: An investigation of the physiological response of the cerebral cortex.* Translated and edited by G. V. Anrep. London: Oxford University Press.
Pearlin, L. and Schooler, C. (1978). 'Mastery scale', *Psychology Journal of Health and Social Behavior*, March 1, 1978.
Pelligrino, C. (2005). *Ghosts of Vesuvius.* New York, NY: Harper Perennial.
Perls, F. (1969). *Gestalt therapy verbatim.* Lafayette, CA: Real People Press.
Pepys, S. (1958). *The diary of Samuel Pepys.* New Haven, Cn: Yale University Press.
Perrotttet, T. (2002). *Route 66 A.D.*, New York, NY: Random House, Inc.
Perry, A. (1990). *Callender Square.* New, NY: Ballantine Books.
Piaget, J. and Inhelder, B. (1962). *The psychology of the child.* New York, NY: Basic Books.
Pincus, A. and Minahan, A. (1974). *Social work practice: model and method.* Itasca, ILL: F.E. Peacock.
Pine, K. (2011). 'Sheconomics: why more women on boards boosts company performance', *The Royal Statistical Society,* (June 2011), 80–81.
Pinker, S. (1997). *How the mind works.* New York, NY: W. W. Norton & Co.
Pinker, S. (2008). 'The moral instinct', *Sunday New York Times Magazine,* (January 13, 2008).
Pipher, M. (2009). 'Stopping for Joshua Bell', *Psychotherapy Networker.* March/April 2009, 50–59.
Pirsig, R. (1974). *Zen and the art of motorcycle maintenance.* New York, NY: Harper Collins.
Plath, S. (1971). *The bell jar.* New York, NY: Harper Perennial.
Porreca, F. and Price, T. (2009). 'When pain lingers', *Scientific American Mind,* 20, 34–41.
Powell, R. (1981). *Return to meaningfulness.* New York, NY: Avant Books.
Prigogine, I & Stengers, I. (1984). *Order out of chaos: Man's new dialogues with nature.* Toronto: Bantam Books.
Pribram, K. (ed.). (1993). *Rethinking neural networks: Quantum fields and biological data.* Hillsdale, N. J.: Erlbaum Publishing.
Pribram, K. (2003). Like Bohm, Karl Pribram sees the holographic nature of reality. *The Ground of Faith,* October 2003.
Progoff, I. (1953). *Jung's psychology and its social meaning.* New York, NY: The Julian Press.
Putnam, A. (1962). *Books and their makers during the Middle Ages. Vol.1.* New York, NY: Hillary House.
Rabin, A. (1975 to 1977). *Behavior viewed from three perspectives: patient, significant other, and treatment personnel.* Workshop notes.
Ralph, L. (1973). *The Renaissance in perspective,* New York, NY: St. Martin's Press.
Reeves, P. (1981). 'The shadow: a vital and revitalizing aspect of the psyche', *Pilgrimage,* (Fall/Winter, 1981), **9**, 3.

Ricard, M. (2007). *Happiness: A guide to developing life's most important skill.* New York, NY: Little, Brown and Co.

Rice, E. (1970). *The foundations of early modern Europe, 1460–1559.* New York, NY: W. W. Norton & Company, Inc.

Riley-Smith, J. (2005). *The Crusades: a short history.* (Second Edition). New Haven, CT: Yale University Press.

Rilke, R.M. (1929). *Letters to a young poet/Briefe an eine jungen Dichter.* Leipzig: Insel Verlag.

Roazen, P. (1997). *Erik H. Erikson: The power and limits of a vision.* London: Collier Macmillan Publishers.

Robinet, I. (1997). *Taoism: growth of a religion.* Stanford, CA: Stanford University Press.

Rockman, P. (2017). 'The downward spiral of shame', *Mindful,* (October 2017), 52–59.

Rockmore, D. (2019). 'The myth of magic of generating new ideas', *Getpocket.com*, 1–9.

Rodgers, J. (2014). 'Go forth in anger', *Psychology Today*, (March/April 2014), 72–79.

Rogers, C. (1957). 'The necessary and sufficient conditions of therapeutic personality change', *Journal of Consulting Psychology*, **21**, 95–103.

Rogers, C. (1974). *A client-centered, person-centered approach to therapy.* Handout received as student at USIU.

Rogers, C. (1975). 'A way of being: An interview with Dr. Carl R. Rogers', *Practical Psychology for Physicians,* (August 1975), 2**(8)**, 16–24.

Rosen, M. (1998) (ed.). 'Continental philosophy from Hegel', in A.C. Grayling, *Philosophy 2: Further through the Subject,* 665.

Rosen, S. (1991). '*My voice will go with you: The teaching tales of Milton H. Erickson',* New York, NY: W. W. Norton & Company.

Rosenberg, M. (2003). *Nonviolent communication: A language of life.* Encinitas, Ca.: Puddle Dancer Press.

Rousseau, M. (1778). *Reveries of the solitary walker.* New York, NY: Penguin Books

Rucker, W. R. (1969). 'A value-oriented framework for education and the behavioral sciences', *Journal for Value Inquiry*, **3 (4)**, 270–280.

Rucker, W. R. (1973). *Value clarification.* New York, NY: Sage Publications.

Ruffin, J., Frankl, V, and Bugental, J. (1984). 'The anxiety of meaninglessness', *Journal of Counseling and Development,* (September 1984), **63**, 40–42.

Ruskin, J. (1843). *Modern painters, parts I and II, of general principles and truth.* New York, NY: Knopf.

Russell, B. (1912). *The problems of philosophy.* London: Williams and Norgate.

Russell, P. (2003). 'The essence of self', *From science to God.* Novato, CA: New World Library.

Ryff, C.D. & Singer, B. (1998). 'The contours of positive human health', *Psychological Inquiry*, **9**, 1, 1–28.

Rychlak, J. (1973). 'The analytical psychology of Carl Jung', *Introduction to Personality and Psychotherapy.* Boston: Houghton Mufflin Co., 132–199.

Salk, J. (1983). *Anatomy of reality: Merging of intuition and reason.* New York, NY: Columbia University Press.

Salzberg, S. (2017). 'Nice guys finish first', *Mindful,* (October 2017), 30–33.

Sampson, P. (2000). *Six modern myths about Christianity & western civilization.* Downers Grove, IL: InterVarsity Press.

Sandmaier, M. (2017). 'Doorways to the embodied self: Eugene Gendlin and the felt sense', *Psychotherapy Networker*, (July/August 2017), 39–46.

Sandford, K. (2017). *Papers and works of art.* Santa Barbara, CA: Opus Archives and Research Center.

Sapolsky, R. & Pulsinelli, W. (1985). 'Glucocorticoid toxicity in the hippocampus: Temporal aspects of neuronal vulnerability', *Brain Research,* (December), **59**, 1–2, 300–305.

Sapolsky, R. (1994). *Why zebras don't get ulcers*. New York, NY: W.H. Freeman and Co.

Sapolsky, R. (1997). *The aging of the brain, the aging of the mind*. Stanford, CA: Institute for CorTexT Research and Development.

Sartre, J.P. (1943). *Being and nothingness.* Paris: *Editions Gallimard.*

Sartre, J.P. (1966). *Situation VI: Problems of Marxism*. Paris: *Editions Galimard*

Satir, V. (1972). *Peoplemaking.* Palo Alto, CA: Science and Behavior Books.

Satir, V. (1976). *Making contact*. Millbrae, CA: Celestial Arts.

Satir, V. (1983). *Conjoint family therapy.* Palo Alto, CA: Science and Behavior Books.

Savistsky, K. & Gilovich, T. (2003). 'The Illusion of transparency and the alleviation of speech anxiety', *Journal of Experimental Social Psychology,* **29**, (6), 618–625.

Saykong Mipham Rinpoche. (2002). 'Taking the first step', *Shambhala Sun,* (November 2002), 15.

Saykong Mipham Rinpoche. (2005). 'No real winners', *Shambhala Sun,* (July 2005), 13–14.

Saykong Mipham Rinpoche. (2007). 'From seed to bloom', *Shambhala Sun*, (January 2007).

Schapira, L. (1988). *The Casandra complex: Living with disbelief.* Toronto, Canada: Inner City Books.

Schleimann, H, (1996). *Golden treasures of Troy*. Eastbourne, UK: Gardners Books.

Schlein, S. (1994). 'Reminiscences in Honor of Erik Erikson: Contributions to Psychotherapeutic Method and Configurations of Human Potential', *Journal of Adult Development,* **Vol. 1, No. 3**, 1994, 149–151.

Schneider, D. (2002). 'Awakening the Sacred', *Turning Wheel.* Summer, 2002, P. 18–22.

Schrodinger (1925) *Seek for the Road*. Cambridge, England: Cambridge University Press.

Schwartz, J. (1999). *Cassandra's daughter: A history of psychoanalysis.* New York, NY: Viking Press.

Searby, S. (1986). The effects of parental loss by death or divorce on children. Unpublished manuscript, PSY 645, San Diego: National University.

Sebes, J. and Ford, D. (1984). 'Moral development and self-regulation: Research and Intervention Planning', *The Personnel and Guidance Journal,* March 1984, 379–381.

Seligman, M. (1975). *Helplessness: on depression, development, and death.* San Francisco: W.H. Freeman.
Seligman, M. (2012). *Flourish.* New York, NY: Atria Books.
Seymour, M. (1989). *A ring of conspirators: Henry James and his literary circle, 1895–1915.* New York, NY: Houghton Mifflin.
Shapiro, R. (2007). 'A simpler origin for life', *Scientific American*, (June 2007), 47.
Shaw, R. & Colimore, K. (1988). 'Humanistic psychology as ideology: As analysis of Maslow's contradictions', *Journal of Humanistic Psychology*, **28, 3**, 51–74.
Shedler, J. (2010). 'The efficacy of psychodynamic psychotherapy', *American Psychologist*, **65**, 2, 98–109.
Shedler, J. (2010). 'Getting to know me', *Scientific American Mind*, November/December 2010, 52–57.
Sheehy, G. (1976). *Passages: predictable crises of adult life.* New York, NY: Dutton Books.
Sheehy (1995a). *New passages: mapping your life across time.* New York, NY: Random House Publishing Group.
Sheehy, G. (1995b) 'New Passages', *US News & World Report.* June 12, 1995, 62–70.
Sheng Yen. Rinpoche, (2006). *Tricycle*, 2006, 16.
Shepherd (2014) 'Emotional regulation, physiological arousal, and PTSD symptoms in trauma exposed individuals', *Journal of Behavior Therapy and Experimental Psychiatry.* (September 2014), **45, 3**, 360–367.
Sherwood, M. (1974). *The new chemistry.* New York, NY: Basic Books.
Shostrom, E. (1964). *Personal orientation inventory.* San Diego, CA: EdITS.
Shostrom, E. (1967). *Man, the manipulator: The inner journey from manipulation to actualization.* Nashville, TN: Abingdon Press.
Siegel, D. (1999). *The developing mind: toward a neurobiology of interpersonal experience.* New York, NY: Guilford Press.
Siegel, D. (2007). *The mindful brain: Reflection and attunement in the cultivation of well-being.* NY: W. W. Norton & Co.
Siegel, D. and Bryson, T. (2011). *The whole-brain child.* NY: Delacorte Press.
Siegel, M. (2005). Can we cure fear? *Scientific American Mind.* 16, 4.
Siegel, R. (2011). 'West Meets East', *Psychotherapy Networker.* September/October 2011, 20.
Siegel, R. and Yapko, M. (2012). 'Has mindfulness been oversold?', *Psychotherapy Networker.* March/April 2012, p. 44–57.
Silver, L. (2007). 'Neuroscience 101', *ADDitude.* December/January 2007.
Simon, R. (2012). 'Still crazy after all these years?' *Psychotherapy Networker*, March/April 2012, 32–56.
Simon, R. & Dockett, L. (2017). 'The addict in all of us: Gabor Mate's unflinching vision', *Psychotherapy Networker.* July/August 2017, 33–46.
Simon, R. (2017). 'An interview with Tony Robbins', *Psychotherapy Networker.* November/December 2017, 47–51.
Simonton, D.K. (2019). 'If you think you're a genius, you're crazy', *Getpocket.com.* 11/15/2010, 1–6.
Singer, June. (1972). *Boundaries of the soul: The practice of Jung's psychology.* Hamburg, Germany: Anchor Academic Publishing.

Skinner, B.F. (1971). *Beyond freedom and dignity.* New York, NY: Alfred A. Knopf.
Smiley, J. (1995). *Moo.* Paris, France: *Rivages Publishers.*
Smith, H. (1958). *The world's religions.* New York, NY: HarperOne.
Snyder, R. (1967). *On becoming human.* Nashville, Tenn: Abbingdon Press.
Snyder, S. (1985). The molecular basis of communication between cells. *The biology of the brain from neurons to networks. Readings from Scientific American*, 1985. New York, NY: W.H. Freeman and Co.
Sobel, R. (1987). *Role of emotional expression, selected personality factors, and early childhood experience in the development of cancer, rheumatoid arthritis, and coronary heart disease and health.* Dissertation. The Professional School of Psychological Studies, San Diego, CA.
Solomon, S. and Teagno, L. (2007). 'Assessing infidelities and their treatment', *SDPA*. (June 2007).
Sparta, S. & Kinscherff, R. (2013). 'The assessment of childhood trauma', *The national register of health service psychologists: The Register Report*, Fall, 2013, 10–17.
Spielberger, C. (1983). *State-Trait Anxiety Inventory.* New York, NY: Routledge.
Spinoza, B. (1677). *Ethics.* Amsterdam.
Spitz, R. (1945). 'Hospitalism—an inquiry into the genesis of psychiatric conditions in early childhood', *Psychoanalytic Study of the Child*, **1**, 53–74.
Sri Ram, N. (1957). *Thoughts for aspirants.* Wheaton, Ill: Theosophical Publishing House.
Sri Ram, N. (1993). *The way of wisdom.* Wheaton, Ill: Theosophical Publishing House.
Staines, N., Brostoff, J., & James, K. (1993). *Introducing immunology.* London: Times Mirror International Publishers.
Steidinger, J. (2016). *Sisterhood in Sports: How female athletes collaborate and compete.* Lanham, MD: Rowman and Littlefield.
Stein, G. (2008). *The art of racing in the rain.* New York, NY: HarperCollins Publishers.
Steiner, C. (1979). *Scripts people live.* New York, NY: Grove Press.
Stephanie E. (1986). *Shame faced.* Center City, MN: Hazeldon Foundation.
Stern, D. (1985). *The interpersonal world of the infant.* New York, NY: Basic Books.
Sternberg, R. (2007). 'Triangulating love', In Oord, T. J. *The altruism reader: Selections from writings on love, religion, and science.* West Conshohocken, PA: Templeton Foundation.
Stevens, J. (1975). '*Gestalt is',* Moah, Utah: Real People Press.
Stewart, I. (1987). *Today: An introduction to Transactional Analysis.* Chapel Hill, NC: Lifespace Publishing.
Stickgold, R. and Ellenbogen, J. (2008). 'Quiet! Sleeping brain at work', *Scientific American Brain*. **19**, 22–29.
Stosny, S. (2003). 'Male-friendly couples counseling', *Psychotherapy Networker*. March/April 2009, 63–70.
Stuart, R. (1980). *Helping couples change.* New York, NY: Guildford Press.
Sullivan, H. S. (1953). *The interpersonal theory of psychiatry.* New York, New York: Norton.

Sullivan, M. (1986). *Suicide and youth.* Unpublished manuscript, PSY 645, San Diego: National University.
Summers, J. and Haradon, J. (2007). Personal communication.
Sumner, Wm. (1906). *The study of the sociological usages, manners, customs, mores, and morals.* New York, NY: Ginn and Company.
Swartz, R. (2011). 'When meditation isn't enough', *Psychotherapy Networker.* September/October 2011), 35.
Swedenborg, E. (1749). *The heavenly doctrine of the Lord.* Whitefish, MT: Kessinger Publishing.
Tagore, R. Chakravarty, A. ed. (1961). The Call of Truth. in *A Tagore Reader.* New York, NY: Beacon Press.
Taitetus Unno. (2002). 'Shin Buddhism', *Tricycle.* Fall, 2002, p. 5.
Tajerian, M. (2011). 'DNA Methylation of SPARC and Chronic Low Back Pain', *Molecular Pain.* 7: pp. 65–74.
Tarrant, J. (2005). 'Paradox, Breakthrough, and the Zen Koan', *Shift.* 3–5/2005, **No. 6,** 24–27.
Tart, C. (2008). 'What Death Tells Us about Life', *Shift.* 12/07–2/08, **No. 17,** P. 30–35.
Taylor, J. (2011). 'Dreams: The Magic Mirror that Never Lies', Talk at UU, San Diego, CA.
Tedeschi, R. and Calhoun, L. (1996). 'The traumatic stress inventory: Measuring the positive legacy of trauma', *Journal of Traumatic Stress,* 1966, July 9*,* **3,** *455–71.*
Teilhard de Chardin, P. (1959). *The Phenomenon of Man.* NY: Harper & Row, Publishers.
Tennov, D. (1979). *Love and Limerence.* Lanham, Maryland: Scarborough House.
TeSelle, E. (1970). *Augustine, the Theologian.* London: Burns and Oates.
Teresi, D. (1986). *The Three Pound Universe.* New York, NY: MacMillan Publishing Company.
Thayer, H.D. (1953). *Principia, Book III;* cited in; Newton's Philosophy of Nature: Selections from his writings, p. 42). New York, NY: Hafner Library of Classics.
Thayer, H. S. (1952). *The Logic of Pragmaticism.* London: Routledge and Kegan Paul.
Thomas, A. and Chess, S. (1977). *Temperament and Development.* New York, NY: Brunner/Mazel.
Thomas, A. and S. Chess. (1987). 'Temperamentally Individuality from Childhood to Adolescence', *Journal of Child Psychiatry,* **16,** 218–226.
Thomas, Lewis. (1974). *The lives of a cell: Notes of a biology watcher.* New York, NY: Viking Press.
Tillich, P. (1952). *The courage to be.* New Haven: Yale University Press.
Tobias, J. (1987). *The integral being.* New York, NY: Henry Holt & Co, Inc.
Tolman, E.C. (1945). 'A stimulus-expectancy need-cathexis psychology', *Science,* 2/16/1945.
Tolman, E. (1951). *Behavior and psychological man: Essays in motivation and learning.* Berkeley: University of California Press.
Treace, B. M. (2005). *The wise woman who talked back to God.* Escondido, CA: Lions Roar Publishing.

Tulku Thubten Rinpoche. (2006). 'Nirvana: Three takes', *Tricycle*. Fall, 2006, p. 99.

Tweed, R. and Lehman, D. (2003). 'The core of Confucian learning: Review of *Jin Li—Confucian and Socratic learning*', *American Psychologist*. (February 2003), 148–149.

Vachss, A. (1994). 'You carry the cure in your own heart', *Parade Magazine*, (August 28, 1994), 4–6.

Valliant, G. (1977). *Adaptations to life*. Boston: Little, Brown.

van der Kolk. B. (1987). *Psychological trauma*. Washington: American Psychiatric Press.

Van Doren, C. (1991). *A history of knowledge*. New York, NY: Random House.

Van Dusen, W. (1971). *The natural depth in man*. New York, NY: Harper & Row, Publishers.

Varela, F. (2004). 'Intimate distances', *Shambhala Sun*. September 2004, 42–50.

Vaskovic, J. (2021). 'Neurotransmitters: Types, functions and disorders', *Kenhub*.

Voltaire. (1756). *Ancient and modern history*, New York, NY: Barnes and Noble, (reprint) **Vol. 13**.

Von Franz, M. (1984). *On dreams and death: A Jungian interpretation*. Chicago: Open Court.

Von Franz, M. (2002). *Animus and Anima in fairy tales*. Toronto, Canada: Inner City Books.

Wachel, E. (2018). 'Keeping couples therapy upbeat', *Psychotherapy Networker*. January/February 2018, 17–20.

Wallace, B. A. and Shapiro, S. (2006). 'Mental balance and well-being: Building Bridges between Buddhism and Western psychology', *American Psychologist*. (October 2006), 690–701.

Wallace, B. A. (2011). *Minding closely: The four applications of mindfulness*. Ithaca, NY: Snow Lion Publications.

Watson, J. (1924). *Behaviorism*. New Brunswick, New Jersey: Transaction Publishing.

Watts, A. (1951). *The Wisdom of insecurity*. New York, NY: Pantheon Books.

Watts, A. (1960). *The meaning of happiness*. New York, NY: Harper & Row, Publishers.

Watts, A. (1961). *Psychotherapy East and West*. New York, NY: Ballantine Books.

Watts, A. (1970). *Does it matter? Essays on man's relation to materiality*. New York, NY: Pantheon Books.

Weber, E. (1989). *Western tradition*. UCLA: WGBH Broadcasting.

Weinberg, S. (2001). 'Can science explain everything? Anything?', *The New York Review*. **5/31**, 47–50.

Weinberg, S. (2001). 'The future of science and the universe', *The New York Review*. 11/15/2001, 58–63.

Weir, K. (2011). 'Memory keepers', *Monitor on Psychology*, June 2011, 32–35.

Weir, K. (2011). 'Golden rule redux', *Monitor on Psychology*. July/August 2011, pp. 42–45.

Weir, K. (2014). 'Mind games', *Monitor on Psychology*. October 2014, pp. 43–46.

Weir, K. (2016). 'Moral minds', *Monitor on Psychology*. September 2016, pp. 41–46.

Weir, K. (2017). 'Keeping dementia at bay', *Monitor on Psychology,* July/August 2017, pp. 44–52.

Weir, K. (2018). 'Life-Saving Relationships', *Monitor on Psychology*, **Vol. 49, No. 3**, 2018.

Werkmeister, W.H. (1967) *Man and his values.* Lincoln, NE: University of Nebraska Press.

Werner, H. (1967). 'Adler, Freud, and American Social Work', *Journal of Individual Psychology*, (May 1967), 11–12.

Westbury, G. (1962). *Good grief.* New York, NY: Fortress Press.

Westen, D., Lohr, N. et. al. (1990). 'Object relations and social cognition in borderlines, major depressives, and normals: A Thematic Apperception Test analysis', *Psychological Assessment*, **Vol. 2, No 4**, 355–354.

Westfall, R. S. (2007). *Isaac Newton*. Cambridge: Cambridge University Press.

Wexler, D. (2003). 'Guy Talk', *SDPA Monthly Newsletter*, June 2003, **Vol. 13 No. 6**, 1–8.

Wikipedia: Epigenetics, 5/30/2008
    Felix culpa, 2/9/2011
    Informatics, 8/19/2021
    Linde, Andrei, 3/21/2014
    Martin Luther, 3/29/2015
    Mirror neurons, 12/9/2008
    Noetics, 9/11/2013
    Physics of Aristole versus The Physics of Galileo, 8/29/2021
    Psychneuroimmunology, 12/4/2007
    Tesla, Nikola, 8/29/2014
    Tolman, Edward, 2/26/2015
    Valence bond theory, 8/25/2014

Wilber, K. (1998). *The essential Ken Wilber*. Boston: Shambhala.

Wilber, K. (2000). *A Theory of Everything*. Boston: Shambhala.

Williams, K. (2001). *Ostracism: The power of silence, emotions, and social behavior*. New York NY: Guilford Press.

Wilson. M. (2002). 'Six views of embodied cognition', *Psychonomic Bulletin and Review*, **9**, 625–636.

Winnicott, D.W. (1971). *Playing and reality.* London: Tavistock.

Wolf, M.S., Gazmararian, J.A. & Baker, D.W. (2005). 'Health literacy and functional health status among older adults', *Archives of Internal Medicine* **165**, 1946–1952.

Wolfram, Stephen (2012). 'The father of fractals', *Wall Street Journal*, 22 November 2012.

Wood, R. (1969). *Martin Buber's ontology: An analysis of I and Thou*. Chicago: Northwestern University Press.

Wright, K. (2008). 'Dare to be yourself: Authenticity', *Psychology Today*. (May/June 2008), 74–77.

Wurmser, L. (1978). *The hidden dimension*. New York, NY: Jason Aronson, Inc.

Yalom, I. (1995ed.). *The theory and practice of group psychotherapy*. New York, NY: Basic Books.

Yapko, M. (2011). 'Suggesting mindfulness', *Psychotherapy Networker.* (September/October 2011), 28.

Yoder, J. (1982). 'Teilhard De Chardin: Phenomenology and implications for counseling', *The Personnel and Guidance Journal,* (March 1982), 431–435.

Young, J. (1994). *Reinventing Your Life.* New York, NY: Penguin.

Zaccaro, St. (2007). 'Trait-based perspectives of leadership', *American Psychologist*, **62**, 1, 1–16.

Zadra, A. (2021). 'Theater of the mind', *Psychology Today*, January/February 2021, 35–42, 62.

Zhong-Yue, W. (2016). 'Modern theory for electromagnetic Metamaterials', *Plasmonics.* **11 (2),** 503–508.

Zilcha-Mano, Si. (2017). 'Is the alliance really therapeutic? Revisiting this question in light of recent methodological advances', *American Psychologist*, **72, 4**, 311–325.

Zohar (2008) 'Changing the story of our future', *Shift*. San Francisco: Institute of Noetic Sciences.

Zukav, G. (1989). *The seat of the soul*. New York, NY: Fireside.

Zukav, G. (2003). *The mind of the Soul*. New York, NY: Simon & Schuster.

Zweig, C. & Abrams, J. eds. (1991). *Meeting the shadow: The hidden power of the dark side of human nature*. New York, NY: Penguin Group.

Index

12-step programs 11, 26, 186, 197, 267, 394, 406

Abandonment 196, 208, 271, 313, 325, 387, 401, 426, 436, 439, 453, 498, 499
Abdill, E. 69, 409
Acceptance 54, 77, 123, 207, 209, 210, 219, 220, 221, 222, 225, 272, 273, 339, 352, 398, 405, 406, 407, 428, 447, 458, 459, 472, 474, 476, 482, 483, 494, 495, 522, 523, 524
Accommodation…theory (assimilation) .11, 135, 258, 461
Ackroyd, P 41
Acting out 66, 310, 311, 364, 365, 368, 373, 386, 391
Active imagination (Jung) 434, 442, 443, 446, 447
Addiction 26, 208, 244, 265, 266, 267, 369, 383, 384, 386, 387, 388, 389, 390, 391, 392, 394, 396, 397, 398, 399, 400, 402, 403, 405, 406, 436, 437
Adler, A 74, 75, 76, 185, 317, 318, 319, 401, 473, 507
ADLs 471, 473
Adolescence 309, 312, 358, 362, 363, 364, 417, 432, 490, 491
Adverse effects 16, 279
Affirmations 217, 218, 462, 501
African History 100, 101, 147, 189
Aging and older adults 196, 245, 256, 275, 277, 378, 379
Agricultural development 97, 98
Ainsworth, M...........313, 314, 315
Alchemy 126, 139, 412, 413, 419, 512

Alcoholics Anonymous... 117, 401
Alexander the Great 102, 103, 105, 106
Alienation 50, 60, 71, 325, 326, 344, 368, 387, 396, 451, 471, 488
Allodynia 263
Allostasis........................ 236, 242
Allport, G. 53, 343, 344
Alzheimer's disease 274, 275, 276
Alzheimer's disease 273, 274, 275, 276, 277, 378
American revolution 22, 27, 143, 146, 151, 152, 153
Amodeo, J 336, 509
Amygdala 229, 230, 232, 248, 263, 264, 266, 269, 273, 367
Anatta/no fear 214
Anima/animus 56, 414, 416, 417, 421, 425, 432, 435, 436, 437, 438, 440, 442, 445, 463
Anticipatory anxiety 72, 332, 346, 474, 475
Antigens 258
Apocrypha...................... 187, 191
Arabs............................... 111, 115
Archetypes 26, 82, 83, 181, 215, 410, 411, 413, 415, 416, 419, 420, 421, 424, 425, 426, 428, 429, 430, 439, 442, 443
Archetypes. 412
Aristotle 20, 31, 36, 38, 65, 74, 102, 103, 104, 105, 106, 136, 223, 283
Assagioli, R 27, 194, 319, 331, 406, 464
Asymmetry 24, 55, 61, 62, 90, 297, 299, 301, 302, 303, 427, 461
Atomic bomb 168
Attachment failure 363

Authenticity 219, 320, 352, 427, 436, 460, 486, 500, 501, 502, 526
Authoritarian 192, 271, 354, 355, 364, 365
Authoritative 354, 355, 364, 365, 404
Autoimmune 23, 236, 258, 262, 275, 392, 515
Autoimmune Deficiency Syndrome (AIDS) 262
Autonomic Nervous System (ANS) 229, 242, 265, 423
 Parasympathetic (PNS) 242, 248
 Sympathetic (SNS) 242, 248
Avoidance 82, 140, 248, 300, 334, 392, 400, 437, 452, 453, 474, 481, 499, 528

Baby boomers 168, 379
Bach, G. 478, 479
Bacon, F 29, 30, 41, 126, 127
Bair, D 331, 421, 422, 423
Barbarian period 107, 109, 110, 111, 112, 113
Bateson Gregory 89, 309, 370, 484
Beattie, M 290, 353
Beck, A 243, 330, 473
Behary, W. 354, 355, 356, 357, 359, 368
Behavioral 391, 405, 491, 492
Belongingness 349, 361, 370, 406, 461, 485
Benevolence 210, 492
Berkeley, G 29, 32, 59
Berman, M. 29, 411, 412
Berne, E 16, 451, 452, 479
Bible 30, 38, 44, 45, 113, 114, 117, 133, 137, 150, 184, 187, 188, 191, 193, 430
Big Bang theory 281, 292
Bill of Rights 152
Birth order 444
Black holes 298, 299
Blake, Wm 40, 41, 434

Blanck, G. & Blanck, R 307, 401, 472, 495, 496
Bloomfield, H. 272, 273, 403
Bolen, J. 386, 416, 440, 489
Boone, D. 146
Boorstin, D. 113, 116, 128, 131, 137, 144, 255, 509
Borderline personality disorder 118, 385, 406, 491
Borgese, E. 37
Boston Tea Party 151
Boundaries 25, 27, 55, 118, 142, 148, 203, 223, 271, 302, 303, 308, 310, 320, 334, 336, 337, 338, 345, 352, 355, 358, 363, 366, 369, 372, 374, 376, 377, 390, 392, 419, 455, 467, 471, 521, 522
Bowlby, J. 312, 313, 314, 315, 316, 357, 365, 385, 458
Brain health 250, 274, 277
Breathing technique 210, 403
Brown, B. 460, 528
Bruner, J. 347
Buber, M. 18, 37, 415
Buck, P. 37
Buddha/Siddhartha Gautama/Buddhism 103, 192, 194, 201, 203, 205, 206, 210, 217, 425, 494, 495, 511
Bugental, J 470, 487

Calvin, J. 47, 133, 148, 193
Campbell, J 103, 176, 192, 222, 373, 412, 422, 423, 424, 425, 426, 427, 428, 430, 431, 433, 434, 435, 438, 479, 505, 510, 511, 512, 514
Capitalism 35, 154, 158, 160
Capra, F 79, 301
Cassandra complex 438, 439
Cell memory 257
Cells and molecules 258, 262
Cerebral cortex 274, 518

Chaos/chaotic logic 34, 49, 62, 72, 89, 175, 176, 177, 194, 236, 293, 301, 303, 426, 427, 472, 507, 513
Charlemagne.... 113, 114, 116, 119
Chaucer, G. 116, 117, 125
Chess, A. & Thomas, S. 311, 324, 397
Chessick, R 85
Chodron, P. 202, 206, 209, 210, 224, 225
Chomsky, N. 43, 89
Chopra, D. & Kafatos, M 34, 287, 289, 294, 507, 508, 513, 514, 515, 517, 518
Christianity 60, 66, 100, 101, 102, 134, 154, 177, 187, 188, 189, 409, 447, 449
Chronic disease 242, 279
Cicero 100, 102, 106
Civil Rights movement 170
Civil War 145, 148, 155, 156, 157, 158
Civilization building 41, 60, 79, 94, 95, 97, 98, 99, 101, 103, 104, 105, 107, 116, 118, 143, 509, 513, 526
Classical period 38, 41, 102, 103, 105, 107, 108, 118, 123, 124, 125, 134, 137, 142, 178, 187, 417, 498, 508
Client-Centered Therapy 480
Codependency 63, 78, 254, 365, 375, 398, 399, 427, 436, 453, 457
Cognitive development 320, 321, 327, 331, 444
Cognitive therapy (CBT) 220, 246, 452
Colarusso, C. & Nemiroff, R ... 352
Cold war 168, 510
Collective Unconscious 99, 178, 317, 318, 331, 408, 411, 413, 418, 421, 426, 432, 444, 446, 447, 448, 449, 505, 521

Colonial times 144, 147, 148, 150, 152, 162, 164, 172
Committee meeting is one's head 20, 26, 386, 429
Communism 144, 166, 169, 170, 509
Compassion and loving kindness 20, 62, 78, 80, 82, 92, 178, 186, 199, 202, 208, 210, 211, 216, 218, 219, 220, 221, 222, 223, 225, 235, 247, 262, 263, 278, 339, 362, 392, 398, 407, 436, 454, 460, 469, 475, 476, 479, 481, 488, 489, 504, 522, 523, 528, 530
Complexification 21, 86, 87
Compulsions 20, 385, 387, 392, 396, 424, 430, 472
Confucius 33, 103, 471, 472
Constantinople 30, 110, 112, 115, 116, 123, 128, 193
Continental Congress 152, 153
Copernicus 127, 136, 137, 138, 139, 146, 227, 283, 293
Corsini, R. 77
Cosmic 12, 22, 26, 30, 65, 82, 105, 123, 127, 171, 174, 194, 293, 296, 298, 304, 384, 506, 508, 514, 517
Cosmology 30, 91, 283, 291, 296, 299
Courage 20, 21, 33, 36, 58, 62, 67, 77, 78, 107, 206, 217, 223, 266, 332, 335, 373, 395, 407, 422, 446, 470, 472, 473, 483, 507, 511, 527, 531
COVID-19 173
Cravings 266, 390, 398
Creativity 24, 25, 27, 41, 54, 56, 67, 73, 79, 121, 135, 141, 214, 216, 218, 224, 248, 266, 288, 350, 371, 372, 374, 384, 428, 459, 462, 467, 470, 471, 481, 497, 507, 525, 526
Crick, F. 92, 227, 237, 514

Crisis 133, 170, 188, 307, 308, 310, 312, 315, 364, 391, 392, 399, 402, 424, 426, 466, 480, 481, 482, 511
Crusades 110, 114, 115, 122
Culture 19, 28, 97, 419
Cybernetics 53, 89, 90, 525
Cytokines 258, 259, 260, 261, 269, 275

Da Vinci, L. 21, 56, 123, 128, 129, 199
Dalai Lama (His Holiness) 11, 91, 176, 204, 216, 219, 296, 512, 527
Dante, A. 117, 118, 130
Dark ages 28, 30, 45, 47, 102, 103, 104, 106, 109, 110, 111, 113, 116, 118, 134, 136, 141, 188
Dark energy 300, 301, 302
Darwin, C. 159, 196, 201, 227, 234, 241, 346, 347, 429, 515, 526
Dawkins, R 255, 256
D-Day WWII 14, 167
de Broglie, L. 287, 290, 419
de Castillejo, I. 15, 395
de Saint-Exupery, A. 217
de Tocqueville, A 154
Dead Sea Scrolls 188, 191
Death and dying 40, 59, 73, 74, 75, 77, 78, 173, 174, 204, 219, 225, 233, 248, 277, 278, 346, 432, 447, 449, 457, 495, 512
Defensiveness 49, 320, 335, 339, 392, 460, 500
Dementia 228, 241, 273, 378
Dependency 54
Depression 14, 160, 163, 165, 167, 223, 243, 405, 425, 437, 451, 473, 533, 546
Descartes, R 16, 29, 32, 46, 47, 73, 138, 139, 208, 286, 538
Despair 47, 85, 174, 307, 310, 315, 373, 401, 464, 465, 470, 492

Detachment 73, 74, 95, 206, 313, 342, 348, 351, 384, 390, 426, 464, 492
Dharma 62, 68, 186, 194, 196, 197, 199, 205, 206, 221, 323, 422, 425, 426, 427, 463
Diagnostic and Statistical Manual (DSM-5) 405
Dialectical Behavior Therapy (DBT) .. 213, 356, 405, 491, 522
Dialectics 59, 505, 506
Diaspora 190
Dignity 43, 44, 124, 152, 310, 395, 529
Divorce 132, 187, 346, 369, 402, 466
DNA 255, 256, 262, 275, 278, 396, 514
Double bind 89, 91, 455
Dream themes and dreaming .. 418, 429, 446
Drob, S. 176, 178, 412, 432, 435, 443
Dual diagnosis 405, 492
Dualism 15, 29, 46, 66, 88, 132, 188, 194, 201, 234, 409, 443, 467, 498, 504, 526
Duality in waves 419
Dyer, W. 218, 219
Dynamics/Mechanics 175, 284, 291, 301, 302, 309, 361, 365, 369, 371, 374, 379, 388, 415, 430, 480, 518, 524, 542, 547

East India Company 151
Eating disorders 455
Efficiency 159
Ego psychology 331, 392, 517
Egocentric ... 61, 82, 222, 409, 444
Ego-strength 308, 331, 365
Egyptian
　History 99, 100, 106
　Religion 106, 179, 189, 377, 448
Eightfold path .. 103, 205, 340, 427

Einstein, A 78, 137, 280, 281, 286, 289, 293, 298, 464, 529, 539
Electron field 26, 520
Electrons 34, 254, 256, 285, 287, 289, 294, 300, 518, 520
Ellis, A 241, 323, 324
Emerson, R.W 11, 70, 136, 145, 146, 149, 154, 171, 194, 215, 218, 338, 477, 539
Emotional development 16, 53, 325, 334
Emotional intelligence (EQ) 35, 247, 351
Empathy 75, 154, 172, 211, 212, 245, 246, 262, 270, 278, 279, 304, 325, 327, 328, 338, 350, 351, 355, 357, 362, 363, 368, 374, 385, 407, 441, 475, 476, 481, 487, 488, 507, 509, 533
English monarchy 147
Enlightenment period 22
Enmeshment 325, 326
Entanglement 285, 292
Epicurean philosophers . 20, 38, 65
Epigenetics 25, 257, 390, 409, 419
Epistemology 39
Erasmus, D 45, 53, 125, 132
Erikson, E 89, 306, 307, 308, 311, 341, 345, 348, 401, 457, 467, 483, 539
Eros 410, 467
Escape behaviors 353
Essentialism 60
Ethnocentrism 530
Eudaimonia 20, 241
European power struggle 120
Event horizon 298, 299
Evolution 37, 60, 66, 68, 85, 86, 87, 89, 91, 94, 99, 144, 159, 178, 187, 194, 212, 229, 237, 255, 256, 278, 282, 299, 301, 306, 329, 347, 410, 418, 428, 429, 432, 435, 484, 507, 512, 515, 518, 533, 547
Existentialism 70, 71, 91

Explorers 35, 125, 128, 131, 134, 135, 146
Externalizing 149, 372
Extroversion 296, 426

Families 53, 70, 84, 89, 126, 147, 150, 156, 158, 159, 167, 169, 200, 279, 339, 364, 445, 458, 461, 465, 519
Fascism 165, 166
Femininity 453
Ferenczi, S. 196
Ferguson, C 93
Feudal system 46, 94, 111, 114, 119, 121, 125
Fight/Flight/Freeze 197, 209, 229, 232, 242, 258, 262, 307, 436, 437, 468, 470
Food density areas 97
Forgiveness 140, 184, 186, 198, 199, 214, 266, 504
Foucault, M 61
Four noble truths 194, 201, 203, 206, 207, 224, 303
Four Noble Truths of Buddhism 201, 303
Fox, E 171, 195, 477
Fractals 302
Franklin, B 143, 150
Free will 52, 53, 62, 88, 93, 125, 132, 154, 233, 234, 280, 463, 508
French revolution 143, 151, 509
Freud, S. 16, 25, 74, 133, 171, 194, 306, 307, 341, 345, 348, 412, 415, 420, 504, 520, 540, 557
Fromm, E 96, 217, 306, 309, 319, 341, 342, 388, 419, 457, 469, 478, 483, 504, 508
Fulgrum, R 540

Galileo, G 53, 129, 137, 138, 139, 146, 227, 282, 283, 284, 286, 540, 557
Gate control theory 264

Gender differences 354
Genetics 89, 237, 255, 270, 456, 461, 529
George III 145, 146, 151
Gershon, R 515, 540
Gestalt therapy 302, 479, 525, 550
Gibbon, E. 112
Gilligan, C. 185
Glial cells 279
Global equity 11, 12, 14, 22, 28, 67, 86, 125, 168, 172, 173, 373, 434, 449, 462, 496, 503, 506, 509, 510, 512, 519, 521, 526, 528, 529, 530
Glucocorticoid 230, 239, 242, 265
Glutamate 264, 277
Gnostics 22, 109, 177, 179, 188, 331, 412, 413
Goble, F .. 341, 342, 349, 521, 540
Goddesses 179, 440, 534
Goldstein, H. 319, 344, 347, 348, 466
Grace 38, 69, 105, 116, 132, 140, 185, 470
Grant, U.S 157, 158, 541, 542
Gratitude 209, 212, 460, 471, 504, 513, 520, 529
Great Depression 14, 163
Great Migration 158
Greed 140, 141, 171, 193, 205, 511
Greenwald, H 225
  Direct Decision Therapy 477
Grief 210, 346, 366, 367, 368, 369, 377, 383, 401, 441, 451, 496, 499, 557
Guilt 64, 76, 77, 140, 154, 156, 171, 209, 271, 308, 309, 311, 319, 329, 349, 364, 367, 393, 394, 395, 396, 405, 451, 452, 459, 471, 499, 528
Gutenberg bible and printing .. 193

Habits 21, 26, 172, 224, 232, 241, 268, 273, 329, 349, 398, 403, 500, 511, 515, 522, 528

Haeckel, E 86, 306, 429, 541
Hamilton, A 152, 153
Happiness 20, 23, 39, 42, 50, 51, 57, 65, 69, 143, 144, 151, 152, 183, 200, 205, 216, 220, 241, 247, 270, 323, 470, 481, 498, 528, 529, 537, 541, 556
Harding, D 214, 215, 216, 218
Hardy, J 216, 243, 331
Harlow, H 329, 341, 542
Harper's Ferry 154
Hayman, R 17, 418, 433, 448
Hegel, G.W.F 16, 55, 58, 59, 60, 61, 77, 90, 173, 299, 344, 394, 434, 435, 446, 467, 489, 506, 508, 509, 541, 542, 551
Heisenberg, W 19, 23, 24, 34, 35, 62, 81, 83, 135, 203, 207, 230, 235, 259, 280, 282, 283, 285, 286, 287, 289, 290, 291, 292, 299, 306, 328, 413, 427, 461, 505, 508, 509, 510, 512, 513, 514, 542, 547
Helplessness 49, 248, 249, 300, 315, 325, 334, 369, 384, 389, 397, 401, 437, 453, 472, 473, 482
Henry VIII 131, 132, 149, 187
Heraclitus 35, 59, 176, 443
Heron Dance 184, 463, 474, 547, 549
Heschel, A 34, 94, 307, 472, 505, 509, 512, 519, 542
Hesse, H. 90, 433, 489, 490, 521, 524, 542
Higgs' particle/CERN 296, 300
Higher Power 26, 57, 62, 141, 172, 175, 182, 183, 186, 190, 195, 197, 199, 297, 308, 332, 336, 395, 397, 420, 427, 469, 495, 498, 499, 501
Hippocampus and memory 181, 230, 248, 249, 268, 269, 271, 274, 317, 552
Hippocrates 35, 103, 104

History 32, 36, 43, 55, 89, 127
Hitler, A... 120, 163, 165, 166, 167
Hobbes, T29, 30, 38, 46, 53, 82, 144, 152, 543
Hoffman, E 388, 480, 484, 489
Holism/holistic 15, 79
Hollis, J432, 433, 434, 435, 436, 437, 438, 467, 468, 543
Holmes, E 477
Holocaust 12, 166, 167, 345
Hormones229, 230, 235, 239, 241, 242, 248, 250, 259, 261, 265, 275, 325, 370, 516
Horney, K67, 207, 306, 341, 342, 343, 348, 496
Humanism20, 67, 122, 124, 126, 127, 133, 136, 142, 148, 149, 174, 508
Hume, D 92, 145
Huxley, A21, 85, 86, 185, 313, 528, 543
Hypersensitivity syndrome 260, 262, 385
Hypnosis 16, 225, 403, 477

Ideal23, 29, 33, 34, 36, 37, 38, 42, 53, 60, 65, 102, 141, 159, 179, 241, 306, 327, 334, 339, 348, 353, 363, 427, 430, 443, 457, 489, 506, 541
Identification20, 66, 75, 213, 224, 236, 273, 327, 348, 353, 371, 421, 435, 436, 440, 464, 467
Illuminated manuscripts 117
Illumination 288, 428
Immigration 150, 155, 526, 530
Immune system80, 227, 241, 242, 244, 250, 251, 257, 259, 261, 265, 409, 516
Immunosuppressive 242
Impermanence63, 90, 202, 206, 223, 236, 303, 464
India18, 24, 66, 97, 100, 101, 103, 106, 142, 151, 175, 188, 193, 204, 213, 296, 387, 417, 422, 427, 512, 519, 545
Indigenous people/"Indian Wars" 107, 142, 147
Individuation18, 37, 53, 126, 312, 368, 390, 411, 412, 413, 415, 416, 419, 423, 424, 425, 431, 432, 433, 434, 436, 439, 442, 445, 446, 447, 448, 449, 512, 544, 547
Industrial revolution148, 160, 307, 508
Inflammation236, 243, 250, 251, 252, 257, 259, 260, 276
Informatics 279, 557
Inner directedness/Outer directedness... 72, 140, 272, 403
Inner work. 78, 180, 221, 448, 501
Instincts/drives22, 62, 75, 88, 118, 149, 178, 228, 229, 266, 295, 307, 328, 332, 372, 388, 409, 412, 415, 417, 418, 424, 442, 480, 520
Interdependence87, 88, 205, 223, 353, 365, 406, 509
Internal Family Systems Therapy (IFS) 221
Internalizing 88, 149, 207, 327
Intimacy130, 217, 307, 309, 373, 398, 429
Introversion 296, 331, 420, 426
Intuition11, 29, 35, 36, 67, 69, 181, 211, 214, 230, 247, 334, 338, 347, 372, 406, 414, 430, 489, 514, 517, 519
Isis/Osiris 98, 179
Islam/Muslim 69, 101, 192, 193
Isolation24, 48, 50, 98, 113, 258, 267, 270, 325, 326, 329, 346, 356, 364, 373, 382, 399, 402, 407, 428, 431, 451, 474, 493, 498, 499, 500, 515, 516, 542

James, H 12

James, Wm 27, 179, 392, 406, 498, 504, 511, 543, 554
Jamestown 146, 147, 148
Jefferson, T 48, 155, 505
Jesus Christ 109, 111, 112, 132, 176, 192
Jourard, S 344, 521
Judaic studies 176, 179, 199
Jung, C.G 16, 25, 27, 171, 194, 307, 317, 331, 341, 345, 401, 412, 413, 415, 416, 418, 419, 421, 424, 425, 431, 432, 433, 437, 443, 446, 447, 448, 457, 483, 496, 509, 533, 544, 547

Kammersgard, E 400
Kant, E 17, 20, 34, 59, 72, 73, 85, 299, 428, 506, 517, 544
Karma 93, 194, 196, 197, 201, 202, 205, 407, 517
Katherine, A. 115, 145, 334, 337, 338, 352, 545
Kepler, J 137, 138, 139, 283
Kierkegaard, S 66, 474
King David 190
Klein, M 27, 306, 314
Koestler, W 25, 29, 141, 209, 306, 328, 332, 413, 418, 419, 498, 504, 545
Kohlberg, L 25, 82, 83, 185, 327, 328, 330, 371, 466
Koob, G 236, 242, 249, 267, 268, 269, 324, 545
Kushner, H 62, 190

Language development 305, 321, 497
Leadership 111, 116, 120, 161, 174, 434, 519, 534, 558
Learning disability 391
Leibniz, G.W 47, 139
Lewy-body disease 276, 378
Libido 67, 85, 242, 308, 410, 414, 415, 419, 420, 435, 438, 453
Life review 63, 381

Lifestyle 101, 171, 195, 275, 302, 310, 319, 327, 379, 401, 452, 470
Limbic system 228
Limerence/love addiction 372, 386, 416
Lincoln, A 155, 156, 157
Literacy 99, 100, 118, 122, 135, 159, 172, 187, 191, 378
Liturgy 95, 112, 117, 183, 184, 448
Locke, J. 32
Loneliness 57, 67, 174, 203, 226, 290, 337, 358, 394, 396, 407, 436, 464, 465, 469, 498, 511
Lorenz, K 53, 313
Loss 46, 95, 121, 126, 170, 174, 186, 193, 197, 201, 208, 209, 238, 241, 242, 252, 254, 264, 267, 271, 273, 274, 276, 277, 287, 303, 309, 311, 314, 315, 334, 346, 351, 354, 357, 358, 359, 364, 366, 367, 368, 369, 372, 373, 374, 381, 383, 387, 388, 390, 395, 398, 399, 401, 405, 407, 428, 436, 439, 440, 451, 452, 453, 457, 460, 463, 464, 465, 467, 470, 476, 480, 493, 496, 499, 522, 523, 530, 532, 552
Luther, M 47, 116, 125, 131, 132, 133, 134, 135, 141, 146, 149, 169, 170, 174, 187, 191, 193, 557

Machiavelli 38, 39, 124, 125, 130, 131, 547
Madeo, R 43, 61, 72, 73, 90, 249, 256, 300, 302, 461, 507, 547
Magna Carta 108, 115, 125
Mahler, M 25, 306, 309, 312, 314, 327, 333, 337, 341, 342, 345, 348, 353, 358, 362, 368, 392, 432, 433, 437, 441, 547
Male psychology 320, 331, 344, 457

Maltz, M ..349, 370, 484, 520, 547
Mandala 431, 446
Mandel, B 26, 406, 504, 526
Mandelbrot, B 301
Manipulation 25, 42, 176, 377, 542, 553
Marcus Aurelius 56, 85, 100, 107, 108, 207, 546, 549
Marital crises 90
Marks-Tarlow, T 247, 271, 301, 303, 547
Marx, K. 61, 82, 105, 144, 161, 174, 506, 509, 527, 547
Mary Catherine 281, 314, 477
Maslow, A 26, 53, 67, 92, 241, 307, 328, 329, 332, 341, 342, 344, 345, 348, 349, 350, 351, 354, 361, 363, 367, 370, 373, 388, 471, 472, 473, 475, 479, 484, 485, 488, 489, 500, 506, 527, 531, 543, 547, 548, 553
Massachusetts Bay/Puritans 148
Maxwell, J.C 282, 285, 286, 290
May, R 469
McQuaide, S 458, 459
Meaningfulness 17, 57, 296, 349, 524, 550
Medici 122, 128, 129, 130, 132
Medieval period ... 38, 39, 125, 193
Meditation 16, 19, 29, 30, 93, 176, 180, 197, 199, 200, 201, 202, 206, 207, 209, 210, 211, 212, 213, 221, 222, 224, 226, 243, 246, 248, 272, 387, 394, 403, 404, 407, 427, 441, 442, 448, 489, 490, 492, 505, 513, 514, 524, 533, 534, 537, 549, 555
Memory 13, 36, 39, 40, 41, 50, 56, 93, 99, 126, 180, 181, 222, 227, 231, 233, 236, 241, 244, 246, 248, 249, 251, 252, 258, 261, 264, 269, 271, 273, 274, 275, 276, 291, 312, 334, 349, 355, 378, 389, 410, 464, 473, 487, 508, 527, 535, 541

Messiah/Savior 109, 179
Metaphysics 11, 44, 58, 59, 85, 117, 124, 280, 409, 427
Methylation 233, 256, 257
Michelangelo 122, 125, 127, 129, 132
Middle Ages 20, 44, 113, 115, 118, 121, 122, 123, 127, 132, 140, 141, 171, 317, 536, 550
Middle East 28, 106, 110, 112, 115, 162, 163, 167, 170, 172, 192
Milkman, H. & Sunderwith, S 383, 384, 385, 386, 396, 398, 408, 548
Miller, A 165, 390, 437, 439
Miller, D 147, 148, 150, 154, 157, 164, 167
Mind-body problem 29, 32
Mindful brain 210
Mindfulness training 223
Mirror neurons/empathy neurons 211, 269, 270, 271, 278
Monasteries 113
Montagu, A 37
Montesquieu, C 48
Moore, T 53, 54, 55, 56, 91, 407, 431, 439, 441, 496, 497, 548
Moral development ... 25, 185, 327
Moring, G 287, 294, 295, 296, 297, 304
Moring, G. 282, 284
Motivation and motivational Interviewing 491
MRI/PET scans 248
Muhammad 103, 192
Multiverse 297, 511
Mutuality 82, 222, 312
Mysticism 39, 67, 177, 217, 272, 409, 412, 415, 435, 479, 506, 512, 538
Mythology 35, 41, 103, 373, 412, 420, 447, 449, 510

Nag Hammadi 188
Napolean/Napoleonic wars 144

Narcissism 74, 82, 171, 309, 310, 312, 351, 352, 354, 356, 357, 362, 366, 368, 369, 372, 396, 407, 426, 431, 441, 467, 491, 519, 537, 545
Nationalism 110, 163, 173, 519
Neff, C 219, 523
Neocortex 96, 180, 181, 229, 231, 233, 274, 361
Neoplatonic influences 15, 36
Neuroendocrine 14, 261
Neurophenomena 272
Neuroplasticity 230, 233, 235, 236, 257, 273, 529
Neuroscience 14, 20, 25, 29, 35, 127, 230, 234, 236, 252, 271, 296, 306, 334, 335, 396, 517, 535, 537
Neurotransmitters 181, 228, 230, 233, 236, 237, 239, 240, 244, 245, 246, 247, 248, 250, 251, 259, 262, 264, 268, 273, 291, 299, 304, 385, 515
New Deal 165
Newton, I 137, 139, 145, 282, 283, 284, 287, 289, 293, 294, 549, 555, 557
Nietzsche, F 16, 20, 22, 53, 66, 67, 71, 86, 144, 174, 433, 441, 468, 549
Nirvana 207
Noetics 278, 495
Nonviolent communication 338
Noumena 428
Nutrition 36, 195, 242, 252, 269, 277, 493, 515

Obesity and addiction 539
Ontosophy and holistic therapy 506
Opioid dependence 265, 266
Origin of life 256
Ostrowski-Sachs, M 412, 415, 441, 448, 449, 549
Ouroboros 44, 181, 205, 439

Outliers 18, 24, 61, 74, 83, 95, 146, 148, 149, 267, 290, 367, 409, 464, 473
Overactive brain 545
Oxidation 252, 257, 269, 275
Oxytocin 235, 246, 263, 289, 295, 371

Pain and pain management 238, 244, 245, 246, 256, 265, 266, 273, 388, 513
Paine, T 151
Pantheism 139, 177
Papacy 53, 112, 113, 116, 122, 192
Parenting style 374
Pascal, B 15, 47, 138, 474, 549, 550
Pathogenesis 257, 260
Pauli, W 507
Pavlov, I.P 295
Peak experience 329
Pearl Harbor 167
Penn, Wm 146, 149
Perfectionism 456
Personal Orientation Inventory (POI) 272, 403
Personality types 243, 302, 414
Phenomenology 52, 79, 475
Physical development 283
Piaget, J 25, 82, 90, 228, 230, 258, 260, 313, 320, 321, 322, 324, 327, 337, 345, 346, 347, 353, 394, 398, 444, 517, 550
Pinker, S. 33, 34, 62, 72, 88, 92, 171, 227, 228, 229, 232, 233, 234, 235, 249, 255, 264, 268, 279, 284, 287, 293, 295, 296, 321, 322, 327, 366, 550
Plague 46, 113, 116, 119, 120, 130, 131
Planck, M 285
Plasticity (see Neuroplasticity) 227, 236, 241, 273, 516, 517
Plato 16, 20, 23, 29, 31, 32, 33, 34, 35, 38, 42, 54, 59, 65, 66, 91, 96, 103, 104, 105, 123, 128, 129,

130, 177, 185, 283, 331, 339, 377, 430, 435, 498, 506, 508, 533, 541
Play 22, 29, 114, 182, 237, 243, 249, 250, 255, 263, 266, 297, 302, 314, 321, 328, 330, 344, 352, 360, 370, 379, 385, 389, 393, 397, 423, 436, 438, 455, 479, 498, 499, 534, 541
Poetry 16, 41, 56, 80, 183, 447, 463, 474, 521, 543
Pompeii 41
Post traumatic stress disorder (PTSD) 248, 389, 445, 493
Prajna (wisdom) 36, 202, 204, 206
Prefrontal cortex 237, 247, 266, 269, 271
Prehistory period 96
Primate development . 96, 180, 229
Principle of complementarity . 289, 290
Probability waves 24, 43, 210, 235, 237, 254, 267, 282, 288, 289, 291, 292, 297, 299, 330
Projection 16, 171, 196, 317, 353, 359, 367, 372, 388, 400, 411, 427, 431, 443, 486, 502, 527, 530
Psyche 20, 21, 27, 29, 40, 74, 171, 197, 244, 271, 295, 307, 310, 317, 411, 413, 414, 416, 420, 421, 424, 425, 428, 443, 447, 459, 506, 507, 526, 541, 544, 550
Psychoanalysis 22, 27, 342, 508, 536, 537, 543, 544
Psychoneuroimmunology 14, 25, 258, 261, 533, 543, 549
Psychosexual development 364
Psychosocial development 227, 341
Ptolemy 31, 100, 127, 128, 136, 187

Quadrium 126

Quantum mechanics 249, 283, 285, 290, 291, 293, 294, 295, 300, 302, 306, 513, 534
Quarks 300
Quintessence 136, 298, 299

Radiation 256, 285, 286, 290, 294, 298
Radical acceptance 405, 494
Rapprochement 312, 353, 362, 366, 392, 433, 438, 441
Rationalists 47, 67, 70, 144
Recursive 91, 244, 245
Reformation 47, 113, 116, 125, 132, 133, 134, 141, 142, 149, 506
Reframing 191, 220, 324, 464
Relational 27, 39, 40, 42, 185, 186, 195, 200, 211, 245, 254, 270, 271, 289, 292, 307, 311, 352, 353, 367, 369, 375, 383, 388, 454, 459, 461, 489, 508
Relational meditation 210
Relativity 59, 129, 137, 235, 255, 282, 284, 286, 287, 293, 299, 300, 309, 327, 415, 467, 486, 526, 544
Relaxation 16, 220, 246, 260, 265, 384, 397, 403, 404, 494, 541
Religion ... 212, 377, 412, 417, 499
Religious influences 18
Renaissance
  influences and perspective 7, 9, 15, 20, 28, 35, 38, 46, 52, 77, 79, 103, 104, 106, 113, 116, 121, 122, 123, 124, 125, 127, 128, 129, 131, 134, 137, 140, 141, 142, 296, 339, 390, 410, 412, 462, 508, 509, 512, 520, 527, 540, 541, 550
Resentment 198, 202, 206, 349, 367, 453
Resilience 124, 227, 236, 252, 269, 316, 380, 457, 458, 460, 481, 492, 509, 522, 533

Rituals 22, 26, 29, 61, 62, 97, 144, 190, 192, 226, 328, 387, 447, 468
Roaring Twenties............ 163, 164
Robbins, T 523
Rockefeller, J.D 159, 160, 172, 279
Roman Catholic Church 38
Roman empire 28, 106, 108, 109, 111, 113, 116, 118, 191, 192, 527
Romantic love.................. 130, 372
Rousseau, M 48, 49, 50, 51, 52, 143, 144, 171, 417, 551
Rucker, R 185, 329, 330, 484, 485, 486, 487, 488, 525, 551
Rugged individualism........ 74, 146
Russell, B 36, 73, 551

Sacred 19, 54, 104, 189, 196, 237, 322, 373, 420, 428, 438, 468, 474, 500, 538
Safety 23, 61, 107, 113, 211, 219, 306, 317, 334, 349, 355, 358, 361, 363, 368, 374, 376, 379, 381, 389, 391, 410, 427, 455, 458, 475, 479, 527, 549
Salk, J 11, 25, 218, 387, 446, 507, 510, 551
Sangha 23, 26, 62, 67, 77, 84, 179, 186, 197, 199, 205, 206, 223, 470, 488, 497
Sapolsky, R 236, 239, 240, 241, 242, 243, 246, 250, 251, 253, 257, 261, 264, 265, 274, 275, 277, 370, 552
Sartre, J.P 34, 40, 54, 67, 71, 72, 174, 241, 501, 552
Satir, V.... 302, 336, 361, 465, 552
Schemas 90, 224, 230, 231, 258, 321, 322, 324, 325, 326, 327, 355, 412, 521
Schopenhauer, A.......... 53, 66, 409
Schrodinger, E 70, 92, 254, 282, 291, 552

Science of Mind/Religious Science Church 80, 171, 195, 477, 499, 501
Self-awareness 16, 52, 73, 207, 230, 260, 323, 328, 336, 342, 350, 376, 394, 404, 416, 427, 429, 462, 467, 480, 484, 510, 523
Self-compassion............... 186, 549
Self-control 14, 20, 36, 42, 47, 260, 309, 325, 326, 396, 405
Self-deception 196, 315, 519
Self-denial 54, 148
Self-determination 42, 309, 500, 511
Self-discovery 69
Self-esteem 183, 219, 220, 221, 273, 329, 356, 358, 386, 394, 452, 455, 456, 459, 460, 462, 469, 472, 473, 482
Self-help 41, 160, 391, 399, 451, 452, 477, 500
Self-knowledge 27, 60, 67, 72, 152, 212, 219, 376, 395, 487
Self-loathing 219, 401, 423, 460, 475, 528
Self-love 51, 66, 329, 406
Self-monitoring 241
Self-recursive 90, 91
Self-regulation 225, 244, 260, 328, 355, 373, 396, 415, 552
Self-soothing 16, 24, 209, 224, 317, 336, 355, 368, 369, 383, 385, 442, 522
Self-sufficiency . 65, 342, 433, 496
Seligman, M 216, 241, 384, 473, 482, 528, 529, 553
Sensorimotor theory of development........................ 321
Sentience 88, 213
Septuagint 187
Serenity 30, 48, 183, 195, 201, 207, 210, 211, 243, 246, 440, 469, 501, 506, 540

Sermon on the Mount 109, 191, 195, 477, 511
Seven Years War 142
Sexual development/behavior .364
Shadow 26, 71, 78, 178, 209, 318, 408, 414, 416, 421, 424, 425, 426, 433, 434, 440, 441, 442, 444, 445, 446, 463, 469, 496, 509, 521
Shakespeare, Wm. 16, 80, 114, 130, 184
Shame 118, 156, 219, 220, 221, 222, 223, 271, 303, 325, 326, 328, 337, 355, 357, 369, 394, 395, 396, 397, 398, 399, 422, 460, 461, 463, 464, 467, 472, 499, 509, 522, 528, 551
Shapiro, R 216, 220, 255, 256, 553, 556
Siegel, D 210, 211, 224, 225, 226, 233, 235, 243, 246, 249, 324, 325, 337, 355, 356, 368, 482, 553
Siegel, R 225, 230, 492
Skinner, B.F 42, 43, 44, 53, 278, 295, 342, 536, 554
Slavery 29, 37, 60, 105, 118, 148, 152, 153, 154, 155, 156, 158
Sleep 196, 236, 275, 541
Smith, A 82, 115, 142, 143, 147, 154, 164, 506, 509, 536, 551, 554
Smith, H 82
Social instinct 74, 317, 507
Socrates 20, 31, 35, 38, 39, 91, 103, 104, 283, 340, 471, 500
Spielberger, C 423
Spinoza, B 32, 47, 139, 288, 508, 554
Spirituality and spiritual fitness 182, 185, 196, 495, 510, 514
Splitting in narcissism 29, 209, 300, 308, 358, 433
Sri Ram, N 66
St. Aquinas 39

St. Augustine 32, 39, 66, 113, 174, 433, 447, 482
St. Benedict 116
Steidinger, J 372
Stoic philosophers 20, 38, 64, 85, 105, 116, 129, 508
Stone Age/Bronze Age/Iron Age 97, 147, 189
Stress disorder (SD) 367, 390, 493, 522
String theory 80, 289, 292, 293, 294
Styron, W 401
Suffering 49, 198, 209
Suicide 67, 168, 186, 203, 368, 369, 422, 465, 492
Sullivan, H.S 11, 27, 318, 369, 405, 554, 555
Superstring theory 300
Survival 15, 16, 20, 37, 43, 46, 52, 64, 77, 95, 118, 126, 147, 148, 150, 152, 159, 171, 172, 174, 189, 196, 201, 210, 232, 233, 236, 241, 243, 256, 260, 264, 266, 271, 278, 306, 309, 315, 316, 346, 348, 358, 365, 367, 372, 387, 401, 469, 492, 493, 516, 526
Sutras 206, 207
Swedenborg, E 79, 503, 529, 530, 555
Synapse 233, 239, 240, 244, 250, 264
Synchronicity 422, 448
Synthesis 13, 16, 18, 19, 24, 25, 26, 27, 29, 34, 41, 53, 55, 58, 59, 60, 61, 77, 78, 85, 129, 133, 173, 249, 259, 290, 300, 307, 308, 344, 379, 404, 406, 432, 434, 439, 443, 464, 467, 474, 483, 504, 505, 524
Systems theory 89, 525

T cells 243, 261, 262, 265, 275
Tagore, R.C 37

Tanakh 187
Taoism and the Tao Te Ching . 18, 175, 200, 201, 203, 290, 377, 412, 484, 489, 551
Teamwork 518, 519
Technology 21, 43, 140, 157, 173, 257, 304, 379, 417, 508, 540
Teilhard de Chardin, P 21, 85, 86, 87, 88, 89, 249, 507, 555
Temperament 71, 78, 149, 222, 248, 316, 324, 325, 333, 343, 351, 355, 361, 397, 423, 515, 545
Tesla, N 160, 297, 298
Theory of Relativity 137, 235, 282, 283, 287, 293, 300, 518
Theory of the Universe 86
Therapeutic alliance 26, 312, 359, 458, 474, 476, 477
Third Force in psychology 67, 345
Third World 67, 172
Thirty Years wars 132, 162
Three jewels 23, 206
Tibetan 24, 55, 104, 174, 176, 200, 201, 202, 203, 204, 217, 219, 277, 430
Tillich, P 56, 78, 470, 474, 475
Time dilation 287
Tolerance 55, 112, 133, 141, 148, 149, 169, 204, 263, 266, 267, 324, 368, 376, 405, 460, 465, 491
Tolman, E.C 67, 217, 313, 330, 555, 557
Tonglen 210, 220
Torah 109, 176, 187, 190
Transactional Analysis (TA) ... 67, 308, 336, 451, 479, 484, 525, 546, 554
Transcendence 16, 21, 36, 53, 179, 183, 194, 319, 328, 332, 346, 420, 428, 442, 467, 479
Transference 315, 334, 359, 419, 439, 458, 476, 544

Transformation 11, 13, 34, 83, 87, 88, 143, 202, 221, 222, 282, 293, 302, 310, 342, 407, 411, 425, 426, 442, 476, 479, 495, 528
Treatment for the untreatable .. 491
Treaty of Versailles 165
Triangulation 301, 302, 309, 377, 452
Tribal/familial units 28, 60, 98, 105, 118, 135, 168, 205, 308, 376, 444, 510, 519
Triumvirate 38, 481
Triune brain 228, 229, 547

Uncertainty Principle 19, 23, 230, 259, 285, 289, 290, 291, 292, 295, 297, 299, 306
Unicosm 19
Unified Field Theory in physics 18
United Nations 168
Unity of Spirit 156, 490
Universals 19, 39, 84, 305, 327, 328, 505
Urbanization 98

Values and value clarification 329, 484, 485, 486
Van Doren, C. 94, 95, 106, 111, 118, 121, 125, 127, 128, 130, 131, 134, 138, 141, 149, 160, 164, 172, 173, 556
Varela, F 79, 92, 213
Victimhood 469, 473
Viet Nam war 157, 170
Vikings 114
Voltaire, M 143, 145
Vulnerability 226, 316, 331, 352, 375, 430, 451, 452, 458, 460, 461, 478, 481, 496, 497, 509, 516, 536, 552

Wallace, B.A 216, 241
Washington, G 151, 152, 153, 155, 156, 157, 491
Watson, J 92, 227, 514

Watts, A 40, 44, 67, 217
Wave packet 292
Weapons 97, 114, 119, 150, 168, 174, 529
Weber, E 95, 97, 98, 100, 102, 105, 106, 107, 110, 111, 112, 114, 125, 127, 131, 133, 144, 145, 154, 160, 161, 172, 173, 193, 194, 556
Weir, K 220, 232, 327, 379, 516
Wellness 13, 244, 397, 462, 482
Wilber, K 22, 41, 80, 81, 82, 83, 84, 87, 92, 93, 557
Will of God 47, 113, 174
William of Ockham 118

Wilson, W 161, 164
Winnicott, D.W 363, 370
WWI 162, 164
WWII 14, 165

Yapko, M 225, 492
Yoga 67, 68, 195, 196, 197, 512, 549
Young, J. 322, 326, 327

Zen Buddhism 23, 202, 203, 217, 532, 545
Zen/koan practice 202, 203, 214
Zeno 102, 105
Zukav, G 392, 393, 394, 398